Commercial Arbitration: Theory and Practice

Commercial Arbitration: Theory and Practice

By

Nicholas R. Weiskopf
Professor of Law, St. John's University School of Law

(with Jacob Singer, St. John's University School of Law, Class of 2010)

VANDEPLAS PUBLISHING, LLC
UNITED STATES OF AMERICA

Commercial Arbitration: Theory and Practice

Weiskopf, Nicholas R.

Published by:

Vandeplas Publishing LLC – February 2011

801 International Parkway, 5th Floor
Lake Mary, FL. 32746
USA

www.vandeplaspublishing.com

ISBN: 978-1-60042-134-1

ABOUT THIS BOOK

In the several years that I have taught Commercial Arbitration at St. John's University School of Law, I have gradually compiled a set of materials for use in a two or three credit course. In the interim, several good texts have been released on the subject, but what I attempt to do here is to develop a litigation perspective to accompany the theory. After all, a student who does not know the proof requirements for a certain type of claim can hardly appreciate issues of arbitrability, or the pros and cons of discovery limitations. Practitioners should find materials of value to them here as well.

In the past several years, St. John's has greatly enhanced its alternate dispute resolution curriculum and programs. Our student teams compete nationally in negotiation, mediation, and arbitration competitions. The school annually sponsors a Triathlon competition in these areas attended by schools from around the country. We also have a Securities Arbitration Clinic.

Our Triathlon, and various related activities, are under the auspices of the (former New York Governor) Hugh L. Carey Center for Dispute resolution which is directed by Professor Elayne Greenberg and advised by Associate Dean Paul Kirgis.

Most critically, this book reflects the efforts of several former or present senior editors of the St. John's *Law Review*. Jacob Singer, class of 2010, worked on this project from inception. He is listed as a "Collaborator" because he has been just that, at times adding text and critical other substantive input while also supervising his student colleagues. Kirsten Ennis, class of 2011, dedicated enormous time and energy to various researching projects as well as the mechanics. I also thank Christopher Linden, class of 2010, and Scott Ross, class of 2011, for their valuable help.

It is my hope that in the years to come, our *Law Review* editors will track new developments in this subject area, and be instrumental in periodically supplementing these materials. The law is changing and evolving so quickly, as our society comes to grips with the many benefits, but also the potential pitfalls, of compulsory arbitration.

New York, N.Y. 2011

PREFACE

Dispute resolution mechanisms are integral to what we would consider to be even somewhat civilized societies. Long before there were courts, there were non-violent means of resolving private claims. Typically, the nature of the power structure within some sort of grouping would dictate who would be looked to for the requisite "wisdom" and power to resolve controversies—tribal leaders, religious leaders, or respected members of ethnic groups sometimes quartered far from home. Later on, with the growth of industrialization, leading members of mercantile guilds would be expected to resolve commercial disputes.

With the centralization of government came organized judiciaries. Those courts were empowered to resolve civil disputes under common law. Then, in this country, with the swell of legislative enactments in the past century, the jurisdiction of courts, at times specialized courts, would expand to cover statutory disputes as well. In resolving disputes, courts applied a host of traditional case precedents and statutory precepts known as "the law," but they were also recognized to have a residuum of equitable discretion, particularly in connection with the award of certain remedies. To this day, every time there is a new nominee for the United States Supreme Court, we hear distinctions made between "applying the law," as opposed to "making the law." Experience tells us that which is which is often linked to the attitudes of the beholder. The intricacies of societal interactions are not always susceptible to talismanic ground rules.

However active were the courts, there was still alternate dispute resolution. In the United States, those who voluntarily resorted to arbitration could expect the courts to enforce awards by giving them the force of judgments. What the courts would not do would be to compel arbitration even under pre-dispute agreements to do so. This 'revocability" approach would change, starting in the 1920's, with the enactment of federal and state arbitration statutes. These statutes gave pre-dispute arbitral agreements the force of contract so as to require the courts to enforce them, subject only to traditional contract law defenses. So too, the courts were to give arbitral awards the force of judgments absent gross infirmities of arbitral process.

What has ensued has been a veritable revolution. Most civil disputes, common law and statutory, are now arbitral. Using Congress's power to regulate interstate commerce as its tool, the federal judiciary, under the Federal Arbitration Act ("FAA") of 1920, has not only fashioned a very pro-arbitral "federal law of arbitration," but imposed it on the states via preemption under the Supremacy Clause of the United States Constitution. Arbitral procedures have, as needed, become increasingly sophisticated. The law of arbitration has evolved with speed, often leaving lack of full resolution in its wake.

Perhaps most fundamentally of all, there is disagreement as to whether arbitrators, particularly but not exclusively in statutory cases, are expected strictly to follow established legal rules. If the answer is essentially affirmative, but awards are not reviewable for legal error, what difference does it make? Also, what of the traditional perception that, at least in certain trade, ethnic, religious and cultural contexts, arbitral process is controlled by "insiders" and thus flawed? Where there is money and standing involved, there is self-interest which, left unbridled, can corrupt. By what standards does a court determine when an arbitral mechanism is too flawed to have statutory protection?

The materials which follow are designed to provoke thought on these and other weighty subjects, but there is also emphasis on how arbitration works in practice. First, however, there is the need for context. We turn early on to the enactment of the federal and state arbitration statutes. We then trace the expansion of arbitrability to most types of statutory disputes, which often pose more sophisticated issues of law then do the commercial disputes which, earlier on, were the main components of the arbitral docket. We also focus on the evolution of the strong federal policies in favor of arbitration that fueled the expansion of arbitrability, and the use of preemption by the federal courts to bring recalcitrant state courts and legislatures into line. Only then do we look at the policing of arbitral processes.

This book is about commercial arbitration, as opposed to labor arbitration which is very different in essential ways, not the least of which is that labor awards, unlike commercial ones, are typically precedential and based on "the law of the shop" under collective bargaining agreements. Similarly, there is little focus on arbitration of consumer grievances. The hope is that by imparting a practical understanding of how arbitral procedures work, this volume will explore some very fascinating issues from a practical as well as a theoretical viewpoint. Certainly based on my experience outside the classroom, a firm knowledge of both the law and how different sorts of arbitrations actually function can be invaluable. Increasingly, the legal academy in emphasizing the imparting of practice skills to students, and I am a believer. Without understanding case presentation and arbitral procedures, for instance, how does one evaluate whether a particular sort of dispute should be arbitrable? Along the same lines, how does the private attorney decide whether a particular contract should have an arbitration clause, or what it should or should not say? So too, most litigators encounter situations where they must choose whether to seek resolution of a particular case in court or by arbitration.

First as to the classroom, this book is designed for use in a two- or three-point course. In many topic areas, such as unconscionability limitations on enforcement of arbitral agreements, and review of awards, there are cases which can be eliminated for a two-point offering. So too, this book, because of its editing and explanatory notes, lends itself to somewhat longer reading assignments than would be practical in a first-year course.

This book is intended as an aid to practitioners as well. Both in the text and the appendices, there are materials concerning the actual handling of arbitrations at the American Arbitration Association, FINRA (securities) and elsewhere. There are outlines of typical arbitral pre-hearing, hearing and post-award procedures. There is focus ranging from pre-hearing discovery to how to preserve issues of arbitrability for subsequent judicial determination. There are discussions of different types of statutory claims, including — securities, discrimination and antitrust, starting with overviews of applicable legal principles, and then going on to burdens of proof and various tactical matters designed to highlight potential differences between arbitration and court. Readers are also brought very much up to date on "hot" topics such as availability of arbitral class actions and potential means of broadening post-award review. Appendices contain statutes, the main treaty of international enforcement of agreements to arbitrate and awards (the "New York Convention"), the ABA-AAA Code of Ethics for Arbitrators, the AAA Commercial Rules and FINRA Rules for Customer Disputes. After all, the class room and the hearing room should not be all that far apart.

New York, N.Y. 2011

TABLE OF CONTENTS

CHAPTER 2: ARBITRABILITY OF STATUTORY CLAIMS 69

CHAPTER 4: ARBITRATION PROVISIONS — CONTRACT FORMATION AND UNCONSCIONABILITY 215

CHAPTER 5: CONSTRUING ARBITRATION PROVISIONS TO DETERMINE ARBITRABILITY AND A LOOK AT RELATED ISSUES INVOLVING POTENTIAL CLASS ACTIONS AND MULTI-PARTY DISPUTES 325

TABLE OF AUTHORITIES

CASES

OTHER AUTHORITIES

Chapter 1

INTRODUCTORY MATERIALS

§ 1.01 SOME HISTORICAL PERSPECTIVE

Arbitration is an alternative to the courts for the resolution of civil disputes. These materials deal almost exclusively with those arbitral processes used to resolve disputes which arise in connection with commercial dealings between businesses, between businesses and their customers, and between businesses and their own employees. While it was not always so, commercial arbitration today is essentially a creature of statute requiring courts to enforce agreements to arbitrate and resulting arbitral awards. While arbitration is seen as an alternative to judicial resolution of party disputes, it is the courts that, particularly in more modern times, have provided a limited but vital superstructure.

Commercial arbitration was a common voluntary dispute mechanism long before its modern day involvement with the legislative and judicial branches of government. Arbitration, for example, was an integral part of the very early Western forms of organized mercantile activity. By the thirteenth century, guilds in England had arbitral mechanisms, and the British courts often referred commercial matters to merchant arbitration.[1] Arbitration carried over to the American colonies, and was often conducted under the auspices of various chambers of

[1] For a broad historical perspective, see Soia Mentshikoff, *Commercial Arbitration*, 61 COLUM. L. REV. 846 (1961).

commerce, including the one in New York.[2]

Several advantages were thought to attach to using arbitrators in mercantile disputes, and these perceived advantages to judicial resolution will repeatedly come up for consideration and analysis in these materials. They are:

> 1. Arbitrators can be chosen for their expertise in matters merchant, including unwritten custom and usage.
>
> 2. Arbitrators, at least in certain types of cases, are typically considered less strictly bound by legal precedent than are the courts, so they have greater flexibility to reach a result fitting the specific circumstances of a case, if need be by compromise or untraditional remedy.
>
> 3. Arbitration is supposed to be less hostile, less costly, less time-consuming, and less entrenched than court litigation and can be a far less unsettling process than litigation among group members whose relationships are designed to remain mutually beneficial despite occasional disagreements.

Arbitration would also flourish in other types of groups, particularly those not entirely comfortable with having their members judged by a governmental arm applying its conceptions of law rather than their own. Various religious groups would refer disputes for resolution by their leaders in keeping with religious laws and custom. Foreign ethnic groups would do likewise in an effort to preserve their heritage.

In the uses of arbitration just described, group pressure and practices can go a long way towards compelling members to arbitrate. A member of a trade or business association, for example, may have its membership conditioned on compliance with its arbitration rules and awards. In other groupings, the threat of commercial ostracism may well be enough to force participation in arbitration. Nonetheless, to repeat, the key to the explosive expansion of arbitration in the last century were the statutory provisions requiring judicial enforcement of agreements to arbitrate. Prior to those enactments, the common law courts would not enforce arbitral agreements with respect to subsequently arising disputes.

---

[2] *See generally* B. Mann, *The Formalization of Informal Law: Arbitration before the American Revolution,* 59 N.Y.U. L. REV. 443 (1984).

Another critical development, most of which has taken place in the past few decades, is that arbitration has been extended to non-mercantile claims arising under various civil rights, securities and other statutes designed to protect so-called "public rights" rather than private contractual ones. With this expansion, which has often been under the lead of the United States Supreme Court, businesses today often receive from their customers and employees contractual undertakings to arbitrate all disputes which may arise between them. As arbitration becomes common not only in the relatively arms-length mercantile setting but also in employment, broker-customer and consumer relationships which are often adhesory, the courts, and at times regulatory agencies, have had to expand their supervisory role to avoid oppression of the weaker party.

To understand fully just how entrenched modern arbitral systems have become, one must also focus on how the United States Supreme Court, under principles of federalism, has largely deprived the states of the power to limit arbitrability on grounds of their own public policy. Much attention will be paid to what has, over the past decades, become a fascinating exercise in constitutional law—the sweeping federal preemption principles which often require state courts to honor the so-called "federal law of arbitration" with its underlying strong pro-arbitration policy.

§ 1.02 THE STATUTORY FRAMEWORK

New York has long been a leading center for arbitral resolution of commercial disputes. These materials thus contain a substantial number of New York cases. In 1920, New York enacted its Arbitration Act. That statute, now found in articles 7501 thru 7514 of the New York Civil Practice Law and Rules (Appendix 1), became the prototype for arbitral statutes adopted by Congress and many states. The Federal Arbitration Act ("FAA") (Appendix 2) was enacted in 1925 and, as we shall see, is designed to cover virtually all disputes "involving interstate commerce," a traditional realm of congressional regulation under the Commerce Clause in the United States Constitution. These materials will also reference the Uniform Arbitration Act (Appendix 3), which is patterned after the New York statute and has been enacted, in either original or amended form, in a majority of states.

All but two states have arbitration statutes. The typical arbitration statute does several critical things. First, it provides specifically for judicial enforcement of agreements to arbitrate existing or future disputes, irrespective of whether said disputes appear to be judicially cognizable or meritorious.[3] Indeed, Section 2 of the FAA is explicit that such arbitral agreements "shall be valid, irrevocable, and enforceable, save upon such grounds as exist at law or inequity for the revocation of any contract." The United States Supreme Court has taken this to mean that the equitable bases of avoidance applicable to other contracts apply to agreements to arbitrate as well. *See* Doctors Associates v. Casarotto, 517 U.S. 681, 686 (1996) ("Generally applicable contract defenses, such as fraud, duress, or unconscionability, may be applied to invalidate arbitration agreements without contravening § 2."). The typical pre-dispute provision, if broad, requires "arbitration of any disputes to arise under or in connection with this agreement."

Second, the typical arbitration statute provides the courts with express authorization to stay court litigation of claims subject to agreement to arbitrate and to refer such claims to arbitration—essentially, then, valid agreements to arbitrate are specifically enforceable. At this time, review the contents of Sections 3 and 4 of the FAA (Appendix 2). Also, take a careful look at their counterparts in N.Y. C.P.L.R. 7503(a) and Section 2 of the Uniform Arbitration Act ("UAA"). It is also either explicit (N.Y. C.P.L.R. 7503(a) and Section 2(b) of the UAA) or, with respect to the FAA, implicit, that a court is empowered to stay arbitral proceedings not authorized by contract.

Third, success in arbitration might be pyrrhic unless the resulting awards were judicially enforceable. While the need to maintain good standing within a group or association may provide the requisite incentive to honor awards, in many situations the prevailing party must petition for judicial confirmation to give the award the full force of a judgment with the accompanying enforcement tools. *See* FAA, 9 U.S.C. § 9; N.Y. C.P.L.R. 7501; UAA, § 11. As such, the judgment will be fully enforceable in the courts (compulsory disclosure of assets, attachment, foreclosure, etc.).

---

[3] *See, e.g.*, N.Y. C.P.L.R. 7501 (the dispute need not even be "tenable"); *see also* UAA, § 1.

We will be making constant references to the other types of statutory provisions which govern the critical interaction of arbitral processes with the courts. Before we leave that subject for now, check each of the Acts referenced above for what they provide concerning judicial grounds for overturning awards and refusing to give them the force of judgments. Are arbitral awards subject to full judicial review? What about upsetting awards predicated on erroneous factual determinations or failures to apply established rules of law? Apparently, there is a policy of attaching finality to awards, even if they are "wrong," so long as certain essential fairness criteria are met in the hearing of the case. As you will see, arbitrators are not generally bound by rules of evidence. Can you identify certain types of arbitral claims deserving of closer judicial scrutiny? What about statutory claims covering so called "public" or "mandatory" rights against discrimination, securities fraud and the like?

Before proceeding, a word about editing. All case opinions are edited, and many are substantially abbreviated. Deletions of entire paragraphs are marked with asterisks. Many citations are eliminated as well. Retained footnotes to opinions are designated by their numbers.

§ 1.03 INTRODUCTORY CASES: OVERCOMING THE REVOCABILITYOF PRE-DISPUTE ARBITRATION AGREEMENTS

U.S. Asphalt Refining Co. v. Trinidad Lake Petroleum Co.

United States District Court, S.D.N.Y., 1915.
222 F. 1006.

- HOUGH, DISTRICT JUDGE.

One of these actions is brought for the alleged breach of the charter party of the steamship Russian Prince, and the other for a similar breach of a like charter party relating to the steamship Roumanian Prince. Libelant is a corporation of South Dakota. Respondent was the chartered owner of the steamships above named. It is a British corporation, and the vessels are of British registry.

The charter parties by which libelant took the steamers from respondent were made in London, and granted libelant the right to use the vessels in any lawful traffic in most parts of the world. As matter of fact the steamers were employed between Trinidad and United States ports until the outbreak of war in August, 1914, when it is alleged that the vessels were wrongfully withdrawn from charterer's service. These actions in personam were begun with clause of foreign attachment, and appearance enforced by seizure of funds within this jurisdiction. Before any steps in the actions other than appearing and giving security for the seized property had been taken, these motions were made.

The charter party of each steamer contained the following very ordinary clause:

> Any dispute arising under this charter shall be settled in London by arbitration, the owners and charters each appointing an arbitrator, and the two so chosen, if they do not agree, shall appoint an umpire, the decision of whom shall be final. Should either party refuse or neglect to appoint an arbitrator within 21 days of being required to do so by the other party, the arbitrator appointed may make a final decision alone, and this decision shall be binding upon both parties. For the purpose of enforcing any award, this agreement shall be made a rule of court.

There can be no doubt that this was a submission to arbitration, and for that reason was a contract between the parties to this action. Under the law of the contract—i.e. England—this arbitration agreement was at the time of making the charter parties entirely valid, and any endeavor to do exactly what libelant has done by bringing these suits would have been restrained by the English courts, acting under authority of the English Arbitration Act of 1889 (chapter 49–, 52–53 Victoria).

The contentions of the parties litigant may therefore be summed up as follows: Respondent urges that the contract for arbitration contained in the charter parties was valid and enforceable when and where it was made, and must consequently be enforced everywhere, unless some positive rule of the law of the forum prevents such recognition and enforcement. Libelant asserts that, whether the contract was or was not good at the time and place of making, it has always been invalid under the law of the United States and most of the states thereof, with the admitted and asserted result that an American may make a solemn contract of this nature in England and repudiate it at will in America with the approbation of the courts of his own country.

There has long been a great variety of available reasons for refusing to give effect to the agreements of men of mature age, and presumably sound judgment, when the intended effect of the agreements was to prevent proceedings in any and all courts and substitute therefor the decision of arbitrators. The remarkably simple nature of this libelant's contract breaking has led me to consider at some length the nature and history of the reasons adduced to justify the sort of conduct, by no means new, but remarkably well illustrated by these libels.

It has never been denied that the hostility of English-speaking courts to arbitration contracts probably originated (as Lord Campbell said in *Scott v. Avery*, 4 H.L.Cas. 811)—

> in the contests of the courts of ancient times for extension of jurisdiction—all of them being opposed to anything that would altogether deprive every one of them of jurisdiction.

A more unworthy genesis cannot be imagined. Since (at the latest) the time of Lord Kenyon, it has been customary to stand rather upon the antiquity of the rule than upon its excellence or reason:

"It is not necessary now to say how this point ought to have been determined if it were res integra—it having been decided again and again," etc. Per Kenyon. J., in Thompson v. Charnock, 8 T.R. 139.

There is little difference between Lord Kenyon's remark and the words of Cardozo, J., uttered within a few months in *Meacham v. Jamestown, etc., R.R. Co.*, 211 N.Y. at page 354.

'It is true that some judges have expressed the belief that parties ought to be free to contract about such matters as they please. In this state the law has long been settled to the contrary.'

Nevertheless the legal mind must assign some reason in order to decide anything with spiritual quiet, and the causes advanced for refusing to compel men to abide by their arbitration contracts may apparently be subdivided as follows:

> (a) The contract is in its nature revocable.
>
> (b) Such contracts are against public policy.
>
> (c) The covenant to refer is but collateral to the main contract, and may be disregarded, leaving the contract keeper to his action for damages for breach of such collateral covenant.
>
> (d) Any contract tending to wholly oust the courts of jurisdiction violates the spirit of the laws creating the courts, in that it is not competent for private persons either to increase or diminish the statutory juridical power.

Doctrine of Revocability.

This seems to rest on *Vynior's Case*, 8 Coke, 81b, and is now somewhat old-fashioned, although it appears in *Oregon, etc., Bank v. American, etc., Co.* (C.C.) 35 Fed. 23, with due citations of authority; and in *Tobey v. County of Bristol*, 3 Story, 800, Fed. Cas. No. 14,065, it is treated at great length.

The Public Policy Doctrine.

No reason for the simple statement that arbitration agreements are against public policy has ever been advanced, except that it must be against such policy to oust the courts of jurisdiction. This is hardly a variant of the reasoning ascribed by Lord Campbell to the "courts of ancient times":

> "Such stipulations (for arbitration) are regarded as against the policy of the common law, as having a tendency to exclude the jurisdiction of the courts."

Hurst v. Litchfield, 39 N.Y. 377.

"Such agreements have repeatedly been held to be against public policy and void." Prince Co. v. Lehman (D.C.) 39 Fed. 704."

The above are two examples of the cruder forms of statement; but of late years the higher courts have been somewhat chary of the phrase "public policy," and in *Insurance Co. v. Morse*, 20 Wall. 457, Hunt, J., quotes approvingly from Story's Commentaries, thus:

> Where the stipulation, though not against the policy of the law, yet is an effort to divest the ordinary jurisdiction of the common tribunals of justice, such as an agreement in case of dispute to refer the same to arbitration, a court of equity will not, any more than a court of law, interfere to enforce the agreement, but will leave the parties to their own good pleasure in regard to such agreements.

But neither the court nor the commentator pointed out any other method by which an arbitration agreement could be against the policy of the law, unless it were by seeking to divest the 'ordinary jurisdiction of the common tribunals of justice.'

Having built up the doctrine that any contract which involves an "ouster of jurisdiction" is invalid, the Supreme Court of the United States has been able of late years to give decision without ever going behind that statement. Thus in *Insurance Co. v. Morse*, supra, it is said:

> "Agreements in advance to oust the courts of the jurisdiction conferred by law are illegal and void."

In *Doyle v. Continental Insurance Co.*, 94 U.S. 535, the case last cited is distinctly reaffirmed. The lower courts have followed, and in *Perkins v. United States*, etc., Co. (C.C.) 16 Fed. 513, Wallace, J., said:

> "It is familiar doctrine that a simple agreement inserted in a contract, that the parties will refer any dispute arising thereunder to arbitration, will not oust courts of law of their ordinary jurisdiction."

* * * *

Whatever form of statement the rule takes, the foregoing citations show that it always amounts to the same thing, viz.: The courts will scarcely permit any other body of men to even partially perform judicial work, and will never permit the absorption of all the business growing out of disputes over a contract by anybody of arbitrators, unless compelled to such action by statute.

* * * *

The English Arbitration Act, supra, is such a statute. It has compelled the courts of that country to abandon the doctrine that it is wrong or wicked to agree to stay away from the courts when disputes arise. It is highly characteristic of lawyers that, when thus coerced by the Legislature, the wisdom of previous decisions begins to be doubted. In *Hamlyn v. Talisker Distillery* (1894) App. Cas. 202, Lord Watson said:

> "The rule that a reference to arbitrators not named cannot be enforced does not appear to me to rest on any essential considerations of public policy. Even if an opposite inference were deducible from the authorities by which it was established, the rule has been so largely trenched upon by the legislation of the last 50 years . . . that I should hesitate to affirm that the policy upon which it was originally based could now be regarded as of cardinal importance."

Neither the Legislature of New York nor the Congress has seen fit thus to modernize the ideas of the judges of their respective jurisdictions.

* * * *

Finally it has been well said by Cardozo, J., in *Meacham v. Jamestown*, etc., R.R. Co., supra, that:

> "An agreement that . . . differences arising under a contract shall be submitted to arbitration relates to the law of remedies, and the law that governs remedies is the law of the forum."

It follows that the final question for determination under these motions is whether the law as laid down by the Supreme Court of the United States permits the enforcement as a remedy of the arbitration clause contained in a contract, assuming that such clause (as here) is intended to oust the courts and all courts of their jurisdiction.

I think the decisions cited show beyond question that the Supreme Court has laid down the rule that such a complete ouster of jurisdiction as is shown by the clause quoted from the charter parties is void in a federal forum. It was within the power of that tribunal to make this rule. Inferior courts may fail to find convincing reasons for it; but the rule must be obeyed, and these motions be severally denied.

NOTES

1. Why is arbitration, according to the preceding case, a "remedy?" What is the source of new remedies? New York's statute was enacted about five years after the last case was decided.

2. The English Arbitration Act of 1889 was designed to overcome hostility to arbitration shown by the British courts. Unlike its subsequent American counterparts, the British statute did provide for judicial review for errors of law.

Kulukundis Shipping Co. v. Amtorg Trading Corp.

United States Court of Appeals, Second Circuit, 1942.
126 F.2d 978.

- FRANK, CIRCUIT JUDGE.

In considering these contentions in the light of the precedents, it is necessary to take into account the history of the judicial attitude towards arbitration: The English courts, while giving full effect to agreements to submit controversies to arbitration after they had ripened into arbitrators' awards, would—over a long period beginning at the end of the 17th century—do little or nothing to prevent or make irksome the breach of such agreements when they were still executory. Prior to 1687, such a breach could be made costly: a penal bond given to abide the result of an arbitration had a real bite, since a breach of the bond's condition led to a judgment for the amount of the penalty. It was so held in 1609 in *Vynoir's Case*, 8 Coke Rep. 81b. To be sure, Coke there, in a dictum, citing precedents, dilated on the inherent revocability of the authority given to an arbitrator; such a revocation was not too important, however, if it resulted in a stiff judgment on a penal bond. But the Statute of Fines and Penalties (8 & 9 Wm.III c. 11, § 8), enacted in 1687, provided that, in an action on any bond given for performance of agreements, while judgment would be entered for the penalty, execution should issue only for the damages actually sustained. Coke's dictum as to revocability, uttered seventy-eight years earlier, now took on a new significance, as it was now held that for breach of an undertaking to arbitrate the damages were only nominal. Recognizing the effect of the impact of this statute on executory arbitration agreements, Parliament, eleven years later, enacted a statute, 9 Wm.III c. 15 (1698), designed to remedy the situation by providing that, if an agreement to arbitrate so provided, it could be made a 'rule of court' (i.e., a court order), in which event it became irrevocable, and one who revoked it would be subject to punishment for contempt of court; but the submission was revocable until such a rule of court had been obtained. This statute, limited in scope, was narrowly construed and was of little help. The ordinary executory arbitration agreement thus lost all real efficacy since it was not specifically enforceable in equity, and was held not to constitute the basis of a plea in bar in, or a stay of, a suit on the original cause of action. In admiralty, the rulings were much the same.

It has been well said that "the legal mind must assign some reason in order to decide anything with spiritual quiet." And so, by way of rationalization, it became fashionable in the middle of the 18th century to say that such agreements were against public policy because they "oust the jurisdiction" of the courts. But that was a quaint explanation, inasmuch as an award, under an arbitration agreement, enforced both at law and in equity, was no less an ouster; and the same was true of releases and covenants not to sue, which were given full effect. Moreover, the agreement to arbitrate was not illegal, since suit could be maintained for its breach. Here was a clear instance of what Holmes called a 'right' to break a contract and to substitute payment of damages for non-performance; as, in this type of case, the damages were only nominal, that 'right' was indeed meaningful.

An effort has been made to justify this judicial hostility to the executory arbitration agreement on the ground that arbitrations, if unsupervised by the courts, are undesirable, and that legislation was needed to make possible such supervision. But if that was the reason for unfriendliness to such executory agreements, then the courts should also have refused to aid arbitrations when they ripened into awards. And what the English courts, especially the equity courts, did in other contexts, shows that, if they had the will, they could have devised means of protecting parties to arbitrations. Instead, they restrictively interpreted successive statutes intended to give effect to executory arbitrations. No similar hostility was displayed by the Scotch courts. Lord Campbell explained the English attitude as due to the desire of the judges, at a time when their salaries came largely from fees, to avoid loss of income. Indignation has been voiced at this suggestion; perhaps it is unjustified. Perhaps the true explanation is the hypnotic power of the phrase, "oust the jurisdiction." Give a bad dogma a good name and its bite may become as bad as its bark.

In 1855, in *Scott v. Avery*, 5 H.C.L. 811, the tide seemed to have turned. There it was held that if a policy made an award of damages by arbitrators a condition precedent to a suit on the policy, a failure to submit to arbitration would preclude such a suit, even if the policy left to the arbitrators the consideration of all the elements of liability. But, despite later legislation, the hostility of the English courts to executory arbitrations resumed somewhat after *Scott v. Avery*, and seems never to have been entirely dissipated.

That English attitude was largely taken over in the 19th century by most courts in this country. Indeed, in general, they would not go as far as *Scott v. Avery*, supra, and continued to use the "ouster of jurisdiction" concept: An executory agreement to arbitrate would not be given specific performance or furnish the basis of a stay of proceedings on the original cause of action. Nor would it be given effect as a plea in bar, except in limited instances, i.e., in the case of an agreement expressly or impliedly making it a condition precedent to litigation that there be an award determining some preliminary question of subsidiary fact upon which any liability was to be contingent. Hamilton v. Liverpool, 1890, etc., Ins. Co., 136 U.S. 242. In the case of broader executory agreements, no more than nominal dangers would be given for a breach.

Generally speaking, then, the courts of this country were unfriendly to executory arbitration agreements. The lower federal courts, feeling bound to comply with the precedents, nevertheless became critical of this judicial hostility. There were intimations in the Supreme Court that perhaps the old view might be abandoned, but in the cases hinting at that newer attitude the issue was not raised. Effective state arbitration statutes were enacted beginning with the New York Statute of 1920.

The United States Arbitration Act of 1925 was sustained as constitutional, initially in its application to cases arising in admiralty. Marine Transit Corp. v. Dreyfus, 1932, 284 U.S. 263. The purpose of that Act was deliberately to alter the judicial atmosphere previously existing. The report of the House Committee stated, in part:

> Arbitration agreements are purely matters of

> contract, and the effect of the bill is simply to make the contracting party live up to his agreement. He can no longer refuse to perform his contract when it becomes disadvantageous to him. An arbitration agreement is placed upon the same footing as other contracts, where it belongs . . . . The need for the law arises from an anachronism of our American law. Some centuries ago, because of the jealousy of the English courts for their own jurisdiction, they refused to enforce specific agreements to arbitrate upon the ground that the courts were thereby ousted from their jurisdiction. This jealousy survived for so long a period that the principle became firmly embedded in the English common law and was adopted with it by the American courts. The courts have felt that the precedent was too strongly fixed to be overturned without legislative enactment, although they have frequently criticized the rule and recognized its illogical nature and the injustice which results from it. The bill declares simply that such agreements for arbitration shall be enforced, and provides a procedure in the Federal courts for their enforcement . . . . It is particularly appropriate that the action should be taken at this time when there is so much agitation against the costliness and delays of litigation. These matters can be largely eliminated by agreements for arbitration, if arbitration agreements are made valid and enforceable.

* * * *

NOTES

1. Before the enacting of the modern arbitral statutes, awards arising from voluntary submission to arbitration tended to be automatically enforced in the law courts, but could be, and were occasionally challenged for denial of essential due process ("fraud") in courts of equity. *E.g.*, Davy v. Faw, 11 U.S. 171, 175 (1812); Brush v. Fuller, 38 N.W. 446, 448 (Mich. 1888); Newland v. Douglass, 2 Johns.

62, 63 (N.Y. 1806) ("[A] suit at law will not lie to re-examine the merits of an award."). The old equitable grounds for rejection of an award—fraud, bias, and corruption—were those which found their way into the modern arbitration statutes.

2. If the courts have traditionally enforced arbitral awards issued after the parties voluntarily participate in arbitration through the award stage, what policy distinctions would cause reluctance to enforce pre-dispute agreements to arbitrate?

3. Under Article III, section 2 of the United States Constitution, it is Congress that creates federal trial and intermediate appellate courts and sets their subject matter jurisdiction. Was the main planned role for the federal courts the resolution of private civil disputes? *See* Federalist Papers Nos. 78 and 80, both of which were penned by Alexander Hamilton.

4. The federal and state courts commonly exert the power to review legislative enactments and exercise of executive power for constitutional compliance. The courts, then, perform a vital and unique governmental "checks and balances" function through the issuance of decisions concerning actual or proposed exercises of power by their sister branches. These decisions carry the force of precedent. The overlap between courts and arbitration is in the area of private disputes. Here too, court decisions set precedents while commercial arbitral awards, which are very often unreasoned and wholly summary, do not. To what extent has Congress empowered the federal courts to hear private disputes? Federal subject matter jurisdiction is generally based on "federal questions" arising under federal statutory or admiralty law, or on diversity of citizenship. *See* 28 U.S.C. §§ 1331–32. Arbitrations are typically conducted at a location selected by the parties. Arbitrations conducted at private locations such as a law office are called "ad hoc." Most arbitrations are conducted before specialized tribunals which have their own procedural rules, so-called panels of eligible neutral arbitrators, hearing rooms, and administrative personnel to handle scheduling and related matters. These materials often refer to the American Arbitration Association (the "AAA"), the largest such organization in the United States. The AAA, which is non-profit, has specialized rules for different types of disputes including international, construction, employment, and the like. The AAA, which is discussed further in section 1.10 *infra*, has Commercial Rules which apply to most mercantile disputes (Appendix

4). Almost all arbitrations in the securities industry are handled by the Financial Industry Regulatory Authority ("FINRA"), which is discussed further in section 1.11, *infra*. Excerpts from its Rules are in Appendix 6. The largest private arbitral organization is JAMS, which is known for a roster of neutral arbitrators including many retired judges. JAMS is worldwide, and handles about ten thousand cases per year, many of which are successfully mediated before going to binding arbitral determinations. Parties to a contract can limit arbitration to specific disputes (*e.g.*, the amount of royalties payable under a license versus whether the license has been violated), but often use a broad clause like this:

> Any dispute arising under or relating to this agreement shall be submitted to binding and final arbitration before the American Arbitration Association (New York City location) pursuant to its Commercial Rules then in effect. Any award shall be subject to confirmation in any court having jurisdiction thereof.

Remember, however, that arbitration is a creature of contract. The parties can make their own rules in lieu of those which an arbitral tribunal would otherwise apply. *See* AAA, COMMERCIAL RULES, Rule 1(a), found in Appendix 4. Principles of contractual unconscionability may limit party discretion in this regard, as we shall see.

Berkovitz v. Arbib & Houlberg, Inc.

New York Court of Appeals, 1921.
230 N.Y. 261.

- CARDOZO, J.

* * * *

2. *The validity of the statute remains to be considered.*

(a) The statute is assailed as inconsistent with article 1, § 2, of the Constitution of the state, which secures the right of trial by jury. The right is one that may be waived .... It was waived by the consent to arbitrate. We are told that the consent must be disregarded as illusory because the parties could not be held to it till this statute was adopted. A consent, none the less, it was, however deficient may once have been the remedy to enforce it. Those who gave it, did so in view of the possibility that a better remedy might come. They took the chances of the future. They must abide by its vicissitudes.

(b) The statute is assailed again as abridging the general jurisdiction of the Supreme Court, which article 6, § 1, of the Constitution of the state continues unimpaired.

Jurisdiction exists that rights may be maintained. Rights are not maintained that jurisdiction may exist. The people, in establishing a Supreme Court to administer the law, did not petrify the law which the court is to administer. . . . Article 6, § 1, preserves the existence of the court "with general jurisdiction in law and equity," but the same article in section 3 secures to the Legislature "the same power to alter and regulate the jurisdiction and proceedings in law and in equity that it has heretofore exercised." When change shall be held to trench on jurisdiction in a prohibited degree cannot be known with certainty in advance of the event as the result of general definition. "The process of judicial inclusion and exclusion" must serve to trace the line. Power lodged in the Supreme Court is not to be withdrawn merely that it may be transferred and established somewhere else. Power, though not transferred, is still not to be withdrawn, if fundamental or inherent in the conception of a court with general jurisdiction in equity and law. Changes, we may assume, will be condemned if subversive of historic traditions of dignity and power. Such is not the change effected by this statute. The Supreme Court does not lose a power inherent in its very being when it loses power to give aid in the repudiation of a contract, concluded without fraud or error, whereby differences are to be settled without resort to litigation. For the right to nullify is substituted the duty to enforce. Contending parties have contracted that the merits of their controversy shall be conditioned upon the report of arbitrators, as upon any other extrinsic fact which agreement might prescribe. Whether they have so contracted is a question which the court must still determine for itself. Arbitration Law, § 3. If the contract has not been made or is invalid, the court will proceed, as in any other case, to a determination of the merits. If it has been made and is valid, the court will stay its hand till the extrinsic fact is ascertained, and the condition thus fulfilled. That done, its doors are open for whatever measure of relief the situation may exact. The award will be enforced if valid, and for cause will be annulled. "In common language where no attempt is made at logical accuracy," it is sometimes said that the contract of arbitration 'ousts the jurisdiction' of the judges. *Wilson v. Glasgow Tramways & O. Co.*, supra. "In strictness, however, it does not oust the jurisdiction, but merely introduces a new plea into the cause" on which the judge as at common law is under a duty to decide. *Wilson v. Glasgow Tramways & O. Co.*, supra. The situation is the same in substance as when effect is given to a release or to a covenant not to sue. Jurisdiction is not renounced, but the time and manner of its exercise are adapted to the convention of the parties restricting the media of proof. Long before the statute there was a like withholding of relief whenever the subject-matter of arbitration, instead of extending to all differences, was limited to some . . . . There was a like refusal to permit the litigation of the merits when the contract, though general, was no longer executory but had ripened into an award. The change resulting from the statute is one of measure and degree.

We think there is no departure from constitutional restrictions in this legislative declaration of the public policy of the state. The ancient rule, with its exceptions and refinements, was criticized by many judges as anomalous and unjust. Its hold even upon the common law was hesitating and feeble. We are now asked to declare it so imbedded in the very foundations of our jurisprudence and the structure of our courts that nothing less than an amendment of the Constitution is competent to change it. We will not go so far. The judges might have changed the rule themselves if they had abandoned some early precedents, as at times they seemed inclined to do.

(c) Finally, the statute is said to violate article 1, § 10, of the Constitution of the United States, on the ground that it impairs the obligation of a contract. There is no merit in the contention. The obligation of the contract is strengthened, not impaired.

NOTE

1. The federal and typical state constitution preserves the right to trial by jury. By agreeing to arbitrate, a party waives any otherwise applicable jury procedure. Should this consideration ever create reluctance to enforce certain types of agreements to arbitrate? Various types of contracts, while not providing for arbitration, do contain

reciprocal waivers of right to trial by jury, and these waivers are typically enforced. There is some authority that they must be "knowingly" made. *See* Nat'l Equip. Rental, Ltd. v. Hendrix, 565 F.2d 255, 258 (2d Cir. 1977). For discussion and comparison of consent standards for enforcement of contractual jury waivers and enforcement of contractual agreements to arbitrate, see Stephen J. Ware, *Arbitration Clauses, Jury-Waiver Clauses, and Other Contractual Waivers of Constitutional Rights*, 67 L. & CONTEMP. PROBS. 167 (2004). Given the requirement in section 2 of the FAA that arbitration agreements be made as enforceable as other contracts, what standard of assent would appear to apply? Must contractual assent, in general, be "knowing?" What about arbitral provisions in standardized agreements? Under section 211(3) of the RESTATEMENT SECOND OF CONTRACTS, for instance, if the proponent of the form has reason to understand that the typical counterparty would not consent to a particular provision if he knew about it, that term drops out of the agreement. Are arbitral provisions in this category? Perhaps it is this possibility which explains why form agreements with arbitration clauses often contains a disclosure of that fact on the first page, sometimes in large print. A FINRA regulation requires such disclosure on brokerage form agreements with customers. *See* FINRA MANUAL § 2263 (2009). Is awareness of an arbitral provision the same as "knowing" assent to it? In non-jury cases, and in connection with appeals, courts often issue reasoned opinions which have the force of stare decisis. We shall see that arbitral awards can have res judicata and collateral estoppel effects, but it should again be emphasized that such awards, at least outside the labor area where decisions are more formal and reasoned do not generally have even limited precedential impact. Does this relax lingering concerns about ouster of judicial jurisdiction?

§ 1.04 INTRODUCTORY CASES: ARBITRAL DISCRETION TO DEPART FROM "THE LAW"

In re Arbitration Between SCM Corp. & Fisher Park Lane Comp.

New York Court of Appeals, 1976.
40 N.Y.2d 788.

- JONES, J.

* * * *

Finally, because the issue has been briefed and argued expansively by the parties in this action, was explicitly addressed by the court below, and is one on which lower courts have differed, we take this occasion to express our disagreement with the position articulated by the Appellate Division that arbitrators have no power under a broad arbitration clause to grant what we would think of as the remedy of reformation. Arbitrators have power to fashion remedies appropriate to the resolution of the dispute between the parties before them. To the extent that relief in the nature of reformation might be deemed an appropriate remedy for the controversies existing between this tenant and this landlord, the award of such a remedy would fall within the authority of arbitrators acting under a broad arbitration clause. "It is customary and appropriate for arbitrators to pass upon claims for reformation for mutual mistake, often applying principles more liberal than judicial equity" (International Union of Operating Engrs. v. Carl A. Morse, Inc., 7 Cir., 529 F.2d 574, 580; American Home Assur. Co. v. American Fid. & Cas. Co., 2 Cir., 356 F.2d 690; Elkouri and Elkouri, How Arbitration Works, p. 346). The function of arbitrators is to "find a just solution" to the controversy between the parties (Lentine v. Fundaro, 29 N.Y.2d 382, 385); to that end it will be for them to "fashion the remedy appropriate to the wrong" (*Matter of Paver & Wildfoerster (Catholic High School Assn.)*, 38 N.Y.2d 669, 677, Supra). Moreover, the rules of the American Arbitration Association adopted by the parties now before the court expressly provide that "(t)he Arbitrator may grant any remedy or relief which he deems just and equitable and within the scope of the agreement of the parties."

In arbitration parties seek the resolution of differences which have arisen between them in concrete factual settings free from the requirements and expectations familiar to judicial proceedings with respect both to the formulation of pleadings and causes of action and to historical and current legal theories as to the availability of remedies. The awards of arbitrators are not subject to judicial review for errors of law or of fact. Nor should there be the control which would flow from the exercise of such power of review. Submissions are for determinations based on the Ad hoc application of broad principles of justice and fairness in the particular instance. Reliance is not placed on continuity of tribunal personnel or operation. Predictability is not an objective and awards do not have, nor is it intended that they should have, the precedential value that we attach to judicial determinations. Thus analytical structure and synthesis take on a different function. In the present context, for instance, it would be unimportant whether an arbitrator were to formulate his resolution of the landlord's claim for increased additional rent in a conclusion that the initial intent of the parties was that the percentage figure in the lease be higher and accordingly that the lease should be rewritten to manifest that intent, or, on the other hand, in a determination that in all the circumstances justice dictated that the differences between the parties should be disposed as though the percentage figure had been higher. This is not to suggest that awards are not based on analysis, logic and experience. It is to say that the channels of legal procedure and thought understandably may often be found to be lacking, or at least not determinative.

* * * *

▪ FUCHSBERG, J., concurring.

I too vote for affirmance; however, I cannot concur with the majority's suggestion that reformation is an arbitral issue.

With the exception of a contrary dictum contained in *Matter of Agora Development Corp.* (Low) (19 A.D.2d 126), and a Federal case relying upon the dictum (American Home Assur. Co. v. American Fid. & Cas. Co., 2d Cir., 356 F.2d 690), the courts of this State have consistently held that unless the parties confer the authority upon him, an arbitrator lacks power to reform or change the contract itself (Stewart-Scott Constr. Co. v. Schaefer Brewing Co., 41 A.D.2d 788; Matter of Glenwood Jewish Center (Marard Caterers), 39 A.D.2d 536).

These decisions, involving arbitration clauses broader than those in the case before us, are based upon the settled rule "that a party may not be required to submit to arbitration matters which he has not agreed to arbitrate" (Matter of Macy & Co. (National Sleep Prods.), 39 N.Y.2d 268, 270). Manifestly, it violates this fundamental principle to suggest, as the majority does, that SCM by agreeing to arbitrate one aspect of potential disputes that might arise between the parties, i.e., those arising out of the explicit escalation provisions, also agreed to confer upon the arbitrator authority to rewrite the contract. "It is not the function of an arbitrator . . . to decide in what respects the contract in question should be modified . . . . Contract modifications are not traditionally matters for arbitration" (City Elec. v. Local Union 77, Int. Brotherhood of Elec. Workers, 9 Cir., 517 F.2d 616, 619).

Moreover, reliance upon prior decisions of this court holding that arbitrators may 'fashion the remedy appropriate to the wrong' (e.g., Matter of Paver & Wildfoerster (Catholic High School Assn.), 38 N.Y.2d 669, 677) begs the question of whether the claim to be arbitrated is within the scope of the arbitration clause. Only if the claim is encompassed by the clause do the arbitrators have discretion to grant the relief they deem proper. Thus, Rule 42 of the American Arbitration Association provides that the arbitrator may "grant any remedy or relief which he deems just and equitable and within the scope of the agreement."

"(G)iven the eminently desirable freedom from judicial overview of law and facts" prevailing in arbitration, the caution against making the proceedings a "trap for the unwary," recently expressed by this court in holding that arbitrators lack the power to award punitive damages (Garrity v. Lyle Stuart, Inc., 40 N.Y.2d 354, 359), is equally applicable here. The power of reformation would likewise "mean that the scope of determination by arbitrators . . . would be both unpredictable and uncontrollable."

NOTES

1. In *SCM,* six of the seven participating judges approved of the dictum concerning arbitral reformation of contracts. When parties provide broadly for arbitration of "all disputes arising from or in connection" with their contract, are they empowering the arbitrator to reform absent traditional fraud or mistake grounds? Is such grant of reformation a mere error of law, or is it an act exceeding the power of the arbitrator? Why might such characterization matter under N.Y. C.P.L.R. 7511, or under Section 10 of the FAA?

2. *SCM* involved arbitral adjustment of a rental escalation clause which apparently failed to track the landlord's increased costs. Under traditional contract law, is an unintended failure to provide adequately for increased costs of performance a "mistake?" How often do

unanticipated cost increases yield impracticability? Courts, it is said, have the power in certain types of situations to reform so as to "divide the baby" in the Solomonic sense. *See, e.g.*, U.C.C. § 2-615 cmt. 6 (2003), which permits a court to make compromise adjustments to contractual obligations where there is borderline impracticability. *See also* RESTATEMENT (SECOND) OF CONTRACTS § 272(2) (1981), which, in cases of impracticability, empowers courts to "grant relief on such terms as justice requires."

3. Given that so many commercial arbitral awards are written but unreasoned, how easy would it be to challenge a monetary award as a reformatory "compromise" between the competing contractual constructions or other positions advanced by the parties?

4. Based on *SCM's* dictum about "reformation," and given the lack of judicial review for errors of fact or law, who has more power—trial judges or arbitrators?

5. Note the Majority's and Dissent's references to the AAA Commercial Rules, which, once again, are in Appendix 4. The Rule cited by the Court is Rule 43(a).

§ 1.05 ADDITIONAL MATERIALS CONCERNING WHETHER ARBITRATORS MUST APPLY "THE LAW"

In Appendix 5, you will find The Code of Ethics for Arbitrators in Commercial Disputes, which is the joint work-product of the American Bar Association and the American Arbitration Association. It references the arbitrator's obligation to be "fair," and Canon V provides that "An Arbitrator Should Make Decisions In A Just, Independent And Deliberate Matter." The Code does not specifically mention adherence to established rules of law.

In what is still perhaps the most important empirical study on the subject, it was found that the great majority of commercial arbitrators thought themselves bound to apply established law, but also at liberty to depart from legal rules to do equity. *See* Soia Mentschikoff, *Commercial*

Arbitration, 61 COLUM. L. REV. 846, 881 (1961). Does that make sense? Would the attitude of jurors in civil cases be any different? Do judges sometimes result-orient? Does the fact that many arbitrators are not lawyers explain the results of the Mentschikoff survey? When a lawyer participates in the selection of arbitrators, what sort of arbitrator might be best for a "good facts, bad law" case and vice versa?

It is generally recognized that labor arbitrators are expected to compromise on disagreements between management and labor, in part because collective bargaining agreements typically designate specific arbitrators concerned with maintaining peaceful coexistence between the two sides. This is particularly true when there are disputes not covered by agreement, disciplinary matters, and the like. However, there are also instances in which labor arbitrators have applied precisely the same labor agreement language in opposite ways. What result? *See, e.g.*, Consolidation Coal Co. v. United Mine Workers, 213 F.3d 404 (7th Cir. 2000). There is a difference, is there not, between "the law" a court would be bound to apply to a civil commercial dispute, and the "law of the shop" as defined and applied by labor arbitrators. Also, once again, is partial departure from contract language to do equity equivalent to purposeful departure from rules of law?

What about where the parties invite the arbitrators to "do equity?" In international arbitrations, the parties are often free to stipulate by contract or otherwise to decision "ex aequo et bono"—that is, according to what is called "natural justice and equity." Arbitrators may also sense that the parties desire compromise, particularly if their relationship is ongoing. Still, arbitrators are not mediators, and are not expected to become involved in settlement negotiations.

What of choice of law provisions as typically found in significant international (which country's law) and domestic (which state's law) contracts? For reasons which will become clear when we return in detail to limitations on judicial review of arbitral awards, and while arbitrators are undoubtedly influenced by such provisions, arbitral departure from a body of law chosen by the parties to govern their dispute would rarely provide a basis for a court to vacate an award.

§ 1.06 "Ex Aequo et Bono"

There is general recognition that courts, as opposed to arbitrators, cannot decide cases "ex aequo et bono" because courts cannot deliberately depart from the law. Yet, today's law courts have inherited the traditional power of courts of equity as they existed first in England and then in this country. The distinction appears to be that courts do equity within established, precedential parameters but cannot simply decide cases as they please. The grant of "ex aeqo et bono" powers to arbitrators, then, would be seen as authorization to do what courts cannot—to decide cases "outside the law." For a fascinating discussion of the distinction between judicial equity powers and those of "ex aequo" decision makers, see the five to four United States Supreme Court decision in *Grupo Mexicano v. Alliance Bond Fubd, Inc.*, 527 U.S. 308 (1999), which deals with whether a court can enjoin pre-judgment transfers of funds which are not illegal. The case quotes the famous equity expert Justice Joseph Story regarding his view that the Court of Equity in England did not have the power resolve controversies "ex aequo et bono":

> If, indeed, a Court of Equity in England did possess the unbounded jurisdiction . . . of correcting, controlling, moderating, and even superseding the law . . . , it would be the most gigantic in its sway, and the most formidable instrument of arbitrary power, that could well be devised. It would literally place the whole rights and property of the community under the arbitrary will of the judge . . . .

1 Commentaries on Equity Jurisprudence § 19, at 21 (Beard Books, 13th ed. 2000).

Does limiting the grant of such broad powers to arbitrators in the context of resolution of contractual controversies raise the same concerns? The fact is that the rules of important international arbitral tribunals, like the International Chamber of Commerce headquartered in Paris, specifically provide for it—in French, the concept is the service of arbitratrors as "amiables compositeurs."

Willemijn Houdstermaatschappij, v. Standard Microsystems Corp.

United States Court of Appeals, Second Circuit, 1997.
103 F.3d 9.

▪ MESKILL, J.

The issue presented on appeal is whether the district court properly vacated an arbitration award. Plaintiff Willemijn Houdstermaatschappij, BV (Willemijn) appeals from an order of the United States District Court for the Southern District of New York, Owen, J., vacating Willemijn's arbitration award and denying Willemijn's petition to confirm the award. The district court found that the arbitrators manifestly disregarded the law. We disagree and accordingly vacate the order of the district court and remand the case with directions to confirm the award.

* * * *

DISCUSSION

We have appellate jurisdiction pursuant to 9 U.S.C. § 16(a)(1)(E), and we review de novo a district court's review of arbitration awards under the "manifest disregard of law" standard, see Merrill Lynch, Pierce, Fenner & Smith v. Bobker, 808 F.2d 930 (2d Cir. 1986).

A. *Manifest Disregard of the Law*

The showing required to avoid summary confirmation of an arbitration award is high and a party moving to vacate the award has the burden of proof. Moreover, "arbitration awards are subject to very limited review in order to avoid undermining the twin goals of arbitration, namely, settling disputes efficiently and avoiding long and expensive litigation."

The "manifest disregard" test requires "something beyond and different from a mere error in the law or failure on the part of the arbitrators to understand or apply the law." "Manifest disregard of the law may be found . . . if the arbitrator 'understood and correctly stated the law but proceeded to ignore it.'" *Siegel*, 779 F.2d at 893 rev'd on other grounds, 500 F.2d 921 (2d Cir. 1974).

It is difficult to apply this standard of review when arbitrators give no explanation for their decision. However, since arbitrators are not required to provide an explanation for their decision a reviewing court must still perform the difficult task of evaluating the conduct and conclusions of the arbitrators.

In such a case we must confirm the arbitrators' decision "if a ground for the arbitrator[s'] decision can be inferred from the facts of the case." This is so even if the ground for their decision is based on an error of fact or an error of law.

Conversely, a court may infer that the arbitrators manifestly disregarded the law if it finds that the error made by the arbitrators is so obvious that it would be instantly perceived by the average person qualified to serve as an arbitrator. However, determining whether to make this inference is not an easy task and a reviewing court must proceed with caution. If there is "even a barely colorable justification for the outcome reached," the court must confirm the arbitration award.

NOTES

1. In both federal and state systems, it is the trial courts which initially confirm, vacate or modify awards. Whether an award should be confirmed, vacated or modified is an issue of law, and hence reviewable de novo at the intermediate appellate level.

2. To the extent courts review awards at all, should the focus be on issues of law, issues of fact, or both?

3. We will return to judicial review of awards in Chapter 6. In the interim, however, note that "manifest disregard" is defined above to require deliberate arbitral departure from what is known to be established legal principle.

§ 1.07 INTRODUCTORY CASES: RIGHT TO BE HEARD AND ARBITRAL NEUTRALITY

Georgina Cheng-Canindin v. Renaissance Hotel Associates

Court of Appeals of California, First Appellate District, Division Two, 1996.
50 Cal. App. 4th 676.

▪ HAERLE, J.

* * * *

Respondent was hired by the Hotel on January 30, 1985, and was employed in its human resources department. In February 1987, she signed a document entitled "Receipt of Employee Handbook." That document states, in part: "I have this day received a copy of the Renaissance Employee Handbook. I agree to fully and completely read the Employee Handbook and to abide by the rules and regulations contained therein. I agree to resolve all disputes concerning my employment with the Hotel by the procedures outlined in this Handbook."

* * * *

On March 10, 1994, respondent, who was five months pregnant, was terminated from her employment. Respondent filed a wrongful termination complaint alleging, among other things, sex and race discrimination, violations of public policy and defamation. Instead of answering the complaint, respondents filed a "petition to compel plaintiff's compliance with contractual alternative dispute resolution, including arbitration pursuant to California Code of Civil Procedure § 1281.2" (the petition).

* * * *

At the hearing on their petition, appellants argued that respondent, by agreeing to comply with the terms of the Handbook, did not simply agree to participate in the review committee procedure before filing suit, but that she effectively waived her right to a judicial forum with respect to any claim relating to her employment. Appellants also challenged any notion that the review committee procedure was "inherently biased."

* * * *

All of this authority confirms our strong view that a third party decision maker and some decree of impartiality must exist for a dispute resolution mechanism to constitute arbitration. This conclusion is reinforced by authority from several other states which define the arbitration process as requiring an impartial third party decision maker with authority to render a final and binding decision. (See Gary Excavating, Inc. v. Town of North Haven (1972) 164 Conn. 119 [318 A.2d 84, 85] [" 'the voluntary submission . . . of an existing or future dispute to a disinterested person or persons for final determination' "].

For the foregoing reasons, we conclude that, although arbitration can take many procedural forms, a dispute resolution procedure is not an arbitration unless there is a third party decision maker, a final and binding decision, and a mechanism to assure a minimum level of impartiality with respect to the rendering of that decision.

2. *The Review Committee Procedure Is Not an Arbitration Procedure*

Arbitration is the submission of a dispute to a third party. Under the review committee procedure at issue in this case, the Hotel is the sole decision maker. Everyone involved in the decisionmaking process is employed by, selected by, and under the control of the Hotel. Employees of the Hotel sit on the committee; the general manager of the Hotel breaks tie votes; the committee is chaired by an employee from the personnel department. The employee does not select any committee member and must accept the roles that the Hotel has assigned to the general manager and the personnel department.

For a procedure to constitute arbitration there must be some mechanism for ensuring a minimum level of impartiality. As we have seen, this mechanism can take many different forms. Party-affiliated representatives or otherwise partial decision makers can play a role in an arbitration when the procedure also contains some impartial means of resolving those disagreements which cannot be resolved by the partial decision makers. In the present case, the effective decision makers are not simply party-affiliated; they are one of the parties to the dispute. The other party, the employee, has no representative among the decision makers to counterbalance the Hotel's inherent, substantial and obvious power. Nor is there any provision in the review committee procedure which even purports to afford, much less assure, impartiality.

Indeed, contrary to the Hotel's contentions on appeal, the entire review committee procedure is inherently slanted in management's direction. The general manager decides, according to some unknown standards, the jurisdiction of the committee, breaks tie votes and makes the final decision about whether a witness should be required to testify. The personnel department chooses the committee members, makes relevancy decisions and also has control over who may testify. It is even suggested that committee members need not to be objective; their job is to "ensure that major decisions affecting the employment of individual employees is [sic] made in accordance with Hotel policy." Hotel policies may never be challenged by employees or altered by the committee.

Arbitration should give both parties an opportunity to be heard. Contrary to appellants' contention on appeal, the review committee procedure does not guarantee the employee such an opportunity. Indeed we are dismayed by appellants' bold contention that their procedures "provide all of the procedures that Plaintiff would have in a trial court, without the consequent delay or expense." A terminated employee is expressly precluded from challenging Hotel policy, procedure or rules. She is strongly discouraged from retaining counsel and is advised to seek assistance from the personnel department if she needs help presenting her case. And, in stark contrast to the trial procedures with which we are familiar, under Hotel procedure the jurisdiction of the committee, the relevancy of evidence and the presentation of witnesses are all matters within the unfettered discretion of one of the parties to the dispute, the Hotel.

NOTE

1. Was it correct to conclude that the serious shortcomings of the review committee procedure caused it to fall outside the statutory definition of "arbitration"? Might it be said, instead, that the "review procedure" provisions were not contractually enforceable for reasons of substantive and procedural unconscionability? Remember that, under Section 2 of the FAA, contractual arbitral provisions are no more enforceable than other contracts.

Morris v. New York Football Giants, Inc.

Supreme Court of New York, New York County, 1991.
575 N.Y.S.2d 1013.

- CAHN, J.

* * * *

This action arises out of a dispute between two professional football players and their former football clubs over the amount of compensation owed to the players for their services in 1990 prior to the start of the football season (1990 preseason).

A very serious issue is raised as to who the arbitrator should be. The contracts expressly provide that the disputes be submitted to the Commissioner of the NFL. Plaintiffs allege (in support of their cross motion) that Tagliabue, the Commissioner of the NFL, has an inherent interest in the outcome of the dispute, and is therefore biased and, consequently, should be replaced by a neutral and impartial arbitrator in advance of arbitration proceedings. As shall be discussed below, under both Federal and State law, it is this court's view that a neutral arbitrator should be substituted for the Commissioner in order to insure a fair and impartial hearing.

Regarding the Commissioner of the NFL, the Constitution of the NFL provides, in article VIII, § 8.1, that the NFL (an unincorporated association of 28 individual teams) shall select and employ the Commissioner and shall determine his period of employment and his compensation. Article VIII, §8.4 (b) provides that the Commissioner is the chief executive officer of the NFL. Article II, § 2.1 provides that the purposes and objectives for which the NFL is organized are to promote and foster the primary businesses of NFL members, each member being an owner of a professional football club. Moreover, prior to becoming Commissioner, Tagliabue was the chief outside counsel for the NFL and its members (as well as legal advisor to the NFLMC). In that capacity, he frequently represented NFL owners in disputes with players and advocated the positions of the owners. In particular relevance to this case, in *Powell v National Football League* (888 F.2d 559 [8th Cir 1989]), Tagliabue advocated on behalf of the NFL owners the proposition that the terms of the CBA had continuing legal effect after its expiration (the very issue he would have to decide here). Indeed, even when Tagliabue became Commissioner of the NFL, he advocated this position during meetings with the office of the Solicitor General of the United States in connection with a certiorari petition filed with the Supreme Court of the United States by plaintiffs in *Powell.* In addition, the complaint names Tagliabue as a defendant in connection with a claim of tortious interference of contract in issuing an edict "that no members of the NFL may pay their players the contractually provided 10% of the players negotiated salary for pre-season services, but instead must pay the fixed per diem wage contained in the expired 1982 CBA."

In opposition to plaintiffs' cross motion, defendants allege, inter alia, that the Commissioner would not be arbitrating plaintiffs' suit against the NFL, but only the breach of contract claims alleged against the two teams. As a result, defendants contend, resolution of the underlying claims against the N. Y. Jets and the N. Y. Giants would have no direct financial impact on the NFL.

The court finds that Tagliabue's position as Commissioner, together with his past advocacy of a position in opposition to plaintiffs' position herein, deprive him of the necessary neutrality to arbitrate these claims. To find for plaintiffs herein, the Commissioner would have to reverse certain positions he previously strongly advocated, and declare nonbinding or void a certain directive he, through his office, issued to NFL clubs. Further, the determination of plaintiffs' claims may have a major financial impact on various NFL teams which pay their players on a per diem basis for preseason services. All of these factors dictate that the Commissioner cannot be a neutral arbitrator herein.

Based upon the record now before it, the court finds that plaintiffs have shown evidence of lack of neutrality and "evident partiality" and bias on the part of the Commissioner with respect to this specific matter. (See, Matter of Cross & Brown Co. v. Nelson, 4 A.D.2d 501 [1st Dept 1957]; Florasynth, Inc. v. Pickholz, 750 F.2d 171 [2d Cir. 1984].)

Further, this court's authority to select a neutral arbitrator is "inherent when the potential bias of a designated arbitrator would make arbitration proceedings simply a prelude to later judicial proceedings challenging the arbitration award" (Masthead Mac Drilling Corp. v. Fleck, 549 F Supp 854, 856 [SDNY 1982]). Therefore, this court finds that the Commissioner should not serve as arbitrator herein.

§ 1.08 DESIGNATED ARBITRATORS

In re Arbitration Between Astoria Medical Group & Health Insurance Plan of Greater New York

New York Court of Appeals, 1962.
11 N.Y.2d 128.

- FULD, J.

The intende[d] practical question presented by this appeal revolves about the attempt of one party to a typical tripartite arbitration agreement to have the court intervene, before an award has been made, and disqualify the arbitrator designated by the other party because of his asserted personal interest and partiality.

The appellant Health Insurance Plan (HIP), a nonprofit corporation organized under this State's Insurance Law (art. IX-C), is engaged in writing policies of insurance which provide complete medical care. And, to assure such care to its policyholders, HIP enters into contracts with a number of partnerships of physicians, called Medical Groups, whereby they agree to furnish the necessary medical services. In identical contracts made by HIP with those Medical Groups which are the respondents herein, it was agreed that each of them would be paid a fixed sum, or "capitation," for each insured person receiving the services of the particular Group. In addition to such "capitation," HIP agreed to pay each Group an additional sum termed "supplemental capitation" in an amount depending upon criteria and standards which were to be established in the future.

The contract further recited that, if the parties were unable to agree upon such criteria by a specified date, "the unresolved issues (were) to go to arbitration" in accordance with the arbitration clause of the contract. This provided, in part that "One arbitrator shall be appointed by HIP and another by the GROUP, who jointly shall appoint a third arbitrator" and that, if the third arbitrator could not be agreed upon, either party was to request the American Arbitration Association to select him. The decision of two of the three arbitrators was to be final and binding upon both parties.

When the parties failed to agree on the essential criteria for "supplemental capitation," the Medical Groups demanded arbitration and appointed an attorney, Samuel Seligsohn, Esq., as their arbitrator. HIP, in turn, designated, as its arbitrator, Dr. George Baehr, a physician with a long and distinguished career in medicine. The Groups objected to the designation of Dr. Baehr. Noting that he was one of the incorporators of HIP and its president from 1950 to 1957 and that he is, currently, a member of its board of directors and one of its paid consultants, they moved for an order (1) disqualifying him on the ground of personal interest, bias and partiality arising out of his relationship with HIP and (2) requiring HIP "to designate an impartial arbitrator." The justice at Special Term granting the motion and the Appellate Division affirmed by a divided court . . . .

In order to determine, therefore, whether HIP's choice of Dr. Baehr was permissible or impermissible, we look to the agreement between the parties. It provides, as we have seen, that "One arbitrator shall be appointed by HIP and another by the GROUP, who jointly shall appoint a third arbitrator."

This type of tripartite arbitration provision, requiring each side to name its own arbitrator and such party-designated arbitrators to agree upon a third neutral arbitrator, is one which has been widely used in both labor and commercial arbitration. Arising out of the repeated use of the tripartite arbitral board, there has grown a common acceptance of the fact that the party-designated arbitrators are not and cannot be "neutral," at least in the sense that the third arbitrator or a judge is. And, as might be expected, the literature is replete with references both to arbitrators who are 'neutrals' and those who are "partial," "partisan" or "interested" and to arbitration boards composed entirely of "neutrals" and those contrastingly denominated "tripartite in their membership."

Turning to the case before us, there can be no doubt that, when HIP and the Medical Groups agreed upon the use of a tripartite tribunal, they must be taken to have contracted with reference to established practice and usage in the field of arbitration. In the light of accepted practice, which sanctions and contemplates two non-neutral arbitrators on a tripartite board, the parties must be deemed to have intended that each was to be free to appoint any arbitrator desired, however close his relationship to it or to the dispute. Moreover, this conclusion is reinforced by the fact that the provision relating to arbitration contains no word of limitation on the identity, status or qualifications of the arbitrators; had the parties intended that their appointees be completely impartial or disinterested, they could have readily so provided.

It is hardly necessary to observe that we enforce the tripartite arbitration clause before us because it is the one chosen by the parties, not because we favor it or regard it as ideal or even desirable. We are, in effect, mandated by the policy, no less than by the terms, of our statute to give life to the tribunal which the parties themselves create. If they choose to have their disputes resolved by a body consisting of two partisan arbitrators, and a third neutral arbitrator, that is their affair. We may not rewrite their contract . . . .

Nor do we perceive any public policy which condemns or forbids this arrangement. On the contrary, this court many years ago recognized that, although every arbitrator must act fairly and impartially in arriving at a decision and making an award, "a known interest does not disqualify, and the parties may not complain merely because the arbitrators named were known to be chosen with a view to a particular relationship to their nominator or to the subject-matter of the controversy". . . . In point of fact, even in cases where the contract expressly designated a single arbitrator who was employed by one of the parties or intimately connected with him, the courts have refused to disqualify the arbitrator on the ground of either interest or partiality.

* * * *

Our decision that an arbitrator may not be disqualified solely because of a relationship to his nominator or to the subject matter of the controversy does not, however, mean that he may be deaf to the testimony or blind to the evidence presented. Partisan he may be, but not dishonest. Like all arbitrators, the arbitrator selected by a party must (unless the requirement is waived) take the prescribed oath that he will "faithfully and fairly . . . hear and examine the matters in controversy and . . . make a just award according to the best of (his) understanding" (Civ.Prac.Act, s 1455). And, if either one of the party-appointed arbitrators fails to act in accordance with such oath, the award may be attacked on the ground that it is the product of "evident partiality or corruption" (Civ.Prac.Act, § 1462, subd. 2). Such an attack, however, must be based on something overt, some misconduct on the part of an arbitrator, and not simply on his interest in the subject matter of the controversy or his relationship to the party who selected him.

It may well be that there is greater danger that party- designated arbitrators will overstep the bounds of propriety than will those who are disinterested neutrals. But this risk, quite apart from being one to which the parties submitted, is thought by many to be more than offset by certain benefits gained from use of the tripartite board. One such benefit is that arbitrators selected by the parties are, generally speaking, experts on the subject in controversy and bring to their task a wealth of specialized knowledge. As one commentator has indicated, "the expert guidance" furnished by "partisan" arbitrators "can be of assistance to the neutral member, who is not in a position to appreciate the problem and the fine points of its setting." (Lesser, Tripartite Boards or Single Arbitrators in Voluntary Labor Arbitration? 5 Arb. J. (N.S.) 276, 279; see, also, *Bell Aircraft Corp.*, 13 L.A. 813, 820–21, supra; Note, 68 Harv. L. Rev. 293, 297 et seq.) Consequently, to disqualify an arbitrator because of his relationship to, or association with, his nominator would be to withhold from the arbitration board a source of the specialized knowledge which contributes to the unique value of the arbitration process. Moreover, any personal advantage to be derived from the power to select as arbitrator anyone he wishes is available to each party and, experience tells us, is ordinarily availed of by both.

In brief, it is our view that, since both parties, by agreeing upon tripartite arbitration, have necessarily accepted the idea of "partisan" appointees, neither may object to the other's designation of someone associated with his interest or related to him.

The order appealed from should be reversed, and the petitioners' motion denied with costs in all courts. The questions certified are not answered.

- DESMOND, C.J., dissenting.

On these facts the arbitrator was correctly held to be disqualified and subject to removal. The appeal does not present the broader and more general question as to whether a party may validly nominate as one of three arbitrators a person whose business or personal relationship to the party is so close as presumably to predispose him in favor of his sponsor. Here the interest of the nominee is not presumed but actual, the conflict direct. It is ancient wisdom not lightly to be discarded that "No one should be judge in his own cause" (Maxims of Publilius Syrus, 42

B.C.). Dr. Baehr is a director and paid consultant and former president of HIP. As the Appellate Division majority wrote: "He is, therefore, essentially a 'party' to the dispute because he is now asked to sit as an arbitrator to determine the propriety or fairness of a decision in the making of which he participated." If there is anything left of the idea that a director is an agent of and trustee for his corporation (Continental Securities Co. v. Belmont, 206 N.Y. 7, 16) or anything left of the concept that an arbitrator is "a judge appointed by the partie" (Fudickar v. Guardian Mut. Life Ins. Co., 62 N.Y. 392, 399) and that he "acts in a quasi-judicial capacity" (Matter of American Eagle Fire Ins. Co. v. New Jersey Ins. Co., 240 N.Y. 398, 405), Dr. Baehr is as matter of law not qualified to sit on this arbitration board. Only by so holding can we preserve a concept which is rooted not in naiveté or impracticality but in integrity and principle. If Dr. Baehr can be an arbitrator when his own corporation is a party, then an individual party can name himself as his own arbitrator-judge and the whole affair becomes a cynical travesty of the arbitral process, "calculated to bring the system of enforced arbitrations into disrepute" (*Matter of American Eagle Fire Ins. Co. v. New Jersey Ins. Co.*, supra).

* * * *

We are, of course, not dealing here with arbitration agreements, if any such there be, where the parties have expressly or by necessary implication consented that a party's nominee may be a director, officer, employee, agent or attorney of that party.

The order should be affirmed, with costs.

NOTES

1. In many construction projects, questions of compliance with specifications are left to the final decision of an architect who is typically employed by the owner. Such provisions often make no reference to judicial review. State courts typically impose a "good faith" test on the architect's determinations, but many such states require only subjective good faith (honesty in fact rather than commercial reasonableness). *Compare* Nolan v. Whitney, 88 N.Y. 648 (1982) (objective "reasonableness" test to avoid unjust forfeiture), *with* Laurel Race Course, Inc. v. Regal Constr. Co., 274 Md. 142, 333 A.2d 319 (1975) (architect's determination is final absent fraud or collusion). How does

this comport with the judicial approach by the New York Court of Appeals on the issue of arbitral neutrality?

2. It is generally agreed that arbitrators enjoy full judicial immunity. *E.g.*, Hoosac Tunnel Dock & Elevator Co. v. O'Brien, 137 Mass. 424 (1884). *See* AAA, COMMERCIAL RULES, Rule 48(d). Should this be so?

3. Arbitral tribunals maintain "panels" or "rosters" of neutral arbitrators which can be the basis for selection by the parties. *See* AAA, COMMERCIAL RULES, Rule 11. The arbitration clause, however, particularly in large business contracts, often covers arbitral selection, so as to "contract out" of otherwise applicable tribunal rules for selection. A common scheme is that each party selects an arbitrator, and the two designees select the third. *See* AAA, COMMERCIAL RULES, Rule 12.

4. Where the parties contract for their own selection of a neutral arbitrator, either directly by them or by their designates, the typical tribunal will choose the neutral in the event of a stalemate. *See* AAA COMMERCIAL RULES, Rule 12(d) in Appendix 4. The same holds true if the parties are to select a neutral from a list of arbitrators supplied by the tribunal but fail to do so. *See* AAA COMMERCIAL RULES, Rule 11. Arbitral tribunals, when providing a list of neutrals to choose from, provide background data including work history, arbitrator experience and, sometimes, the candidate's votes in earlier cases. In addition, particularly absent a tribunal mechanism, the typical arbitral statute provides for judicial appointment of a neutral when the parties cannot or will not agree. *See* N.Y. C.P.L.R. 7504.

5. Arbitral tribunals require arbitrators, including designated ones, to make full disclosure of any past or present party contacts. *See also* Canon 2 of the very influential Code of Ethics for Commercial Arbitrators (Appendix 5). A failure to disclose prior or particularly ongoing business or social contacts can, if meaningful, lead to vacation of an award. *E.g.*, Crow Constr. Co. v. Jeffrey M. Brown Assoc., 264 F. Supp.2d 217 (E.D. Pa. 2003).

6. Attitudes as to the types of disclosed relationships requiring replacement or recusal vary somewhat, at least theoretically. The Supreme Court's majority opinion by Justice Hugo Black in *Commonwealth Coatings Corp. v. Continental Casualty Co.*, 393 U.S. 145, 148 (1968) says:

> It is true that arbitrators cannot sever all their ties with the business world, since they are not expected to get all their income from their work deciding cases, but we should, if anything, be even more scrupulous to safeguard the impartiality of arbitrators than judges, since the former have completely free rein to decide the law as well as the facts and are not subject to appellate review. We can perceive no way in which the effectiveness of the arbitration process will be hampered by the simple requirement that arbitrators disclose to the parties any dealings that might create an impression of possible bias.

7. Judge Richard Posner would not impose a neutrality requirement of the type applicable to judges on any arbitrator:

> [P]eople who arbitrate do so because they prefer a tribunal knowledge about the subject matter of their dispute to a generalist court with its austere impartiality but limited knowledge of the subject matter . . . . The expert adjudicator is more likely than a judge or juror not only to be precommitted to a particular substantive position but to know or have heard of the parties.

Merit Ins. Co. v. Leathley Ins. Co., 714 F.2d 673, 679 (7th Cir. 1983).

8. At least absent adhesion, commercial parties can jointly waive objection to a neutral's contacts with one of them. *E.g.*, Kendall Builders, Inc. v. Chesson, 149 S.W.3d 796, 804–06 (Tex. App. 2004). Absent waiver, arbitral tribunals like the AAA often use extreme caution to preserve their own reputations for neutrality. In highly specialized proceedings before trade tribunals, there may be a practical need to tolerate a certain degree of prior contact in order to secure an arbitrator with the requisite industry background.

9. Problematic prior contacts with arbitrators can arise during a hearing as well. For instance, there can be an unlisted witness who knows the arbitrator. What should happen then?

10. What does the fact that arbitrators need not be attorneys suggest about the arbitral process, and judicial supervision of that process?

11. What about an arbitrator who belongs to the same social club as

counsel for one of the parties? A review of the cases suggests that an arbitrator's failure to disclose even the type of party contact which would not require recusal can be treated as evidence of possible bias.

12. Collective Bargaining Agreements between employers and unions typically name the person(s) to serve as arbitrator of underlying disputes and grievances. How would such an approach work in commercial contracts?

§ 1.09 MORE ON DESIGNATED ARBITRATORS

The use of party designated arbitration is very common, particularly in larger disputes. A designated arbitrator may fill the role of party advocate, and sometimes is chosen for the technical skills and knowledge requisite to effective advancement of the party's cause. In international disputes, parties sometimes designate based on an arbitrator's nationality. It is the arbitrators designated by the respective parties which are usually empowered to choose the neutral arbitrator.

As a general matter, a party does not designate an arbitrator without having a discussion of what the case is about, and how the candidate "might see it" assuming a given set of facts. How much of this ought to be disclosed? Does this create predisposition? Bias? Also, at least in this country, each party often pays its own designated arbitrator directly. Good idea?

The so-called American view, as set forth in the *Astoria* case, no longer sits well in the international community in which the emerging practice is to have all party designated arbitrators serve as neutrals. This typically bars direct compensation by the designating party, and substantive *ex parte* discussion between party and designee about the case or selection of the third arbitrator. *See generally* Thomas E. Carbonneau, *The Exercise of Contract Freedom in the Making of Arbitration Agreements*, 26 VAND. J. TRANSNAT'L L. 1189, 1211–13 (2003).

Under new Commercial Rules 17–18 added in 2004, the American Arbitration Association requires designated arbitrators to serve as neutrals and, upon designation, to avoid ex parte substantive exchange with the appointing party, all subject, however, to the parties agreeing otherwise in writing. Even where such substantive exchanges are permitted, arbitration panels typically agree, or will in any event understand, that substantive discussion among them must be kept confidential.

The American Bar Association and the American Arbitration Association jointly prepared a Code of Ethics for Arbitrators in Commercial Disputes which has different requirements for neutrals than for designated arbitrators. Review them in Appendix 5. The vernacular is that a designated arbitrator may be "predisposed," but must still be "fair" and "unbiased." What does that mean?

What about arbitration clauses providing that all arbitrators must be physicians in the event of a malpractice claim? Is that a "neutrality" problem, or something else?

§ 1.10 MAJOR INSTITUTIONAL TRIBUNALS: THE AMERICAN ARBITRATION ASSOCIATION AND AN OUTLINE OF CASE PROCEDURES

This book focuses on commercial arbitrations. These arbitrations often are held before institutional arbitral tribunals which have their preset rules and procedures, even though the parties have latitude to modify them per contract. *See* AAA, COMMERCIAL RULES, Rule 1. As already noted, arbitrations can also be held at any location chosen by the parties (held ad hoc), under such established or party devised ground-rules as the parties select.

While these materials place great emphasis on the American Arbitration Association as the major domestic institutionalized tribunal, there are other established tribunals as well. One is "FINRA" (the Financial Industry Regulatory Authority), which oversees a 2007 combination of departments of the New York Stock Exchange and the National Association of Securities Dealers. FINRA handles customer disputes with brokers and securities industry disputes as well. As for the

AAA, it has sets of rules for various types of disputes (*e.g.*, construction, labor), and an international presence as well. The AAA Commercial Rules also provide special case management and procedures for "Large Complex Commercial Disputes." *See* Appendix 4. Such cases are defined in Commercial Rule 1(c) as those involving claims or counterclaims of at least $500,000. Many cases are significantly larger than that, and some require many months of hearings.

The AAA describes itself as follows:

> **The American Arbitration Association Today**
>
> The American Arbitration Association has, for more than seventy years, pioneered the alternative dispute resolution movement to its present level of acceptability and application in virtually every area of public and private life. A not-for-profit, public service organization, the Association has maintained its integrity throughout its history by providing a fair and equitable process for all users of its services.
>
> The Association does not decide cases. Rather, it provides a forum for the hearing of disputes—tested rules and procedures that have broad acceptance and an extensive roster of impartial experts to hear and resolve cases. Recognized for their standing and expertise in their fields, and their dispute resolution skills, arbitrators and mediators are nominated to the Association's National Panel of Construction Industry Neutrals by leaders in the construction industry. Their conduct is guided by the Association's Code of Ethics, prepared by a joint committee of the American Arbitration Association and the American Bar Association.
>
> While the vast majority of cases administered by the Association are arbitrated, less formal methods of dispute resolution—such as mediation, fact-finding, partnering, and dispute review boards—are clearly coming into wider use.
>
> With a nationwide network of offices and cooperative agreements with arbitral institutions in 54 other nations, the Association is the largest

> single repository of information on alternative dispute resolution law and practice.

The AAA's Commercial Arbitration Rules are referenced throughout these materials. Remember that under Rule 1, parties designating AAA as a tribunal are deemed to accept its Rules unless they "contract out" of them, which they may do in whole or, more likely, in part. The AAA's typical procedures in a commercial case, as reflected in Appendix 4, contemplate:

- Statement of claims and responses—the "pleadings" in an informal sense. The Statement of Claim follows or can accompany the Demand for Arbitration. *See, e.g.*, N.Y. C.P.L.R. 7503(c), requiring that such Demand (or Notice of Intent to Arbitrate) be served like a summons in a civil action.
- Selection of arbitrators, which can be from candidates provided by AAA or otherwise.
- Prehearing conference(s) to arrange exchanges of information by the parties—interrogatories and depositions are atypical except in major cases.
- Prehearing written submissions which also identify witnesses and proposed exhibits. The parties, in connection with their exchange of exhibits, are typically expected to note any evidentiary objections to the adversary's proposed exhibits in advance of the hearing.
- Evidentiary hearings, which must provide full opportunity to present a case but need not comply with rules of evidence applicable in courts—in many states, arbitrators and/or the attorneys have subpoena power. *E.g.*, N.Y. C.P.L.R. 7505.

Compare the FAA to the N.Y. C.P.L.R. provisions concerning procedures. As is typical, the state statute has more to say than the FAA about the arbitral process itself. Still, when a tribunal is used, its rules are the most detailed. A useful exercise is to trace the case stages just identified through the AAA Commercial Rules.

§ 1.11 SECURITIES ARBITRATIONS — THE FINANCIAL INDUSTRY REGULATORY AUTHORITY

For the past two decades or so, virtually all securities industry disputes, including those between customers and stock brokerage firms, have been arbitrated. FINRA regulates the almost 5,000 brokerage firms with trading privileges on the NYSE and/or NASDAQ (the so-called "over the counter" market), as well as the brokers in those firms. These brokers must qualify for licensing and registration under established FINRA processes. FINRA has rule-making and disciplinary powers, as well as a Department of Arbitration and its own Arbitration Code (Exhibit 6 has extracts). Customer disputes are arbitrable where account agreements so provide or, even absent that, at the option of the customer.

Under Rule 12401, customer disputes of $25,000 or less are heard by one arbitrator, and disputes over $25,000 and up to $100,000 are also heard by one arbitrator unless both parties request a panel of three. For disputes over $100,000, three arbitrators are provided unless both parties request only a single arbitrator. That part of the FINRA Code dealing with such arbitrations is found in Appendix 6. Customer disputes of over $100,000 are typically heard by two "public" and one "industry" arbitrators, and this system has provoked considerable controversy. Under section 12 of the Code, an "industry" arbitrator is somebody who has been associated with a stock brokerage firm within the past five years. Advocates of the use of industry representatives claim that they bring knowledge of applicable norms and customs of trade to the resolution of disputes, which, at times, can be technical.

There are detailed "Panel Sheets" for each arbitrator—arbitrators are not "designated" but rather chosen by the parties from a list provided to both of them. The "Panel Sheets" list each securities case arbitrated by a given individual by type and result, together with the person's education and training. FINRA also keeps a public record of each of its awards which is available on the internet. Typical case procedures at FINRA are similar to those at AAA.

While customer disputes take many forms, the typical such dispute, on the non-institutional customer level, is based on so-called "suitability" of investment. Such claims typically sound in breach of contract, fraud or breach of fiduciary duty. While their use is diminishing, there are also customer accounts giving the broker discretion to initiate stock trades in an account. A broker is obligated not to overtrade or "churn" such accounts to generate excessive commissions. Churning claims also are brought in contract, as fraud allegations, or as breach of fiduciary duty allegations. While all brokers making recommendations owe a duty of due care, it is the brokers with discretion which are treated as true fiduciaries.

FINRA's own Rules require recommendations to be suitable in terms of investor objectives and financial circumstances. They also impose duties of supervision on the so-called "principals" of brokerage firms. Both firms and individual brokers must report most customer complaints to FINRA as well as adverse determinations. Notably, these reports become matters of public record.

The use of mandatory customer arbitration clauses is so prevalent in the securities industry that it is almost impossible to find reported court cases brought by customers against their brokers. However, situations in which alleged wrongdoers have gone out of business are unfortunately quite common, and the FINRA Code, under Rule 12202, exempts claims against such respondents from mandatory arbitration.

In 2008, FINRA funded a study of the securities arbitral process conducted by the Securities Industry Conference on Arbitration. The study found widespread customer dissatisfaction with the system based on cost, use of industry arbitrators, perceived bias, and the issuance of unreasoned awards. *See* JILL GROSS & BARBARA BLACK, PERCEPTIONS OF FAIRNESS OF SECURITIES ARBITRATION (2008). Certain other reports are more positive.

Presumably as a result of stock market upheaval, the number of FINRA arbitrations filed in 2009 was over 7,000, as compared to about 5,000 in 2008 and about 3,200 in 2007. The typical case still takes approximately 15 months to resolve, even though the great majority of cases are resolved before the making of awards—sometimes through FINRA mediation processes, and sometimes through negotiated settlements. In cases actually decided in 2009, claimants prevailed 48%

of the time, a six point increase from the prior year. *See* http://www.stockbrokerfraudblog.com/2010/01 (last visited Sept. 1, 2010). However, claimants often receive significantly less than the amount they claim. When a brokerage respondent loses, it is often assessed with all or part of the filing and hearing fees incident to the proceedings. Check the filing and hearing fees associated with a $100,000 claim in Appendix 6.

What might happen if customer claims went to court? Arguably, customers would fare little better. Unless a broker has discretion over an account, she is not a fiduciary. While, the broker still owes some duty of due professional care in dealing with an account, the dominant judicial yardstick would almost certainly be one of "fraud" in connection with the purchase and sale of securities under the federal securities laws, most notably section 10(b) of the 1934 Exchange Act and SEC Rule 10b-5 enacted pursuant thereto. In securities fraud, one is subject to the pleading particularity requirements of Rule 9(b) of the Federal Rules of Civil Procedure, and a plaintiff must both plead and show that she was misled by the broker's material misstatements or omissions. *E.g.*, *In re* Burlington Coat Factory Litigation, 114 F.3d 1410, 1417–18 (3d Cir. 1997). Moreover, there must be pleading and proof permitting a "strong inference of scienter." *Id.* at 1410. *Accord* Acito v. IMCERA Group, Inc., 47 F.3d 47, 53 (2d Cir. 2005). It has been said that "mere irrationality" is not enough for stock fraud. *DiLeo v. Ernst & Young*, 901 F.2d 624, 629 (7th Cir. 1990).

It should also be noted that there is quite extensive documentary discovery in securities arbitrations, including automatic preliminary disclosures which may then be supplemented by specific requests for information. These Discovery Guidelines, which cover exchanges of documents, are set forth below. To further protect customers, the FINRA Rules are very restrictive on grants of pre-hearing motions to dismiss. *See* FINRA Rules § 12206(b). "Failure to state a claim" is not a basis for dismissal until the Claimant has put in her case, and the Panel must, in its award, include an explanation of the basis for the dismissal.

Under FINRA Rule 12904(g), the parties may jointly request a reasoned award. Nonetheless, even reasoned awards tend to be cryptic. An example of one that was not, and that is now a matter of record, appears after the Discovery Guidelines.

Increasingly, customers make their own trades online. Whether arbitrators might be prepared to find that a brokerage firm has the duty to intervene in so-called "financial suicide" cases is unclear.

[A] FINRA Discovery Guide

In evaluating the adequacy of FINRA arbitral procedures to protect customer claimants, a critical factor would be the adequacy of documentary discovery. The following is an edited reproduction of the FINRA Discovery Guide.

This Discovery Guide and Document Production Lists supplement the discovery rules contained in NASD Code of Arbitration Procedure for Customer Disputes ("NASD Customer Code.") (See Rules 12505–11.)

No requirement under the Discovery Guide supersedes any record retention requirement of any federal or state law or regulation or any rule of a self-regulatory organization.

The Discovery Guide, including the Document Production Lists serves as a guide for the parties and the arbitrators; it is not intended to remove flexibility from arbitrators or parties in a given case. Arbitrators can order the production of documents not provided for by the Document Production Lists or alter the production schedule described in the Discovery Guide. Nothing in the Discovery Guide precludes the parties from voluntarily agreeing to an exchange of documents in a manner different from that set forth in the Discovery Guide. NASD encourages the parties to agree to the voluntary exchange of documents and information and to stipulate to various matters. The fact that an item appears on a Document Production List does not shift the burden of establishing or defending any aspect of a claim.

The arbitrators and the parties should consider the documents described in Document Production Lists 1 and 2 presumptively discoverable. Absent a written objection, documents on Document Production Lists 1 and 2 shall be exchanged by the parties within the time frames set forth in the NASD Customer Code. The arbitrators and parties also should consider the additional documents identified in Document Production Lists 3 through 14, respectively, discoverable, as indicated, for cases alleging the following causes of action: churning, failure to supervise, misrepresentation/omission, negligence/breach of fiduciary duty, unauthorized trading, and unsuitability. For the general document production and for each of these causes of action, there are separate Document Production Lists for firms/Associated Person(s) and for customers.

Confidentiality

If a party objects to document production on grounds of privacy or confidentiality, the arbitrator(s) or one of the parties may suggest a stipulation between the parties that the document(s) in question will not be disclosed or used in any manner outside of the arbitration of the particular case, or the arbitrator(s) may issue a confidentiality order. The arbitrator(s) shall not issue an order or use a confidentiality agreement to require parties to produce documents otherwise subject to an established privilege. Objections to the production of documents, based on an established privilege, should be raised in accordance with the time frame for objections set forth in the NASD Customer Code.

Affirmation In The Event That There Are No Responsive Documents or Information

If a party responds that no responsive information or documents exist, the customer or the appropriate person in the brokerage firm who has personal knowledge (i.e., the person who has conducted a physical search), upon the request of the requesting party, must: 1) state in writing that he/she conducted a good faith search for the requested information or documents; 2) describe the extent of the search; and 3) state that, based on the search, no such information or documents exist.

Admissibility

Production of documents in discovery does not create a presumption that the documents are admissible at the hearing. A party may state objections to the introduction of any document as evidence at the hearing to the same extent that any other objection may be raised in arbitration.

DOCUMENT PRODUCTION LISTS

LIST 1 DOCUMENTS TO BE PRODUCED IN ALL CUSTOMER CASES: FIRM/ASSOCIATED PERSON(S):

1) All agreements with the customer, including, but not limited to, account opening documents, cash, margin, and option agreements, trading authorizations, powers of attorney, or discretionary authorization agreements, and new account forms.

2) All account statements for the customer's account(s) during the time period and/or relating to the transaction(s) at issue.

3) All confirmations for the customer's transaction(s) at issue. As an alternative, the firm/Associated Person(s) should ascertain from the claimant and produce those confirmations that are at issue and are not within claimant's possession, custody, or control.

4) All "holding (posting) pages" for the customer's account(s) at issue or, if not available, any electronic equivalent.

5) All correspondence between the customer and the firm/Associated Person(s) relating to the transaction(s) at issue.

6) All notes by the firm/Associated Person(s) or on his/her behalf, including entries in any diary or calendar, relating to the customer's account(s) at issue.

7) All recordings and notes of telephone calls or conversations about the customer's account(s) at issue that occurred between the Associated Person(s) and the customer (and any person purporting to act on behalf of the customer), and/or between the firm and the Associated Person(s).

8) All Forms RE-3, U-4, and U-5, including all amendments, all customer complaints identified in such forms, and all customer complaints of a similar nature against the Associated Person(s) handling the account(s) at issue.

9) All sections of the firm's Compliance Manual(s) related to the claims alleged in the statement of claim, including any separate or supplemental manuals governing the duties and responsibilities of the Associated Person(s) and supervisors, any bulletins (or similar notices) issued by the compliance department, and the entire table of contents and index to each such Manual.

10) All analyses and reconciliations of the customer's account(s) during

the time period and/or relating to the transaction(s) at issue.

Only named parties must produce documents pursuant to the guidelines set forth herein. However, non-parties may be required to produce documents pursuant to a subpoena or an arbitration panel order to direct the production of documents (see Rule 12513). In addition, the arbitration chairperson may use the Document Production Lists as guidance for discovery issues involving non-parties.

11) All records of the firm/Associated Person(s) relating to the customer's account(s) at issue, such as, but not limited to, internal reviews and exception and activity reports which reference the customer's account(s) at issue.

12) Records of disciplinary action taken against the Associated Person(s) by any regulator or employer for all sales practices or conduct similar to the conduct alleged to be at issue.

LIST 2 DOCUMENTS TO BE PRODUCED IN ALL CUSTOMER CASES: CUSTOMER:

1) All customer and customer-owned business (including partnership or corporate) federal income tax returns, limited to pages 1 and 2 of Form 1040, Schedules B, D, and E, or the equivalent for any other type of return, for the three years prior to the first transaction at issue in the statement of claim through the date the statement of claim was filed.

2) Financial statements or similar statements of the customer's assets, liabilities and/or net worth for the period(s) covering the three years prior to the first transaction at issue in the statement of claim through the date the statement of claim was filed.

3) Copies of all documents the customer received from the firm/Associated Person(s) and from any entities in which the customer invested through the firm/Associated Person(s), including monthly statements, opening account forms, confirmations, prospectuses, annual and periodic reports, and correspondence.

4) Account statements and confirmations for accounts maintained at securities firms other than the respondent firm for the three years prior to the first transaction at issue in the statement of claim through the date the statement of claim was filed.

5) All agreements, forms, information, or documents relating to the account(s) at issue signed by or provided by the customer to the firm/Associated Person(s).

6) All account analyses and reconciliations prepared by or for the customer relating to the account(s) at issue.

7) All notes, including entries in diaries or calendars, relating to the account(s) at issue.

8) All recordings and notes of telephone calls or conversations about the customer's account(s) at issue that occurred between the Associated Person(s) and the customer (and any person purporting to act on behalf of the customer).

9) All correspondence between the customer (and any person acting on behalf of the customer) and the firm/Associated Person(s) relating to the account(s) at issue.

10) Previously prepared written statements by persons with knowledge of the facts and circumstances related to the account(s) at issue, including those by accountants, tax advisors, financial planners, other Associated Person(s), and any other third party.

11) All prior complaints by or on behalf of the customer involving securities matters and the firm's/Associated Person(s') response(s).

12) Complaints/Statements of Claim and Answers filed in all civil actions involving securities matters and securities arbitration proceedings in which the customer has been a party, and all final decisions and awards entered in these matters.

13) All documents showing action taken by the customer to limit losses in the transaction(s) at issue.

LIST 3 CHURNING: FIRM/ASSOCIATED PERSON(S)

1) All commission runs relating to the customer's account(s) at issue or, in the alternative, a consolidated commission report relating to the customer's account(s) at issue.

2) All documents reflecting compensation of any kind, including commissions, from all sources generated by the Associated Person(s) assigned to the customer's account(s) for the two months preceding

through the two months following the transaction(s) at issue, or up to 12 months, whichever is longer. The firm may redact all information identifying customers who are not parties to the action, except that the firm/Associated Person(s) shall provide at least the last four digits of the non-party customer account number for each transaction.

3) Documents sufficient to describe or set forth the basis upon which the Associated Person(s) was compensated during the years in which the transaction(s) or occurrence(s) in question occurred, including: a) any bonus or incentive program; and b) all compensation and commission schedules showing compensation received or to be received based upon volume, type of product sold, nature of trade (e.g., agency v. principal), etc.

LIST 4 CHURNING: CUSTOMER No additional documents identified.

LIST 5 FAILURE TO SUPERVISE: FIRM/ASSOCIATED PERSON(S):

1) All commission runs and other reports showing compensation of any kind relating to the customer's account(s) at issue or, in the alternative, a consolidated commission report relating to the customer's account(s) at issue.

2) All exception reports and supervisory activity reviews relating to the Associated Person(s) and/or the customer's account(s) that were generated not earlier than one year before or not later than one year after the transaction(s) at issue, and all other documents reflecting supervision of the Associated Person(s) and the customer's account(s) at issue.

3) Those portions of internal audit reports at the branch in which the customer maintained his/her account(s) that: (a) focused on the Associated Person(s) or the transaction(s) at issue; and (b) were generated not earlier than one year before or not later than one year after the transaction(s) at issue and discussed alleged improper behavior in the branch against other individuals similar to the improper conduct alleged in the statement of claim.

4) Those portions of examination reports or similar reports following an

examination or an inspection conducted by a state or federal agency or a self-regulatory organization that focused on the Associated Person(s) or the transaction(s) at issue or that discussed alleged improper behavior in the branch against other individuals similar to the improper conduct alleged in the statement of claim.

LIST 6 FAILURE TO SUPERVISE: CUSTOMER

No additional documents identified.

LIST 7 MISREPRESENTATION/OMISSIONS: /ASSOCIATED PERSON(S)

Copies of all materials prepared or used by the firm/Associated Person(s) relating to the transactions or products at issue, including research reports, prospectuses, and other offering documents, including documents intended or identified as being "for internal use only," and worksheets or notes indicating the Associated Person(s) reviewed or read such documents. As an alternative, the firm/Associated Person(s) may produce a list of such documents that contains sufficient detail for the claimant to identify each document listed. Upon further request by a party, the firm/Associated Person(s) must provide any documents identified on the list.

LIST 8 MISREPRESENTATION/OMISSIONS: CUSTOMER

1) Documents sufficient to show the customer's ownership in or control over any business entity, including general and limited partnerships and closely held corporations.

2) Copy of the customer's resume.

3) Documents sufficient to show the customer's complete educational and employment background or, in the alternative, a description of the customer's educational and employment background if not set forth in a resume produced under item 2.

LIST 9 NEGLIGENCE/BREACH OF FIDUCIARY DUTY: FIRM/ASSOCIATED PERSON(S)

Copies of all materials prepared or used by the firm/Associated Person(s) relating to the transactions or products at issue, including research reports, prospectuses, and other offering documents, including documents intended or identified as being "for internal use only," and worksheets or notes indicating the Associated Person(s) reviewed or read such documents. As an alternative, the firm/Associated Person(s) may produce a list of such documents that contains sufficient detail for the claimant to identify each document listed. Upon further request by a party, the firm/Associated Person(s) must provide any documents identified on the list.

LIST 10 NEGLIGENCE/BREACH OF FIDUCIARY DUTY: CUSTOMER

1) Documents sufficient to show the customer's ownership in or control over any business entity, including general and limited partnerships and closely held corporations.

2) Copy of the customer's resume.

3) Documents sufficient to show the customer's complete educational and employment background or, in the alternative, a description of the customer's educational and employment background if not set forth in a resume produced under item 2.

LIST 11 UNAUTHORIZED TRADING: FIRM/ASSOCIATED PERSON(S)

1) Order tickets for the customer's transaction(s) at issue.

2) Copies of all telephone records, including telephone logs, evidencing telephone contact between the customer and the firm/Associated Person(s).

3) All documents relied upon by the firm/Associated Person(s) to establish that the customer authorized the transaction(s) at issue.

LIST 12 UNAUTHORIZED TRADING: CUSTOMER

1. Copies of all telephone records, including telephone logs, evidencing

telephone contact between the customer and the firm/Associated Person(s).

2. All documents relied upon by the customer to show that the transaction(s) at issue was made without his/her knowledge or consent.

LIST 13 UNSUITABILITY: FIRM/ASSOCIATED PERSON(S)

1) Copies of all materials prepared, used, or reviewed by the firm/Associated Person(s) related to the transactions or products at issue, including but not limited to research reports, prospectuses, other offering documents, including documents intended or identified as being "for internal use only," and worksheets or notes indicating the Associated Person(s) reviewed or read such documents. As an alternative, the firm/Associated Person(s) may produce a list of such documents. Upon further request by a party, the firm/Associated Person(s) must provide any documents identified on the list.

2) Documents sufficient to describe or set forth the basis upon which the Associated Person(s) was compensated in any manner during the years in which the transaction(s) or occurrence(s) in question occurred, including, but not limited to: a) any bonus or incentive program; and b) all compensation and commission schedules showing compensation received or to be received based upon volume, type of product sold, nature of trade (e.g., agency v. principal), etc.

LIST 14 UNSUITABILITY: CUSTOMER

1) Documents sufficient to show the customer's ownership in or control over any business entity, including general and limited partnerships and closely held corporations.

2) Written documents relied upon by the customer in making the investment decision(s) at issue.

3) Copy of the customer's resume.

4) Documents sufficient to show the customer's complete educational and employment background or, in the alternative, a description of the customer's educational and employment background if not set forth in a resume produced under item 3.

[B] A Sample FINRA Arbitration Award

As previously noted, FINRA awards are typically unreasoned unless the parties join in requesting otherwise. What follows is an example of a reasoned award showing a careful weighting of the parties' respective contributions to what occurred. The result is an interesting exercise in arbitral flexibility.

In re Arbitration Between Chang v. Mcginn, Smith & Co., Inc.

2009 WL 5224588 (FINRA).

CASE SUMMARY: Claimants asserted the following causes of action: unsuitable investments, negligence, negligent supervision, breach of contract, violations of industry rules, failure to diversify, respondeat superior, breach of fiduciary duty, fraud, misrepresentations, and omissions. The causes of action relate to unspecified private placement products, notes, and trusts.

Unless specifically admitted in their Answer, Respondents MS & Co., Smith, and Lex denied the allegations made in the Statement of Claim and asserted various affirmative defenses.

RELIEF REQUESTED: In the Statement of Claim, Claimants requested compensatory damages in the amount of $2,577,000.00, commissions, interest, attorneys' fees, costs, and punitive damages.

Respondents MS & Co., Smith, and Lex requested Claimants' claims be denied in their entirety.

OTHER ISSUES CONSIDERED AND DECIDED: The Panel acknowledges that they have each read the pleadings and other materials filed by the parties.

Respondents Lex & Smith, MS Advisors, and MS Capital are not members or associated persons of FINRA and did not voluntarily submit to arbitration. Therefore, the Panel made no determination with respect to Claimants' claims against Respondents Lex & Smith, MS Advisors, and MS Capital.

On or about June 30, 2009, Claimants filed a Motion in Support for Default Judgment against Respondents Timothy M. McGinn and Thomas E. Livingston. On or about July 10, 2009, Respondents filed an Opposition to Claimants' Motion. On August 4, 2009 a pre-hearing conference was conducted to address the Motion and the Panel, having considered the submissions and oral arguments of the parties and after due deliberation, denied the Motion.

The parties have agreed that the Award in this matter may be executed in counterpart copies or that a handwritten, signed Award may be entered.

ARBITRATORS' FINDINGS: The arbitrators have provided an explanation of their decision in this Award, the explanation is for the information of the parties only and is not precedential in nature.

Dr. Chang and his wife as individuals and Dr. Chang in his role as trustee of Cumberland Pathology pension accounts appear to be intelligent, accomplished people. However, the Arbitration Panel finds no logical carryover from being very experienced at the practice of medicine or music theory or the use of Quicken software programs to account for small-business accounts receivable and accounts payable to any understanding of private placement prospectus.

Furthermore, Mr. Lex seems to be a conscientious broker and insurance salesman who is congenial. McGinn, Smith & Company as the supervisor of Mr. Lex had necessary procedures and policies in place to carry out its duties to potential customers as they had standard education programs for brokers and industry-standard supervision procedures for individual broker accounts.

The Panel has come to a unanimous decision that there is some definitive fault by Dr. Chang and some fault by three of the Respondents-Mr. Lex, Mr. David Smith, and McGinn, Smith & Co. As a preface to this decision, the Panel finds there was no role by the two individuals-Mr. Thomas Livingston or Mr. McGinn. However, in light of this finding being joint and several, and, in light of McGinn, Smith & Co. being liable, it is entirely a matter of the contractual ownership and employment relationship between either Mr. Livingston or Mr. McGinn and McGinn, Smith & Co. as to any contribution these two gentlemen may owe McGinn, Smith & Co. At the risk of being redundant, this arbitration decision does not affect any contractual responsibility Mr. Livingston and Mr. McGinn may have, if any, to reimburse McGinn, Smith & Co. for damages McGinn, Smith & Co. ultimately provides the Claimants. Furthermore, while neither party requested any expungement action by the Panel, after a review of the entire record, which included direct and cross-examination of Mr. Livingston and Mr. McGinn, on its own initiative, the Panel unanimously finds, as a matter of justice and equity, that any mention of this claim, including all allegations originating from this claim, be stricken from all FINRA records and those records FINRA may advise upon concerning both Mr. Thomas Livingston and Mr. McGinn.

The quantitative reasoning and reason for the assignment of fault is set out immediately below.

Dr. Chang and Kee Mann Chang are found to be responsible for the consequences of their own investment decisions after their stating repeatedly verbally and in writing that they had the opportunity to read investment literature and query resources such as Mr. Lex about the risks and rewards of the subject private placement notes.

The fault of Mr. Lex, Mr. Smith, and McGinn, Smith & Company is derived from the overconcentration of the Claimants' investments in these private placement notes. While Mr. Lex is certainly not responsible for preventing the Claimants from investing all of their funds into a single instalment, Mr. Lex and McGinn, Smith & Co. through Mr. David Smith <because Mr. David Smith oversaw Mr. Lex as the compliance officer for a large majority of the time period in question> could have just told Dr. Chang and Kee Mann Chang that McGinn, Smith & Co. would not play a part in these disproportionate investment actions as they developed. Mr. Lex and/or McGinn, Smith & Co. could have declined to conduct the sale of any more of these notes once the over-concentration reached a critical mass.

As to some counter-arguments presented to the arbitration Panel, the Panel finds the line of reasoning that these private placement notes were both diversified within each note, and the five or more notes were separately varied so there was not concentration, to be disingenuous. There are about a dozen or maybe two dozen small to moderately capitalized LLCs within these notes that are all either consumer service companies like residential alarm companies or discretionary-consumer goods companies like swimming pool supply firms or golf club accessory supply firms. A truly diversified portfolio would have some selections of small, mid and large capitalized businesses among the number of business areas such as some greater number of the 98 categories of businesses that Value Line created. Another counterpoint raised in the arbitration hearing with colored "pie-charts" depicting the percentage of the Chang's assets that were invested in these private placements, was that the Respondents concluded that the subject private placement notes were only 40 to 60% of the Claimants' total assets; this statement by the Respondents rings hollow. Of the liquid or near liquid assets Dr. Chang and Kee Mann Chang had, these subject notes were close to 90% of their net worth, and this aspect of the over-concentration is exacerbated by Mr. Lex only knowing a fraction of Dr. Chang's and Kee Mann Chang's total liquid/near liquid assets.

As to one other counterpoint raised by the Respondents in this case, the Panel finds that the Respondents' argument, that rescission is impossible because the "wrong" parties were sued, to be a fiction. Even while the Respondents referenced briefly and vaguely to regulatory prohibitions at the end of the Arbitration Hearing, this Panel finds that it is within regulatory parameters for Mr. Lex and/or Mr. David Smith to own the notes as individuals if McGinn, Smith & Co. believes it cannot do so. As a result of the Panel's award being joint and several, McGinn, Smith & Co. could compensate Mr. Lex and/or Mr. David Smith if McGinn, Smith & Co. chose to do so in the possible ownership interest in the subject notes ordered here to be returned by the Claimants.

In determining the Award of $805,110.00, the Arbitration Panel has accounted for in a partial rescission of the purchase of the subject notes: (1) the interest earned by the notes while the Claimants actually held these notes, (2) an imputed interest the Claimants would have conservatively earned with the $805,110.00 if they had never purchased some of these notes, and (3) there is no purposeful assault on the public good by the Respondents so NO punitive damages are awarded.

AWARD: After considering the pleadings, the testimony and evidence presented at the hearing, the Panel has decided in full and final resolution of the issues submitted for determination as follows:

> 1. Respondents McGinn, Smith & Co., Inc., William Lex, and David Smith are jointly and severally liable for and shall pay to Claimants $805,110.00 in compensatory damages. Concurrently Dr. Chang, Kee Mann Chang, and Cumberland Pathology Associates are to provide ownership rights to the Respondents of 45% of the face value of the initial value of private placement notes as defined below.
>
> a. Payment of $805,110.00 shall be made within 30 days of the issuance of this Award, and any amount paid after 30 days from the Award issuance date will be subject to post-judgment interest of 6% per Pennsylvania statutes.
>
> b. Concurrently with the payment of the full amount of funds to the Claimants in the amount of $805,110.00, the Claimants shall sign over to the specific Respondent party(s) <designated before hand by the Respondents> all ownership rights the Claimants have to 45% of the face value of the "notes" to the Respondents <the particular private placement notes will be chosen by the Claimants>.

* * * *

4. Any and all relief not specifically addressed herein, including punitive damages, is denied.

FEES: Pursuant to the Code, the following fees are assessed:

Filing Fees: FINRA Dispute Resolution assessed a filing fee for each claim:

Initial claim filing fee = $1,800.00

Member Fees: Member fees are assessed to each member firm that is a party in these proceedings or to the member firm that employed the associated persons at the time of the events giving rise to the dispute. Accordingly, as a party, McGinn, Smith & Co., Inc., is assessed the following:

Member surcharge = $2,800.00

Pre-hearing process fee = $ 750.00

Hearing process fee = $5,000.00

Hearing Session Fees and Assessments: The Panel has assessed hearing session fees for each session conducted. A session is any meeting between the parties and the arbitrators, including a pre-hearing conference with the arbitrators, that lasts four (4) hours or less. 1. The Panel has assessed $14,025.00 of the hearing session fees jointly and severally to Claimants.

2. The Panel has assessed $14,025.00 of the hearing session fees jointly and severally to Respondents McGinn, Smith & Co., Inc., William F. Lex, and David L Smith.

All balances are payable to FINRA Dispute Resolution and are due upon receipt.

§ 1.12 THE PERIPHERIES OF ARBITRATION

Avitzur v. Avitzur

New York Court of Appeals, 1983.
58 N.Y.2d 108.

- WACHTLER, J.

This appeal presents for our consideration the question of the proper role of the civil courts in deciding a matter touching upon religious concerns. At issue is the enforceability of the terms of a document, known as a Ketubah, which was entered into as part of the religious marriage ceremony in this case. The Appellate Division, 86 A.D.2d 133, held this to be a religious covenant beyond the jurisdiction of the civil courts. However, we find nothing in law or public policy to prevent judicial recognition and enforcement of the secular terms of such an agreement. There should be a reversal.

Plaintiff and defendant were married on May 22, 1966 in a ceremony conducted in accordance with Jewish tradition. Prior to the marriage ceremony, the parties signed both a Hebrew/Aramaic and an English version of the "Ketubah." According to the English translation, the Ketubah evidences both the bridegroom's intention to cherish and provide for his wife as required by religious law and tradition and the bride's willingness to carry out her obligations to her husband in faithfulness and affection according to Jewish law and tradition. By signing the Ketubah, the parties declared their "desire to . . . live in accordance with the Jewish law of marriage throughout [their] lifetime" and further agreed as follows:

> [W]e, the bride and bridegroom . . . hereby agree to recognize the Beth Din of the Rabbinical Assembly and the Jewish Theological Seminary of America or its duly appointed representatives, as having authority to counsel us in the light of Jewish tradition which requires husband and wife to give each other complete love and devotion, and to summon either party at the request of the other, in order to enable the party so requesting to live in accordance with the standards of the Jewish law of marriage throughout his or her lifetime. We authorize the Beth Din to impose such terms of compensation as it may see fit for failure to respond to its summons or to carry out its decision.

Defendant husband was granted a civil divorce upon the ground of cruel and inhuman treatment on May 16, 1978. Notwithstanding this civil divorce, plaintiff wife is not considered divorced and may not remarry pursuant to Jewish law, until such time as a Jewish divorce decree, known as a "Get", is granted. In order that a Get may be obtained plaintiff and defendant must appear before a "Beth Din", a rabbinical tribunal having authority to advise and pass upon matters of traditional Jewish law. Plaintiff sought to summon defendant before the Beth Din pursuant to the provision of the Ketubah recognizing that body as having authority to counsel the couple in the matters concerning their marriage.

Defendant has refused to appear before the Beth Din, thus preventing plaintiff from obtaining a religious divorce. Plaintiff brought this action, alleging that the Ketubah constitutes a marital contract, which defendant has breached by refusing to appear before the Beth Din, and she seeks relief both in the form of a declaration to that effect and an order compelling defendant's specific performance of the Ketubah's requirement that he appear before the Beth Din. Defendant moved to dismiss the complaint upon the grounds that the court lacked subject matter jurisdiction and the complaint failed to state a cause of action, arguing that resolution of the dispute and any grant of relief to plaintiff would involve the civil court in impermissible consideration of a purely religious matter. Plaintiff, in addition to opposing the motion, cross-moved for summary judgment.

* * * *

Defendant argues, in this connection, that enforcement of the terms of the Ketubah by a civil court would violate the constitutional prohibition against excessive entanglement between church and State, because the court must necessarily intrude upon matters of religious doctrine and practice. It is urged that the obligations imposed by the Ketubah arise solely from Jewish religious law and can be interpreted only with reference to religious dogma. Granting the religious character of the Ketubah, it does not necessarily follow that any recognition of its obligations is foreclosed to the courts.

The present case can be decided solely upon the application of neutral principles of contract law, without reference to any religious principle. Consequently, defendant's objections to enforcement of his promise to appear before the Beth Din, based as they are upon the religious origin of the agreement, pose no constitutional barrier to the relief sought by plaintiff. The fact that the agreement was entered into as part of a religious ceremony does not render it unenforceable. Solemnization of the marital relationship often takes place in accordance with the religious beliefs of the participants, and this State has long recognized this religious aspect by permitting duly authorized pastors, rectors, priests, rabbis and other religious officials to perform the ceremony (Domestic Relations Law, § 11, subds. 1, 7). Similarly, that the obligations undertaken by the parties to the Ketubah are grounded in religious belief and practice does not preclude enforcement of its secular terms. Nor does the fact that all of the Ketubah's provisions may not be judicially recognized prevent the court from enforcing that portion of the agreement by which the parties promised to refer their disputes to a nonjudicial forum (see Ferro v. Bologna, 31 N.Y.2d 30, 36). The courts may properly enforce so much of this agreement as is not in contravention of law or public policy.

In short, the relief sought by plaintiff in this action is simply to compel defendant to perform a secular obligation to which he contractually bound himself. In this regard, no doctrinal issue need be passed upon, no implementation of a religious duty is contemplated, and no interference with religious authority will result. Certainly nothing the Beth Din can do would in any way affect the civil divorce. To the extent that an enforceable promise can be found by the application of neutral principles of contract law, plaintiff will have demonstrated entitlement to the relief sought. Consideration of other substantive issues bearing upon plaintiff's entitlement to a religious divorce, however, is appropriately left to the forum the parties chose for resolving the matter.

Accordingly, the order of the Appellate Division should be reversed, with costs, and defendant's motion to dismiss the complaint denied.

- JONES, J., dissenting.

We are of the opinion that to grant the relief plaintiff seeks in this action, even to the limited extent contemplated by the majority, would necessarily violate the constitutional prohibition against entanglement of our secular courts in matters of religious and ecclesiastical content. Accordingly, we would affirm the order of the Appellate Division.

* * * *

At the outset we observe that the complaint contains no allegation that the parties intended that the Ketubah should manifest secular promises or have any civil or secular status or any legal significance independent of the religious ceremony between them of which it was an integral part. Nor is any such assertion advanced in the papers submitted by the wife in support of her cross motion for summary judgment.

Moreover, it appears evident to us that any determination of the content and particulars of the rights of the wife or the obligations of the husband under this document cannot be made without inquiry into and resolution of questions of Jewish religious law and tradition. We think it inaccurate to identify the relief sought by plaintiff, as does the majority, as "simply to compel defendant to perform a secular obligation to which he contractually bound himself."

* * * *

Finally, the evident objective of the present action—as recognized by the majority and irrefutably demonstrated by the complaint—even if procedural jurisdiction were to be assumed, is to obtain a religious divorce, a matter well beyond the authority of any civil court. (Again supplying her own interpretation of the Ketubah, the wife alleges: "That pursuant to the terms of the Ketubah, the plaintiff and defendant agreed that in the event of any civil divorce decree that the husband grant and the wife accept a Jewish divorce decree in accordance with the authority vested in the Beth Din of the Rabbinical Assembly".) As was noted at the Appellate Division, the interest of the civil authorities of the State of New York in the status of the marriage between these parties was concluded when the final judgment of divorce was entered in 1978.

Order reversed, etc.

NOTES

1. It is sometimes the fear of social ostracism, rather than a motion to compel, which "forces" adherence to the arbitral procedures of a traditional religious or national group. One New York court had this to say about "shunning" practices in Orthodox Jewish Communities:

> Both parties are members of the orthodox Jewish community. Respondent's denial of the existence of any disputable issue between themselves and petitioner convinced them to refuse to appear for a *Din Torah* and they would not have done so had they not received the threat of a "sirov." Rabbis testifying for respondents stated that a sirov, literally translated as contempt of court, is a prohibitionary decree that subjects the recipient to shame, scorn, ridicule and ostracism by his coreligionists, fellow members of his community. Ostensibly, he is ostracized and scorned. Other Jews refuse to eat or speak with him. He is discredited and dishonored. The respondents maintain that the draconian measures of a sirov are sufficiently threatening so as to compel their compliance with the demand to appear. They claim they would have become outcasts among their friends and coreligionists. However, from other

> testimony, it appears that the sirov, while most assuredly ominous in its potential power, is honored in its breach. The court cannot, of course, know the actual state of mind of respondents and it may be that their fear of a sirov decree was real. However, it seems more plausible that if respondents believed the consequences so fearful, they would not, at this point, be willing to defy the rabbinical court by refusing to accept the arbitrator's determination. Undoubtedly, pressure was brought to bear to have them participate in the *Din Torah*, but pressure is not duress. Their decision to acquiesce to the rabbinical court's urgings was made without the coercion that would be necessary for the agreement to be void.

In re Arbitration Between Mickel & Shart, 105 Misc. 2d 548, 553, *aff'd*, 85 A.D.2d 604 (N.Y. App. Div., 2d Dep't 1981).

2. The *Mickel* opinion traces the Jewish rabbinical courts, which it recognizes as arbitral tribunals, back to the second century.

3. To what extent would an award from a religious arbitral tribunal be reviewable, either on matters of substance or procedural fairness? Can such review implicate the constitutionally mandated separation of church and state? Or is it impermissible for religious groups to "oust" the courts of their jurisdiction over civil disputes? What about judicial enforcement of awards by religious tribunals?

Joseph Martin, Jr., Delicatessen, Inc. v. Schumacher

New York Court of Appeals, 1981.
52 N.Y.2d 105.

- FUCHSBERG, J.

This case raises an issue fundamental to the law of contracts. It calls upon us to review a decision of the Appellate Division, 70 A.D.2d 1, which held that a realty lease's provision that the rent for a renewal period was "to be agreed upon" may be enforceable.

* * * *

It also follows that, before the power of law can be invoked to enforce a promise, it must be sufficiently certain and specific so that what was promised can be ascertained. Otherwise, a court, in intervening, would be imposing its own conception of what the parties should or might have undertaken, rather than confining itself to the implementation of a bargain to which they have mutually committed themselves. Thus, definiteness as to material matters is of the very essence in contract law. Impenetrable vagueness and uncertainty will not do (1 Corbin, Contracts, § 95, p. 394; 6 Encyclopedia of New York Law, Contracts, § 301; Restatement, Contracts 2d, § 32, Comment a).

Dictated by these principles, it is rightfully well settled in the common law of contracts in this State that a mere agreement to agree, in which a material term is left for future negotiations, is unenforceable. The rule applies all the more, and not the less, when, as here, the extraordinary remedy of specific performance is sought (11 Williston, Contracts (Jaeger 3d ed.), § 1424; Pomeroy, Equity Jurisprudence, § 1405).

This is not to say that the requirement for definiteness in the case before us now could only have been met by explicit expression of the rent to be paid. The concern is with substance, not form. It certainly would have sufficed, for instance, if a methodology for determining the rent was to be found within the four corners of the lease, for a rent so arrived at would have been the end product of agreement between the parties themselves.

But the renewal clause here in fact contains no such ingredients. Its unrevealing, unamplified language speaks to no more than "annual rentals to be agreed upon." Its simple words leave no room for legal construction or resolution of ambiguity. Neither tenant nor landlord is bound to any formula. There is not so much as a hint at a commitment to be bound by the "fair market rental value" which the tenant's expert reported or the "reasonable rent" the Appellate Division would impose, much less any definition of either. Nowhere is there an inkling that either of the parties directly or indirectly assented, upon accepting the clause, to subordinate the figure on which it ultimately would insist, to one fixed judicially, as the Appellate Division decreed be done, or, for that matter, by an arbitrator or other third party.

NOTES

1. What does the *Martin* case add to your knowledge of proceedings which fall under the arbitration umbrella?

2. Arbitral mechanisms are often set forth in contracts calling for appraisals and other quantified determinations which are highly expertized. Once such clause:

> Dispute Resolution Mechanism. Buyer and Seller shall submit any dispute concerning the Purchase Price or the allocation thereof to a jointly selected accounting firm (the "Settlement Firm") for resolution. If Buyer and Seller cannot jointly agree on an accounting firm to serve as the Settlement Firm, each Party shall submit the name of a national accounting firm (which firm shall not be either party's accountants) to Buyer's and Sellers' counsel, who shall select one of such firms by lot. The decision of the Settlement Firm shall be final and binding on the parties and the award of the Settlement Firm (as arbitrator) may be entered in any court of competent jurisdiction. The fees and expenses of the Settlement Firm shall be borne equally by Buyer and Seller.

Chapter 2

ARBITRABILITY OF STATUTORY CLAIMS

At the time of enactment of arbitration statutes in the 1920's, the disputes sent to arbitration were generally mercantile, and involved traditional common law claims such as breach of contract. As years went on, Congress would enact more and more legislation to protect "public rights," such as freedom from racial and other forms of employment discrimination, and protection against securities fraud. Were the pro-arbitral policies behind the FAA to extend to claims arising under statutes that, for the most part, did not even exist in 1925 when the FAA was enacted? Predictably, the earlier judicial answers to this question were in the negative. "Judicial ouster" concerns were particularly tenacious here. One reason was that statutory claims were seen to pose issues of law requiring legal training to resolve—resolving a securities fraud claim was thought to be far different than deciding whether a fabric met trade standards. A second reason was that the protection of "public rights" under statutes enacted for the protection of the populace was seen as having broader societal implications than would private common law disputes.

But what of the statutory mandates to treat pre-dispute arbitral agreements the same as other contracts? Well, weren't public policy considerations always a potential part of the mix when a court was asked to enforce contractual agreement?

The judicial processes leading to the ultimate expansion of arbitrability to most statutory claims make a fascinating study. We see the radical growth in the internationalization of economic activity at work, with parties unwilling to submit to the sovereign power of another country's courts and legal system—private dispute resolution, sometimes by international tribunals, will fill a critical void. Even more generally, we see the ever-accelerating adoption of increasingly pro-arbitration policies under the lead of the United States Supreme Court—the cases enunciating these policies are often those which reverse many years of prior judicial refusals to compel arbitration of various types of statutory claims. These pro-arbitral policies will be put to use in many other ways, as we shall soon see.

§ 2.01 SECURITIES CLAIMS AND THE "OLD" VIEW

Wilko v. Swan

Supreme Court of the United States, 1953.
346 U.S. 427.

- REED, JUSTICE.

This action by petitioner, a customer, against respondents, partners in a securities brokerage firm, was brought in the United States District Court for the Southern District of New York, to recover damages under § 12(2) of the Securities Act of 1933. The complaint alleged that on or about January 17, 1951, through the instrumentalities of interstate commerce, petitioner was induced by Hayden, Stone and Company to purchase 1,600 shares of the common stock of Air Associates, Incorporated, by false representations.

* * * *

The question is whether an agreement to arbitrate a future controversy is a "condition, stipulation, or provision binding any person acquiring any security to waive compliance with any provision" of the Securities Act which § 14 declares "void."

* * * *

The United States Arbitration Act establishes by statute the desirability of arbitration as an alternative to the complications of litigation. The reports of both Houses on that Act stress the need for avoiding the delay and expense of litigation . . . . This hospitable attitude of legislatures and courts toward arbitration, however, does not solve our question as to the validity of petitioner's stipulation . . . to submit to arbitration controversies that might arise from the transactions.

Petitioner argues that § 14, shows that the purpose of Congress was to assure that sellers could not maneuver buyers into a position that might weaken their ability to recover under the Securities Act. He contends that arbitration lacks the certainty of a suit at law under the Act to enforce his rights. He reasons that the arbitration paragraph of the margin agreement is a stipulation that waives "compliance with" the provision of the Securities Act conferring jurisdiction of suits and special powers.

Respondent asserts that arbitration is merely a form of trial to be used in lieu of a trial at law and therefore no conflict exists between the Securities Act and the United States Arbitration Act either in their language or in the congressional purposes in their enactment. Each may function within its own scope, the former to protect investors and the latter to simplify recovery for actionable violations of law by issuers or dealers in securities.

* * * *

Even though the provisions of the Securities Act, advantageous to the buyer, apply, their effectiveness in application is lessened in arbitration as compared to judicial proceedings. Determination of the quality of a commodity or the amount of money due under a contract is not the type of issue here involved. This case requires subjective findings on the purpose and knowledge of an alleged violator of the Act. They must be not only determined but applied by the arbitrators without judicial instruction on the law. As their award may be made without explanation of their reasons and without a complete record of their proceedings, the arbitrators' conception of the legal meaning of such statutory requirements as "burden of proof," "reasonable care" or "material fact," cannot be examined. Power to vacate an award is limited. While it may be true, as the Court of Appeals thought, that a failure of the arbitrators to decide in accordance with the provisions of the Securities Act would "constitute grounds for vacating the award pursuant to section 10 of the Federal Arbitration Act," that failure would need to be made clearly to appear. In unrestricted submissions, such as the present margin agreements envisage, the interpretations of the law by the arbitrators in contrast to manifest disregard are not subject, in the federal courts, to judicial review for error in interpretation. The United States Arbitration Act contains no provision for judicial determination of legal issues such as is found in the English law. As the protective provisions of the Securities Act require the exercise of judicial direction to fairly assure their effectiveness, it seems to us that Congress must have intended § 14 to apply to waiver of judicial trial and review.

* * * *

Two policies, not easily reconcilable, are involved in this case. Congress has afforded participants in transactions subject to its legislative power an opportunity generally to secure prompt, economical and adequate solution of controversies through arbitration if the parties are willing to accept less certainty of legally correct adjustment. On the other hand, it has enacted the Securities Act to protect the rights of investors and has forbidden a waiver of any of those rights. Recognizing the advantages that prior agreements for arbitration may provide for the solution of commercial controversies, we decide that the intention of Congress concerning the sale of securities is better carried out by holding invalid such an agreement for arbitration of issues arising under the Act.

Reversed.

- JACKSON, J., concurring.

I agree with the Court's opinion insofar as it construes the Securities Act to prohibit waiver of a judicial remedy in favor of arbitration by agreement made before any controversy arose. I think thereafter the parties could agree upon arbitration. However, I find it unnecessary in this case, where there has not been and could not be any arbitration, to decide that the Arbitration Act precludes any judicial remedy for the arbitrators' error of interpretation of a relevant statute.

- FRANKFURTER, J. dissenting (with whom MINTON, J., joins).

If arbitration inherently precluded full protection of the rights § 12(2) of the Securities Act affords to a purchaser of securities, or if there were no effective means of ensuring judicial review of the legal basis of the arbitration, then, of course, an agreement to settle the controversy by arbitration would be barred by § 14, the antiwaiver provision, of that Act.

* * * *

Arbitrators may not disregard the law. Specifically they are, as Chief Judge Swan pointed out, "bound to decide in accordance with the provisions of section 12(2)." On this we are all agreed. It is suggested, however, that there is no effective way of assuring obedience by the arbitrators to the governing law. But since their failure to observe this law "would . . . constitute grounds for vacating the award pursuant to section 10 of the Federal Arbitration Act," appropriate means for judicial scrutiny must be implied, in the form of some record or opinion, however informal, whereby such compliance will appear, or want of it will upset the award.

We have not before us a case in which the record shows that the plaintiff in opening an account had no choice but to accept the arbitration stipulation, thereby making the stipulation an unconscionable and unenforceable provision in a business transaction. The Securities and Exchange Commission, as amicus curiae, does not contend that the stipulation which the Court of Appeals respected, under the appropriate safeguards defined by it, was a coercive practice by financial houses against customers incapable of self-protection. It is one thing to make out a case of overreaching as between parties bargaining not at arm's length. It is quite a different thing to find in the anti-waiver provision of the Securities Act a general limitation on the Federal Arbitration Act.

On the state of the record before us, I would affirm the decision of the Court of Appeals.

NOTES

1. Are the issues in a case like *Wilko* any different than those that could be posed by a common law case for fraud, misrepresentation, or

breach of warranty? Why should what the claim is called determine arbitrability?

2. If the *Wilko* dissent is correct, arbitral awards in a statutory case would be subject to judicial review sufficient to insure arbitral compliance with the 1933 Securities Act. Do the bases in the arbitration statutes for overturning awards contemplate such an approach? Is there effective review for fundamental arbitral error in applying, or attempting to apply, statutes directed at protection of the public? What does it mean to say that arbitrators are expected to apply a statute?

3. Note the majority's rejection of the idea that arbitration is simply a different method of dispute resolution. Wasn't that what Cardozo meant when, in *Berkovitz, supra* at 16, he portrayed arbitration as a type of "remedy"?

4. What happens when an arbitrable common law claim and a non-arbitrable statutory claim are combined? We shall see that there could have to be two proceedings that substantially overlap. More on this later.

§ 2.02 INTERNATIONAL CASES — THE CHANGING TIDE

In retrospect, it is not surprising that when the Supreme Court started to strike barriers to the arbitrability of statutory claims, it chose to focus on international disputes between significant business entities. No longer would claims "arising under or in connection with contracts"—the typical wording of a deliberately "broad" arbitration clause—be limited to breach of contract or other common law claims. Foreign entities, after all, might refuse to submit to the jurisdiction of our domestic courts, and vice versa. At certain times, foreign entities would have insufficient "contacts" to be subject to long-arm jurisdiction. A judicial refusal to send statutory claims to arbitration could spell the "death knell" of legitimate grievances, or else, even where there was jurisdiction, set off the sort of judicial forum-shopping and distrust which led to the establishing by Congress of diversity jurisdiction between parties from different states.

Scherk v. Alberto-Culver Co.

Supreme Court of the United States, 1974.
417 U.S. 506.

▪ STEWART, J.

Alberto-Culver Co., the respondent, is an American company incorporated in Delaware with its principal office in Illinois. It manufactures and distributes toiletries and hair products in this country and abroad. During the 1960's Alberto-Culver decided to expand its overseas operations, and as part of this program it approached the petitioner Fritz Scherk, a German citizen residing at the time of trial in Switzerland. Scherk was the owner of three interrelated business entities, organized under the laws of Germany and Liechtenstein, that were engaged in the manufacture of toiletries and the licensing of trademarks for such toiletries. An initial contact with Scherk was made by a representative of Alberto-Culver in Germany in June 1967, and negotiations followed at further meetings in both Europe and the United States during 1967 and 1968. In February 1969 a contract was signed in Vienna, Austria, which provided for the transfer of the ownership of Scherk's enterprises to Alberto-Culver, along with all rights held by these enterprises to trademarks in cosmetic goods. The contract contained a number of express warranties whereby Scherk guaranteed the sole and unencumbered ownership of these trademarks. In addition, the contract contained an arbitration clause providing that "any controversy or claim (that) shall arise out of this agreement or the breach thereof" would be referred to arbitration before the International Chamber of Commerce in Paris, France, and that "(t)he laws of the State of Illinois, U.S.A. shall apply to and govern this agreement, its interpretation and performance."

The closing of the transaction took place in Geneva, Switzerland, in June 1969. Nearly one year later Alberto-Culver allegedly discovered that the trademark rights purchased under the contract were subject to substantial encumbrances that threatened to give others superior rights to the trademarks and to restrict or preclude Alberto-Culver's use of them. Alberto-Culver thereupon tendered back to Scherk the property that had been transferred to it and offered to rescind the contract. Upon Scherk's refusal, Alberto-Culver commenced this action for damages and other relief in a Federal District Court in Illinois, contending that Scherk's fraudulent representations concerning the status of the trademark rights constituted violations of § 10(b) of the Securities Exchange Act of 1934 and Rule 10b-5 promulgated thereunder.

In response, Scherk filed a motion to dismiss the action for want of personal and subject-matter jurisdiction as well as on the basis of forum non conveniens, or, alternatively, to stay the action pending arbitration in Paris pursuant to the agreement of the parties. Alberto-Culver, in turn, opposed this motion and sought a preliminary injunction restraining the prosecution of arbitration proceedings. On December 2, 1971, the District Court denied Scherk's motion to dismiss, and, on January 14, 1972, it granted a preliminary order enjoining Scherk from proceeding with arbitration. In taking these actions the court relied entirely on this Court's decision in *Wilko v. Swan*, 346 U.S. 427, which held that an agreement to arbitrate could not preclude a buyer of a security from seeking a judicial remedy under the Securities Act of 1933, in view of the language of § 14 of that Act, barring "(a)ny condition, stipulation, or provision binding any person acquiring any security to waive compliance with any provision of this subchapter . . . ." The Court of Appeals for the Seventh Circuit, with one judge dissenting, affirmed, upon what it considered the controlling authority of the *Wilko* decision. 484 F.2d 611. Because of the importance of the question presented we granted Scherk's petition for a writ of certiorari.

The United States Arbitration Act, reversing centuries of judicial hostility to arbitration agreements, was designed to allow parties to avoid "the costliness and delays of litigation, and to place arbitration agreements 'upon the same footing as other contracts . . . .' " H.R.Rep.No.96, 68th Cong., 1st Sess., 1, 2 (1924); see also S.Rep.No.536, 68th Cong., 1st Sess. (1924). Accordingly the Act provides that an arbitration agreement such as is here involved "shall be valid, irrevocable, and enforceable, save upon such grounds as exist at law or in equity for the revocation of any contract." 9 U.S.C. § 2. The Act also provides in § 3 for a stay of proceedings in a case where a court is satisfied that the issue before it is arbitrable under the agreement, and § 4 of the Act directs a federal court to order parties to proceed to arbitration if there has been a "failure, neglect, or refusal" of any party to honor an agreement to arbitrate.

In *Wilko v. Swan*, supra, this Court acknowledged that the Act reflects a legislative recognition of the "desirability of arbitration as an alternative to the complications of litigation," 346 U.S. at 431, but nonetheless declined to apply the Act's provisions. That case involved an agreement between Anthony Wilko and Hayden, Stone & Co., a large brokerage firm, under which Wilko agreed to purchase on margin a number of shares of a corporation's common stock. Wilko alleged that his purchase of the stock was induced by false representations on the part of the defendant concerning the value of the shares, and he brought suit for damages under § 12(2) of the Securities Act of 1933, 15 U.S.C. § 77l. The defendant responded that Wilko had agreed to submit all controversies arising out of the purchase to arbitration, and that this agreement, contained in a written margin contract between the parties, should be given full effect under the Arbitration Act.

The Court found that "(t)wo policies, not easily reconcilable, are involved in this case." 346 U.S. at 438. On the one hand, the Arbitration Act stressed "the need for avoiding the delay and expense of litigation," id. at 431, and directed that such agreements be "valid, irrevocable, and enforceable" in federal courts. On the other hand, the Securities Act of 1933 was "(d)esigned to protect investors" and to require "issuers, underwriters, and dealers to make full and fair disclosure of the character of securities sold in interstate and foreign commerce and to prevent fraud in their sale," by creating "a special right to recover for misrepresentation . . . ." 346 U.S. at 431 (footnote omitted). In particular, the Court noted that § 14 of the Securities Act, 15 U.S.C. § 77n, provides:

> Any condition, stipulation, or provision binding any person acquiring any security to waive compliance with any provision of this subchapter or of the rules and regulations of the Commission shall be void.

The Court ruled that an agreement to arbitrate "is a "stipulation," and (that) the right to select the judicial forum is the kind of "provision" that cannot be waived under § 14 of the Securities Act." 346 U.S. at 434–43. Thus, Wilko's advance agreement to arbitrate any disputes subsequently arising out of his contract to purchase the securities was unenforceable under the terms of § 14 of the Securities Act of 1933.

Alberto-Culver, relying on this precedent, contends that the District Court and Court of Appeals were correct in holding that its agreement to arbitrate disputes arising under the contract with Scherk is similarly unenforceable in view of its contentions that Scherk's conduct constituted violations of the Securities Exchange Act of 1934 and rules promulgated thereunder. For the reasons that follow, we reject this contention and hold that the provisions of the Arbitration Act cannot be ignored in this case.

Accepting the premise, however, that the operative portions of the language of the 1933 Act relied upon in *Wilko* are contained in the Securities Exchange Act of 1934, the respondent's reliance on *Wilko* in this case ignores the significant and, we find, crucial differences between the agreement involved in *Wilko* and the one signed by the parties here. Alberto-Culver's contract to purchase the business entities belonging to Scherk was a truly international agreement. Alberto-Culver is an American corporation with its principal place of business and the vast bulk of its activity in this country, while Scherk is a citizen of Germany whose companies were organized under the laws of Germany and Liechtenstein. The negotiations leading to the signing of the contract in Austria and to the closing in Switzerland took place in the United States, England, and Germany, and involved consultations with legal and trademark experts from each of those countries and from Liechtenstein. Finally, and most significantly, the subject matter of the contract concerned the sale of business enterprises organized under the laws of and primarily situated in European countries, whose activities were largely, if not entirely, directed to European markets.

Such a contract involves considerations and policies significantly different from those found controlling in *Wilko*. In *Wilko*, quite apart from the arbitration provision, there was no question but that the laws of the United States generally, and the federal securities laws in particular, would govern disputes arising out of the stock-purchase agreement. The parties, the negotiations, and the subject matter of the contract were all situated in this country, and no credible claim could have been entertained that any international conflict-of-laws problems would arise. In this case, by contrast, in the absence of the arbitration provision considerable uncertainty existed at the time of the agreement, and still exists, concerning the law applicable to the resolution of disputes arising out of the contract.

Such uncertainty will almost inevitably exist with respect to any contract touching two or more countries, each with its own substantive laws and conflict-of-laws rules. A contractual provision specifying in advance the forum in which disputes shall be litigated and the law to be applied is, therefore, an almost indispensable precondition to achievement of the orderliness and predictability essential to any international business transaction. Furthermore, such a provision obviates the danger that a dispute under the agreement might be submitted to a forum hostile to the interests of one of the parties or unfamiliar with the problem area involved.

A parochial refusal by the courts of one country to enforce an international arbitration agreement would not only frustrate these purposes, but would invite unseemly and mutually destructive jockeying by the parties to secure tactical litigation advantages. In the present case, for example, it is not inconceivable that if Scherk had anticipated that Alberto-Culver would be able in this country to enjoin resort to arbitration he might have sought an order in France or some other country enjoining Alberto-Culver from proceeding with its litigation in the United States. Whatever recognition the courts of this country might ultimately have granted to the order of the foreign court, the dicey atmosphere of such a legal no-man's-land would surely damage the fabric of international commerce and trade, and imperil the willingness and ability of businessmen to enter into international commercial agreements.

The exception to the clear provisions of the Arbitration Act carved out by *Wilko* is simply inapposite to a case such as the one before us. In *Wilko* the Court reasoned that "(w)hen the security buyer, prior to any violation of the Securities Act, waives his right to sue in courts, he gives up more than would a participant in other business transactions. The security buyer has a wider choice of courts and venue. He thus surrenders one of the advantages the Act gives him . . . ." 346 U.S. at 43. In the context of an international contract, however, these advantages become chimerical since, as indicated above, an opposing party may by speedy resort to a foreign court block or hinder access to the American court of the purchaser's choice.

Two Terms ago in *The Bremen v. Zapata Off-Shore Co.*, 407

U.S. 1, we rejected the doctrine that a forum-selection clause of a contract, although voluntarily adopted by the parties, will not be respected in a suit brought in the United States "unless the selected state would provide a more convenient forum than the state in which suit is brought." Id. at 7. Rather, we concluded that a "forum clause should control absent a strong showing that it should be set aside." Id. at 15. We noted that "much uncertainty and possibly great inconvenience to both parties could arise if a suit could be maintained in any jurisdiction in which an accident might occur or if jurisdiction were left to any place (where personal or in rem jurisdiction might be established). The elimination of all such uncertainties by agreeing in advance on a forum acceptable to both parties is an indispensable element in international trade, commerce, and contracting." Id. at 13–14.

An agreement to arbitrate before a specified tribunal is, in effect, a specialized kind of forum-selection clause that posits not only the situs of suit but also the procedure to be used in resolving the dispute. The invalidation of such an agreement in the case before us would not only allow the respondent to repudiate its solemn promise but would, as well, reflect a "parochial concept that all disputes must be resolved under our laws and in our courts . . . ." We cannot have trade and commerce in world markets and international waters exclusively on our terms, governed by our laws, and resolved in our courts." Id. at 9.

For all these reasons we hold that the agreement of the parties in this case to arbitrate any dispute arising out of their international commercial transaction is to be respected and enforced by the federal courts in accord with the explicit provisions of the Arbitration Act.

Accordingly, the judgment of the Court of Appeals is reversed and the case is remanded to that court with directions to remand to the District Court for further proceedings consistent with this opinion.

NOTES

1. The parties in *Scherk* selected Illinois law to govern in arbitration. What does that mean, as a practical matter, if arbitral awards are not reviewed for ordinary errors of law? Would Illinois law control the validity of foreign intellectual property rights purportedly transferred as part of the sale of the foreign entities? Not likely.

2. Again with reference to choice of law, what if the parties, as is common in international disputes, choose the law of a foreign country to govern arbitration? Does that defeat the right of a party from the United States to press a claim governed by American statute? The next case suggests not, assuming there is sufficient transactional nexus with this country for there to be territorial and/or extraterritorial subject matter jurisdiction which would permit a United States court to apply the securities, antitrust or other statute in question. Is this expectation realistic, particularly in arbitrations before foreign arbitrators in a foreign forum?

3. What does *Scherk* suggest about the need for foreign arbitrators outside the United States to apply its federal securities statutes?

4. One of the problems created when certain statutory claims cannot be arbitrated is that a claimant will "stretch" to assert such a claim along with common law claims in an effort to induce the opposition to agree to litigate everything in court, or else to secure "two bites of the apple"—arbitration for common law claims and court for statutory ones. In the last case, the patents were covered by express warranties, so all the purchaser had to prove, at common law, was that the patents were not valid. The Securities Exchange Act claim was seemingly superfluous, and required additional proof of intent to deceive.

Mitsubishi Motor Corp. v. Soler Chrysler-Plymouth, Inc.

Supreme Court of the United States, 1985.
473 U.S. 614.

- BLACKMUN, J.

The principle question . . . is the arbitrability, pursuant to the FAA and the Convention on the Recognition and Enforcement of Awards, of claims arising under the Sherman Act, and encompassed within a valid arbitration clause in an international commercial transaction.

I.

Petitioner-cross-respondent Mitsubishi Motors Corporation (Mitsubishi) is a Japanese corporation which manufactures automobiles and has its principal place of business in Tokyo, Japan. Mitsubishi is the product of a joint venture between, on the one hand, Chrysler International, S.A. (CISA), a Swiss corporation registered in Geneva and wholly owned by Chrysler Corporation, and, on the other, Mitsubishi Heavy Industries, Inc., a Japanese corporation. The aim of the joint venture was the distribution through Chrysler dealers outside the continental United States of vehicles manufactured by Mitsubishi and bearing Chrysler and Mitsubishi trademarks. Respondent-cross-petitioner Soler Chrysler-Plymouth, Inc. (Soler), is a Puerto Rico corporation with its principal place of business in Pueblo Viejo, Guaynabo, Puerto Rico.

On October 31, 1979, Soler entered into a Distributor Agreement with CISA which provided for the sale by Soler of Mitsubishi-manufactured vehicles within a designated area, including metropolitan San Juan. On the same date, CISA, Soler, and Mitsubishi entered into a Sales Procedure Agreement (Sales Agreement) which, referring to the Distributor Agreement, provided for the direct sale of Mitsubishi products to Soler and governed the terms and conditions of such sales. Paragraph VI of the Sales Agreement, labeled "Arbitration of Certain Matters," provides:

> All disputes, controversies or differences which may arise between [Mitsubishi] and [Soler] out of or in relation to Articles I-B through V of this Agreement or for the breach thereof, shall be finally settled by arbitration in Japan in accordance with the rules and regulations of the Japan Commercial Arbitration Association.

Initially, Soler did a brisk business in Mitsubishi-manufactured vehicles. As a result of its strong performance, its minimum sales volume, specified by Mitsubishi and CISA, and agreed to by Soler, for the 1981 model year was substantially increased. In early 1981, however, the new-car market slackened. Soler ran into serious difficulties in meeting the expected sales volume, and by the spring of 1981 it felt itself compelled to request that Mitsubishi delay or cancel shipment of several orders. About the same time, Soler attempted to arrange for the transshipment of a quantity of its vehicles for sale in the continental United States and Latin America. Mitsubishi and CISA, however, refused permission for any such diversion, citing a variety of reasons, and no vehicles were transshipped. Attempts to work out these difficulties failed. Mitsubishi eventually withheld shipment of 966 vehicles, apparently representing orders placed for May, June, and July 1981 production, responsibility for which Soler disclaimed in February 1982.

The following month, Mitsubishi brought an action against Soler in the United States District Court for the District of Puerto Rico under the Federal Arbitration Act and the Convention. Mitsubishi sought an order, pursuant to 9 U.S.C. §§ 4 and 201, to compel arbitration in accord with the Sales Agreement. Shortly after filing the complaint, Mitsubishi filed a request for arbitration before the Japan Commercial Arbitration Association.

Soler denied the allegations and counterclaimed against both Mitsubishi and CISA. It alleged numerous breaches by Mitsubishi of the Sales Agreement. In the counterclaim premised on the Sherman Act, Soler alleged that Mitsubishi and CISA had conspired to divide markets in restraint of trade. To effectuate the plan, according to Soler, the manufacturers had refused to permit Soler to resell to buyers in North, Central, or South America vehicles it had obligated itself to purchase from Mitsubishi; had refused to ship ordered vehicles or the parts, such as heaters and defoggers, that would be necessary to permit Soler to make its vehicles suitable for resale outside Puerto Rico; and had coercively attempted to replace Soler and its other Puerto Rico distributors with a wholly owned subsidiary which would serve as the exclusive Mitsubishi distributor in Puerto Rico.

* * * *

At the outset, we address the contention raised in Soler's cross-petition that the arbitration clause at issue may not be read to encompass the statutory counterclaims stated in its answer to the complaint. In making this argument, Soler does not question the Court of Appeals' application of ¶ VI of the Sales Agreement to the disputes involved here as a matter of standard contract interpretation. Instead, it argues that as a matter of law a court may not construe an arbitration agreement to encompass claims arising out of statutes designed to protect a class to which the party resisting arbitration belongs "unless [that party] has expressly agreed" to arbitrate those claims, by which Soler presumably means that the arbitration clause must specifically mention the statute giving rise to the claims that a party to the clause seeks to arbitrate. Soler reasons that, because it falls within the class for whose benefit the federal and local antitrust laws and dealers' Acts were passed, but the arbitration clause at issue does not mention these statutes or statutes in general, the clause cannot be read to contemplate arbitration of these statutory claims.

We do not agree, for we find no warrant in the Arbitration Act for implying in every contract within its ken a presumption against arbitration of statutory claims. The Act's centerpiece provision makes a written agreement to arbitrate "in any maritime transaction or a contract evidencing a transaction involving commerce . . . valid, irrevocable, and enforceable, save upon such grounds as exist at law or in equity for the revocation of any contract." 9 U.S.C. § 2. The "liberal federal policy favoring arbitration agreements," Memorial Hospital v. Mercury Construction Corp., 460 U.S. 1, 24 (1983), manifested by this provision and the Act as a whole, is at bottom a policy guaranteeing the enforcement of private contractual arrangements: the Act simply "creates a body of federal substantive law establishing and regulating the duty to honor an agreement to arbitrate." Id. at 25 n.32. As this Court recently observed, "[t]he preeminent concern of Congress in passing the Act was to enforce private agreements into which parties had entered," a concern which "requires that we rigorously enforce agreements to arbitrate." Dean Witter Reynolds Inc. v. Byrd, 470 U.S. 213, 221 (1985).

Accordingly, the first task of a court asked to compel arbitration of a dispute is to determine whether the parties agreed to arbitrate that dispute. The court is to make this determination by applying the "federal substantive law of arbitrability, applicable to any arbitration agreement within the coverage of the Act." *Moses H. Cone Memorial Hospital*, 460 U.S. at 24. See Prima Paint Corp. v. Flood & Conklin Mfg. Co., 388 U.S. 395, 400–04 (1967); Southland Corp. v. Keating, 465 U.S. 1, 12 (1984). And that body of law counsels

> that questions of arbitrability must be addressed with a healthy regard for the federal policy favoring arbitration . . . . The Arbitration Act

> establishes that, as a matter of federal law, any doubts concerning the scope of arbitrable issues should be resolved in favor of arbitration, whether the problem at hand is the construction of the contract language itself or an allegation of waiver, delay, or a like defense to arbitrability.

Moses H. Cone Memorial Hospital, 460 U.S. at 24–25.

* * * *

That is not to say that all controversies implicating statutory rights are suitable for arbitration. There is no reason to distort the process of contract interpretation, however, in order to ferret out the inappropriate. Just as it is the congressional policy manifested in the Federal Arbitration Act that requires courts liberally to construe the scope of arbitration agreements covered by that Act, it is the congressional intention expressed in some other statute on which the courts must rely to identify any category of claims as to which agreements to arbitrate will be held unenforceable. For that reason, Soler's concern for statutorily protected classes provides no reason to color the lens through which the arbitration clause is read. By agreeing to arbitrate a statutory claim, a party does not forgo the substantive rights afforded by the statute; it only submits to their resolution in an arbitral, rather than a judicial, forum. It trades the procedures and opportunity for review of the courtroom for the simplicity, informality, and expedition of arbitration. We must assume that if Congress intended the substantive protection afforded by a given statute to include protection against waiver of the right to a judicial forum, that intention will be deducible from text or legislative history.

* * * *

We now turn to consider whether Soler's antitrust claims are nonarbitrable even though it has agreed to arbitrate them. In holding that they are not, the Court of Appeals followed the decision of the Second Circuit in *American Safety Equipment Corp. v. J.P. Maguire & Co.*, 391 F.2d 821 (1968). Notwithstanding the absence of any explicit support for such an exception in either the Sherman Act or the Federal Arbitration Act, the Second Circuit there reasoned that "the pervasive public interest in enforcement of the antitrust laws, and the nature of the claims that arise in such cases, combine to make . . . antitrust claims . . . inappropriate for arbitration." Id. at 827–28. We find it unnecessary to assess the legitimacy of the *American Safety* doctrine as applied to agreements to arbitrate arising from domestic transactions. As in *Scherk v. Alberto-Culver Co.*, 417 U.S. 506 (1974), we conclude that concerns of international comity, respect for the capacities of foreign and transnational tribunals, and sensitivity to the need of the international commercial system for predictability in the resolution of disputes require that we enforce the parties' agreement, even assuming that a contrary result would be forthcoming in a domestic context.

Even before *Scherk*, this Court had recognized the utility of forum-selection clauses in international transactions. In *The Bremen*, supra, an American oil company, seeking to evade a contractual choice of an English forum and, by implication, English law, filed a suit in admiralty in a United States District Court against the German corporation which had contracted to tow its rig to a location in the Adriatic Sea. Notwithstanding the possibility that the English court would enforce provisions in the towage contract exculpating the German party which an American court would refuse to enforce, this Court gave effect to the choice-of-forum clause. It observed:

> The expansion of American business and industry will hardly be encouraged if, notwithstanding solemn contracts, we insist on a parochial concept that all disputes must be resolved under our laws and in our courts . . . . We cannot have trade and commerce in world markets and international waters exclusively on our terms, governed by our laws, and resolved in our courts.

407 U.S. at 9.

* * * *

Identical considerations governed the Court's decision in *Scherk*, which categorized "[a]n agreement to arbitrate before a specified tribunal [as], in effect, a specialized kind of forum-selection clause that posits not only the situs of suit but also the procedure to be used in resolving the dispute." 417 U.S. at 519. In *Scherk*, the American company Alberto-Culver purchased several interrelated business enterprises, organized under the laws of Germany and Liechtenstein, as well as the rights held by those enterprises in certain trademarks, from a German citizen who at the time of trial resided in Switzerland. Although the contract of sale contained a clause providing for arbitration before the International Chamber of Commerce in Paris of "any controversy or claim [arising] out of this agreement or the breach thereof," Alberto-Culver subsequently brought suit against Scherk in a Federal District Court in Illinois, alleging that Scherk had violated § 10(b) of the Securities Exchange Act of 1934 by fraudulently misrepresenting the status of the trademarks as unencumbered. The District Court denied a motion to stay the proceedings before it and enjoined the parties from going forward before the arbitral tribunal in Paris. The Court of Appeals for the Seventh Circuit affirmed, relying on this Court's holding in *Wilko v. Swan*, 346 U.S. 427, that agreements to arbitrate disputes arising under the Securities Act of 1933 are nonarbitrable. This Court reversed, enforcing the arbitration agreement even while assuming for purposes of the decision that the controversy would be nonarbitrable under the holding of *Wilko* had it arisen out of a domestic transaction.

* * * *

At the outset, we confess to some skepticism of certain aspects of the *American Safety* doctrine. As distilled by the First Circuit, 723 F.2d at 162, the doctrine comprises four ingredients. First, private parties play a pivotal role in aiding governmental enforcement of the antitrust laws by means of the private action for treble damages. Second, "the strong possibility that contracts which generate antitrust disputes may be contracts of adhesion militates against automatic forum determination by contract." Third, antitrust issues, prone to complication, require sophisticated legal and economic analysis, and thus are "ill-adapted to strengths of the arbitral process, i.e., expedition, minimal requirements of written rationale, simplicity, resort to basic concepts of common sense and simple equity." Finally, just as "issues of war and peace are too important to be vested in the generals . . . decisions as to antitrust regulation of business are too important to be lodged in arbitrators chosen from the business community-particularly those from a foreign community that has had no experience with or exposure to our law and values." See *American Safety*, 391 F.2d at 826–27.

Initially, we find the second concern unjustified. The mere appearance of an antitrust dispute does not alone warrant invalidation of the selected forum on the undemonstrated assumption that the arbitration clause is tainted. A party resisting arbitration of course may attack directly the validity of the agreement to arbitrate. Moreover, the party may attempt to make a showing that would warrant setting aside the forum-selection clause-that the agreement was "[a]ffected by fraud, undue influence, or overweening bargaining power;" that "enforcement would be unreasonable and unjust;" or that proceedings "in the contractual forum will be so gravely difficult and inconvenient that [the resisting party] will for all practical purposes be deprived of his day in court." *The Bremen*, 407 U.S. at 12, 15, 18. But absent such a showing—and none was attempted here—there is no basis for assuming the forum inadequate or its selection unfair.

Next, potential complexity should not suffice to ward off arbitration. We might well have some doubt that even the courts following *American Safety* subscribe fully to the view that antitrust matters are inherently insusceptible to resolution by arbitration, as these same courts have agreed that an undertaking to arbitrate antitrust claims entered into *after* the dispute arises is acceptable. See, e.g., Coenen v. R.W. Pressprich & Co., 453 F.2d 1209, 1215 (2d Cir. 1972), Cobb v. Lewis, 488 F.2d 41, 48 (5th Cir. 1974). And the vertical restraints which most frequently give birth to antitrust claims covered by an arbitration agreement will not often occasion the monstrous proceedings that have given antitrust litigation an image of intractability. In any event, adaptability and access to expertise are hallmarks of arbitration. The anticipated subject matter of the dispute may be taken into account when the arbitrators are appointed, and arbitral rules typically provide for the participation of experts either employed by the parties or appointed by the tribunal. Moreover, it is often a judgment that streamlined proceedings and expeditious results will best serve their needs that causes parties to agree to arbitrate their disputes; it is typically a desire to keep the effort and expense required to resolve a dispute within manageable bounds that prompts them mutually to forgo access to judicial remedies. In sum, the factor of potential complexity alone does not persuade us that an arbitral tribunal could not properly handle an antitrust matter.

For similar reasons, we also reject the proposition that an arbitration panel will pose too great a danger of innate hostility to the constraints on business conduct that antitrust law imposes. International arbitrators frequently are drawn from the legal as well as the business community; where the dispute has an important legal component, the parties and the arbitral body with whose assistance they have agreed to settle their dispute can be expected to select arbitrators accordingly. We decline to indulge the presumption that the parties and arbitral body conducting a proceeding will be unable or unwilling to retain competent, conscientious, and impartial arbitrators.

We are left, then, with the core of the *American Safety* doctrine-the fundamental importance to American democratic capitalism of the regime of the antitrust laws. As the Court of Appeals pointed out:

> A claim under the antitrust laws is not merely a private matter. The Sherman Act is designed to promote the national interest in a competitive economy; thus, the plaintiff asserting his rights under the Act has been likened to a private attorney-general who protects the public's interest. 723 F.2d at 168.

The treble-damages provision wielded by the private litigant is a chief tool in the antitrust enforcement scheme, posing a crucial deterrent to potential violators. See, e.g., Perma Life Mufflers, Inc. v. Int'l Parts Corp., 392 U.S. 134, 138–39 (1968).

* * * *

There is no reason to assume at the outset of the dispute that international arbitration will not provide an adequate mechanism. To be sure, the international arbitral tribunal owes no prior allegiance to the legal norms of particular states; hence, it has no direct obligation to vindicate their statutory dictates. The tribunal, however, is bound to effectuate the intentions of the parties. Where the parties have agreed that the arbitral body is to decide a defined set of claims which includes, as in these cases, those arising from the application of American antitrust law, the tribunal therefore should be bound to decide that dispute in accord with the national law giving rise to the claim. And so long as the prospective litigant effectively may vindicate its statutory cause of action in the arbitral forum, the statute will continue to serve both its remedial and deterrent function.

* * * *

- STEVENS, J., dissenting (with whom BRENNAN, J., joins, and with whom MARSHALL, J., joins, except as to Part II).

* * * *

The federal policy favoring arbitration cannot sustain the weight that the Court assigns to it. A clause requiring arbitration of all claims "relating to" a contract surely could not encompass a claim that the arbitration clause was itself part of a contract in restraint of trade. Cf. Paramount Famous Lasky Corp. v. United States, 282 U.S. 30 (1930); see also United States v. Paramount Pictures, Inc., 334 U.S. 131, 176 (1948). Nor in my judgment should it be read to encompass a claim that relies, not on a failure to perform the contract, but on an independent violation of federal law. The matters asserted by way of defense do not control the character, or the source, of the claim that Soler has asserted. Accordingly, simply as a matter of ordinary contract interpretation, I would hold that Soler's antitrust claim is not arbitrable.

* * * *

Until today all of our cases enforcing agreements to arbitrate under the Arbitration Act have involved contract claims. In one, the party claiming a breach of contractual warranties also claimed that the breach amounted to fraud actionable under § 10(b) of the Securities Exchange Act of 1934. But this is the first time the Court has considered the question whether a standard arbitration clause referring to claims arising out of or relating to a contract should be construed to cover statutory claims that have only an indirect relationship to the contract. In my opinion, neither the Congress that enacted the Arbitration Act in 1925, nor the many parties who have agreed to such standard clauses, could have anticipated the Court's answer to that question.

* * * *

This Court would be well advised to endorse the collective wisdom of the distinguished judges of the Courts of Appeals who have unanimously concluded that the statutory remedies fashioned by Congress for the enforcement of the antitrust laws render an agreement to arbitrate antitrust disputes unenforceable. Arbitration awards are only reviewable for manifest disregard of the law and the rudimentary procedures which make arbitration so desirable in the context of a private dispute often mean that the record is so inadequate that the arbitrator's decision is virtually unreviewable. Despotic decision making of this kind is fine for parties who are willing to agree in advance to settle for a best approximation of the correct result in order to resolve quickly and inexpensively any contractual dispute that may arise in an ongoing commercial relationship. Such informality, however, is simply unacceptable when every error may have devastating consequences for important businesses in our national economy and may undermine their ability to compete in world markets. Instead of "muffling a grievance in the cloakroom of arbitration," the public interest in free competitive markets would be better served by having the issues resolved "in the light of impartial public court adjudication." See Merrill Lynch, Pierce, Fenner & Smith, Inc. v. Ware, 414 U.S. 117, 136 (1973).

NOTES

1. As far as the Second Circuit's *American Safety* case is concerned, that Court no longer follows it. *E.g.*, JLM Industries, Inc. v. Stolt-Nielsen, 387 F.3d 163 (2d Cir. 2004). A number of other federal courts have read *Mitsubishi*'s criticism of *American Safety* as indication that the Supreme Court would treat domestic antitrust claims as arbitrable. *E.g.*, Nghiem v. NEC Elec., Inc., 25 F.3d 1437 (9th Cir. 1994).

2. One of the United States Supreme Court's footnotes in *Scherk* makes reference to the key international treaty, known as the United Nations (New York) Convention for Recognition and Enforcement of Foreign Arbitral Awards, requiring member states to enforce arbitral agreements and awards arising out of transactions between nationals of those different countries. In *Mitsubishi*, the application to compel arbitration was based both on the FAA and the Convention. Under Article V(2)(b) of the Convention, a domestic court may refuse enforcement of a foreign award which "would be contrary to the public policy of that country." If the arbitrators in Japan refuse to consider the antitrust claim in *Mitsubishi*, what happens? What if they purport to consider it, but reject it despite its merit?

3. The text of the U.N. Convention is in Appendix 7. The FAA provisions implementing it are in its Chapter 2, §§ 201–08. *See* Appendix 2. That is why the Court in the last case refers both to

Sections 4 and 204 of the FAA. There are now over 140 countries party to the U.N. Convention which permits participation limited to reciprocity—*i.e.*, if Country A will not enforce Country B's awards, Country B need not, upon reciprocity reservation, respect Country A's awards. Is this approach based on sovereignty considerations? Caselaw strongly suggests that even what the Supreme Court in *Wilko* termed "manifest disregard" is not a basis to vacate an award under the Convention. We will return to this later, but the Convention makes no provision for the overturning of awards for even the most fundamental legal error.

4. In a *Mitsubishi* footnote, the Supreme Court states that if the parties' choice of a foreign forum and foreign law resulted in a waiver of its antitrust protection, "we would have little hesitation in condemning the agreement as against public policy." Actually, Article II of the U.N. Convention has no "public policy" exception to enforcement of agreements to arbitrate. Compare Article V of the Convention regarding award enforcement, which has a "public policy" exception. If the arbitrators in *Mitsubishi* refused to hear the antitrust counterclaim, could it then be brought in an American court? Actually, by the time of oral argument in *Mitsubishi*, the Japanese arbitrators had accepted submission of Soler's antitrust claims.

5. Are foreign court judgments enforceable in the United States as a matter of right, other than as a matter of treaty? Of comity? *See* N.Y. C.P.L.R. 5301.

6. Note the Court's rejection of any requirement that the arbitral agreement make specific reference to statutory claims if they are to be covered. Do antitrust claims "arise under" a contract because one of the parties engages in activity which, while not expressly barred by the contract, is an undue restraint of trade, and hence, an antitrust violation?

7. Are the majority and dissenting justices in accord as to standard of judicial review for an international antitrust award?

8. There are references in *Mitsubishi* to certain Supreme Court cases referencing the "federal law of arbitration," which stems from federal caselaw under the FAA, and contains a very strong pro-arbitration policy. It is this policy that is relied upon in deciding whether a given type of claim is arbitrable from a policy standpoint, and that also

influences how broadly the language of arbitral agreements (such as "arising under") is construed.

9. The Court in *Mitsubishi* first references the concept than an American entity may have to relinquish application of American law in order to have a foreign arbitral mechanism available. Later on, however, the Court references the parties' intent here, discerned in its interpretation of their arbitration agreement, to have antitrust protections under the United States' statute apply. This is the predicate for what the Court finds to be the obligation of the foreign arbitrations to take cognizance of the American antitrust claims. What party intent? How was such intent manifested when the clause did not mention statutory claims of any sort? What effect should the choice of Swiss law clause have? Unlike in the *Sherk* case, where the transactional nexus with the United States was very peripheral, Soler's claims arose from the transaction of business in the United States, so that, absent an arbitration requirement, the District Court should have had both in personam and subject matter jurisdiction.

[A] Evaluating Mitsubishi — The American Sherman Antitrust Act

Many students (and practitioners) have not had an antitrust course. They should have a basic understanding of the antitrust laws found in the Sherman Act and other statutes. Section 2 of the Sherman Act condemns monopolistic practices that are unduly anticompetitive. Such claims are often brought by the federal government rather than private litigants.

More important from the private claim perspective are Section 1 prohibitions against concerted actions by two or more parties in restraint of trade. Restraints may be "vertical," such as when a manufacturer successfully dictates maximum or minimum pricing to a distributor or retailer. Restraints may also be by agreement between parties at the same level in the distributive chain—two or more retailers, for example. Such "horizontal" restraints may include price fixing or concerted refusals to deal with a third party. In *Mitsubishi*, two auto manufacturers in a joint venture were alleged by a distributor to have conspired to divide markets in violation of Section 1 of the Sherman Act, in part by refusing to permit it to sell cars outside its territory—the perceived ill would be in the "horizontal" agreement between the two manufacturers—a single manufacturer is normally entitled to limit distributors of its products to specified territories. There are also other antitrust provisions, including those concerning pricing found in the Robinson-Patman Act of 1936, 15 U.S.C. § 13.

The "public" nature of the antitrust laws is apparent. Private claimants, if successful, get treble damages and attorney's fees. Such private actions are sometimes said to be *parens patriae*—to be on behalf of the citizenry as a whole. *Parens patriae* literally means "parent of the country," and is often considered by the Supreme Court as "necessary to be exercised in the interest of humanity, and for the prevention of injury to those who cannot protect themselves. Alfred L. Snapp & Son, Inc. v. Puerto Rico *ex rel.* Baez, 458 U.S. 592, 600 (1982) (quoting Mormon Church v. United States, 136 U.S. 1, 57 (1890)). Also, the Department of Justice may bring both civil and criminal proceedings to stop antitrust violations.

Most types of Sherman Act violations have, over the years, been subjected by the United States Supreme Court to the "rule of reason" doctrine identified in *Standard Oil Co. of New Jersey v. United States*, 221 U.S. 1 (1911). On the other hand, certain agreements in restraint of trade have been held to be illegal per se—these include price fixing and group boycotts. As the pendulum moves back and forth, the more recent trend has been for the Supreme Court to restrict per se illegality. The alleged non-price concerted vertical restraint in *Mitsubishi* would appear to be subject, under American law, to a "rule of reason" analysis. *See* Continental TV v. GTE Sylvania, 433 U.S. 36 (1977). The "rule of reason" focuses on the economic consequences of the restraint at issue.

Would the Japanese arbitrators in *Mitsubishi* be equipped to make an economic impact analysis under a "rule of reason" analysis? What about domestic arbitrators?

§ 2.03 THE UNITED NATIONS (NEW YORK) CONVENTION

The New York Convention (Appendix 7) requires member states to enforce both agreements to arbitrate (Article II) and resulting awards (Article III). In Article V, the Convention specifies when enforcement of an award may be refused. Review Article V. Nothing is said regarding a refusal to recognize an award because it is wrong. Under Section 2(b) of Article V, however, a court of a member state may refuse to enforce an award that is "contrary to the public policy" of the state in which the court is located. That exception, however, is sparingly used. The Second Circuit Court of Appeals, in *Parsons & Whittemore Overseas Co., Inc. v. Societe General de l'Industrie du Papier*, 508 F.2d 969, 974 (2d Cir. 1974), would limit the "public policy" exception under the Convention to awards violating the "most basic notions of morality and justice." Is that consonant with what the Supreme Court said in *Mitsubishi* about not accepting a foreign tribunal's refusal to entertain the antitrust claims? Is it germane that choice of law principles permit sophisticated commercial parties to contract for application of a body of law from a forum having little, if anything, to do with the transaction at hand. *See* RESTATEMENT (SECOND) OF CONFLICT OF LAWS § 187 (1971).

The fact is, however, that certain statutory laws may be said to be "mandatory," so that they must be applied to conduct taking place, or impacting, within the country that has those laws. See Mayer, *Mandatory Rules of Law in International Arbitration*, 2 ARB. INT'L 274 (1986). In *PPG Indus., Inc. v. Pilkington PLC*, 825 F. Supp. 1465 (D. Ariz. 1993), the Court directed that arbitrators, asked to proceed under British law, nonetheless apply the United States antitrust laws to Sherman Act claims. At the same time, it is clear that if a forum's remedies are sufficient to protect perceived statutory interests, the remedies under the foreign law selected need not duplicate those available in the American system. *Haynesworth v. The Corp.*, 121 F.3d 956, 969 (5th Cir. 1997). *See also* Lipcon v. Underwriters of Lloyd's London, 148 F.3d 1285, 1297–98 (11th Cir. 1998) (foreign remedies do not have to be as broad). Does any of this fall under the Convention's "public policy" exception to enforcement?

§ 2.04 SECURITIES CLAIMS REVISITED – THE "NEW" VIEW

With *Scherk* and *Mitsubishi* behind it, the Supreme Court now forges ahead to extend FAA coverage to federal statutory claims in domestic cases. While part of the focus to date has been on the practicalities imposed by international transactions involving an American and a foreign entity, there has also been reference in the cases to a strong federal policy in favor of arbitration and rejection in *Mitsubishi* of any argument that such policy should not apply to contracts of adhesion. So too, it is already established that an arbitration clause normally need not expressly reference "statutory claims" for them to be covered. Gone too is the notion that arbitrators can handle fact issues, and breach of contract issues, but not the issues of law posed by statute. The stage is set.

Shearson/American Express, Inc. v. McMahon

Supreme Court of the United States, 1987.
482 U.S. 220.

- O'CONNOR, J.

* * * *

The Arbitration Act, standing alone, therefore mandates enforcement of agreements to arbitrate statutory claims. Like any statutory directive, the Arbitration Act's mandate may be overridden by a contrary congressional command. The burden is on the party opposing arbitration, however, to show that Congress intended to preclude a waiver of judicial remedies for the statutory rights at issue. If Congress did intend to limit or prohibit waiver of a judicial forum for a particular claim, such an intent "will be deducible from [the statute's] text or legislative history," or from an inherent conflict between arbitration and the statute's underlying purposes.

To defeat application of the Arbitration Act in this case, therefore, the McMahons must demonstrate that Congress intended to make an exception to the Arbitration Act for claims arising under RICO and the Exchange Act, an intention discernible from the text, history, or purposes of the statute. We examine the McMahons' arguments regarding the Exchange Act and RICO in turn.

When Congress enacted the Exchange Act in 1934, it did not specifically address the question of the arbitrability of § 10(b) claims. The McMahons contend, however, that congressional intent to require a judicial forum for the resolution of § 10(b) claims can be deduced from § 29(a) of the Exchange Act, 15 U.S.C. § 78cc(a), which declares void "[a]ny condition, stipulation, or provision binding any person to waive compliance with any provision of [the Act]."

First, we reject the McMahons' argument that § 29(a) forbids waiver of § 27 of the Exchange Act, 15 U.S.C. § 78aa. Section 27 provides in relevant part:

> The district courts of the United States . . . shall have exclusive jurisdiction of violations of this title or the rules and regulations thereunder, and of all suits in equity and actions at law brought to enforce any liability or duty created by this title or the rules and regulations thereunder.

The McMahons contend that an agreement to waive this jurisdictional provision is unenforceable because § 29(a) voids the waiver of "any provision" of the Exchange Act. The language of § 29(a), however, does not reach so far. What the antiwaiver provision of § 29(a) forbids is enforcement of agreements to waive "compliance" with the provisions of the statute. But § 27 itself does not impose any duty with which persons trading in securities must "comply." By its terms, § 29(a) only prohibits waiver of the substantive obligations imposed by the Exchange Act. Because § 27 does not impose any statutory duties, its waiver does not constitute a waiver of "compliance with any provision" of the Exchange Act under § 29(a).

We do not read *Wilko* as compelling a different result. In *Wilko*, the Court held that a predispute agreement could not be enforced to compel arbitration of a claim arising under § 12(2) of the Securities Act, 15 U.S.C. § 77l(2). The basis for the ruling was § 14 of the Securities

Act, which, like § 29(a) of the Exchange Act, declares void any stipulation "to waive compliance with any provision" of the statute. At the beginning of its analysis, the *Wilko* Court stated that the Securities Act's jurisdictional provision was "the kind of 'provision' that cannot be waived under § 14 of the Securities Act." 346 U.S. at 435. This statement, however, can only be understood in the context of the Court's ensuing discussion explaining why arbitration was inadequate as a means of enforcing "the provisions of the Securities Act, advantageous to the buyer." Ibid. The conclusion in *Wilko* was expressly based on the Court's belief that a judicial forum was needed to protect the substantive rights created by the Securities Act: "As the protective provisions of the Securities Act require the exercise of judicial direction to fairly assure their effectiveness, it seems to us that Congress must have intended § 14 . . . to apply to waiver of judicial trial and review." Id. at 437. *Wilko* must be understood, therefore, as holding that the plaintiff's waiver of the "right to select the judicial forum," id. at 435, was unenforceable only because arbitration was judged inadequate to enforce the statutory rights created by § 12(2).

Indeed, any different reading of *Wilko* would be inconsistent with this Court's decision in *Scherk v. Alberto-Culver Co.*, 417 U.S. 506 (1974). In *Scherk*, the Court upheld enforcement of a predispute agreement to arbitrate Exchange Act claims by parties to an international contract. The *Scherk* Court assumed for purposes of its opinion that *Wilko* applied to the Exchange Act, but it determined that an international contract "involve[d] considerations and policies significantly different from those found controlling in *Wilko*." The Court reasoned that arbitration reduced the uncertainty of international contracts and obviated the danger that a dispute might be submitted to a hostile or unfamiliar forum. At the same time, the Court noted that the advantages of judicial resolution were diminished by the possibility that the opposing party would make "speedy resort to a foreign court." Id. at 518. The decision in *Scherk* thus turned on the Court's judgment that under the circumstances of that case, arbitration was an adequate substitute for adjudication as a means of enforcing the parties' statutory rights. *Scherk* supports our understanding that *Wilko* must be read as barring waiver of a judicial forum only where arbitration is inadequate to protect the substantive rights at issue. At the same time, it confirms that where arbitration does provide an adequate means of enforcing the provisions of the Exchange Act, § 29(a) does not void a predispute waiver of § 27—*Scherk* upheld enforcement of just such a waiver.

The second argument offered by the McMahons is that the arbitration agreement effects an impermissible waiver of the substantive protections of the Exchange Act. Ordinarily, "[b]y agreeing to arbitrate a statutory claim, a party does not forgo the substantive rights afforded by the statute; it only submits to their resolution in an arbitral, rather than a judicial, forum." *Mitsubishi Motors Corp. v. Soler Chrysler-Plymouth, Inc.*, 473 U.S. at 628. The McMahons argue, however, that § 29(a) compels a different conclusion. Initially, they contend that predispute agreements are void under § 29(a) because they tend to result from broker overreaching. They reason, as do some commentators, that *Wilko* is premised on the belief "that arbitration clauses in securities sales agreements generally are not freely negotiated." See, e.g., Sterk, Enforceability of Agreements to Arbitrate: An Examination of the Public Policy Defense, 2 CARDOZO L. REV. 481, 519 (1981). According to this view, *Wilko* barred enforcement of predispute agreements because of this frequent inequality of bargaining power, reasoning that Congress intended for § 14 generally to ensure that sellers did not "maneuver buyers into a position that might weaken their ability to recover under the Securities Act." 346 U.S. at 432. The McMahons urge that we should interpret § 29(a) in the same fashion.

We decline to give *Wilko* a reading so far at odds with the plain language of § 14, or to adopt such an unlikely interpretation of § 29(a). The concern that § 29(a) is directed against is evident from the statute's plain language: it is a concern with whether an agreement "waive[s] compliance with [a] provision" of the Exchange Act. The voluntariness of the agreement is irrelevant to this inquiry: if a stipulation waives compliance with a statutory duty, it is void under § 29(a), whether voluntary or not. Thus, a customer cannot negotiate a reduction in commissions in exchange for a waiver of compliance with the requirements of the Exchange Act, even if the customer knowingly and voluntarily agreed to the bargain. Section 29(a) is concerned, not with whether brokers "maneuver[ed customers] into" an agreement, but with whether the agreement "weaken[s] their ability to recover under the [Exchange] Act." 346 U.S. at 432. The former is grounds for revoking the contract under ordinary principles of contract law; the latter is grounds for voiding the agreement under § 29(a).

The other reason advanced by the McMahons for finding a waiver of their § 10(b) rights is that arbitration does "weaken their ability to recover under the [Exchange] Act." That is the heart of the Court's decision in *Wilko*, and respondents urge that we should follow its reasoning. *Wilko* listed several grounds why, in the Court's view, the "effectiveness [of the Act's provisions] in application is lessened in arbitration." 346 U.S. at 435. First, the *Wilko* Court believed that arbitration proceedings were not suited to cases requiring "subjective findings on the purpose and knowledge of an alleged violator." Id. at 435–36. *Wilko* also was concerned that arbitrators must make legal determinations "without judicial instruction on the law," and that an arbitration award "may be made without explanation of [the arbitrator's] reasons and without a complete record of their proceedings." Id. at 436. Finally, *Wilko* noted that the "[p]ower to vacate an award is limited," and that "interpretations of the law by the arbitrators in contrast to manifest disregard are not subject, in the federal courts, to judicial review for error in interpretation." Id. at 436–37. *Wilko* concluded that in view of these drawbacks to arbitration, § 12(2) claims "require[d] the exercise of judicial direction to fairly assure their effectiveness." Id. at 437.

As Justice Frankfurter noted in his dissent in *Wilko*, the Court's opinion did not rest on any evidence, either "in the record . . . [or] in the facts of which [it could] take judicial notice," that "the arbitral system . . . would not afford the plaintiff the rights to which he is entitled." Id. at 439. Instead, the reasons given in *Wilko* reflect a general suspicion of the desirability of arbitration and the competence of arbitral tribunals—most apply with no greater force to the arbitration of securities disputes than to the arbitration of legal disputes generally. It is difficult to reconcile *Wilko*'s mistrust of the arbitral process with this Court's subsequent decisions involving the Arbitration Act. See, e.g., *Mitsubishi Motors Corp.*

Indeed, most of the reasons given in *Wilko* have been rejected subsequently by the Court as a basis for holding claims to be nonarbitrable. In *Mitsubishi*, for example, we recognized that arbitral tribunals are readily capable of handling the factual and legal complexities of antitrust claims, notwithstanding the absence of judicial instruction and supervision. See 473 U.S. at 633–34. Likewise, we have concluded that the streamlined procedures of arbitration do not entail any consequential restriction on substantive rights. Id. at 628. Finally, we have indicated that there is no reason to assume at the outset that arbitrators will not follow the law; although judicial scrutiny of arbitration awards necessarily is limited, such review is sufficient to ensure that arbitrators comply with the requirements of the statute. See id. at 636–37, and n.19 (declining to assume that arbitration will not be resolved in accordance with statutory law, but reserving consideration of "effect of an arbitral tribunal's failure to take cognizance of the statutory cause of action on the claimant's capacity to reinstate suit in federal court").

The suitability of arbitration as a means of enforcing Exchange Act rights is evident from our decision in *Scherk*. Although the holding in that case was limited to international agreements, the competence of arbitral tribunals to resolve § 10(b) claims is the same in both settings. Courts likewise have routinely enforced agreements to arbitrate § 10(b) claims where both parties are members of a securities exchange or the National Association of Securities Dealers (NASD), suggesting that arbitral tribunals are fully capable of handling such matters. And courts uniformly have concluded that *Wilko* does not apply to the submission to arbitration of existing disputes, see, e.g., Gardner v. Shearson, Hammill & Co., 433 F.2d 367 (CA5 1970); Moran v. Paine, Webber, Jackson & Curtis, 389 F.2d 242 (CA3 1968), even though the inherent suitability of arbitration as a means of resolving § 10(b) claims remains unchanged.

Thus, the mistrust of arbitration that formed the basis for the *Wilko* opinion in 1953 is difficult to square with the assessment of arbitration that has prevailed since that time. This is especially so in light of the intervening changes in the regulatory structure of the securities laws. Even if *Wilko*'s assumptions regarding arbitration were valid at the time *Wilko* was decided, most certainly they do not hold true today for arbitration procedures subject to the SEC's oversight authority.

In 1953, when *Wilko* was decided, the Commission had only limited authority over the rules governing self-regulatory organizations (SROs)—the national securities exchanges and registered securities associations—and this authority appears not to have included any authority at all over their arbitration rules. Since the 1975 amendments to § 19 of the Exchange Act, however, the Commission has had expansive power to ensure the adequacy of the arbitration procedures employed by the SROs. No proposed rule change may take effect unless the SEC finds that the proposed rule is consistent with the requirements of the Exchange Act, and the Commission has the power, on its own initiative, to "abrogate, add to, and delete from" any SRO rule if it finds such changes necessary or appropriate to further the objectives of the Act. In short, the Commission has broad authority to oversee and to regulate the rules adopted by the SROs relating to customer disputes, including the power to mandate the adoption of any rules it deems necessary to ensure that arbitration procedures adequately protect statutory rights.

In the exercise of its regulatory authority, the SEC has specifically approved the arbitration procedures of the New York Stock Exchange, the American Stock Exchange, and the NASD, the organizations mentioned in the arbitration agreement at issue in this case. We conclude that where, as in this case, the prescribed procedures are subject to the Commission's § 19 authority, an arbitration agreement does not effect a waiver of the protections of the Act. While stare decisis concerns may counsel against upsetting *Wilko*'s contrary conclusion under the Securities Act, we refuse to extend *Wilko*'s reasoning to the Exchange Act in light of these intervening regulatory developments. The McMahons' agreement to submit to arbitration therefore is not tantamount to an impermissible waiver of the McMahons' rights under § 10(b), and the agreement is not void on that basis under § 29(a).

* * * *

NOTES

1. *McMahon* involves customer claims against their securities broker. Is such a case more or less suitable for arbitration than *Scherk*? What if customer claims, which typically allege unsuitability of investment under a "know your customer" industry requirement, were heard instead by judges? By juries?

2. *McMahon* rejects the argument that even extreme adhesion invalidates arbitration provisions. Assuming all stock brokerage houses use customer agreements requiring arbitration of customer claims, is that rejection sound? Under current brokerage industry regulation, broker dealers would have to arbitrate if the customer so elected even absent

agreement to do so.

3. *McMahon*, heavily relying on *Mitsubishi*, holds that private treble damage RICO claims are also arbitrable, in part because they are no more complicated than antitrust claims. Is that also indication that the Supreme Court sees domestic antitrust claims as being arbitrable?

§ 2.05 WORKPLACE DISCRIMINATION

Gilmer v. Interstate/Johnson Lane Corp.

Supreme Court of the United States, 1991.
500 U.S. 20.

- WHITE, J.

The question presented in this case is whether a claim under the Age Discrimination in Employment Act of 1967 (ADEA), 29 U.S.C. § 621 et seq., can be subjected to compulsory arbitration pursuant to an arbitration agreement in a securities registration application. The Court of Appeals held that it could, 895 F.2d 195 (CA4 1990), and we affirm.

Respondent Interstate/Johnson Lane Corporation (Interstate) hired petitioner Robert Gilmer as a Manager of Financial Services in May 1981. As required by his employment, Gilmer registered as a securities representative with several stock exchanges, including the New York Stock Exchange (NYSE). His registration application, entitled "Uniform Application for Securities Industry Registration or Transfer," provided, among other things, that Gilmer "agree[d] to arbitrate any dispute, claim or controversy" arising between him and Interstate "that is required to be arbitrated under the rules, constitutions or by-laws of the organizations with which I register." Of relevance to this case, NYSE Rule 347 provides for arbitration of "[a]ny controversy between a registered representative and any member or member organization arising out of the employment or termination of employment of such registered representative."

Interstate terminated Gilmer's employment in 1987, at which

time Gilmer was 62 years of age. After first filing an age discrimination charge with the Equal Employment Opportunity Commission (EEOC), Gilmer subsequently brought suit in the United States District Court for the Western District of North Carolina, alleging that Interstate had discharged him because of his age, in violation of the ADEA. In response to Gilmer's complaint, Interstate filed in the District Court a motion to compel arbitration of the ADEA claim. In its motion, Interstate relied upon the arbitration agreement in Gilmer's registration application, as well as the Federal Arbitration Act (FAA), 9 U.S.C. § 1 et seq.

It is by now clear that statutory claims may be the subject of an arbitration agreement, enforceable pursuant to the FAA. Indeed, in recent years we have held enforceable arbitration agreements relating to claims arising under the Sherman Act, 15 U.S.C. §§ 1–7; § 10(b) of the Securities Exchange Act of 1934, 15 U.S.C. § 78j(b); the civil provisions of the Racketeer Influenced and Corrupt Organizations Act (RICO), 18 U.S.C. § 1961 et seq.; and § 12(2) of the Securities Act of 1933, 15 U.S.C. § 77l(2). See Mitsubishi Motors Corp. v. Soler Chrysler-Plymouth, Inc., 473 U.S. 614 (1985); Shearson/American Express, Inc. v. McMahon, 482 U.S. 220 (1987); Rodriguez de Quijas v. Shearson/American Express, Inc., 490 U.S. 477 (1989). In these cases we recognized that "[b]y agreeing to arbitrate a statutory claim, a party does not forgo the substantive rights afforded by the statute; it only submits to their resolution in an arbitral, rather than a judicial, forum." *Mitsubishi*, 473 U.S. at 628.

Although all statutory claims may not be appropriate for arbitration, "[h]aving made the bargain to arbitrate, the party should be held to it unless Congress itself has evinced an intention to preclude a waiver of judicial remedies for the statutory rights at issue." Ibid. In this regard, we note that the burden is on Gilmer to show that Congress intended to preclude a waiver of a judicial forum for ADEA claims. See *McMahon*, 482 U.S. at 227. If such an intention exists, it will be discoverable in the text of the ADEA, its legislative history, or an "inherent conflict" between arbitration and the ADEA's underlying purposes. See ibid. Throughout such an inquiry, it should be kept in mind that "questions of arbitrability must be addressed with a healthy regard for the federal policy favoring arbitration." *Moses H. Cone*, supra, 460 U.S. at 24.

Gilmer concedes that nothing in the text of the ADEA or its legislative history explicitly precludes arbitration. He argues, however, that compulsory arbitration of ADEA claims pursuant to arbitration agreements would be inconsistent with the statutory framework and purposes of the ADEA. Like the Court of Appeals, we disagree.

Congress enacted the ADEA in 1967 "to promote employment of older persons based on their ability rather than age; to prohibit arbitrary age discrimination in employment; [and] to help employers and workers find ways of meeting problems arising from the impact of age on employment." 29 U.S.C. § 621(b). To achieve those goals, the ADEA, among other things, makes it unlawful for an employer "to fail or refuse to hire or to discharge any individual or otherwise discriminate against any individual with respect to his compensation, terms, conditions, or privileges of employment, because of such individual's age." § 623(a)(1). This proscription is enforced both by private suits and by the EEOC. In order for an aggrieved individual to bring suit under the ADEA, he or she must first file a charge with the EEOC and then wait at least 60 days. § 626(d). An individual's right to sue is extinguished, however, if the EEOC institutes an action against the employer. § 626(c)(1). Before the EEOC can bring such an action, though, it must "attempt to eliminate the discriminatory practice or practices alleged, and to effect voluntary compliance with the requirements of this chapter through informal methods of conciliation, conference, and persuasion." § 626(b); see also 29 CFR § 1626.15 (1990).

As Gilmer contends, the ADEA is designed not only to address individual grievances, but also to further important social policies. We do not perceive any inherent inconsistency between those policies, however, and enforcing agreements to arbitrate age discrimination claims.

We also are unpersuaded by the argument that arbitration will undermine the role of the EEOC in enforcing the ADEA. An individual ADEA claimant subject to an arbitration agreement will still be free to file a charge with the EEOC, even though the claimant is not able to institute a private judicial action. Indeed, Gilmer filed a charge with the EEOC in this case. In any event, the EEOC's role in combating age discrimination is not dependent on the filing of a charge; the agency may receive information concerning alleged violations of the ADEA "from any source," and it has independent authority to investigate age discrimination.

In arguing that arbitration is inconsistent with the ADEA, Gilmer also raises a host of challenges to the adequacy of arbitration procedures. Initially, we note that in our recent arbitration cases we have already rejected most of these arguments as insufficient to preclude arbitration of statutory claims. Such generalized attacks on arbitration "res[t] on suspicion of arbitration as a method of weakening the protections afforded in the substantive law to would-be complainants," and as such, they are "far out of step with our current strong endorsement of the federal statutes favoring this method of resolving disputes." *Rodriguez de Quijas*, supra, 490 U.S. at 481. Consequently, we address these arguments only briefly.

Gilmer first speculates that arbitration panels will be biased. However, "[w]e decline to indulge the presumption that the parties and arbitral body conducting a proceeding will be unable or unwilling to retain competent, conscientious and impartial arbitrators." *Mitsubishi*, supra, 473 U.S. at 634. In any event, we note that the NYSE arbitration rules, which are applicable to the dispute in this case, provide protections against biased panels. The rules require, for example, that the parties be informed of the employment histories of the arbitrators, and that they be allowed to make further inquiries into the arbitrators' backgrounds. In addition, each party is allowed one peremptory challenge and unlimited challenges for cause. Moreover, the arbitrators are required to disclose "any circumstances which might preclude [them] from rendering an objective and impartial determination." The FAA also protects against bias, by providing that courts may overturn arbitration decisions "[w]here there was evident partiality or corruption in the arbitrators." 9 U.S.C. § 10(b). There has been no showing in this case that those provisions are inadequate to guard against potential bias.

Gilmer also complains that the discovery allowed in arbitration is more limited than in the federal courts, which he contends will make it difficult to prove discrimination. It is unlikely, however, that age discrimination claims require more extensive discovery than other claims that we have found to be arbitrable, such as RICO and antitrust claims. Moreover, there has been no showing in this case that the NYSE discovery provisions, which allow for document production, information requests, depositions, and subpoenas will prove insufficient to allow ADEA claimants such as Gilmer a fair opportunity to present their claims. Although those procedures might not be as extensive as in the federal courts, by agreeing to arbitrate, a party "trades the procedures and opportunity for review of the courtroom for the simplicity, informality, and expedition of arbitration." *Mitsubishi*, supra, 473 U.S. at 628. Indeed, an important counterweight to the reduced discovery in NYSE arbitration is that arbitrators are not bound by the rules of evidence.

A further alleged deficiency of arbitration is that arbitrators often will not issue written opinions, resulting, Gilmer contends, in a lack of public knowledge of employers' discriminatory policies, an inability to obtain effective appellate review, and a stifling of the development of the law. The NYSE rules, however, do require that all arbitration awards be in writing, and that the awards contain the names of the parties, a summary of the issues in controversy, and a description of the award issued.

An additional reason advanced by Gilmer for refusing to enforce arbitration agreements relating to ADEA claims is his contention that there often will be unequal bargaining power between employers and employees. Mere inequality in bargaining power, however, is not a sufficient reason to hold that arbitration agreements are never enforceable in the employment context. Relationships between securities dealers and investors, for example, may involve unequal bargaining power, but we nevertheless held in *Rodriguez de Quijas* and *McMahon* that agreements to arbitrate in that context are enforceable. As discussed above, the FAA's purpose was to place arbitration agreements on the same footing as other contracts. Thus, arbitration agreements are enforceable "save upon such grounds as exist at law or in equity for the revocation of any contract." 9 U.S.C. § 2. "Of course, courts should remain attuned to well-supported claims that the agreement to arbitrate resulted from the sort of fraud or overwhelming economic power that would provide grounds 'for the revocation of any contract.' " *Mitsubishi*, supra, 473 U.S. at 627. There is no indication in this case, however, that Gilmer, an experienced businessman, was coerced or defrauded into agreeing to the arbitration clause in his registration application. As with the claimed procedural inadequacies discussed above, this claim of unequal bargaining power is best left for resolution in specific cases.

* * * *

- STEVENS, J., dissenting (with whom MARSHALL, J., joins).

* * * *

Not only would I find that the FAA does not apply to employment-related disputes between employers and employees in general, but also I would hold that compulsory arbitration conflicts with the congressional purpose animating the ADEA, in particular. As this Court previously has noted, authorizing the courts to issue broad injunctive relief is the cornerstone to eliminating discrimination in society. The ADEA, like Title VII of the Civil Rights Act of 1964, authorizes courts to award broad, class-based injunctive relief to achieve the purposes of the Act. 29 U.S.C. § 626(b). Because commercial arbitration is typically limited to a specific dispute between the particular parties and because the available remedies in arbitral forums generally do not provide for class-wide injunctive relief . . . I would conclude that an essential purpose of the ADEA is frustrated by compulsory arbitration of employment discrimination claims.

* * * *

When the FAA was passed in 1925, I doubt that any legislator who voted for it expected it to apply to statutory claims, to form contracts between parties of unequal bargaining power, or to the arbitration of disputes arising out of the employment relationship. In recent years, however, the Court "has effectively rewritten the statute," and abandoned its earlier view that statutory claims were not appropriate subjects for arbitration.

NOTES

1. In *Gilmer*, the Supreme Court, repeating its earlier formulation in *McMahon*, creates a presumption in favor of statutory claims to be overcome in one of three ways—by statutory prohibition of arbitration, by legislative history showing intended prohibition, or by an "inherent conflict" between arbitration and underlying statutory purpose. The burden of making such a showing is on the party resisting arbitration.

What sort of statute might fall in the last category?

2. Few federal statutes expressly bar arbitration. One that does is the 2002 Motor Vehicle Franchise Contract Arbitration Act, 15 U.S.C. § 1226(a)(2), which only permits arbitration with written dealer consent secured post-dispute. Why are motor vehicle franchises singled out—effective lobbying?

3. A statute can also limit the preclusive effect of an arbitral award. A 1982 law authorizes arbitration of patent claims, but provides that awards are not preclusive in subsequent cases involving one of the parties. 35 U.S.C. § 294. An arbitral determination of patent invalidity will not bar an infringement claim by the same holder of the same patent against a third party.

4. For a case rejecting arbitrability under federal statute despite lack of explicit statutory language to that effect, see *Alexander v. U.S. Credit Mgmt., Inc.*, 384 F. Supp.2d 1003 (N.D. Tex. 2005), which deals with the Credit Repair Organization Act, a consumer protection piece of legislation.

5. One area of confusion has to do with claims against debtors in bankruptcy. *See generally* Mette H. Kurth, *An Unstoppable Mandate and an Immovable Policy: The Arbitration Act and the Bankruptcy Code Collide*, 43 UCLA L. REV. 999 (1996). The caselaw consensus is that a bankruptcy court may stay arbitration of so-called "core proceedings," especially those proceedings which are unique to the Bankruptcy Act. *E.g.*, Gandy Ltd. v. Sarma Gandy, 299 F.3d 489 (5th Cir. 2002); *see* § 2.08, *infra*.

Desiderio v. National Ass'n of Securities Dealers, Inc.

United States Court of Appeals, Second Circuit, 1999.
191 F.3d 198.

- CARDAMONE, CIRCUIT JUDGE.

Plaintiff, Susan A. Desiderio, received an offer of employment from Florida's Suntrust Bank (Suntrust or bank) to become a securities broker. Her employment was conditioned on registration with defendant National Association of Securities Dealers, Inc. (NASD). To register with the NASD, Desiderio was asked to sign Form U-4 that contained a provision making all employment related disputes subject to arbitration. Desiderio said she would sign the form only if the mandatory arbitration provision was stricken from it. When the NASD refused to accept an altered form, the bank's offer of employment to plaintiff was revoked.

In her complaint, Desiderio asserts that the mandatory arbitration provision in Form U-4 violates her statutory rights under Title VII, 42 U.S.C. §§ 2000e to e-17, her constitutional rights under the Fifth Amendment Due Process Clause to an Article III judicial forum, and her right to a jury trial under the Seventh Amendment. She seeks a declaratory judgment invalidating the mandatory arbitration provision in Form U-4, and also asks for compensatory damages through her pendent state law tort claims.

* * * *

I. Statutory Rights Under Title VII

A. *Views of Other Circuits*

Whether a pre-dispute agreement requiring compulsory arbitration, such as Form U-4, is enforceable with regard to Title VII claims is an issue that has divided the circuits and is one of first impression in this Court. Practically every circuit that has addressed the question has held that the arbitration clause in Form U-4 validly applies to Title VII claims. See Rosenberg v. Merrill Lynch, Pierce, Fenner & Smith, Inc., 170 F.3d 1, 7 (1st Cir. 1999).

In a notable exception to this unanimity, the Ninth Circuit has ruled that the Form U-4 compulsory arbitration clause is unenforceable with regard to Title VII claims. See Duffield v. Robertson Stephens & Co., 144 F.3d 1182, 1190 (9th Cir. 1998), cert. denied, 525 U.S. 982, 982 (1998). Further, the EEOC has issued a policy statement that supports the conclusion found in Duffield. See EEOC, Notice No. 915.002, Policy Statement on Mandatory Binding Arbitration of Employment Discrimination Disputes as a Condition of Employment (1997), available in LEXIS, 2NDARY Library, EEOMAN FILE.

The circuit conflict stems from varying interpretations of *Gilmer v. Interstate/Johnson Lane Corp.*, 500 U.S. 20 (1991). In *Gilmer*, the Supreme Court held that employees could be required under Form U-4 and New York Stock Exchange Rule 347 to arbitrate age discrimination claims brought under the Age Discrimination in Employment Act (ADEA). Id. at 23. Most circuits have found the analytical framework used in *Gilmer* with respect to the ADEA applies to Title VII as well. Thus, we proceed to examine *Gilmer*'s application to Title VII claims.

* * * *

C. *What Gilmer and the FAA Require*

Gilmer states the general principle that arbitration agreements are enforceable with regard to statutory claims, "unless Congress itself has evinced an intention to preclude a waiver of judicial remedies for the statutory rights at issue [as indicated] in the text of the [statute], its legislative history, or an inherent conflict between arbitration and the [statute's] underlying purposes." 500 U.S. at 26. *Gilmer* found nothing in the text, legislative history, statutory framework or purposes of the ADEA demonstrated a congressional aim to preclude arbitration, and hence concluded that mandatory arbitration clauses were enforceable under the FAA with respect to claims under the ADEA. 500 U.S. at 26–27; see also Shearson/Am. Express, Inc. v. McMahon, 482 U.S. 220, 226–27 (1987) (applying the same searching test to RICO and the Securities Exchange Act of 1934); Bird v. Shearson Lehman/Am. Express, Inc., 926 F.2d 116, 118 (2d Cir. 1991) (same with respect to claims under ERISA).

Although many circuits have attempted to simplify the Gilmer inquiry by assuming that Title VII and ADEA share parallel objectives because they are similar civil rights statutes, see *Cole*, 105 F.3d at 1468; *Alford*, 939 F.2d at 230; *Metz*, 39 F.3d at 1487; *Patterson*, 113 F.3d at 837; *Bender*, 971 F.2d at 700, reliance on such an assumption does not accord with the detailed analysis of statutory text, history, and purposes required by *Gilmer* on a statute-by-statute basis. Thus, we undertake this same statute-by-statute analysis with regard to Title VII. We begin by noting that the burden is on Desiderio to show that Congress intended to preclude a waiver of a judicial forum for her statutory claims, see *Gilmer*, 500 U.S. at 26, keeping in mind that "questions of arbitrability must be addressed with a healthy regard for the federal policy favoring arbitration," Moses H. Cone Mem'l Hosp. v. Mercury Const. Corp., 460 U.S. 1, 24 (1983). We pass to an in-depth look at Title VII.

II. Title VII's Text, Legislative History, & Purposes

A. *Text*

The first step in interpreting a statute is to determine whether the language at issue has a "plain and unambiguous meaning with regard to the particular dispute in the case." Robinson v. Shell Oil Co., 519 U.S. 337, 340 (1997). "The plainness or ambiguity of statutory language is determined by reference to the language itself, the specific context in which that language is used, and the broader context of the statute as a whole." Id. at 341. If the text is unambiguous, the inquiry is at an end and we need proceed no further. See id. at 340.

The relevant text in Title VII states that "[w]here appropriate and to the extent authorized by law, the use of . . . arbitration[ ] is encouraged to resolve disputes arising under the Acts or provisions of Federal law amended by this Title." Civil Rights Act of 1991, § 118. We conclude—as did the Third, Fourth, and Seventh Circuits—that the text of § 118 evinces a plain Congressional purpose of encouraging arbitration of Title VII claims and not one of precluding such arbitration. See *Koveleskie*, 167 F.3d at 365; *Seus*, 146 F.3d at 182; *Austin*, 78 F.3d at 881–83. It follows that barring the application of mandatory arbitration agreements to Title VII claims would conflict with the express statutory term "encouraged" in § 118.

The Ninth Circuit in *Duffield* suggested, to the contrary, that the text of § 118 is ambiguous when viewed in light of the general purpose of the Civil Rights Act of 1991, namely, to provide "additional remedies" against intentional discrimination, such as more expansive fee-shifting provisions and added rights to a jury trial and to compensatory and punitive damages. 144 F.3d at 1193 (citing § 2 of the Act). *Duffield* then concluded that the goal of expanding remedies was at odds with compulsory arbitration, which would effectively limit a plaintiff's options. 144 F.3d at 1192–93.

We are unable to adopt the view expressed in *Duffield*. Compulsory arbitration does not defeat the right to compensatory and punitive damages, or fee shifting because an arbitrator is also empowered to grant this kind of relief. Moreover, it is untenable to contend that compulsory arbitration conflicts with the Act's provision for the right to a jury trial, because *Gilmer* ruled that compulsory arbitration clauses could be enforced in claims under the ADEA, a statute that explicitly provides for jury trials. See *Rosenberg*, 170 F.3d at 11. Nor are we convinced that the underlying purposes of Title VII and the 1991 Civil Rights Act inherently conflict with the imposition of compulsory arbitration. We conclude therefore that the word "encouraged" is free of ambiguity when viewed in the context of the purpose of the statute.

NOTE

1. We shall see that attempts have been made to bolster due process safeguards in arbitration of employee workplace claims of discrimination. *See* Due Process Protocol, *infra* at pages 304–309. We will also look at court opinions that use prohibitions against contractual unconscionability in attempting to regulate the fairness of such arbitrations. *See, e.g.*, *Cole*, *infra* at 278.

Equal Employment Opportunity Commission v. Waffle House, Inc.

Supreme Court of the United States, 2002.
534 U.S. 279.

- STEVENS, J.

The question presented is whether an agreement between an employer and an employee to arbitrate employment-related disputes bars the Equal Employment Opportunity Commission (EEOC) from pursuing victim-specific judicial relief, such as backpay, reinstatement, and damages, in an enforcement action alleging that the employer has violated Title I of the Americans with Disabilities Act of 1990 (ADA), 104 Stat. 328, 42 U.S.C. § 12101 et seq. (1994 ed. and Supp. V).

* * * *

Several Courts of Appeals have considered this issue and reached conflicting conclusions. Compare EEOC v. Frank's Nursery & Crafts, Inc., 177 F.3d 448 (C.A.6 1999) (employee's agreement to arbitrate does not affect the EEOC's independent statutory authority to pursue an enforcement action for injunctive relief, backpay, and damages in federal court), with EEOC v. Kidder, Peabody & Co., 156 F.3d 298 (2d Cir. 1998) (allowing the EEOC to pursue injunctive relief in federal court, but precluding monetary relief); Merrill Lynch, Pierce, Fenner Smith, Inc. v. Nixon, 210 F.3d 814 (8th Cir.), cert. denied, 531 U.S. 958 (2000) (same). We granted the EEOC's petition for certiorari to resolve this conflict, 532 U.S. 941 (2001), and now reverse.

* * * *

The Court of Appeals based its decision on its evaluation of the "competing policies" implemented by the ADA and the FAA, rather than on any language in the text of either the statutes or the arbitration agreement between Baker and respondent. 193 F.3d at 812. It recognized that the EEOC never agreed to arbitrate its statutory claim, id. at 811 ("We must also recognize that in this case the EEOC is not a party to any arbitration agreement"), and that the EEOC has "independent statutory authority" to vindicate the public interest, but opined that permitting the EEOC to prosecute Baker's claim in court "would significantly trample" the strong federal policy favoring arbitration because Baker had agreed to submit his claim to arbitration. Id. at 812. To effectuate this policy, the court distinguished between injunctive and victim-specific relief, and held that the EEOC is barred from obtaining the latter because any public interest served when the EEOC pursues "make whole" relief is outweighed by the policy goals favoring arbitration. Only when the EEOC seeks broad injunctive relief, in the Court of Appeals' view, does the public interest overcome the goals underpinning the FAA.

If it were true that the EEOC could prosecute its claim only with Baker's consent, or if its prayer for relief could be dictated by Baker, the court's analysis might be persuasive. But once a charge is filed, the exact opposite is true under the statute—the EEOC is in command of the process. The EEOC has exclusive jurisdiction over the claim for 180 days. During that time, the employee must obtain a right-to-sue letter from the agency before prosecuting the claim. If, however, the EEOC files suit on its own, the employee has no independent cause of action, although the employee may intervene in the EEOC's suit. 42 U.S.C. § 2000e-5(f)(1) (1994 ed.). In fact, the EEOC takes the position that it may pursue a claim on the employee's behalf even after the employee has disavowed any desire to seek relief. The statute clearly makes the EEOC the master of its own case and confers on the agency the authority to evaluate the strength of the public interest at stake. Absent textual support for a contrary view, it is the public agency's province—not that of the court—to determine whether public resources should be committed to the recovery of victim-specific relief. And if the agency makes that determination, the statutory text unambiguously authorizes it to proceed in a judicial forum.

* * * *

The compromise solution reached by the Court of Appeals turns what is effectively forum selection clause into a waiver of a nonparty's statutory remedies. But if the federal policy favoring arbitration trumps the plain language of Title VII and the contract, the EEOC should be barred from pursuing any claim outside the arbitral forum. If not, then the statutory language is clear; the EEOC has the authority to pursue victim-specific relief regardless of the forum that the employer and employee have chosen to resolve their disputes. Rather than attempt to split the difference, we are persuaded that, pursuant to Title VII and the ADA, whenever the EEOC chooses from among the many charges filed each year to bring an enforcement action in a particular case, the agency may be seeking to vindicate a public interest, not simply provide make-whole relief for the employee, even when it pursues entirely victim-specific relief. To hold otherwise would undermine the detailed enforcement scheme created by Congress simply to give greater effect to an agreement between private parties that does not even contemplate the EEOC's statutory function.

* * * *

But no question concerning the validity of his claim or the character of the relief that could be appropriately awarded in either a judicial or an arbitral forum is presented by this record. Baker has not sought arbitration of his claim, nor is there any indication that he has entered into settlement negotiations with respondent. It is an open question whether a settlement or arbitration judgment would affect the validity of the EEOC's claim or the character of relief the EEOC may seek. The only issue before this Court is whether the fact that Baker has signed a mandatory arbitration agreement limits the remedies available to the EEOC. The text of the relevant statutes provides a clear answer to that question. They do not authorize the courts to balance the competing policies of the ADA and the FAA or to second-guess the agency's judgment concerning which of the remedies authorized by law that it shall seek in any given case.

Moreover, it simply does not follow from the cases holding that the employee's conduct may affect the EEOC's recovery . . . . We have recognized several situations in which the EEOC does not stand in the employee's shoes. See *Occidental*, 432 U.S. at 368 (EEOC does not have to comply with state statutes of limitations); *General Telephone*, 446 U.S. at 326 (EEOC does not have to satisfy Rule 23 requirements); *Gilmer*, 500 U.S. at 32 (EEOC is not precluded from seeking classwide and equitable relief in court on behalf of an employee who signed an arbitration agreement). And, in this context, the statute specifically grants the EEOC exclusive authority over the choice of forum and the prayer for relief once a charge has been filed. The fact that ordinary principles of res judicata, mootness, or mitigation may apply to EEOC claims, does not contradict these decisions, nor does it render the EEOC a proxy for the employee.

The judgment of the Court of Appeals is reversed, and the case is remanded for further proceedings consistent with this opinion.

NOTE

1. What happens if a discrimination claimant loses in arbitration before the EEOC case on that person's behalf is heard in court? The Supreme Court raises that question just above, but does not answer it.

§ 2.06 ENFORCEABILITY OF ARBITRATION PROVISIONS UNDER COLLECTIVE BARGAINING AGREEMENTS—STATUTORY DISCRIMINATION AND OTHER FEDERAL STATUTORY CLAIMS

Wright v. Universal Maritime Service Corp.

Supreme Court of the United States, 1998.
525 U.S. 70.

- SCALIA, J.

* * * *

II.

In this case, the Fourth Circuit concluded that the general arbitration provision in the CBA [Collective Bargaining Agreement vs. individual contract of employment] governing Wright's employment was sufficiently broad to encompass a statutory claim arising under the ADA [Americans with Disabilities Act], and that such a provision was enforceable. The latter conclusion brings into question two lines of our case law. The first is represented by *Alexander v. Gardner-Denver Co.*, 415 U.S. 36 (1974), which held that an employee does not forfeit his right to a judicial forum for claimed discriminatory discharge in violation of Title VII of the Civil Rights Act of 1964, as amended, 42 U.S.C. § 2000e et seq., if "he first pursues his grievance to final arbitration under the nondiscrimination clause of a collective-bargaining agreement." 415 U.S. at 49. In rejecting the argument that the doctrine of election of remedies barred the Title VII lawsuit, we reasoned that a grievance is designed to vindicate a "contractual right" under a CBA, while a lawsuit under Title VII asserts "independent statutory rights accorded by Congress." Id. at 49–50. The statutory cause of action was not waived by the union's agreement to the arbitration provision of the CBA, since "there can be no prospective waiver of an employee's rights under Title VII." Id. at 51. We have followed the holding of *Gardner-Denver* in deciding the effect of CBA arbitration upon employee claims under other statutes. See McDonald v. West Branch, 466 U.S. 284 (1984) (claim under 42 U.S.C. § 1983); Barrentine v. Arkansas-Best Freight System, Inc., 450 U.S. 728 (1981) (claim under Fair Labor Standards Act, 29 U.S.C. § 201 et seq.).

The second line of cases implicated here is represented by *Gilmer v. Interstate/Johnson Lane Corp.*, supra, which held that a claim brought under the Age Discrimination in Employment Act of 1967 (ADEA), as amended, 29 U.S.C. § 621 et seq., could be subject to compulsory arbitration pursuant to an arbitration provision in a securities registration form. Relying upon the federal policy favoring arbitration embodied in the Federal Arbitration Act (FAA), we said that "statutory claims may be the subject of an arbitration agreement, enforceable pursuant to the FAA."

There is obviously some tension between these two lines of cases. Whereas *Gardner-Denver* stated that "an employee's rights under Title VII are not susceptible of prospective waiver," 415 U.S. at 51–52, *Gilmer* held that the right to a federal judicial forum for an ADEA claim could be waived. Petitioner and the United States as amicus would have us reconcile the lines of authority by maintaining that federal forum rights cannot be waived in union-negotiated CBAs even if they can be waived in individually executed contracts—a distinction that assuredly finds support in the text of *Gilmer*, see 500 U.S. at 26, 35. Respondents and their amici, on the other hand, contend that the real difference between *Gardner-Denver* and *Gilmer* is the radical change, over two decades, in the Court's receptivity to arbitration, leading *Gilmer* to affirm that "questions of arbitrability must be addressed with a healthy regard for the federal policy favoring arbitration," 500 U.S. at 26 (internal quotation marks and citation omitted); *Gilmer*, they argue, has sufficiently undermined *Gardner-Denver* that a union can waive employees' rights to a judicial forum. Although, as will appear, we find *Gardner-Denver* and *Gilmer* relevant for various purposes to the case before us, we find it unnecessary to resolve the question of the validity of a union-negotiated waiver, since it is apparent to us, on the facts and arguments presented here, that no such waiver has occurred.

In asserting the existence of an agreement to arbitrate the ADA claim, respondents rely upon the presumption of arbitrability this Court has found in § 301 of the Labor Management Relations Act, 1947 (LMRA), 29 U.S.C. § 185.

That presumption, however, does not extend beyond the reach of the principal rationale that justifies it, which is that arbitrators are in a better position than courts to interpret the terms of a CBA . . . . The dispute in the present case, however, ultimately concerns not the application or interpretation of any CBA, but the meaning of a federal statute. The cause of action Wright asserts arises not out of contract, but out of the ADA, and is distinct from any right conferred by the collective-bargaining agreement.

Not only is petitioner's statutory claim not subject to a presumption of arbitrability; we think any CBA requirement to arbitrate it must be particularly clear.

The Fourth Circuit relied upon the fact that the equivalently broad arbitration clause in *Gilmer*—applying to "any dispute, claim or controversy"—was held to embrace federal statutory claims. But *Gilmer* involved an individual's waiver of his own rights, rather than a union's waiver of the rights of represented employees—and hence the "clear and unmistakable" standard was not applicable.

We hold that the collective-bargaining agreement in this case does not contain a clear and unmistakable waiver of the covered employees' rights to a judicial forum for federal claims of employment discrimination. We do not reach the question whether such a waiver would be enforceable. The judgment of the Fourth Circuit is vacated, and the case is remanded for further proceedings consistent with this opinion.

It is so ordered.

NOTE

1. In the so-called *Gardner-Denver* line of cases preceding *Wright*, the Supreme Court emphasized that CBAs are negotiated by unions with objectives which can vary materially from that of its members, that labor arbitrators have expertise in the "law of the shop" versus public laws, and that labor arbitrators are bound by CBA provisions when reaching decisions. *See* McDonald v. City of West Branch, 466 U.S. 284, 290–92 (1984). *McDonald* holds that a labor arbitrator's decision is not preclusive in a federal case between the same parties based on 42 U.S.C. § 1983 claims for constitutional violations. *See Gardner-Denver*, 415 U.S. at 36 (Title VII); *see also* Barrentine v. Ark.-Best Freight Sys., Inc., 450 U.S. 728 (1981) (Fair Labor Standards Act). After these cases were decided, trial courts sometimes would take non-preclusive CBA awards on statutory claims as evidence.

14 Penn Plaza LLC v. Pyett

Supreme Court of the United States, 2009.
---- U.S. ----, 129 S. Ct. 1456.

▪ THOMAS, J.

The question presented by this case is whether a provision in a collective-bargaining agreement that clearly and unmistakably requires union members to arbitrate claims arising under the Age Discrimination in Employment Act of 1967 (ADEA) is enforceable. The United States Court of Appeals for the Second Circuit held that this Court's decision in *Alexander v. Gardner-Denver Co.*, 415 U.S. 36 (1974), forbids enforcement of such arbitration provisions. We disagree and reverse the judgment of the Court of Appeals.

I.

Respondents are members of the Service Employees International Union, Local 32BJ (Union). Under the National Labor Relations Act (NLRA), the Union is the exclusive bargaining representative of employees within the building-services industry in New York City, which includes building cleaners, porters, and doorpersons. In this role, the Union has exclusive authority to bargain on behalf of its members over their "rates of pay, wages, hours of employment, or other conditions of employment." Since the 1930's, the Union has engaged in industry-wide collective bargaining with the Realty Advisory Board on Labor Relations, Inc. (RAB), a multiemployer bargaining association for the New York City real-estate industry. The agreement between the Union and the RAB is embodied in their Collective Bargaining Agreement for Contractors and Building Owners (CBA). The CBA requires union members to submit all claims of employment discrimination to binding arbitration under the CBA's grievance and dispute resolution procedures:

> § 30 NO DISCRIMINATION. There shall be no discrimination against any present or future employee by reason of race, creed, color, age, disability, national origin, sex, union membership, or any other characteristic protected by law, including, but not limited to, claims made pursuant to Title VII of the Civil

> Rights Act, the Americans with Disabilities Act, the Age Discrimination in Employment Act, the New York State Human Rights Law, the New York City Human Rights Code . . . or any other similar laws, rules, or regulations. All such claims shall be subject to the grievance and arbitration procedures (Articles V and VI) as the sole and exclusive remedy for violations. Arbitrators shall apply appropriate law in rendering decisions based upon claims of discrimination.

* * * *

Respondents thereafter filed suit against petitioners in the United States District Court for the Southern District of New York, alleging that their reassignment violated the ADEA and state and local laws prohibiting age discrimination. Petitioners filed a motion to compel arbitration of respondents' claims pursuant to § 3 and § 4 of the Federal Arbitration Act (FAA), 9 U.S.C. §§ 3, 4. The District Court denied the motion because under Second Circuit precedent, "even a clear and unmistakable union-negotiated waiver of a right to litigate certain federal and state statutory claims in a judicial forum is unenforceable." Respondents immediately appealed the ruling under § 16 of the FAA, which authorizes an interlocutory appeal of "an order . . . refusing a stay of any action under section 3 of this title" or "denying a petition under section 4 of this title to order arbitration to proceed." 9 U.S.C. §§ 16(a)(1)(A)-(B).

The Court of Appeals affirmed. 498 F.3d 88. According to the Court of Appeals, it could not compel arbitration of the dispute because *Gardner-Denver*, which "remains good law," held "that a collective bargaining agreement could not waive covered workers' rights to a judicial forum for causes of action created by Congress." 498 F.3d at 92, 91 n.3 (citing *Gardner-Denver*, 415 U.S. at 49–51). The Court of Appeals observed that the *Gardner-Denver* decision was in tension with this Court's more recent decision in *Gilmer v. Interstate/Johnson Lane Corp.*, 500 U.S. 20 (1991), which "held that an individual employee who had agreed individually to waive his right to a federal forum *could* be compelled to arbitrate a federal age discrimination claim." 498 F.3d at 91 n.3 (citing *Gilmer*, supra, at 33–35; emphasis in original). The Court of Appeals also noted that this Court previously declined to resolve this tension in *Wright v. Universal Maritime Service Corp.*, 525 U.S. 70, 82 (1998), where the waiver at issue was not "clear and unmistakable." 498 F.3d at 91 n.3.

The Court of Appeals attempted to reconcile *Gardner-Denver* and *Gilmer* by holding that arbitration provisions in a collective-bargaining agreement, "which purport to waive employees' rights to a federal forum with respect to statutory claims, are unenforceable." 498 F.3d, at 93–94. As a result, an individual employee would be free to choose compulsory arbitration under *Gilmer*, but a labor union could not collectively bargain for arbitration on behalf of its members. We granted certiorari, to address the issue left unresolved in *Wright*, which continues to divide the Courts of Appeals, and now reverse.

II.

The NLRA governs federal labor-relations law. As permitted by that statute, respondents designated the Union as their "exclusive representativ[e] . . . for the purposes of collective bargaining in respect to rates of pay, wages, hours of employment, or other conditions of employment." 29 U.S.C. § 159(a). As the employees' exclusive bargaining representative, the Union "enjoys broad authority . . . in the negotiation and administration of [the] collective bargaining contract." *Communications Workers v. Beck*, 487 U.S. 735, 739 (1988) (internal quotation marks omitted). But this broad authority "is accompanied by a responsibility of equal scope, the responsibility and duty of fair representation." Humphrey v. Moore, 375 U.S. 335, 342 (1964). The employer has a corresponding duty under the NLRA to bargain in good faith "with the representatives of his employees" on wages, hours, and conditions of employment. 29 U.S.C. § 158(a)(5); see also § 158(d).

In this instance, the Union and the RAB, negotiating on behalf of 14 Penn Plaza, collectively bargained in good faith and agreed that employment-related discrimination claims, including claims brought under the ADEA, would be resolved in arbitration. This freely negotiated term between the Union and the RAB easily qualifies as a "conditio[n] of employment" that is subject to mandatory bargaining under § 159(a).

Respondents, however, contend that the arbitration clause here is outside the permissible scope of the collective-bargaining process because it affects the "employees' individual, non-economic statutory rights." Brief for Respondents 22; see also *Post*, at 1478–80 (Souter, J., dissenting). We disagree. Parties generally favor arbitration precisely because of the economics of dispute resolution. See Circuit City Stores, Inc. v. Adams, 532 U.S. 105, 123 (2001) ("Arbitration agreements allow parties to avoid the costs of litigation, a benefit that may be of particular importance in employment litigation, which often involves smaller sums of money than disputes concerning commercial contracts"). As in any contractual negotiation, a union may agree to the inclusion of an arbitration provision in a collective-bargaining agreement in return for other concessions from the employer. Courts generally may not interfere in this bargained-for exchange. "Judicial nullification of contractual concessions . . . is contrary to what the Court has recognized as one of the fundamental policies of the National Labor Relations Act-freedom of contract." NLRB v. Magnavox Co., 415 U.S. 322, 328 (1974) (Stewart, J., concurring in part and dissenting in part).

* * * *

The *Gilmer* Court's interpretation of the ADEA fully applies in the collective-bargaining context. Nothing in the law suggests a distinction between the status of arbitration agreements signed by an individual employee and those agreed to by a union representative. This Court has required only that an agreement to arbitrate statutory antidiscrimination claims be "explicitly stated" in the collective-bargaining agreement. *Wright*, 525 U.S. at 801 (internal quotation marks omitted). The CBA under review here meets that obligation.

* * * *

The CBA's arbitration provision is also fully enforceable under the *Gardner-Denver* line of cases. Respondents interpret *Gardner-Denver* and its progeny to hold that "a union cannot waive an employee's right to a judicial forum under the federal antidiscrimination statutes" because "allowing the union to waive this right would substitute the union's interests for the employee's antidiscrimination rights." The "combination of union control over the process and inherent conflict of interest with respect to discrimination claims," they argue, "provided the foundation for the Court's holding [in *Gardner-Denver*] that arbitration under a collective-bargaining agreement could not preclude an individual employee's right to bring a lawsuit in court to vindicate a statutory discrimination claim." We disagree.

* * * *

The facts underlying *Gardner-Denver*, *Barrentine*, and *McDonald* reveal the narrow scope of the legal rule arising from that trilogy of decisions. Summarizing those opinions in *Gilmer*, this Court made clear that the *Gardner-Denver* line of cases "did not involve the issue of the enforceability of an agreement to arbitrate statutory claims." 500 U.S. at 35. Those decisions instead "involved the quite different issue whether arbitration of contract-based claims precluded subsequent judicial resolution of statutory claims. Since the employees there had not agreed to arbitrate their statutory claims, and the labor arbitrators were not authorized to resolve such claims, the arbitration in those cases understandably was held not to preclude subsequent statutory actions." *Gardner-Denver* and its progeny thus do not control the outcome where, as is the case here, the collective-bargaining agreement's arbitration provision expressly covers both statutory and contractual discrimination claims.

We recognize that apart from their narrow holdings, the *Gardner-Denver* line of cases included broad dicta that was highly critical of the use of arbitration for the vindication of statutory antidiscrimination rights. That skepticism, however, rested on a misconceived view of arbitration that this Court has since abandoned.

First, the Court in *Gardner-Denver* erroneously assumed that an agreement to submit statutory discrimination claims to arbitration was tantamount to a waiver of those rights. See 415 U.S. at 51. ("[T]here can be no prospective *waiver* of an employee's rights under Title VII" (emphasis added)). For this reason, the Court stated, "the rights conferred [by Title VII] can form no part of the collective-bargaining process since waiver of these rights would defeat the paramount congressional purpose behind Title VII." Ibid; see also id. at 56 ("we have long recognized that 'the choice of forums inevitably affects the scope of the substantive right to be vindicated' " (quoting U.S. Bulk Carriers, Inc. v. Arguelles, 400 U.S. 351, 359–60 (1971) (Harlan, J., concurring)).

The Court was correct in concluding that federal antidiscrimination rights may not be prospectively waived, see 29 U.S.C. § 626(f)(1)(C); see supra, at 1465, but it confused an agreement to arbitrate those statutory claims with a prospective waiver of the substantive right. The decision to resolve ADEA claims by way of arbitration instead of litigation does not waive the statutory right to be free from workplace age discrimination; it waives only the right to seek relief from a court in the first instance. See *Gilmer*, supra, at 26 (" '[B]y agreeing to arbitrate a statutory claim, a party does not forgo the substantive rights afforded by the statute; it only submits to their resolution in an arbitral, rather than a judicial, forum' " (quoting *Mitsubishi Motors Corp.*, 473 U.S. at 628)). This "Court has been quite specific in holding that arbitration agreements can be enforced under the FAA without contravening the policies of congressional enactments giving employees specific protection against discrimination prohibited by federal law." *Circuit City Stores, Inc.*, 532 U.S. at 123. The suggestion in *Gardner-Denver* that the decision to arbitrate statutory discrimination claims was tantamount to a substantive waiver of those rights, therefore, reveals a distorted understanding of the compromise made when an employee agrees to compulsory arbitration.

In this respect, *Gardner-Denver* is a direct descendant of the Court's decision in *Wilko v. Swan*, 346 U.S. 427 (1953), which held that an agreement to arbitrate claims under the Securities Act of 1933 was unenforceable. See id. at 438. The Court subsequently overruled *Wilko* and, in so doing, characterized the decision as "pervaded by . . . 'the old judicial hostility to arbitration.' " Rodriguez de Quijas v. Shearson/American Express, Inc., 490 U.S. 477, 480 (1989). The Court added: "To the extent that *Wilko* rested on suspicion of arbitration as a method of weakening the protections afforded in the substantive law to would-be complainants, it has fallen far out of step with our current strong endorsement of the federal statutes favoring this method of resolving disputes." Id. at 481; see also *Mitsubishi Motors Corp.*, supra, at 626–27 ("[W]e are well past the time when judicial suspicion of the desirability of arbitration and of the competence of arbitral tribunals inhibited the development of arbitration as an alternative means of dispute resolution"). The timeworn "mistrust of the arbitral process" harbored by the Court in *Gardner-Denver* thus weighs against reliance on anything more than its core holding. Shearson/American Express Inc.

v. McMahon, 482 U.S. 220, 231–32 (1987); see also *Gilmer*, 500 U.S. at 34 n.5 (reiterating that *Gardner-Denver*'s view of arbitration "has been undermined by [the Court's] recent arbitration decisions"). Indeed, in light of the "radical change, over two decades, in the Court's receptivity to arbitration," *Wright*, 525 U.S. at 77, reliance on any judicial decision similarly littered with *Wilko*'s overt hostility to the enforcement of arbitration agreements would be ill advised.

Second, *Gardner-Denver* mistakenly suggested that certain features of arbitration made it a forum "well suited to the resolution of contractual disputes," but "a comparatively inappropriate forum for the final resolution of rights created by Title VII." 415 U.S. at 56. According to the Court, the "factfinding process in arbitration" is "not equivalent to judicial factfinding" and the "informality of arbitral procedure . . . makes arbitration a less appropriate forum for final resolution of Title VII issues than the federal courts." Id. at 57, 58. The Court also questioned the competence of arbitrators to decide federal statutory claims. See id. at 57 ("[T]he specialized competence of arbitrators pertains primarily to the law of the shop, not the law of the land"); *Barrentine*, 450 U.S. at 743 ("Although an arbitrator may be competent to resolve many preliminary factual questions, such as whether the employee 'punched in' when he said he did, he may lack competence to decide the ultimate legal issue whether an employee's right to a minimum wage or to overtime pay under the statute has been violated"). In the Court's view, "the resolution of statutory or constitutional issues is a primary responsibility of courts, and judicial construction has proved especially necessary with respect to Title VII, whose broad language frequently can be given meaning only by reference to public law concepts." *Gardner-Denver*, supra, at 57; see also *McDonald*, 466 U.S. at 290 ("An arbitrator may not . . . have the expertise required to resolve the complex legal questions that arise in § 1983 actions").

These misconceptions have been corrected. For example, the Court has "recognized that arbitral tribunals are readily capable of handling the factual and legal complexities of antitrust claims, notwithstanding the absence of judicial instruction and supervision" and that "there is no reason to assume at the outset that arbitrators will not follow the law." *McMahon*, supra, at 232; *Mitsubishi Motors Corp.*, 473 U.S. at 634 ("We decline to indulge the presumption that the parties and arbitral body conducting a proceeding will be unable or unwilling to retain competent, conscientious, and impartial arbitrators"). An arbitrator's capacity to resolve complex questions of fact and law extends with equal force to discrimination claims brought under the ADEA. Moreover, the recognition that arbitration procedures are more streamlined than federal litigation is not a basis for finding the forum somehow inadequate; the relative informality of arbitration is one of the chief reasons that parties select arbitration. Parties "trad[e] the procedures and opportunity for review of the courtroom for the simplicity, informality, and expedition of arbitration." Id. at 628. In any event, "[i]t is unlikely . . . that age discrimination claims require more extensive discovery than other claims that we have found to be arbitrable, such as RICO and antitrust claims." *Gilmer*, 500 U.S. at 31. At bottom, objections centered on the nature of arbitration do not offer a credible basis for discrediting the choice of that forum to resolve statutory antidiscrimination claims.

Third, the Court in *Gardner-Denver* raised in a footnote a "further concern" regarding "the union's exclusive control over the manner and extent to which an individual grievance is presented." 415 U.S. at 58 n.19. The Court suggested that in arbitration, as in the collective-bargaining process, a union may subordinate the interests of an individual employee to the collective interests of all employees in the bargaining unit. Ibid.; see also *McDonald*, supra, at 291 ("The union's interests and those of the individual employee are not always identical or even compatible. As a result, the union may present the employee's grievance less vigorously, or make different strategic choices, than would the employee"); see also *Barrentine*, supra, at 742; *Post,* at 1480–81 n.4 (Souter, J., dissenting).

We cannot rely on this judicial policy concern as a source of authority for introducing a qualification into the ADEA that is not found in its text. Absent a constitutional barrier, "it is not for us to substitute our view of . . . policy for the legislation which has been passed by Congress." Florida Dept. of Revenue v. Piccadilly Cafeterias, Inc., 554 U.S. ----, ----, 128 S. Ct. 2326, 2338–39 (2008) (internal quotation marks omitted). Congress is fully equipped "to identify any category of claims as to which agreements to arbitrate will be held unenforceable." *Mitsubishi Motors Corp.*, supra, at 627. Until Congress amends the

ADEA to meet the conflict-of-interest concern identified in the *Gardner-Denver* dicta, and seized on by respondents here, there is "no reason to color the lens through which the arbitration clause is read" simply because of an alleged conflict of interest between a union and its members.

* * * *

We hold that a collective-bargaining agreement that clearly and unmistakably requires union members to arbitrate ADEA claims is enforceable as a matter of federal law. The judgment of the Court of Appeals is reversed, and the case is remanded for further proceedings consistent with this opinion.

It is so ordered.

▪ STEVENS, J., dissenting.

Justice SOUTER'S dissenting opinion, which I join in full, explains why our decision in *Alexander v. Gardner-Denver Co.*, 415 U.S. 36 (1974), answers the question presented in this case. My concern regarding the Court's subversion of precedent to the policy favoring arbitration prompts these additional remarks.

Notwithstanding the absence of change in any relevant statutory provision, the Court has recently retreated from, and in some cases reversed, prior decisions based on its changed view of the merits of arbitration. Previously, the Court approached with caution questions involving a union's waiver of an employee's right to raise statutory claims in a federal judicial forum. After searching the text and purposes of Title VII of the Civil Rights Act of 1964, the Court in *Gardner-Denver* held that a clause of a collective-bargaining agreement (CBA) requiring arbitration of discrimination claims could not waive an employee's right to a judicial forum for statutory claims. See 415 U.S. at 51. The Court's decision rested on several features of the statute, including the individual nature of the rights it confers, the broad remedial powers it grants federal courts, and its expressed preference for overlapping remedies. See id. at 44–48. The Court also noted the problem of entrusting a union with certain arbitration decisions given the potential conflict between the collective interest and the interests of an individual employee seeking to assert his rights. See id. at 58 n.19. That concern later provided a basis for our decisions in *Barrentine v. Arkansas-Best Freight System, Inc.*, 450 U.S. 728, 742 (1981), and *McDonald v. West Branch*, 466 U.S. 284, 291 (1984), which similarly held that a CBA may not commit enforcement of certain rights-creating statutes exclusively to a union-controlled arbitration process. Congress has taken no action signaling disagreement with those decisions.

The statutes construed by the Court in the foregoing cases and in *Wilko v. Swan*, 346 U.S. 427 (1953), have not since been amended in any relevant respect. But the Court has in a number of cases replaced our predecessors' statutory analysis with judicial reasoning espousing a policy favoring arbitration and thereby reached divergent results. I dissented in those cases to express concern that my colleagues were making policy choices not made by Congress.

Today the majority's preference for arbitration again leads it to disregard our precedent. Although it purports to ascertain the relationship between the Age Discrimination in Employment Act of 1967 (ADEA), the National Labor Relations Act, and the Federal Arbitration Act, the Court ignores our earlier determination of the relevant provisions' meaning. The Court concludes that "[i]t was Congress' verdict that the benefits of organized labor outweigh the sacrifice of individual liberty" that the system of organized labor "necessarily demands," even when the sacrifice demanded is a judicial forum for asserting an individual statutory right. *Ante*, at 1472–73. But in *Gardner-Denver* we determined that "Congress' verdict" was otherwise when we held that Title VII does not permit a CBA to waive an employee's right to a federal judicial forum. Because the purposes and relevant provisions of Title VII and the ADEA are not meaningfully distinguishable, it is only by reexamining the statutory questions resolved in *Gardner-Denver* through the lens of the policy favoring arbitration that the majority now reaches a different result.

Under the circumstances, I believe a passage from one of my earlier dissents merits repetition. The Court in *Rodriguez de Quijas* overruled our decision in *Wilko* and held that predispute agreements to arbitrate claims under the Securities Act of 1933 are enforceable. 490 U.S. at 484; see also id. at 481 (noting *Wilko*'s reliance on "the outmoded presumption of disfavoring arbitration proceedings"). I observed in dissent:

> In the final analysis, a Justice's vote in a case like this depends more on his or her views about the respective lawmaking responsibilities of Congress and this Court than on conflicting policy interests. Judges who have confidence in their own ability to fashion public policy are less hesitant to change the law than those of us who are inclined to give wide latitude to the views of the voters' representatives on nonconstitutional matters. Cf. Boyle v. United Technologies Corp., 487 U.S. 500 (1988). As I pointed out years ago, Alberto-Culver Co. v. Scherk, 484 F.2d 611 (C.A.7 1973) (dissenting opinion), rev'd, 417 U.S. 506 (1974), there are valid policy and textual arguments on both sides regarding the interrelation of federal securities and arbitration Acts. None of these arguments, however, carries sufficient weight to tip the balance between judicial and legislative authority and overturn an interpretation of an Act of Congress that has been settled for many years.

As was true in *Rodriguez de Quijas*, there are competing arguments in this case regarding the interaction of the relevant statutory provisions. But the Court in *Gardner-Denver* considered these arguments, including "the federal policy favoring arbitration of labor disputes," 415 U.S. at 59, and held that Congress did not intend to permit the result petitioners seek. In the absence of an intervening amendment to the relevant statutory language, we are bound by that decision. It is for Congress, rather than this Court, to reassess the policy arguments favoring arbitration and revise the relevant provisions to reflect its views.

* * * *

§ 2.07 ADDITIONAL MATERIALS ON WORKPLACE DISCRIMINATION

[A] Job-Discrimination Cases Tend to Fare Poorly in Federal Court

- THE WALL STREET JOURNAL, Feb. 19, 2009, at page A16 , ©2009, reprinted with permission.

By NATHAN KOPPEL

Workers recently gained new ammunition to file job-discrimination cases in federal court, but they still face long odds against emerging victorious.

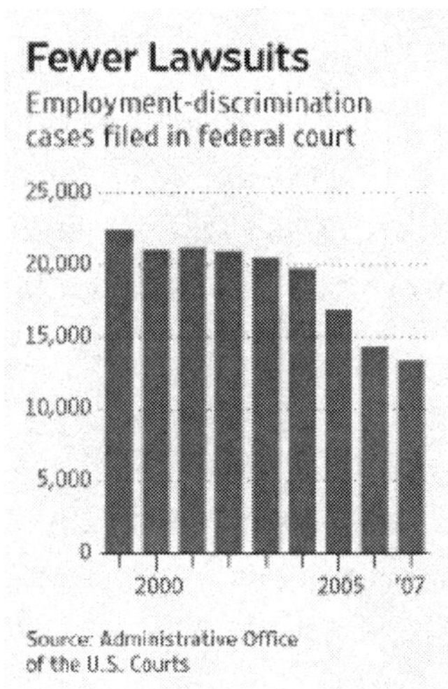

A battery of recent studies shows that employees who sue over discrimination lose at a higher rate in federal court than other types of plaintiffs. They also get less time in court, with judges quicker to throw out their cases.

Many employee advocates hope the Obama administration will herald a better climate for discrimination claims. President Barack Obama last month signed the Lilly Ledbetter Fair Pay Act, which makes it easier for workers to sue over pay discrimination on the basis of gender, race, age or disability by extending the legal deadline to file suit. Experts think the act will lead to a surge in employment cases in federal court.

Just because more workers have standing to sue doesn't mean that they will receive a better reception in court, if previous patterns hold steady. From 1979 through 2006, federal plaintiffs won 15% of job-discrimination cases. By comparison, in all other civil cases, the win rate was 51%, according to a study to be published this month by the Harvard Law & Policy Review. "Judges demand more of discrimination cases than other types of cases," says Stewart Schwab, a co-author of the study and the dean of Cornell University Law School.

The odds against winning discrimination cases have some

employee lawyers reluctant even to try. "We will no longer take individual employment-discrimination cases, because there's such a high likelihood of losing," New York plaintiffs' attorney Joe Whatley Jr. says. Job-discrimination case filings declined by 40% from 1999 to 2007, federal court records show.

The bad track record for discrimination cases has been ascribed to everything from a dearth of minorities on the bench to inherent difficulties in proving job discrimination, which is rarely overt.

Another reason why discrimination suits might fare poorly, say lawyers who represent employers, is that companies can be quick to settle suits that appear credible. Cases that aren't settled, says Dallas defense attorney Michael Maslanka, often are frivolous and should be dismissed. Adds Lawrence Lorber, a defense lawyer in Washington: "If it's a real case, they settle. Employers aren't dumb."

The case of Vicky Crawford illustrates the challenges faced by some workers in federal court, critics say. A Tennessee government employee, Ms. Crawford in 2002 was asked whether she had witnessed inappropriate behavior by a colleague. Ms. Crawford reported that the colleague had on one occasion grabbed her head and pulled it to his crotch.

Ms. Crawford was later fired, but her retaliation claim was tossed out by a Tennessee federal judge, and later upheld by the Sixth U.S. Circuit Court of Appeals. Since Ms. Crawford hadn't instigated a complaint, but had merely answered investigators' questions, she didn't qualify to bring a retaliation suit, the courts held. The U.S. Supreme Court unanimously reversed the rulings in January, calling the lower courts' interpretation of federal law "freakish." The Supreme Court's ruling in the Crawford case, however, applies only to a narrow sliver of employment claims.

Even the federal courts have detected the pattern of more dismissals in discrimination cases, though they surmise different reasons for it than do plaintiffs' lawyers. A report last year by the Federal Judicial Center, the research arm of the federal courts, found that judges nationwide terminated 12.5% of employment-discrimination cases through summary judgments, before the suits reached trial. In 90% of those cases, it was the employers who requested the summary judgment. In contrast, the study found, 3% of contract cases and 1.7% of personal-injury and property-damage suits were dismissed via summary judgments.

One possible explanation, says David Hittner, a U.S. District Court judge in Houston, is that employers generally have become more careful to avoid discriminatory behavior. They also are better at documenting the reasons behind firings. "Companies often have an extensive record that this [employee] was not doing their job well and that is the reason for the termination," Judge Hittner says.

Equally troubling to critics, though, is that federal judges also now routinely terminate employment-discrimination cases through motions to dismiss, meaning that the plaintiffs aren't allowed to conduct fact finding to support their claims, according to a law-review study due to be published in August by the University of Illinois College of Law.

The study analyzed the impact of the U.S. Supreme Court's 2007 ruling in *Bell Atlantic Corp. v. Twombly*, which authorized federal judges to dismiss cases unless plaintiffs can detail enough facts in their initial complaints to state a "plausible" claim—a higher standard than previously existed. Although the *Twombly* case involved an antitrust dispute, it has since been applied broadly to discrimination cases, says Joseph Seiner, a professor at the University of South Carolina School of Law, who wrote the study.

As an example of the kind of case that has suffered, Mr. Seiner pointed to *Mangum v. Town of Holly Springs*, in which a North Carolina federal judge last year dismissed a female firefighter's claim that she had been subjected to a hostile work environment. The judge cited *Twombly* in dismissing the sexual-harassment claim. Mr. Seiner says "such a harassment allegation should at least get to the stage where you take depositions."

[B] What Will Congress Do?

In part because of the problems discussed in the forgoing article, two members of Congress, Senator Feingold (D-Wisc.) and

Representative Johnson (D-Ga.), have co-sponsored proposed legislation called The Arbitration Fairness Act of 2009. The statute would bar judicial enforcement of mandatory predispute arbitration clauses in employment contracts, as well as in consumer and franchise transactions. While consumer arbitration is essentially outside the scope of this book, there are obvious issues presented by it. An argument in favor is that consumer claims are generally small, and impossible to litigate economically. Arguments against are that tribunals used by sellers to consumers can be "stacked decks" and/or beholden to corporate "repeat players" which fund the process. A further potential issue, to be addressed later in this book, has to do with the relative lack of availability of class action procedures in arbitration. We shall see that there are decisions striking down class action waivers in arbitration clauses as unconscionable, but the status of those decisions is in doubt—in April 2010, in *Stolt-Nielsen v. Animal-Feeds Int'l Corp.*, ---- U.S. ----, 130 S. Ct. 1758 (2010) discussed *infra* at 362, the Supreme Court held that where an arbitration clause is simply silent as to maintainability of class actions, an arbitrator lacks power to permit such a procedure. Some commentators expect that this decision will further encourage Congress to act in some fashion. As for employment claims, the NASD, and hence, now FINRA, exempt employment discrimination claims from mandatory arbitration unless a brokerage firm provides for it in a separate employment contract with the employee seeking to assert such a claim. *See* FINRA Rule 13201.

[C] The Workplace Discrimination Claimant – Court or Arbitration?

The United States Supreme Court has spelled out, in considerable detail, how federal trial courts are to deal with claims of discrimination. In *McDonnell Douglas v. Green*, 411 U.S. 792 (1973), the Court spelled out the shifting burden of proof, which applies to an individual claimant. Initially, the claimant need only establish that she belongs to a protected class (race, gender, religion, national origin, ethnicity), that she was refused employment, terminated from employment, or treated negatively while on the job without justification, and that others not within the protected category were not so treated. At that point, the burden shifts to the employer to produce evidence of a legitimate non-discriminatory basis for its actions concerning the plaintiff—perhaps, lack of qualification, insubordination, or business necessity affecting all those similarly situated without regard to race, gender, ethnicity, or religion. The burden then shifts back to the plaintiff to show that the employer's proffered justification is pretextual. This can be done by disproving the purportedly neutral justification the employer has put forth for what it did, or by specific proof of a prohibited animus. The latter sort of proof is difficult to come by these days because of the organized efforts made, at least by larger employers, to avoid liabilities of this sort by workplace training, careful recording keeping and documentation, and the disciplining of misbehaving employees. Effectively, under *McDonnell*, an employer found to assert only pretextual reasons for the employment action taken is assumed to have acted with discriminatory intent.

Even where employer action is not driven by discriminatory animus, the Supreme Court, starting in *Griggs v. Duke Power Co.*, 401 U.S. 424 (1971), has made it clear that employment action neutral on its face, unless driven by overriding "business necessity," also violates Title VII of the 1964 Civil Rights Act if the practice at issue disparately impacts on a protected class of employee. In this sort of case, plaintiff's proof will be statistical—*i.e.*, a test for job promotion produces significantly racially skewed results. At this point, the burden shifts to the employer to either undermine plaintiff's statistical analysis (perhaps through one of its own), or else, in the words of the statute, as amended, to show that the challenged practice or procedure is "job-related for the position in question and consistent with business necessity." This defense, however, is still subject to claimant's showing that an alternative practice can accomplish the legitimate employment objective without the sort of disparate impact otherwise produced.

"Disparate impact" cases are, or can be, very detailed and sophisticated, and also very expensive. Furthermore, plaintiff's statistical proof typically is generated by extensive pretrial discovery of documents from which statistics can be compiled. Arbitration of such claims, as opposed to the *McDonnell* sort of claim, might be particularly hindered in arbitration, either because of more limited documentary discovery than available in court, or because of lack of availability of class action procedures, as more fully discussed later in these materials.

Age discrimination is not covered by Title VII, but by the Age Discrimination in Employment Act. The "protected class" begins at age 40. Most of the caselaw under this statute is consistent with Title VII caselaw, but there is a notable exception. In *Gross v. FBL Financial Services, Inc.*, 129 S.Ct. 2343 (2009), the Supreme Court held that an age claimant must prove more than that age was a "motivating factor," which theretofore had been the test used. Instead, age had to be the "but for" motivation behind the challenged employer decision. Corrective legislation is pending in Congress as the proposed "Protecting Older Workers Against Discrimination Act."

Under the *Penn Plaza* holding, *supra*, provisions specifying statutory discrimination claims in collective bargaining agreements are now unquestionably enforceable. CBAs often designate the arbitrator to hear all disputes arising under its provisions. Alternatively, employers, unionized or not, often incorporate internal arbitral procedures for employment disputes of all types into employment manuals.

While the securities industry no longer covers employment discrimination disputes under the mandatory arbitration provisions of its broker registration provisions, arbitration can still be the subject of private employment contract with an individual worker. This sort of arbitration requirement is found in other industries as well, particularly in the contracts of senior executives and in employee handbooks.

The American Arbitration Association has its own Employment Arbitration Rules, and also encourages mediation of employment disputes. The AAA has mediator and arbitrator Panels required to have substantial experience in the employment field. The AAA has expedited procedures before one arbitrator for employment claims not exceeding $50,000, which will also be applied to larger claims by consent of the parties. Arbitrators have subpoena power over witnesses and documents, as do attorneys in some jurisdictions, such as New York—see N.Y. C.P.L.R. 7505. Under Rule 6 of the AAA Employment Rules, much as under its Commercial Rules, there is provision for pretrial discovery:

> In large or complex cases, at the request of any party or at the discretion of the Arbitrator or the AAA, a preliminary hearing . . . may be scheduled . . . . Consistent with the expedited

> nature of arbitration of arbitration, the arbitrator may, at the preliminary hearing, establish (i) the extent and schedule for the production [of] relevant documents and other information . . . .

Is such pretrial discovery adequate, particularly in a "disparate impact" case to be proven, if at all, by statistical evidence? How does a claimant verify or undercut opposing statistical offerings? What about depositions, including of those not subject to subpoena because of location or some other reason? Later in this book, there is discussion of a Due Process Protocol developed by a Joint Task Force of the American Bar Association and AAA to govern workplace discrimination claims (*see* pages 304–309, *infra*). The Protocol provides for "[n]ecessary depositions consistent with the expedited nature of arbitration," and, presumably, the AAA's Rule 6 is construed accordingly. It is, one would expect, unlikely that arbitral procedures constructed by employers would provide for prehearing depositions.

Must arbitrators follow the law given the "public" nature of workplace discrimination claims? The Due Process Protocol provides that arbitrators are "bound . . . by applicable statute." We shall see, however, that vacating an award in this area still imposes a very high burden, and the Protocol itself provides for only "limited" judicial review. Given that, if arbitrators refused to use the "but for" test recently mandated by the Supreme Court for age discrimination cases, instead applying the more relaxed "motivating factor" test, how likely would judicial intervention be? Remember that employment awards do not have to be reasoned any more than other types of awards.

Then there is the issue of arbitration costs. The Due Process Protocol encourages arrangements for the employer to pay the greater share of the fees as required.

§ 2.08 BANKRUPTCY AND BANKRUPTCY MATTERS

In a number of Supreme Court decisions compelling arbitration of federal statutory claims, the point is made that arbitration should not be ordered where compelling arbitration would be "hostile" to the underlying statutory purpose. In the bankruptcy area we sometimes see such situations. Bankruptcy proceedings are designed to centralize administration and distribution of debtor assets in one place, the bankruptcy court, which have subject matter jurisdiction under 13 U.S.C. § 1334. To prevent fragmentation, a bankruptcy filing imposes an automatic stay on all pending and future proceedings seeking all or part of the filer's remaining funds. Claims on behalf of the filer, once bankruptcy is declared, are typically seen as assets of the debtor's estate available for distribution to creditors in keeping with priority and, sometimes, the percentage of the remaining assets of the estate to go to each member of each class of creditors. One can readily see the need to keep certain claims involving the debtor in one place so as to permit orderly administration.

MBNA America Bank, N.A. v. Hill

United States Court of Appeals, Second Circuit, 2006.
436 F.3d 104.

- GIBSON, CIRCUIT JUDGE.

Hill filed the adversary proceeding [in bankruptcy court] against MBNA on February 7, 2002, as a putative class action on behalf of herself and others similarly situated, alleging violations of section 362(h) of the Bankruptcy Code and unjust enrichment. MBNA moved to dismiss or stay the proceeding in favor of arbitration under the Federal Arbitration Act, claiming that an account agreement between MBNA and Hill mandated arbitration of the claims. We hold that the bankruptcy court did not have discretion to refuse to stay the proceeding pending arbitration, and we reverse the district court judgment.

On October 9, 2001, Hill filed a petition for relief under Chapter 7 of the Bankruptcy Code. In December 2001, the trustee appointed for Hill's bankruptcy estate filed a report concluding that "there is no property available for distribution from the estate over and above that exempted by law" and declaring that the estate had "been fully administered." The bankruptcy case was concluded in March 2003, when the bankruptcy court granted Hill a discharge.

Hill filed this adversary proceeding in February 2002, based on events that occurred shortly after she sought bankruptcy relief. Before filing for bankruptcy, Hill had authorized MBNA to withdraw monthly payments of $159.01 from her bank account to pay down the balance she owed MBNA on a consumer loan. MBNA made the first of these withdrawals days before Hill filed her bankruptcy petition. Hill included MBNA in the schedule of creditors she filed with the bankruptcy court, and the bankruptcy court mailed notices to all creditors on October 10, 2001. In addition, Hill's counsel sent MBNA notice of the bankruptcy filing on October 23, 2001. In spite of these notices, MBNA withdrew another $159.01 installment from Hill's bank account on November 5, 2001. Hill claimed that MBNA continued to attempt to collect monthly payments and argued that MBNA's actions constituted a willful violation of the automatic stay provision in section 362(a) of the Bankruptcy Code, and that MBNA was thereby unjustly enriched.

Hill styled her complaint as a class action, setting forth allegations specific to her situation and asserting that a class of persons exist who are similarly situated. She alleged common issues, including whether MBNA has engaged in conduct that violates automatic stays in bankruptcy, whether MBNA's conduct is willful, and whether MBNA should be required to make restitution. Hill requested class certification.

MBNA filed a motion seeking to stay or dismiss the adversary proceeding in favor of arbitration, based on an arbitration clause contained in an amendment to Hill's credit account agreement. Hill's original account agreement with MBNA included a provision that authorized MBNA to amend the agreement. In December 1999, MBNA amended the agreements of the class of account holders that included Hill, and notified all account holders of the amendment by mail. The amended agreements contained a mandatory arbitration provision. Hill's notice was not returned as undeliverable, and she did not exercise her opt-out right as set forth in the amendment. The arbitration amendment became effective February 1, 2000, and it provides:

> Any claim or dispute ("claim") by either you or us against the other ... arising from or relating in any way to this Account Agreement or ... your account (whether under a statute, in contract, tort, or otherwise and whether for money damages, penalties or declaratory or equitable relief) ... shall be resolved by binding arbitration.

MBNA contends that this provision required the bankruptcy court to stay or dismiss Hill's claims pending arbitration.

In a thorough opinion and order, the bankruptcy court denied MBNA's motion, concluding that the bankruptcy court was the "most appropriate forum to adjudicate the matter." MBNA appealed the order to the district court. The district court affirmed in part and reversed in part, holding that the bankruptcy court did not abuse its discretion by refusing to dismiss or stay the adversary proceeding in favor of arbitration of the section 362 claim. The district court concluded that permitting arbitration of the alleged automatic stay violation would "seriously jeopardize the objectives of the Bankruptcy Code." The district court held that the bankruptcy court abused its discretion by denying arbitration of the unjust enrichment claim because it was "arbitrable and non-core." However, because Hill had stated that she would abandon the unjust enrichment claim if it were held to be arbitrable, the district court dismissed the claim, and Hill does not appeal that dismissal. MBNA appeals the district court's order denying arbitration of the alleged violation of the automatic stay.

I.

Our jurisdiction to hear this appeal is authorized by the Federal Arbitration Act, which states, "An appeal may be taken from ... an order ... refusing a stay" in proceedings where an issue is referable to arbitration. 9 U.S.C. §§ 3, 16(a); Aceros Prefabricados, S.A. v. TradeArbed, Inc., 282 F.3d 92, 97 (2d Cir.2002).

We review de novo a district court's order issued in an appeal from the bankruptcy court. Gulf States Exploration Co. v. Manville Forest Prods. Corp. (In re Manville Forest Prods. Corp.), 896 F.2d 1384, 1388 (2d Cir.1990). The bankruptcy court's conclusions with respect to enforcement of the arbitration clause raise mixed questions of law and fact. We review the bankruptcy court's factual determinations for clear error and its legal conclusions de novo. U.S. Lines, Inc. v. Am. S.S. Owners Mut. Prot. & Indem. Ass'n, Inc. (In re U.S. Lines, Inc.), 197 F.3d 631, 640–41 (2d Cir.1999). If the bankruptcy court "has properly considered the conflicting policies in accordance with law, we acknowledge its exercise of discretion and show due deference to its determination that arbitration will seriously jeopardize a particular core bankruptcy proceeding." Id. at 641.

II.

The Federal Arbitration Act establishes a "federal policy favoring arbitration agreements," Moses H. Cone Mem'l Hosp. v. Mercury Constr. Corp., 460 U.S. 1, 24 (1983), and mandates the enforcement of contractual arbitration provisions. The Act provides that written agreements to arbitrate "shall be valid, irrevocable, and enforceable, save upon such grounds as exist at law or in equity for the revocation of any contract." 9 U.S.C. § 2. A court has a duty to stay its proceedings if it is satisfied that the issue before it is arbitrable, and "[t]his duty ... is not diminished when a party bound by an agreement raises a claim founded on statutory rights." Shearson/Am. Express, Inc. v. McMahon, 482 U.S. 220, 226, (1987).

However, as the Supreme Court acknowledged in *McMahon,* "[l]ike any statutory directive, the Arbitration Act's mandate may be overridden by a contrary congressional command." Id. The party opposing arbitration has the burden of showing that Congress intended to preclude arbitration of the statutory rights at issue. Congressional intent can be deduced from the statute's text or legislative history, or from "an inherent conflict between arbitration and the statute's underlying purposes." Id. at 227.

Disputes that involve both the Bankruptcy Code and the Arbitration Act often present conflicts of "near polar extremes: bankruptcy policy exerts an inexorable pull towards centralization while arbitration policy advocates a decentralized approach toward dispute resolution." *In re U.S. Lines, Inc.*, 197 F.3d at 640.

In resolving these conflicts, courts distinguish between claims over which bankruptcy judges have discretion to refuse arbitration and those that they must send directly to arbitration. Bankruptcy courts generally do not have discretion to refuse to compel arbitration of "non-core" bankruptcy matters, or matters that are simply "related to" bankruptcy cases. Crysen/Montenay Energy Co. v. Shell Oil Co. (In re Crysen/Montenay Energy Co.), 226 F.3d 160, 166 (2d Cir.2000). As to these matters, the presumption in favor of arbitration usually trumps the lesser interest of bankruptcy courts in adjudicating non-core proceedings.

Id.; *In re U.S. Lines, Inc.*, 197 F.3d at 640.

Bankruptcy courts are more likely to have discretion to refuse to compel arbitration of core bankruptcy matters, which implicate "more pressing bankruptcy concerns." *In re U.S. Lines, Inc.*, 197 F.3d at 640. However, even as to core proceedings, the bankruptcy court will not have discretion to override an arbitration agreement unless it finds that the proceedings are based on provisions of the Bankruptcy Code that "inherently conflict" with the Arbitration Act or that arbitration of the claim would "necessarily jeopardize" the objectives of the Bankruptcy Code. Id. This determination requires a particularized inquiry into the nature of the claim and the facts of the specific bankruptcy. The objectives of the Bankruptcy Code relevant to this inquiry include "the goal of centralized resolution of purely bankruptcy issues, the need to protect creditors and reorganizing debtors from piecemeal litigation, and the undisputed power of a bankruptcy court to enforce its own orders." Ins. Co. of N. Am. v. NGC Settlement Trust & Asbestos Claims Mgmt. Corp. (In re Nat'l Gypsum Co.), 118 F.3d 1056, 1069 (5th Cir.1997). If a severe conflict is found, then the court can properly conclude that, with respect to the particular Code provision involved, Congress intended to override the Arbitration Act's general policy favoring the enforcement of arbitration agreements.

In this case, Hill's claim under § 362(h) of the Bankruptcy is properly characterized as a "core" bankruptcy proceeding. Claims that clearly invoke substantive rights created by federal bankruptcy law necessarily arise under Title 11 and are deemed core proceedings. Banque Nationale de Paris v. Murad (In re Housecraft Indus. USA, Inc.), 310 F.3d 64, 70 (2d Cir.2002). So too are proceedings that, by their nature, could arise only in the context of a bankruptcy case. Wood v. Wood (In re Wood), 825 F.2d 90, 96-97 (5th Cir.1987). Actions brought under 11 U.S.C. § 362(h) are therefore core proceedings because they derive directly from the Bankruptcy Code and can be brought only in the context of a bankruptcy case.

In addressing the question of whether Hill's core proceeding should be arbitrated, both the bankruptcy court and the district court provided thoughtful analysis and addressed the relevant competing interests. The bankruptcy court recognized that "Code § 362(h) presents a conundrum in the context of a conflict between the jurisdiction of bankruptcy courts and arbitral fora." The bankruptcy court concluded that its court was the most appropriate forum for Hill's claim because a section 362(h) cause of action is strictly a product of the Bankruptcy Code. It is derived from the rights of a debtor, and recovery under it inures to the debtor rather than to the bankruptcy estate. Moreover, at the time of the bankruptcy court's ruling, Hill's bankruptcy case was open and she continued to require the protection of the automatic stay. Finally, the bankruptcy court noted that automatic stay provisions are the equivalent of an injunctive order of the bankruptcy court.

The district court held that the bankruptcy court did not abuse its discretion by denying MBNA's motion. The district court recognized it as a close case, but ultimately was persuaded by the fact that a ruling on Hill's claim did not require the bankruptcy court to address the terms of the agreement between Hill and MBNA. Instead, the court would decide whether MBNA violated the automatic stay provision. The district court also emphasized that to allow arbitration to go forward would seriously jeopardize the objectives of the Code in light of the fact that the automatic stay serves the same function as an injunction.

Although we reach the same conclusion as the lower courts that Hill's § 362(h) claim is a core proceeding, we hold that arbitration of her claim would not seriously jeopardize the objectives of the Bankruptcy Code because: (1) Hill's estate has now been fully administered and her debts have been discharged, so she no longer requires protection of the automatic stay and resolution of the claim would have no effect on her bankruptcy estate; (2) as a purported class action, Hill's claims lack the direct connection to her own bankruptcy case that would weigh in favor of refusing to compel arbitration; and (3) a stay is not so closely related to an injunction that the bankruptcy court is uniquely able to interpret and enforce its provisions.

First, and most importantly, arbitration of Hill's § 362(h) claim would not jeopardize the important purposes that the automatic stay serves: providing debtors with a fresh start, protecting the assets of the estate, and allowing the bankruptcy court to centralize disputes concerning the estate. See SEC v. Brennan, 230 F.3d 65, 70 (2d Cir.2000). District courts have often reversed bankruptcy decisions refusing to compel arbitration of core bankruptcy matters and granted motions to arbitrate core claims on the grounds that arbitration would not interfere with or affect the distribution of the estate. See, e.g., Cibro Petroleum Prods., Inc. v. City of Albany (In re Winimo Realty Corp.).

* * * *

Chapter 3

FEDERAL PREEMPTION — THE INTERPLAY OF FEDERAL AND STATE LAWS OF ARBITRATION

The "arbitration explosion" led by the United States Supreme Court has several components. So far, we have largely focused on that Court's extension of arbitrability to almost all types of federal statutory claims. Now we go far beyond that. Section 2 of the FAA makes it applicable to all matters "involving commerce," and the Supreme Court, relying on this formulation, has held the FAA to have application coextensive with the broadest possible coverage of the United States Constitution's Commerce Clause, so that it reaches not only federal claims, but a large proportion of state law claims as well. It does not matter whether such claims are common law or statutory, just so long as they "involve commerce." The court has then taken the boldest step of all in deciding, not without controversy, that, by virtue of the United States Constitution's Supremacy Clause, the states and their courts, in dealing with arbitral matters involving interstate commerce, must, under the concept of preemption, apply the almost overriding presumption of arbitrability said to be set by the FAA and the "federal law of arbitration" created by the federal courts to implement it. We shall see that preemption is a multi-faceted concept.

How else do you see pro-arbitration policies at work in the materials that follow? What, for instance, are the ramifications of requiring courts to send even ostensibly absurd claims to arbitration if they fall under the arbitration clause? *See* Chapter 4, *infra*.

Nowhere does the law of arbitration get more confusing than in the area of preemption. The FAA does not vest exclusive subject matter jurisdiction in the federal courts. Unless there is a "federal question" or diversity predicate, it is up to the state courts, when dealing with matters affecting arbitrability, to apply the FAA and the federal caselaw standards for its implementation in any case "involving" interstate commerce. Hence, in a matter covered by the FAA, a state rule restricting arbitrability or imposing special requirements for arbitration agreements would be trumped by federal statutory and caselaw policies that proscribe such limitations. Note how frequently state courts cite federal caselaw in FAA cases.

§ 3.01 BASIC PRINCIPLES OF PREEMPTION

Moses H. Cone Memorial Hospital v. Mercury Construction Corp.

Supreme Court of the United States, 1983.
460 U.S. 1.

- BRENNAN, J.

* * * *

The basic issue presented in Mercury's federal suit was the arbitrability of the dispute between Mercury and the Hospital. Federal law in the terms of the Arbitration Act governs that issue in either state or federal court. Section 2 is the primary substantive provision of the Act, declaring that a written agreement to arbitrate "in any maritime transaction or a contract evidencing a transaction involving commerce . . . shall be valid, irrevocable, and enforceable, save upon such grounds as exist at law or in equity for the revocation of any contract." 9 U.S.C. § 2. Section 2 is a congressional declaration of a liberal federal policy favoring arbitration agreements, notwithstanding any state substantive or procedural policies to the contrary. The effect of the section is to create a body of federal substantive law of arbitrability, applicable to any arbitration agreement within the coverage of the Act. In *Prima Paint Corp. v. Flood & Conklin Mfg. Corp.*, 388 U.S. 395 (1967), for example, the parties had signed a contract containing an arbitration clause, but one party alleged that there had been fraud in the inducement of the entire contract (although the alleged fraud did not go to the arbitration clause in particular). The issue before us was whether the issue of fraud in the inducement was itself an arbitrable controversy. We held that the language and policies of the Act required the conclusion that the fraud issue was arbitrable. Id., at 402–04. Although our holding in *Prima Paint* extended only to the specific issue presented, the courts of appeals have since consistently concluded that questions of arbitrability must be addressed with a healthy regard for the federal policy favoring arbitration. We agree. The Arbitration Act establishes that, as a matter of federal law, any doubts concerning the scope of arbitrable issues should be resolved in favor of arbitration, whether the problem at hand is the construction of the contract language itself or an allegation of waiver, delay, or a like defense to arbitrability.

The Arbitration Act is something of an anomaly in the field of federal-court jurisdiction. It creates a body of federal substantive law establishing and regulating the duty to honor an agreement to arbitrate, yet it does not create any independent federal-question jurisdiction under 28 U.S.C. § 1331 or otherwise. Section 4 provides for an order compelling arbitration only when the federal district court would have jurisdiction over a suit on the underlying dispute; hence, there must be diversity of citizenship or some other independent basis for federal jurisdiction before the order can issue. E.g., Commercial Metals Co. v. Balfour, Guthrie, & Co., 577 F.2d 264, 268–69 (CA5 1978), and cases cited. Section 3 likewise limits the federal courts to the extent that a federal court cannot stay a suit pending before it unless there is such a suit in existence. Nevertheless, although enforcement of the Act is left in large part to the state courts, it nevertheless represents federal policy to be vindicated by the federal courts where otherwise appropriate.

NOTE

1. Can judicial construction of arbitral agreements really ever be

fully a matter of federal law? What about state law principles of contract interpretation, and those governing defenses to enforcement, such as unconscionability? Illusoriness? Section 2 of the FAA permits defenses to enforcement of arbitration agreements if such defenses are available to enforcement of other contracts as well. It is read, however, to prohibit use of special restrictions aimed only at arbitral provisions.

Prima Paint Corp. v. Flood & Conklin Manufacturing Co.

Supreme Court of the United States 1967.
388 U.S. 395.

- FORTAS, J.

This case presents the question whether the federal court or an arbitrator is to resolve a claim of "fraud in the inducement," under a contract governed by the United States Arbitration Act of 1925, where there is no evidence that the contracting parties intended to withhold that issue from arbitration.

The question arises from the following set of facts. On October 7, 1964, respondent, Flood & Conklin Manufacturing Company, a New Jersey corporation, entered into what was styled a "Consulting Agreement," with petitioner, Prima Paint Corporation, a Maryland corporation. This agreement followed by less than three weeks the execution of a contract pursuant to which Prima Paint purchased F & C's paint business. The consulting agreement provided that for a six-year period F & C was to furnish advice and consultation "in connection with the formulae, manufacturing operations, sales and servicing of Prima Trade Sales accounts." These services were to be performed personally by F & C's chairman, Jerome K. Jelin, "except in the event of his death or disability." F & C bound itself for the duration of the contractual period to make no "Trade Sales" of paint or paint products in its existing sales territory or to current customers. To the consulting agreement were appended lists of F & C customers, whose patronage was to be taken over by Prima Paint. In return for these lists, the covenant not to compete, and the services of Mr. Jelin, Prima Paint agreed to pay F & C certain percentages of its receipts from the listed customers and from all others, such payments not to exceed $225,000 over the life of the agreement. The agreement took into account the possibility that Prima Paint might encounter financial difficulties, including bankruptcy, but no corresponding reference was made to possible financial problems which might be encountered by F & C. The agreement stated that it "embodies the entire understanding of the parties on the subject matter." Finally, the parties agreed to a broad arbitration clause, which read in part:

> Any controversy or claim arising out of or relating to this Agreement, or the breach thereof, shall be settled by arbitration in the City of New York, in accordance with the rules then obtaining of the American Arbitration Association . . . .

The first payment by Prima Paint to F & C under the consulting agreement was due on September 1, 1965. None was made on that date. Seventeen days later, Prima Paint did pay the appropriate amount, but into escrow. It notified attorneys for F & C that in various enumerated respects their client had broken both the consulting agreement and the earlier purchase agreement. Prima Paint's principal contention, so far as presently relevant, was that F & C had fraudulently represented that it was solvent and able to perform its contractual obligations, where as it was in fact insolvent and intended to file a petition under Chapter XI of the Bankruptcy Act. Prima Paint noted that such a petition was filed by F & C on October 14, 1964, one week after the contract had been signed. F & C's response, on October 25, was to serve a "notice of intention to arbitrate." On November 12, three days before expiration of its time to answer this "notice," Prima Paint filed suit in the United States District Court for the Southern District of New York, seeking rescission of the consulting agreement on the basis of the alleged fraudulent inducement. The complaint asserted that the federal court had diversity jurisdiction.

The District Court, 262 F. Supp. 605, granted F & C's motion to stay the action pending arbitration, holding that a charge of fraud in the inducement of a contract containing an arbitration clause as broad as this one was a question for the arbitrators and not for the court. The Court of Appeals for the Second Circuit dismissed Prima Paint's appeal, 2 Cir., 360 F.2d 315. It held that the contract in question evidenced a transaction involving interstate commerce; [and] that a claim of fraud in the inducement of the contract generally—as opposed to the arbitration clause itself—is for the arbitrators and not for the courts; and that this rule—one of "national substantive law"—governs even in the face of a contrary state rule. We agree, albeit for somewhat different reasons, and we affirm the decision below.

* * * *

Having determined that the contract in question is within the coverage of the Arbitration Act, we turn to the central issue in this case: Whether a claim of fraud in the inducement of the entire contract is to be resolved by the federal court, or whether the matter is to be referred to the arbitrators. The courts of appeals have differed in their approach to this question. The view of the Court of Appeals for the Second Circuit, as expressed in this case and in others, is that—except where the parties otherwise intend—arbitration clauses as a matter of federal law are "separable" from the contracts in which they are embedded, and that where no claim is made that fraud was directed to the arbitration clause itself, a broad arbitration clause will be held to encompass arbitration of the claim that the contract itself was induced by fraud. The Court of Appeals for the First Circuit, on the other hand, has taken the view that the question of "severability" is one of state law, and that where a State regards such a clause as inseparable a claim of fraud in the inducement must be decided by the court. Lummus Co. v. Commonwealth Oil Ref. Co., 280 F.2d 915, 923–24 (1st Cir.).

With respect to cases brought in federal court involving maritime contracts or those evidencing transactions in "commerce," we think that Congress has provided an explicit answer. That answer is to be found in § 4 of the Act, which provides a remedy to a party seeking to compel compliance with an arbitration agreement. Under section 4, with respect to a matter within the jurisdiction of the federal courts save for the existence of an arbitration clause, the federal court is instructed to order arbitration to proceed once it is satisfied that "the making of the agreement for arbitration or the failure to comply (with the arbitration agreement) is not in issue." Accordingly, if the claim is fraud in the inducement of the arbitration clause itself—an issue which goes to the "making" of the agreement to arbitrate—the federal court may proceed to adjudicate it. But the statutory language does not permit the federal court to consider claims of fraud in the inducement of the contract generally.

There remains the question whether such a rule is constitutionally permissible. The point is made that, whatever the nature of the contract involved here, this case is in federal court solely by reason of diversity of citizenship, and that since the decision in *Erie R. Co. v. Tompkins*, 304 U.S. 64 (1938), federal courts are bound in diversity cases to follow state rules of decision in matters which are " 'substantive' rather than 'procedural,' or where the matter is 'outcome determinative.' " Guaranty Trust Co. of New York v. York, 326 U.S. 99 (1945). The question in this case, however, is not whether Congress may fashion federal substantive rules to govern questions arising in simple diversity cases. Rather, the question is whether Congress may prescribe how federal courts are to conduct themselves with respect to subject matter over which Congress plainly has power to legislate. The answer to that can only be in the affirmative. And it is clear beyond dispute that the federal arbitration statute is based upon and confined to the incontestable federal foundations of "control over interstate commerce and over admiralty."

In the present case no claim has been advanced by Prima Paint that F & C fraudulently induced it to enter into the agreement to arbitrate "(a)ny controversy or claim arising out of or relating to this Agreement, or the breach thereof." This contractual language is easily broad enough to encompass Prima Paint's claim that both execution and acceleration of the consulting agreement itself were procured by fraud. Indeed, no claim is made that Prima Paint ever intended that "legal" issues relating to the contract be excluded from arbitration, or that it was not entirely free so to contract. Federal courts are bound to apply rules enacted by Congress with respect to matters—here, a contract involving commerce—over which it has legislative power. The question which Prima Paint requested the District Court to adjudicate preliminarily to allowing arbitration to proceed is one not intended by Congress to delay the granting of a § 3 stay. Accordingly, the decision below dismissing Prima Paint's appeal is affirmed.

Affirmed.

- BLACK, J. dissenting (with whom DOUGLAS, J., and STEWART, J., join).

The Court here holds that the United States Arbitration Act, as a matter of federal substantive law, compels a party to a contract containing a written arbitration provision to carry out his "arbitration agreement" even though a court might, after a fair trial, hold the entire contract—including the arbitration agreement—void because of fraud in the inducement. The Court holds, what is to me fantastic, that the legal issue of a contract's voidness because of fraud is to be decided by persons designated to arbitrate factual controversies arising out of a valid contract between the parties. And the arbitrators who the Court holds are to adjudicate the legal validity of the contract need not even be lawyers, and in all probability will be nonlawyers, wholly unqualified to decide legal issues, and even if qualified to apply the law, not bound to do so. I am by no means sure that thus forcing a person to forgo his opportunity to try his legal issues in the courts where, unlike the situation in arbitration, he may have a jury trial and right to appeal, is not a denial of due process of law. I am satisfied, however, that Congress did not impose any such procedures in the Arbitration Act. And I am fully satisfied that a reasonable and fair reading of that Act's language and history shows that both Congress and the framers of the Act were at great pains to emphasize that nonlawyers designated to adjust and arbitrate factual controversies arising out of valid contracts would not trespass upon the courts' prerogative to decide the legal question of whether any legal contract exists upon which to base an arbitration.

NOTES

1. At times, it is unclear whether a claim for avoidance is addressed to the arbitration clause or to the entire contract. What about a customer asked to sign an instrument with an arbitration clause "because the document is a mere formality and contains nothing of importance?" *See* Rosenthal v. Great W. Fin. Sec. Corp., 926 P.2d 1061 (Cal. 1996).

2. *Prima Paint* reasons that in a diversity case, the federal court is to apply the federal law of arbitration, not state law. Is that because the federal law of arbitration is "merely procedural?" Is it because interstate commerce is involved? Isn't interstate commerce always involved in diversity cases? When Congress enacted the FAA, did it have any intent as to whether state or federal law would govern arbitrability and related issues in a diversity case? *Erie* was not decided until 1938—prior to

that, the "federal common law" governed substantive issues in diversity cases.

3. We have seen references to "federal question" jurisdiction arise under federal statutes, which typically vest jurisdiction over violations in the federal courts—*e.g.*, securities laws, antitrust, Title VII, other discrimination statutes, RICO, etc. The FAA has no such provision.

4. A lasting influence of *Prima Paint* is referred to as the "severability doctrine." In deciding an application to compel arbitration, the court's focus is to be on the arbitration clause itself, and not on the remainder of the contract. Hence, the only issue of fraud going to arbitrability is fraud in the securing of the agreement to arbitrate. Any claim that the contract containing the arbitration agreement was induced by fraud is for the arbitrator under the typically broad clause. The severability concept leads to a conclusion that arbitrability is to be determined without regard to whether a claim has merit or is otherwise defeated by contractual provisions in the rest of the overall agreement.

5. In an arbitral matter involving interstate commerce, would a state court have to apply *Prima Paint*?

6. Is "severability" pro-arbitration because it gets the issue of fraudulent inducement of the contract containing the arbitration clause out of the court and before the arbitrator?

§ 3.02 AN EARLY FOCUS ON "SEVERABILITY"

In *Prima Paint*, the holding is that, as a matter of substantive federal law which preempts state law to the contrary in an arbitration covered by the FAA, a claim of fraudulent inducement of the contract containing an arbitration clause is for the arbitrator, not the court being asked to compel arbitration. Only a claim of fraud directed at the arbitration clause itself is for the court. Hence, for purposes of allocating responsibility between judge and arbitrator, the arbitration clause is severable from the rest of the contract containing it. If that clause alone is subject to a defense applicable to contracts in general, then, under FAA Section 2, the court should not enforce it.

In this context, severability makes certain sense, because a party seeking to avoid arbitration can always assert "fraudulent inducement" and delay matters in court. Also, if the court were to find that the entire contract was fraudulently induced, that would typically dispose of the entire controversy on the merits so that the arbitration clause would be rendered nugatory. A cardinal principle is that a court, asked to rule on arbitrability, is not supposed to pass on the merits of the underlying dispute. See N.Y. C.P.L.R. 7501. There is caselaw to this effect as well. In *AT&T Technologies, Inc. v. Communication Workers of America*, 475 U.S. 643, 649 (1986), the Court explains that "in deciding whether the parties have agreed to submit a particular grievance to arbitration, a court is not to rule on the potential merits of the underlying claims." This rule, says the Court, applies even when claims are "frivolous."

The possible counterargument, of course, is that a party who has been fraudulently induced into a contract should not face enforcement of any part of it. While courts will, at times, sever unenforceable provisions from enforceable ones—in restrictive covenant cases, for example—a fraud or other predicate for avoidability directed at an entire contract would rarely, if ever, present this sort of situation. Pleading rules do require that fraud be pleaded with specificity, *see* FED. R. CIV. P. 9(b), so that knee-jerk fraud allegations aimed at simply avoiding arbitration might not work very well.

The United States Supreme Court has referenced the holding of *Prima Paint* in later cases, and it is entrenched law. In an adhesion situation involving an arguably unconscionable contract, how likely is it that the party resisting a possibly "stacked deck" will be able to fashion a defense which goes directly to the arbitration clause rather than to the overall agreement? If not, the arbitrator will be the one to rule on contractual unconscionability.

More on this topic later.

§ 3.03 THE BROAD REACH OF THE PREEMPTIVE EFFECT OF THE FAA BECAUSE OF THE COMMERCE CLAUSE

Allied-Bruce Terminix Cos. v. Dobson*

Supreme Court of the United States, 1995.
513 U.S. 265.

- BREYER, J.

This case concerns the reach of § 2 of the Federal Arbitration Act. That section makes enforceable a written arbitration provision in "a contract *evidencing* a transaction *involving* commerce." 9 U.S.C. § 2 (emphasis added). Should we read this phrase broadly, extending the Act's reach to the limits of Congress' Commerce Clause power? Or, do the two italicized words—"involving" and "evidencing"—significantly restrict the Act's application? We conclude that the broader reading of the Act is the correct one, and we reverse a State Supreme Court judgment to the contrary.

I.

In August 1987, Steven Gwin, a respondent who owned a house in Birmingham, Alabama, bought a lifetime "Termite Protection Plan" (Plan) from the local office of Allied-Bruce Terminix Companies, a franchise of Terminix International Company. In the Plan, Allied-Bruce promised "to protect" Gwin's house "against the attack of subterranean termites," to reinspect periodically, to provide any "further treatment found necessary," and to repair, up to $100,000, damage caused by new termite infestations. App. 69. Terminix International "guarantee[d] the fulfillment of the terms" of the Plan. The Plan's contract document provided in writing that

> *any controversy or claim* . . . arising out of or relating to the interpretation, performance or breach of any provision of this agreement *shall be settled exclusively by arbitration.*

---

* The dissenting opinion of this case appears *infra* at page 185.

Id. at 70 (emphasis added).

In the spring of 1991, Mr. and Mrs. Gwin, wishing to sell their house to Mr. and Mrs. Dobson, had Allied-Bruce reinspect the house. They obtained a clean bill of health. But no sooner had they sold the house and transferred the Plan to Mr. and Mrs. Dobson than the Dobsons found the house swarming with termites. Allied-Bruce attempted to treat and repair the house, but the Dobsons found Allied-Bruce's efforts inadequate. They therefore sued the Gwins, and (along with the Gwins, who cross-claimed) also sued Allied-Bruce and Terminix in Alabama state court. Allied-Bruce and Terminix, pointing to the Plan's arbitration clause and § 2 of the Federal Arbitration Act, immediately asked the court for a stay, to allow arbitration to proceed. The court denied the stay. Allied-Bruce and Terminix appealed.

The Supreme Court of Alabama upheld the denial of the stay on the basis of a state statute, Ala. Code § 8-1-41(3) (1993), making written, predispute arbitration agreements invalid and "unenforceable." 628 So.2d 354, 355 (1993). To reach this conclusion, the court had to find that the Federal Arbitration Act, which pre-empts conflicting state law, did not apply to the termite contract. It made just that finding. The court considered the federal Act inapplicable because the connection between the termite contract and interstate commerce was too slight. In the court's view, the Act applies to a contract only if " 'at the time [the parties entered into the contract] and accepted the arbitration clause, they *contemplated* substantial interstate activity.' " Ibid. (emphasis in original) (quoting Metro Industrial Painting Corp. v. Terminal Constr. Co., 287 F.2d 382, 387 (CA2) (Lumbard, C.J., concurring), cert. denied, 368 U.S. 817 (1961)). Despite some interstate activities (e.g., Allied-Bruce, like Terminix, is a multistate firm and shipped treatment and repair material from out of state), the court found that the parties "contemplated" a transaction that was primarily local and not "substantially" interstate.

Several state courts and Federal District Courts, like the Supreme Court of Alabama, have interpreted the Act's language as requiring the parties to a contract to have "contemplated" an interstate commerce connection. Several federal appellate courts, however, have interpreted the same language differently, as reaching to the limits of Congress' Commerce Clause power. We granted certiorari to resolve this conflict, and, as we said, we conclude that the broader reading of the statute is the right one.

Before we can reach the main issues in this case, we must set forth three items of legal background.

First, the basic purpose of the Federal Arbitration Act is to overcome courts' refusals to enforce agreements to arbitrate.

Second, some initially assumed that the Federal Arbitration Act represented an exercise of Congress' Article III power to "ordain and establish" federal courts, U.S. Const., Art. III, § 1. See Southland Corp. v. Keating, 465 U.S. 1, 28, n. 16 (1984) (O'Connor, J., dissenting) (collecting cases). In 1967, however, this Court held that the Act "is based upon and confined to the incontestable federal foundations of 'control over interstate commerce and over admiralty.' " Prima Paint Corp. v. Flood & Conklin Mfg. Co., 388 U.S. 395, 405 (1967) (quoting H.R. Rep. No. 96, 68th Cong., 1st Sess., 1 (1924)). The Court considered the following complicated argument: (1) The Act's provisions (about contract remedies) are important and often outcome determinative, and thus amount to "substantive," not "procedural," provisions of law; (2) *Erie R. Co. v. Tompkins*, 304 U.S. 64, 71–80 (1938), made clear that federal courts must apply state substantive law in diversity cases, see also Hanna v. Plumer, 380 U.S. 460, 465 (1965); therefore (3) federal courts must not apply the Federal Arbitration Act in diversity cases. This Court responded by agreeing that the Act set forth substantive law, but concluding that, nonetheless, the Act applied in diversity cases because Congress had so intended. The Court wrote: "Congress may prescribe how federal courts are to conduct themselves with respect to subject matter over which Congress plainly has power to legislate."

Third, the holding in *Prima Paint* led to a further question. Did Congress intend the Act also to apply in state courts? Did the Federal Arbitration Act pre-empt conflicting state antiarbitration law, or could state courts apply their anti-arbitration rules in cases before them, thereby reaching results different from those reached in otherwise similar federal diversity cases? In *Southland Corp. v. Keating*, supra, this Court decided that Congress would not have wanted state and federal courts to reach different outcomes about the validity of arbitration in similar cases. The Court concluded that the Federal Arbitration Act pre-empts state law; and it held that state courts cannot apply state statutes that invalidate arbitration agreements. Id., 465 U.S., at 15–16.

We therefore proceed to the basic interpretive questions aware that we are interpreting an Act that seeks broadly to overcome judicial hostility to arbitration agreements and that applies in both federal and state courts. We must decide in this case whether that Act used language about interstate commerce that nonetheless limits the Act's application, thereby carving out an important statutory niche in which a State remains free to apply its antiarbitration law or policy. We conclude that it does not.

The Federal Arbitration Act, § 2, provides that a

> written provision in any maritime transaction or a contract evidencing a transaction involving commerce to settle by arbitration a controversy thereafter arising out of such contract or transaction . . . shall be valid, irrevocable, and enforceable, save upon such grounds as exist at law or in equity for the revocation of any contract.

After examining the statute's language, background, and structure, we conclude that the word "involving" is broad and is indeed the functional equivalent of "affecting." For one thing, such an interpretation, linguistically speaking, is permissible. The dictionary finds instances in which "involve" and "affect" sometimes can mean about the same thing. V Oxford English Dictionary 466 (1st ed. 1933) (providing examples dating back to the mid-19th century, where "involve" means to "include or affect in . . . operation"). For another, the Act's legislative history, to the extent that it is informative, indicates an expansive congressional intent.

Further, this Court has previously described the Act's reach expansively as coinciding with that of the Commerce Clause. See, e.g., Perry v. Thomas, 482 U.S. 483, 490, (1987) (the Act "embodies Congress' intent to provide for the enforcement of arbitration agreements within the full reach of the Commerce Clause"); *Southland Corp. v. Keating*, 465 U.S., at 14–15, (the " 'involving commerce' " requirement is a constitutionally "necessary qualification" on the Act's reach, marking its permissible outer limit); see also *Prima Paint Corp. v. Flood*

& Conklin Mfg. Co., 388 U.S., at 407 (Harlan, J., concurring) (endorsing Robert Lawrence Co. v. Devonshire Fabrics, Inc., 271 F.2d 402, 407 (CA2 1959) (Congress, in enacting the FAA, "took pains to utilize as much of its power as it could").

Finally, a broad interpretation of this language is consistent with the Act's basic purpose, to put arbitration provisions on "the same footing" as a contract's other terms. *Scherk v. Alberto-Culver Co.*, 417 U.S., at 511. Conversely, a narrower interpretation is not consistent with the Act's purpose, for (unless unreasonably narrowed to the flow of commerce) such an interpretation would create a new, unfamiliar test lying somewhere in a no man's land between "in commerce" and "affecting commerce," thereby unnecessarily complicating the law and breeding litigation from a statute that seeks to avoid it.

Section 2 applies where there is "a contract evidencing a transaction involving commerce." 9 U.S.C. § 2 (emphasis added). The second interpretive question focuses on the italicized words. Does "evidencing a transaction" mean only that the transaction (that the contract "evidences") must turn out, in fact, to have involved interstate commerce? Or, does it mean more?

Many years ago, Second Circuit Chief Judge Lumbard said that the phrase meant considerably more. He wrote:

> The significant question . . . is not whether, in carrying out the terms of the contract, the parties did cross state lines, but whether, at the time they entered into it and accepted the arbitration clause, they contemplated substantial interstate activity. Cogent evidence regarding their state of mind at the time would be the terms of the contract, and if it, on its face, evidences interstate traffic . . . the contract should come within § 2. In addition, evidence as to how the parties expected the contract to be performed and how it was performed is relevant to whether substantial interstate activity was contemplated.

Metro Industrial Painting Corp. v. Terminal Constr. Co., 287 F.2d 382, 387 (CA2 1961) (concurring opinion).

The Supreme Court of Alabama and several other courts have

followed this view, known as the "contemplation of the parties" test.

We find the interpretive choice difficult, but for several reasons we conclude that the first interpretation ("commerce in fact") is more faithful to the statute than the second ("contemplation of the parties"). First, the "contemplation of the parties" interpretation, when viewed in terms of the statute's basic purpose, seems anomalous. That interpretation invites litigation about what was, or was not, "contemplated." Why would Congress intend a test that risks the very kind of costs and delay through litigation (about the circumstances of contract formation) that Congress wrote the Act to help the parties avoid? See *Moses H. Cone Memorial Hospital*, 460 U.S., at 29 (the Act "calls for a summary and speedy disposition of motions or petitions to enforce arbitration clauses").

Moreover, that interpretation too often would turn the validity of an arbitration clause on what, from the perspective of the statute's basic purpose, seems happenstance, namely, whether the parties happened to think to insert a reference to interstate commerce in the document or happened to mention it in an initial conversation. After all, parties to a sales contract with an arbitration clause might naturally think about the goods sold, or about arbitration, but why should they naturally think about an interstate commerce connection?

We are uncertain, however, just how the "objective" version of the "contemplation" test would help consumers. Sometimes, of course, it would permit, say, a consumer with potentially large damages claims to disavow a contract's arbitration provision and proceed in court. But, if so, it would equally permit, say, local business entities to disavow a contract's arbitration provisions, thereby leaving the typical consumer who has only a small damages claim (who seeks, say, the value of only a defective refrigerator or television set) without any remedy but a court remedy, the costs and delays of which could eat up the value of an eventual small recovery.

In any event, § 2 gives States a method for protecting consumers against unfair pressure to agree to a contract with an unwanted arbitration provision. States may regulate contracts, including arbitration clauses, under general contract law principles and they may invalidate an arbitration clause "upon such grounds as exist at law or in equity for the revocation of *any* contract." 9 U.S.C. § 2 (emphasis added). What States may not do is decide that a contract is fair enough to enforce all its basic terms (price, service, credit), but not fair enough to enforce its arbitration clause. The Act makes any such state policy unlawful, for that kind of policy would place arbitration clauses on an unequal "footing," directly contrary to the Act's language and Congress' intent. See *Volt Info. Sciences, Inc.*, 489 U.S., at 474.

For these reasons, we accept the "commerce in fact" interpretation, reading the Act's language as insisting that the "transaction" in fact "involv[e]" interstate commerce, even if the parties did not contemplate an interstate commerce connection.

The parties do not contest that the transaction in this case, in fact, involved interstate commerce. In addition to the multistate nature of Terminix and Allied-Bruce, the termite-treating and house-repairing material used by Allied-Bruce in its (allegedly inadequate) efforts to carry out the terms of the Plan, came from outside Alabama.

Consequently, the judgment of the Supreme Court of Alabama is reversed, and the case is remanded for further proceedings not inconsistent with this opinion.

NOTE

1. It is getting increasingly difficult to conjure a mercantile dispute that does not involve interstate commerce. In the next case, the Supreme Court applies the FAA to an essentially localized loan transaction because the funds were to be used in different states, but also because "Congress' Commerce Clause power may be exercised in individual cases without showing any specific effect upon interstate commerce if in the aggregate the economic activity in question would represent 'a general practice . . . subject to federal control.' "

Citizens Bank v. Alafabco, Inc.

Supreme Court of the United States, 2003.
539 U.S. 52.

▪ PER CURIAM.

The question presented is whether the parties' debt-restructuring agreement is "a contract evidencing a transaction involving commerce" within the meaning of the Federal Arbitration Act (FAA). 9 U.S.C. § 2. As we concluded in Allied-Bruce Terminix Cos. v. Dobson, 513 U.S. 265 (1995), there is a sufficient nexus with interstate commerce to make enforceable, pursuant to the FAA, an arbitration provision included in that agreement.

Petitioner The Citizens Bank—an Alabama lending institution—seeks to compel arbitration of a financial dispute with respondents Alafabco, Inc.—an Alabama fabrication and construction company—and its officers. According to a complaint filed by respondents in Alabama state court, the dispute among the parties arose out of a series of commercial loan transactions made over a decade-long course of business dealings. In 1986, the complaint alleges, the parties entered into a quasi-contractual relationship in which the bank agreed to provide operating capital necessary for Alafabco to secure and complete construction contracts. That relationship began to sour in 1998, when the bank allegedly encouraged Alafabco to bid on a large construction contract in Courtland, Alabama, but refused to provide the capital necessary to complete the project. In order to compensate for the bank's alleged breach of the parties' implied agreement, Alafabco completed the Courtland project with funds that would otherwise have been dedicated to repaying existing obligations to the bank. Alafabco in turn became delinquent in repaying those existing obligations.

On two occasions, the parties attempted to resolve the outstanding debts. On May 3, 1999, Alafabco and the bank executed "renewal notes" in which all previous loans were restructured and redocumented. The debt-restructuring arrangement included an arbitration agreement covering "all disputes, claims, or controversies." That agreement provided that the FAA "shall apply to [its] construction, interpretation, and enforcement." Alafabco defaulted on its obligations under the renewal notes and sought bankruptcy protection in federal court in September 1999.

In return for the dismissal of Alafabco's bankruptcy petition, the bank agreed to renegotiate the outstanding loans in a second debt-restructuring agreement. On December 10, 1999, the parties executed new loan documents encompassing Alafabco's entire outstanding debt, approximately $430,000, which was secured by a mortgage on commercial real estate owned by the individual respondents, by Alafabco's accounts receivable, inventory, supplies, fixtures, machinery, and equipment, and by a mortgage on the house of one of the individual respondents. As part of the second debt-restructuring agreement, the parties executed an arbitration agreement functionally identical to that of May 3, 1999.

Within a year of the December 1999 debt restructuring, Alafabco brought suit in the Circuit Court of Lawrence County, Alabama, against the bank and its officers. Alafabco alleged, among other causes of action, breach of contract, fraud, breach of fiduciary duties, intentional infliction of emotional distress, and interference with a contractual or business relationship. Essentially, the suit alleged that Alafabco detrimentally "incur[red] massive debt" because the bank had unlawfully reneged on its agreement to provide capital sufficient to complete the Courtland project. Invoking the arbitration agreements, the bank moved to compel arbitration of the parties' dispute. The Circuit Court ordered respondents to submit to arbitration in accordance with the arbitration agreements.

The Supreme Court of Alabama reversed over Justice See's dissent. Applying a test it first adopted in *Sisters of the Visitation v. Cochran Plastering Co.*, 775 So.2d 759 (2000), the court held that the debt-restructuring agreements were the relevant transactions and proceeded to determine whether those transactions, by themselves, had a "substantial effect on interstate commerce." 872 So.2d, at 800–01, 803. Because there was no showing "that any portion of the restructured debt was actually attributable to interstate transactions; that the funds comprising that debt originated out-of-state; or that the restructured debt was inseparable from any out-of-state projects," the court found an insufficient nexus with interstate commerce to establish FAA coverage of the parties' dispute.

* * * *

We have interpreted the term "involving commerce" in the FAA as the functional equivalent of the more familiar term "affecting commerce"—words of art that ordinarily signal the broadest permissible exercise of Congress' Commerce Clause power. *Allied-Bruce Terminix Cos.*, 513 U.S., at 273–74. Because the statute provides for "the enforcement of arbitration agreements within the full reach of the Commerce Clause," Perry v. Thomas, 482 U.S. 483, 490 (1987), it is perfectly clear that the FAA encompasses a wider range of transactions than those actually "in commerce"—that is, "within the flow of interstate commerce," *Allied-Bruce Terminix Cos.*, supra, at 273 (internal quotation marks, citation, and emphasis omitted).

The Supreme Court of Alabama was therefore misguided in its search for evidence that a "portion of the restructured debt was actually attributable to interstate transactions" or that the loans "originated out-of-state" or that "the restructured debt was inseparable from any out-of-state projects." Such evidence might be required if the FAA were restricted to transactions actually " 'in commerce,' " Gulf Oil Corp. v. Copp Paving Co., 419 U.S. 186, 195–96 (1974), but, as we have explained, that is not the limit of the FAA's reach.

Nor is application of the FAA defeated because the individual debt-restructuring transactions, taken alone, did not have a "substantial effect on interstate commerce." 872 So.2d, at 803. Congress' Commerce Clause power "may be exercised in individual cases without showing any specific effect upon interstate commerce" if in the aggregate the economic activity in question would represent "a general practice . . . subject to federal control." Mandeville Island Farms, Inc. v. American Crystal Sugar Co., 334 U.S. 219, 236, (1948). See also Perez v. United States, 402 U.S. 146, 154 (1971); Wickard v. Filburn, 317 U.S. 111, 127–28 (1942). Only that general practice need bear on interstate commerce in a substantial way. Maryland v. Wirtz, 392 U.S. 183, 196–97, n. 27 (1968).

This case is well within our previous pronouncements on the extent of Congress' Commerce Clause power. Although the debt-restructuring agreements were executed in Alabama by Alabama residents, they nonetheless satisfy the FAA's "involving commerce" test for at least three reasons. First, Alafabco engaged in business throughout the southeastern United States using substantial loans from the bank that were renegotiated and redocumented in the debt-restructuring agreements. Indeed, the gravamen of Alafabco's state-court suit was that it had incurred " 'massive debt' " to the bank in order to keep its business afloat, and the bank submitted affidavits of bank officers establishing that its loans to Alafabco had been used in part to finance large construction projects in North Carolina, Tennessee, and Alabama.

Second, the restructured debt was secured by all of Alafabco's business assets, including its inventory of goods assembled from out-of-state parts and raw materials. If the Commerce Clause gives Congress the power to regulate local business establishments purchasing substantial quantities of goods that have moved in interstate commerce, Katzenbach v. McClung, 379 U.S. 294, 304–05 (1964), it necessarily reaches substantial commercial loan transactions secured by such goods.

Third, were there any residual doubt about the magnitude of the impact on interstate commerce caused by the particular economic transactions in which the parties were engaged, that doubt would dissipate upon consideration of the "general practice" those transactions represent. *Mandeville Island Farms*, supra, at 236. No elaborate explanation is needed to make evident the broad impact of commercial lending on the national economy or Congress' power to regulate that activity pursuant to the Commerce Clause.

The decision below therefore adheres to an improperly cramped view of Congress' Commerce Clause power. That view, first announced by the Supreme Court of Alabama in *Sisters of the Visitation v. Cochran Plastering Co.*, 775 So.2d 759 (2000), appears to rest on a misreading of our decision in *United States v. Lopez*, 514 U.S. 549 (1995). *Lopez* did not restrict the reach of the FAA or implicitly overrule *Allied-Bruce Terminix Cos.*—indeed, we did not discuss that case in *Lopez*. Nor did *Lopez* purport to announce a new rule governing Congress' Commerce Clause power over concededly economic activity such as the debt-restructuring agreements before us now. 514 U.S. at 561. To be sure, "the power to regulate commerce, though broad indeed, has limits," *Maryland v. Wirtz*, supra, at 196, but nothing in our decision in *Lopez* suggests that those limits are breached by applying the FAA to disputes arising out of the commercial loan transactions in this case.

Accordingly, the petition for writ of certiorari is granted, the judgment of the Supreme Court of Alabama is reversed, and the case is remanded for further proceedings not inconsistent with this opinion.

NOTES

1. In the cited *Lopez* case, 514 U.S. 549 (1995), the Supreme Court held that a federal criminal statute preventing firearm possession in school zones did not involve "commerce" and hence, was unconstitutional. A reason given was that there was no "substantial effect" on interstate commerce, and certain courts saw this statement as a basis to be somewhat more restrictive than theretofore in applying the FAA to commercial transactions. Note, however, that in the last case, the Court says that *Lopez* was not intended to restrict the scope of the FAA. Given that a "substantial effect" test is overly restrictive when construing the FAA's "involving commerce," what type of contractual transaction would not "involve commerce" under the FAA? What about a pay dispute under a product researcher's employment contract where the employer sells to out of state buyers? Would it be enough if the employer had offices out of state? Did some business out of state? What about a dispute regarding the perfection of a lien where the sole interstate nexus is that part of the security is located in another state? A malpractice claim based on an overdose of an FDA approved drug? There are not all that many cases holding disputes to fall outside the FAA. For two that do, see *Saneii v. Robards*, 289 F. Supp.2d 855 (W.D. Ky. 2003) (sale of single family house) and *Brown v. Hyatt Corp.*, 128 F. Supp. 2d 697 (D. Haw. 2000) (hotel guest fall on water slide).

2. Based on the cases we have just seen, interstate commerce is "involved" even if the underlying transaction is not in the flow of interstate commerce, even though the parties do not focus on interstate activity in connection with the performance of the contract, and even if there is no "direct" effect on interstate commerce. It is enough that essentially localized activity falls within the traditional ambit of federal regulation.

[A] Some Thoughts About Congressional Intent

In Chapter 3, we have seen the United States Supreme Court

construe the Commerce Clause to extend to matters where there is no flow of commerce, no contemplation of an impact on interstate commerce, and not even any direct connection with interstate commerce, so long as the involved activity is one in which the federal government has shown significant regulatory interest. Working from these premises, the Court has employed preemption with equal breadth—if interstate commerce is "involved," preemption applies. The Court has thus struck down arbitration bans in state statutes regulating wages and franchising.

It is not conceivable that Congress could have foreseen these developments when it enacted the FAA in 1925. At that time, the Supreme Court had not departed all that significantly from the definition of the Commerce Power in the landmark opinion by Chief Justice Marshall in *Gibbons v. Ogden*, 9 Wheat. 1 (1824), in which it was held that commerce involved actual commercial "traffic" between two or more states, but not internal commercial activity giving rise to interstate trade, and not commerce with incidental impact outside state lines. Indeed, as late as 1935, in *A.I.A. Schecter Poultry Corp. v. United States*, 295 U.S. 495 (1935), the Court ruled that the compensation of those employed by an interstate business had too "indirect" a relationship to interstate commerce to be regulated at the federal level.

§ 3.04 THE NARROWNESS OF THE SECTION 1 "EMPLOYEE" EXCLUSION

Circuit City Stores, Inc. v. Adams

Supreme Court of the United States, 2001.
532 U.S. 105.

- KENNEDY, J.

Section 1 of the Federal Arbitration Act (FAA) excludes from the Act's coverage "contracts of employment of seamen, railroad employees, or any other class of workers engaged in foreign or interstate commerce." 9 U.S.C. § 1. All but one of the Courts of Appeals which have addressed the issue interpret this provision as exempting contracts of employment of transportation workers, but not other employment contracts, from the FAA's coverage. A different interpretation has been adopted by the Court of Appeals for the Ninth Circuit, which construes the exemption so that all contracts of employment are beyond the FAA's reach, whether or not the worker is engaged in transportation. It applied that rule to the instant case. We now decide that the better interpretation is to construe the statute, as most of the Courts of Appeals have done, to confine the exemption to transportation workers.

In October 1995, respondent Saint Clair Adams applied for a job at petitioner Circuit City Stores, Inc., a national retailer of consumer electronics. Adams signed an employment application which included the following provision:

> I agree that I will settle any and all previously unasserted claims, disputes or controversies arising out of or relating to my application or candidacy for employment, employment and/or cessation of employment with Circuit City, *exclusively* by final and binding *arbitration* before a neutral Arbitrator. By way of example only, such claims include claims under federal, state, and local statutory or common law, such as the Age Discrimination in Employment Act, Title VII of the Civil Rights Act of 1964, as amended, including the amendments of the Civil Rights Act of 1991, the Americans with Disabilities Act, the law of contract and the law of tort.

Adams was hired as a sales counselor in Circuit City's store in Santa Rosa, California.

Two years later, Adams filed an employment discrimination lawsuit against Circuit City in state court, asserting claims under California's Fair Employment and Housing Act, and other claims based on general tort theories under California law. Circuit City filed suit in the United States District Court for the Northern District of California, seeking to enjoin the state-court action and to compel arbitration of respondent's claims pursuant to the FAA. The District Court entered the requested order. Respondent, the court concluded, was obligated by the arbitration agreement to submit his claims against the employer to binding arbitration. An appeal followed.

While respondent's appeal was pending in the Court of Appeals for the Ninth Circuit, the court ruled on the key issue in an unrelated case. The court held the FAA does not apply to contracts of employment. See Craft v. Campbell Soup Co., 177 F.3d 1083 (C.A. 9 1999). In the instant case, following the rule announced in *Craft*, the Court of Appeals held the arbitration agreement between Adams and Circuit City was contained in a "contract of employment," and so was not subject to the FAA. 194 F.3d 1070 (C.A.9 1999). Circuit City petitioned this Court, noting that the Ninth Circuit's conclusion that all employment contracts are excluded from the FAA conflicts with every other Court of Appeals to have addressed the question . . . .

Congress enacted the FAA in 1925. As the Court has explained, the FAA was a response to hostility of American courts to the enforcement of arbitration agreements, a judicial disposition inherited from then-longstanding English practice. See, e.g., Allied-Bruce Terminix Cos. v. Dobson, 513 U.S. 265, 270–71 (1995); Gilmer v. Interstate/Johnson Lane Corp., 500 U.S. 20, 24 (1991). To give effect to this purpose, the FAA compels judicial enforcement of a wide range of written arbitration agreements. The FAA's coverage provision, § 2, provides that

> [a] written provision in any maritime transaction or a contract evidencing a transaction involving commerce to settle by arbitration a controversy thereafter arising out of such contract or transaction, or the refusal to perform the whole or any part thereof, or an agreement in writing to submit to arbitration an existing controversy arising out of such a contract, transaction, or refusal, shall be valid, irrevocable, and enforceable, save upon such grounds as exist at law or in equity for the revocation of any contract.

9 U.S.C. § 2.

We had occasion in *Allied-Bruce* to consider the significance of Congress' use of the words "involving commerce" in § 2. The analysis began with a reaffirmation of earlier decisions concluding that the FAA was enacted pursuant to Congress' substantive power to regulate interstate commerce and admiralty, see Prima Paint Corp. v. Flood &

Conklin Mfg. Co., 388 U.S. 395, 405 (1967), and that the Act was applicable in state courts and pre-emptive of state laws hostile to arbitration, see Southland Corp. v. Keating, 465 U.S. 1 (1984). Relying upon these background principles and upon the evident reach of the words "involving commerce," the Court interpreted § 2 as implementing Congress' intent "to exercise [its] commerce power to the full." *Allied-Bruce*, supra, at 277.

The instant case, of course, involves not the basic coverage authorization under § 2 of the Act, but the exemption from coverage under § 1. The exemption clause provides the Act shall not apply "to contracts of employment of seamen, railroad employees, or any other class of workers engaged in foreign or interstate commerce." 9 U.S.C. § 1. Most Courts of Appeals conclude the exclusion provision is limited to transportation workers, defined, for instance, as those workers "actually engaged in the movement of goods in interstate commerce." As we stated at the outset, the Court of Appeals for the Ninth Circuit takes a different view and interprets the § 1 exception to exclude all contracts of employment from the reach of the FAA. This comprehensive exemption had been advocated by amici curiae in *Gilmer*, where we addressed the question whether a registered securities representative's employment discrimination claim under the Age Discrimination in Employment Act of 1967 could be submitted to arbitration pursuant to an agreement in his securities registration application. Concluding that the application was not a "contract of employment" at all, we found it unnecessary to reach the meaning of § 1. See *Gilmer*, supra, at 25, n. 2. There is no such dispute in this case; while Circuit City argued in its petition for certiorari that the employment application signed by Adams was not a "contract of employment," we declined to grant certiorari on this point. So the issue reserved in *Gilmer* is presented here.

In sum, the text of the FAA forecloses the construction of § 1 followed by the Court of Appeals in the case under review, a construction which would exclude all employment contracts from the FAA. While the historical arguments respecting Congress' understanding of its power in 1925 are not insubstantial, this fact alone does not give us basis to adopt, "by judicial decision rather than amendatory legislation," an expansive construction of the FAA's exclusion provision that goes beyond the meaning of the words Congress used. While it is of course possible to speculate that Congress might have chosen a different jurisdictional formulation had it known that the Court would soon embrace a less restrictive reading of the Commerce Clause, the text of § 1 precludes interpreting the exclusion provision to defeat the language of § 2 as to all employment contracts. Section 1 exempts from the FAA only contracts of employment of transportation workers.

We see no paradox in the congressional decision to exempt the workers over whom the commerce power was most apparent. To the contrary, it is a permissible inference that the employment contracts of the classes of workers in § 1 were excluded from the FAA precisely because of Congress' undoubted authority to govern the employment relationships at issue by the enactment of statutes specific to them. By the time the FAA was passed, Congress had already enacted federal legislation providing for the arbitration of disputes between seamen and their employers, see Shipping Commissioners Act of 1872, 17 Stat. 262. When the FAA was adopted, moreover, grievance procedures existed for railroad employees under federal law, see Transportation Act of 1920, §§ 300–16, 41 Stat. 456, and the passage of a more comprehensive statute providing for the mediation and arbitration of railroad labor disputes was imminent, see Railway Labor Act of 1926, 44 Stat. 577, 46 U.S.C. § 651 (repealed). It is reasonable to assume that Congress excluded "seamen" and "railroad employees" from the FAA for the simple reason that it did not wish to unsettle established or developing statutory dispute resolution schemes covering specific workers.

Various amici, including the attorneys general of 22 States, object that the reading of the § 1 exclusion provision adopted today intrudes upon the policies of the separate States. They point out that, by requiring arbitration agreements in most employment contracts to be covered by the FAA, the statute in effect pre-empts those state employment laws which restrict or limit the ability of employees and employers to enter into arbitration agreements. It is argued that States should be permitted, pursuant to their traditional role in regulating employment relationships, to prohibit employees like respondent from contracting away their right to pursue state-law discrimination claims in court.

It is not our holding today which is the proper target of this criticism. The line of argument is relevant instead to the Court's decision in *Southland Corp. v. Keating*, 465 U.S. 1 (1984), holding that Congress intended the FAA to apply in state courts, and to pre-empt state antiarbitration laws to the contrary. See id., at 16.

Furthermore, for parties to employment contracts not involving the specific exempted categories set forth in § 1, it is true here, just as it was for the parties to the contract at issue in *Allied-Bruce*, that there are real benefits to the enforcement of arbitration provisions. We have been clear in rejecting the supposition that the advantages of the arbitration process somehow disappear when transferred to the employment context. See *Gilmer*, 500 U.S., at 30–32. Arbitration agreements allow parties to avoid the costs of litigation, a benefit that may be of particular importance in employment litigation, which often involves smaller sums of money than disputes concerning commercial contracts . . . .

- SOUTER, J., dissenting (with whom STEVENS, J., GINSBURG, J., and BREYER, J., join).

Section 2 of the Federal Arbitration Act (FAA or Act) provides for the enforceability of a written arbitration clause in "any maritime transaction or a contract evidencing a transaction involving commerce," 9 U.S.C. § 2, while § 1 exempts from the Act's coverage "contracts of employment of seamen, railroad employees, or any other class of workers engaged in foreign or interstate commerce." Whatever the understanding of Congress's implied admiralty power may have been when the Act was passed in 1925, the commerce power was then thought to be far narrower than we have subsequently come to see it. As a consequence, there are two quite different ways of reading the scope of the Act's provisions. One way would be to say, for example, that the coverage provision extends only to those contracts "involving commerce" that were understood to be covered in 1925; the other would be to read it as exercising Congress's commerce jurisdiction in its modern conception in the same way it was thought to implement the more limited view of the Commerce Clause in 1925. The first possibility would result in a statutory ambit frozen in time, behooving Congress to amend the statute whenever it desired to expand arbitration clause enforcement beyond its scope in 1925; the second would produce an elastic reach, based on an understanding that Congress used language intended to go as far as Congress could go, whatever that might be over time.

Again looking to the context of the time, I reach the same conclusion about the phrase "engaged in commerce" as a description of employment contracts exempted from the Act. When the Act was passed (and the commerce power was closely confined) our case law indicated that the only employment relationships subject to the commerce power were those in which workers were actually engaged in interstate commerce . . . . Thus, by using "engaged in" for the exclusion, Congress showed an intent to exclude to the limit of its power to cover employment contracts in the first place, and it did so just as clearly as its use of "involving commerce" showed its intent to legislate to the hilt over commercial contracts at a more general level.

NOTES

1. The Supreme Court has construed the "involving commerce" coverage of the FAA as broadly as possible, but the "employee . . . engaged in commerce" exception to coverage as narrowly as possible. Sound reasoning or result-oriented?

2. Based on how the Commerce Clause was viewed when the FAA was enacted in 1925, did Congress have reason to believe that worker claims, in general, would fall under "involving commerce" so as to be governed by the new statute?

§ 3.05 FEDERAL PREEMPTION OF STATE LAW RESTRICTIONS ON ARBITRABILITY BASED ON THE SUBJECT MATTER OF THE UNDERLYING DISPUTE

In the *Cone* case at the beginning of this chapter, the Supreme Court references the provision in Section 2 of the FAA that arbitral provisions in maritime transactions and transactions involving interstate commerce are "valid, irrevocable, and enforceable, save upon such grounds as exist at law or in equity for the revocation of any contract." This section is said to create "a body of federal substantive law of arbitrability, applicable to any arbitration agreement within the coverage of the Act." This so-called federal law of arbitration, in turn, must govern "notwithstanding any state substantive or procedural policies to the contrary." 460 U.S. at 24.

What does all this mean? Is the force of preemption such that a state cannot apply its own public policies to issues of arbitrability of claims under its own laws?

Southland Corp. v. Keating

Supreme Court of the United States, 1984.
465 U.S. 1.

- BURGER, C.J.

* * * *

The California Franchise Investment Law provides:

> Any condition, stipulation or provision purporting to bind any person acquiring any franchise to waive compliance with any provision of this law or any rule or order hereunder is void.

Cal. Corp. Code Ann. § 31512 (West 1977).

The California Supreme Court interpreted this statute to require judicial consideration of claims brought under the state statute and accordingly refused to enforce the parties' contract to arbitrate such claims. So interpreted the California Franchise Investment Law directly conflicts with § 2 of the Federal Arbitration Act and violates the *Supremacy Clause*.

In enacting § 2 of the federal Act, Congress declared a national policy favoring arbitration and withdrew the power of the states to require a judicial forum for the resolution of claims which the contracting parties agreed to resolve by arbitration. The Federal Arbitration Act provides:

> A written provision in any maritime transaction or a contract evidencing a transaction involving commerce to settle by arbitration a controversy thereafter arising out of such contract or transaction, or the refusal to perform the whole or any part thereof, or an agreement in writing to submit to arbitration an existing controversy arising out of such a contract, transaction, or refusal, shall be valid, irrevocable, and enforceable, save upon such grounds as exist at law or in equity for the revocation of any contract.

9 U.S.C. § 2.

Congress has thus mandated the enforcement of arbitration agreements.

We discern only two limitations on the enforceability of arbitration provisions governed by the Federal Arbitration Act: They must be part of a written maritime contract or a contract "evidencing a transaction involving commerce" and such clauses may be revoked upon "grounds as exist at law or in equity for the revocation of any contract." We see nothing in the Act indicating that the broad principle of enforceability is subject to any additional limitations under State law.

The Federal Arbitration Act rests on the authority of Congress to enact substantive rules under the Commerce Clause. In *Prima Paint Corp. v. Flood & Conklin Manufacturing Corp.*, 388 U.S. 395 (1967), the Court examined the legislative history of the Act and concluded that the statute "is based upon . . . the incontestable federal foundations of 'control over interstate commerce and over admiralty.' " The contract in *Prima Paint*, as here, contained an arbitration clause. One party in that case alleged that the other had committed fraud in the inducement of the contract, although not of arbitration clause in particular, and sought to have the claim of fraud adjudicated in federal court. The Court held that, notwithstanding a contrary state rule, consideration of a claim of fraud in the inducement of a contract "is for the arbitrators and not for the courts."

At least since 1824 Congress' authority under the Commerce Clause has been held plenary. Gibbons v. Ogden, 22 U.S. 1 (1824). In the words of Chief Justice Marshall, the authority of Congress is "the power to regulate; that is, to prescribe the rule by which commerce is to be governed." The statements of the Court in *Prima Paint* that the Arbitration Act was an exercise of the Commerce Clause power clearly implied that the substantive rules of the Act were to apply in state as well as federal courts. As Justice Black observed in his dissent, when Congress exercises its authority to enact substantive federal law under the Commerce Clause, it normally creates rules that are enforceable in state as well as federal courts. *Prima Paint*, 388 U.S., at 420 (Black, J., dissenting).

* * * *

Justice O'Connor argues that Congress viewed the Arbitration Act "as a procedural statute, applicable only in federal courts." If it is correct that Congress sought only to create a procedural remedy in the federal courts, there can be no explanation for the express limitation in the Arbitration Act to contracts "involving commerce." 9 U.S.C. § 2. For example, when Congress has authorized this Court to prescribe the rules of procedure in the federal Courts of Appeals, District Courts, and bankruptcy courts, it has not limited the power of the Court to prescribe rules applicable only to causes of action involving commerce. We would expect that if Congress, in enacting the Arbitration Act, was creating what it thought to be a procedural rule applicable only in federal courts, it would not so limit the Act to transactions involving commerce. On the other hand, Congress would need to call on the Commerce Clause if it intended the Act to apply in state courts. Yet at the same time, its reach would be limited to transactions involving interstate commerce. We therefore view the "involving commerce" requirement in § 2, not as an inexplicable limitation on the power of the federal courts, but as a necessary qualification on a statute intended to apply in state and federal courts.

Under the interpretation of the Arbitration Act urged by Justice O'Connor, claims brought under the California Franchise Investment Law are not arbitrable when they are raised in state court. Yet it is clear beyond question that if this suit had been brought as a diversity action in a federal district court, the arbitration clause would have been enforceable. *Prima Paint*, supra. The interpretation given to the Arbitration Act by the California Supreme Court would therefore encourage and reward forum shopping. We are unwilling to attribute to Congress the intent, in drawing on the comprehensive powers of the

Commerce Clause, to create a right to enforce an arbitration contract and yet make the right dependent for its enforcement on the particular forum in which it is asserted. And since the overwhelming proportion of all civil litigation in this country is in the state courts, we cannot believe Congress intended to limit the Arbitration Act to disputes subject only to federal court jurisdiction. Such an interpretation would frustrate Congressional intent to place "[a]n arbitration agreement . . . upon the same footing as other contracts, where it belongs."

In creating a substantive rule applicable in state as well as federal courts, Congress intended to foreclose state legislative attempts to undercut the enforceability of arbitration agreements. We hold that § 31512 of the California Franchise Investment Law violates the Supremacy Clause.

It is so ordered.

▪ STEVENS, J., concurring in part and dissenting in part.

The Court holds that an arbitration clause that is enforceable in an action in a federal court is equally enforceable if the action is brought in a state court. I agree with that conclusion. Although Justice O'Connor's review of the legislative history of the Federal Arbitration Act demonstrates that the 1925 Congress that enacted the statute viewed the statute as essentially procedural in nature, I am persuaded that the intervening developments in the law compel the conclusion that the Court has reached. I am nevertheless troubled by one aspect of the case that seems to trouble none of my colleagues.

For me it is not "clear beyond question that if this suit had been brought as a diversity action in a Federal District Court, the arbitration clause would have been enforceable." The general rule prescribed by § 2 of the Federal Arbitration Act is that arbitration clauses in contracts involving interstate transactions are enforceable as a matter of federal law. That general rule, however, is subject to an exception based on "such grounds as exist at law or in equity for the revocation of any contract." I believe that exception leaves room for the implementation of certain substantive state policies that would be undermined by enforcing certain categories of arbitration clauses.

A state policy excluding wage claims from arbitration or a state policy of providing special protection for franchisees, such as that expressed in California's Franchise Investment Law, can be recognized without impairing the basic purposes of the federal statute. Like the majority of the California Supreme Court, I am not persuaded that Congress intended the pre-emptive effect of this statute to be "so unyielding as to require enforcement of an agreement to arbitrate a dispute over the application of a regulatory statute which a state legislature, in conformity with analogous federal policy, has decided should be left to judicial enforcement."

Thus, although I agree with most of the Court's reasoning and specifically with its jurisdictional holdings, I respectfully dissent from its conclusion concerning the enforceability of the arbitration agreement. On that issue, I would affirm the judgment of the California Supreme Court.

- O'CONNOR, J., dissenting (with whom REHNQUIST, J., joins).

* * * *

The majority opinion decides three issues. First, it holds that § 2 creates federal substantive rights that must be enforced by the state courts. Second, though the issue is not raised in this case, the Court states that § 2 substantive rights may not be the basis for invoking federal court jurisdiction under 28 U.S.C. § 1331. Third, the Court reads § 2 to require state courts to enforce § 2 rights using procedures that mimic those specified for federal courts by FAA §§ 3 and 4. The first of these conclusions is unquestionably wrong as a matter of statutory construction; the second appears to be an attempt to limit the damage done by the first; the third is unnecessary and unwise.

One rarely finds a legislative history as unambiguous as the FAA's. That history establishes conclusively that the 1925 Congress viewed the FAA as a procedural statute, applicable only in federal courts, derived, Congress believed, largely from the federal power to control the jurisdiction of the federal courts.

In 1925 Congress emphatically believed arbitration to be a matter of "procedure." At hearings on the Act congressional subcommittees were told: "The theory on which you do this is that you have the right to tell the Federal courts how to proceed." The House

Report on the FAA stated: "Whether an agreement for arbitration shall be enforced or not is a question of procedure . . . ."

A month after the Act was signed into law the American Bar Association Committee that had drafted and pressed for passage of the federal legislation wrote:

> The statute establishes a procedure in the Federal courts for the enforcement of arbitration agreements . . . . A Federal statute providing for the enforcement of arbitration agreements does relate solely to procedure in the Federal courts . . . . [W]hether or not an arbitration agreement is to be enforced is a question of the law of procedure and is determined by the law of the jurisdiction wherein the remedy is sought. That the enforcement of arbitration contracts is within the law of procedure as distinguished from substantive law is well settled by the decisions of our courts.

If characterizing the FAA as procedural was not enough, the draftsmen of the Act, the House Report, and the early commentators all flatly stated that the Act was intended to affect only federal court proceedings. Mr. Cohen, the American Bar Association member who drafted the bill, assured two congressional subcommittees in joint hearings:

> Nor can it be said that the Congress of the United States, directing its own courts . . . would infringe upon the provinces or prerogatives of the States . . . . [T]he question of the enforcement relates to the law of remedies and not to substantive law. The rule must be changed for the jurisdiction in which the agreement is sought to be enforced . . . . There is no disposition therefore by means of the Federal bludgeon to force an individual State into an unwilling submission to arbitration enforcement.

* * * *

The structure of the FAA itself runs directly contrary to the reading the Court today gives to § 2. §§ 3 and 4 are the implementing provisions of the Act, and they expressly apply only to federal courts. § 4 refers to the "United States district court[s]," and provides that it can be invoked only in a court that has jurisdiction under Title 28 of the United States Code. As originally enacted, § 3 referred, in the same terms as § 4, to "courts [or court] of the United States."

* * * *

Today's decision is unfaithful to congressional intent, unnecessary, and, in light of the FAA's antecedents and the intervening contraction of federal power, inexplicable. Although arbitration is a worthy alternative to litigation, today's exercise in judicial revisionism goes too far. I respectfully dissent.

NOTES

1. The majority in this case suggests that, under Justice O'Connor's approach, arbitrability of the state law claim would depend on whether the issue arose in state or federal court by virtue of diversity of citizenship. Is that what Justice O'Connor says in her dissent, or is she contending that state policy with respect to arbitrability of state law claims should control irrespective of the forum? What does the next case suggest? Should a federal court blind itself to state restrictions on arbitrability of claims arising under state law?

2. The Justice O'Connor position is that the FAA should not apply in state courts, even if the dispute at hand involves interstate commerce. Part of her argument is that while Section 2 of the FAA extends its coverage to transactions involving commerce of an interstate or foreign nature, the basic judicial mechanisms in Sections 3 and 4 for specific enforcement of arbitration agreements reference "courts of the United States" exclusively. In fact, Section 4 sets forth detailed procedures to be used by federal courts in determining arbitrability. What is the response to the majority's contention that if O'Connor were right about the FAA applying only in the federal courts, statutory reference to "interstate commerce" would be superfluous? How could any claim finding its way into federal court not involve interstate commerce?

3. As Justices O'Connor and Stevens point out, even if state courts are bound by the federal law of arbitration under the FAA, that need not foreclose some degree of deference to state policy restrictions on

arbitrability. Are there applications of federalism that account for state policy preferences?

4. In contract law, unconscionability principles are used to restrict enforcement of agreements to arbitrate certain types of disputes. What about the "public policy" exception to enforcement of contracts? Doesn't Section 2 of the FAA preserve these contract law defenses to enforcement of an arbitration provision? Why should that not extend to state public policies concerning arbitration of claims under its own statutes?

5. Does the majority here say that state courts, in implementing the FAA, must use the same procedures as federal courts do? Must state courts "mimic" FAA Sections 3 and 4, as Justice O'Connor suggests is the result of the majority's conclusion here? It would appear that Justice O'Connor overstates. See generally *Volt Information Sciences, Inc. v. Board of Trustees of Leland Stanford Junior University*, 489 U.S. 468, 477 (1989), which makes it clear that the FAA preempts only those state laws and procedures which are in conflict with it and its pro-arbitrability policies. *See also In re* Arbitration Between Propulsora Ixtapa Sur, S.A. De C.V. & Omni Hotels Franchising Corp., 621 N.Y.S.2d 569 (1st Dep't 1995)—FAA does not preempt the statutory provision in Section 7503(c) of New York's Arbitration Law permitting a claimant to require a respondent to object in court to arbitrability within 20 days or be barred from doing so.

Perry v. Thomas

Supreme Court of the United States, 1987.
482 U.S. 483.

- MARSHALL, J.

In this appeal we decide whether § 2 of the Federal Arbitration Act, 9 U.S.C. § 1 et seq., which mandates enforcement of arbitration agreements, pre-empts § 229 of the California Labor Code, which provides that actions for the collection of wages may be maintained "without regard to the existence of any private agreement to arbitrate." Cal. Lab. Code Ann. § 229 (West 1971).

Appellee, Kenneth Morgan Thomas, brought this action in California Superior Court against his former employer, Kidder, Peabody & Co. (Kidder, Peabody), and two of its employees, appellants Barclay Perry and James Johnston. His complaint arose from a dispute over commissions on the sale of securities. Thomas alleged breach of contract, conversion, civil conspiracy to commit conversion, and breach of fiduciary duty, for which he sought compensatory and punitive damages. After Thomas refused to submit the dispute to arbitration, the defendants sought to stay further proceedings in the Superior Court. Perry and Johnston filed a petition in the Superior Court to compel arbitration; Kidder, Peabody invoked diversity jurisdiction and filed a similar petition in Federal District Court. Both petitions sought arbitration under the authority of §§ 2 and 4 of the Federal Arbitration Act.

The demands for arbitration were based on a provision found in a Uniform Application for Securities Industry Registration form, which Thomas completed and executed in connection with his application for employment with Kidder, Peabody. That provision states:

> I agree to arbitrate any dispute, claim or controversy that may arise between me and my firm, or a customer, or any other person, that is required to be arbitrated under the rules, constitutions or by-laws of the organizations with which I register . . . .

Rule 347 of the New York Stock Exchange, Inc. (1975), with which Thomas registered, provides that

> [a]ny controversy between a registered representative and any member or member organization arising out of the employment or termination of employment of such registered representative by and with such member or member organization shall be settled by arbitration, at the instance of any such party.

Kidder, Peabody sought arbitration as a member organization of the New York Stock Exchange (NYSE). Perry and Johnston relied on Thomas' allegation that they had acted in the course and scope of their employment and argued that, as agents and employees of Kidder, Peabody, they were beneficiaries of the arbitration agreement.

Thomas opposed both petitions on the ground that § 229 of the California Labor Code authorized him to maintain an action for wages, defined to include commissions, despite the existence of an agreement to arbitrate.

* * * *

"Section 2 is a congressional declaration of a liberal federal policy favoring arbitration agreements, notwithstanding any state substantive or procedural policies to the contrary. The effect of the section is to create a body of federal substantive law of arbitrability, applicable to any arbitration agreement within the coverage of the Act." Moses H. Cone Memorial Hospital v. Mercury Construction Corp., 460 U.S. 1, 24 (1983). Enacted pursuant to the Commerce Clause, U.S. Const., Art. I, § 8, cl. 3, this body of substantive law is enforceable in both state and federal courts. Southland Corp. v. Keating, 465 U.S. 1, 11–12 (1984). As we stated in *Keating*, "[i]n enacting § 2 of the federal Act, Congress declared a national policy favoring arbitration and withdrew the power of the states to require a judicial forum for the resolution of claims which the contracting parties agreed to resolve by arbitration." Id., at 10. "Congress intended to foreclose state legislative attempts to undercut the enforceability of arbitration agreements." Id., at 16 (footnote omitted). Section 2, therefore, embodies a clear federal policy of requiring arbitration unless the agreement to arbitrate is not part of a contract evidencing interstate commerce or is revocable "upon such grounds as exist at law or in equity for the revocation of any contract." "We see nothing in the Act indicating that the broad principle of enforceability is subject to any additional limitations under state law." *Keating*, supra, at 11.

* * * *

[T]he present appeal addresses the pre-emptive effect of the Federal Arbitration Act, a statute that embodies Congress' intent to provide for the enforcement of arbitration agreements within the full reach of the Commerce Clause. Its general applicability reflects that "[t]he preeminent concern of Congress in passing the Act was to enforce private agreements into which parties had entered . . . ." *Byrd*, 470 U.S., at 221. We have accordingly held that these agreements must be "rigorously enforce[d]." Ibid.; see Shearson/American Express Inc. v.

McMahon, 482 U.S. 220, 226. This clear federal policy places § 2 of the Act in unmistakable conflict with California's § 229 requirement that litigants be provided a judicial forum for resolving wage disputes. Therefore, under the Supremacy Clause, the state statute must give way.

- O'CONNOR, J., dissenting.

The Court today holds that § 2 of the Federal Arbitration Act (Act), 9 U.S.C. § 1 et seq., requires the arbitration of appellee's claim for wages despite clear state policy. This Court held in *Southland Corp. v. Keating*, 465 U.S. 1 (1984), that the Act applies to state court as well as federal court proceedings. Because I continue to believe that this holding was "unfaithful to congressional intent, unnecessary, and in light of the [Act's] antecedents and the intervening contraction of federal power, inexplicable," id., at 36 (O'Connor, J., dissenting), I respectfully dissent.

Even if I were not to adhere to my position that the Act is inapplicable to state court proceedings, however, I would still dissent. We have held that Congress can limit or preclude a waiver of a judicial forum, and that Congress' intent to do so will be deduced from a statute's text or legislative history, or "from an inherent conflict between arbitration and the statute's underlying purposes." Shearson/American Express Inc. v. McMahon, 482 U.S. 220, 227 (1987). As Justice Stevens has observed, the Court has not explained why state legislatures should not also be able to limit or preclude waiver of a judicial forum:

> We should not refuse to exercise independent judgment concerning the conditions under which an arbitration agreement, generally enforceable under the Act, can be held invalid as contrary to public policy simply because the source of the substantive law to which the arbitration agreement attaches is a State rather than the Federal Government. I find no evidence that Congress intended such a double standard to apply, and I would not lightly impute such an intent to the 1925 Congress which enacted the Arbitration Act.

Southland Corp. v. Keating, supra, 465 U.S., at 21.

Under the standards we most recently applied in *Shearson/American Express Inc. v. McMahon*, supra, there can be little doubt that the California Legislature intended to preclude waiver of a judicial forum; it is clear, moreover, that this intent reflects an important state policy. Section 229 of the California Labor Code specifically provides that actions for the collection of wages may be maintained in the state courts "without regard to the existence of any private agreement to arbitrate." The California Legislature thereby intended "to protect the worker from the exploitative employer who would demand that a prospective employee sign away in advance his right to resort to the judicial system for redress of an employment grievance," and § 229 has "manifested itself as an important state policy through interpretation by the California courts." Merrill Lynch, Pierce, Fenner & Smith v. Ware, 414 U.S. 117, 131–33 (1973).

In my view, therefore, even if the Act applies to state court proceedings, California's policy choice to preclude waivers of a judicial forum for wage claims is entitled to respect. Accordingly, I would affirm the judgment of the California Court of Appeal.

NOTES

1. What should happen if an arbitration proscription is found in a state statute that parallels a federal one under which claims are non-arbitrable?

2. At least two of the Supreme Court members who were in the majority in *Keating* and *Perry* have since stated that were the issue of the FAA's applicability in state courts to come up again, they would change their votes to adopt Justice O'Connor's position that it does not. See below.

Allied-Bruce Terminix Cos. v. Dobson*

Supreme Court of the United States, 1995.
513 U.S. 265.

▪ SCALIA, J., dissenting (with whom THOMAS, J., joins).

I have previously joined two judgments of this Court that rested upon the holding of Southland Corp. v. Keating, 465 U.S. 1 (1984). See Volt Information Sciences, Inc. v. Board of Trustees of Leland Stanford Junior Univ., 489 U.S. 468 (1989); Perry v. Thomas, 482 U.S. 483 (1987). In neither of those cases, however, did any party ask that Southland be overruled, and it was therefore not necessary to consider the question. In the present case, by contrast, one of respondents' central arguments is that *Southland* was wrongly decided, and their request for its overruling has been supported by an amicus brief signed by the attorneys general of 20 States. For the reasons set forth in JUSTICE THOMAS' opinion, which I join, I agree with the respondents (and belatedly with JUSTICE O'CONNOR) that *Southland* clearly misconstrued the Federal Arbitration Act.

I do not believe that proper *application of stare decisis prevents* correction of the mistake. Adhering to *Southland* entails a permanent, unauthorized eviction of state-court power to adjudicate a potentially large class of disputes. Abandoning it does not impair reliance interests to a degree that justifies this evil. Primary behavior is not affected: No rule of conduct is retroactively changed, but only (perhaps) the forum in which violation is to be determined and remedied. I doubt that many contracts with arbitration clauses would have been forgone, or entered into only for significantly higher remuneration, absent the *Southland* guarantee. Where, moreover, reliance on *Southland* did make a significant difference, rescission of the contract for mistake of law would often be available. See 3 A. Corbin, Corbin on Contracts § 616 (1960 ed. and Supp. 1992); Restatement (Second) of Contracts § 152 (1979).

I shall not in the future dissent from judgments that rest on *Southland*. I will, however, stand ready to join four other Justices in overruling it, since *Southland* will not become more correct over time, the course of future lawmaking seems unlikely to be affected by its

---

* Only the dissenting opinion is displayed here. The majority opinion appears *supra* at page 155.

existence, cf. Pennsylvania v. Union Gas Co., 491 U.S. 1, 34–35 (1989) (SCALIA, J., concurring in part and dissenting in part), and the accumulated private reliance will not likely increase beyond the level it has already achieved (few contracts not terminable at will have more than a 5-year term).

For these reasons, I respectfully dissent from the judgment of the Court.

- THOMAS, J., dissenting (with whom SCALIA, J., joins).

I disagree with the majority at the threshold of this case, and so I do not reach the question that it decides. In my view, the Federal Arbitration Act (FAA) does not apply in state courts. I respectfully dissent.

I.

In *Southland Corp. v. Keating*, 465 U.S. 1 (1984), this Court concluded that § 2 of the FAA "appl[ies] in state as well as federal courts," id., at 12, and "withdr[aws] the power of the states to require a judicial forum for the resolution of claims which the contracting parties agreed to resolve by arbitration," id., at 10. In my view, both aspects of Southland are wrong.

Section 2 of the FAA declares that an arbitration clause contained in "a contract evidencing a transaction involving commerce" shall be "valid, irrevocable, and enforceable, save upon such grounds as exist at law or in equity for the revocation of any contract." 9 U.S.C. § 2; see also § 1 (defining "commerce," as relevant here, to mean "commerce among the several States or with foreign nations"). On its face, and considered out of *context, § 2 draws* no apparent distinction between federal courts and state courts. But not until 1959 —nearly 35 years after Congress enacted the FAA—did any court suggest that § 2 applied in state courts. See Robert Lawrence Co. v. Devonshire Fabrics, Inc., 271 F.2d 402, 407 (CA2 1959), cert. dism'd, 364 U.S. 801 (1960). No state court agreed until the 1960's. See, e. g., REA Express v. Missouri Pacific R. Co., 447 S.W.2d 721, 726 (Tex. Civ. App. 1969) (stating that the FAA applies but noting that it had been waived in the case at hand);

cf. Rubewa Products Co. v. Watson's Quality Turkey Products, Inc., 242 A.2d 609, 613 (D. C. *1968)* (same). This Court waited until 1984 to conclude, over a strong dissent by JUSTICE O'CONNOR, that § 2 extends to the States. See *Southland,* supra, at 10–16.

The explanation for this delay is simple: The statute that Congress enacted actually applies only in federal courts. At the time of the FAA's passage in 1925, laws governing the enforceability of arbitration agreements were generally thought to deal purely with matters of procedure rather than substance, because they were directed solely to the mechanisms for resolving the underlying disputes. As then-Judge Cardozo explained: "Arbitration is a form of procedure whereby differences may be settled. It is not a definition of the rights and wrongs out of which differences grow." Berkovitz v. Arbib & Houlberg, Inc., 230 N.Y. 261, 270 (1921) (holding the New York arbitration statute of 1920, from which the FAA was copied, to be purely procedural).[4] It would have been extraordinary for Congress to attempt to prescribe procedural rules for state courts. See, e. g., Ex parte Gounis, 263 S. W. 988, 990 (1924) (describing the rule that Congress cannot "regulate or control [state courts'] modes of procedure" as one of the "general principles which have come to be accepted as settled constitutional law"). And because the FAA was enacted against this general

[4] See also, e. g., Atlantic Fruit Co. v. Red Cross Line, 276 F. 319, 323 (SDNY 1921) ("Arbitration statutes or judicial recognition of the enforceability of such provisions do not confer a substantive right, but a remedy for the enforcement of the right which is created by the agreement of the parties"), aff'd, 5 F.2d 218 (CA2 1924); Cohen & Dayton, The New Federal Arbitration Law, 12 Va. L. Rev. 265, 276 (1926) ("Whether or not an arbitration agreement is to be enforced is a question of the law of procedure and is determined by the law of the jurisdiction wherein the remedy is sought. That the enforcement of arbitration contracts is within the law of procedure as distinguished from substantive law is well settled by the decisions of our courts" (footnote omitted)); Baum & Pressman, The Enforcement of Commercial Arbitration Agreements in the Federal Courts, 8 N.Y.U. L. Q. Rev. 428, 430 (1931) (referring uncritically to "the prevalent notions that arbitration legislation affects merely the remedy or procedural aspects and not substance"); 2 J. Beale, Conflict of Laws 1245–46 (1935) ("American courts, without exception, hold that arbitration agreements pertain to remedy or procedure. Consequently, the law of the forum determines their enforceability . . ." (footnote omitted)); cf. Alexandria Canal Co. v. Swann, 46 U.S. 83 (1847) (whether a court should grant the parties' motion to refer a lawsuit to a panel of arbitrators, and then should enter judgment on the arbitrators' award, was "not [a question] upon the rights of the respective parties, but upon the mode of proceeding by which they were determined," and hence was governed by the law of the forum).

* * * *

background, no one read it as such an attempt. See, *e. g.*, Baum & Pressman, The Enforcement of Commercial Arbitration Agreements in the Federal Courts, 8 N. Y. U. L. Q. Rev. 428, 459 (1931) (noting that the FAA "does not purport to extend its teeth to state proceedings," though arguing that it constitutionally could have done so); 6 S. Williston & G. Thompson, Law of Contracts 5368 (rev. ed. 1938) ("Inasmuch as arbitration acts are deemed procedural, the [FAA] applies only to deed, to judge from the reported cases, it appears that no state court was even *asked* to enforce the statute for many years after the passage of the FAA. Federal courts, for their part, refused to apply state arbitration statutes in cases to which the FAA was inapplicable. See, e. g., California Prune & Apricot Growers' Assn. v. Catz American Co., 60 F.2d 788 (CA9 1932). It is easy to understand why lawyers in 1925 classified arbitration statutes as procedural. An arbitration agreement is a species of forum-selection clause: Without laying down any rules of decision, it identifies the adjudicator of disputes. A strong argument can be made that such forum-selection clauses concern procedure rather than substance. Cf. Fed. Rules Civ. Proc. 73 (district court, with consent of the parties, may refer case to magistrate for resolution), 53 (district court may refer issues to special master). And if a contractual provision deals purely with matters of judicial procedure, one might well conclude that questions about whether and how it will be enforced also relate to procedure.

The context of § 2 confirms this understanding of the FAA's original meaning. Most sections of the statute plainly have no application in state courts, but rather prescribe rules either for federal courts or for arbitration proceedings themselves. Thus, § 3 provides:

Section 4 addresses the converse situation, in which a party breaches an arbitration agreement not by filing a lawsuit but rather by refusing to submit to arbitration:

> "A party aggrieved by the alleged failure, neglect, or refusal of another to arbitrate under a written agreement for arbitration may petition *any United States district court which, save for such agreement, would have jurisdiction under title 28, in a civil action or in admiralty of the subject matter of a suit arising out of the controversy between the parties*, for an order

> directing that such arbitration proceed in the manner provided for in such agreement. . . . The court shall hear the parties, and upon being satisfied that the making of the agreement for arbitration or the failure to comply therewith is not in issue, the court shall make an order directing the parties to proceed to arbitration in accordance with the terms of the agreement." (Emphasis added.)

The Act then turns its attention to the covered arbitration proceedings themselves, treating the arbitration forum as an extension of the federal courts. Section 7, for instance, provides that the fees for witnesses "shall be the same as the fees of witnesses before masters of the United States courts"; it adds that if a witness neglects a summons to appear at an arbitration hearing,

> "upon petition the United States district court for the district in which such arbitrators . . . are sitting may compel the attendance of such person . . . or punish said person . . . for contempt in the same manner provided by law for securing the attendance of witnesses or their punishment for neglect or refusal to attend in the courts of the United States."

Likewise, when the arbitrator eventually issues an award, either party (absent contrary directions in the agreement) may apply to "the United States court in and for the district within which such award was made" for an order confirming the award. § 9. The district court may also vacate or modify the award in a few specified circumstances, §§ 10–11, but generally it will simply enter a confirmatory judgment, § 9, which is then docketed and given the same effect as a judgment in an ordinary civil case, § 13.

Despite the FAA's general focus on the federal courts, of course, § 2 itself contains no such explicit limitation. But the text of the statute nonetheless makes clear that § 2 was not meant as a statement of substantive law binding on the States. After all, if § 2 really was understood to "create federal substantive law requiring the parties to honor arbitration agreements," *Southland*, supra, at 15, n. 9, then the breach of an arbitration agreement covered by § 2 would give rise to a federal question within the subject-matter jurisdiction of the federal district courts. See 28 U.S.C. § 1331. Yet the ensuing provisions of the Act, without expressly taking away this jurisdiction, clearly rest on the assumption that federal courts have jurisdiction to enforce arbitration agreements only when they would have had jurisdiction over the underlying dispute. See 9 U.S.C. §§ 3, 4, 8. In other words, the FAA treats arbitration simply as one means of resolving disputes that lie within the jurisdiction of the federal courts; it makes clear that the breach of a covered arbitration agreement does not itself provide any independent basis for such jurisdiction. Even the *Southland* majority was forced to acknowledge this point, conceding that § 2 "does not create any independent federal-question jurisdiction under 28 U.S.C. § 1331 or otherwise." 465 U.S. at 15, n. 9. But the reason that § 2 does not give rise to federal-question jurisdiction is that it was enacted as a purely procedural provision. For the same reason, it applies only in the federal courts.

* * * *

When JUSTICE O'CONNOR pointed out the FAA's original meaning in her *Southland* dissent, see 465 U.S. at 25–30, the majority offered only one real response. If § 2 had been considered a purely procedural provision, the majority reasoned, Congress would have extended it to *all* contracts rather than simply to maritime transactions and "contract[s] evidencing a transaction involving [interstate or foreign] commerce." See id., at 14. Yet Congress might well have thought that even if it *could* have called upon federal courts to enforce arbitration agreements in every single case that came before them, there was no federal interest in doing so unless interstate commerce or maritime transactions were involved. This conclusion is far more plausible than *Southland*'s idea that Congress both viewed § 2 as a statement of substantive law and believed that it created no federal-question jurisdiction.

Even if the interstate commerce requirement raises uncertainty about the original meaning of the statute, we should resolve the uncertainty in light of core principles of federalism. While "Congress may legislate in areas traditionally regulated by the States" as long as it "is acting within the powers granted it under the Constitution," we assume that "Congress does not exercise [this power] lightly." Gregory

v. Ashcroft, 501 U.S. 452, 460 (1991). To the extent that federal statutes are ambiguous, we do not read them to displace state law. Rather, we must be "absolutely certain" that Congress intended such displacement before we give pre-emptive effect to a federal statute. Id., at 464. In 1925, the enactment of a "substantive" arbitration statute along the lines envisioned by *Southland* would have displaced an enormous body of state law: Outside of a few States, predispute arbitration agreements either were wholly unenforceable or at least were not subject to specific performance. See generally Note to Williams v. Branning Mfg. Co., 47 L. R. A. (n.s.) 337 (1914) (detailed listing of state cases). Far from being "absolutely certain" that Congress swept aside these state rules, I am quite sure that it did not.

B

Suppose, however, that the first aspect of *Southland* was correct: § 2 requires States to enforce the covered arbitration agreements and pre-empts all contrary state law. There still would be no textual basis for *Southland*'s suggestion that § 2 requires the States to enforce those agreements through the remedy of specific performance -- that is, by forcing the parties to submit to arbitration. A contract surely can be "valid, irrevocable, and enforceable" even though it can be enforced only through actions for damages. Thus, on the eve of the FAA's enactment, this Court described executory arbitration agreements as being "valid" and as creating "a perfect obligation" under federal law even though federal courts refused to order their specific performance. See Red Cross Line v. Atlantic Fruit Co., 264 U.S. 109, 120–23 (1924).

To be sure, §§ 3 and 4 of the FAA require that *federal* courts specifically enforce arbitration agreements. These provisions deal, respectively, with the potential plaintiffs and the potential defendants in the underlying dispute: § 3 holds the plaintiffs to their promise not to take their claims straight to court, while § 4 holds the defendants to their promise to submit to arbitration rather than making the other party sue them. Had this case arisen in one of the "courts of the United States," it is § 3 that would have been relevant. Upon proper motion, the court would have been obliged to grant a stay pending arbitration, unless the contract between the parties did not "evidence a transaction involving [interstate] commerce." See *Bernhardt*, supra, at 202 (holding that § 3 is limited to the arbitration agreements that § 2 declares valid). Because this case arose in the courts of Alabama, however, petitioners are forced to contend that § 2 imposes precisely the same obligation on *all* courts (both federal and state) that § 3 imposes solely on *federal* courts. Though *Southland* supports this argument, it simply cannot be correct, or § 3 would be superfluous.

Alabama law brings these issues into sharp focus. Citing "public policy" grounds that reach back to Bozeman v. Gilbert, 1 Ala. 90 (1840), Alabama courts have declared that predispute arbitration agreements are "void." See, e. g., Wells v. Mobile County Bd. of Realtors, 387 So. 2d 140, 144 (Ala. 1980). But a separate state statute also includes "an agreement to submit a controversy to arbitration" among the obligations that "cannot be specifically enforced" in Alabama. *Ala. Code § 8-1-41* (1975). Especially in light of the *Gregory* v. *Ashcroft* presumption, § 2—even if applicable to the States—is most naturally read to pre-empt only Alabama's common-law rule and not the state statute; the statute does not itself make executory arbitration agreements invalid, revocable, or unenforceable, any more than the inclusion of "an obligation to render personal service" in the same statutory provision means that employment contracts are invalid in Alabama. In the case at hand, the specific-enforcement statute appears to provide an adequate ground for the denial of petitioners' motion for a stay.

II.

Rather than attempting to defend *Southland* on its merits, petitioners rely chiefly on the doctrine of stare decisis in urging us to adhere to our mistaken interpretation of the FAA. See Reply Brief for Petitioners 3–6. In my view, that doctrine is insufficient to save *Southland.*

The majority (ante, at 272–73) and JUSTICE O'CONNOR (ante, at 283–84) properly focus on whether overruling *Southland* would frustrate the legitimate expectations of people who have drafted and executed contracts in the belief that even state courts will strictly enforce arbitration clauses. I do not doubt that innumerable contracts containing arbitration clauses have been written since 1984, or that arbitrable disputes might yet arise out of a large proportion of these contracts.

Some of these contracts might well have been written differently in the absence of *Southland.* Still, I see no reason to think that the costs of overruling *Southland* are unacceptably high. Certainly no reliance interests are involved in cases like the present one, where the applicability of the FAA was not within the contemplation of the parties at the time of contracting. In many other cases, moreover, the parties will simply comply with their arbitration agreement, either on the theory that they should live up to their promises or on the theory that arbitration is the cheapest and best way of resolving their dispute. In a fair number of the remaining cases, the party seeking to enforce an arbitration agreement will be able to get into federal court, where the FAA will apply. And even if access to federal court is impossible (because § 2 creates no independent basis for federal-question jurisdiction), many cases will arise in States whose own law largely parallels the FAA. Only Alabama, Mississippi, and Nebraska still hold all executory arbitration agreements to be unenforceable, though some other States refuse to enforce particular classes of such agreements. See Strickland, The Federal Arbitration Act's Interstate Commerce Requirement: What's Left for State Arbitration Law?, 21 Hofstra L. Rev. 385, 401–03, and n. 93 (1992).

Quoting Arizona v. Rumsey, 467 U.S. 203, 212 (1984), JUSTICE O'CONNOR nonetheless acquiesces in the majority's judgment "because there is no 'special justification' to overrule *Southland.*" Ante, at 284. Even under this approach, the necessity of "preserving state autonomy in state courts," ibid., seems sufficient to me.

But suppose that stare decisis really did require us to abide by *Southland*'s holding that § 2 applies to the States. The doctrine still would not require us to follow *Southland* 's suggestion that § 2 requires the specific enforcement of the arbitration agreements that it covers. We accord no precedential weight to mere dicta, and this latter suggestion was wholly unnecessary to the decision in *Southland.* The arbitration agreement at issue there, if valid at all with respect to the particular claims in dispute, clearly was subject to specific performance under state law; indeed, the state trial court had already compelled arbitration for all the other claims raised in the complaint. See *Southland*, 465 U.S. at 4; Cal. Civ. Proc. Code Ann. §§ 1281.2, 1281.4 (West 1982). Accordingly, the only question properly before the *Southland* Court was whether *§ 2* pre-empted a separate state law declaring the arbitration agreement "void" as applied to the remaining claims. See 465 U.S. at 10 (discussing Cal. Corp. Code Ann. § 31512 (West 1977)). The same can be said for Perry v. Thomas, 482 U.S. 483 (1987), *in which we again held that § 2 pre-empted* a California statute that (as we had observed in a prior case, see Merrill Lynch, Pierce, Fenner & Smith, Inc. v. Ware, 414 U.S. 117, 133 (1973)) made certain arbitration clauses "unenforceable." We have subsequently reserved judgment about the extent to which state courts must enforce arbitration agreements through the mechanisms that §§ 3 and 4 of the FAA prescribe for the federal courts. See Volt Information Sciences, Inc. v. Board of Trustees of Leland Stanford Junior Univ., 489 U.S. 468, 477 (1989). Cf. McDermott Int'l, Inc. v. Lloyds Underwriters of London, 944 F.2d 1199, 1210 (CA5 1991) ("We conclude from the Supreme Court's opinions that state courts do not necessarily have to grant stays of conflicting litigation or compel arbitration in compliance with the FAA's sections 3 and 4"). In short, we have never actually held, as opposed to stating or implying in dicta, that the FAA requires a state court to stay lawsuits brought in violation of an arbitration agreement covered by § 2.

Because I believe that the FAA imposes no such obligation on state courts, and indeed that the statute is wholly inapplicable in those courts, I would affirm the Alabama Supreme Court's judgment.

§ 3.06 FEDERAL PREEMPTION OF STATE LAW RESTRICTIONS ON ARBITRABILITY NOT BASED ON THE UNDERLYING SUBJECT MATTER

Doctor's Associates, Inc. v. Casarotto

Supreme Court of the United States, 1996.
517 U.S. 681.

- GINSBURG, J.

This case concerns a standard form franchise agreement for the operation of a Subway sandwich shop in Montana. When a dispute arose between parties to the agreement, franchisee Paul Casarotto sued franchisor Doctor's Associates, Inc. (DAI), and DAI's Montana development agent, Nick Lombardi, in a Montana state court. DAI and Lombardi sought to stop the litigation pending arbitration pursuant to the arbitration clause set out on page nine of the franchise agreement.

The Federal Arbitration Act (FAA or Act) declares written provisions for arbitration "valid, irrevocable, and enforceable, save upon such grounds as exist at law or in equity for the revocation of any contract." 9 U.S.C. §2. Montana law, however, declares an arbitration clause unenforceable unless "[n]otice that [the] contract is subject to arbitration" is "typed in underlined capital letters on the first page of the contract." Mont. Code Ann. § 27-5-114(4) (1995). The question here presented is whether Montana's law is compatible with the federal Act. We hold that Montana's first-page notice requirement, which governs not "any contract," but specifically and solely contracts "subject to arbitration," conflicts with the FAA and is therefore displaced by the federal measure.

* * * *

DAI and Lombardi unsuccessfully argued before the Montana Supreme Court that § 27-5-114(4) was preempted by § 2 of the FAA. DAI and Lombardi dominantly relied on our decisions in *Southland Corp. v. Keating*, 465 U.S. 1 (1984), and *Perry v. Thomas*, 482 U.S. 483 (1987). In *Southland*, we held that § 2 of the FAA applies in state as well as federal courts, see 465 U.S., at 12, and "withdr[aws] the power of the states to require a judicial forum for the resolution of claims which the contracting parties agreed to resolve by arbitration," id., at 10. We noted in the pathmarking *Southland* decision that the FAA established a "broad principle of enforceability," id., at 11, and that § 2 of the federal Act provided for revocation of arbitration agreements only upon "grounds as exist at law or in equity for the revocation of any contract." In *Perry*, we reiterated: "[S]tate law, whether of legislative or judicial origin, is applicable if that law arose to govern issues concerning the validity, revocability, and enforceability of contracts generally. A state-law principle that takes its meaning precisely from the fact that a contract to arbitrate is at issue does not comport with [the text of § 2]." 482 U.S., at 492, n. 9.

* * * *

Section 2 of the FAA provides that written arbitration agreements "shall be valid, irrevocable, and enforceable, save upon such grounds as exist at law or in equity for the revocation of *any* contract." 9 U.S.C. § 2 (emphasis added). Repeating our observation in *Perry*, the text of § 2 declares that state law may be applied "if that law arose to govern issues concerning the validity, revocability, and enforceability of contracts generally." 482 U.S., at 492, n.9. Thus, generally applicable contract defenses, such as fraud, duress, or unconscionability, may be applied to invalidate arbitration agreements without contravening § 2.

Courts may not, however, invalidate arbitration agreements under state laws applicable only to arbitration provisions. See *Allied-Bruce*, 513 U.S., at 281; *Perry*, 482 U.S., at 492, n. 9. By enacting § 2, we have several times said, Congress precluded States from singling out arbitration provisions for suspect status, requiring instead that such provisions be placed "upon the same footing as other contracts." Scherk v. Alberto-Culver Co., 417 U.S. 506, 511 (1974) (internal quotation marks omitted). Montana's § 27-5-114(4) directly conflicts with § 2 of the FAA because the State's law conditions the enforceability of arbitration agreements on compliance with a special notice requirement not applicable to contracts generally. The FAA thus displaces the Montana statute with respect to arbitration agreements covered by the Act.

NOTES

1. What if the Montana court had simply said that this particular arbitration clause should have been in bolder print? What of a court decision that principles of contractual unconscionability require only those arbitration clauses in form agreements to be in block capitals, large print, or both?

2. What of a statute requiring that all contract provisions dealing with forum selection, whether judicial or arbitral, be in large print? The SEC has long had requirements that brokerage firms use large print disclosure of arbitration provisions in customer agreements on the front pages of such instruments.

§ 3.07 THE EXTENSION OF PREEMPTION OF STATE LAW ON ISSUES WHICH POTENTIALLY IMPACT ON ARBITRABILITY—CONSTRUCTION OF ARBITRATION PROVISIONS AND WAIVER OF THE RIGHT TO ARBITRATE

Singer v. Jefferies & Co.

New York Court of Appeals, 1991.
78 N.Y.2d 76.

- WACHTLER, C.J.

Plaintiff commenced an action to recover damages from his former employer and its former chief executive officer, claiming that they caused injury to his reputation and career when they used him as an unwitting pawn in an illegal stock trading scheme. The defendants claim the dispute should be resolved by arbitration pursuant to the rules of the National Association of Securities Dealers (NASD), to which all the parties subscribe, and which provide for arbitration of any dispute "arising out of or in connection with the business" of the employer.

Plaintiff was employed by Jefferies & Co. from 1983 to 1986. The firm is a member of the NASD, and after being hired by the firm, plaintiff applied for registration with the Association. On the uniform application (form U-4), he stated that he agreed to arbitrate "any dispute, claim or controversy that may arise between me and my firm, or a customer, or any other person, that is required to be arbitrated under the rules, constitutions, or by-laws of the organizations with which I register." The NASD has a Code of Arbitration Procedure (NASD Code) which provides for arbitration of "any dispute, claim or controversy arising out of or in connection with the business of any member of the Association . . . between or among members and public customers, or others" (Part I, § 1).

The dispute here focuses on an invoice which the firm sent to Ivan F. Boesky Corp. in March of 1985, seeking payment in the amount of $3 million for "investment, advisory and corporate finance services."

The invoice was prepared and signed by the plaintiff, a senior vice-president and manager of the firm's corporate finance department, at the direction of Boyd Jefferies, who was then the firm's chief executive officer.

The plaintiff left Jefferies in the fall of 1986, to take a position with another firm, Salomon Brothers. On November 14 of that year, the Securities and Exchange Commission and the United States Attorney's office announced to the media that Ivan Boesky had pleaded guilty to illegal stock/market activities and that an investigation was under way to determine who participated in the schemes. That same day plaintiff received a summons from the Securities and Exchange Commission, which was investigating Boesky's financial dealings with Jefferies & Co., including the invoice signed by the plaintiff in March of 1985. Several days after receiving that subpoena, plaintiff left the employ of Salomon Brothers.

No criminal action was taken against plaintiff as a result of the Federal investigation. However, defendant Boyd Jefferies was charged with violating the Federal securities laws and pleaded guilty to two felony counts. On March 19, 1987, Jefferies & Co. issued a press release stating that the criminal charges against Boyd Jefferies related to a transaction in which he agreed on behalf of the firm to purchase certain stock from Boesky entities and later resell the stock to those entities. Under the agreement Boesky was obligated to reimburse the defendant firm for any loss. When the stock declined in value, the defendant Boyd Jefferies ordered that Boesky be sent a bill for $3 million, ostensively for investment services, but actually intended and used to cover the loss. This enabled the Boesky entities to make false entries on their books for which defendant Boyd Jefferies was charged with aiding and abetting. The release states that Boyd Jefferies accepts sole responsibility for the transactions.

On November 13, 1987, plaintiff commenced this action, alleging that he had been ordered to prepare the fraudulent invoice without knowledge of the true facts, that he was thereby made to appear a party to the crime, and that this caused him to suffer damage to his finances and professional reputation. Defendants moved to dismiss on the ground, among others, that the complaint failed to state a cause of action and that the suit was barred by the Statute of Limitations. They also claimed that the dispute was subject to arbitration, and asserted arbitration as an affirmative defense in their answer. The motion to dismiss was denied, defendants filed an appeal and then moved to compel arbitration. The trial court granted that motion and plaintiff appealed. On the appeals the Appellate Division agreed with the trial court that the complaint should not be dismissed, but disagreed with the trial court's holding that the dispute was arbitrable and concluded that it was not within the scope of the arbitration agreement. Defendants have appealed, claiming that the Appellate Division's interpretation of the arbitration agreement is inconsistent with Federal law.

Here, plaintiff contends that the dispute is not arbitrable because it arose out of illegal activity and not out of the lawful business of the firm.

* * * *

To hold that such a dispute does not arise out of the firm's business is unrealistic and inconsistent with the Federal policy requiring liberal, indeed generous, interpretation of arbitration agreements (cf., *Pearce v. E.F. Hutton Group*, supra [claim that employer's criminal acts damaged employee's reputation because of implication in public reports that he participated presents arbitrable controversy]). Such a narrow approach to arbitrability could only diminish the value of arbitration agreements in highly regulated industries where civil wrongs caused by improper business practices are often criminal offenses as well.

* * * *

Plaintiff contends that defendants waived their right to arbitration because they actively participated in the litigation. He refers specifically to their motion to dismiss the complaint and the appeal from the order denying the motion.

There is a threshold question as to whether Federal or State law applies. Plaintiff urges that the waiver issue is governed by State law because the Federal Arbitration Act creates only substantive rights and this is a procedural question (compare, Matter of Vigo S.S. Corp. [Marship Corp.], 26 N.Y.2d 157 [consolidation of arbitration proceedings governed by State law], with Matter of Rederi [Dow Chem. Co.], 25 N.Y.2d 576, 581 [claim that arbitration is barred by Statute of Limitations governed by Federal law]). He then relies on several recent decisions in which this Court found a waiver under other circumstances, but ignores an earlier case directly on point in which the Court held that a motion to dismiss does not amount to a waiver (Matter of Haupt v. Rose, 265 N.Y. 108). In any event, it appears that Federal law is controlling. As the Supreme Court noted in *Cone Mem. Hosp. v. Mercury Constr. Corp.*, (supra, 460 U.S. at 24–25): "The Arbitration Act establishes that, as a matter of federal law, any doubts concerning the scope of arbitrable issues should be resolved in favor of arbitration, whether the problem at hand is the construction of the contract language itself or an allegation of waiver, delay, or a like defense to arbitrability." (See also, Rush v. Oppenheimer & Co., 779 F.2d 885; Brener v. Becker Paribas, 628 F. Supp. 442.)

The United States Supreme Court has never considered under what circumstances a party may be said to have waived the right to have an arbitration agreement enforced pursuant to the Federal Arbitration Act. The Federal courts that have considered the point seem to be in agreement that substantial resort to the judicial process, such as moving for summary judgment after extensive discovery, reflects an intention to relinquish the right to arbitrate (see, e.g., Peterson v. Shearson/American Express, 849 F.2d 464; National Found. for Cancer Research v. Edwards & Sons, 821 F.2d 772), but that making a motion to dismiss the complaint before moving to compel arbitration should not be considered a waiver unless the opposing party demonstrates prejudice (see, e.g., *Rush v. Oppenheimer & Co.*, supra; Sweater Bee by Banff v. Manhattan Indus., 754 F.2d 457; cf., Allied Bldg. Inspectors v. Office of Labor Relations, 45 N.Y.2d 735) . . . .

Bearing in mind that a waiver should not be lightly inferred in light of the liberal Federal policy favoring arbitration (*Mitsubishi Motors v. Soler Chrysler-Plymouth*, supra, 473 U.S. at 624–25; *Rush v. Oppenheimer & Co.*, supra, at 887), we have concluded, as did the trial court, that defendants timely asserted their right to arbitrate and that their preliminary and minimal resort to court for relief should not be viewed as an abandonment of their right to enforce the arbitration agreement.

NOTE

1. A claimant brings an arbitral case to court. The defendant may

have a key advantage if the case's legal foundation is shaky—first move to dismiss in court, because dismissal is likelier there than in arbitration. If the motion loses, then move to compel arbitration. Fair?

In re Arbitration Between Propulsora Ixtapa Sur, S.A. De C.V. & Omni Hotels Franchising Corp.

New York Supreme Court, Appellate Division, 1st Dep't, 1995.
211 A.D.2d 546.

- LIPPMANN, J.

* * * *

In 1993, a dispute arose concerning petitioner's failure to pay respondent certain fees for services rendered over a period of time. On November 5, 1993, petitioner commenced an action against Omni in the Superior Court of Justice for the Federal District of Mexico asserting, inter alia, that the Agreement was illegal, invalid and void under Mexican law because it had not been notarized and because Omni did not have a license to engage in commercial activity in Mexico.

On January 21, 1994, Omni served Propulsora with a notice of intention to arbitrate in New York, which notice was in compliance with CPLR 7503(c) and specifically advised petitioner that it had twenty days after service of the notice to apply for a stay of arbitration. On March 7, 1994, Omni commenced an arbitration proceeding before the American Arbitration Association in New York.

On March 16, 1994, fifty-four days after the service of Omni's notice of intention to arbitrate, petitioner filed a Notice of Petition and Petition commencing the underlying action seeking to stay the arbitration proceeding. Omni subsequently moved to dismiss the petition, pursuant to CPLR 404(a), as it had been filed more than thirty days after the expiration of the twenty day limitations period. Petitioner cross-moved to stay arbitration pending the determination of the action in Mexico and to deem the petition filed nunc pro tunc.

The IAS court denied respondent's motion to dismiss the petition and granted petitioner's cross-motion to the extent of staying the arbitration pending the outcome of the action in Mexico. The court held that: "[a]s a matter of comity, the determination of the alleged illegality of the contract should be left with the Mexican court in the pending lawsuit." Omni appeals and we now reverse.

The IAS court erred when it permitted petitioner to commence the underlying proceeding fifty-four days after being served with Omni's notice of intention to arbitrate. The twenty-day limitations period set forth in CPLR 7503(c) is to be strictly enforced and the court has no jurisdiction, unless there was never an agreement to arbitrate, to entertain an untimely application

The petitioner herein invokes two grounds for a stay of arbitration: that the Agreement was unlawful because Omni was not licensed to do business in Mexico; and that the Agreement was unenforceable because it was not notarized as required by Mexican law. Initially we note that the IAS court correctly recognized the obvious infirmities of the foregoing arguments in that the Agreement, pursuant to its own terms, was to be construed and interpreted pursuant to New York, not Mexican, law. Further, both arguments go to the validity of the contract and as such are precluded if not brought within the twenty-day limitations period (CPLR 7503[c]).

Equally devoid of merit is petitioner's contention, which is raised for the first time on appeal, that the twenty-day limitations period set forth in CPLR 7503(c) is pre-empted by the Federal Arbitration Act (the "FAA"). Federal law in the field of arbitration pre-empts state law only to the extent that the two bodies of law conflict (Volt Information Sciences v. Stanford Univ., 489 U.S. 468, 477). In the matter at bar, no conflict exists as the FAA is silent on the issue of a limitations period whereas CPLR 7503(c), the applicability of which was specifically endorsed by both parties, provides that a petition must be brought within twenty days, and in such a circumstance, a court applying federal law would utilize the restrictive period (Morgan v. Nikko Sec. Co. Int'l, 691 F. Supp. 792, 794, n. 1).

In view of the strong policy of this State favoring the arbitration of disputes, coupled with the Agreement's plain language providing that any controversies arising out of the Agreement be resolved by arbitration conducted in a New York forum pursuant to the law of New York State, it was error to stay the within proceeding pending the resolution of the

Mexican action.

NOTES

1. For a conflicting decision on whether the federal law of arbitration preempts New York's "20 day rule," see *Sandivik, Ins. v. Libby*, 762 F. Supp. 596 (S.D.N.Y. 1991). Distinguishable?

2. Absent the New York rule, one can arbitrate, preserve the lack of arbitrability argument, and then raise that issue post-award if the counterparty wins the arbitration. Is it not pro-arbitration to stop that from happening? Should the N.Y. C.P.L.R. 7503(c) procedure apply in federal courts located in New York?

§ 3.08 FEDERAL PREEMPTION AND CHOICE OF LAW

The state law of arbitration is not preempted under the FAA when it comes to matters that are essentially procedural. A state court, for instance, need not use federal procedures on motions to stay or compel arbitration. That might explain the express references, in Sections 3 and 4 of the FAA, to procedures in federal courts. We also have seen and will see, however, that state laws and rules that violate the pro-arbitrability policies enunciated by the federal courts are subject to preemption—a state rule against severability, which would permit a fraud claim directed at the entire contract containing the agreement to arbitrate to be heard by the court, would be preempted, as we know from *Prima Paint*.

Potentially in conflict with full applications of preemption is the fundamental idea that arbitration is a creature of contract, so that the parties have considerable latitude to adopt their own ground rules. That is why arbitral procedural rules, at AAA, FINRA, and elsewhere, each provide that their contents are subject to contrary agreement of the parties. Thus, if the parties want to broaden the discovery envisioned by tribunal rules, so be it. If they want an arbitrator with a degree in nuclear physics, so be it.

Going a step further, what if the parties, based on their arbitral agreement, are understood to want their arbitration governed not only by a given state forum's substantive law, but also its "law of arbitration." The New York "law of arbitration," for instance, provides in N.Y. C.P.L.R. 7503(C), that a court shall pass on a statute of limitations defense in deciding arbitrability. The federal case law rule is that the arbitrator decides. What happens in an FAA case if the parties are understood to want New York law to apply not only to the substance of any dispute, but to "law of arbitration" matters as well? Should it matter whether the matter is in state or federal court?

As the case below shows, the typical choice of law clause, which says that a dispute is "governed" by a particular law, would not normally be read to incorporate that jurisdiction's "law of arbitration," so that a state rule restricting arbitrability would not apply. This is so even where choice of law is set forth in an arbitration clause. What if the choice of law clause can, however, be more broadly construed because it may be read to reference "the state law of arbitration." The cases are confusing.

Mastrobuono v. Shearson Lehman Hutton, Inc.

Supreme Court of the United States, 1995.
514 U.S. 52.

▪ STEVENS, J.

New York law allows courts, but not arbitrators, to award punitive damages. In a dispute arising out of a standard-form contract that expressly provides that it "shall be governed by the laws of the State of New York," a panel of arbitrators awarded punitive damages. The District Court and Court of Appeals disallowed that award. The question presented is whether the arbitrators' award is consistent with the central purpose of the Federal Arbitration Act to ensure "that private agreements to arbitrate are enforced according to their terms." Volt Information Sciences, Inc. v. Board of Trustees of Leland Stanford Junior Univ., 489 U.S. 468, 479 (1989).

In 1985, petitioners, Antonio Mastrobuono, then an assistant professor of medieval literature, and his wife Diana Mastrobuono, an artist, opened a securities trading account with respondent Shearson Lehman Hutton, Inc. (Shearson), by executing Shearson's standard-form Client's Agreement. Respondent Nick DiMinico, a vice president of Shearson, managed the Mastrobuonos' account until they closed it in 1987. In 1989, petitioners filed this action in the United States District Court for the Northern District of Illinois, alleging that respondents had mishandled their account and claiming damages on a variety of state and federal law theories.

Paragraph 13 of the parties' agreement contains an arbitration provision and a choice-of-law provision. Relying on the arbitration provision and on §§ 3 and 4 of the Federal Arbitration Act (FAA), 9 U.S.C. §§ 3, 4, respondents filed a motion to stay the court proceedings and to compel arbitration pursuant to the rules of the National Association of Securities Dealers. The District Court granted that motion, and a panel of three arbitrators was convened. After conducting hearings in Illinois, the panel ruled in favor of petitioners.

In the arbitration proceedings, respondents argued that the arbitrators had no authority to award punitive damages. Nevertheless, the panel's award included punitive damages of $400,000, in addition to compensatory damages of $159,327. Respondents paid the compensatory portion of the award but filed a motion in the District Court to vacate the award of punitive damages. The District Court granted the motion, 812 F. Supp. 845 (ND Ill.1993), and the Court of Appeals for the Seventh Circuit affirmed, 20 F.3d 713 (1994). Both courts relied on the choice-of-law provision in paragraph 13 of the parties' agreement, which specifies that the contract shall be governed by New York law. Because the New York Court of Appeals has decided that in New York the power to award punitive damages is limited to judicial tribunals and may not be exercised by arbitrators, Garrity v. Lyle Stuart, Inc., 40 N.Y.2d 354 (1976), the District Court and the Seventh Circuit held that the panel of arbitrators had no power to award punitive damages in this case.

We granted certiorari, 513 U.S. 921 (1994), because the Courts of Appeals have expressed differing views on whether a contractual choice-of-law provision may preclude an arbitral award of punitive damages that otherwise would be proper. Compare Barbier v. Shearson Lehman Hutton Inc., 948 F.2d 117 (CA2 1991), and Pierson v. Dean,

Witter, Reynolds, Inc., 742 F.2d 334 (CA7 1984), with Bonar v. Dean Witter Reynolds, Inc., 835 F.2d 1378, 1386–88 (CA11 1988), Raytheon Co. v. Automated Business Systems, Inc., 882 F.2d 6 (CA1 1989), and Lee v. Chica, 983 F.2d 883 (CA8 1993). We now reverse.

* * * *

Respondents answer that the choice-of-law provision in their contract evidences the parties' express agreement that punitive damages should not be awarded in the arbitration of any dispute arising under their contract. Thus, they claim, this case is distinguishable from *Southland* and *Perry*, in which the parties presumably desired unlimited arbitration but state law stood in their way. Regardless of whether the FAA preempts the *Garrity* decision in contracts not expressly incorporating New York law, respondents argue that the parties may themselves agree to be bound by *Garrity*, just as they may agree to forgo arbitration altogether. In other words, if the contract says "no punitive damages," that is the end of the matter, for courts are bound to interpret contracts in accordance with the expressed intentions of the parties-even if the effect of those intentions is to limit arbitration.

Shearson's standard-form "Client Agreement," which petitioners executed, contains 18 paragraphs. The two relevant provisions of the agreement are found in paragraph 13. The first sentence of that paragraph provides, in part, that the entire agreement "shall be governed by the laws of the State of New York." The second sentence provides that "any controversy" arising out of the transactions between the parties "shall be settled by arbitration" in accordance with the rules of the National Association of Securities Dealers (NASD), or the Boards of Directors of the New York Stock Exchange and/or the American Stock Exchange. Ibid. The agreement contains no express reference to claims for punitive damages. To ascertain whether paragraph 13 expresses an intent to include or exclude such claims, we first address the impact of each of the two relevant provisions, considered separately. We then move on to the more important inquiry: the meaning of the two provisions taken together. See Restatement (Second) of Contracts § 202(2) (1979) ("A writing is interpreted as a whole").

The choice-of-law provision, when viewed in isolation, may reasonably be read as merely a substitute for the conflict-of-laws analysis that otherwise would determine what law to apply to disputes arising out of the contractual relationship. Thus, if a similar contract, without a choice-of-law provision, had been signed in New York and was to be performed in New York, presumably "the laws of the State of New York" would apply, even though the contract did not expressly so state. In such event, there would be nothing in the contract that could possibly constitute evidence of an intent to exclude punitive damages claims. Accordingly, punitive damages would be allowed because, in the absence of contractual intent to the contrary, the FAA would pre-empt the *Garrity* rule.

Even if the reference to "the laws of the State of New York" is more than a substitute for ordinary conflict-of-laws analysis and, as respondents urge, includes the caveat, "detached from otherwise-applicable federal law," the provision might not preclude the award of punitive damages because New York allows its courts, though not its arbitrators, to enter such awards. In other words, the provision might include only New York's substantive rights and obligations, and not the State's allocation of power between alternative tribunals. Respondents' argument is persuasive only if "New York law" means "New York decisional law, including that State's allocation of power between courts and arbitrators, notwithstanding otherwise-applicable federal law." But, as we have demonstrated, the provision need not be read so broadly. It is not, in itself, an unequivocal exclusion of punitive damages claims.

The arbitration provision (the second sentence of paragraph 13) does not improve respondents' argument. On the contrary, when read separately this clause strongly implies that an arbitral award of punitive damages is appropriate. It explicitly authorizes arbitration in accordance with NASD rules, the panel of arbitrators in fact proceeded under that set of rules. The NASD's Code of Arbitration Procedure indicates that arbitrators may award "damages and other relief." NASD Code of Arbitration Procedure ¶ 3741(e) (1993). While not a clear authorization of punitive damages, this provision appears broad enough at least to contemplate such a remedy.

NOTE

1. What happens if contractual parties to an FAA dispute have specified that a given state's law is to govern not only disputes arising

under the contract, but arbitral procedures as well? In *Volt Information Sciences, Inc. v. Board of Trustees of Leland Stanford Junior University*, 489 U.S. 468, (1989), under reasoning that probably does not survive the last case, the parties were deemed to have incorporated into their contract not only California substantive law, but also the California law of arbitration. A California statute, in turn, authorized a court to refuse to compel arbitration where one of the parties was also involved in court litigation centered on the same transaction, but with a different party who had not agreed to arbitrate. The idea was to avoid conflicting rulings on common issues, and to permit the party in common to both disputes to resolve everything in one proceeding. The *Volt* Court held that the paramount FAA policy was that arbitration was a matter of contract. If parties could exclude certain types of disputes from arbitration, so too could they embrace specific ground rules which, otherwise, would be subject to preemption. Were there limits? Yes, said the Court, but only when the incorporated state procedure "would undermine the goals and policies of the FAA." 489 U.S. at 478. Under the federal law of arbitration, a claim must be sent to arbitration even if this creates the potential for inconsistent resolutions in multiparty disputes because one or more parties has not agreed to arbitrate. The California rule, while normally subject to preemption, was not sufficiently hostile to the policies behind the FAA to be preempted where the parties opted to have state law govern their arbitration as well as its merits. It would thus appear that the parties' contractual arrangements for arbitration would be considerably less subject to preemption than are arbitral rules set by state legislatures and state courts.

In re Diamond Waterproofing Systems, Inc. v. 55 Liberty Owners Corp.

Court of Appeals of New York, 2005.
4 N.Y.3d 247.

▪ CIPARICK, J.

On this appeal, the issues presented are whether the Federal Arbitration Act (9 USC § 1 et [FAA]) governs the parties' contract dispute and, if so, whether the question as to the timeliness of the subject arbitration demand is an issue for the arbitrator or the courts. We conclude that the FAA is applicable here as the contract had an effect on interstate commerce. We further conclude that the timeliness question and all other related questions are for the arbitrator to determine because the contract's choice of law provision does not provide that New York law shall govern the enforcement of the parties' agreement.

* * * *

Here, Diamond Systems and Liberty agreed to submit "[a]ny controversy or Claim arising out of or related to the Contract" for arbitration. Their choice of law provision provides only that "[t]he Contract shall be governed by the law of the place where the Project is located." The parties did not express intent to have New York law govern their agreement's enforcement. Therefore, the timeliness issue should be determined by the arbitrator.

* * * *

Goldman, Sachs & Co. v. Griffin

United States District Court, S.D.N.Y., 2007.
2007 WL 1467430.

- McKenna, J.

* * * *

A Trust, Estate and Guardian Account Agreement between respondent and Goldman that "[t]his agreement and its enforcement shall be governed by the laws of the State of New York . . . " that "[t]he parties are waiving their right to seek remedies in court, including the right to a jury trial," and that "[a]ny controversy between you . . . or any of your . . . employees on the one hand, and Client . . . on the other hand, arising out of or relating to this agreement, the transactions contemplated hereby, or the accounts established hereunder, shall be settled by arbitration, in accordance with the rules then obtaining of any one of [various organizations including the NASD], as Client may elect."

Petitioners contend that the last trade in respondent's Goldman account occurred on December 19, 2000, and that the arbitration was commenced on December 27, 2006, more than six years later, so that all of respondent's claims are barred by limitations, and that this Court, under *Diamond Waterproofing Systems, Inc. v. 55 Liberty Owners Corp.*, 4 N.Y.3d 247 (2005), should so decide, and permanently stay the arbitration.

* * * *

Petitioners emphasize the fact that the language of the Agreement provides that both the Agreement "*and its enforcement*" are to be governed by New York law

These facts, however, are not persuasive of petitioners' position.

In *Bybyk*, a choice of law clause in substantially the same terms as those in the Agreement here—" '[t]his agreement and its enforcement shall be construed and governed by the laws of the State of New York,' " *Bybyk*, 81 F.3d at 1196—did not persuade the Second Circuit that the applicability of an NASD time limitation should be decided by the court.

Nor does the fact that, here, it is state law time limitations that petitioners seek to enforce, suggest that a court, rather than the arbitrator, should decide the issue. In *Shearson Lehman Hutton, Inc. v. Wagoner*, 944 F.2d 114 (2d Cir. 1991), an arbitration was commenced against a brokerage firm, which obtained an order from the district court permanently enjoining the plaintiff from instituting or pursuing arbitration of his claim against the brokerage firm; the district court based its decision on the running of a three year state tort statute of limitations. 944 F.2d at 117. The Second Circuit found the district court's decision (granting summary judgment on a churning claim on the ground that it was time-barred) somewhat unclear, but said that, if the district court "decided the statute of limitations question itself—before examining the scope of the agreement—that conflicts with the rule that it is up to the arbitrators, not the court, to decide the validity of time-bar defenses." 944 F.2d at 120–21.

* * * *

In sum, the FAA applies to the arbitration agreement and *Diamond* does not govern. Under the FAA and the governing case law, the issue of whether respondent's claims are barred by any New York statute of limitation is for the arbitrator, not this Court.

NOTES

1. Given the conflict in the last two cases about whether a choice of law provision expressly said to govern "enforcement" of the underlying contract incorporates the chosen state's "law of arbitration," how would a drafter make clear a party intent to have state rules trump the normal allocation of power between court and arbitrator in an FAA matter?

2. Would a provision in an arbitration clause specifically directing arbitrators to adhere to the substantive law of a given state require judicial review for the "mere" errors of law that typically do not provide a basis to vacate? If arbitrators do not comply with such a directive, haven't they impermissibly "exceeded their powers" within the meaning of the typical arbitration statute? Apparently not. *See, e.g.*, BEM I, L.L.C. v. Anthropologie, Inc., 301 F.3d 548 (7th Cir. 2002).

§ 3.09 PREEMPTION AND AWARD CONFIRMATION

While confirmation of awards—the judicial process which turns awards into judgments, is covered later in Chapter 6, confirmation is fast becoming a significant piece of the preemption puzzle. *See, e.g.*, Weiskopf & Mulqueen, *Hall Street, Judicial Review of Arbitral Awards, and Federal Preemption*, 29 REV. LITIG. 361 (2010). This is so even though the "law of arbitration" on the state level provides bases to vacate awards that are often as restrictive as those set forth in the FAA. Where the federal and a state's "law of arbitration" may differ is on the issue of whether the parties themselves can effectively contract for broader, or full, judicial review.

Section 9 of the FAA states that a reviewing court "must" confirm an award absent grounds set forth in Sections 10 or 11. This has caused the United States Supreme Court, in *Hall Street Associates, L.L.C. v. Mattel, Inc.*, 552 U.S. 576 (2008) (discussed *infra* at 459), to hold that where the review procedures of the FAA apply, they provide the exclusive bases for judicial intervention, even where the parties have provided in their arbitration agreement for broader judicial review. The Court added, however:

> The FAA is not the only way into courts for parties wanting review of arbitration awards: They may contemplate enforcement under state statutory or common law, for example, where judicial review of different scope is arguable. But here we speak only to the scope of expeditious judicial review under [the FAA], deciding nothing about other possible avenues for judicial enforcement of arbitration awards.

552 U.S. at 557.

FAA Section 9, in dealing with post-award proceedings, references only federal District Courts. Are the restrictions on review in FAA Sections 10 and 11 "procedural," so as to have no application in state courts, even in so-called "FAA cases," just as with FAA Sections 3 and 4? Or are the FAA limitations on review "substantive," so that they apply to state court review of awards in cases "involving" interstate commerce within the FAA's ambit? Assuming the latter, what happens if the arbitral agreement is construed to invite review pursuant to state statute? Do the state statutory ground rules for review apply absent manifest "hostility" to federal arbitral policy under the *Volt* analysis, discussed at page 209, *supra*? What if a state's courts have ruled that party agreement to expand the scope of review is permitted by state arbitral statute? Is that preempted in an FAA case under the *Volt* standard? For a holding that it is not, see *Cable Connection, Inc. v. Direct TV, Inc.*, 190 P.3d 586 (Cal. 2008) (discussed *infra* at page 471). The quote from *Hall Street* set forth above suggests that the Supreme Court, in holding FAA grounds for review were exclusive and could not be contractually expanded, was ruling more as a matter of strict statutory construction of the FAA than as a matter of policy, does it not? If so, that weakens the argument for preemption at the state level, at least where review is pursuant to state statute.

Chapter 4

ARBITRATION PROVISIONS — CONTRACT FORMATION AND UNCONSCIONABILITY

§ 4.01 CONTRACT FORMATION

Under federal and state law, the threshold issue of whether there is an enforceable agreement to arbitrate has traditionally been for the court. It typically arises in the context of a motion to compel arbitration and/or to stay a court proceeding in favor of arbitration.

We have seen in *Gilmer*, *Shearson*, and other cases that the fact that an arbitration provision appears in a non-negotiated contract of adhesion does not invalidate it. We have also seen that state law attempts to limit enforcement of such provisions according to the type of dispute are invariably preempted, as are other restrictions not based on general contract law. Nonetheless, none of this goes to the issue of whether the parties actually contracted to arbitrate, under a "battle of the forms" or otherwise.

The most common "battle of the forms" for our purposes is a mercantile exchange of forms, with the "last shot" response by seller to a buyer's offer containing an arbitration clause. Under § 2-207(2) of the

UCC, even if there is no objection to the clause, it will quite possibly be found to be a proposed "material" addition to the offer, which does not become part of the contract absent the express consent of the counterparty. There are also cases, however, showing that "materiality" can be defeated if arbitration is a trade or recurrent party practice.

It is very important to understand that arbitral statutes require written agreements to arbitrate, but say nothing about the need for a signature, even by the party against whom enforcement of an arbitral undertaking is sought. It is true that many cases mention that an arbitral agreement was signed, or set forth in a broader agreement that was signed. That, however, is because signature is a manifestation of assent, and not because assent to an arbitration provision cannot be found or manifested in some other fashion. The "battle of the forms" can lead to charging a party with the obligation to arbitrate based on a counterparty form providing for arbitration. *E.g.*, Genesco, Inc. v. T. Kakiuchi & Co., 815 F.2d 840, 846 (2d Cir. 1987) (party bound to arbitrate by other's unsigned sales confirmations). Also, one can accept by conduct a contractual proposal containing an obligation to arbitrate. *E.g.*, Brown v. St. Paul Travelers Cos., 331 F. App'x 68 (2d Cir. 2009) (employee bound to arbitral provision in employee handbook despite lack of employee signature).

Dorton v. Collins & Aikman Corp.

United States Court of Appeals, Sixth Circuit, 1972.
453 F.2d 1161.

- CELEBREZZE, CIRCUIT JUDGE.

This is an appeal from the District Court's denial of Defendant-Appellant's motion for a stay pending arbitration, pursuant to *Section 3* of the United States Arbitration Act of 1925, *9 U.S.C. § 3*. The suit arose after a series of over 55 transactions during 1968, 1969, and 1970 in which Plaintiffs-Appellees [hereinafter The Carpet Mart], carpet retailers in Kingsport, Tennessee, purchased carpets from Defendant-Appellant [hereinafter Collins & Aikman], incorporated under the laws of the State of Delaware, with its principal place of business in New York, New York, and owner of a carpet manufacturing plant located in Dalton, Georgia. The Carpet Mart originally brought this action in a Tennessee state trial court, seeking compensatory and punitive damages in the amount of $450,000 from Collins & Aikman for the latter's alleged fraud, deceit, and misrepresentation in the sale of what were supposedly carpets manufactured from 100% Kodel polyester fiber. The Carpet Mart maintains that in May, 1970, in response to a customer complaint, it learned that not all of the carpets were manufactured from 100% Kodel polyester fiber but rather some were composed of a cheaper and inferior carpet fiber. After the cause was removed to the District Court on the basis of diversity of citizenship, Collins & Aikman moved for a stay pending arbitration, asserting that The Carpet Mart was bound to an arbitration agreement which appeared on the reverse side of Collins & Aikman's printed sales acknowledgment forms. Holding that there existed no binding arbitration agreement between the parties, the District Court denied the stay. For the reasons set forth below, we remand the case to the District Court for further findings.

We initially note that the denial of a motion to stay pending arbitration, although interlocutory in nature, is appealable to this Court. In *Shanferoke Coal & Supply Corp. v. Westchester Service Corp.*, 293 U.S. 449 (1935), the Supreme Court held that a motion to stay pending arbitration under 9 U.S.C. § 3 is, in effect, an application for an interlocutory injunction, the denial of which is appealable under Section 9 of the Judicial Code [now, as amended, 28 U.S.C. § 1292.] See also Hoover Motor Express Co., Inc. v. Teamsters, Chauffeurs, Helpers and Taxicab Drivers, Local No. 327, 217 F.2d 49, 51 (6th Cir. 1954).

We also find that there is no conflict of law problem in the present case, the Uniform Commercial Code having been enacted in both Georgia and Tennessee at the time of the disputed transactions.

The primary question before us on appeal is whether the District Court, in denying Collins & Aikman's motion for a stay pending arbitration, erred in holding that The Carpet Mart was not bound by the arbitration agreement appearing on the back of Collins & Aikman's acknowledgment forms. In reviewing the District Court's determination, we must look closely at the procedures which were followed in the sales transactions which gave rise to the present dispute over the arbitration agreement.

In holding that no binding arbitration agreement was created between the parties through the transactions above, the District Court relied on T.C.A. § 47-2-207 [UCC § 2-207], which provides:

> (1) A definite and seasonable expression of acceptance or a written confirmation which is sent within a reasonable time operates as an acceptance even though it states terms additional to or different from those offered or agreed upon, unless acceptance is expressly made conditional on assent to the additional or different terms.
>
> (2) The additional terms are to be construed as proposals for addition to the contract. Between merchants such terms become part of the contract unless: (a) the offer expressly limits acceptance to the terms of the offer; (b) they materially alter it; or (c) notification of objection to them has already been given or is given within a reasonable time after notice of them is received.

Assuming, for purposes of analysis, that the arbitration provision was an addition to the terms of The Carpet Mart's oral offers, we must next determine whether or not Collins & Aikman's acceptances were "expressly made conditional on assent to the additional . . . terms" therein, within the proviso of Subsection 2-207(1).

Although Collins & Aikman's use of the words "subject to" suggests that the acceptances were conditional to some extent, we do not believe the acceptances were "expressly made conditional on [the buyer's] assent to the additional or different terms," as specifically required under the Subsection 2-207(1) proviso. In order to fall within this proviso, it is not enough that an acceptance is expressly conditional on additional or different terms; rather, an acceptance must be *expressly* conditional on the offeror's *assent* to those terms. Viewing the Subsection (1) proviso within the context of the rest of that Subsection and within the policies of Section 2-207 itself, we believe that it was intended to apply only to an acceptance which clearly reveals that the offeree is unwilling to proceed with the transaction unless he is assured of the offeror's assent to the additional or different terms therein. See 1 W. Hawkland, supra. That the acceptance is predicated on the offeror's assent must be "directly and distinctly stated or expressed rather than implied or left to inference." Webster's Third International Dictionary (defining "express").

Because Collins & Aikman's acceptances were not expressly conditional on the buyer's assent to the additional terms within the proviso of Subsection 2-207(1), a contract is recognized under Subsection (1), and the additional terms are treated as "proposals" for addition to the contract under Subsection 2-207(2). Since both Collins & Aikman and The Carpet Mart are clearly "merchants" as that term is defined in Subsection 2-104(1), the arbitration provision will be deemed to have been accepted by The Carpet Mart under Subsection 2-207(2) unless it materially altered the terms of The Carpet Mart's oral offers. We believe that the question of whether the arbitration provision materially altered the oral offer under Subsection 2-207(2) (b) is one which can be resolved only by the District Court on further findings of fact in the present case. If the arbitration provision did in fact materially alter The Carpet Mart's offer, it could not become a part of the contract "unless expressly agreed to" by The Carpet Mart.

We therefore conclude that if on remand the District Court finds that Collins & Aikman's acknowledgments were in fact acceptances and that the arbitration provision was additional to the terms of The Carpet Mart's oral orders, contracts will be recognized under Subsection 2-207(1). The arbitration clause will then be viewed as a "proposal" under Subsection 2-207(2) which will be deemed to have been accepted by The Carpet Mart unless it materially altered the oral offers.

If the District Court finds that Collins & Aikman's acknowledgment forms were not acceptances but rather were confirmations of prior oral agreements between the parties, an application of Section 2-207 similar to that above will be required. Subsection 2-207(1) will require an initial determination of whether the arbitration provision in the confirmations was "additional to or different from" the terms orally agreed upon. Assuming that the District Court finds that the arbitration provision was not a term of the oral agreements between the parties, the arbitration clause will be treated as a "proposal" for addition to the contract under Subsection 2-207(2), as was the case when Collins & Aikman's acknowledgments were viewed as acceptances above. The provision for arbitration will be deemed to have been accepted by The Carpet Mart unless the District Court finds that it materially altered the prior oral agreements, in which case The Carpet Mart could not become bound thereby absent an express agreement to that effect.

As a result of the above application of Section 2-207 to the limited facts before us in the present case, we find it necessary to remand the case to the District Court for the following findings: (1) whether oral agreements were reached between the parties prior to the sending of Collins & Aikman's acknowledgment forms; if there were no such oral agreements, (2) whether the arbitration provision appearing in Collins & Aikman's "acceptances" was additional to the terms of The Carpet Mart's oral offers; and, if so, (3) whether the arbitration provision materially altered the terms of The Carpet Mart's oral offers. Alternatively, if the District Court does find that oral agreements were reached between the parties before Collins & Aikman's acknowledgment forms were sent in each instance, it will be necessary for the District Court to make the following findings: (1) whether the prior oral agreements embodied the arbitration provision appearing in Collins & Aikman's "confirmations"; and, if not, (2) whether the arbitration provision materially altered the prior oral agreements. Regardless of whether the District Court finds Collins & Aikman's acknowledgment forms to have been acceptances or confirmations, if the arbitration provision was additional to, and a material alteration of, the offers or prior oral agreements, The Carpet Mart will not be bound to that provision absent a finding that it expressly agreed to be bound thereby.

* * * *

NOTES

1. Why is it that most mercantile cases involve arbitration provisions sought by sellers, not buyers?

2. Does *Dorton* really involve a "battle of the forms?" The case is unusual in involving only one form, which the court says is in response to either an oral offer, or in confirmation of an oral agreement. It does not matter which, because 2-207(1) treats form acceptances, and post-contractual form confirmations or acknowledgments, the same. Both have the potential to add to the contract, but subject to the significant limitations of 2-207(2).

3. What if one form provides for all disputes to be litigated "in the federal or state courts of New York County," but the other provides for AAA arbitration in Cleveland, Ohio? What result under the so-called "knockout doctrine"? *See generally* Northrop Corp. v. Litronic Inds., 29 F.3d 1173 (7th Cir. 1994). Is there a UCC Article 2 "gap filler" to provide for location of arbitration where the parties have conflicting provisions in that regard? Do Article 2 "gap fillers" say anything at all about arbitration?

4. Which law governs whether there is an agreement to arbitrate in *Dorton*? Is *Cone* reconcilable?

5. Still on the books in New York is *Marlene Industries Corp. v. Carnac Textiles, Inc.*, 45 N.Y.2d 327 (1978), holding that the proposed addition of an arbitration clause is *per se* material. *Marlene* has been read by some courts as creating only a rebuttable presumption of materiality. *See* Avedon Eng'g, Inc. v. Seatex, 126 F.3d 1279, 1285 n.15 (10th Cir. 1997).

6. If the proponent of the "first shot" communication uses an arbitration clause, and the counterparty's "last shot" is silent on that subject, the contract resulting, under UCC section 2-207(1), will contain the clause, irrespective of materiality.. Fair? Why should the party receiving the first form be expected to study it, but not the party receiving the so-called 'last shot." Section 2-207 has been criticized for creating a "first shot" presumption which is just as arbitrary as the "last shot" common law rule it replaced. *See* Nicholas Weiskopf, *Standard Forms and Standard Terms: Revising Article 2 of the UCC*, 29 UCC L.J. 257 (1997).

Colorado-Arkansas-Texas Distributing, L.L.C. v. American Eagle Food Products, Inc.

United States District Court, S.D.N.Y, 2007.
2007 WL 4233010.

- KAPLAN, DISTRICT JUDGE.

* * * *

Section 2-207 of the New York Uniform Commercial Code governs disputes involving the additional terms in written confirmations. It provides that, as between merchants, additional terms included in a written confirmation become part of the contract unless (1) the offer expressly limits the acceptance to the terms of the offer, (2) they materially alter it, or (3) notification of objection to them is given within a reasonable time. In this case, the parties are merchants who reached oral agreements that were confirmed by AEF's sales orders dated February 10 and 23. Thus, additional terms contained in the sales orders were incorporated unless they materially altered the oral agreements.

Whether the inclusion of an arbitration clause materially alters the oral agreement must be determined on a case-by-case basis with "the burden of proving the materiality . . . on the party that opposes inclusion." "A material alteration is one that would 'result in surprise or hardship if incorporated without express awareness by the other party.' " To show a material alteration, the non-assenting party "must establish that, under the circumstances, it cannot be presumed that a reasonable merchant would have consented to the additional term." Evidence of industry custom and the parties' course of dealings often are relevant to determining whether an additional term is material.

In this case, there is no evidence that incorporation of the arbitration clauses without CAT's express assent would result in surprise or hardship. CAT does not deny that it was familiar with the arbitration language contained in AEF's standard sales order or that it received the sales orders at issue here. Nor does it claim to have objected to the arbitration clauses in these or prior transactions. CAT's actions, prior to the filing of this suit, were consistent with an expectation that it had agreed to arbitration. And arbitration clauses are common, if not customary, in the nut industry. I, therefore, find that the parties agreed to arbitrate any disputes arising out of the February 10 and 23 sales orders. This conclusion is consistent with those reached by other courts faced with merchants who received, without objection, unsigned confirmation forms containing arbitration agreements that were consistent with prior courses of dealing.

NOTES

1. Can a mercantile agreement to arbitrate be established solely by a repeated course of dealings? Industry custom? Or are custom and course of dealings relevant only to "materiality" of a proposed additional term in a written form? What of the requirement of a writing?

2. The general learning under UCC Section 2-207 is that the acting out of a transaction, unlike at common law, is not impliedly assenting to a counterparty's terms. Why, then, should repeated use of a clause in form documents, as referenced in the last case, be relevant to the issue of "materiality"?

Itoh & Co. v. Jordan International Co.

United States Court of Appeals, Seventh Circuit, 1977.
552 F.2d 1228.

- SPRECHER, CIRCUIT JUDGE.

* * * *

The pertinent facts may be briefly restated. Itoh sent its purchase order for steel coils to Jordan which contained no provision for arbitration. Subsequently, Jordan sent Itoh its acknowledgment form which included, inter alia, a broad arbitration term on the reverse side of the form. On the front of Jordan's form, the following statement also appears:

> Seller's acceptance is . . . expressly conditioned on Buyer's assent to the additional or different terms and conditions set forth below and printed on the reverse side. If these terms and

> conditions are not acceptable, Buyer should notify Seller at once.

After the exchange of documents, Jordan delivered and Itoh paid for the steel coils. Itoh never expressly assented or objected to the additional arbitration term in Jordan's form.

* * * *

What are the terms of a contract created by conduct under Section 2-207(3) rather than by an exchange of forms under Section 2-207(1)? As noted above, at common law the terms of the contract between Jordan and Itoh would be the terms of the Jordan counter-offer. However, the Code has effectuated a radical departure from the common law rule. The second sentence of Section 2-207(3) provides that where, as here, a contract has been consummated by the conduct of the parties, "the terms of the particular contract consist of those terms on which the writings of the parties agree, together with any supplementary terms incorporated under any other provisions of this Act." Since it is clear that the Jordan and Itoh forms do not "agree" on arbitration, the only question which remains under the Code is whether arbitration may be considered a supplementary term incorporated under some other provision of the Code.

* * * *

Accordingly, we find that the "supplementary terms" contemplated by Section 2-207(3) are limited to those supplied by the standardized "gap-filler" provisions of Article Two. Since provision for arbitration is not a necessary or missing term which would be supplied by one of the Code's "gap-filler" provisions unless agreed upon by the contracting parties, there is no arbitration term in the Section 2-207(3) contract which was created by the conduct of Jordan and Itoh in proceeding to perform even though no contract had been established by their exchange of writings.

We are convinced that this conclusion does not result in any unfair prejudice to a seller who elects to insert in his standard sales acknowledgement form the statement that acceptance is expressly conditional on buyer's assent to additional terms contained therein. Such a seller obtains a substantial benefit under Section 2-207(1) through the inclusion of an "expressly conditional" clause. If he decides after the exchange of forms that the particular transaction is not in his best interest, Subsection (1) permits him to walk away from the transaction without incurring any liability so long as the buyer has not in the interim expressly assented to the additional terms. Moreover, whether or not a seller will be disadvantaged under Subsection (3) as a consequence of inserting an "expressly conditional" clause in his standard form is within his control. If the seller in fact does not intend to close a particular deal unless the additional terms are assented to, he can protect himself by not delivering the goods until such assent is forthcoming. If the seller does intend to close a deal irrespective of whether or not the buyer assents to the additional terms, he can hardly complain when the contract formed under Subsection (3) as a result of the parties' conduct is held not to include those terms. Although a seller who employs such an "expressly conditional" clause in his acknowledgement form would undoubtedly appreciate the dual advantage of not being bound to a contract under Subsection (1) if he elects not to perform and of having his additional terms imposed on the buyer under Subsection (3) in the event that performance is in his best interest, we do not believe such a result is contemplated by Section 2-207. Rather, while a seller may take advantage of an "expressly conditional" clause under Subsection (1) when he elects not to perform, he must accept the potential risk under Subsection (3) of not getting his additional terms when he elects to proceed with performance without first obtaining buyer's assent to those terms. Since the seller injected ambiguity into the transaction by inserting the "expressly conditional" clause in his form, he, and not the buyer, should bear the consequence of that ambiguity under Subsection (3).

NOTES

1. Remember that the use of an "expressly conditional acceptance" does not serve as an acceptance at all. That is why no contract forms based on the use of such an instrument in response to a form offer. There is no contract until the parties act out the transaction contemplated. At that point, there is a contract by "conduct" and one turns to 2-207(3), which covers situations where there is no contract created by an exchange of forms. The last case involves precisely that situation.

Under subsection (3), one takes those written terms that both parties have put forth, and "gap fills" the rest by resort to Article 2 "gap fillers" such as implied warranties, price, time of delivery, time of payment, and so forth. There is no Article 2 "gap filler" providing for arbitration. Hence, both the form offer and the 'expressly conditional acceptance" would have to provide for it.

2. There is no battle of the forms in the next case—it is a consumer transaction.

Hill v. Gateway 2000, Inc.

United States Court of Appeals, Seventh Circuit, 1997.
105 F.3d 1147.

▪ EASTERBROOK, CIRCUIT JUDGE.

A customer picks up the phone, orders a computer, and gives a credit card number. Presently a box arrives, containing the computer and a list of terms, said to govern unless the customer returns the computer within 30 days. Are these terms effective as the parties' contract, or is the contract term-free because the order-taker did not read any terms over the phone and elicit the customer's assent?

One of the terms in the box containing a Gateway 2000 system was an arbitration clause. Rich and Enza Hill, the customers, kept the computer more than 30 days before complaining about its components and performance. They filed suit in federal court arguing, among other things, that the product's shortcomings make Gateway a racketeer (mail and wire fraud are said to be the predicate offenses), leading to treble damages under RICO for the Hills and a class of all other purchasers. Gateway asked the district court to enforce the arbitration clause; the judge refused, writing that "[t]he present record is insufficient to support a finding of a valid arbitration agreement between the parties or that the plaintiffs were given adequate notice of the arbitration clause." Gateway took an immediate appeal, as is its right. 9 U.S.C. § 16(a)(1)(A).

The Hills say that the arbitration clause did not stand out: they concede noticing the statement of terms but deny reading it closely enough to discover the agreement to arbitrate, and they ask us to conclude that they therefore may go to court. Yet an agreement to arbitrate must be enforced "save upon such grounds as exist at law or in equity for the revocation of any contract." 9 U.S.C. § 2. *Doctor's Associates, Inc. v. Casarotto*, 517 U.S. 681 (1996), holds that this provision of the Federal Arbitration Act is inconsistent with any requirement that an arbitration clause be prominent. A contract need not be read to be effective; people who accept take the risk that the unread terms may in retrospect prove unwelcome. Carr v. CIGNA Securities, Inc., 95 F.3d 544, 547 (7th Cir. 1996); Chicago Pacific Corp. v. Canada Life Assurance Co., 850 F.2d 334 (7th Cir. 1988). Terms inside Gateway's box stand or fall together. If they constitute the parties' contract because the Hills had an opportunity to return the computer after reading them, then all must be enforced.

ProCD, Inc. v. Zeidenberg, 86 F.3d 1447 (7th Cir. 1996), holds that terms inside a box of software bind consumers who use the software after an opportunity to read the terms and to reject them by returning the product. Likewise, *Carnival Cruise Lines, Inc. v. Shute*, 499 U.S. 585 (1991), enforces a forum-selection clause that was included among three pages of terms attached to a cruise ship ticket. *ProCD* and *Carnival Cruise Lines* exemplify the many commercial transactions in which people pay for products with terms to follow; *ProCD* discusses others. 86 F.3d at 1451–52. The district court concluded in *ProCD* that the contract is formed when the consumer pays for the software; as a result, the court held, only terms known to the consumer at that moment are part of the contract, and provisos inside the box do not count. Although this is one way a contract could be formed, it is not the only way: "A vendor, as master of the offer, may invite acceptance by conduct, and may propose limitations on the kind of conduct that constitutes acceptance. A buyer may accept by performing the acts the vendor proposes to treat as acceptance." Gateway shipped computers with the same sort of accept-or-return offer ProCD made to users of its software. *ProCD* relied on the Uniform Commercial Code rather than any peculiarities of Wisconsin law; both Illinois and South Dakota, the two states whose law might govern relations between Gateway and the Hills, have adopted the UCC; neither side has pointed us to any atypical doctrines in those states that might be pertinent; *ProCD* therefore applies to this dispute.

Plaintiffs ask us to limit *ProCD* to software, but where's the sense in that? *ProCD* is about the law of contract, not the law of software. Payment preceding the revelation of full terms is common for air transportation, insurance, and many other endeavors. Practical considerations support allowing vendors to enclose the full legal terms with their products. Cashiers cannot be expected to read legal documents to customers before ringing up sales. If the staff at the other end of the phone for direct-sales operations such as Gateway's had to read the four-page statement of terms before taking the buyer's credit card number, the droning voice would anesthetize rather than enlighten many potential buyers. Others would hang up in a rage over the waste of their time. And oral recitation would not avoid customers' assertions (whether true or feigned) that the clerk did not read term X to them, or that they did not remember or understand it. Writing provides benefits for both sides of commercial transactions. Customers as a group are better off when vendors skip costly and ineffectual steps such as telephonic recitation, and use instead a simple approve-or-return device. Competent adults are bound by such documents, read or unread. For what little it is worth, we add that the box from Gateway was crammed with software. The computer came with an operating system, without which it was useful only as a boat anchor. See Digital Equipment Corp. v. Uniq Digital Technologies, Inc., 73 F.3d 756, 761 (7th Cir. 1996). Gateway also included many application programs. So the Hills' effort to limit *ProCD* to software would not avail them factually, even if it were sound legally-which it is not.

For their second sally, the Hills contend that ProCD should be limited to executory contracts (to licenses in particular), and therefore does not apply because both parties' performance of this contract was complete when the box arrived at their home. This is legally and factually wrong: legally because the question at hand concerns the *formation* of the contract rather than its *performance*, and factually because both contracts were incompletely performed. *ProCD* did not depend on the fact that the seller characterized the transaction as a license rather than as a contract; we treated it as a contract for the sale of goods and reserved the question whether for other purposes a "license" characterization might be preferable. 86 F.3d at 1450. All debates about characterization to one side, the transaction in *ProCD* was no more executory than the one here: Zeidenberg paid for the software and walked out of the store with a box under his arm, so if arrival of the box with the product ends the time for revelation of contractual terms, then the time ended in *ProCD* before Zeidenberg opened the box. But of course ProCD had not completed performance with delivery of the box, and neither had Gateway. One element of the transaction was the warranty, which obliges sellers to fix defects in their products. The Hills have invoked Gateway's warranty and are not satisfied with its response, so they are not well positioned to say that Gateway's obligations were fulfilled when the motor carrier unloaded the box. What is more, both ProCD and Gateway promised to help customers to use their products. Long-term service and information obligations are common in the computer business, on both hardware and software sides. Gateway offers "lifetime service" and has a round-the-clock telephone hotline to fulfil this promise. Some vendors spend more money helping customers use their products than on developing and manufacturing them. The document in Gateway's box includes promises of future performance that some consumers value highly; these promises bind Gateway just as the arbitration clause binds the Hills.

Next the Hills insist that *ProCD* is irrelevant because Zeidenberg was a "merchant" and they are not. Section 2-207(2) of the UCC, the infamous battle-of-the-forms section, states that "additional terms [following acceptance of an offer] are to be construed as proposals for addition to a contract. Between merchants such terms become part of the contract unless . . ." Plaintiffs tell us that *ProCD* came out as it did only because Zeidenberg was a "merchant" and the terms inside ProCD's box were not excluded by the "unless" clause. This argument pays scant attention to the opinion in *ProCD,* which concluded that, when there is only one form, "sec. 2-207 is irrelevant." 86 F.3d at 1452. The question in *ProCD* was not whether terms were added to a contract after its formation, but how and when the contract was formed-in particular, whether a vendor may propose that a contract of sale be formed, not in the store (or over the phone) with the payment of money or a general "send me the product," but after the customer has had a chance to inspect both the item and the terms. *ProCD* answers "yes," for merchants and consumers alike. Yet again, for what little it is worth we observe that the Hills misunderstand the setting of *ProCD.* A "merchant" under the UCC "means a person who deals in goods of the kind or otherwise by his occupation holds himself out as having knowledge or skill peculiar to the practices or goods involved in the transaction," § 2-104(1). Zeidenberg bought the product at a retail store, an uncommon place for merchants to acquire inventory. His corporation put ProCD's database on the Internet for anyone to browse, which led to the litigation but did not make Zeidenberg a software merchant.

Perhaps the Hills would have had a better argument if they were first alerted to the bundling of hardware and legal-ware after opening the box and wanted to return the computer in order to avoid disagreeable terms, but were dissuaded by the expense of shipping. What the remedy would be in such a case-could it exceed the shipping charges?—is an interesting question, but one that need not detain us because the Hills knew before they ordered the computer that the carton would include *some* important terms, and they did not seek to discover these in advance. Gateway's ads state that their products come with limited warranties and lifetime support. How limited was the warranty-30 days, with service contingent on shipping the computer back, or five years, with free onsite service? What sort of support was offered? Shoppers have three principal ways to discover these things. First, they can ask the vendor to send a copy before deciding whether to buy. The Magnuson-Moss Warranty Act requires firms to distribute their warranty terms on request, 15 U.S.C. § 2302(b)(1)(A); the Hills do not contend that Gateway would have refused to enclose the remaining terms too. Concealment would be bad for business, scaring some customers away and leading to excess returns from others. Second, shoppers can consult public sources (computer magazines, the Web sites of vendors) that may contain this information. Third, they may inspect the documents after the product's delivery. Like Zeidenberg, the Hills took the third option. By keeping the computer beyond 30 days, the Hills accepted Gateway's offer, including the arbitration clause.

The Hills' remaining arguments, including a contention that the arbitration clause is unenforceable as part of a scheme to defraud, do not require more than a citation to *Prima Paint Corp. v. Flood & Conklin Mfg. Co.*, 388 U.S. 395 (1967). Whatever may be said pro and con about the cost and efficacy of arbitration (which the Hills disparage) is for Congress and the contracting parties to consider. Claims based on RICO are no less arbitrable than those founded on the contract or the law of torts. *Shearson/American Express, Inc. v. McMahon*, 482 U.S. 220, 238–42 (1987). The decision of the district court is vacated, and this case is remanded with instructions to compel the Hills to submit their dispute to arbitration.

§ 4.02 BINDING THIRD PARTIES

We have seen that arbitral statutes require written arbitral agreements, not ones *signed by* the parties or either of them. Still, that is a very different question than that of permitting or requiring third parties to arbitrate even though they are not party to the contract setting forth the undertaking to arbitrate. Such third parties will have some sort of relationship with at least one of the parties to the arbitral agreement.

Contract law governs here. Despite a pro-arbitrability bent, courts will not require a party to arbitrate who has not agreed in fact or by operation of law to do so. The fact that it would be efficient to bring an involved third party into an arbitration, in an impleader situation for example, is by no means enough to do so. Nonetheless, arbitral entitlements are relatively routinely extended to third-party beneficiaries and to those with "derivative" entitlements. Also, under principles of "piercing the corporate veil," a party may find itself obligated to honor the arbitral undertaking of a dominated closely held company or that of a highly controlled subsidiary. As a general proposition, it appears easier for a related third party to enforce an agreement to arbitrate than it is to enforce such an agreement against a related third party which does not wish to arbitrate. Can you see why?

Confusingly, cases sometimes reference third parties who may become bound to arbitrate as "non-signatories." It would be better to reference them as "non-parties" to the contract containing the agreement to arbitrate. The lack of signature, we have seen, is not really the issue.

TNS Holdings, Inc. v. MKI Securities Corp.

New York Court of Appeals, 1998.
92 N.Y.2d 335.

- CIPARICK, J.

At issue on this appeal is whether a corporation that is related to, but not itself, a party to an agreement containing an arbitration clause can be compelled to arbitrate a dispute arising from an alleged breach of that agreement. We conclude that, absent a showing of abuse of the corporate form, the nonsignatory corporation cannot be compelled to arbitrate.

* * * *

Although arbitration is favored as a matter of public policy, equally important is the policy that seeks to avoid the unintentional waiver of the benefits and safeguards which a court of law may provide in resolving disputes. Indeed, unless the parties have subscribed to an arbitration agreement it would be "unfair to infer such a significant waiver on the basis of anything less than a clear indication of intent" (Matter of Marlene Indus. Corp. [Carnac Textiles], 45 NY2d 327, 333–34). While CPLR 7501 requires that an agreement to arbitrate be in writing, this Court has recognized in certain limited circumstances the need to impute the intent to arbitrate to a nonsignatory.

Other courts have created an "alter ego" exception, compelling the "alter egos" of a signatory to arbitrate (see, e.g., Pile Found. Constr. Co. [Howell Co.], 159 A.D.2d 352; Glasser v Price, 35 A.D.2d 98). Akin to piercing the corporate veil to "prevent fraud or to achieve equity" (International Aircraft Trading Co. v Manufacturers Trust Co., 297 NY 285, 292), this exception applies as well in determining whether a nonsignatory to an arbitration agreement should be bound by it (see, Matter of Sbarro Holding [Shiaw Tien Yuan], 91 AD2d 613). Those seeking to pierce a corporate veil of course bear a heavy burden of showing that the corporation was dominated as to the transaction attacked and that such domination was the instrument of fraud or otherwise resulted in wrongful or inequitable consequences (Matter of Morris v New York State Dept. of Taxation & Fin., 82 NY2d 135; see, Walkovszky v Carlton, 18 NY2d 414). Evidence of domination alone does not suffice without an additional showing that it led to inequity, fraud or malfeasance (*Matter of Morris v New York State Dept. of Taxation & Fin.*, supra, at 141–42).

Applying the "alter ego" test here, plaintiffs have failed to show that, even if MKI dominated Batchnotice, that control resulted in some fraud or wrong mandating disregard of the corporate form in this case.

Far from seeking to avoid obligations by vesting title to the software in Batchnotice—a step allegedly motivated by the corporation's tax considerations—MAI agreed to assume Batchnotice's financial obligations if Batchnotice failed to fulfill them. An inference of abuse does not arise from this record where a corporation was formed for legal purposes or is engaged in legitimate business. There is no showing that through its domination MKI misused the corporate form for its personal ends so as to commit a fraud or wrongdoing or avoid any of its obligations.

Thomson-CSF v. American Arbitration Ass'n

United States Court of Appeals, Second Circuit, 1995.
64 F.3d 773.

- ALTIMARI, CIRCUIT JUDGE.

Plaintiff-appellant Thomson-CSF, S.A. ("Thomson") appeals from a judgment entered in the United States District Court for the Southern District of New York (Keenan, J.), denying its request for declaratory and injunctive relief and granting defendant-appellee Evans & Sutherland Computer Corporation's ("E & S") cross-motion to compel arbitration. Thomson asserts that the district court improvidently compelled it to arbitrate against E & S based upon an arbitration agreement between E & S and Thomson's subsidiary, to which Thomson was not a signatory. Because, under ordinary principles of contract and agency law, Thomson cannot be said to have voluntarily submitted to arbitrate its disputes with E & S, we reverse the judgment of the district court and remand for proceedings consistent with this opinion.

BACKGROUND

Rediffusion Simulation Limited ("Rediffusion") was a British company engaged in the business of building flight simulators for the training of pilots. In 1986, Rediffusion entered into a "Working Agreement" with E & S, located in Salt Lake City, Utah. Under the Working Agreement, Rediffusion agreed to purchase computer-generated image equipment (the computer "brain" of the flight simulator) exclusively from E & S and to use its best efforts to market those systems containing E & S equipment; in return, E & S agreed to supply its imaging equipment only to Rediffusion.

Subsequent to entering into the Working Agreement, Rediffusion was sold to Hughes Aircraft Company. Hughes amended and extended the Working Agreement between Rediffusion and E & S. On December 31, 1993, Hughes sold Rediffusion to Thomson, which renamed it Thomson Training and Simulation Limited. Prior to purchasing Rediffusion, Thompson maintained a division engaged in the business of building flight simulation equipment (the Training and Simulation Systems Division) into which it began integrating Rediffusion.

At the time Thomson began publicly contemplating the acquisition of Rediffusion, E & S informed Thomson that, if it purchased Rediffusion, E & S intended to bind Thomson and its flight simulation division to the Working Agreement. Specifically, E & S told Thomson that upon purchasing Rediffusion both Rediffusion and Thomson's Training and Simulation Systems Division would be required to purchase all needed computer-generated image equipment from E & S. In response, Thomson wrote to E & S seeking to have it waive those provisions of the Working Agreement that E & S believed to be binding upon Thomson. Thomson did not, however, concede that it would be bound by Rediffusion's Working Agreement. In fact, when it became clear that Thomson and E & S could reach no agreement prior to Thomson's acquisition of Rediffusion, Thomson explicitly informed E & S that it was not adopting the Working Agreement and did not consider itself bound by Rediffusion's Agreement which it had neither negotiated nor signed.

The Working Agreement

Section 6.1 of the Working Agreement provides for the arbitration of all disputes between the "parties" to the Agreement. While the Agreement provides no explicit definition of "parties," it does define "E & S" and "Rediffusion:"

> 1.14 the term "E & S," wherever used in this Working Agreement, shall include the affiliates of E & S.
>
> The term "Rediffusion" wherever used in this Working Agreement, shall . . . mean Rediffusion and each of its affiliates.

* * * *

> 1.6 An "affiliate" of a party hereto shall mean any person, firm or corporation that, directly or indirectly, through one or more intermediaries, controls, or is controlled by, or is under common control with, such party.

Despite the lack of definition for "parties" in the Working Agreement, the district court found that the term "parties" was intended to mean "E & S and Rediffusion" and, therefore, was also intended to include the affiliates of the parties. Accordingly, the arbitration clause in the Working Agreement purported to bind not only Rediffusion, but also its affiliates--namely, Thomson (given that Thomson indisputably controlled Rediffusion).

Injunctive Relief

While under Thomson's ownership, Rediffusion's share of the flight simulator market drastically decreased. On August 8, 1994, E & S filed a demand for arbitration under the Working Agreement against both Rediffusion and its parent-company Thomson, asserting a breach of their obligations arising out of the Working Agreement. Despite Thomson's insistence that it was not bound by the Working Agreement (and the arbitration clause contained therein), E & S filed a demand for arbitration against both Rediffusion and Thomson on August 8, 1994. While Rediffusion did not contest the applicability of the arbitration clause to it, Thomson refused to answer E & S's demand for arbitration. On August 29, 1994, Thomson commenced this action in the Southern District of New York, seeking 1) a declaration that it was not bound by the arbitration clause of the Working Agreement and 2) an injunction prohibiting further proceedings against it under the Working Agreement. E & S cross-moved to compel Thomson to arbitrate.

The district court granted E & S's cross-motion to compel arbitration. In doing so, the district court stated that while E & S's claims did not fall under any of the traditional categories for binding a nonsignatory to an arbitration clause, Thomson was bound nonetheless. Adopting a hybrid approach to binding a nonsignatory to an arbitration agreement, the district court accepted E & S's assertion that "the Court may bind Thomson based on its conduct in voluntarily becoming . . . an affiliate, on the degree of control Thomson exercises over [Rediffusion], and on the interrelatedness of the issues."

Thomson now appeals the judgment of the district court.

DISCUSSION

Arbitration is contractual by nature--"a party cannot be required to submit to arbitration any dispute which he has not agreed so to submit." United Steelworkers of America v. Warrior & Gulf Navigation Co., 363 U.S. 574, 582 (1960). Thus, while there is a strong and "liberal federal policy favoring arbitration agreements," Mitsubishi Motors Corp. v. Soler Chrysler-Plymouth, Inc., 473 U.S. 614, 625 (1985) (quotations omitted), such agreements must not be so broadly construed as to encompass claims and parties that were not intended by the original contract. "It does not follow, however, that under the [Federal Arbitration] Act an obligation to arbitrate attaches only to one who has personally signed the written arbitration provision." Fisser v. International Bank, 282 F.2d 231, 233 (2d Cir. 1960); see also Deloitte Noraudit A/S v. Deloitte Haskins & Sells, U.S., 9 F.3d 1060, 1064 (2d Cir. 1993). This Court has made clear that a nonsignatory party may be bound to an arbitration agreement if so dictated by the "ordinary principles of contract and agency." McAllister Bros., Inc. v. A & S Transp. Co., 621 F.2d 519, 524 (2d Cir. 1980); see also A/S Custodia v. Lessin Int'l, Inc., 503 F.2d 318, 320 (2d Cir. 1974).

A. *Traditional Bases for Binding Nonsignatories.*

This Court has recognized a number of theories under which nonsignatories may be bound to the arbitration agreements of others. Those theories arise out of common law principles of contract and agency law. Accordingly, we have recognized five theories for binding nonsignatories to arbitration agreements: 1) incorporation by reference; 2) assumption; 3) agency; 4) veil-piercing/alter ego; and 5) estoppel. The district court properly rejected each of these traditional theories as sufficient justification for binding Thomson to the arbitration agreement of its subsidiary.

1. Incorporation by Reference.

A nonsignatory may compel arbitration against a party to an arbitration agreement when that party has entered into a separate contractual relationship with the nonsignatory which incorporates the existing arbitration clause. See Import Export Steel Corp. v. Mississippi Valley Barge Line Co., 351 F.2d 503, 505–06 (2d Cir. 1965) (separate agreement with nonsignatory expressly "assum[ing] all the obligations and privileges of [signatory party] under the . . . subcharter" constitutes grounds for enforcement of arbitration clause by nonsignatory); Matter of Arbitration Between Keystone Shipping Co. and Texport Oil Co., 782 F. Supp. 28, 31 (S.D.N.Y. 1992). As the district court noted, E & S has not attempted to show that the Working Agreement was incorporated into any document which Thomson adopted. Thus, Thomson cannot be bound under an incorporation theory.

2. Assumption.

In the absence of a signature, a party may be bound by an arbitration clause if its subsequent conduct indicates that it is assuming the obligation to arbitrate. See Gvozdenovic v. United Air Lines, Inc., 933 F.2d 1100, 1105 (2d Cir.) (flight attendants manifested a clear intention to arbitrate by sending a representative to act on their behalf in arbitration process), cert. denied, 502 U.S. 910 (1991); Keystone Shipping, 782 F. Supp. at 31; In re Transrol Navegacao S.A., 782 F. Supp. 848, 851 (S.D.N.Y. 1991). While Thomson was aware that the Working Agreement purported to bind it as an "affiliate" of Rediffusion, at no time did Thomson manifest an intention to be bound by that Agreement. In fact, Thomson explicitly disavowed any obligations arising out of the Working Agreement and filed this action seeking a declaration of non-liability under the Agreement. Accordingly, it cannot be said that Thomson assumed the obligation to arbitrate.

3. Agency.

Traditional principles of agency law may bind a nonsignatory to an arbitration agreement. See Interbras Cayman Co. v. Orient Victory Shipping Co., S.A., 663 F.2d 4, 6–7 (2d Cir. 1981). Because the Working Agreement was entered into well before Thomson purchased Rediffusion, Thomson could not possibly be bound under an agency theory.

4. Veil Piercing/Alter Ego.

In some instances, the corporate relationship between a parent and its subsidiary are sufficiently close as to justify piercing the corporate veil and holding one corporation legally accountable for the actions of the other. As a general matter, however, a corporate relationship alone is not sufficient to bind a nonsignatory to an arbitration agreement. See *Keystone Shipping*, 782 F.Supp. at 30–31. Nonetheless, the courts will pierce the corporate veil "in two broad situations: to prevent fraud or other wrong, or where a parent dominates and controls a subsidiary." Carte Blanche (Singapore) Pte., Ltd. v. Diners Club Int'l, Inc., 2 F.3d 24, 26 (2d Cir. 1993); see also Wm. Passalacqua Builders, Inc. v. Resnick Developers S., Inc., 933 F.2d 131, 138–39 (2d Cir. 1991) ("Liability . . . may be predicated either upon a showing of fraud or upon complete control by the dominating corporation that leads to a wrong against third parties."). While the district court below noted that, "[c]ounsel for E & S also denied at oral-argument that its claim was properly articulated as veil-piercing," E & S now asserts that an alter ego relationship between Thomson and Rediffusion may exist. While E & S concedes that it can make no showing of fraud, it argues that Thomson sufficiently dominated Rediffusion as to justify veil piercing.

Veil piercing determinations are fact specific and "differ[ ] with the circumstances of each case." *American Protein Corp. v. AB Volvo*, 844 F.2d 56, 60 (2d Cir.). This Court has determined that a parent corporation and its subsidiary lose their distinct corporate identities when their conduct demonstrates a virtual abandonment of separateness. See *Carte Blanche*, 2 F.3d at 29 ("No bank accounts, offices, stationery, transactions, or any other activities were maintained or carried on in the name of [the subsidiary]."); *Wm. Passalacqua*, 933 F.2d at 139 (corporate veil is pierced where, among other things, parent and subsidiary 1) share common office and staff; 2) are run by common officers; 3) intermingle funds; 4) do not deal at arm's length with each other; and 5) are not treated as separate profit centers); see also Walter E. Heller & Co. v. Video Innovations, Inc., 730 F.2d 50, 53 (2d Cir. 1984) (absence of corporate formalities relevant factor in piercing corporate veil). "[T]he factors that determine the question of control and domination are less subjective than 'good faith'; they relate to how the corporation was actually operated." *Carte Blanche*, 2 F.3d at 28–29.

E & S has not demonstrated that Thomson exerted the degree of control over Rediffusion necessary to justify piercing the corporate veil. While the district court found that "Thomson has common ownership with [Rediffusion]; that Thomson actually controls

[Rediffusion]; . . . [and] that Thomson incorporated [Rediffusion] into its own organizational and decision-making structure," the district court did not find an abandonment of the corporate structure. E & S has not shown an absence of corporate formalities, nor has it shown an intermingling of corporate finances and directorship. Rather, as the district court found, Rediffusion continued to function as a distinct entity closely incorporated into the existing corporate structure of its parent company, Thomson. Accordingly, in light of the totality of the circumstances, Thomson cannot be bound by Rediffusion's arbitration agreement under a veil piercing/alter ego theory.

5. Estoppel.

This Court has also bound nonsignatories to arbitration agreements under an estoppel theory. In *Deloitte Noraudit A/S v. Deloitte Haskins & Sells, U.S.*, 9 F.3d 1060, 1064 (2d Cir. 1993), a foreign accounting firm received a settlement agreement concerning the use of the trade name "Deloitte" in association with accounting practices. Under the agreement--containing an arbitration clause--local affiliates of the international accounting association Deloitte Haskins & Sells International were entitled to use the trade name "Deloitte" in exchange for compliance with the dictates of the agreement. A Norwegian accounting firm received the agreement, made no objection to the terms of the agreement, and proceeded to utilize the trade name. This Court held that by knowingly exploiting the agreement, the accounting firm was estopped from avoiding arbitration despite having never signed the agreement. *See* 9 F.3d at 1064 ("Noraudit failed to object to the Agreement when it received it . . . . In addition, Noraudit knowingly accepted the benefits of the Agreement . . . . Thus, Noraudit is estopped from denying its obligation to arbitrate under the 1990 Agreement.").

* * * *

As these cases indicate, the circuits have been willing to estop a *signatory* from avoiding arbitration with a nonsignatory when the issues the nonsignatory is seeking to resolve in arbitration are intertwined with the agreement that the estopped party has signed. As the district court pointed out, however, "[t]he situation here is inverse: E & S, as signatory, seeks to compel Thomson, a non-signatory." While E & S suggests that this is a non-distinction, the nature of arbitration makes it important. Arbitration is strictly a matter of contract; if the parties have not agreed to arbitrate, the courts have no authority to mandate that they do so. *United Steelworkers*, 363 U.S. at 582. In the line of cases discussed above, the courts held that the parties were estopped from avoiding arbitration because they had entered into written arbitration agreements, albeit with the affiliates of those parties asserting the arbitration and not the parties themselves. Thomson, however, cannot be estopped from denying the existence of an arbitration clause to which it is a signatory because no such clause exists. At no point did Thomson indicate a willingness to arbitrate with E & S. Therefore, the district court properly determined these estoppel cases to be inapposite and insufficient justification for binding Thomson to an agreement that it never signed.

* * * *

B. *The District Court's Hybrid Approach.*

Despite properly determining that E & S's claims did not fall within any of the traditional theories for binding a nonsignatory, the district court stated, "[n]evertheless, E & S asserts that the Court may bind Thomson based on its conduct in 'voluntarily bec[oming] . . . an affiliate,' on the degree of control Thomson exercises over [Rediffusion], and on the interrelatedness of the issues. This Court agrees." (citations omitted). In so doing, the district court improperly extended the law of this Circuit and diluted the protections afforded nonsignatories by the "ordinary principles of contract and agency." *McAllister*, 621 F.2d at 524. A nonsignatory may not be bound to arbitrate except as dictated by some accepted theory under agency or contract law.

* * * *

The district court below improperly extended the limited theories upon which this Court is willing to enforce an arbitration agreement against a nonsignatory. The district court's hybrid approach dilutes the safeguards afforded to a nonsignatory by the "ordinary principles of contract and agency" and fails to adequately protect parent companies, the subsidiaries of which have entered into arbitration agreements. Anything short of requiring a *full* showing of some accepted theory under agency or contract law imperils a vast number of parent corporations. This Court did not intend such an outcome in *Deloitte* or *McAllister* and does not adopt such an approach here.

CONCLUSION

Accordingly, the judgment of the district court is reversed and remanded for proceedings consistent with the foregoing.

NOTE

1. Had Rediffusion been merged into Thomson through a stock sale, Thomson would, by operation of law, become a successor in interest to Rediffusion's outstanding contractual obligations, including that of having to arbitrate under the contract at issue. Successor liability is also sometimes found absent a stock acquisition by the surviving entity when, in connection with acquisition of its assets, the acquired entity, as a practical matter, loses all independence as an operating entity—this is covered by the "de facto merger" doctrine. In the last case, there was no actual or de facto merger, presumably because Rediffusion, despite its integration into Thompson's structure, continued a *bona fide* separate operating existence.

Shaffer v. Stratton Oakmont, Inc.

United States District Court, N.D. Ill., 1991.
765 F. Supp. 365.

- NORGLE, DISTRICT JUDGE.

Before the court is the motion of defendants Stratton Oakmont, Inc. and Robert Koch for a stay pending arbitration and for a protective order staying discovery. For the reasons discussed below, this motion is denied.

FACTS

In February of 1990, plaintiff John E. Shaffer ("Shaffer") opened an account with Stratton Oakmont, Inc. ("Stratton"), a securities broker and dealer, through Robert Koch ("Koch"), an employee of Shaffer. Unlike those securities brokers known in the industry as "self-clearing" brokers, Stratton is an "introducing" broker (also known as a "corresponding" broker), and does not perform its own "clearing" services. Stratton must contract with a "clearing broker" in order to consummate the securities transactions which it recommends to its customers. Pursuant to opening his account with Stratton, Shaffer signed a brokerage account agreement (the "Brokerage Agreement") provided by Ameritrade, Inc., Stratton's clearing broker.

The Brokerage Agreement consists of several pages of pre-printed forms. The top of the first page of the Brokerage Agreement contains Ameritrade's name in large letters and bold print and provides a space for identification of the introducing broker. This space, however, is left blank on the form. On the bottom of the page, immediately above the signature line on which Shaffer's signature appears, is printed: "This brokerage account agreement contains a pre-dispute arbitration clause in form AM-9-89, section 1, paragraph 7." The arbitration clause referred to in this notice appears subsequently in the agreement, and reads, in relevant part:

> Any controversy between *Ameritrade, Inc. and me* arising out of or relating to this Agreement or the breach thereof may be settled by arbitration . . . . If I do not make such election by registered mail addressed to Ameritrade, Inc. at its main office within five days after the mailing by Ameritrade, Inc. of a notice requesting such election, I authorize Ameritrade, Inc. to make such election in behalf of myself. [Emphasis added.]

Neither defendant's name appears anywhere in the agreement.

* * * *

Plaintiff contends that on June 27, 1990, without his express consent, defendants purchased 30,000 shares of Ventura Motion Picture Group Stock on his account, at $8 per share. Defendants contend that plaintiff had agreed to purchase the stock but failed to make a timely margin deposit payment in order to secure the acquisition. Defendants then sold the stock at $7 per share, resulting in a loss of $30,000 on the deal. In order to cover the loss, defendants liquidated the remaining stocks in plaintiff's account and returned to plaintiff the remaining balance.

On October 10, 1990, plaintiff filed this action, alleging claims for federal securities fraud, as well as pendant state claims for breach of fiduciary duty and violations of the Illinois Consumer Fraud and Deceptive Practices Act. On December 13, 1990, defendants filed this motion for a stay pending arbitration and for a protective order staying discovery.

DISCUSSION

The parties agree that the sole question at issue here is whether defendants Stratton and Koch have standing to compel plaintiff to arbitrate his grievances with them pursuant to the arbitration provision in the Ameritrade Brokerage Agreement. In the memorandum in support of its motion for stay, defendants acknowledge that there is some division of authority on this question. They argue that the better rule resolves all doubts in favor of arbitration. Defendants further argue that they should be permitted to invoke the arbitration provision under either an agency theory or a third party beneficiary theory. Plaintiff, on the other hand, argues that the defendants are not parties to the Brokerage Agreement and have no standing to benefit from its arbitration provision. He cites to a number of cases in which courts have refused to apply the third party beneficiary doctrine or the principles of agency to permit an introducing broker to benefit from an arbitration agreement signed only by the clearing broker and the investor. As a policy issue, plaintiff also argues that it would be unfair for the court to compel him to arbitrate his dispute with defendants when he never consented to relinquish his right to be heard in federal court.

* * * *

Although all relevant authorities will not compel arbitration absent evidence of the parties' agreement to arbitrate, they appear somewhat divided on whether to imply such an agreement in the absence of an express contract or understanding. Most courts addressing this issue have held that a securities investor will not be deemed to have agreed to arbitration (and thus, to have waived its right to federal jurisdiction) absent evidence of its actual intent to be so bound. Other courts, however, appear to hold that consent may be implied in law, either because the introducing broker is deemed to be the disclosed agent of the clearing broker, *see Okcuoglu*, or because the introducing broker is viewed as a third party beneficiary to the written agreement between the investor and the clearing broker. See Cauble v. Mabon, Nugent & Co., 594 F. Supp. 985 (S.D.N.Y. 1984).

Although these cases initially appear to be irreconcilable, they may also be viewed as merely factually distinguishable. Each of the four cases cited in support of defendants' position, *Okcuoglu*, *Cauble*, *Scher*, and Nesslage v. York Securities, Inc., 823 F.2d 231, 233 (8th Cir. 1987), either are factually distinguishable from the cases which support plaintiff's position, or are inapplicable to the narrow issue presented here.

For example, in *Nesslage*, which held that the introductory broker could enforce the arbitration clause contained in the clearing broker's account agreement with the plaintiff, the Eight Circuit arguably relied on a factual finding by the trial court that all parties concerned intended the margin agreement between the plaintiff and the clearing broker to apply to the introducing broker as well. The court stated that:

> the district court found that the Nesslages [investors], York Securities [introducing brokerage firm] and Samson [employee of York Securities] *intended* that the margin agreement, including the arbitration provision, would govern their brokerage relationship, even though York Securities and Samson were not parties to the margin agreement, and that York Securities and Samson could enforce the margin agreement. [Emphasis added.]

Nesslage, 823 F.2d at 233.

Similarly, in *Okcuoglu*, the district court held that the conduct of the parties expressed their intention for a nonsignatory to the securities agreement to benefit from the arbitration clause contained therein. "Although it [the agreement] was not signed by Pershing's representatives, unquestionably, by their conduct all parties adopted the terms thereof governing the relationships. For over five (5) years, each operated under it in complete mutual reliance . . . ." *Okcuoglu*, 580 F. Supp. at 751.

In the *Scher* opinion, the district court held that a nonsignatory to a customer account agreement was entitled to benefit from the arbitration clause contained therein under the principles of agency. However, in that case, unlike the present case, the broker who had not signed the agreement was merely an individual employee (assistant director) of the brokerage company which had entered into the brokerage agreement with the plaintiff. The *Scher* court held that: "Acts by employees of one of the parties to a customer agreement are equally arbitrable as acts of the principals as long as the challenged acts fall within the scope of the customer agreement." *Scher*, 723 F. Supp. at 216. In *Scher* it was obvious that the parties to the customer agreement intended it to apply to both the brokerage firm and the individual employees through which the firm acted. Because neither Stratton nor Koch are employees of Ameritrade, Inc., the *Scher* holding does not apply here.

Finally, the fourth case cited in support of defendants' position, *Cauble*, is inapplicable to the narrow question at issue here. That case addressed the issue of whether an introducing broker had the authority to liquidate a customer's account, and not whether it had standing to enforce an arbitration provision. Thus, *Cauble* does not present relevant authority on the limited issue presented here.

In *Mowbray*, the First Circuit noted that:

> the difference between this case and *Cauble* is that, unlike the *liquidation* provisions at issue there, it does not follow from the introducing broker's *de facto* control over a client's account that the client originally or subsequently intended that the introducing broker be able to invoke [the clearing broker's] power to compel *arbitration.* [Emphasis in original.]

Id.

The *Mowbray* court also pointed out that a lesser showing of intent is necessary for the court to find that a broker has authority to enforce a liquidation provision than would be necessary to find that a broker has the authority to compel arbitration. Unlike a liquidation provision which "can be characterized as an 'obvious' (and hence, intended) incident of an introducing broker's administrative or supervisory powers over a customer's account," an arbitration provision involves important procedural rights and is not an obvious incident of an introducing broker's supervisory power. Id. This court finds the reasoning of the *Mowbray* court persuasive on this issue. The power to compel arbitration will not be deemed to be part of an introducing broker's supervisory power absent a substantial factual showing that the investor knowingly consented to such an exercise of power.

In the present case, there has been no showing that Shaffer knowingly consented to give Stratton and Koch the power to compel arbitration which it gave to Ameritrade. The fact that Shaffer never communicated directly with Ameritrade does not establish that Shaffer intended for the terms of the Ameritrade Brokerage Agreement, which made no mention of defendants, to apply equally to them. Significantly, nothing in defendants' pleadings indicates an *intention* by Shaffer to consent to arbitrate his disputes with defendants. Rather, defendants merely argue that constructive consent must be implied from defendants' relationship with Ameritrade. Significantly, none of the cases cited by defendants support the position that a court may imply constructive consent in the absence of an investor's actual intention (either express-i.e., a written or oral statement, or implied-i.e., from conduct) to be bound by arbitration. Because an agreement to arbitrate entails the abrogation of an investor's important procedural right to be heard in federal court, the court will not imply an investor's "constructive" consent based solely upon the relationship between the introducing and clearing brokers.

IT IS SO ORDERED.

* * * *

§ 4.03 SECURITIES DISPUTES — INTRODUCING AND CLEARING BROKERS

The relationships between customer, introducing, and clearing broker provide fertile grounds for third party beneficiary analysis. Under RESTATEMENT (SECOND) OF CONTRACTS § 302, the recognition of third party intended beneficiary status is governed by two considerations—whether the promisee has put the promisor on notice of its intent to have rights of enforcement vest in a third party, and whether such recognition would be "appropriate." Thus, the inquiry in the last case was whether the customer, in promising to arbitrate with the clearing broker, had reason to understand, under so-called "objective theory," that the clearing broker intended to extend this right to arbitrate to the introducing broker (and its personnel) as well. Unlike in the last case, the typical brokerage customer agreement, while prepared by the clearing broker for standard use by each of the introducing firms it represents, will bear the name of both the introducing and the clearing broker. Such agreements sometimes expressly provide that the introducing broker is to have third-party status.

By regulation, the introducing and clearing broker are required to have a detailed Clearing Agreement which, inter alia, assigns designated responsibilities to each. At times, there are indemnification or cross-indemnification provisions so that the party with direct responsibility for a certain activity will bear the brunt of successful customer claims arising from those activities. The issue of agency, despite disclaimers when used, can be confusing—for instance, while margin loans, and margin "house rules," come from the clearing broker, implementation of margin calls to post additional collateral are typically the responsibility of the introducing broker, who maintains direct customer contact. Who should the customer claim against in a margin dispute? A customer will likely want to claim against both brokers. What happens if only one of the brokers is entitled to arbitrate?

As to whether it is "appropriate," in the context of this tripartite relationship, to make the introducing broker a third party intended beneficiary of the arbitration agreement between clearing broker and customer, litigation efficiencies strongly suggest that it is. Adopting the contrary course may well leave the customer with "two bites at the apple." A pending court case against the introducing broker may lead to broader discovery of clearing broker materials the introducing broker receives in due course than would otherwise be available in arbitration. As an offset, district courts will sometimes stay court cases in favor of arbitration, even against different parties, when both litigations involve the same securities transactions and underlying operative facts. For instance, a finding by arbitrators in the last case that there were no margin violations would likely preclude the customer from attempting to show otherwise in its suit against the introducing broker.

What happens when it is a clearing broker, perhaps one not around when the original customer agreement was signed with its introducing broker, which seeks to arbitrate under the arbitration clause in the customer agreement? For a case holding that a determination of arbitrability in favor of the introducing broker extends to its clearing broker as a "privy," see *Walzer v. Muriel Siebert*, 2005 WL 1541054 (D.N.J. 2005), *aff'd*, 221 F. App'x 153 (3d Cir. 2007).

§ 4.04 AVOIDANCE OF AN ARBITRATION PROVISION — UNCONSCIONABILITY

Those who think back to the unconscionability illustrations in their contracts casebooks will probably remember that certain of them involved arbitration provisions. Once again, the law of contracts and that of commercial arbitration intersect. Why?

The critical concept in the modern arbitration statute is that arbitral provisions ought to be as enforceable as other contractual arrangements. As such, arbitral provisions are subject to enforceability limitations applying to all types of agreements, but none other. Such limitations may be based on traditional contract theory requiring an objectively manifested assent to the other's terms, academic lingo for the idea that a person should only be bound by material she has reason to know is contractual, and applies to her. Such prevention of "unfair surprise" takes on special force when dealing with form contracts of adhesion. It can, and often does, fall under the "procedural unconscionability" umbrella.

Following the lead of the United States Supreme Court in cases like *Shearson* and *Gilmer*, the courts repeatedly emphasize that showing adhesion—that arbitration was part of a "take it or leave it" proposition—is not enough to refuse enforcement, even in the patterned sort of form consumer transaction. Any experienced contract lawyer will tell you, however, that courts are more concerned about adequate notice and unfairness in these situations than where the party relationship is one of "arm's length." In the latter situation, we are likely to run into the maxim that a party is responsible for reading and understanding what she signs. Cases in which there is adhesion, however, tend to focus sharply on the type of arbitration procedure provided for in terms of neutrality, fairness, and costs. This broad subset of considerations invokes considerations of "unconscionability," which, since they apply somewhat to all contracts, may be used to defeat enforcement of arbitral provisions. Residual uneasiness with compulsory arbitration sometimes bubbles to the surface under the guise of "unconscionability."

In the cases to follow, see whether you agree that the lower courts have not fully accommodated to the notion that arbitration clauses do not merit special scrutiny, at least more scrutiny than typically received by other sorts of "non-dickered" terms. Why might that be so? Should it be? Are courts not more likely to find objections in connection with pre-dispute provisions that push some ill-defined envelope? Does all this have anything to do with the repeated judicial reminders that one cannot be compelled to arbitrate absent specific written agreement—that there is still something very important about the right to go to court?

[A] Adequate Notice

Specht v. Netscape Communications Corp.

United States Court of Appeals, Second Circuit, 2002.
306 F.3d 17.

- SOTOMAYOR, CIRCUIT JUDGE.

This is an appeal from a judgment of the Southern District of New York denying a motion by defendants-appellants Netscape Communications Corporation and its corporate parent, America Online, Inc. (collectively, "defendants" or "Netscape"), to compel arbitration and to stay court proceedings. In order to resolve the central question of arbitrability presented here, we must address issues of contract formation in cyberspace. Principally, we are asked to determine whether plaintiffs-appellees ("plaintiffs"), by acting upon defendants' invitation to download free software made available on defendants' webpage, agreed to be bound by the software's license terms (which included the arbitration clause at issue), even though plaintiffs could not have learned of the existence of those terms unless, prior to executing the download, they had scrolled down the webpage to a screen located below the download button. We agree with the district court that a reasonably prudent Internet user in circumstances such as these would not have known or learned of the existence of the license terms before responding to defendants' invitation to download the free software, and that defendants therefore did not provide reasonable notice of the license terms. In consequence, plaintiffs' bare act of downloading the software did not unambiguously manifest assent to the arbitration provision contained in the license terms.

* * * *

I. The Reasonably Prudent Offeree of Downloadable Software.

Defendants argue that plaintiffs must be held to a standard of reasonable prudence and that, because notice of the existence of SmartDownload license terms was on the next scrollable screen, plaintiffs were on "inquiry notice" of those terms. We disagree with the proposition that a reasonably prudent offeree in plaintiffs' position would necessarily have known or learned of the existence of the SmartDownload license agreement prior to acting, so that plaintiffs may be held to have assented to that agreement with constructive notice of its terms.

* * * *

Most of the cases cited by defendants in support of their inquiry-notice argument are drawn from the world of paper contracting. See, e.g., Taussig v. Bode & Haslett, 134 Cal. 260, 66 P. 259 (1901) (where party had opportunity to read leakage disclaimer printed on warehouse receipt, he had duty to do so); In re First Capital Life Ins. Co., 34 Cal. App. 4th 1283, 1288, 40 Cal. Rptr. 2d 816, 820 (1995) (purchase of insurance policy after opportunity to read and understand policy terms creates binding agreement); King v. Larsen Realty, Inc., 175 Cal. Rptr. 226, 231 (1981) (where realtors' board manual specifying that party was required to arbitrate was "readily available," party was "on notice" that he was agreeing to mandatory arbitration); Cal. State Auto. Ass'n Inter-Ins. Bureau v. Barrett Garages, Inc., 64 Cal. Rptr. 699, 703 (1967) (recipient of airport parking claim check was bound by terms printed on claim check, because a "ordinarily prudent" person would have been alerted to the terms); Larrus v. First Nat'l Bank, 266 P.2d 143, 147 (1954) ("clearly printed" statement on bank card stating that depositor agreed to bank's regulations provided sufficient notice to create agreement, where party had opportunity to view statement and to ask for full text of regulations, but did not do so); *see also* Hux v. Butler, 339 F.2d 696, 700 (6th Cir. 1964) (constructive notice found where "slightest inquiry" would have disclosed relevant facts to offeree); Walker v. Carnival Cruise Lines, 63 F.Supp.2d 1083, 1089 (N.D. Cal.1999) (under California and federal law, "conspicuous notice" directing the attention of parties to existence of contract terms renders terms binding) (quotation marks omitted); Shacket v. Roger Smith Aircraft Sales, Inc., 651 F. Supp. 675, 691 (N.D. Ill. 1986) (constructive notice found where "minimal investigation" would have revealed facts to offeree).

As the foregoing cases suggest, receipt of a physical document containing contract terms or notice thereof is frequently deemed, in the world of paper transactions, a sufficient circumstance to place the offeree on inquiry notice of those terms. "Every person who has actual notice of circumstances sufficient to put a prudent man upon inquiry as to a particular fact, has constructive notice of the fact itself in all cases in which, by prosecuting such inquiry, he might have learned such fact." Cal. Civ. Code § 19. These principles apply equally to the emergent world of online product delivery, pop-up screens, hyperlinked pages, clickwrap licensing, scrollable documents, and urgent admonitions to "Download Now!" What plaintiffs saw when they were being invited by defendants to download this fast, free plug-in called SmartDownload was a screen containing praise for the product and, at the very bottom of the screen, a "Download" button. Defendants argue that under the principles set forth in the cases cited above, a "fair and prudent person using ordinary care" would have been on inquiry notice of SmartDownload's license terms.

* * * *

We are not persuaded that a reasonably prudent offeree in these circumstances would have known of the existence of license terms.

Plaintiffs were responding to an offer that did not carry an immediately visible notice of the existence of license terms or require unambiguous manifestation of assent to those terms. Thus, plaintiffs' "apparent manifestation of . . . consent" was to terms "contained in a document whose contractual nature [was] not obvious." *Windsor Mills*, 101 Cal. Rptr. at 351. Moreover, the fact that, given the position of the scroll bar on their computer screens, plaintiffs may have been aware that an unexplored portion of the Netscape webpage remained below the download button does not mean that they reasonably should have concluded that this portion contained a notice of license terms.

We conclude that in circumstances such as these, where consumers are urged to download free software at the immediate click of a button, a reference to the existence of license terms on a submerged screen is not sufficient to place consumers on inquiry or constructive notice of those terms. The SmartDownload webpage screen was "printed in such a manner that it tended to conceal the fact that it was an express acceptance of [Netscape's] rules and regulations." *Larrus*, 266 P.2d at 147. Internet users may have, as defendants put it, "as much time as they need" to scroll through multiple screens on a webpage, but there is no reason to assume that viewers will scroll down to subsequent screens simply because screens are there. When products are "free" and users are invited to download them in the absence of reasonably conspicuous notice that they are about to bind themselves to contract terms, the transactional circumstances cannot be fully analogized to those in the paper world of arm's-length bargaining. In the next two sections, we discuss caselaw and other legal authorities that have addressed the circumstances of computer sales, software licensing, and online transacting. Those authorities tend strongly to support our conclusion that plaintiffs did not manifest assent to SmartDownload's license terms.

II. Shrinkwrap Licensing and Related Practices.

Defendants cite certain well-known cases involving shrinkwrap licensing and related commercial practices in support of their contention that plaintiffs became bound by the SmartDownload license terms by virtue of inquiry notice. For example, in *Hill v. Gateway 2000, Inc.*, 105 F.3d 1147 (7th Cir. 1997), the Seventh Circuit held that where a purchaser had ordered a computer over the telephone, received the order in a shipped box containing the computer along with printed contract terms, and did not return the computer within the thirty days required by the terms, the purchaser was bound by the contract. *Id.* at 1148–49. In *ProCD, Inc. v. Zeidenberg*, the same court held that where an individual purchased software in a box containing license terms which were displayed on the computer screen every time the user executed the software program, the user had sufficient opportunity to review the terms and to return the software, and so was contractually bound after retaining the product. *ProCD*, 86 F.3d at 1452; *cf. Moore v. Microsoft Corp.*, 293 A.D.2d 587, 587 (2d Dep't 2002) (software user was bound by license agreement where terms were prominently displayed on computer screen before software could be installed and where user was required to indicate assent by clicking "I agree") Brower v. Gateway 2000, Inc., 246 A.D.2d 246, 251 (1st Dep't 1998) (buyer assented to arbitration clause shipped inside box with computer and software by retaining items beyond date specified by license terms); M.A. Mortenson Co. v. Timberline Software Corp., 970 P.2d 803, 809 (1999) (buyer manifested assent to software license terms by installing and using software), *aff'd*, 998 P.2d 305 (2000); *see also I. Lan Sys.*, 183 F. Supp. 2d at 338 (business entity "explicitly accepted the clickwrap license agreement [contained in purchased software] when it clicked on the box stating 'I agree' ").

These cases do not help defendants. To the extent that they hold that the purchaser of a computer or tangible software is contractually bound after failing to object to printed license terms provided with the product, *Hill* and *Brower* do not differ markedly from the cases involving traditional paper contracting discussed in the previous section. Insofar as the purchaser in *ProCD* was confronted with conspicuous, mandatory license terms every time he ran the software on his computer, that case actually undermines defendants' contention that downloading in the absence of conspicuous terms is an act that binds plaintiffs to those terms. In *Mortenson*, the full text of license terms was printed on each sealed diskette envelope inside the software box, printed again on the inside cover of the user manual, and notice of the terms appeared on the computer screen every time the purchaser executed the program. *Mortenson*, 970 P.2d at 806. In sum, the foregoing cases are clearly distinguishable from the facts of the present action.

III. Online Transactions.

Cases in which courts have found contracts arising from Internet use do not assist defendants, because in those circumstances there was much clearer notice than in the present case that a user's act would manifest assent to contract terms. See, e.g., Hotmail Corp. v. Van$ Money Pie Inc., 47 U.S.P.Q.2d 1020, 1025 (N.D. Cal. 1998) (granting preliminary injunction based in part on breach of "Terms of Service" agreement, to which defendants had assented); America Online, Inc. v. Booker, 781 So.2d 423, 425 (Fla. Dist. Ct. App. 2001) (upholding forum selection clause in "freely negotiated agreement" contained in online terms of service); Caspi v. Microsoft Network, L.L.C., 732 A.2d 528, 530, 532-33 (N.J. Super. Ct. App. Div. 1999) (upholding forum selection clause where subscribers to online software were required to review license terms in scrollable window and to click "I Agree" or "I Don't Agree") . . . .

* * * *

NOTE

1. In *Doctor's Associates*, *infra* at page 195, the Supreme Court overturned a Montana statute requiring that arbitration provisions be set forth *in large type*. Was it correct to use preemption in that case? Or was the statute simply a tool aimed at avoiding generic contractual "notice" problems?

[B] Burden

Brower v. Gateway 2000, Inc.

New York Supreme Court, Appellate Division, 1st Dep't, 1998.
246 A.D.2d 246.

- MILONAS, J.

* * * *

Appellants are among the many consumers who purchased computers and software products from defendant Gateway 2000 through a direct-sales system, by mail or telephone order. As of July 3, 1995, it was Gateway's practice to include with the materials shipped to the purchaser along with the merchandise a copy of its "Standard Terms and Conditions Agreement" and any relevant warranties for the products in the shipment. The Agreement begins with a "NOTE TO CUSTOMER," which provides, in slightly larger print than the remainder of the document, in a box that spans the width of the page: "This document contains Gateway 2000's Standard Terms and Conditions. By keeping your Gateway 2000 computer system beyond thirty (30) days after the date of delivery, you accept these Terms and Conditions." The document consists of 16 paragraphs, and, as is relevant to this appeal, paragraph 10 of the agreement, entitled "DISPUTE RESOLUTION," reads as follows:

> Any dispute or controversy arising out of or relating to this Agreement or its interpretation shall be settled exclusively and finally by arbitration. The arbitration shall be conducted in accordance with the Rules of Conciliation and Arbitration of the International Chamber of Commerce. The arbitration shall be conducted in Chicago, Illinois, U.S.A. before a sole arbitrator. Any award rendered in any such arbitration proceeding shall be final and binding on each of the parties, and judgment may be entered thereon in a court of competent jurisdiction.

Plaintiffs commenced this action on behalf of themselves and others similarly situated for compensatory and punitive damages, alleging deceptive sales practices in seven causes of action, including breach of warranty, breach of contract, fraud and unfair trade practices. In particular, the allegations focused on Gateway's representations and advertising that promised "service when you need it," including around-the-clock free technical support, free software technical support and certain on-site services. According to plaintiffs, not only were they unable to avail themselves of this offer because it was virtually impossible to get through to a technician, but also Gateway continued to advertise this claim notwithstanding numerous complaints and reports about the problem.

Insofar as is relevant to appellants, who purchased their computers after July 3, 1995, Gateway moved to dismiss the complaint based on the arbitration clause in the Agreement. Appellants argued that the arbitration clause is invalid under UCC 2-207, unconscionable under UCC 2-302 and an unenforceable contract of adhesion. Specifically, they claimed that the provision was obscure; that a customer could not reasonably be expected to appreciate or investigate its meaning and effect; that the International Chamber of Commerce ("ICC") was not a forum commonly used for consumer matters; and that because ICC headquarters were in France, it was particularly difficult to locate the organization and its rules. To illustrate just how inaccessible the forum was, appellants advised the court that the ICC was not registered with the Secretary of State, that efforts to locate and contact the ICC had been unsuccessful and that apparently the only way to attempt to contact the ICC was through the United States Council for International Business, with which the ICC maintained some sort of relationship.

In support of their arguments, appellants submitted a copy of the ICC's Rules of Conciliation and Arbitration and contended that the cost of ICC arbitration was prohibitive, particularly given the amount of the typical consumer claim involved. For example, a claim of less than $50,000 required advance fees of $4,000 (more than the cost of most Gateway products), of which the $2000 registration fee was nonrefundable even if the consumer prevailed at the arbitration. Consumers would also incur travel expenses disproportionate to the damages sought, which appellants' counsel estimated would not exceed $1,000 per customer in this action, as well as bear the cost of Gateway's legal fees if the consumer did not prevail at the arbitration; in this respect, the ICC rules follow the "loser pays" rule used in England. Also, although Chicago was designated as the site of the actual arbitration, all correspondence must be sent to ICC headquarters in France.

The IAS court dismissed the complaint as to appellants based on the arbitration clause in the Agreements delivered with their computers. We agree with the court's decision and reasoning in all respects but for the issue of the unconscionability of the designation of the ICC as the arbitration body.

First, the court properly rejected appellants' argument that the arbitration clause was invalid under UCC 2-207. Appellants claim that when they placed their order they did not bargain for, much less accept, arbitration of any dispute, and therefore the arbitration clause in the agreement that accompanied the merchandise shipment was a "material alteration" of a preexisting oral agreement. Under UCC 2-207(2), such a material alteration constitutes "proposals for addition to the contract" that become part of the contract only upon appellants' express acceptance. However, as the court correctly concluded, the clause was not a "material alteration" of an oral agreement, but, rather, simply one provision of the sole contract that existed between the parties. That contract, the court explained, was formed and acceptance was manifested not when the order was placed but only with the retention of the merchandise beyond the 30 days specified in the Agreement enclosed in the shipment of merchandise. Accordingly, the contract was outside the scope of UCC 2-207.

In reaching its conclusion, the IAS court took note of the litigation in Federal courts on this very issue, and, indeed, on this very arbitration clause. In *Hill v. Gateway 2000, Inc.*, 105 F.3d 1147, *cert. denied*, 522 U.S. 808, plaintiffs in a class action contested the identical Gateway contract in dispute before us, including the enforceability of the arbitration clause. As that court framed the issue, the "[t]erms inside Gateway's box stand or fall together. If they constitute the parties contract because the Hills had an opportunity to return the computer after reading them, then all must be enforced" (id. at 1148). The court then concluded that the contract was not formed with the placement of a telephone order or with the delivery of the goods. Instead, an enforceable contract was formed only with the consumer's decision to retain the merchandise beyond the 30-day period specified in the agreement. Thus, the agreement as a whole, including the arbitration clause, was enforceable.

This conclusion was in keeping with the same court's decision in *ProCD, Inc. v. Zeidenberg*, 86 F.3d 1447, where it found that detailed terms enclosed within the packaging of particular computer software purchased in a retail outlet constituted the contract between the vendor and the consumer who retained the product. In that case, the Seventh Circuit held that UCC 2-207 did not apply and indeed was "irrelevant" to such transactions, noting that the section is generally invoked where multiple agreements have been exchanged between the parties a classic "battle of the forms," whereas *ProCD* (as well as *Hill* and this case) involves but a single form (id. at 1452).

The *Hill* decision, in its examination of the formation of the contract, takes note of the realities of conducting business in today's world. Transactions involving "cash now, terms later" have become commonplace, enabling the consumer to make purchases of sophisticated merchandise such as computers over the phone or by mail--and even by computer. Indeed, the concept of "[p]ayment preceding the revelation of full terms" is particularly common in certain industries, such as air transportation and insurance (id. at 1149; *ProCD v. Zeidenberg*, supra, at 1451).

* * * *

Second, with respect to appellants' claim that the arbitration clause is unenforceable as a contract of adhesion, in that it involved no choice or negotiation on the part of the consumer but was a "take it or leave it" proposition, we find that this argument, too, was properly rejected by the IAS court. Although the parties clearly do not posses [sic] equal bargaining power, this factor alone does not invalidate the contract as one of adhesion. As the IAS court observed, with the ability to make the purchase elsewhere and the express option to return the goods, the consumer is not in a "take it or leave it" position at all; if any term of the agreement is unacceptable to the consumer, he or she can easily buy a competitor's product instead—either from a retailer or directly from the manufacturer—and reject Gateway's agreement by returning the merchandise. The consumer has 30 days to make that decision. Within that time, the consumer can inspect the goods and examine and seek clarification of the terms of the agreement; until those 30 days have elapsed, the consumer has the unqualified right to return the merchandise, because the goods or terms are unsatisfactory or for no reason at all.

While returning the goods to avoid the formation of the contract entails affirmative action on the part of the consumer, and even some expense, this may be seen as a trade-off for the convenience and savings for which the consumer presumably opted when he or she chose to make a purchase of such consequence by phone or mail as an alternative to onsite retail shopping. That a consumer does not read the agreement or thereafter claims he or she failed to understand or appreciate some term therein does not invalidate the contract any more than such claim would undo a contract formed under other circumstances.

Finally, we turn to appellants' argument that the IAS court should have declared the contract unenforceable, pursuant to UCC 2-302, on the ground that the arbitration clause is unconscionable due to the unduly burdensome procedure and cost for the individual consumer. The IAS court found that while a class-action lawsuit, such as the one herein, may be a less costly alternative to the arbitration (which is generally less costly than litigation), that does not alter the binding effect of the valid arbitration clause contained in the agreement (see, Harris v. Shearson Hayden Stone, 82 A.D.2d 87, 92–93, *aff'd*, 56 N.Y.2d 627 for reasons stated below; see also Matter of Ball, 236 A.D.2d 158.)

As a general matter, under New York law, unconscionability requires a showing that a contract is "both procedurally and substantively unconscionable when made" (Gillman v. Chase Manhattan Bank, 73 N.Y.2d 1, 10). That is, there must be "some showing of 'an absence of meaningful choice on the part of one of the parties together with contract terms which are unreasonably favorable to the other party' [citation omitted]" (Matter of State of New York v. Avco Financial Service, 50 N.Y.2d 383, 389). The *Avco* court took pains to note, however, that the purpose of this doctrine is not to redress the inequality between the parties but simply to ensure that the more powerful party cannot "surprise" the other party with some overly oppressive term (id., at 389).

As to the procedural element, a court will look to the contract formation process to determine if in fact one party lacked any meaningful choice in entering into the contract, taking into consideration such factors as the setting of the transaction, the experience and education of the party claiming unconscionability, whether the contract contained "fine print," whether the seller used "high-pressured tactics" and any disparity in the parties' bargaining power (Gillman v Chase Manhattan Bank, supra, at 11). None of these factors supports appellants' claim here. Any purchaser has 30 days within which to thoroughly examine the contents of their shipment, including the terms of the Agreement, and seek clarification of any term therein (e.g., Matter of Ball, supra, at 161). The Agreement itself, which is entitled in large print "STANDARD TERMS AND CONDITIONS AGREEMENT," consists of only three pages and 16 paragraphs, all of which appear in the same size print. Moreover, despite appellants' claims to the contrary, the arbitration clause is in no way "hidden" or "tucked away" within a complex document of inordinate length, nor is the option of returning the merchandise, to avoid the contract, somehow a "precarious" one . . .

With respect to the substantive element, which entails an examination of the substance of the agreement in order to determine whether the terms unreasonably favor one party (Gillman v. Chase Manhattan Bank, supra, 73 N.Y.2d, at 12), we do not find that the possible inconvenience of the chosen site (Chicago) alone rises to the level of unconscionability. We do find, however, that the excessive cost factor that is necessarily entailed in arbitrating before the ICC is unreasonable and surely serves to deter the individual consumer from invoking the process (see, Matter of Teleserve Systems, 230 A.D.2d 585, 594 App. Div., 1st Dept., Sept. 30, 1997). Barred from resorting to the courts by the arbitration clause in the first instance, the designation of a financially prohibitive forum effectively bars consumers from this forum as well; consumers are thus left with no forum at all in which to resolve a dispute. In this regard, we note that this particular claim is not mentioned in the *Hill* decision, which upheld the clause as part of an enforceable contract.

While it is true that, under New York law, unconscionability is generally predicated on the presence of both the procedural and substantive elements, the substantive element alone may be sufficient to render the terms of the provision at issue unenforceable (see, Gillman v Chase Manhattan Bank, supra, at 12; Matter of State of New York v. Avco Financial Service, supra, at 389; State of New York v. Wolowitz, 96 A.D.2d 47). Excessive fees, such as those incurred under the ICC procedure, have been grounds for finding an arbitration provision unenforceable or commercially unreasonable (see, e.g., Matter of Teleserve Systems, supra, at 593–94).

In the *Filias* case previously mentioned, the Federal District Court stated that it was "inclined to agree" with the argument that selection of the ICC rendered the clause unconscionable, but concluded that the issue was moot because Gateway had agreed to arbitrate before the American Arbitration Association ("AAA") and sought court appointment of the AAA pursuant to Federal Arbitration Act

9 U.S.C. § 5. The court accordingly granted Gateway's motion to compel arbitration and appointed the AAA in lieu of the ICC. Plaintiffs in that action (who are represented by counsel for appellants before us) contend that costs associated with the AAA process are also excessive, given the amount of the individual consumer's damages, and their motion for reconsideration of the court's decision has not yet been decided. While the AAA rules and costs are not part of the record before us, the parties agree that there is a minimum, nonrefundable filing fee of $500, and appellants claim each consumer could spend in excess of $1,000 to arbitrate in this forum.

Gateway's agreement to the substitution of the AAA is not limited to the *Filias* plaintiffs. Gateway's brief includes the text of a new arbitration agreement that it claims has been extended to all customers, past, present and future (apparently through publication in a quarterly magazine sent to anyone who has ever purchased a Gateway product). The new arbitration agreement provides for the consumer's choice of the AAA or the ICC as the arbitral body and the designation of any location for the arbitration by agreement of the parties, which "shall not be unreasonably withheld." It also provides telephone numbers at which the AAA and the ICC may be reached for information regarding the "organizations and their procedures."

As noted, however, appellants complain that the AAA fees are also excessive and thus in no way have they accepted defendant's offer (see, UCC 2-209); because they make the same claim as to the AAA as they did with respect to the ICC, the issue of unconscionability is not rendered moot, as defendant suggests. We cannot determine on this record whether the AAA process and costs would be so "egregiously oppressive" that they, too, would be unconscionable (Avildsen v. Prystay, 171 A.D.2d 13, 14, *appeal dismissed*, 79 N.Y.2d 841). Thus, we modify the order on appeal to the extent of finding that portion of the arbitration provision requiring arbitration before the ICC to be unconscionable and remand to Supreme Court so that the parties have the opportunity to seek appropriate substitution of an arbitrator pursuant to the Federal Arbitration Act (9 U.S.C. § 1 et seq.), which provides for such court designation of an arbitrator upon application of either party, where, for whatever reason, one is not otherwise designated (9 U.S.C. § 5).

NOTE

1. Presumably, courts are free to modify arbitration clauses rather than to reject them outright. When should they refuse such an approach? Cases involving restrictive covenants provide guidance. Is overreaching encouraged by severing unconscionable provisions, but leaving the rest?

[C] Fairness of Process

Graham v. Scissor-Tail, Inc.

Supreme Court of California, 1981.
28 Cal.3d 807.

- TOBRINER, J.

* * * *

Plaintiff Bill Graham is an experienced promoter and producer of musical concerts. Defendant, Russell Bridges, also known as Leon Russell (Russell), is a successful performer and recording artist and the leader of a musical group; he is also a member of the American Federation of Musicians (A.F. of M.). Defendant Scissor-Tail, Inc. (Scissor-Tail) is a California corporation, wholly owned by Russell, which serves as the vehicle by which the services of Russell and his group are marketed. Defendant David Forest Agency, Ltd. (Forest) was, at the time here relevant, acting in the capacity of booking agent for Scissor-Tail.

Early in 1973, Scissor-Tail and Russell decided to formulate and structure a personal appearance tour for the latter and his group. Forest was engaged to assist in this project, and at the suggestion of Dennis Cordell, Russell's personal manager and an officer of Scissor-Tail, contacted plaintiff Graham, who had previously promoted a number of Russell concerts, to request that he provide his services for four of the twelve concerts on the projected tour. A series of four contracts was prepared covering, respectively, concerts at Ontario, Oakland, Long Island, and Philadelphia.

The four contracts in question were all prepared on an identical form known in the industry as an A.F. of M. Form B Contract . . . .

The contracts designated Graham as the "purchaser of music" or "employer," the seven members of the group as "musicians." They did not speak explicitly to the question of who was to bear any eventual net losses. The contract forms also provided: "9. In accordance with the Constitution, By-laws, Rules and Regulations of the Federation, the parties will submit every claim, dispute, controversy or difference involving the musical services arising out of or connected with this contract and the engagement covered thereby for determination by the International Executive Board of the Federation or a similar board of an appropriate local thereof and such determination shall be conclusive, final and binding upon the parties."

The Ontario concert took place as scheduled and had gross receipts of $173,000 (out of a potential gross reflected in the contract of "$450,000 plus"), with expenses of $236,000, resulting in a net loss of some $63,000. The Oakland concert also took place, resulting in a net profit of some $98,000. Following this second concert a dispute arose among the parties over who was to bear the loss sustained in the Ontario concert and whether that loss could be offset against the profits . . . .

On October 29, 1976, a hearing was held at the union's western (Hollywood) office before a "referee" appointed by the union president. The referee was a former executive officer and a long-time member of the union; he had acted as a hearing officer in many previous union matters. All parties (excluding Russell himself) and counsel were present. Graham sought to have the proceedings transcribed by a court reporter brought by him; the request was denied and the reporter excused. The hearing thereupon proceeded. Graham produced considerable evidence consisting of his own testimony, the testimony of another promoter, the stipulated testimony of a third promoter, and three sworn statements by others engaged in the popular music concert field to the effect that under common and widely held custom and practice in the industry, the promoter under a 9 0/10 or 8 5/15 contract was understood to bear no risk of loss because his share of the profits under such contracts was considerably smaller than under the "normal" contract, under which the promoter takes a larger percentage of the profits but is understood to bear the risk of loss; no contrary evidence was offered by Scissor-Tail . . . .

On November 5, 1976, in his report to the union's International Executive Board, the referee recommended that Graham be ordered to pay to Scissor-Tail the amount of its original claim (some $53,000) . . . .

On February 22, 1977, the union's International Executive Board made its award in conformity with the recommendation of the referee.

* * * *

Plaintiff's basic contention in this respect is that the order compelling arbitration was in error because the underlying agreement at least insofar as it required arbitration of disputes before the A.F. of M. was an unenforceable contract of adhesion. Two separate questions are thus presented, each of which requires separate consideration: (1) Is this a contract of adhesion? (2) If so, is it unenforceable?

The term "contract of adhesion," now long a part of our legal vocabulary, has been variously defined in the cases and other legal literature. The serviceable general definition first suggested by Justice Tobriner in 1961, however, has well stood the test of time and will bear little improvement: "The term signifies a standardized contract, which, imposed and drafted by the party of superior bargaining strength, relegates to the subscribing party only the opportunity to adhere to the contract or reject it."

Such contracts are, of course, a familiar part of the modern legal landscape, in which the classical model of "free" contracting by parties of equal or near-equal bargaining strength is often found to be unresponsive to the realities brought about by increasing concentrations of economic and other power. They are an inevitable fact of life for all citizens, businessman and consumer alike. While not lacking in social advantages, they bear within them the clear danger of oppression and overreaching. It is in the context of this tension between social advantage in the light of modern conditions on the one hand, and the danger of oppression on the other that courts and legislatures have sometimes acted to prevent perceived abuses.

We believe that the contract here in question, in light of all of the circumstances presented, may be fairly described as adhesive. Although defendant and its supporting amicus curiae are strenuous in their insistence that Graham's prominence and success in the promotion of popular music concerts afforded him considerable bargaining strength in the subject negotiations, the record before us fairly establishes that he, for all his asserted stature in the industry, was here reduced to the humble role of "adherent." It appears that all concert artists and groups of any significance or prominence are members of the A.F. of M.; that pursuant to express provision of the A.F. of M.'s constitution and bylaws members are not permitted to sign any form of contract other than that issued by the union; that the A.F. of M. Form B. Contract in use at the time here relevant included the arbitration provisions here in question; and that Scissor-Tail insisted upon the use of 8 5/15 and 9 0/10 contractual arrangements. In these circumstances it must be concluded that Graham, whatever his asserted prominence in the industry, was required by the realities of his business as a concert promoter to sign A.F. of M. form contracts with any concert artist with whom he wished to do business and that in the case before us he, wishing to promote the Russell concerts, was presented with the nonnegotiable option of accepting such contracts on an 8 5/15 or 9 0/10 basis or not at all.

* * * *

Generally speaking, there are two judicially imposed limitations on the enforcement of adhesion contracts or provisions thereof. The first is that such a contract or provision which does not fall within the reasonable expectations of the weaker or "adhering" party will not be enforced against him. The second a principle of equity applicable to all contracts generally is that a contract or provision, even if consistent with the reasonable expectations of the parties, will be denied enforcement if, considered in its context, it is unduly oppressive or "unconscionable." We proceed to examine whether the instant contract, and especially that provision thereof requiring the arbitration of disputes before the A.F. of M., should have been denied enforcement under either of these two principles.

* * * *

We cannot conclude on the record before us that the contractual provision requiring arbitration of disputes before the A.F. of M. was in any way contrary to the reasonable expectations of plaintiff Graham. By his own declarations and testimony, he had been a party to literally thousands of A.F. of M. contracts containing a similar provision; indeed it appears that during the 3 years preceding the instant contracts he had promoted 15 or more concerts with Scissor-Tail, on each occasion signing a contract containing arbitration provisions similar to those here in question. It also appears that he had been involved in prior proceedings before the A.F. of M. regarding disputes with other musical groups arising under prior contracts.

* * * *

We are thus brought to the question whether the contract provision requiring the arbitration of disputes before the A.F. of M. because it designates an arbitrator who, by reason of its status and identity, is presumptively biased in favor of one party is for that reason to be deemed unconscionable and unenforceable. Graham, although couching his arguments in other terminology, essentially maintains that it is the thrust of his position being that to allow the A.F. of M. to sit in judgment of a dispute arising between one of its members and a contracting nonmember is so inimical to fundamental notions of fairness as to require nonenforcement. We proceed to a consideration of this contention.

* * * *

The answer to this question, we have concluded, must clearly be yes. Although our review of the record has disclosed nothing which would indicate that A.F. of M. procedures operate to deny any party a fair opportunity to present his position prior to decision, we are of the view that the "minimum levels of integrity" which are requisite to a contractual arrangement for the nonjudicial resolution of disputes are not achieved by an arrangement which designates the union of one of the parties as the arbitrator of disputes arising out of employment especially when, as here, the arrangement is the product of circumstances indicative of adhesion.

NOTE

1. What is the difference between the last case and the ones holding that there can be no arbitration without a neutral? Is the preceding *Graham* case, at least in part, a "subterfuge" rejection of a bad arbitral decision on the merits?

[D] Informed Consent

Broemmer v. Abortion Services of Phoenix

Supreme Court of Arizona, 1992.
173 Ariz. 148.

- MOELLER, J.

Melinda Kay Broemmer (plaintiff) asks this court to review a court of appeals opinion that held that an "Agreement to Arbitrate" which she signed prior to undergoing a clinical abortion is an enforceable, albeit an adhesive, contract.

* * * *

FACTS AND PROCEDURAL HISTORY

In December 1986, plaintiff, an Iowa resident, was 21 years old, unmarried, and 16 or 17 weeks pregnant. She was a high school graduate earning less than $ 100.00 a week and had no medical benefits. The father-to-be insisted that plaintiff have an abortion, but her parents advised against it. Plaintiff's uncontested affidavit describes the time as one of considerable confusion and emotional and physical turmoil for her.

Plaintiff's mother contacted Abortion Services of Phoenix and made an appointment for her daughter for December 29, 1986. During their visit to the clinic that day, plaintiff and her mother expected, but did not receive, information and counseling on alternatives to abortion and the nature of the operation. When plaintiff and her mother arrived at the clinic, plaintiff was escorted into an adjoining room and asked to complete three forms, one of which is the agreement to arbitrate at issue in this case. The agreement to arbitrate included language that "any dispute aris[ing] between the Parties as a result of the fees and/or services" would be settled by binding arbitration and that "any arbitrators appointed by the AAA [American Arbitration Association] shall be licensed medical doctors who specialize in obstetrics/gynecology." The two other documents plaintiff completed at the same time were a 2-page consent-to-operate form and a questionnaire asking for a detailed medical history. Plaintiff completed all three forms in less than 5 minutes and returned them to the front desk. Clinic staff made no attempt to explain the agreement to plaintiff before or after she signed, and did not provide plaintiff with copies of the forms.

After plaintiff returned the forms to the front desk, she was taken into an examination room where pre-operation procedures were performed. She was then instructed to return at 7:00 a.m. the next morning for the termination procedure. Plaintiff returned the following day and Doctor Otto performed the abortion. As a result of the procedure, plaintiff suffered a punctured uterus that required medical treatment.

Plaintiff filed a malpractice complaint in June 1988, approximately 1 1/2 years after the medical procedure. By the time litigation commenced, plaintiff could recall completing and signing the medical history and consent-to-operate forms, but could not recall signing the agreement to arbitrate. Defendants moved to dismiss, contending that the trial court lacked subject matter jurisdiction because arbitration was required.

* * * *

Our conclusion that the contract was one of adhesion is not, of itself, determinative of its enforceability. "[A] contract of adhesion is fully enforceable according to its terms unless certain other factors are present which, under established legal rules—legislative or judicial—operate to render it otherwise." Graham v. Scissor-Tail, Inc., 623 P.2d 165, 172 (1981) (footnotes omitted). To determine whether this contract of adhesion is enforceable, we look to two factors: the reasonable expectations of the adhering party and whether the contract is unconscionable. As the court stated in *Graham*:

> Generally speaking, there are two judicially imposed limitations on the enforcement of adhesion contracts or provisions thereof. The first is that such a contract or provision which does not fall within the reasonable expectations of the weaker or "adhering" party will not be enforced against him. The second—a principle of equity applicable to all contracts generally—is that a contract or provision, even if consistent

> with the reasonable expectations of the parties, will be denied enforcement if, considered in its context, it is unduly oppressive or "unconscionable."

Clearly, the issues of knowing consent and reasonable expectations are closely related and intertwined. In *Darner Motor Sales, Inc. v. Universal Underwriters Ins. Co.*, 140 Ariz. 383 (1984), this court used the Restatement (Second) of Contracts § 211 (Standardized Agreements), as a guide to analyzing, among other things, contracts that contain non-negotiated terms. The comment to subsection (3), quoted with approval in *Darner*, states in part:

> Although customers typically adhere to standardized agreements and are bound by them without even appearing to know the standard terms in detail, they are not bound to unknown terms which are beyond the range of reasonable expectation.

The Restatement focuses our attention on whether it was beyond plaintiff's reasonable expectations to expect to arbitrate her medical malpractice claims, which includes waiving her right to a jury trial, as part of the filling out of the three forms under the facts and circumstances of this case. Clearly, there was no conspicuous or explicit waiver of the fundamental right to a jury trial or any evidence that such rights were knowingly, voluntarily and intelligently waived. The only evidence presented compels a finding that waiver of such fundamental rights was beyond the reasonable expectations of plaintiff.

Plaintiff was under a great deal of emotional stress, had only a high school education, was not experienced in commercial matters, and is still not sure "what arbitration is." Given the circumstances under which the agreement was signed and the nature of the terms included therein, [we conclude] that the contract fell outside plaintiff's reasonable expectations and is, therefore, unenforceable. Because of this holding, it is unnecessary for us to determine whether the contract is also unconscionable.

- MARTONE, J., dissenting.

The court's conclusion that the agreement to arbitrate was outside the plaintiff's reasonable expectations is without basis in law or fact. I fear today's decision reflects a preference for litigation over alternative dispute resolution that I had thought was behind us. I would affirm the court of appeals.

We begin with the undisputed facts that the court ignores. Appendix "A" to this dissent is the agreement to arbitrate. At the top it states in bold capital letters "PLEASE READ THIS CONTRACT CAREFULLY AS IT EFFECTS [sic] YOUR LEGAL RIGHTS." Directly under that in all capital letters are the words "AGREEMENT TO ARBITRATE." The recitals indicate that "the Parties deem it to be in their respective best interest to settle any such dispute as expeditiously and economically as possible." The parties agreed that disputes over services provided would be settled by arbitration in accordance with the rules of the American Arbitration Association. They further agreed that the arbitrators appointed by the American Arbitration Association would be licensed medical doctors who specialize in obstetrics/gynecology. Plaintiff, an adult, signed the document.

Under A.R.S. § 12-1501, a written contract to submit to arbitration *any* controversy that might arise between the parties is "valid, enforceable and irrevocable, save upon such grounds as exist at law or in equity for the revocation of any contract." The statute applies to any controversy. Under A.R.S. § 12-1503, if the arbitration agreement provides a method of appointment of arbitrators, "this method shall be followed." Under A.R.S. § 12-1518, the American Arbitration Association is expressly acknowledged as an entity that the state itself may use in connection with arbitration. There is judicial review of any award. A.R.S. § 12-1512. Thus, on the face of it, the contract to arbitrate is plainly reasonable and enforceable unless there are grounds to revoke it. A.R.S. § 12-1501.

The court seizes upon the doctrine of reasonable expectations to revoke this contract. But there is nothing in this record that would warrant a finding that an agreement to arbitrate a malpractice claim was not within the reasonable expectations of the parties. On this record, the exact opposite is likely to be true. For all we know, both sides in this case might wish to avoid litigation like the plague and seek the more harmonious waters of alternative dispute resolution.[5] Nor is there anything in this record that would suggest that arbitration is bad. Where is the harm? In the end, today's decision reflects a preference in favor of litigation that is not shared by the courts of other states and the courts of the United States.

* * * *

Today's decision sends a mixed message. In light of all of these developments, how can it be that an agreement to arbitrate "fell outside plaintiff's reasonable expectations?" The court's answer, merely confuses the concept of a contract of adhesion with the doctrine of reasonable expectations. The court says it will enforce arbitration agreements "freely and fairly entered," and that "the document involved is a contract of adhesion." Id. But the court's own framework of analysis acknowledges that its "conclusion that the contract was one of adhesion is not, of itself, determinative of its enforceability." It acknowledges that once it is determined that an adhesive contract exists, one looks to (1) reasonable expectations and (2) conscionability. Id. No one doubts that this was a contract of adhesion. And the court holds that because "the contract fell outside plaintiff's reasonable expectations" it is unenforceable, and therefore it is not necessary "to determine whether the contract is also unconscionable." *Ante*, 840 P.2d at 1017. Thus the court does not reach conscionability.

The only basis for the court's decision is "reasonable expectations," but words such as "freely and fairly entered," or "contract of adhesion" are irrelevant to that inquiry. If it is not "free" it is a contract of adhesion. If it is "unfair" it is unconscionable. Nowhere does the court provide the basis for its legal conclusion that this adhesive agreement to arbitrate fell outside of plaintiff's reasonable expectations. In the end we are left to conclude that people reasonably expect litigation over alternative dispute resolution. For all these reasons, I dissent.

---

[5] According to a national survey on American attitudes toward dispute resolution, 82% of the American public, once informed, is willing to use dispute resolution, particularly mediation and arbitration. *NIDR Releases Findings of National Survey on Public Attitudes Towards DR,* Forum, Summer 1992 at 26.

NOTES

1. Was the majority determination encouraged by the provision that any arbitrator had to be a doctor specializing in obstetrics/gynecology?

2. Should a counterparty have to understand what arbitration is before an undertaking to do so becomes enforceable? What might a clinic representative have told the patient to meet such a requirement? Would it have been enough to explain that there would be no entitlement to a jury trial? How do these possibilities comport with the notion that arbitration provisions not be treated differently than others?

Morris v. Metriyakool & South Macomb Hospital

Supreme Court of Michigan, 1984.
418 Mich. 423

- KAVANAGH, J.

These cases concern arbitration of medical malpractice claims. The most significant issue presented is whether the Malpractice Arbitration Act of 1975, M.C.L. § 600.5040 *et seq.*; M.S.A. § 27A.5040 *et seq.*, deprives plaintiffs of constitutional rights to an impartial decisionmaker. We hold that it does not.

* * * *

The malpractice arbitration act provides that a patient "may, if offered, execute an agreement to arbitrate a dispute, controversy, or issue arising out of health care or treatment by a health care provider," M.C.L. § 600.5041(1); M.S.A. § 27A.5041(1), or by a hospital, M.C.L. § 600.5042(1); M.S.A. § 27A.5042(1). A patient executing such an agreement with a health-care provider may revoke it within 60 days after execution, M.C.L. § 600.5041(3); M.S.A. § 27A.5041(3), or, in the case of a hospital, within 60 days after discharge, M.C.L. § 600.5042(3); M.S.A. § 27A.5042(3), options which must be stated in the agreement. All such agreements must provide in 12-point boldface type immediately above the space for the parties' signatures that agreement to arbitrate is not a prerequisite to the receipt of health care. M.C.L. §§ 600.5041(5), 600.5042(4); M.S.A. §§ 27A.5041(5), 27A.5042(4).

For those who have elected arbitration, the act requires a three-member panel composed of an attorney, who shall be chairperson, a physician, preferably from the respondent's medical specialty, and a person who is not a licensee of the health care profession involved, a lawyer, or a representative of a hospital or an insurance company. M.C.L. § 600.5044(2); M.S.A. § 27A.5044(2). Where the claim is against a hospital only, a hospital administrator may be substituted for the physician. If the claim is against a health-care provider other than a physician, a licensee of the health-care profession involved shall be substituted.

Defendants Detroit Memorial Hospital and Dr. Bloom appeal from the holding that the presence of the medical member unconstitutionally created a biased panel . . . .

[W]e have concluded that the composition of the arbitration panel does not offend guarantees of due process.

* * * *

No showing of actual bias on the part of a particular arbitration panel is claimed, the parties having appealed from motions for accelerated judgment and no arbitration panel having been convened. That does not prevent a party from claiming that the risk of actual bias is too high to be constitutionally tolerable. "[O]ur system of law has always endeavored to prevent even the probability of unfairness." *Murchison*, supra, 349 U.S. 136. "In pursuit of this end, various situations have been identified in which experience teaches that the probability of actual bias on the part of the judge or decisionmaker is too high to be constitutionally tolerable." *Withrow*, supra, 421 U.S. 47. Included in those situations is that of a decisionmaker who has a direct or substantial pecuniary interest in the outcome of the controversy. E.g., Gibson v. Berryhill, 411 U.S. 564 (1973); see *Crampton*, 395 Mich. 351–55.

Such a pecuniary interest is claimed here—the decisionmaker's interest in lower malpractice insurance premiums will influence his decision towards reducing the number and size of malpractice awards. In their affidavits, the underwriters averred that physicians and hospital administrators have a vested interest in the medical malpractice claims made against others; the claims made do affect the rate of insurance premiums and the availability of insurance. Premium rates for all doctors, they averred, are generally determined by the number of all claims, settlements, and judgments against physicians and hospitals in Michigan. The effect of an arbitration award on insurance rates is thus said to be direct and substantial.

This situation is aggravated, contends plaintiff Jackson, by the composition of the advisory committee, which selects the pool of candidates from which all members of the arbitration panel are chosen. The statute provides:

> An arbitration advisory committee is created within the bureau of insurance and shall be appointed by the commission and shall consist of 18 members. One-half of the advisory committee shall be broadly composed of licensed physicians and other health care providers, licensed hospital or institutional health care providers, malpractice insurance carriers and licensed legal practitioners. One-half shall be broadly composed of nongovernmental, nonlawyer, nonhealth care provider, and noninsurance carrier persons. The committee may appoint 1 or more specialized subcommittees with the approval of the commissioner."

M.C.L. § 500.3054.

The medical part of the committee, which includes the malpractice insurance carriers and health-care providers, has a direct interest in reducing the number and size of malpractice awards. There is a substantial possibility, plaintiff Jackson insists, that they will select candidates who are similarly inclined.

All that has been shown here with any degree of certainty is that there is a relationship between the number and size of malpractice awards on the one hand, and the cost and availability of malpractice insurance on the other. This may be taken for granted. It may also be assumed that, because physicians and hospital administrators are concerned with the cost and availability of malpractice insurance, they are members of a class which is affected by the decision in a case between other parties. More than that must be shown, however, to make out a case which offends due process.

* * * *

In the present case . . . it has not been demonstrated that the medical members of these panels have a direct pecuniary interest or that their decision may have any substantial effect on the availability of insurance or insurance premiums. We have been shown no grounds sufficient for us to conclude that these decisionmakers will not act with honesty and integrity. We look for a pecuniary interest which creates a probability of unfairness, a risk of actual bias which is too high to be constitutionally tolerable. It has not been shown here.

* * * *

We do not believe that the medical members of these panels are so identified and aligned with respondents in malpractice cases that they may be expected to favor the respondents. Physicians and other health professionals are trained in the medical arts and are oath-bound to treat the ill. Hospital administrators are trained in the proper functioning of hospitals. Neither physicians nor hospital administrators have professional interests that are adverse to patients or even malpractice claimants on a consistent, daily basis. Any identity of interest with respondents is not so strong as to create a subliminal bias for one side and against the other.

* * * *

Plaintiffs next argue that the arbitration agreement waives constitutional rights to a jury trial and access to a court. Because these fundamental rights are waived, they say, the burden should rest with the defendants to show a valid contract, which they can only do by showing that the waiver was made voluntarily, knowingly, and intelligently. The burden of showing a voluntary waiver is not an easy one, argue plaintiffs, because the arbitration agreement was offered at the time of admission to the hospital in an atmosphere infected with implicit coercion. Additionally, plaintiffs argue that a knowing and intelligent waiver will not be easily shown because the defendants are chargeable with constructive fraud. Constructive fraud is said to arise out of the agreement's failure to highlight the fact of waiver, failure to disclose the composition of the arbitration panel (even though this information is contained in an informational booklet accompanying the agreement), and failure to disclose the attitudes of physicians in general, that they and hospital administrators may be biased and the reasonable probability that insurance rates are affected by awards.

* * * *

Answering the merits of plaintiffs' questions, defendants contend that arbitration is a matter of contract and that one who signs a written agreement is presumed to understand it. The act presumes a conforming agreement to be valid. Therefore, the burden of disproving this arbitration agreement rests with plaintiffs. Moreover, say defendants, the burden of establishing a constitutional violation rests with the party asserting it. The arbitration agreement and informational booklet reasonably indicated that arbitration was an exclusive alternative to trial by jury. Plaintiffs expressly waived their rights to trial by jury. Arbitration is voluntary and not required, which the agreement plainly states in capital letters above the signature. The form of the agreement and the information booklet is strictly controlled and was approved by the Michigan Commissioner of Insurance.

Plaintiffs, contend defendants, have failed to demonstrate that they were coerced into signing the agreement. Answering the argument of constructive fraud, defendants say that the information booklet given to plaintiffs states that a doctor or hospital administrator serves on the arbitration panel. A chart in the booklet also states that a court case is heard by a judge and jury while an arbitration case is heard by the three-member panel.

We reject plaintiffs' allocation of the burden of proof to defendants. The burden of avoiding these arbitration agreements, as with other contracts, rests with those who would avoid them . . . .

The burden of showing some ground for rescinding or invalidating a contract is not altered merely because the contract entails eschewal of constitutional rights. Plaintiffs' allegations of coercion, like other contract defenses of mistake, duress, and fraud, must be proven by the party seeking to avoid the contract on such grounds.

Plaintiff Jackson contends that the arbitration agreement is a contract of adhesion, the terms of which exceeded her reasonable expectations. She claims that by not stating explicitly that court access with the right to jury trial was waived, this fact was in effect concealed and hence the contract is unconscionable.

Contracts of adhesion are characterized by standardized forms prepared by one party which are offered for rejection or acceptance without opportunity for bargaining and under the circumstances that the second party cannot obtain the desired product or service except by acquiescing in the form agreement. Regardless of any possible perception among patients that the provision of optimal medical care is conditioned on their signing the arbitration agreement, we believe that the sixty-day rescission period, of which patients must be informed, fully protects those who sign the agreement. The patients' ability to rescind the agreement after leaving the hospital allows them to obtain the desired service without binding them to its terms. As a result, the agreement cannot be considered a contract of adhesion.

We also reject plaintiff's claim that the arbitration agreement is unconscionable. According to the record before us, the arbitration agreement signed by plaintiff Jackson is six paragraphs long. The first sentence of the first paragraph begins, "I understand that this hospital and I by signing this document agree to arbitrate any claims or disputes." The first two sentences of the second paragraph state:

> I understand that Michigan Law gives me the choice of trial by judge or jury or of arbitration. I understand that arbitration is a procedure by which a panel that is either mutually agreed upon or appointed decides the dispute rather than a judge or jury.

This was not a long contract covering different terms, only one of which, obscured among many paragraphs, concerned arbitration. Arbitration was the essential and singular nature of the agreement. We do not believe that an ordinary person signing this agreement to arbitrate would reasonably expect a jury trial. We also reject plaintiffs' argument that the agreement is unconscionable for failure to highlight these terms.

Finally, both plaintiffs ask that we find constructive fraud and hold that the agreements are unconscionable because of failure of the contracts to disclose the composition of the panel, the attitudes of physicians, the fact that the medical member of the panel may be intrinsically biased against plaintiffs, and the reasonable probability that malpractice rates are affected by awards in medical malpractice cases.

We decline. We do not believe that the agreements are

unconscionable for failing to include plaintiffs' recommendations. Nor do we believe that defendants have breached a legal or equitable duty which has had the effect of deceiving plaintiffs, nor have defendants received an unmerited benefit.

* * * *

NOTES

1. *Broemmer* and *Morris* are factually distinguishable in key respects. How? Are these differences enough to change their results?

2. Does the Michigan statute pass muster under federal preemption principles?

3. Jury waivers, according to the cases, have to be "knowing." Does such a showing depend on the sophistication, or the lack of sophistication, of the affected party? Is the test the same for "waiver" of the right to go to court under a pre-dispute arbitral agreement? Are adults, who are not under legal incapacity, considered to understand what they sign, at least absent effort to be misled? Are parties expected to read form agreements carefully, if at all? See discussion and citations in the Note on page 18 *supra*.

§ 4.05 POSSIBLE PROTECTIONS FOR THOSE OBLIGATED TO ARBITRATE STATUTORY CLAIMS

Cole v. Burns International Security Services

United States Court of Appeals, District of Columbia Circuit, 1997.
105 F.3d 1465.

- EDWARDS, J.

I. Summary of Opinion

This case raises important issues regarding whether and to what extent a person can be required, *as a condition of employment*, to (1) waive all rights to a trial by jury in a court of competent jurisdiction with respect to any dispute relating to recruitment, employment, or termination, including claims involving laws against discrimination, and (2) sign an agreement providing that, at the employer's option, any such employment disputes must be arbitrated. At its core, this appeal challenges the enforceability of conditions of employment requiring individuals to arbitrate claims resting on statutory rights. The issues at hand bring into focus the seminal decision of *Gilmer v. Interstate/Johnson Lane Corp.*, 500 U.S. 20 (1991), and call into question the limits of the Supreme Court's holdings in that case.

In this case, the appellant, Clinton Cole, seeks to overturn an order of the District Court dismissing his complaint under Title VII of the Civil Rights Act of 1964, as amended, and compelling arbitration of his disputes with Burns International Security Services ("Burns" or "Burns Security"). Although Cole seemingly raised a viable action under Title VII, the District Court held that his statutory claims of employment discrimination should be dismissed pursuant to the Federal Arbitration Act ("FAA" or "Act").

* * * *

We note that this case raises an issue not directly presented in *Gilmer* or any other Supreme Court case to date: can an employer require an employee to arbitrate all disputes and also require the employee to pay all or part of the arbitrators' fees? We hold that it cannot. In *Gilmer* and other securities industry cases, the employers routinely paid *all* arbitrators' fees, so the matter was not in dispute. However, there is no reason to think that the Court would have approved a program of mandatory arbitration of statutory claims in *Gilmer* in the absence of employer agreement to pay arbitrators' fees. Because public law confers both substantive rights and a reasonable right of access to a neutral forum in which those rights can be vindicated, we find that employees cannot be *required* to pay for the services of a "judge" in order to pursue their statutory rights. In this case, the parties' contract does not address explicitly the payment of the arbitrators' fees; however, because ambiguity in a contract should be resolved against the drafter—here, the employer—and ambiguity should be resolved in favor of a legal construction of the parties' agreement, we interpret the arbitration agreement at issue as requiring Burns to pay all arbitrators' fees associated with the resolution of Cole's claims. So construed, the contract is valid.

Cole has also argued that the arbitration agreement should not be enforced because the arbitrator's rulings, even as to the meaning of public law under Title VII, will not be subject to judicial review. Cole is wrong on this point. The nearly unlimited deference paid to arbitration awards in the context of collective bargaining is not required, and not appropriate, in the context of employees' statutory claims. In this context, the Supreme Court has assumed that arbitration awards are subject to judicial review sufficiently rigorous to ensure compliance with statutory law. Indeed, Burns has conceded such review in this case. Because the courts will always remain available to ensure that arbitrators properly interpret the dictates of public law, an agreement to arbitrate statutory claims of discrimination is not unconscionable or otherwise unenforceable.

II. Background

Clinton Cole used to work as a security guard at Union Station in Washington, D.C. for a company called LaSalle and Partners ("LaSalle"). In 1991, Burns Security took over LaSalle's contract to provide security at Union Station and required all LaSalle employees to sign a "Pre-Dispute Resolution Agreement" in order to obtain employment with Burns. The Pre-Dispute Resolution Agreement ("agreement" or "contract"), in relevant part, provides:

> In consideration of the Company employing you, you and the Company each agrees that, in the event either party (or its representatives, successors or assigns) brings an action in a court of competent jurisdiction relating to your recruitment, employment with, or termination of employment from the Company, the plaintiff in such action agrees to waive his, her or its right to a trial by jury, and further agrees that no demand, request or motion will be made for trial by jury.
>
> In consideration of the Company employing you, you further agree that, in the event that you

> seek relief in a court of competent jurisdiction for a dispute covered by this Agreement, the Company may, at any time within 60 days of the service of your complaint upon the Company, at its option, require all or part of the dispute to be arbitrated by one arbitrator in accordance with the rules of the American Arbitration Association. You agree that the option to arbitrate any dispute is governed by the Federal Arbitration Act, and fully enforceable. You understand and agree that, if the Company exercises its option, any dispute arbitrated will be heard solely by the arbitrator, and not by a court.
>
> This pre-dispute resolution agreement will cover all matters directly or indirectly related to your recruitment, employment or termination of employment by the Company; including, but not limited to, claims involving laws against discrimination whether brought under federal and/or state law, and/or claims involving co-employees but excluding Worker's Compensation Claims.
>
> The right to a trial, and to a trial by jury, is of value.
>
> YOU MAY WISH TO CONSULT AN ATTORNEY PRIOR TO SIGNING THIS AGREEMENT. IF SO, TAKE A COPY OF THIS FORM WITH YOU. HOWEVER, YOU WILL NOT BE OFFERED EMPLOYMENT UNTIL THIS FORM IS SIGNED AND RETURNED BY YOU.

In October 1993, Burns Security fired Cole. After filing charges with the Equal Employment Opportunity Commission, Cole filed the instant complaint in the United States District Court for the District of Columbia, alleging racial discrimination, harassment based on race, retaliation for his writing a letter of complaint regarding sexual harassment of a subordinate employee by another supervisor at Burns, and intentional infliction of emotional distress. Burns moved to compel arbitration of the dispute and to dismiss Cole's complaint pursuant to the terms of the contract.

The District Court found that the arbitration agreement clearly covered Cole's claims. The court also rejected Cole's suggestions (1) that the Pre-Dispute Resolution Agreement was excluded from coverage under the Federal Arbitration Act under 9 U.S.C. § 1, and (2) that the agreement was an unenforceable and unconscionable contract of adhesion. As a result, the trial court granted Burns Security's motion to compel arbitration and dismissed Cole's complaint.

III. Discussion

* * * *

In the context of collective bargaining arbitration, there are also unique protections for both parties built into the arbitration process that minimize the risk of unfairness or error by the arbitrator. For example, because both unions and employers are repeat customers of arbitration and have a hand in selecting the arbitrator to hear their disputes, arbitrators who regularly favor one side or the other will not be hired again. As a result, arbitrators have a strong personal interest in crafting awards that will be respected as fair by both parties regardless of who wins or loses the particular dispute.

Additionally, although arbitration awards are final as far as the courts are concerned, they need not be final for the parties. Because the parties to a collective bargaining agreement maintain an ongoing relationship, they remain free to rewrite their contract and thereby "correct" what they perceive to be "errors" on the part of the arbitrator.

Whereas an arbitrator serves as an agent or "alter ego" for the parties to a collective bargaining agreement, an arbitrator who resolves statutory claims serves simply as a private judge. See Shell, 68 TEX. L. REV. at 512. Yet, unlike a judge, an arbitrator is neither publicly chosen nor publicly accountable.

Arbitration of public law issues is also troubling, on a less abstract level, because the structural protections inherent in the collective bargaining context are not duplicated in cases involving mandatory arbitration of individual statutory claims. Unlike the labor case, in which both union and employer are regular participants in the arbitration process, only the employer is a repeat player in cases involving individual statutory claims. As a result, the employer gains some advantage in having superior knowledge with respect to selection of an arbitrator.

* * * *

Additionally, while a lack of public disclosure of arbitration awards is acceptable in the collective bargaining context, because both employers and unions monitor such decisions and the awards rarely involve issues of concern to persons other than the parties, in the context of individual statutory claims, a lack of public disclosure may systematically favor companies over individuals. Judicial decisions create binding precedent that prevents a recurrence of statutory violations; it is not clear that arbitral decisions have any such preventive effect. The unavailability of arbitral decisions also may prevent potential plaintiffs from locating the information necessary to build a case of intentional misconduct or to establish a pattern or practice of discrimination by particular companies.

Furthermore, as in the instant case, mandatory arbitration agreements in individual employees' contracts often are presented on a take-it-or-leave-it basis; there is no union to negotiate the terms of the arbitration arrangement. Thus, employers are free to structure arbitration in ways that may systematically disadvantage employees.

* * * *

Finally, the competence of arbitrators to analyze and decide purely legal issues in connection with statutory claims has been questioned. Many arbitrators are not lawyers, and they have not traditionally engaged in the same kind of legal analysis performed by judges.

For instance, arbitrators often cite to and rely extensively on treatises . . . . A court is unlikely to rely on a treatise-even . . . a widely respected one. Similarly, arbitrators frequently rely on leading cases on the subject of employment discrimination, such as *Texas Department of Community Affairs v. Burdine (Burdine)*, and *McDonnell Douglas Corp. v. Green (McDonnell Douglas)*, without citing to subsequent lower courts or less publicized cases. This means that an arbitrator's decision may be based on broad stroke principles to the exclusion of cases more analogous to the claim being decided.

Nor do arbitrators always analyze an intentional discrimination case within the judicially accepted three-prong framework articulated by the Supreme Court in *Burdine* and *McDonnell Douglas*.

* * * *

Nonetheless, the Supreme Court now has made clear that, as a general rule, statutory claims are fully subject to binding arbitration, at least outside of the context of collective bargaining. *See Gilmer*, 500 U.S. at 26, 34–35, (collecting cases and distinguishing *Gardner-Denver*). Rejecting "generalized attacks on arbitration" of statutory claims as based " 'on suspicion of arbitration as a method of weakening the protections afforded in the substantive law to would-be complainants' " and " 'far out of step with [the] current strong endorsement' " of arbitration, id. at 30 (quoting Rodriguez de Quijas v. Shearson/American Express, Inc., 490 U.S. 477, 481 (1989)), the Court has emphasized that " '[b]y agreeing to arbitrate a statutory claim, a party does not forego the substantive rights afforded by the statute; it only submits to their resolution in an arbitral, rather than a judicial, forum.' " Id. at 26 (quoting Mitsubishi Motors Corp. v. Soler Chrysler-Plymouth, Inc., 473 U.S. 614, 628, (1985)). The Court has stressed that " '[s]o long as the prospective litigant effectively may vindicate [his or her] statutory cause of action in the arbitral forum, the statute will continue to serve both its remedial and deterrent function.' " Id. at 28 (quoting *Mitsubishi*, 473 U.S. at 637).

* * * *

Despite the Supreme Court's recent endorsement of arbitration of statutory claims, however, concerns remain regarding arbitration's ability to live up to the Court's expectations, particularly in cases involving mandatory arbitration of statutory claims which is imposed as a condition of employment. In fact, the Equal Employment Opportunity Commission has taken the position that such agreements are unenforceable in a number of cases being litigated around the country.

* * * *

The National Labor Relations Board also has expressed some concerns. At one point, officials with the Board took the position that it is an unfair labor practice to require an employee to agree to mandatory arbitration of all claims.

2. *The Validity of the Agreement to Arbitrate in This Case.*

We start with the assumption that, under *Gilmer,* a person may agree to arbitrate statutory claims. We do not assume, however, that an employer has a free hand in requiring arbitration as a condition of employment.

Fortunately, in the instant case, the parties largely agree on the meaning of their arbitration agreement. Each side concurs in the following propositions:

> (1) The agreement allows the employer the option of forcing statutory claims into arbitration for the resolution of public law issues;
>
> (2) The agreement's waiver of a jury trial is absolute, i.e., it operates even if the employer does not seek arbitration;
>
> (3) The agreement does not affect an employee's ability to seek relief from the Equal Employment Opportunity Commission;
>
> (4) The arbitrator is fully bound to apply Title VII and other applicable public law, both as to substance and remedy, in accordance with statutory requirements and prevailing judicial interpretation; and
>
> (5) The agreement provides for appointment of a neutral arbitrator through the American Arbitration Association ("AAA") and for the conduct of the arbitration proceeding in accordance with AAA rules.

The provisions of the AAA [Employment] Rules immediately relevant to our analysis are as follows:

> (1) Rule 7: The arbitrator has "the authority to order such discovery, by way of deposition, interrogatory, document production, or otherwise, as the arbitrator considers necessary to a full and fair exploration of the issues in dispute;"
>
> (2) Rule 32(b): "The award shall be in writing and shall be signed by a majority of the arbitrators and shall provide the written reasons for the award unless the parties agree

> otherwise;"
>
> (3) Rule 32(c): "The arbitrator may grant any remedy or relief that the arbitrator deems just and equitable, including, but not limited to, any remedy or relief that would have been available to the parties had the matter been heard in court;"
>
> (4) Rule 35: A filing fee of $500 must be advanced by the initiating party, subject to final apportionment by the arbitrator in the award, and an administrative fee of $150 per hearing day must be paid by each party, but the AAA "may, in the event of extreme hardship on any party, defer or reduce the administrative fees;"
>
> (5) Rule 36: The expenses of the arbitration, including required travel and other expenses of the arbitrator, AAA representatives, and witnesses, will be shared equally by the parties, unless the parties agree otherwise or the arbitrator directs otherwise in the award;
>
> (6) Rule 37: The parties are to agree with the arbitrator on appropriate compensation for the arbitrator's work, but if the parties cannot agree with the arbitrator on a rate of compensation, the arbitrator's fee will be set by AAA. Payment of the arbitrator's fee is made through AAA, not directly between the parties and the arbitrator.

The parties stipulated that arbitrators' fees are commonly $500 to $1,000 *or more* per day. Significantly, however, the AAA Rules do not prescribe any particular allocation of responsibility for the payment of the arbitrators' fees.

We believe that all of the factors addressed in *Gilmer* are satisfied here. In particular, we note that the arbitration arrangement (1) provides for neutral arbitrators, (2) provides for more than minimal discovery, (3) requires a written award, (4) provides for all of the types of relief that would otherwise be available in court, and (5) does not require employees to pay either unreasonable costs *or* any arbitrators' fees or expenses as a condition of access to the arbitration forum.

* * * *

3. *The Obligation to Pay Arbitrators' Fees*

Although we find that the disputed arbitration agreement is legally valid, there is one point that requires amplification. The arbitration agreement in this case presents an issue not raised by the agreement in *Gilmer*: Can an employer condition employment on acceptance of an arbitration agreement that requires the employee to submit his or her statutory claims to arbitration and then requires the employee to pay all or part of the arbitrators' fees? This was not an issue in *Gilmer* (and other like cases), because, under NYSE Rules and NASD Rules, it is standard practice in the securities industry for employers to pay all of the arbitrators' fees. Employees may be required to pay a filing fee, expenses, or an administrative fee, but these expenses are routinely waived in the event of financial hardship.

Thus, in *Gilmer*, the Supreme Court endorsed a system of arbitration in which employees are not required to pay for the arbitrator assigned to hear their statutory claims. There is no reason to think that the Court would have approved arbitration in the absence of this arrangement. Indeed, we are unaware of any situation in American jurisprudence in which a beneficiary of a federal statute has been required to pay for the services of the judge assigned to hear her or his case. Under *Gilmer*, arbitration is supposed to be a reasonable substitute for a judicial forum. Therefore, it would undermine Congress's intent to prevent employees who are seeking to vindicate statutory rights from gaining access to a judicial forum and then require them to pay for the services of an arbitrator when they would never be required to pay for a judge in court.

There is no doubt that parties appearing in federal court may be required to assume the cost of filing fees and other administrative expenses, so any reasonable costs of this sort that accompany arbitration are not problematic. However, if an employee like Cole is required to pay arbitrators' fees ranging from $500 to $1,000 per day *or more*, in addition to administrative and attorney's fees, is it likely that he will be able to pursue his statutory claims? We think not.

* * * *

4. *Judicial Review*

The final issue in this case concerns the scope of judicial review of arbitral awards in cases of this sort, where an employee is compelled as a condition of employment to arbitrate statutory claims. Cole has argued that the arbitration agreement is unconscionable, because any arbitrator's rulings, even as to the meaning of public law under Title VII, will not be subject to judicial review. Cole is wrong on this point.

Judicial review of arbitration awards covering statutory claims is necessarily focused, but that does not mean that meaningful review is unavailable. The FAA itself recognizes a number of grounds on which arbitration awards may be vacated, including:

> (1) Where the award was procured by corruption, fraud, or undue means.
>
> (2) Where there was evident partiality or corruption in the arbitrators, or either of them.
>
> (3) Where the arbitrators were guilty of misconduct in refusing to postpone the hearing, upon sufficient cause shown, or in refusing to hear evidence pertinent and material to the controversy; or of any other misbehavior by which the rights of any party have been prejudiced.
>
> (4) Where the arbitrators exceeded their powers, or so imperfectly executed them that a mutual, final, and definite award upon the subject matter submitted was not made.

9 U.S.C. § 10(a).

The grounds listed in the FAA, however, are not exclusive. Indeed, even in the context of arbitration in collective bargaining-where judicial review of arbitral awards is extremely limited-awards may be set aside if they are contrary to "some explicit public policy" that is "well defined and dominant" and ascertained "by reference to the laws and legal precedents." See United Paperworkers Int'l Union v. Misco, Inc., 484 U.S. 29, 43 (1987) (internal quotation omitted). There is no doubt that the scope of review of arbitration in cases involving mandatory arbitration of statutory claims is *at least* as great as the judicial review available in the context of collective bargaining.

The Supreme Court has also indicated that arbitration awards can be vacated if they are in "manifest disregard of the law." See First Options of Chicago, Inc. v. Kaplan, 514 U.S. 938 (1995) (citing Wilko v. Swan, 346 U.S. 427, 436–37 (1953), overruled on other grounds in

Rodriguez de Quijas v. Shearson/American Express, Inc., 490 U.S. 477 (1989)). Although this term has not been defined by the Court, and the circuits have adopted various formulations, we believe that this type of review must be defined by reference to the assumptions underlying the Court's endorsement of arbitration. As discussed above, the strict deference accorded to arbitration decisions in the collective bargaining arena may not be appropriate in statutory cases in which an employee has been forced to resort to arbitration as a condition of employment. Rather, in this statutory context, the "manifest disregard of law" standard must be defined in light of the bases underlying the Court's decisions in *Gilmer*-type cases.

Two assumptions have been central to the Court's decisions in this area. First, the Court has insisted that, " '[b]y agreeing to arbitrate a statutory claim, a party does not forego the substantive rights afforded by the statute; it only submits to their resolution in an arbitral, rather than a judicial, forum.' " *Gilmer*, 500 U.S. at 26 (quoting *Mitsubishi*, 473 U.S. at 628); see also *McMahon*, 482 U.S. at 229–30. Second, the Court has stated repeatedly that, " 'although judicial scrutiny of arbitration awards necessarily is limited, such review is sufficient to ensure that arbitrators comply with the requirements of the statute' at issue." *Gilmer*, 500 U.S. at 32 n.4, (quoting *McMahon*, 482 U.S. at 232). These twin assumptions regarding the arbitration of statutory claims are valid only if judicial review under the "manifest disregard of the law" standard is sufficiently rigorous to ensure that arbitrators have properly interpreted and applied statutory law.

The value and finality of an employer's arbitration system will not be undermined by focused review of arbitral legal determinations. Most employment discrimination claims are entirely factual in nature and involve well-settled legal principles. As a result, in the vast majority of cases, judicial review of legal determinations to ensure compliance with public law should have no adverse impact on the arbitration process. Nonetheless, there will be some cases in which novel or difficult legal issues are presented demanding judicial judgment. In such cases, the courts are empowered to review an arbitrator's award to ensure that its resolution of public law issues is correct.

* * * *

IV. Conclusion

We acknowledge the concerns that have been raised regarding arbitration's ability to vindicate employees' statutory rights. However, for all of arbitration's shortcomings, the process, if fairly conducted, is not necessarily inferior to litigation as a mechanism for the resolution of employment disputes.

* * * *

As a result, it is perhaps misguided to mourn the Supreme Court's endorsement of the arbitration of complex and important public law claims. Arbitrators, however, must be mindful that the Court's endorsement has been based on the assumption that "competent, conscientious, and impartial arbitrators" will be available to decide these cases. *Mitsubishi Motors*, 473 U.S. at 634. Therefore, arbitrators must step up to the challenges presented by the resolution of statutory issues and must be vigilant to protect the important rights embodied in the laws entrusted to their care.

* * * *

NOTE

1. When this text, in Chapter 6, turns to the subject of review of awards, it will be critical to see whether the various judicial pronouncements about requiring arbitral fealty to so-called "public" statutes are to be met in practice. To the extent "manifest disregard" requires deliberate departure from the law, that would appear unlikely, would it not?

Green Tree Financial Corp.-Alabama v. Randolph

Supreme Court of the United States, 2000.
531 U.S. 79.

- REHNQUIST, C.J.

* * * *

We now turn to the question whether Randolph's agreement to arbitrate is unenforceable because it says nothing about the costs of arbitration, and thus fails to provide her protection from potentially substantial costs of pursuing her federal statutory claims in the arbitral forum. Section 2 of the FAA provides that "[a] written provision in any maritime transaction or a contract evidencing a transaction involving commerce to settle by arbitration a controversy thereafter arising out of such contract . . . shall be valid, irrevocable, and enforceable, save upon such grounds as exist at law or in equity for the revocation of any contract." 9 U.S.C. § 2. In considering whether respondent's agreement to arbitrate is unenforceable, we are mindful of the FAA's purpose "to reverse the longstanding judicial hostility to arbitration agreements . . . and to place arbitration agreements upon the same footing as other contracts." Gilmer v. Interstate/Johnson Lane Corp., 500 U.S. 20, 24 (1991).

In light of that purpose, we have recognized that federal statutory claims can be appropriately resolved through arbitration, and we have enforced agreements to arbitrate that involve such claims. We have likewise rejected generalized attacks on arbitration that rest on "suspicion of arbitration as a method of weakening the protections afforded in the substantive law to would-be complainants." These cases demonstrate that even claims arising under a statute designed to further important social policies may be arbitrated because " 'so long as the prospective litigant effectively may vindicate [his or her] statutory cause of action in the arbitral forum,' " the statute serves its functions. See *Gilmer*, *supra*, at 28 (quoting *Mitsubishi*, supra, at 637).

In_determining whether statutory claims may be arbitrated, we first ask whether the parties agreed to submit their claims to arbitration, and then ask whether Congress has evinced an intention to preclude a waiver of judicial remedies for the statutory rights at issue. See *Gilmer*, supra, at 26; *Mitsubishi*, supra, at 628. In this case, it is undisputed that the parties agreed to arbitrate all claims relating to their contract, including claims involving statutory rights. Nor does Randolph contend that the [Truth In Lending Act] evinces an intention to preclude a waiver of judicial remedies. She contends instead that the arbitration agreement's silence with respect to costs and fees creates a "risk" that she will be required to bear prohibitive arbitration costs if she pursues her claims in an arbitral forum, and thereby forces her to forgo any claims she may have against petitioners. Therefore, she argues, she is unable to vindicate her statutory rights in arbitration.

It may well be that the existence of large arbitration costs could preclude a litigant such as Randolph from effectively vindicating her federal statutory rights in the arbitral forum. But the record does not show that Randolph will bear such costs if she goes to arbitration. Indeed, it contains hardly any information on the matter. As the Court of Appeals recognized, "we lack . . . information about how claimants fare under Green Tree's arbitration clause." 178 F.3d, at 1158. The record reveals only the arbitration agreement's silence on the subject, and that fact alone is plainly insufficient to render it unenforceable. The "risk" that Randolph will be saddled with prohibitive costs is too speculative to justify the invalidation of an arbitration agreement.

To invalidate the agreement on that basis would undermine the "liberal federal policy favoring arbitration agreements." *Moses H. Cone*, 460 U.S., at 24. It would also conflict with our prior holdings that the party resisting arbitration bears the burden of proving that the claims at issue are unsuitable for arbitration. See *Gilmer*, supra, at 26; *McMahon*, supra, at 227. We have held that the party seeking to avoid arbitration bears the burden of establishing that Congress intended to preclude arbitration of the statutory claims at issue. See *Gilmer*, supra; *McMahon*, supra. Similarly, we believe that where, as here, a party seeks to invalidate an arbitration agreement on the ground that arbitration would be prohibitively expensive, that party bears the burden of showing the likelihood of incurring such costs. Randolph did not meet that burden. How detailed the showing of prohibitive expense must be before the party seeking arbitration must come forward with contrary evidence is a matter we need not discuss; for in this case neither during discovery nor when the case was presented on the merits was there any timely showing at all on the point. The Court of Appeals therefore erred in deciding that the arbitration agreement's silence with respect to costs and fees rendered it unenforceable.

NOTES

1. How can one carry the burden of showing prohibitive arbitral costs other than by introducing fee schedules and the like? The Supreme Court says nothing about requiring the employer to pay arbitrator fees, does it? What about in a case like *Gilmer* involving a presumably highly paid claimant?

2. Where a party cannot prove that costs of arbitration will be excessive until after the proceedings are held, it would appear that the matter of excessive costs could be raised in a post-award challenge. Is that a sensible approach? What if the claimant wins? What if the final tally of a claimant's costs and expenses is based on post-award allocation by the arbitrator(s)?

Armendariz v. Foundation Health Psychcare Services, Inc.

Supreme Court of California, 2000.
24 Cal.4th 83.

- MOSK, J.

In this case, we consider a number of issues related to the validity of a mandatory employment arbitration agreement, i.e., an agreement by an employee to arbitrate wrongful termination or employment discrimination claims rather than filing suit in court, which an employer imposes on a prospective or current employee as a condition of employment. The employees in this case claim that employees may not be compelled to arbitrate antidiscrimination claims brought under the California Fair Employment and Housing Act (FEHA). We conclude that such claims are in fact arbitrable *if* the arbitration permits an employee to vindicate his or her statutory rights. As explained, in order for such vindication to occur, the arbitration must meet certain minimum requirements, including neutrality of the arbitrator, the provision of adequate discovery, a written decision that will permit a limited form of judicial review, and limitations on the costs of arbitration.

The employees further claim that several provisions of the arbitration agreement are unconscionable, both because they fail to meet these minimum requirements and because the arbitration agreement is not bilateral. We conclude that the agreement possesses a damages limitation that is contrary to public policy, and that it is unconscionably unilateral.

[T]he employees contend that the presence of these unconscionable provisions renders the entire arbitration agreement unenforceable. The employer argues that even if some of the provisions are unconscionable or contrary to public policy, the proper remedy is to strike or restrict those clauses, and to enforce the rest of the arbitration agreement. The trial court chose the employees' preferred solution of refusing to enforce the arbitration agreement, but the Court of Appeal sided with the employer and enforced the agreement minus the one provision it found unconscionable. We conclude, for reasons explained below, that the arbitration agreement is unenforceable and that therefore the Court of Appeal's judgment must be reversed.

I. Statement of Facts and Procedural Issues.

Marybeth Armendariz and Dolores Olague-Rodgers (hereafter the employees) filed a complaint for wrongful termination against their former employer, Foundation Health Psychcare Services, Inc. (hereafter the employer). The complaint and certain documents filed in support of the employer's petition to compel arbitration provide us with the basic factual background of this case. In July and August of 1995, the employer hired the employees in the "Provider Relations Group" and they were later given supervisory positions with annual salaries of $38,000. On June 20, 1996, they were informed that their positions were being eliminated and that they were being terminated. During their year of employment, they claim that their supervisors and coworkers engaged in sexually based harassment and discrimination. The employees alleged that they were "terminated . . . because of their perceived and/or actual sexual orientation (heterosexual)."

Both employees had filled out and signed employment application forms, which included an arbitration clause pertaining to any future claim of wrongful termination. Later, they executed a separate employment arbitration agreement, containing the same arbitration clause. The clause states in full: "I agree as a condition of my employment, that in the event my employment is terminated, and I contend that such termination was wrongful or otherwise in violation of the conditions of employment or was in violation of any express or implied condition, term or covenant of employment, whether founded in fact or in law, including but not limited to the covenant of good faith and fair dealing, or otherwise in violation of any of my rights, I and Employer agree to submit any such matter to binding arbitration. I and Employer further expressly agree that in any such arbitration, my exclusive remedies for violation of the terms, conditions or covenants of employment shall be limited to a sum equal to the wages I would have earned from the date of any discharge until the date of the arbitration award. I understand that I shall not be entitled to any other remedy, at law or in equity, including but not limited to reinstatement and/or injunctive relief."

The employees' complaint against the employer alleges a cause of action for violation of the FEHA and three additional causes of action for wrongful termination based on tort and contract theories of recovery. The complaint sought general damages, punitive damages, injunctive relief, and the recovery of attorney fees and costs of suit.

The employer countered by filing a motion for an order to compel arbitration. [T]he trial court denied the motion on the ground that the arbitration provision in question was an unconscionable contract. The trial court first found that the arbitration agreement was an "adhesion contract." It also found that several of the provisions of the contract are "so one-sided as to 'shock the conscience.' " In particular, it singled out the fact that only employees who file claims against an employer are required to arbitrate their claims, but not vice versa. Second, the agreement limits damages to backpay, precluding damages available for statutory antidiscrimination claims and tort damages, such as punitive damages. The trial court also mentioned the supposed lack of discovery under the arbitration agreement. It concluded: "Given the overall unfairness of the provision," this was not an appropriate case for striking the unlawful provisions of the arbitration agreement; instead it invalidated the entire agreement.

After the employer filed a timely appeal, the Court of Appeal reversed. The court concluded that the contract was indeed one of adhesion and that the damages provision was unconscionable and contrary to public policy. But for reasons elaborated below, the Court of Appeal held, contrary to the trial court, that the rest of the arbitration agreement should be enforced.

We granted review.

* * * *

The United States Supreme Court's dictum that a party, in agreeing to arbitrate a statutory claim, "does not forgo the substantive rights afforded by the statute [but] only submits to their resolution in an arbitral . . . forum" (*Mitsubishi Motors*, supra, 473 U.S. at p. 628) is as much prescriptive as it is descriptive. That is, it sets a standard by which arbitration agreements and practices are to be measured, and disallows forms of arbitration that in fact compel claimants to forfeit certain substantive statutory rights.

* * * *

Based on *Gilmer*, and on the basic principle of nonwaivability of statutory civil rights in the workplace, the *Cole* court formulated five minimum requirements for the lawful arbitration of such rights pursuant to a mandatory employment arbitration agreement. Such an arbitration agreement is lawful if it "(1) provides for neutral arbitrators, (2) provides for more than minimal discovery, (3) requires a written award, (4) provides for all of the types of relief that would otherwise be available in court, and (5) does not require employees to pay either unreasonable costs or any arbitrators' fees or expenses as a condition of access to the arbitration forum. Thus, an employee who is made to use arbitration as a condition of employment " 'effectively may vindicate [his or her] statutory cause of action in the arbitral forum.' " (*Cole*, supra, 105 F.3d at 1482, italics omitted.)

Except for the neutral arbitrator requirement, which we have held is essential to ensuring the integrity of the arbitration process (Graham v. Scissor-Tail, Inc. (1981) 28 Cal.3d 807, 825 (*Scissor-Tail*), and is not at issue in this case, the employees claim that the present arbitration agreement fails to measure up to the *Cole* requirements enumerated above. We consider below the validity of those requirements and whether they are met by the employer's arbitration agreement.

1. <u>Limitation of Remedies.</u>

The principle that an arbitration agreement may not limit statutorily imposed remedies such as punitive damages and attorney fees appears to be undisputed.

* * * *

We conclude this damages limitation is contrary to public policy and unlawful.

We are not faced in this case with a petition to confirm an arbitration award, and therefore have no occasion to articulate precisely what standard of judicial review is "sufficient to ensure that arbitrators comply with the requirements of [a] statute." (McMahon, supra, 482 U.S. at p. 232.). All we hold today is that in order for such judicial review to be successfully accomplished, an arbitrator in a FEHA case must issue a written arbitration decision that will reveal, however briefly, the essential findings and conclusions on which the award is based.

* * * *

4. <u>Employee Not to Pay Unreasonable Costs and Arbitration Fees.</u>

Accordingly, consistent with the majority of jurisdictions to consider this issue, we conclude that when an employer imposes mandatory arbitration as a condition of employment, the arbitration agreement or arbitration process cannot generally require the employee to bear any *type* of expense that the employee would not be required to bear if he or she were free to bring the action in court. This rule will ensure that employees bringing FEHA claims will not be deterred by costs greater than the usual costs incurred during litigation, costs that are essentially imposed on an employee by the employer.

E. *Severability of Unconscionable Provisions.*

The employees contend that the presence of various unconscionable provisions or provisions contrary to public policy leads to the conclusion that the arbitration agreement as a whole cannot be enforced. The employer contends that, insofar as there are unconscionable provisions, they should be severed and the rest of the agreement enforced.

* * * *

Two reasons for severing or restricting illegal terms rather than voiding the entire contract appear implicit in caselaw. The first is to prevent parties from gaining undeserved benefit or suffering undeserved detriment as a result of voiding the entire agreement—particularly when there has been full or partial performance of the contract. Second, more generally, the doctrine of severance attempts to conserve a contractual relationship if to do so would not be condoning an illegal scheme. The overarching inquiry is whether " 'the interests of justice . . . would be furthered' " by severance. Moreover, courts must have the *capacity* to cure the unlawful contract through severance or restriction of the offending clause, which, as discussed below, is not invariably the case.

* * * *

In this case, two factors weigh against severance of the unlawful provisions. First, the arbitration agreement contains more than one unlawful provision; it has both an unlawful damages provision and an unconscionably unilateral arbitration clause. Such multiple defects indicate a systematic effort to impose arbitration on an employee not simply as an alternative to litigation, but as an inferior forum that works to the employer's advantage. In other words, given the multiple unlawful provisions, the trial court did not abuse its discretion in concluding that the arbitration agreement is permeated by an unlawful purpose.

* * * *

Second, in the case of the agreement's lack of mutuality, such permeation is indicated by the fact that there is no single provision a court can strike or restrict in order to remove the unconscionable taint from the agreement. Rather, the court would have to, in effect, reform the contract, not through severance or restriction, but by augmenting it with additional terms. Because a court is unable to cure this unconscionability through severance or restriction and is not permitted to cure it through reformation and augmentation, it must void the entire agreement.

Moreover, whether an employer is willing, now that the employment relationship has ended, to allow the arbitration provision to be mutually applicable, or to encompass the full range of remedies, does not change the fact that the arbitration agreement as written is unconscionable and contrary to public policy. Such a willingness "can be seen, at most, as an offer to modify the contract; an offer that was never accepted. No existing rule of contract law permits a party to resuscitate a legally defective contract merely by offering to change it."

* * * *

- BROWN, J. (concurring, with whom CHIN, J., joins).

Although I agree with most of the majority's reasoning, I write separately on the issue of apportioning arbitral costs. The majority takes the simple approach: where the employer imposes mandatory arbitration and the employee asserts a statutory claim, the employer must bear all costs "unique to arbitration." Simplicity, however, is not a proxy for correctness. As explained below, I do not believe that the possible imposition of arbitration forum costs automatically undermines an employee's statutory rights. Accordingly, I see no reason to adopt the majority's preemptive approach. Instead, the issue of apportionment is better left to the arbitrator, and any problems with the arbitrator's decision should be resolved at the judicial review stage.

In adopting the bright-line approach advocated by *Cole v. Burns Intern. Security Services* (D.C. Cir. 1997) 105 F.3d 1465, 1484–85 (*Cole*), the majority argues that the mere risk that an employee may have to bear certain arbitral costs necessarily "chills the exercise" of her statutory rights. Thus, arbitration is not a reasonable substitute for a court if arbitral costs, such as the arbitrator's fees, may be imposed on the employee. (See *Cole*, supra, 105 F.3d at 1484.) The majority, however, assumes too much. "[A]rbitration is often far more affordable to plaintiffs and defendants alike than is pursuing a claim in court." (Rosenberg v. Merrill Lynch, Pierce, Fenner & Smith (1st Cir. 1999) 170 F.3d 1, 16 (*Rosenberg*); see also Koveleskie v. SBC Capital Markets, Inc. (7th Cir. 1999) 167 F.3d 361, 366 (*Koveleskie*)). Because employees may incur fewer costs and attorney fees in arbitration than in court, the potential imposition of arbitration forum costs does not automatically render the arbitral forum more expensive than—and therefore inferior to—the judicial forum. (See Arakawa v. Japan Network Group (S.D.N.Y. 1999) 56 F. Supp. 2d 349, 354 (*Arakawa*)).

The majority's approach also ignores the unique circumstances of each case. Not all arbitrations are costly, and not all employees are unable to afford the unique costs of arbitration. Thus, the imposition of some arbitral costs does not deter or discourage employees from pursuing their statutory claims in every case. (See, e.g., Williams v. Cigna Financial Advisors Inc. (5th Cir. 1999) 197 F.3d 752, 763–65 (*Williams*) [compelling arbitration because the employee did not show that he was unable to pay the arbitral costs or that these costs would deter him from pursuing his claims]; McCaskill v. SCI Management Corp. (N.D. Ill. June 22, 2000, No. 00C1543) 2000 WL 875396 at 3 (*McCaskill*) [compelling arbitration because there was no evidence that the costs of arbitration would be prohibitively expensive for the employee]; Cline v. H.E. Butt Grocery Co. (S.D. Tex. 1999) 79 F. Supp. 2d 730, 733 (*Cline*) [compelling arbitration because there was no evidence that the employee would have to pay any costs or that the employee could not afford to do so]). Indeed, the uniqueness of each case makes impossible for any court to "conclude that the payment of fees will constitute a barrier to the vindication of . . . statutory rights" without knowing the exact amount the employee must pay. (*Arakawa*, supra, 56 F. Supp. 2d at 355).

Accordingly, I would reject the majority's approach and follow the approach suggested by courts in several other jurisdictions. As long as the mandatory arbitration agreement does not require the employee to front the arbitration forum costs or to pay a certain share of these costs, apportionment should be left to the arbitrator. When apportioning costs, the arbitrator should consider the magnitude of the costs unique to arbitration, the ability of the employee to pay a share of these costs, and the overall expense of the arbitration as compared to a court proceeding. Ultimately, any apportionment should ensure that the costs imposed on the employee, if known at the onset of litigation, would *not* have deterred her from enforcing her statutory rights or stopped her from effectively vindicating these rights.

If the employee feels that the arbitrator's apportionment of costs is unreasonable, then she can raise the issue during judicial review of the arbitration award. I believe such an approach is preferable because it accounts for the particular circumstances of each case without sacrificing the employee's statutory rights.

NOTE

1. Why worry about "mutuality" of arbitral remedy in the employment context? What type of claim is an employer likely to have against an at-will employee?

Floss v. Ryan's Family Steak Houses, Inc.

United States Court of Appeals, Sixth Circuit, 2000.
211 F.3d 306.

- GWIN, DISTRICT JUDGE.

With these appeals, consolidated for purposes of decision, the Court reviews whether employees effectively waived their rights to bring actions in federal court under the Americans with Disabilities Act, 42 U.S.C. § 12101, *et seq.* ("ADA"), and the Fair Labor Standards Act, 29 U.S.C. § 201, *et seq.* ("FLSA"). At the district court, the plaintiffs attempted to sue their former employer, Ryan's Family Steak Houses, Inc. ("Ryan's"). However, when applying for employment at Ryan's, both plaintiffs had signed a form indicating they would arbitrate all employment-related disputes. In both cases, Ryan's filed a motion to compel arbitration.

* * * *

In support of its argument that the plaintiffs agreed to waive their right to bring an action in federal court and instead agreed to arbitrate all employment disputes, Ryan's relies upon a document identified as the "Job Applicant Agreement to Arbitration of Employment-Related Disputes." Ryan's includes this purported agreement in its employment application packet. Only those applicants who sign the agreement are considered for employment at Ryan's. Both Daniels and Floss acknowledge signing the agreement.

The employee's agreement to arbitrate is not with Ryan's. Instead, the agreement runs between the employee and a third-party arbitration services provider, Employment Dispute Services, Inc. ("EDSI"). In the agreement, EDSI agrees to provide an arbitration forum in exchange for the employee's agreement to submit any dispute with his potential employer to arbitration with EDSI. Although Ryan's is not explicitly identified as a party to the agreement, the agreement says the employee's potential employer is a third-party beneficiary of the employee's agreement to waive a judicial forum and arbitrate all employment-related disputes.

The agreement gives EDSI complete discretion over arbitration rules and procedures. The agreement says that all arbitration proceedings will be conducted under "EDSI Rules and Procedures." The agreement then gives EDSI the unlimited right to modify the rules without the employee's consent.

* * * *

Both Floss and Daniels argue that the specific arbitration forum provided by the current version of the EDSI Rules and Procedures does not allow them to effectively vindicate their claims under the FLSA and the ADA. They say the procedures allow for the appointment of a biased and incompetent panel of arbitrators, as well as unduly limit the participants' discovery opportunities.

We have serious reservations as to whether the arbitral forum provided under the current version of the EDSI Rules and Procedures is suitable for the resolution of statutory claims. Specifically, the neutrality of the forum is far from clear in light of the uncertain relationship between Ryan's and EDSI. Floss and Daniels suggest that EDSI is biased in favor of Ryan's and other employers because it has a financial interest in maintaining its arbitration service contracts with employers. Though the record does not clearly reflect whether EDSI, in contrast to the American Arbitration Association, operates on a for-profit basis, the potential for bias exists. In light of EDSI's role in determining the pool of potential arbitrators, any such bias would render the arbitral forum fundamentally unfair. See Cole v. Burns Int'l Security Services, 105 F.3d 1465, 1482 (D.C. Cir. 1997) ("At a minimum, statutory rights include both a substantive protection and access to a neutral forum in which to enforce those protections.").

Moreover, EDSI's current rules require an employee to generally pay one-half of the arbitrators' fees as a condition of pursuing a dispute.

Such a fee structure could potentially prevent an employee from prosecuting a federal statutory claim against an employer. Recognizing as much, the District of Columbia Circuit has refused to countenance an employer's requirement that employees submit their disputes to arbitration as a condition of employment absent that employer's agreement to bear the full costs of the arbitrators' fees. See *Cole*, 105 F.3d at 1484–85.

* * * *

In the purported agreement at issue in this case, EDSI offered its promise to provide an arbitral forum as consideration for Floss and Daniels's promise to submit any dispute they may have with their employer to arbitration with EDSI. In ruling in favor of Daniels, the district court found that EDSI's promise did not create a binding obligation. We agree.

EDSI's promise to provide an arbitral forum is fatally indefinite. Though obligated to provide some type of arbitral forum, EDSI has unfettered discretion in choosing the nature of that forum. Specifically, EDSI has reserved the right to alter the applicable rules and procedures without any obligation to notify, much less receive consent from, Floss and Daniels. EDSI's right to choose the nature of its performance renders its promise illusory. As Professor Williston has explained:

> Where a promisor retains an unlimited right to decide later the nature or extent of his performance, the promise is too indefinite for legal enforcement. The unlimited choice in effect destroys the promise and makes it merely illusory.

1 Samuel Williston Contracts § 43, at 140 (3d ed. 1957).

DSI's illusory promise does not create a binding obligation. The purported arbitration agreement therefore lacks a mutuality of obligation. Without a mutuality of obligation, the agreement lacks consideration and, accordingly, does not constitute an enforceable arbitration agreement.

NOTES

1. Selection of a for-profit arbitral forum that has a dependence on a large employer for its existence poses real problems. *See* Lisa B. Bingham, *Control Over Dispute-System Design and Mandatory Commercial Arbitration*, 67 LAW & CONTEMP. PROBS. 221 (2004).

2. What about the discussion of "lack of mutuality" in *Floss*? Is that concept used the same way as in *Armendariz*, *supra* at page 293?

§ 4.06 THE DUE PROCESS PROTOCOL

We have seen judicial opinions requiring various safeguards in arbitral processes used to resolve statutory workplace claims. Several years ago, a Joint Task Force of the American Bar Association and the American Arbitration Association issued the "Due Process Protocol" to govern such arbitrations. Subsequently, the AAA heavily relied upon the Protocol in its Employment Arbitration Rules. The Protocol is reproduced below.

[A] Due Process Protocol for Mediation and Arbitration of Statutory Disputes Arising Out of the Employment Relationship

The following Protocol is offered by the undersigned individuals, members of the Task Force on Alternative Dispute Resolution in Employment, as a means of providing due process in the resolution by mediation and binding arbitration of employment disputes involving statutory rights. The signatories were designated by their respective organizations, but the Protocol reflects their personal views, and should not be construed as representing the policy of the designating organizations.

DUE PROCESS PROTOCOL

Genesis

This Task Force was created by individuals from diverse organizations involved in labor and employment law to examine questions of due process arising out of the use of mediation and arbitration for resolving employment disputes. In this Protocol we confine ourselves to statutory disputes.

The members of the Task Force felt that mediation and arbitration of statutory disputes conducted under proper due process safeguards should be encouraged in order to provide expeditious, accessible, inexpensive and fair private enforcement of statutory employment disputes for the 100 million members of the workforce who might not otherwise have ready, effective access to administrative or judicial relief. They also hope that such a system will serve to reduce the delays which now arise out of the huge backlog of cases pending before administrative agencies and courts and that it will help forestall an even greater number of such cases.

Pre- or Post-Dispute Arbitration

The Task Force recognizes the dilemma inherent in the timing of an agreement to mediate and/or arbitrate statutory disputes.

It did not achieve consensus on this difficult issue. The views in this spectrum are set forth randomly, as follows:

- Employers should be able to create mediation and/or arbitration systems to resolve statutory claims, but any agreement to mediate and/or arbitrate disputes should be informed, voluntary, and not a condition of initial or continued employment.
- Employers should have the right to insist on an agreement to mediate and/or arbitrate statutory disputes as a condition of initial or continued employment. Postponing such an agreement until a dispute actually arises, when there will likely exist a stronger predisposition to litigate, will result in very few agreements to mediate and/or arbitrate, thus negating the likelihood of effectively utilizing alternative dispute resolution and overcoming the problems of administrative and judicial delays which now plague the system.

- Employees should not be permitted to waive their right to judicial relief of statutory claims arising out of the employment relationship for any reason.
- Employers should be able to create mediation and/or arbitration systems to resolve statutory claims, but the decision to mediate and/or arbitrate individual cases should not be made until after the dispute arises.

The Task Force takes no position on the timing of agreements to mediate and/or arbitrate statutory employment disputes, though it agrees that such agreements be knowingly made. The focus of this Protocol is on standards of exemplary due process.

Right of Representation

1. ***Choice of Representative.*** Employees considering the use of or, in fact, utilizing mediation and/or arbitration procedures should have the right to be represented by a spokesperson of their own choosing. The mediation and arbitration procedure should so specify and should include reference to institutions which might offer assistance, such as bar associations, legal service associations, civil rights organizations, trade unions, etc.

2. ***Fees for Representation.*** The amount and method of payment for representation should be determined between the claimant and the representative. We recommend, however, a number of existing systems which provide employer reimbursement of at least a portion of the employee's attorney fees, especially for lower-paid employees. The arbitrator should have the authority to provide for fee reimbursement, in whole or in part, as part of the remedy in accordance with applicable law or in the interests of justice.

3. ***Access to Information.*** One of the advantages of arbitration is that there is usually less time and money spent in pre-trial discovery. Adequate but limited pre-trial discovery is to be encouraged and employees should have access to all information reasonably relevant to mediation and/or arbitration of their claims. The employees' representative should also have reasonable pre-hearing and hearing access to all such information and documentation.

Necessary pre-hearing depositions consistent with the expedited nature of arbitration should be available.

We also recommend that prior to selection of an arbitrator, each side should be provided with the names, addresses and phone numbers of the representatives of the parties in that arbitrator's six most recent cases to aid them in selection.

Mediator and Arbitrator Qualification

1. ***Roster Membership.*** Mediators and arbitrators selected for such cases should have skill in the conduct of hearings, knowledge of the statutory issues at stake in the dispute, and familiarity with the workplace and employment environment. The roster of available mediators and arbitrators should be established on a non-discriminatory basis, diverse by gender, ethnicity, background, experience, etc., to satisfy the parties that their interests and objectives will be respected and fully considered.

Our recommendation is for selection of impartial arbitrators and mediators. We recognize the right of employers and employees to jointly select as mediator and/or arbitrator one in whom both parties have requisite trust, even though not possessing the qualifications here recommended, as most promising to bring finality and to withstand judicial scrutiny.

The existing cadre of labor and employment mediators and arbitrators, some lawyers, some not, although skilled in conducting hearings and familiar with the employment milieu, is unlikely, without special training, to consistently possess knowledge of the statutory environment in which these disputes arise and of the characteristics of the nonunion workplace.

There is a manifest need for mediators and arbitrators with expertise in statutory requirements in the employment field who may, without special training, lack experience in the employment area and in the conduct of arbitration hearings and mediation sessions. Reexamination of rostering eligibility by designating agencies, such as the American Arbitration Association, may permit the expedited inclusion in the pool of this most valuable source of expertise.

The roster of arbitrators and mediators should contain representatives with all such skills in order to meet the diverse needs of this caseload.

Regardless of their prior experience, mediators and arbitrators on the roster must be independent of bias toward either party. They should reject cases if they believe the procedure lacks requisite due process.

2. ***Training.*** The creation of a roster containing the foregoing qualifications dictates the development of a training program to educate existing and potential labor and employment mediators and arbitrators as to the statutes, including substantive, procedural and remedial issues to be confronted and to train experts in the statutes as to employer procedures governing the employment relationship as well as due process and fairness in the conduct and control of arbitration hearings and mediation sessions.

Training in the statutory issues should be provided by the government agencies, bar associations, academic institutions, etc., administered perhaps by the designating agency, such as the AAA, at various locations throughout the country. Such training should be updated periodically and be required of all mediators and arbitrators. Training in the conduct of mediation and arbitration could be provided by a mentoring program with experienced panelists.

Successful completion of such training would be reflected in the resume or panel cards of the arbitrators supplied to the parties for their selection process.

3. ***Panel Selection.*** Upon request of the parties, the designating agency should utilize a list procedure such as that of the AAA or select a panel composed of an odd number of mediators and arbitrators from its roster or pool. The panel cards for such individuals should be submitted to the parties for their perusal prior to alternate striking of the names on the list, resulting in the designation of the remaining mediator and/or arbitrator.

The selection process could empower the designating agency to appoint a mediator and/or arbitrator if the striking procedure is unacceptable or unsuccessful. As noted above, subject to the consent of the parties, the designating agency should provide the names of the parties and their representatives in recent cases decided by the listed arbitrators.

4. ***Conflicts of Interest.*** The mediator and arbitrator for a case has a duty to disclose any relationship which might reasonably constitute or be perceived as a conflict of interest. The designated mediator and/or arbitrator should be required to sign an oath provided by the designating agency, if any, affirming the absence of such present or preexisting ties.

5. ***Authority of the Arbitrator.*** The arbitrator should be bound by applicable agreements, statutes, regulations and rules of procedure of the designating agency, including the authority to determine the time and place of the hearing, permit reasonable discovery, issue subpoenas, decide arbitrability issues, preserve order and privacy in the hearings, rule on evidentiary matters, determine the close of the hearing and procedures for post-hearing submissions, and issue an award resolving the submitted dispute.

The arbitrator should be empowered to award whatever relief would be available in court under the law. The arbitrator should issue an opinion and award setting forth a summary of the issues, including the type(s) of dispute(s), the damages and/or other relief requested and awarded, a statement of any other issues resolved, and a statement regarding the disposition of any statutory claim(s).

6. ***Compensation of the Mediator and Arbitrator.*** Impartiality is best assured by the parties sharing the fees and expenses of the mediator and arbitrator. In cases where the economic condition of a party does not permit equal sharing, the parties should make mutually acceptable arrangements to achieve that goal if at all possible. In the absence of such agreement, the arbitrator should determine allocation of fees. The designating agency, by negotiating the parties' share of costs and collecting such fees, might be able to reduce the bias potential of disparate contributions by forwarding payment to the mediator and/or arbitrator without disclosing the parties' share therein.

Scope of Review

The arbitrator's award should be final and binding and the scope of review should be limited.

NOTES

1. Under Article C-5 of the Protocol, the arbitrator is to comply with statute. Article D, however, provides that "the scope of review should be limited." Reconcilable?

2. Article C-5 of the Protocol, in keeping with various caselaw

discussion, provides that:

> The arbitrator should be bound by applicable agreements, statutes, regulations and rules of procedure of the designating agency, including the authority to determine the time and place of the hearing, permit reasonable discovery, issue subpoenas, decide arbitrability issues, preserve order and privacy in the hearings, rule on evidentiary matters, determine the close of the hearing and procedures for post-hearing submissions, and issue an award resolving the submitted dispute.
>
> The arbitrator should be empowered to award whatever relief would be available in court under the law. The arbitrator should issue an opinion and award setting forth a summary of the issues, including the type(s) of dispute(s), the damages and/or other relief requested and awarded, a statement of any other issues resolved, and a statement regarding the disposition of any statutory claim(s).

Is this sufficient to permit meaningful judicial review, particularly absent a full transcript of the hearings?

3. Should fee allocations by an arbitrator be based at all on the merits, or lack of merits, of the employee's claims?"

4. Unlike in *Cole*, the Protocol is not absolute about the employer having to pay arbitrator fees. The American Arbitration Association's Employment Arbitration Rules require the employer to pay those fees if the claim is brought under an "Employer Promulgated Plan." Unless otherwise agreed, all such cases are heard by one arbitrator. Where, however, the employee claim arises out of an "Individually Negotiated Employment Agreement," arbitrator fees are subject to allocation in the award. In such instance, the *claimant* must also pay an Initial Filing Fee which, for instance, would come to $2,600 in a case seeking between $75,000 and $150,000. The claimant also has the option to pay a lower initial filing fee with an added fee if the matter proceeds to actual hearings. Typically, employees with individual contracts are at the more highly paid executive level.

5. Under the federal discrimination statutes, a prevailing claimant

recovers reasonable attorney fees.

§ 4.07 WHO DECIDES THE ISSUE OF CONSCIONABILITY?

In all of the unconscionability cases we have seen thus far, the court decided that issue as part of the determination of whether there is a legally enforceable agreement to arbitrate. Many took this as axiomatic, but the United States Supreme Court has now created an exception that took many by surprise.

Rent-A-Center, West, Inc., v. Jackson

Supreme Court of the United States, 2010.
130 S. Ct. 2772 (2010).

- SCALIA, J.

We consider whether, under the Federal Arbitration Act (FAA or Act), 9 U.S.C. §§ 1–16, a district court may decide a claim that an arbitration agreement is unconscionable, where the agreement explicitly assigns that decision to the arbitrator.

On February 1, 2007, the respondent here, Antonio Jackson, filed an employment-discrimination suit under 42 U.S.C. § 1981, against his former employer in the United States District Court for the District of Nevada. The defendant and petitioner here, Rent-A-Center, West, Inc., filed a motion under the FAA to dismiss or stay the proceedings, 9 U.S.C. § 3, and to compel arbitration, § 4. Rent-A-Center argued that the Mutual Agreement to Arbitrate Claims (Agreement), which Jackson signed on February 24, 2003 as a condition of his employment there, precluded Jackson from pursuing his claims in court. The Agreement provided for arbitration of all "past, present or future" disputes arising out of Jackson's employment with Rent-A-Center, including "claims for discrimination" and "claims for violation of any federal . . . law." It also provided that "[t]he Arbitrator, and not any federal, state, or local court or agency, shall have exclusive authority to resolve any dispute relating to the interpretation, applicability, enforceability or formation of this Agreement including, but not limited to any claim that all or any part of this Agreement is void or voidable."

Jackson opposed the motion on the ground that "the arbitration agreement in question is clearly unenforceable in that it is unconscionable" under Nevada law. Rent-A-Center responded that Jackson's unconscionability claim was not properly before the court because Jackson had expressly agreed that the arbitrator would have exclusive authority to resolve any dispute about the enforceability of the Agreement. It also disputed the merits of Jackson's unconscionability claims.

The District Court granted Rent-A-Center's motion to dismiss the proceedings and to compel arbitration. The court found that the Agreement " 'clearly and unmistakenly [sic]' " gives the arbitrator exclusive authority to decide whether the Agreement is enforceable, and, because Jackson challenged the validity of the Agreement *as a whole*, the issue was for the arbitrator. The court noted that even if it were to examine the merits of Jackson's unconscionability claims, it would have rejected the claim that the agreement to split arbitration fees was substantively unconscionable under Nevada law. It did not address Jackson's procedural or other substantive unconscionability arguments.

Without oral argument, a divided panel of the Court of Appeals for the Ninth Circuit reversed in part, affirmed in part, and remanded. 581 F.3d 912 (2009). The court reversed on the question of who (the court or arbitrator) had the authority to decide whether the Agreement is enforceable. It noted that "Jackson does not dispute that the language of the Agreement clearly assigns the arbitrability determination to the arbitrator," but held that where "a party challenges an arbitration agreement as unconscionable, and thus asserts that he could not meaningfully assent to the agreement, the threshold question of unconscionability is for the court."

The FAA reflects the fundamental principle that arbitration is a matter of contract. Section 2, the "primary substantive provision of the Act," Moses H. Cone Memorial Hospital v. Mercury Constr. Corp., 460 U.S. 1, 24 (1983), provides:

> "A written provision in . . . a contract evidencing a transaction involving commerce to settle by arbitration a controversy thereafter arising out of such contract . . . shall be valid, irrevocable, and enforceable, save upon such grounds as exist at law or in equity for the revocation of any contract."

9 U.S.C. § 2.

The FAA thereby places arbitration agreements on an equal footing with other contracts, and requires courts to enforce them according to their terms, Volt Information Sciences, Inc. v. Board of Trustees of Leland Stanford Junior Univ., 489 U.S. 468, 478 (1989). Like other contracts, however, they may be invalidated by "generally applicable contract defenses, such as fraud, duress, or unconscionability." Doctor's Associates, Inc. v. Casarotto, 517 U.S. 681, 687 (1996).

The Act also establishes procedures by which federal courts implement § 2's substantive rule. Under § 3, a party may apply to a federal court for a stay of the trial of an action "upon any issue referable to arbitration under an agreement in writing for such arbitration." Under § 4, a party "aggrieved" by the failure of another party "to arbitrate under a written agreement for arbitration" may petition a federal court "for an order directing that such arbitration proceed in the manner provided for in such agreement." The court "shall" order arbitration "upon being satisfied that the making of the agreement for arbitration or the failure to comply therewith is not in issue." Ibid.

The Agreement here contains multiple "written provision[s]" to "settle by arbitration a controversy," § 2. Two are relevant to our discussion. First, the section titled "Claims Covered By The Agreement" provides for arbitration of all "past, present or future" disputes arising out of Jackson's employment with Rent-A-Center. Second, the section titled "Arbitration Procedures" provides that "[t]he Arbitrator . . . shall have exclusive authority to resolve any dispute relating to the . . . enforceability . . . of this Agreement including, but not limited to any claim that all or any part of this Agreement is void or voidable." The current "controversy" between the parties is whether the Agreement is unconscionable. It is the second provision, which delegates resolution of that controversy to the arbitrator, that Rent-A-Center seeks to enforce. Adopting the terminology used by the parties, we will refer to it as the delegation provision.

The delegation provision is an agreement to arbitrate threshold issues concerning the arbitration agreement. We have recognized that parties can agree to arbitrate "gateway" questions of "arbitrability," such as whether the parties have agreed to arbitrate or whether their agreement covers a particular controversy. See, e.g., *Howsam*, 537 U.S., at 83–85; Green Tree Financial Corp. v. Bazzle, 539 U.S. 444, 452 (2003) (plurality opinion). This line of cases merely reflects the principle that arbitration is a matter of contract.[6] See First Options of Chicago, Inc. v. Kaplan, 514 U.S. 938, 943 (1995). An agreement to arbitrate a gateway issue is simply an additional, antecedent agreement the party seeking arbitration asks the federal court to enforce, and the FAA operates on this additional arbitration agreement just as it does on any other. The additional agreement is valid under § 2 "save upon such grounds as exist at law or in equity for the revocation of any contract," and federal courts can enforce the agreement by staying federal litigation under § 3 and compelling arbitration under § 4. The question before us, then, is whether the delegation provision is valid under § 2.

There are two types of validity challenges under § 2: "One type challenges specifically the validity of the agreement to arbitrate," and "[t]he other challenges the contract as a whole, either on a ground that directly affects the entire agreement (e.g., the agreement was fraudulently induced), or on the ground that the illegality of one of the contract's provisions renders the whole contract invalid." In a line of cases neither party has asked us to overrule, we held that only the first type of challenge is relevant to a court's determination whether the arbitration agreement at issue is enforceable. See Prima Paint 388 U.S. 395 (1967). That is because § 2 states that a "written provision" "to settle by arbitration a controversy" is "valid, irrevocable, and

---

[6] There is one caveat. *First Options of Chicago, Inc. v. Kaplan,* 514 U.S. 938, 944 (1995), held that "[c]ourts should not assume that the parties agreed to arbitrate arbitrability unless there is 'clea[r] and unmistakabl[e]' evidence that they did so." The parties agree the heightened standard applies here. The District Court concluded the "Agreement to Arbitrate clearly and unmistakenly [sic] provides the arbitrator with the exclusive authority to decide whether the Agreement to Arbitrate is enforceable." The Ninth Circuit noted that Jackson did not dispute that the text of the Agreement was clear and unmistakable on this point. 581 F.3d 912, 917 (2009). He also does not dispute it here.

enforceable" *without mention* of the validity of the contract in which it is contained. Thus, a party's challenge to another provision of the contract, or to the contract as a whole, does not prevent a court from enforcing a specific agreement to arbitrate . . . .

But that agreements to arbitrate are severable does not mean that they are unassailable. If a party challenges the validity under § 2 of the precise agreement to arbitrate at issue, the federal court must consider the challenge before ordering compliance with that agreement under § 4. In *Prima Paint* for example, if the claim had been "fraud in the inducement of the arbitration clause itself," then the court would have considered it. 388 U.S., at 403–04. "To immunize an arbitration agreement from judicial challenge on the ground of fraud in the inducement would be to elevate it over other forms of contract," id., at 404, n. 12. In some cases the claimed basis of invalidity for the contract as a whole will be much easier to establish than the same basis as applied only to the severable agreement to arbitrate. Thus, in an employment contract many elements of alleged unconscionability applicable to the entire contract (outrageously low wages, for example) would not affect the agreement to arbitrate alone. But even where that is not the case-as in *Prima Paint* itself, where the alleged fraud that induced the whole contract equally induced the agreement to arbitrate which was part of that contract-we nonetheless require the basis of challenge to be directed specifically to the agreement to arbitrate before the court will intervene.

Here, the "written provision . . . to settle by arbitration a controversy," 9 U.S.C. § 2, that Rent-A-Center asks us to enforce is the delegation provision-the provision that gave the arbitrator "exclusive authority to resolve any dispute relating to the . . . enforceability . . . of this Agreement." The "remainder of the contract," is the rest of the agreement to arbitrate claims arising out of Jackson's employment with Rent-A-Center. To be sure this case differs from *Prima Paint*, *Buckeye*, and *Preston*, in that the arbitration provisions sought to be enforced in those cases were contained in contracts unrelated to arbitration . . . . In this case, the underlying contract is itself an arbitration agreement. But that makes no difference. Application of the severability rule does not depend on the substance of the remainder of the contract. Section 2 operates on the specific "written provision" to "settle by arbitration a controversy" that the party seeks to enforce. Accordingly, unless

Jackson challenged the delegation provision specifically, we must treat it as valid under § 2, and must enforce it under §§ 3 and 4, leaving any challenge to the validity of the Agreement as a whole for the arbitrator.

The District Court correctly concluded that Jackson challenged only the validity of the contract as a whole. Nowhere in his opposition to Rent-A-Center's motion to compel arbitration did he even mention the delegation provision . . . .

The arguments Jackson made in his response to Rent-A-Center's motion to compel arbitration support this conclusion. Jackson stated that "the *entire agreement* seems drawn to provide [Rent-A-Center] with undue advantages should an employment-related dispute arise." At one point, he argued that the limitations on discovery "further suppor[t] [his] contention that the *arbitration agreement as a whole* is substantively unconscionable." And before this Court, Jackson describes his challenge in the District Court as follows: He "opposed the motion to compel on the ground that the *entire arbitration agreement,* including the delegation clause, was unconscionable."

Jackson's other two substantive unconscionability arguments assailed arbitration procedures called for by the contract-the fee-splitting arrangement and the limitations on discovery-procedures that were to be used during arbitration under *both* the agreement to arbitrate employment-related disputes *and* the delegation provision. It may be that had Jackson challenged the delegation provision by arguing that these common procedures *as applied* to the delegation provision rendered *that provision* unconscionable, the challenge should have been considered by the court. To make such a claim based on the discovery procedures, Jackson would have had to argue that the limitation upon the number of depositions causes the arbitration of his claim that the Agreement is unenforceable to be unconscionable. That would be, of course, a much more difficult argument to sustain than the argument that the same limitation renders arbitration of his factbound employment-discrimination claim unconscionable. Likewise, the unfairness of the fee-splitting arrangement may be more difficult to establish for the arbitration of enforceability than for arbitration of more complex and fact-related aspects of the alleged employment discrimination. Jackson, however, did not make any arguments specific to the delegation provision; he argued that the fee-sharing and discovery procedures rendered the *entire* Agreement invalid.

- STEVENS, J. (dissenting, with whom GINSBURG, J., BREYER, J., and SOTOMAYOR, J., join).

* * * *

Neither petitioner nor respondent has urged us to adopt the rule the Court does today: Even when a litigant has specifically challenged the validity of an agreement to arbitrate he must submit that challenge *to the arbitrator* unless he has lodged an objection to the particular line in the agreement that purports to assign such challenges to the arbitrator-the so-called "delegation clause."

The Court asserts that its holding flows logically from *Prima Paint* 388 U.S. 395 (1967), in which the Court held that consideration of a contract revocation defense is generally a matter for the arbitrator, unless the defense is specifically directed at the arbitration clause. We have treated this holding as a severability rule: When a party challenges a contract, "but not specifically its arbitration provisions, those provisions are enforceable apart from the remainder of the contract." *Buckeye Check Cashing, Inc. v. Cardegna*, 546 U.S. 440, 446. The Court's decision today goes beyond *Prima Paint*. Its breezy assertion that the subject matter of the contract at issue—in this case, an arbitration agreement and nothing more—"makes no difference," is simply wrong. This written arbitration agreement is but one part of a broader employment agreement between the parties, just as the arbitration clause in *Prima Paint* was but one part of a broader contract for services between those parties. Thus, that the subject matter of the agreement is exclusively arbitration makes *all* the difference in the *Prima Paint* analysis.

Under the Federal Arbitration Act (FAA), parties generally have substantial leeway to define the terms and scope of their agreement to settle disputes in an arbitral forum. "[A]rbitration is," after all, "simply a matter of contract between the parties; it is a way to resolve those disputes-but only those disputes-that the parties have agreed to submit to arbitration." *First Options of Chicago, Inc. v. Kaplan,* 514 U.S. 938, 943 (1995). The FAA, therefore, envisions a limited role for courts asked to stay litigation and refer disputes to arbitration.

Certain issues—the kind that "contracting parties would likely have expected a court to have decided" —remain within the province of judicial review. Howsam v. Dean Witter Reynolds, Inc., 537 U.S. 79, 83, (2002); see also Green Tree Financial Corp. v. Bazzle, 539 U.S. 444, 452 (2003) (plurality opinion); AT & T Technologies, Inc. v. Communications Workers, 475 U.S. 643, 649 (1986). These issues are "gateway matter[s]" because they are necessary antecedents to enforcement of an arbitration agreement; they raise questions the parties "are not likely to have thought that they had agreed that an arbitrator would" decide. *Howsam*, 537 U.S., at 83. Quintessential gateway matters include "whether the parties have a valid arbitration agreement at all," *Bazzle*, 539 U.S., at 452 (plurality opinion); "whether the parties are bound by a given arbitration clause," *Howsam*, 537 U.S., at 84; and "whether an arbitration clause in a concededly binding contract applies to a particular type of controversy," ibid. It would be bizarre to send these types of gateway matters to the arbitrator as a matter of course, because they raise a " 'question of arbitrability.' " See, e.g., ibid.; *First Options*, 514 U.S., at 947.

"[Q]uestion[s] of arbitrability" thus include questions regarding the existence of a legally binding and valid arbitration agreement, as well as questions regarding the scope of a concededly binding arbitration agreement. In this case we are concerned with the first of these categories: Whether the parties have a valid arbitration agreement. This is an issue the FAA assigns to the courts. Section 2 of the FAA dictates that covered arbitration agreements "shall be valid, irrevocable, and enforceable, save upon such grounds as exist at law or in equity for the revocation of any contract." 9 U.S.C. § 2. "[S]uch grounds," which relate to contract validity and formation, include the claim at issue in this case, unconscionability.

Two different lines of cases bear on the issue of *who* decides a question of arbitrability respecting validity, such as whether an arbitration agreement is unconscionable. Although this issue, as a gateway matter, is typically for the court, we have explained that such an issue can be delegated to the arbitrator in some circumstances . . . .

In sum, questions related to the validity of an arbitration agreement are usually matters for a court to resolve before it refers a dispute to arbitration. But questions of arbitrability may go to the arbitrator in two instances: (1) when the parties have demonstrated, clearly and unmistakably, that it is their intent to do so; or (2) when the validity of an arbitration agreement depends exclusively on the validity of the substantive contract of which it is a part.

We might have resolved this case by simply applying the *First Options* rule: Does the arbitration agreement at issue "clearly and unmistakably" evince petitioner's and respondent's intent to submit questions of arbitrability to the arbitrator? The answer to that question is no. Respondent's claim that the arbitration agreement is unconscionable undermines any suggestion that he "clearly" and "unmistakably" assented to submit questions of arbitrability to the arbitrator . . . .

In other words, when a party raises a good-faith validity challenge to the arbitration agreement itself, that issue must be resolved before a court can say that he clearly and unmistakably intended to *arbitrate* that very validity question. This case well illustrates the point: If respondent's unconscionability claim is correct—*i.e.,* if the terms of the agreement are so one-sided and the process of its making so unfair—it would contravene the existence of clear and unmistakable assent to arbitrate the very question petitioner now seeks to arbitrate. Accordingly, it is necessary for the court to resolve the merits of respondent's unconscionability claim in order to decide whether the parties have a valid arbitration agreement under § 2. Otherwise, that section's preservation of revocation issues for the Court would be meaningless.

* * * *

Rather than apply *First Options*, the Court takes us down a different path, one neither briefed by the parties nor relied upon by the Court of Appeals. In applying *Prima Paint*, the Court has unwisely extended a "fantastic" and likely erroneous decision. 388 U.S., at 407 (Black, J., dissenting).

As explained at the outset, this case lies at a seeming crossroads in our arbitration jurisprudence. It implicates cases such as *First Options*, which address whether the parties intended to delegate questions of arbitrability, and also those cases, such as *Prima Paint*, which address the severability of a presumptively valid arbitration agreement from a potentially invalid contract. The question of "Who decides?"—arbitrator or court—animates both lines of cases, but they are driven by different concerns. In cases like *First Options*, we are concerned with the parties' intentions. In cases like *Prima Paint*, we are concerned with *how* the parties challenge the validity of the agreement.

Under the *Prima Paint* inquiry, recall, we consider whether the parties are actually challenging the validity of the arbitration agreement, or whether they are challenging, more generally, the contract within which an arbitration clause is nested. In the latter circumstance, we assume there is no infirmity per se with the arbitration agreement, i.e., there are no grounds for revocation of the arbitration agreement itself under § 2 of the FAA. Accordingly, we commit the parties' general contract dispute to the arbitrator, as agreed.

* * * *

Prima Paint and its progeny allow a court to pluck from a potentially invalid *contract* a potentially valid *arbitration agreement.* Today the Court adds a new layer of severability-something akin to Russian nesting dolls-into the mix: Courts may now pluck from a potentially invalid *arbitration agreement* even narrower provisions that refer particular arbitrability disputes to an arbitrator. See ante, at 2777–78. I do not think an agreement to arbitrate can ever manifest a clear and unmistakable intent to arbitrate its own validity. But even assuming otherwise, I certainly would not hold that the *Prima Paint* rule extends this far.

* * * *

The Court, however, reads the delegation clause as a distinct mini-arbitration agreement divisible from the contract in which it resides-which just so happens also to be an arbitration agreement. Ante, at 2777–78. Although the Court simply declares that it "makes no difference" that the underlying subject matter of the agreement is itself an arbitration agreement, Ante, at 2777–78, that proposition does not follow from—rather it is at odds with—*Prima Paint*'s severability rule.

* * * *

It would seem the Court reads *Prima Paint* to require, as a matter of course, infinite layers of severability: We must always pluck from an arbitration agreement the specific delegation mechanism that would—but for present judicial review—commend the matter to arbitration, even if this delegation clause is but one sentence within one paragraph within a standalone agreement. And, most importantly, the party must identify this one sentence and lodge a specific challenge to its validity. Otherwise, he will be bound to pursue his validity claim in arbitration.

Even if limited to separately executed arbitration agreements, however, such an infinite severability rule is divorced from the underlying rationale of *Prima Paint* The notion that a party may be bound by an arbitration clause in a contract that is nevertheless invalid may be difficult for any lawyer-or any person-to accept, but this is the law of *Prima Paint.* It reflects a judgment that the " 'national policy favoring arbitration,' " *Preston*, 552 U.S., at 353, outweighs the interest in preserving a judicial forum for questions of arbitrability—*but only when questions of arbitrability are bound up in an underlying dispute*. *Prima Paint*, 388 U.S., at 404. When the two are so bound up, there is actually no gateway matter at all: The question "Who decides" is the entire ball game. Were a court to decide the fraudulent inducement question in *Prima Paint*, in order to decide the antecedent question of the validity of the included arbitration agreement, then it would also, necessarily, decide the merits of the underlying dispute. Same, too, for the question of illegality in *Buckeye*; on its way to deciding the arbitration agreement's validity, the court would have to decide whether the contract was illegal, and in so doing, it would decide the merits of the entire dispute.

In this case, however, resolution of the unconscionability question will have no bearing on the merits of the underlying employment dispute. It will only, as a preliminary matter, resolve who should decide the merits of that dispute. Resolution of the unconscionability question will, however, decide whether the arbitration agreement *itself* is "valid" under "such grounds as exist at law or in equity for the revocation of any contract." 9 U.S.C. § 2. As *Prima Paint* recognizes, the FAA commits those gateway matters, specific to the arbitration agreement, to the court. 388 U.S., at 403–04. Indeed, it is clear that the present controversy over whether the arbitration agreement is unconscionable is *itself severable* from the merits of the underlying dispute, which involves a claim of employment discrimination. This is true for all gateway matters, and for this reason *Prima Paint* has no application in this case.

While I may have to accept the "fantastic" holding in *Prima Paint*, id., at 407 (Black, J., dissenting), I most certainly do not accept the

Court's even more fantastic reasoning today. I would affirm the judgment of the Court of Appeals, and therefore respectfully dissent.

NOTE

1. Is the last decision limited to stand alone agreements to arbitrate?

§ 4.08 DEFINING THE SUPERVISORY ROLE OF THE COURTS OVER THE COMMERCIAL ARBITRATION PROCESS

In the last case, you undoubtedly focused on the concerns voiced by the four dissenters that a court enforcing a clear "delegation" to the arbitrator of the traditional judicial function of deciding the enforceability of the arbitration clause is an unfortunate abdication of judicial responsibility. Throughout these materials, we see what can be the very complicated interplay between judges and arbitrators. This is as good a time as any to stop and take stock. File away for later that the courts have a statutory role, in connection with the requested confirmation or vacatur of an award, to insure, at the very least, that the arbitral process was fundamentally fair, and free of fraud.

Under Sections 3 and 4 of the FAA, and under traditionally worded state statutes, it is for the court to determine whether a dispute is arbitrable—within the scope of the agreement to arbitrate—before requiring the parties to arbitrate. We have yet to focus on the ground rules governing such determinations. What is arguably quite curious, however, is that the United States Supreme Court has determined that the parties may, by agreement, delegate to the arbitrator issues of whether particular disputes are arbitral. *E.g.*, AT&T Techs, Inc. v. Comm'ns Workers of Am., 475 U.S. 643 (1986) ("[W]hether a collective-bargaining agreement creates a duty for the parties to arbitrate a particular grievance—is undeniably an issue for judicial determination . . . [u]nless the parties clearly and unmistakably provide otherwise . . . ."). This principle is also found in a non-labor case, *First Options*, [*infra* at page 326] which states that "[c]ourts should not assume that the parties agreed to arbitrate arbitrability unless there is 'clear and unmistakable' evidence that they did so." One could argue that these permissive holdings mark departures from underlying statutory text. It is also true, however, that recalcitrant parties sometimes hold up arbitral processes by challenging arbitrability under so-called "broad" arbitration clauses routinely interpreted by courts to cover any dispute at all related to the substance of the contracts in which they appear.

A second statutory dictate, as set forth precisely in Section 2 of the FAA, is that even though arbitration contracts are on equal footing with other contracts, they are still subject to avoidability defenses applicable to contracts in general, including fraud and unconscionability. The *Prima Paint* case sets forth a cardinal "severability" principle under which a defense such as fraud only goes to the court, as opposed to the arbitrator, when it is addressed specifically to the arbitration agreement rather than the entire contract containing it. The offered justification for this is that fraudulent inducement claims are easy to concoct, and that, aside from delay, requiring courts to hear them would typically require the very determination of the merits of the dispute that the parties have left to the arbitrator. Nonetheless, Justice Black's dissent in *Prima Paint*, as referenced in *Rent-A-Center*, found "fantastic" the notion that a party induced by fraud into a contract would have to adhere to its "severable" arbitration provision.

It is somewhat surprising that, in the face of mounting concerns about use of arbitration in adhesory contexts, the Supreme Court would continue to erode "gateway" protections that even arguably ought to be within the sphere of judicial controls. Does any provision of the FAA permit or contemplate delegating the issue of the conscionability of the agreement to arbitrate to the arbitrator? What if the objections underlying unconscionability protestations are based on arbitral forum ground rules? Is the arbitrator likely to condemn the tribunal under whose auspices she has been appointed? Moreover, what does the majority in *Rent-A-Center* mean by the concept of permitting courts to hear unconscionability objections to the "delegation" itself? How would one establish such a thing without reference to unconscionability of other aspects of the arbitral process at issue? Put another way, does it make sense to extend the concept of severability to different portions of an agreement to arbitrate?

Chapter 5

CONSTRUING ARBITRATION PROVISIONS TO DETERMINE ARBITRABILITY AND A LOOK AT RELATED ISSUES INVOLVING POTENTIAL CLASS ACTIONS AND MULTI-PARTY DISPUTES

We know now that a very broad variety of disputes are arbitrable as a matter of legal policy. Far more frequent is the issue of whether a particular dispute is covered by the actual language of the agreement to arbitrate.

In making such a determination, principles of contractual construction apply. There is also the strong federal policy favoring arbitration. The cases that follow show a mix of both factors—when in doubt, the dispute will probably be found to be arbitrable. What is at work here? State contract law used generally to interpret? A preemptive federally enunciated public policy in favor of arbitration? What do these cases suggest to the drafters of arbitration provisions?

Before proceeding further, have a look at the AAA's suggested wording for an arbitration provision on the first page of Appendix 4. Coverage of disputes "arising out of or relating to" the contract containing the clause is a common formulation of what is called a "broad" clause, which carries with it the presumption that any dispute somehow connected with that contract is arbitrable, even if it involves tort rather than breach of contract. On the other hand, because contractual assent to arbitrate is required, the use of a restrictively worded arbitration provision that singles out specific types of disputes, or specifically exempts certain types of disputes, obviously will provoke a more restrictive approach, and one that at least somewhat blunts the presumption of arbitrability otherwise at work.

The issue of whether a clause is to be construed to cover a particular dispute is typically a threshold issue for a court, because arbitrability is involved. As we have noted, however, the United States Supreme Court, however, has, for some time, starting in the labor arbitration context, shown a willingness to permit arbitrators, if the parties specifically so provide, to determine whether disputes presented to them are, in fact, arbitrable.

§ 5.01 WHO DECIDES? JUDGE OR ARBITRATOR?

First Options of Chicago, Inc. v. Kaplan & MK Investments, Inc.

Supreme Court of the United States, 1995.
514 U.S. 938.

- BREYER, J.

The case concerns several related disputes between, on one side, First Options of Chicago, Inc., a firm that clears stock trades on the Philadelphia Stock Exchange, and, on the other side, three parties: Manuel Kaplan; his wife, Carol Kaplan; and his wholly owned investment company, MK Investments, Inc. (MKI), whose trading account First Options cleared. The disputes center on a "workout" agreement, embodied in four separate documents, which governs the "working out" of debts to First Options that MKI and the Kaplans incurred as a result of the October 1987 stock market crash. In 1989, after entering into the agreement, MKI lost an additional $1.5 million. First Options then took control of, and liquidated, certain MKI assets;

demanded immediate payment of the entire MKI debt; and insisted that the Kaplans personally pay any deficiency. When its demands went unsatisfied, First Options sought arbitration by a panel of the Philadelphia Stock Exchange.

The first question—the standard of review applied to an arbitrator's decision about arbitrability—is a narrow one. To understand just how narrow, consider three types of disagreement present in this case. First, the Kaplans and First Options disagree about whether the Kaplans are personally liable for MKI's debt to First Options. That disagreement makes up the merits of the dispute. Second, they disagree about whether they agreed to arbitrate the merits. That disagreement is about the arbitrability of the dispute. Third, they disagree about who should have the primary power to decide the second matter. Does that power belong primarily to the arbitrators (because the court reviews their arbitrability decision deferentially) or to the court (because the court makes up its mind about arbitrability independently)? We consider here only this third question.

Although the question is a narrow one, it has a certain practical importance. That is because a party who has not agreed to arbitrate will normally have a right to a court's decision about the merits of its dispute (say, as here, its obligation under a contract). But, where the party has agreed to arbitrate, he or she, in effect, has relinquished much of that right's practical value. The party still can ask a court to review the arbitrator's decision, but the court will set that decision aside only in very unusual circumstances. See, e.g., 9 U.S.C. § 10 (award procured by corruption, fraud, or undue means; arbitrator exceeded his powers); Wilko v. Swan, 346 U.S. 427, 436–37 (1953) (parties bound by arbitrator's decision not in "manifest disregard" of the law), overruled on other grounds, Rodriguez de Quijas v. Shearson/American Express, Inc., 490 U.S. 477 (1989). Hence, who—court or arbitrator—has the primary authority to decide whether a party has agreed to arbitrate can make a critical difference to a party resisting arbitration.

We believe the answer to the "who" question (i.e., the standard-of-review question) is fairly simple. Just as the arbitrability of the merits of a dispute depends upon whether the parties agreed to arbitrate that dispute, so the question "who has the primary power to decide arbitrability" turns upon what the parties agreed about that matter. Did the parties agree to submit the arbitrability question itself to arbitration? If so, then the court's standard for reviewing the arbitrator's decision about that matter should not differ from the standard courts apply when they review any other matter that parties have agreed to arbitrate. See AT & T Technologies, Inc. v. Communications Workers, 475 U.S. 643, 649 (1986) (parties may agree to arbitrate arbitrability); Steelworkers v. Warrior & Gulf Nav. Co., 363 U.S. 574, 583, n. 7 (1960) (same). That is to say, the court should give considerable leeway to the arbitrator, setting aside his or her decision only in certain narrow circumstances. See, e.g., 9 U.S.C. § 10. If, on the other hand, the parties did not agree to submit the arbitrability question itself to arbitration, then the court should decide that question just as it would decide any other question that the parties did not submit to arbitration, namely, independently. These two answers flow inexorably from the fact that arbitration is simply a matter of contract between the parties; it is a way to resolve those disputes—but only those disputes—that the parties have agreed to submit to arbitration.

We agree with First Options, therefore, that a court must defer to an arbitrator's arbitrability decision when the parties submitted that matter to arbitration. Nevertheless, that conclusion does not help First Options win this case. That is because a fair and complete answer to the standard-of-review question requires a word about how a court should decide whether the parties have agreed to submit the arbitrability issue to arbitration. And, that word makes clear that the Kaplans did not agree to arbitrate arbitrability here.

When deciding whether the parties agreed to arbitrate a certain matter (including arbitrability), courts generally (though with a qualification we discuss below) should apply ordinary state-law principles that govern the formation of contracts. See, e.g., *Mastrobuono*, supra, at 62–63, and n. 9; *Volt*, 489 U.S. at 475–76; Perry v. Thomas, 482 U.S. 483, 492–93, n. 9 (1987); G. Wilner, 1 Domke on Commercial Arbitration § 4:04, p. 15 (rev. ed. Supp. 1993) (hereinafter Domke). The relevant state law here, for example, would require the court to see whether the parties objectively revealed an intent to submit the arbitrability issue to arbitration. See, e.g., Estate of Jesmer v. Rohlev, 609 N.E.2d 816, 820 (1993) (law of the State whose law governs the workout agreement); Burkett v. Allstate Ins. Co., 534 A.2d 819, 823–

24 (1987) (law of the State where the Kaplans objected to arbitrability).

This Court, however, has (as we just said) added an important qualification, applicable when courts decide whether a party has agreed that arbitrators should decide arbitrability: Courts should not assume that the parties agreed to arbitrate arbitrability unless there is "clea[r] and unmistakabl[e]" evidence that they did so. *AT & T Technologies*, supra, at 649; see *Warrior & Gulf*, supra, at 583, n. 7. In this manner the law treats silence or ambiguity about the question "who (primarily) should decide arbitrability" differently from the way it treats silence or ambiguity about the question "whether a particular merits-related dispute is arbitrable because it is within the scope of a valid arbitration agreement"—for in respect to this latter question the law reverses the presumption. See *Mitsubishi Motors*, supra, at 626 (" '[A]ny doubts concerning the scope of arbitrable issues should be resolved in favor of arbitration' ") (quoting *Moses H. Cone*, 460 U.S. at 24–25); *Warrior & Gulf*, supra, at 582–83.

But, this difference in treatment is understandable. The latter question arises when the parties have a contract that provides for arbitration of some issues. In such circumstances, the parties likely gave at least some thought to the scope of arbitration. And, given the law's permissive policies in respect to arbitration, see, e.g., *Mitsubishi Motors*, supra, at 626, one can understand why the law would insist upon clarity before concluding that the parties did not want to arbitrate a related matter. See Domke § 12.02, p. 156 (issues will be deemed arbitrable unless "it is clear that the arbitration clause has not included" them). On the other hand, the former question—the "who (primarily) should decide arbitrability" question—is rather arcane. A party often might not focus upon that question or upon the significance of having arbitrators decide the scope of their own powers. And, given the principle that a party can be forced to arbitrate only those issues it specifically has agreed to submit to arbitration, one can understand why courts might hesitate to interpret silence or ambiguity on the "who should decide arbitrability" point as giving the arbitrators that power, for doing so might too often force unwilling parties to arbitrate a matter they reasonably would have thought a judge, not an arbitrator, would decide.

§ 5.02 GUIDING PRINCIPLES OF CONSTRUCTION OF ARBITRAL PROVISIONS

Must a court refer a matter to arbitration even if the purported claim is obviously baseless? *See* N.Y. C.P.L.R. 7501, which instructs courts not to consider "the merits of the dispute" or the "tenability" of a claim. The federal standard is the same. *E.g.*, Warren Bros. Co. v. Cardi Corp., 471 F.2d 1304, 1309 (1st Cir. 1973). Sometimes, the ultimate issue of arbitrability depends on whether the dispute falls under a particular section of a contract, and that may require reaching the merits. What then? *See* AT&T Techs., Inc. v. Commc'n Workers of Am., 475 U.S. 643, 650 (1986). Particularly in such cases, a "broad" clause will require a finding of arbitrability if there is some logical nexus between the overall contract and the dispute. The next case presents a similar pattern. The one after it, however, involves a "narrow" arbitration provision in the sense that it specifically excludes certain disputes from arbitration.

Nationwide General Insurance Co. v. Investors Insurance Co. of America

Court of Appeals of New York, 1975.
37 N.Y.2d 91.

- WACHTLER, J.

The question on this appeal is whether the courts below properly stayed arbitration on the ground that the dispute was not within the scope of the arbitration clause.

Appellants (Investors) entered into a reinsurance treaty with the petitioners who agreed to indemnify Investors "for that portion of its General Liability writings which represents the excess of the sum of: (a) $50,000 each person, $50,000 each loss occurrence for Bodily Injury." Investors, in turn, issued a general liability policy to Rova Farms Resort,

Inc. providing coverage up to $50,000 for each person and $100,000 for each accident.

In July, 1965, while both of these agreements were in effect, one Lawrence McLaughlin was injured on Rova Farms' premises McLaughlin and his wife commenced an action in the New Jersey courts and obtained a jury verdict of $225,000. When this judgment was affirmed on appeal to the New Jersey Supreme Court, Investors paid the limit of its policy ($50,000) plus interest and costs, and Rova Farms paid the balance.

Rova Farms then brought a separate action against Investors to recover the balance, on the theory that Investors had, without good cause, refused to settle the McLaughlin action within the limits of its policy. Trial of that action resulted in a judgment against Investors for $175,000 plus interest and costs, which was later affirmed on appeal.

Investors then turned to petitioners for reimbursement claiming that since the judgment arose from an occurrence covered by one of their general liability writings, they were entitled to recover under the reinsurance treaty. Petitioners refused payment stating that the agreement only afforded coverage when Investors issued a policy with limits exceeding $50,000 per person, and not when, as here, the excess liability was based on a failure to settle a claim within the face amount of the policy. To resolve this impasse Investors served a notice of arbitration pursuant to article XII of the reinsurance agreement which provides, in part, as follows: "In case of any question or dispute between (Investors) on the one hand and the Reinsurer (petitioners) on the other touching the construction, meaning or effect of this Agreement or any article therein contained or any fact or matter connected with the carrying out of these presents or the rights or the liabilities of either of the said parties hereto, the same shall in every case be submitted to a court of arbitration."

After receiving the notice petitioners moved to stay arbitration on the ground that the issue is not arbitrable since the contract simply did not provide for any reimbursement under these circumstances. In granting the stay the court stated: "Initially it does not appear that the subject matter of the Notice of Intention to Arbitrate is encompassed within the terms of the agreement, for the reinsurance provisions appear only to afford coverage in cases beyond the limits of the primary coverage herein. Moreover it does not seem that the agreement herein was intended to cover respondent for sums exacted punitively rather than for sums paid as a consequence of its issuing a policy of insurance." The Appellate Division affirmed, without opinion.

It is always useful to bear in mind that the announced policy of this State favors and encourages arbitration as a means of conserving the time and resources of the courts and the contracting parties. "One way to encourage the use of the arbitration forum" we recently noted "would be to prevent parties to such agreements from using the courts as a vehicle to protract litigation. This conduct has the effect of frustrating both the initial intent of the parties as well as legislative policy." Matter of Weinrott (Carp), 32 N.Y.2d 190, 199. To this end the Legislature has assigned the courts a minimal role in supervising arbitration practice and procedures.

Generally it is for the courts to make the initial determination as to whether the dispute is arbitrable . . . . The ultimate disposition of the merits is of course reserved for the arbitrators and the courts are expressly prohibited from considering "whether the claim with respect to which arbitration is sought is tenable, or otherwise pass(ing) upon the merits of the dispute" (CPLR 7501). Ideally then the courts should confine themselves to the arbitration clause and leave the overall contract to the arbitrators. This, of course, is facilitated when the arbitration clause specifies the issues which are subject to arbitration and those which are not.

More typically the parties adopt a "broad" arbitration clause agreeing generally to submit to arbitration all disputes arising out of the contract, or any dispute relating to the meaning and interpretation of the underlying agreement. Then the scope of the arbitration clause and the scope of the underlying agreement are identical, and disputes over interpretation run the hazard of being refined into questions of arbitrability. For instance in this case, the petitioners argue that since the "arbitration clause . . . has no greater scope than does the treaty to which it relates" the courts must first define the limits of the substantive agreement before they can determine whether the dispute is arbitrable.

Thus in order to reach the threshold question, the petitioners would have the courts first resolve the merits of the dispute—the ultimate issue in this case.

The way out of this apparent dilemma of course is to recognize that although the courts and the arbitrators in these cases cover the same field, they perform very different functions. Basically the courts perform the initial screening process designed to determine in general terms whether the parties have agreed that the subject matter under dispute should be submitted to arbitration. Once it appears that there is, or is not a reasonable relationship between the subject matter of the dispute and the general subject matter of the underlying contract, the court's inquiry is ended. Penetrating definitive analysis of the scope of the agreement must be left to the arbitrators whenever the parties have broadly agreed that any dispute involving the interpretation and meaning of the agreement should be submitted to arbitration.

As far as this case is concerned it is sufficient to note that the parties entered into a reinsurance agreement and that the appellant relying on the agreement has submitted a claim for reimbursement of a judgment. Petitioners have refused payment on the ground that the claim does not come within the letter of the agreement and the appellant urges that the agreement is to be liberally construed. This is a dispute "touching the construction meaning or effect of the agreement" and the courts may not stay arbitration by deciding on the merits whether or not the claim is tenable. A claim need not be tenable in order to be arbitrable.

The order appealed from should be reversed and the motion to stay arbitration denied.

Choice Hotels International, Inc. v. BSR Tropicana Resort, Inc.

United States Court of Appeals, Fourth Circuit, 2001.
252 F.3d 707.

- WILKINS, CIRCUIT JUDGE.

SR Tropicana Resort, Incorporated and two affiliated individuals (collectively, "BSR") appeal the denial of their motion to dismiss a lawsuit against them in favor of arbitration. Because the relevant contractual language requires arbitration of one of the two claims against BSR, we vacate the decision of the district court and remand for further proceedings.

This case arises from a franchise agreement ("the Agreement") between BSR and Appellee Choice Hotels International, Incorporated (Choice). Under the Agreement, BSR agreed to open a motel in Davenport, Florida, and Choice authorized BSR to use the "Quality Inn" brand name. Three terms of the Agreement are relevant here. First, BSR was required to pay Choice a nonrefundable $25,000 "affiliation fee" upon signing the Agreement. J.A. 10. Second, in the event of termination, the Agreement allowed Choice to recover liquidated damages. Third, the Agreement contained the following arbitration provision:

> Except for claims for indemnification, actions for collection of moneys owed [to Choice] under this Agreement, or actions seeking to enjoin [BSR] from using [Choice's trademarks] in violation of this Agreement, any controversy or claim relating to this Agreement, or the breach of this Agreement, including any claim that this Agreement or any part of this Agreement is invalid, illegal, or otherwise voidable or void, will be sent to final and binding arbitration . . . .

After less than two years, and before BSR opened its hotel, Choice sued BSR, alleging that: (1) BSR failed to pay the affiliation fee and (2) BSR breached the Agreement, prompting Choice to terminate it and causing damages to Choice of $586,600. BSR moved to dismiss, asserting, inter alia, that the Agreement required arbitration of Choice's claims. The district court denied the motion; as is relevant here, the court ruled that Choice's claims were not arbitrable because they fell within the exception for "actions for collection of moneys owed." After the district court denied reconsideration, BSR took this interlocutory appeal. See 9 U.S.C.A. § 16(a) (West 1999) (authorizing interlocutory appeals from certain orders favoring litigation over arbitration).

* * * *

We now turn to BSR's assertion that the Agreement requires arbitration of both of Choice's claims. Because this appeal involves a matter of contract interpretation, we review the decision of the district court de novo. Agreements to arbitrate are construed according to the ordinary rules of contract interpretation, as augmented by a federal policy requiring that all ambiguities be resolved in favor of arbitration. See First Options of Chicago, Inc. v. Kaplan, 514 U.S. 938, 944–45 (1995).

The Agreement provides for arbitration of "any controversy or claim relating to this Agreement, or the breach of this Agreement," subject to three exceptions. J.A. 20. This appeal requires us to interpret one of these exceptions, which embraces "actions for collection of moneys owed [to Choice] under this Agreement" ("the collection exemption"). Id.

The crucial terms within this phrase are "collection" and "owed." "To collect a debt or claim is to obtain payment or liquidation of it, either by personal solicitation or legal proceedings." Black's Law Dictionary 263 (6th ed. 1990) (emphasis added). To "owe" means "[t]o be bound to do or omit something, especially to pay a debt." Both of these definitions point us to the word "debt," which denotes a "sum of money due by certain and express agreement" or a "fixed and certain obligation to pay money or some other valuable thing or things." In light of these definitions, we hold that the collection exemption applies to actions by Choice to enforce specific payment obligations that are "fixed" by the Agreement and not contingent on additional events. This interpretation of the phrase "actions for collection" accords with the ordinary understanding of the phrase "collection action."

The parties offer two alternative readings of the collection exemption. BSR contends that the exemption is limited to the enforcement of judgments. For its part, Choice asserts that the phrase embraces all actions seeking monetary damages. We find neither of these interpretations persuasive.

Under BSR's interpretation, most disputes between Choice and BSR would proceed to arbitration first, and then Choice could resort to judicial proceedings to recover damages awarded by the arbitrator. This interpretation is inconsistent with the contractual language referring to "moneys owed . . . under this Agreement."

Choice, by contrast, favors an extremely broad reading of the collection exemption. According to Choice, the exemption excludes from arbitration all claims (by Choice) seeking monetary damages. Given the opportunity at oral argument to identify claims that would be arbitrable, counsel for Choice was able to offer only two examples—demands for specific performance and actions for replevin. Choice's interpretation is intuitively unsatisfying, however, because most breach of contract claims seek monetary relief; consequently, most breach of contract claims by Choice would be exempt from arbitration, notwithstanding that the arbitration clause expressly embraces "any controversy or claim relating to . . . the breach of this Agreement." Id. Our discomfort with Choice's interpretation is heightened by the fact that a separate exemption within the arbitration clause excludes certain equitable actions brought by Choice to arrest "violation[s] of this Agreement." Id. Thus, the interpretation urged by Choice effectively transforms the arbitration provision into a unilateral commitment by BSR to arbitrate its claims, while claims by Choice are subject to judicial determination. We are reluctant to give the arbitration provision this effect, as the structure of the provision does not imply such an imbalance in its application.

At best, Choice's construction offers a minimally plausible alternative to the interpretation we set forth above and thereby renders the collection exemption ambiguous. To resolve this ambiguity, we resort to three interpretive guides. First, as noted above, federal policy requires that ambiguities in arbitration clauses be resolved in favor of arbitration. See Am. Recovery Corp. v. Computerized Thermal Imaging, Inc., 96 F.3d 88, 92 (4th Cir. 1996) ("[W]e may not deny a party's request to arbitrate an issue unless it may be said with positive assurance that the arbitration clause is not susceptible of an interpretation that covers the asserted dispute."); see also Armijo v. Prudential Ins. Co., 72 F.3d 793, 800 (10th Cir. 1995) (noting that policy favoring broad construction of arbitration clauses compels narrow construction of exceptions to arbitration clauses). Second, when faced with a general rule and enumerated exceptions, we interpret the exceptions narrowly, lest they overwhelm the rule. See Commissioner v. Clark, 489 U.S. 726, 739 (1989). Third, any doubts in the interpretation of a contract must be resolved against the drafter—in this case, Choice. See *Bankers Ins.*, 245 F.3d, at 321 n. 7. These principles uniformly support a narrow reading of the collection exemption and a correspondingly expansive construction of the general arbitration requirement. Accordingly, we reject Choice's interpretation of the collection exemption and adhere to the conclusion that only traditional collection actions are excluded from the arbitration requirement.

Having determined the scope of the collection exemption, we must now consider the extent to which it applies to Choice's claims. We hold that Choice's effort to recover the affiliation fee is a collection action subject to the collection exemption; the breach of contract claim, however, falls outside the exemption.

The Agreement between Choice and BSR expressly requires BSR to pay the affiliation fee. The fee is part of the contract itself, not a remedy for either party's deviation from the contract. Moreover, the amount of the fee ($25,000) is a sum certain under the Agreement. Thus, Choice's effort to enforce this contractual provision provides a classic example of a collection action. [B]ecause this claim is not arbitrable, BSR was not entitled to dismissal of Choice's complaint in its entirety.

We nevertheless vacate the order of the district court because Choice's breach of contract claim is not within the collection exemption and therefore is subject to arbitration. The Agreement provides for liquidated damages in the event of termination, and Choice specifically invoked this provision in its complaint; thus, the amount of Choice's damage request is, like the affiliation fee, contractually determined. BSR's obligation to pay this amount, however, does not arise from the formation of the contract, but rather from an alleged breach of contract. Because this is not a debt subject to collection, the collection exemption does not apply. By contrast, the general terms of the arbitration clause specifically embrace claims arising from "the breach of this Agreement." BSR is therefore entitled to arbitration of this issue and to a stay of proceedings while the arbitration takes place.

In sum, Choice's complaint is not subject to dismissal, because it contains at least one nonarbitrable claim. However, Choice's breach of contract claim is arbitrable under the Agreement. We therefore vacate the decision of the district court and remand with instructions to stay proceedings on this claim pending arbitration. The court may, in its discretion, stay proceedings on the affiliation fee claim as well.

In re Arbitration Between Denihan & Denihan

New York Supreme Court, Appellate Division, First Dep't, 1986.
119 A.D.2d 144.

- SANDLER, J.

Michael G. Denihan appeals from an order and judgment of the Supreme Court, New York County which granted the petitioners' application to stay an arbitration on his claim that a proposed plan of liquidation of the assets of 3 Mitchell Place Inc. (Corporation) violated his rights under a shareholders' agreement, and dismissed [his] cross-petition for an injunction without prejudice.

The principals in this lawsuit, the latest in a series of ongoing controversies, are Michael G. Denihan, owner of 25% of the shares of the corporation, and his older brother, Benjamin J. Denihan, the effective leader of a group of stockholders who own 75% of the shares. Until April 1970, the two brothers were in effect partners in a group of real estate and other businesses owned and operated by them, in some cases with other members of the family. The older brother was the dominant force in the several enterprises. As a result of disputes between them, and following extended negotiations, a series of transactions were consummated pursuant to which they separated all of their business interests, with the single exception of the Corporation, owner of the Beekman Tower Hotel. As to that Corporation, the parties negotiated a shareholders' agreement, dated January 1, 1969 but executed on or about April 1, 1970, which appears to have been meticulously drafted to protect Michael's interests as a minority shareholder.

As relevant to the issue with which we are concerned, paragraph 4 of the shareholders agreement sets forth promises that the Corporation would not undertake certain actions without Michael's "prior express written approval." In particular it was agreed that the Corporation would not, without such approval, "(v) sell all or substantially all of Corporation's assets, or merge, consolidate or liquidate except . . . pursuant to a transaction in which MG shares in any direct or indirect benefit accruing to the other shareholders in the same proportion as MG's share of Common Stock bear to all of Corporation's Common Stock then issued and outstanding, including, but not limited to, formation of a partnership as successor to the business and property of the Corporation."

Paragraph 11 of the agreement provided that "[a]ny claims, difference, dispute or question of interpretation arising under this agreement shall be determined solely and exclusively by arbitration pursuant to the rules then obtaining of the American Arbitration Association in New York City."

The years that followed were marked by repeated claims by Michael (two of which were the subject of completed arbitrations) that the majority shareholders were persistently violating his rights under the shareholders agreement. In the two arbitrations addressing such claims that have been completed, both sustained, in essence, his claims that the majority shareholders had violated his rights. On another occasion, a proposal, without his consent, to refinance an existing mortgage was abandoned after a court enjoined the proposed refinancing pending arbitration of the claim. In addition, an earlier proposed plan to sell the assets of the Corporation, alleged without contradiction to be essentially the same as that with which we are now concerned, was abandoned by the majority shareholders after Michael demanded arbitration. Another arbitration addressed to other claims of Michael is now pending.

The immediate issue was precipitated when the petitioners, by notice of a shareholders meeting, dated May 20, 1985 (approved by the Board of Directors, but without the consent of Michael), called a special meeting of the shareholders of the Corporation for the purpose of approving a resolution to dissolve and liquidate the Corporation and sell its assets and properties at public auction at which the shareholders would be permitted to bid.

By notice dated June 20, 1985, Michael demanded arbitration of his claim that the proposed liquidation of the Corporation and sale of its assets and properties constituted "a scheme to improperly 'squeeze out' the claimant as a minority shareholder of the Corporation, in derogation of respondents' fiduciary duties and obligations under the Shareholders Agreement." He further alleged that the petitioners intended to " 'buy' the Corporation's assets and properties at a price far less than the fair market value, and then to resume operation of the Beekman Tower, albeit without the constraints of the Shareholders Agreement."

Petitioners then commenced this proceeding to stay the arbitration maintaining that the plan did not require Michael's prior express written approval since it met the alternative requirement of being "a transaction in which MG shares in any direct or indirect benefit accruing to the other shareholders in the same proportion as MG's shares of Common Stock bear to all of the Corporation's Common Stock." Michael cross-petitioned for a preliminary injunction in aid of arbitration, detailing in the accompanying papers what he claimed to be the history of petitioners' persistent efforts to violate his rights under the shareholders agreement.

Concluding that the proposed plan of liquidation was in accord with the procedure authorized under the shareholders agreement for selling the assets of the Corporation without the consent of the minority shareholder, and that the requested injunctive relief was based on apprehensions of misconduct in carrying out the plan that had not yet occurred and was, accordingly, at best premature, Special Term granted the petition staying the arbitration and denying the cross-petition seeking an injunction against the proposed auction sale.

What becomes apparent from a study of Special Term's opinion is that the issues were decided on the basis of a determination, not that an arbitrable issue had not been presented, but rather on the basis of the court's judgment that the issue presented lacked merit. In so deciding the questions presented, Special Term departed from the statutory direction in CPLR 7501 that: "In determining any matter arising under this article, the court shall not consider whether the claim with respect to which arbitration is sought is tenable, or otherwise pass upon the merits of the dispute."

The definitive statement of the court's role in determining whether or not an issue is arbitrable was set forth in *Matter of Nationwide General Insurance Co. v. Investors Insurance Co. of America*, 37 N.Y.2d 91. The court there said (at 95):

> Generally it is for the courts to make the initial

> determination as to whether the dispute is arbitrable . . . . The ultimate disposition of the merits is of course reserved for the arbitrators and the courts are expressly prohibited from considering 'whether the claim with respect which arbitration is sought is tenable, or otherwise pass[ing] upon the merits of the dispute . . . .' Ideally then the courts should confine themselves to the arbitration clause and leave the overall contract to the arbitrators.

Going on to discuss the responsibilities of courts confronted with a broad arbitration clause, the court stated (at 96):

> [A]lthough the courts and the arbitrators in these cases cover the same field, they perform very different functions. Basically the courts perform the initial screening process designed to determine in general terms whether the parties have agreed that the subject matter under dispute should be submitted to arbitration. Once it appears that there is, or is not a reasonable relationship between the subject matter of the dispute and the general subject matter of the underlying contract, the court's inquiry is ended. Penetrating definitive analysis of the scope of the agreement must be left to the arbitrators whenever the parties have broadly agreed that any dispute involving the interpretation and meaning of the agreement should be submitted to arbitration.

In a more recent Court of Appeals decision, the essence of the principle set forth in the Nationwide case was succinctly phrased as follows: "Since the parties agreed to submit the merits of their disputes to arbitration, the courts should not stay arbitration on the ground that a claim is meritless for it is precisely that issue that the arbitrator is to decide." Matter of Franklin Cent. School, [Franklin Teachers Association], 51 N.Y.2d 348, 356.

As Special Term's opinion makes clear, he decided the issue presented by the petition for a stay by looking, not at the arbitration clause, but rather at the substantive provisions of the agreement in issue, and concluding that the proposed plan was authorized under the agreement. In deciding the issue in this manner, clearly contrary to the specific mandate of CPLR 7501 . . . that "the court shall not consider whether the claim with respect to which arbitration is sought is tenable . . . ." (C.P.L.R. 7501).

When the issue is approached in accordance with the now well-established controlling principles, it seems to me clear that the claim that the proposed plan of liquidation violated Michael's rights under the shareholders agreement bears "a reasonable relationship between the subject matter of the dispute and the general subject matter of the contract." (See, *Nationwide Insurance Co.*, supra, 37 N.Y.2d at 96). Or looked at in terms of the broad arbitration clause in the shareholders agreement, it is clear that Michael has set forth a "claim" arising under the agreement, that it states a "difference" or "dispute" arising under the agreement, and that it presents a "question of interpretation" arising under the agreement. Indeed, contrary to Special Term's apparent view, it is by no means an extraordinary notion that the relevant clause of the agreement might reasonably be interpreted as interdicting a public auction, without Michael's consent, at which the majority shareholders would be permitted to make a bid for the assets of the corporation, on the view that such a procedure has a significant potential for impairing rights that were intended to be preserved under the contract.

Once it is accepted that the issue posed is arbitrable and that it was an error to stay the arbitration, it follows under the circumstances presented that an injunction in aid of the arbitration process is warranted. It is clear that in the absence of an injunction pending the arbitration, the award to which Michael may be entitled "may be rendered ineffectual." (See, CPLR 7502[c]).

* * * *

- MILONAS, J., dissenting.

In my opinion, the order and judgment of the Supreme Court should be affirmed.

Paragraph 11 of the Shareholders Agreement provides that any "claims, difference, dispute or question of interpretation" arising thereunder shall be determined through arbitration. However, the inclusion of an arbitration clause does not mean that an interested party is entitled to avail himself of such a procedure merely on demand regardless of whether or not there is a genuine matter to be arbitrated. In the instant situation, petitioners moved to stay arbitration on the ground that there is no arbitrable issue involved. The existence of an arbitrable issue is generally for the courts to determine. In that connection, the majority concludes that Special Term's decision was based upon a finding that respondent's claim is without substantive merit rather than upon an assessment that no issue has been presented which can be arbitrated. I disagree. In my view, the Supreme Court did indeed rule that there is no issue to be arbitrated, and there is, in fact, none.

According to paragraph 4(b) of the agreement, the shareholders will not authorize the subject corporation to undertake the following without respondent's express written approval:

> (v) sell all or substantially all of Corporation's assets, or merge, consolidate or liquidate except pursuant to or in furtherance of transactions permitted under paragraph 4(c) or pursuant to a transition in which MG shares in any direct or indirect benefit accruing to the other shareholders in the same proportion as MG's shares of Common Stock bear to all of Corporation's Common Stock then issued and outstanding, including, but not limited to, formation of a partnership as successor to the business and property of the Corporation.

Thus, it is clear that the agreement expressly authorizes the sale of all or most of the corporate assets so long as respondent shares in the benefits of the liquidation in the same proportion as his interest in the corporation. Although circumstances might conceivably arise in which respondent would be warranted in applying to the courts for an injunction to prevent the sale—as, for example, were he to obtain evidence of the other shareholders' intent to defraud him, or to dissipate the corporation's property—none have been shown to exist at this time. Similarly, the Shareholders Agreement does not establish particular guidelines to be followed in the event of a sale, so the arbitrator could not direct the manner of the auction. Indeed, the procedural details of the sale have not even been established.

By demanding arbitration, respondent merely suggests that because of petitioners' conduct in the past, and the extensive history of litigation between the parties herein, he has reason to believe that the future will only bring more of the same and that his interests will not be protected. No breach of the Shareholders Agreement has been demonstrated or even alleged. Certainly, he has not shown that petitioners do not plan to pay him the proportionate share of the liquidation proceeds to which he is entitled or that he has not been afforded full disclosure of the actions of the majority shareholders. He is merely speculating as to what might happen in the future. Consequently, any damages to respondent are, at best, prospective, and an arbitrator cannot determine something that has not yet occurred. However, if his worst fears do materialize, and petitioners, once the liquidation has been effected, fail to distribute the proceeds as mandated under the agreement or can be shown to have engaged in any other improper or fraudulent practices, there is nothing to preclude him from obtaining full relief at that time either through arbitration or, where appropriate, in the courts. Moreover, he will also be able to procure all relevant financial information concerning the assets and property of the corporation, as well as the data surrounding the sale. Since there is no issue to be arbitrated and nothing has yet taken place which would in any way compromise respondent's interests, arbitration is premature.

NOTES

1. Who decides whether a dispute is "ripe" for determination, court or arbitrator? Or is the point of the dissent here that there is no dispute at all? Is that the same as a finding of lack of merit?

2. A party requiring an emergency temporary restraining order and/or a preliminary injunction can often avail itself of a state statutory procedure whereby a court is asked to provisionally "freeze" matters so that arbitration will not prove an empty exercise. *See, e.g.*, N.Y. C.P.L.R. 7502(c). Do you see how this sort of judicial involvement can jeopardize the traditional division of functions between judge and arbitrator? Various tribunals have special procedures for emergency relief. The AAA Commercial Rules O-1 to O-8 (Appendix 4) so

provide, but their use is optional, and requires prior or post-dispute consent of both parties. Absent special provision in advance, is a respondent likely to submit to these procedures or to instead invite a presumably more cumbersome court application?

3. Arbitrators are, of course, empowered to grant preliminary and final injunctive relief. How are such awards enforced? Arbitrators may sometimes retain jurisdiction to do so, but often will not. Arbitrators do not have contempt power. If there is violation of an arbitral injunction, one could presumably apply for expedited confirmation by Order to Show Cause seeking interim restraint. That would appear to be the preferable course.

§ 5.03 PROCEDURAL ASPECTS OF LITIGATING WHETHER A PARTICULAR DISPUTE IS COVERED BY AN ARBITRAL PROVISION — TACTICS AND APPEALABILITY OF JUDICIAL DETERMINATIONS

In the last case, *Choice Hotels*, the Court of Appeals for the Fourth Circuit reviewed a District Court decision refusing to send claims to arbitration. Section 16(a)(1) of the FAA, added by Congress in 1988, is a pro-arbitration provision designed to permit immediate appeal of a trial court refusal to stay an action in favor of arbitration under FAA Section 3, or a similar refusal to simply compel arbitration under FAA Section 4. Otherwise, a trial court decision against arbitration could only be heard on appeal after a lower court resolution of the merits of the dispute in question. That could pose all sorts of problems, including issues of preclusion.

Conversely, Section 16(b) of the FAA further provides that, subject to a special certification under 28 U.S.C. § 1292(b), an "interlocutory" order in favor of arbitration under FAA Sections 3 or 4 is not appealable, the idea presumably being that once a lower court directs arbitration, there should be no further delay. Post-arbitration, in a challenge to an adverse award, the party originally resisting arbitration may raise the issue again on the theory that the arbitrator exceeded her powers within the meaning of FAA Section 10.

A problem arises, however, when, as would not be unusual, the District Court order sending a claim to arbitration dismisses that claim. That action can then be deemed "final" so as to permit immediate appeal, because it would not come within FAA Section 16(b)'s prohibition against appeal of "interlocutory" orders in favor of appealability. *E.g.*, Salim Oleochemicals v. M/V Shropshire, 278 F.3d 90 (2d Cir. 2002). Congress may have overlooked this factor when it enacted FAA Section 16, but that provision has remained on the books as is for over twenty years.

Where, for whatever reason, a party plans to challenge arbitrability only in the event of an adverse award, care must be taken to preserve that objection before the arbitrator, who has the sparingly utilized power to dismiss for this reason. That approach, however, would be insufficient in New York under N.Y. C.P.L.R. 7503(c), which requires that when an arbitration demand contains the requisite notice, a party claiming lack of arbitrability must seek judicial relief within twenty days, or be deemed to have waived objection.

There will be times when an arbitrator purports to pass on a matter not set forth in the notice of claim. Where a party has no reason to foresee this, and the contention is that the additional matter was not arbitrable at all, the twenty-day rule under N.Y. C.P.L.R. 7503(c) does not apply. In such instances, or in other permitted post-award challenges to the scope of an award, the typical contention is that the arbitrator acted in "excess of its powers" under the applicable statute. This, of course, is a traditional basis for vacation of an award.

§ 5.04 More on Provisional Relief

Teradyne, Inc. v. Mostek Corp.

United States Court of Appeals, First Circuit, 1986.
797 F.2d 43.

- Tauro, District Judge.

Defendant-appellant, Mostek Corporation (Mostek), now known as CTU of Delaware, Inc., appeals from a district court interlocutory order issued in favor of plaintiff-appellee, Teradyne, Inc. (Teradyne), in an ongoing breach of contract action by Teradyne against Mostek. The order enjoins Mostek from disposing of or encumbering $4,000,000 of its assets and directs it to set that amount aside in an interest bearing account to satisfy any judgment or arbitration award obtained by Teradyne. Teradyne is claiming approximately $3,500,000 for cancellation charges, alleged failure to pay unearned price discounts on goods delivered, for goods and services invoiced, and for incidental and consequential damages.

Changes in Mostek's corporate status complicated matters when United Technologies Corporation, which had acquired Mostek in 1980, announced, on October 17, 1985, that Mostek would cease operations. On October 30, United and Mostek entered into a Memorandum of Understanding with Thomson Semiconductors, Inc., under which Thomson agreed to buy substantially all of Mostek's assets for approximately $71 million in cash, subject to certain offsets and debits. The sale was executed in November and Teradyne was contemporaneously notified that it had occurred. The proceeds of the sale were deposited in a separate bank account in Mostek's name and dedicated to the payment of the claims of Mostek's creditors. Prompted by this change in Mostek's status, Teradyne commenced this action on January 17, 1986, seeking, inter alia, an injunction requiring Mostek to set aside sufficient funds to satisfy a Teradyne judgment pending the outcome of arbitration.

* * * *

THE EFFECT OF THE FEDERAL ARBITRATION ACT, *9 U.S.C. §§ 1-14*, ON THE DISTRICT COURT'S POWER TO GRANT PRELIMINARY INJUNCTIVE RELIEF

Mostek contends that the policy of the Arbitration Act precludes the grant of preliminary injunctive relief in an arbitrable dispute. The district court has not yet determined whether or not this dispute is arbitrable. If Mostek's argument is correct, then it clearly would have been an abuse of discretion for the court to issue this injunction before deciding the arbitrability question. If Mostek's argument is not correct, however, and the Arbitration Act poses no bar to the grant of a preliminary injunction, then whether or not the dispute is arbitrable is irrelevant. Accordingly, the initial question to be determined is whether or not a preliminary injunction can be issued in an arbitrable dispute.

The Arbitration Act does not address this issue specifically and it has not previously been ruled upon by this circuit. Other circuits, however, have examined the issue in some detail. The Second, Fourth and Seventh Circuits all take the view that a court can, and should, grant a preliminary injunction in an arbitrable dispute whenever an injunction is necessary to preserve the status quo pending arbitration.

In *Roso-Lino Beverage Distributors, Inc. v. The Coca-Cola Bottling Company of New York*, 749 F.2d 124 (2d Cir. 1984), the Second Circuit reversed the district court's denial of a preliminary injunction because it "appeared, from the record . . . that the district court believed its decision to refer the dispute to arbitration stripped the court of the power to grant injunctive relief." Id. at 125. Relying on its decision in *Erving v. Virginia Squires Basketball Club*, 468 F.2d 1064 (2d Cir. 1972), the Second Circuit held that the fact that the dispute was to be arbitrated did not "absolve the court of its obligation to consider the merits of a requested preliminary injunction," and that the proper course for the district court was to determine whether the dispute was a "proper case" for an injunction. 749 F.2d at 125.

Erving v. Virginia Squires Basketball Club, 468 F.2d 1064, involved a suit by a basketball player for rescission of his contract with a professional club. The club counterclaimed, asserting a right to arbitration, and sought injunctive relief. The district court granted a preliminary injunction enjoining the plaintiff from playing for any other club pending determination of the dispute by arbitration. The Second Circuit affirmed, noting that the injunction was the only way to preserve the status quo during the pendency of the arbitration proceeding. Id. at 1067.

The Fourth Circuit's examination of this issue, in *Merrill Lynch, Pierce, Fenner & Smith, Inc. v. Bradley*, 756 F.2d 1048 (4th Cir. 1985), focused on the effect of § 3 of the Arbitration Act on the court's power to issue preliminary injunctive relief. Section 3 provides that the court shall, upon determination that a dispute is arbitrable, and on application of one of the parties, "stay the trial of the action until such arbitration has been had." Merrill Lynch sued Bradley, a former account executive, for damages for alleged breach of contract, and sought injunctive relief to prevent Bradley from using its records and soliciting its clients. The district court granted Merrill Lynch a preliminary injunction, denied Bradley's motion to stay the injunction, and ordered expedited arbitration, both parties having agreed that the dispute was arbitrable. Bradley appealed, claiming that the injunction was an abuse of discretion because § 3 of the Arbitration Act precluded a court from considering the merits of an arbitrable dispute. The Fourth Circuit rejected this argument, holding that nothing in § 3 abrogated the equitable power of district courts to enter preliminary injunctions to preserve the status quo pending arbitration . . . .

The issue was addressed by the Seventh Circuit in *Sauer Getriebe KG v. White Hydraulics, Inc.*, 715 F.2d 348 (7th Cir. 1983). The dispute in that case arose when the defendant announced that it was negotiating for the sale of its assets. The plaintiff claimed this announcement amounted to a repudiation of a previous agreement the defendant had made with the plaintiff to buy certain of the defendant's manufacturing rights. The complaint alleged that plaintiff intended to exercise its contractual right to arbitrate the dispute and contained a request for a preliminary injunction barring the defendant from transferring any manufacturing rights pending the arbitration. The district court denied injunctive relief on the grounds that the defendant had not repudiated the contract. The Seventh Circuit reversed. In doing so, it expressly rejected the defendant's argument that the plaintiff had waived its right to arbitrate by filing the suit. The court held that the right to arbitrate and to seek injunctive relief were not incompatible and that the plaintiff was not obliged to abandon one in order to pursue the other. 715 F.2d at 350. It held, further, that the plaintiff was entitled to an injunction pending the arbitration, noting that the plaintiff's contractual right to arbitrate the dispute would not be worth much if the defendant transferred the manufacturing rights before the arbitration was settled. Id.

Running counter to the approach taken by the Second, Fourth and Seventh Circuits is that taken by the Eighth Circuit in *Merrill Lynch, Pierce, Fenner & Smith, Inc. v. Hovey*, 726 F.2d 1286 (8th Cir. 1984) . . . . *Hovey* involved a petition by Merrill Lynch for an injunction against five former employees to prevent them from using Merrill Lynch's records and from soliciting Merrill Lynch clients. The employees counterclaimed, seeking to compel arbitration pursuant to New York Stock Exchange rules regulating dispute resolution procedures. The district court granted Merrill Lynch a preliminary injunction and refused to submit the dispute to arbitration. The employees appealed, claiming that the dispute was arbitrable. The Eighth Circuit held that the dispute was arbitrable and that issuing a preliminary injunction was, therefore, precluded by § 3 of the Arbitration Act. The court took the view that granting preliminary injunctive relief in an arbitrable dispute ran counter to the "unmistakably clear congressional purpose that the arbitration procedure, when selected by the parties to a contract, be speedy and not subject to delay and obstruction in the courts." Id. at 1292 (quoting *Prima Paint Corp.*).

* * * *

Having thus outlined our disagreement with both the reasoning and approach of the Eighth Circuit, we are persuaded that the approach taken by the Second, Fourth and Seventh Circuits should be followed. We hold, therefore, that a district court can grant injunctive relief in an arbitrable dispute pending arbitration, provided the prerequisites for injunctive relief are satisfied. We believe this approach reinforces rather than detracts from the policy of the Arbitration Act . . . .

THE PROPRIETY OF PRELIMINARY INJUNCTIVE RELIEF

In *Planned Parenthood League of Massachusetts v. Bellotti*, 641 F.2d 1006 (1st Cir. 1981), we listed four criteria that must be established to warrant preliminary injunctive relief. The court must find: (1) that plaintiff will suffer irreparable injury if the injunction is not granted; (2) that such injury outweighs any harm which granting injunctive relief would inflict on the defendant; (3) that plaintiff has exhibited a likelihood of success on the merits; and (4) that the public interest will not be adversely affected by the granting of the injunction.

The district court here clearly articulated its reasons for finding that Teradyne had satisfied the prerequisites for injunctive relief. It held that Mostek's freedom to dispose of its assets created a substantial risk of irreparable harm to Teradyne, given that Mostek was in the process of winding down after selling the bulk of its assets, that it had failed to provide adequate assurances to alleviate Teradyne's concerns, and that it could at any time make itself judgment proof. Further, the court found that the affidavits submitted to it showed a likelihood that Teradyne would succeed on its contractual claims, and that the balance of hardships was in Teradyne's favor . . . .

* * * *

<u>NOTE</u>

1. An obvious cross-current here is that a court asked for preliminary relief would typically make an assessment of the merits of the underlying claims—"probability of success on the merits" is a typical prerequisite to preliminary injunctive relief. That assessment is tentative, but might well prejudice the outcome of the arbitration to follow. The absence of preliminary judicial relief in anticipation of arbitration would also cause problems—picture an arbitral claim for violation of a restrictive covenant involving ongoing prohibited solicitation of customers. By the time of an award, irreparable damage could well be done, but with monetary damages difficult to quantify or else uncollectable.

§ 5.05 ENFORCEMENT OF ARBITRATION AGREEMENTS IN TRIPARTITE DISPUTES

We have seen that absent special situations, such as those justifying the piercing of a corporate veil, a party cannot be forced to arbitrate absent a contractual undertaking to do so. Obviously, there will be times when disputes will involve multiple parties under different contracts, one or more with an arbitration provision and one or more without. This can cause inefficient fragmentation between court and arbitration.

We often see this pattern arise in what would normally be an impleader situation if a tripartite dispute were to all be heard in court—a defendant wants to implead a third party on the theory that if defendant is liable to plaintiff, the third party is liable to it for its loss. Take this situation:

Contractor sues Owner for delaying its work so as to increase cost of performance, and demands arbitration pursuant to their contract. Owner, in turn, sues its Architect, claiming that faulty architectural plans caused the delay. The Owner-Architect contract has no arbitration clause. The Architect cannot be required to arbitrate. May a court deny application by Contractor to compel arbitration against Owner so as to permit a tripartite unitary court action in which Owner may implead the Architect? If not, may a court at least stay arbitration until completion of the court litigation between Owner and Architect? The general answer is "No." The right to arbitrate takes precedence, this despite the obvious potential overlaps. One could argue, however, that were the rule different, a party seeking to avoid arbitration would simply implead a third party not bound to arbitrate, whether justified to do so or otherwise. The next case deals with a tripartite situation.

Moses H. Cone Memorial Hospital v. Mercury Construction Corp.

Supreme Court of the United States, 1983.
460 U.S. 1.

▪ BRENNAN, J.

Petitioner Moses H. Cone Memorial Hospital (Hospital) is located in Greensboro, N.C. Respondent Mercury Construction Corp. (Mercury), a construction contractor, has its principal place of business in Alabama. In July 1975, Mercury and the Hospital entered into a contract for the construction of additions to the Hospital building. . . . With certain stated exceptions, any dispute decided by the Architect (or not decided by it within a stated time) could be submitted by either party to binding arbitration under a broad arbitration clause in the contract. . . .

The Hospital points out that it has two substantive disputes here—one with Mercury, concerning Mercury's claim for delay and impact costs, and the other with the Architect, concerning the Hospital's claim for indemnity for any liability it may have to Mercury. The latter dispute cannot be sent to arbitration without the Architect's consent, since there is no arbitration agreement between the Hospital and the Architect. It is true, therefore, that if Mercury obtains an arbitration order for its dispute, the Hospital will be forced to resolve these related disputes in different forums . . . .

Under the Arbitration Act, an arbitration agreement must be enforced notwithstanding the presence of other persons who are parties to the underlying dispute but not to the arbitration agreement. If the dispute between Mercury and the Hospital *is* arbitrable under the Act, then the Hospital's two disputes will be resolved separately—one in arbitration, and the other (if at all) in state-court litigation . . . .

§ 5.06 JOINDER OF ARBITRAL AND NON-ARBITRAL CLAIMS

Now take a related situation involving multiple interrelated claims rather than multiple parties. A securities brokerage executive sues her firm both for breach of employment contract and sexual discrimination. Under FINRA Rules, the discrimination claim does not have to be arbitrated absent a separate contractual undertaking to do so. Assume there is none. What happens? The answer is that we have parallel proceedings. What a court would have the power to do here, however, is to stay the court action pending completion of the arbitration, this on the theory that arbitral findings might be preclusive in the court case—an arbitral determination that the executive was terminated for cause, for instance, would probably be the death knell of the discrimination claim.

Prior to the Supreme Court's 1987 decision in *Shearson*, remember, a brokerage firm could not compel arbitration of customer claims under the federal securities laws even though state law claims based on the same transactions were, in fact, arbitrable. In *Dean Witter Reynolds, Inc. v. Byrd*, 470 U.S. 213 (1985), with respect to a federal complaint asserting federal securities violations and pendent state claims, the Supreme Court held that the pendent claims had to be sent to arbitration irrespective of resulting inefficiencies. Were this pattern to persist today, it could readily be one in which the court stays the federal claims before it, pending results of arbitration which might be preclusive or else render hearing of the federal claims unnecessary if the customer is given a full recovery.

§ 5.07 ARBITRAL CLASS ACTIONS AND WAIVERS

When it comes to the maintainability of class actions in arbitration, the law, to say the least, is in a state of rapid flux. The question takes on special force in the area of consumer arbitration, where costs and potential costs to the customer are thought to immunize merchants from most claims. Were it not for availability of class actions, the same would be true in the courts as well.

Arbitrators usually have the power to allocate fees after the fact, but that has not been enough to make consumers comfortable with the process. *See generally* Mark E. Budnitz, *Mandatory Arbitration: The High Cost of Mandatory Consumer Arbitration*, 67 LAW & CONTEMP. PROBS. 133 (2004).

It is only in the past several years that the class action device has been used in arbitration. The AAA adopted special class action rules in 2003, but FINRA still expressly prohibits class action proceedings. In any event, it is not unusual, in contracts of adhesion, for the stronger party to provide against class actions in arbitration clauses. The literature often advances use of unconscionability to overcome such class action waivers in contracts of adhesion. *See generally* Jean R. Sternlight & Elizabeth J. Jensen, *Using Arbitration to Eliminate Consumer Class Actions: Efficient Business Practice or Unconscionable Abuse?*, 67 LAW & CONTEMP. PROBS. 75 (2004). Still, somebody must spend the money to mount such a challenge. A number of decisions, both federal and state, have adopted an unconscionability approach. *E.g.*, Ting v. AT&T, 182 F. Supp. 2d 902 (N.D. Cal. 2002), *aff'd in relevant part*, 319 F.3d 1126 (9th Cir. 2003). The following case uses a cost analysis to strike down a class action waiver.

In re American Express Merchants' Litigation

United States Court of Appeals, Second Circuit, 2009.
554 F.3d 300.

- POOLER, CIRCUIT JUDGE.

On this appeal we are asked to consider the enforcement of a mandatory arbitration clause in a commercial contract that also contains a "class action waiver," also referred to as a "collective action waiver," that is, a provision which forbids the parties to the contract from pursuing anything other than individual claims in the arbitral forum. This is a matter of first impression in our Court.

One commentator has recently contended that "[t]he outright banning of class action in mandatory arbitration clauses has become a standard policy for many corporations that transact with consumers." Bryan Allen Rice, "Comment: Enforceable or Not?: Class Action Waivers in Mandatory Arbitration Clauses and the Need for a Judicial Standard," 45 Hous. L. Rev. 215, 224 (2008). We acknowledge at the outset, as have other courts that have considered questions arising from the enforcement of class action waivers, in both consumer and commercial contracts, that the wisdom and utility of these provisions have become the subject of intense debate. See Skirchak v. Dynamics Research Corp., 508 F.3d 49, 63 (1st Cir. 2007) ("We recognize that there is a policy debate about whether class action waivers essentially act as exculpatory clauses, allowing for violations of laws where individual cases involve low dollar amounts and so will not adequately address or prevent illegality."). The opposing positions in this frequently impassioned debate have been dispassionately described as follows:

> Companies' use of class action waivers is motivated by the view that plaintiffs exploit the class action procedure in order to wrest large and unfair settlements from defendants . . . . Class action waivers are viewed by these companies as a way to defend themselves from consumers who are ganging up on companies through the leverage inherent in the aggregation of large numbers of claims. In further support of these waivers, corporations argue that the many (perceived) advantages of arbitration to a plaintiff make up for any disadvantages or inconveniences that the plaintiff may incur by sacrificing the ability to be part of a class action.
>
> Opponents of class action waivers contend that the ability to aggregate claims is crucial to protect the rights of those individuals . . . who do not have the resources to litigate individual claims. Further, many individual claims are only viable if brought on a classwide basis. Indeed, by prohibiting class actions in . . . lawsuits[ ] where the expected recovery is dwarfed by the cost of litigating or arbitrating the claim, individuals are effectively prevented from pursuing their claims. As a result, businesses are able to engage in unchecked market misbehavior . . . .

J. Maria Glover, "Beyond Unconscionability: Class Action Waivers and Mandatory Arbitration Agreements," 59 Vand. L. Rev. 1735, 1746–47 (2006) (footnotes and internal quotation marks omitted).

While we are conscious of this debate, we are thankful that we need not resolve it on this appeal. That is, we do not decide whether class action waiver provisions are either void or enforceable per se. Rather, we are concerned solely with the class action waiver contained in the contract between the parties before us on this appeal. We conclude that, on the record before us, the plaintiffs have adequately demonstrated that the class action waiver provision at issue should not be enforced because enforcement of the clause would effectively preclude any action seeking to vindicate the statutory rights asserted by the plaintiffs.

The named plaintiffs seek to represent the following class, pursuant to Rule 23 of the Federal Rules of Civil Procedure.

At the heart of the instant appeal is the fact that the Agreement also contains the following provision:

> IF ARBITRATION IS CHOSEN BY ANY PARTY WITH RESPECT TO A CLAIM, NEITHER YOU NOR WE WILL HAVE THE RIGHT TO LITIGATE THAT CLAIM IN COURT OR HAVE A JURY TRIAL ON THAT CLAIM . . . . FURTHER, YOU WILL NOT HAVE THE RIGHT TO PARTICIPATE IN A REPRESENTATIVE CAPACITY OR AS A MEMBER OF ANY CLASS OF CLAIMANTS PERTAINING TO ANY CLAIM SUBJECT TO ARBITRATION. THE ARBITRATOR'S DECISION WILL BE FINAL AND BINDING. NOTE THAT OTHER RIGHTS THAT YOU WOULD HAVE IF YOU WENT TO COURT MAY ALSO NOT BE AVAILABLE IN ARBITRATION.
>
> There shall be no right or authority for any Claims to be arbitrated on a class action basis or on any basis involving Claims brought in a purported representative capacity on behalf of the general public, other establishments which

> accept the Card (Service Establishments), or other persons or entities similarly situated. Furthermore, Claims brought by or against a Service Establishment may not be joined or consolidated in the arbitration with Claims brought by or against any other Service Establishment(s), unless otherwise agreed to in writing by all parties.

The plaintiffs argue and we do not see that Amex posits any argument to the contrary that the district court erred in holding that the question of the class action waiver's enforceability is a matter for the arbitrator, not the court. This is plainly correct.

The plaintiffs are plainly challenging the Card Acceptance Agreement's arbitration clause insofar as they dispute the enforceability of its class action waiver and, by extension, the validity of the parties' agreement to arbitrate. Their "challenge is to the arbitration clause itself," id., rather than to the entirety of the Card Acceptance. This appeal therefore involves "a gateway dispute about whether the parties are bound by a given arbitration clause," a dispute which "raises a question of arbritrability for a court to decide." Howsam v. Dean Witter Reynolds, Inc., 537 U.S. 79, 84 (2002). We will therefore proceed to consider whether the class action waiver contained in the Card Acceptance Agreement is enforceable.

We begin by recognizing that insofar as a plaintiff may be said to possess a "right" to litigate an action in federal court as a class action under Rule 23 of the Federal Rules of Civil Procedure, the right "is a procedural right only, ancillary to the litigation of substantive claims." Deposit Guar. Nat'l Bank v. Roper, 445 U.S. 326, 332 (1980). Nevertheless, the Supreme Court has repeatedly recognized the utility of the class action as a vehicle for vindicating statutory rights. This is especially true with respect to the Court's recognition that the class action device is the only economically rational alternative when a large group of individuals or entities has suffered an alleged wrong, but the damages due to any single individual or entity are too small to justify bringing an individual action.

* * * *

The record abundantly supports the plaintiffs' argument that they would incur prohibitive costs if compelled to arbitrate under the class action waiver. This argument is compellingly set forth in an affidavit filed in the district court by Gary L. French, Ph.D., an economist associated with Nathan Associates Inc., a financial consulting firm retained by the plaintiffs. Dr. French states that the purpose of his affidavit is "to provide an expert opinion concerning the likely costs and complexity of an expert economic study concerning the liability and damages" relating to this action, and to compare this with "the potential recovery of damages by an American Express Card merchant with annual sales volume of $10 million or less, such as most if not all of the named plaintiffs in this litigation, and to provide my opinion as to whether it would be economically rational for such a merchant to pursue recovery of damages given the likely out-of-pocket costs of the arbitration or litigation proceeding." Dr. French continues:

> Due to the complexity and analytical intensity of an antitrust study, total expert fees and expenses usually are substantial, even in a nonclass action involving an individual plaintiff. In my experience, even a relatively small economic antitrust study will cost at least several hundred thousand dollars, while a larger study can easily exceed $1 million . . . . In summary, the cost of [Nathan Associates'] expert assistance in individual plaintiff antitrust cases has ranged from about $300 thousand to more than $2 million. However, after reviewing the complaint and doing some preliminary research in this case, it is my opinion that . . . the cost for this case will fall in the middle of the range of [Nathan Associates'] experience.

An economic antitrust study . . . is necessarily complex and costly because it involves investigating several antitrust liability and damages issues and, potentially involves numerous tasks and services. The antitrust liability and damages issues that an expert economist will study in this matter will likely include:

> • defining the relevant tying and tied product markets and determining whether they are distinct;

> • determining whether the defendant has market (monopoly) power in the tying product market;
>
> • determining whether the defendant has exercised its market (monopoly) power to enforce the tying arrangement;
>
> • determining whether the tying arrangement has an anticompetitive effect in the tied product market;
>
> • determining what the merchant fees would have been but for the alleged anticompetitive tying; and
>
> • quantifying the dollar amount of damages to the plaintiffs as a consequence of the tying arrangement.

Dr. French then proceeds to consider the economic rationality of bringing an individual action against Amex in light of these substantial expert witness costs:

> Based upon publicly available information . . . . I have estimated that a small merchant with $10 million of annual sales, on average, might calculate and expect $754 of economic damages for the year 2001, which is roughly the midpoint of the damage period covered by this litigation . . . . Multiplying the $754 damage figure by four, gives a rough estimate of $3,015 total damages for the whole four-year damage period, or $9,046 when trebled, assuming that the merchant's sales remain constant at $10 million for the four-year period. The median volume merchant, with half of the named plaintiffs having more and half having less American Express charge volume, and having reported $230,343 American Express Card volume in 2003, might expect four-year damages of $1,751, or $5,252 when trebled . . . . The largest volume named plaintiff merchant, with reported American Express Card volume of $1,690,749 in 2003, might expect four-year damages of $12,850, or $38,549 when trebled. In my opinion as a professional economist . . . it would not be worthwhile for an individual plaintiff . . . to pursue individual

> arbitration or litigation where the out-of-pocket costs, just for the expert economic study and services, would be at least several hundred thousand dollars, and might exceed $1 million.

Concluding that Amex has brought no serious challenge to the plaintiffs' demonstration that their claims cannot reasonably be pursued as individual actions, whether in federal court or in arbitration, we find ourselves in agreement with the plaintiffs' contention that enforcement of the class action waiver in the Card Acceptance Agreement "flatly ensures that no small merchant may challenge American Express's tying arrangements under the federal antitrust laws." The effective negation of a private suit under the antitrust laws is troubling because such "private suits provide a significant supplement to the limited resources available to the Department of Justice for enforcing the antitrust laws and deterring violations."

We therefore hold that the class action waiver in the Card Acceptance Agreement cannot be enforced in this case because to do so would grant Amex de facto immunity from antitrust liability by removing the plaintiffs' only reasonably feasible means of recovery. As already set forth, Section 2 of the FAA, 9 U.S.C. § 2, provides that an agreement to arbitrate "shall be valid, irrevocable, and enforceable, save upon such grounds as exist at law or in equity for the revocation of any contract." Given that we believe that a valid ground exists for the revocation of the class action waiver, it cannot be enforced under the FAA.

§ 5.08 ARBITRAL CLASS ACTIONS ABSENT EXPRESS WAIVER

We have yet to focus on what happens if an arbitral provision is silent as to class actions, but an arbitral matter comes before a tribunal, such as AAA, which does have class action procedures available. Is arbitration like a court case in the sense that the plaintiff's decision to seek class certification need not be based on contractual authorization?

It would appear not. In April 2010, the United States Supreme Court, in the decision to follow, passes on a Panel's decision that arbitration as a class action may proceed, assuming procedural requirements are met, in a price-fixing case brought by charterers against owners of parcel tankers.

The majority holding appears to be that it violates the federal law of arbitration under the FAA to treat party "silence" as permitting arbitrators (and, presumably courts) from allowing an arbitration to proceed as a class action unless the parties have subsequently so agreed. In this regard, the Court held that the Panel had "exceeded it powers" under FAA Section 10(a)(4) by agreeing to determine whether the arbitral action was suitable for class treatment, the class to consist of those party to arbitral agreements with the owners.

On the strength of the decision in this next case, the Supreme Court has, upon a grant of certiorari at 130 S.Ct. 2401, remanded the last case to the Second Circuit for further consideration. No further explanation was provided. What might the explanation be?

Stolt-Nielsen v. Animal-Feeds International Corp.

Supreme Court of the United States, 2010.
130 S. Ct. 1758.

- ALITO, J.

We granted certiorari in this case to decide whether imposing class arbitration on parties whose arbitration clauses are "silent" on that issue is consistent with the Federal Arbitration Act (FAA), 9 U.S.C. § 1 et seq.

Petitioners are shipping companies that serve a large share of the world market for parcel tankers seagoing vessels with compartments that are separately chartered to customers wishing to ship liquids in small quantities. One of those customers is Animal-Feeds International Corp. (hereinafter Animal-Feeds), which supplies raw ingredients, such as fish oil, to animal-feed producers around the world. Animal-Feeds ships its goods pursuant to a standard contract known in the maritime trade as a charter party. Numerous charter parties are in regular use, and the charter party that Animal-Feeds uses is known as the "Vegoilvoy" charter party. Petitioners assert, without contradiction, that charterers like Animal-Feeds, or their agents not the ship owners typically select the particular charter party that governs their shipments.

Adopted in 1950, the Vegoilvoy charter party contains the following arbitration clause:

> Arbitration. Any dispute arising from the making, performance or termination of this Charter Party shall be settled in New York, Owner and Charterer each appointing an arbitrator, who shall be a merchant, broker or individual experienced in the shipping business; the two thus chosen, if they cannot agree, shall nominate a third arbitrator who shall be an Admiralty lawyer. Such arbitration shall be conducted in conformity with the provisions and procedure of the United States Arbitration Act [i.e., the FAA], and a judgment of the Court shall be entered upon any award made by said arbitrator.

In 2005, Animal-Feeds served petitioners with a demand for class arbitration, designating New York City as the place of arbitration and seeking to represent a class of "[a]ll direct purchasers of parcel tanker transportation services globally for bulk liquid chemicals, edible oils, acids, and other specialty liquids from [petitioners] at any time during the period from August 1, 1998, to November 30, 2002." The parties entered into a supplemental agreement providing for the question of class arbitration to be submitted to a panel of three arbitrators who were to "follow and be bound by Rules 3 through 7 of the American Arbitration Association's Supplementary Rules for Class Arbitrations (as effective Oct. 8, 2003)." These rules (hereinafter Class Rules) were developed by the American Arbitration Association (AAA) after our decision in *Green Tree Financial Corp. v. Bazzle*, 539 U.S. 444., and Class Rule 3, in accordance with the plurality opinion in that case, requires an arbitrator, as a threshold matter, to determine "whether the applicable arbitration clause permits the arbitration to proceed on behalf of or against a class."

The parties selected a panel of arbitrators and stipulated that the arbitration clause was "silent" with respect to class arbitration. Counsel for Animal-Feeds explained to the arbitration panel that the term "silent" did not simply mean that the clause made no express reference to class arbitration. Rather, he said, "[a]ll the parties agree that when a contract is silent on an issue there's been no agreement that has been reached on that issue."

After hearing argument and evidence, including testimony from petitioners' experts regarding arbitration customs and usage in the maritime trade, the arbitrators concluded that the arbitration clause allowed for class arbitration. They found persuasive the fact that other arbitrators ruling after *Bazzle* had construed "a wide variety of clauses in a wide variety of settings as allowing for class arbitration," but the panel acknowledged that none of these decisions was "exactly comparable" to the present dispute. Petitioners' expert evidence did not show an "inten[t] to preclude class arbitration," the arbitrators reasoned, and petitioners' argument would leave "no basis for a class action absent express agreement among all parties and the putative class members.

Petitioners contend that the decision of the arbitration panel must be vacated, but in order to obtain that relief, they must clear a high hurdle. It is not enough for petitioners to show that the panel committed an error or even a serious error[s] his own brand of industrial justice' that his decision may be unenforceable." Major League Baseball Players Assn. v. Garvey, 532 U.S. 504, 509 (2001) (per curiam) (quoting Steelworkers v. Enterprise Wheel & Car Corp., 363 U.S. 593, 597 (1960)). In that situation, an arbitration decision may be vacated under § 10(a)(4) of the FAA on the ground that the arbitrator "exceeded [his] powers," for the task of an arbitrator is to interpret and enforce a contract, not to make public policy. In this case, we must conclude that what the arbitration panel did was simply to impose its own view of sound policy regarding class arbitration.

Rather than inquiring whether the FAA, maritime law, or New York law contains a "default rule" under which an arbitration clause is construed as allowing class arbitration in the absence of express consent, the panel proceeded as if it had the authority of a common law court to develop what it viewed as the best rule to be applied in such a situation. The conclusion is inescapable that the panel simply imposed its own conception of sound policy.

* * * *

We think it is clear from our precedents and the contractual nature of arbitration that parties may specify with whom they choose to arbitrate their disputes. See EEOC v. Waffle House, Inc., 534 U.S. 279, 289 (2002) ("[N]othing in the [FAA] authorizes a court to compel arbitration of any issues, *or by any parties*, that are not already covered in the agreement" (emphasis added)); Moses H. Cone Memorial Hospital v. Mercury Constr. Corp., 460 U.S. 1, 20 (1983) ("[A]n arbitration agreement must be enforced notwithstanding the presence of other persons who are parties to the underlying dispute but not to the arbitration agreement"); *Steelworkers*, 80 S. Ct. 1358 (an arbitrator "has no general charter to administer justice for a community which transcends the parties" (internal quotation marks omitted)); accord, First Options of Chicago, Inc. v. Kaplan, 514 U.S. 938, 943 (1995) ("[A]rbitration is simply a matter of contract *between the parties*; it is a way to resolve those disputes but only those disputes . . . that the *parties* have agreed to submit to arbitration" (emphasis added)).

From these principles, it follows that a party may not be compelled under the FAA to submit to class arbitration unless there is a contractual basis for concluding that the party agreed to do so. In this case, however, the arbitration panel imposed class arbitration even though the parties concurred that they had reached "no agreement" on that issue.

An implicit agreement to authorize class-action arbitration, is not a term that the arbitrator may infer solely from the fact of the parties' agreement to arbitrate. This is so because class-action arbitration changes the nature of arbitration to such a degree that it cannot be presumed the parties consented to it by simply agreeing to submit their disputes to an arbitrator. In bilateral arbitration, parties forgo the procedural rigor and appellate review of the courts in order to realize the benefits of private dispute resolution: lower costs, greater efficiency and speed, and the ability to choose expert adjudicators to resolve specialized disputes.

Consider just some of the fundamental changes brought about by the shift from bilateral arbitration to class-action arbitration. An arbitrator chosen according to an agreed-upon procedure, no longer resolves a single dispute between the parties to a single agreement, but instead resolves many disputes between hundreds or perhaps even thousands of parties. Under the Class Rules, "the presumption of privacy and confidentiality" that applies in many bilateral arbitrations "shall not apply in class arbitrations," see Addendum to Brief for American Arbitration Association as Amicus Curiae 10a (Class Rule 9(a)), thus potentially frustrating the parties' assumptions when they agreed to arbitrate. The arbitrator's award no longer purports to bind just the parties to a single arbitration agreement, but adjudicates the rights of absent parties as well. We think that the differences between bilateral and class-action arbitration are too great for arbitrators to presume, consistent with their limited powers under the FAA, that the parties' mere silence on the issue of class-action arbitration constitutes consent to resolve their disputes in class proceedings.

NOTES

1. The majority opinion says that there was no evidence of a state law default rule that class action treatment could be accorded where the arbitral agreement was "silent" on the matter. Given that the majority speaks about overriding FAA policies trumping state law principles of contractual construction, would the existence of such a state law default rule make any difference? The Court has granted certiorari on a related matter—whether the FAA preempts state courts from rejecting class action waivers on unconscionability grounds. *See* AT&T Mobility LLC v. Concepcion, 130 S. Ct. 3322 (2010).

2. Given all the concern about mandatory arbitration in consumer cases, has the Supreme Court adding fuel to the fire?

3. The issue of consolidation of similar claims has also provoked controversy. Consolidation in courts is used when multiple claimants

wish to proceed against a common defendant on essentially similar claims. *See* FED. R. CIV. P. 20(a)). The AAA bars consolidation unless all parties agree. Unlike class actions pursued by one or more representative claimants, in a consolidation each claimant actively pursues its claim.

4. For one of several cases holding that courts cannot order consolidation of arbitrations unless the parties have provided for it, see *Glencore, Ltd. v. Schnitzer Steel Products Co.*, 189 F.3 264 (2d Cir. 1999). Certain state arbitral statutes, such as those in California and Texas, specifically permit such consolidation, but these statutes may be subject to preemption.

5. In *Stolt*, the parties specifically assigned the class action issue to the arbitrators. Otherwise, is the issue of whether class action treatment is proper one of arbitrability for the court or one of construction of the arbitration clause for the arbitrators? In *Green Tree Financial Corp. v. Bazzle*, 339 U.S. 444 (2003), the Supreme Court concluded the latter. However, since that time, and particularly given the rationale of *Stolt* that imposing class action treatment where the arbitral provision is silent requires a party to arbitrate without its consent, it is unclear whether the *Bazzle* approach is still viable. Whether a party has consented to arbitrate is traditionally a matter for judicial determination. Notably, *Stolt* refers to the *Bazzle* analysis as "obscure." The issue of the appropriateness of class action treatment should not be confused with that of whether a class action waiver is unconscionable. That issue, presumably, would normally be for the court to decide under the severability approach. See *In re American Express Merchants' Litigation*, *supra* at page 355.

Study of AAA Consumer Cases Yields Positive Results

- *In-Depth Study of AAA Consumer Arbitration Caseload Released by the Searle Civil Justice Institute.*
- NEW YORK, March 11, 2009.

An independent study by the Searle Civil Justice Institute (SCJI) at the Northwestern University School of Law has found that the majority of consumer arbitration cases administered by the American Arbitration Association (AAA) are cost efficient, expeditious and in full compliance with Due Process Protocols.

According to the study, *Consumer Arbitration Before the American Arbitration Association,* due process protocols "commonly require independent and impartial arbitrators, reasonable costs, and remedies comparable to those available in court."

"We are gratified that this independent study demonstrates the value and efficacy of the commitment of the American Arbitration Association to due process and quality administration and that arbitration can deliver a fair and efficient forum for consumers and employees," said Richard Naimark, Senior Vice President of the AAA.

"The SCJI study illustrates that arbitration can provide consumers and employees access to justice when the process is carefully balanced with the Due Process Protocols. Most consumers and employees have difficulty accessing court if their claims are of modest size. Some studies have indicated that individuals with claims smaller than $65,000 may have difficulty engaging legal counsel. Arbitration can be a remedy in that setting. But it is essential that Due Process Protocols, or some comparable safeguards, be integral, to ensure a level playing field with no undue advantage to either party," Mr. Naimark continued.

SCJI reviewed a sample of 301 AAA cases involving consumer arbitrations closed by an award between April and December of 2007. This sample was analyzed for approximately 200 variables in the arbitration process.

The study revealed that consumer claimants paid an average of $96 ($1 in administrative fees and $95 in arbitrator fees) in cases seeking less than $10,000 and $219 ($15 in administrative fees and $204 in arbitrator fees) for claims between $10,000 and $75,000.

The average time from filing to final award for the consumer arbitrations studied was 6.9 months, SCJI found.

In 98.2 percent of cases in the sample subject to AAA protocol compliance review, the arbitration clause either complied with the Due Process Protocol, or AAA properly identified the non-compliance and responded to it.

Chapter 6

CONFIRMATION AND VACATUR OF AWARDS

With all the historical opposition and reservations about compulsory arbitration, one would expect the courts to be somewhat intrusive at the post-award stage if, as is often the case, they are asked to adopt awards ("confirm") as court judgments. Somewhat curiously, even with respect to awards determining statutory cases in which the public is deemed to have an interest, courts rarely disturb arbitral decisions.

Historically, where the parties agreed post-dispute to arbitrate, courts would confirm awards virtually automatically absent some truly critical infirmity in the proceedings. However, as courts came to reject "ouster" as a basis to refuse enforcement of pre-dispute agreements, there would be constant assurances that the judiciary would supervise, particularly where arbitral adherence to statute was "mandatory." Under the federal law of arbitration, awards would be rejected not only if a party was denied a fundamentally fair opportunity to be heard, but also where there was "manifest disregard" of the law. See the *Willemijn* case, supra at 26. The state courts often claim the power to reject awards which are "arbitrary and capricious," but rarely do. Recall that the key arbitral statutes do not provide for vacation of awards because of material legal or factual error. Review N.Y. C.P.L.R. 7509–11

(Appendix 2) and FAA §§ 9–12 (Appendix 1). As for modification, that is typically limited to mistakes such as calculative errors appearing on the face of the award. *Id.*

Typically, the application to vacate or modify must be brought fairly quickly (within three months of delivery of the award under FAA § 12; within 90 days under N.Y. C.P.L.R. 7511(a)). However, the prevailing party has a full year to seek confirmation, with such application extending the time in New York for the counterparty to cross-apply for relief from the award. There is no such extension under the FAA, but courts are sometimes known to disregard this limitation in practice. *See* FAA § 9 and N.Y. C.P.L.R. 7509.

§ 6.01 LACK OF FUNDAMENTAL FAIRNESS

As explicitly set forth in the New York and Uniform Model statutes (N.Y. C.P.L.R. 7506(c)), "[t]he parties are entitled to be heard, to present evidence material to the controversy and to cross-examine witnesses appearing at the hearing." In this regard, weigh the following crosscurrents:

- Arbitrators, and often the attorneys, are empowered to subpoena witnesses and documents (records")
- Discovery is limited
- Rules of evidence do not apply (does that temper reduce pre-hearing discovery?)
- Arbitrators may accept testimony by affidavit
- Awards are very often unreasoned

[A] Discovery Matters

Superadio Ltd. P'ship v. Winstar Radio Prods., LLC

Supreme Judicial Court of Massachusetts, 2006.
844 N.E.2d 246.

- GREANEY, J.

The background of the case is as follows. In May, 1995, Superadio and Baby Love entered a radio network agreement (agreement) wherein Superadio became the exclusive advertising sales agent for an existing radio program and a proposed new radio program produced by Baby Love. Under the agreement, the net revenues collected from the sale of advertising airing on the radio programs were to be divided equally between Superadio and Baby Love. The agreement provided that it "shall be interpreted" under Massachusetts law and that "[a]ny dispute arising under the [a]greement, including but not limited to any dispute concerning payments due, shall be arbitrated under the rules of the American Arbitration Association [AAA] before a panel of the [AAA] sitting in Boston, Massachusetts." After an extension, the agreement terminated on December 31, 1998.

A few months later, Superadio filed a demand for arbitration, alleging that Baby Love had withheld approximately $150,000 in advertising revenues that should have been shared with Superadio. The disputed revenue allegedly derived from advertisements that had been booked by Superadio during the term of the agreement, but had not aired until after the agreement had terminated. Baby Love filed an answer and a counterclaim asserting that Superadio had violated the agreement by refusing to turn over advertising revenues that Superadio had collected on Baby Love's behalf for advertisements that had aired before the agreement terminated. Baby Love sought $841,239 in damages. Superadio agreed that Baby Love was entitled to approximately $75,000 of those revenues, but held the money to offset the amount which Superadio claimed it was owed.

The parties selected a panel of three arbitrators (panel). By agreement of the parties, the Commercial Arbitration Rules of the AAA (AAA rules), would govern the proceeding. The panel entered a partial summary judgment award, finding that Superadio had no right to offset, and ordering Superadio to pay the withheld amount to Baby Love.

The parties proceeded with discovery on the remaining claims to be arbitrated. Baby Love claimed that Superadio was not complying with its discovery requests and sought intervention from the panel. On August 21, 2000, the panel entered an order directing Superadio either to satisfy certain discovery requests "by September 22, 2000," or to pay Baby Love "$1,000 per day until Superadio is either in compliance or until the date of the [h]earing, whichever shall occur first." The parties were notified that the failure to produce discovery would result in the exclusion of such discovery as evidence at the arbitration hearing. Superadio did not comply with the discovery order and, on September 28, 2000, withdrew its demand for arbitration. Baby Love proceeded to arbitrate its counterclaim.

The panel conducted a hearing on the case in June, 2001, and did not permit either party to introduce documents or witnesses that it had not produced in response to a reasonable discovery request. On July 23, 2001, the panel entered its award. The panel concluded that Baby Love had supported its claim that Superadio had underreported the amount of advertising revenues owed. The panel, however, could not enter an award for contract damages because of Baby Love's inability to prove its damages, an inability attributable to Superadio's failure in discovery to produce documents relevant to the damages issue. The panel concluded that, under Rule 23(c) of the AAA rules, it had the authority to impose a sanction on Superadio for violating the panel's August 21, 2000, discovery order, and imposed a sanction in the amount of $271,000. The amount represented an assessment of $1,000 a day from September 23, 2000 (the day following the deadline for discovery compliance), to June 20, 2001 (the day that the arbitration hearing commenced). The panel noted that Superadio could have tolled the accrual of sanctions by producing the ordered discovery, which Superadio admitted was in its possession. The panel added to its award certain costs and prejudgment interest, amounts not in dispute, for a total award of $287,566.83. In addition, the panel noted that Superadio, by filing its demand for arbitration, had agreed to abide by the AAA rules, which permit nonlawyers to represent parties at an arbitration proceeding. In view of the applicable AAA rules, the panel rejected Superadio's argument that the representation of Baby Love by a licensed out-of-State attorney constituted the unauthorized practice of law.

* * * *

[T]he AAA rules provide arbitrators with broad authority to fashion remedies during arbitration proceedings and to oversee discovery. Rule 45 (a) provides:

> The arbitrator may grant *any remedy or relief that the arbitrator deems just and equitable* and within the scope of the agreement of the parties, including, but not limited to, specific performance of a contract. (emphasis added).

Rule 23 provides:

> (a) At the request of any party or at the discretion of the arbitrator, consistent with the expedited nature of arbitration, the arbitrator may direct (i) the production of documents and other information, and (ii) the identification of any witnesses to be called.
> (b) At least five (5) business days prior to the hearing, the parties shall exchange copies of all exhibits they intend to submit at the hearing.
> (c) *The arbitrator is authorized to resolve any disputes concerning the exchange of information.* (emphasis added).

Noteworthy in these rules is the absence of any language limiting the means by which an arbitrator or arbitration panel may resolve discovery disputes, or language restricting the application of the broad remedial relief of rule 45 (a) to final awards (and precluding the grant of broad remedial relief to interim awards). The rules, construed together, and supported by the broad arbitration provision in the agreement and the absence of any limiting language prohibiting a monetary sanction for discovery violations, authorized the panel to resolve discovery dispute by imposing monetary sanctions.... To give arbitrators control over discovery and discovery disputes without the authority to impose monetary sanctions for discovery violations and noncompliance with appropriate discovery orders, would impede the arbitrators' ability to adjudicate claims effectively in the manner contemplated by the arbitration process.

NOTE

1. What practical difference is there between a "fine" for failure to make discovery, and a negative inference conclusive on the merits? Just as courts can do, arbitrators have the power to treat a failure to produce as an admission that the contents of withheld materials are adverse to the defaulting party. In more extreme circumstances, arbitrators can actually preclude a party from presenting evidence on a matter dealt with in withheld materials. The ultimate sanction, as in court, would be an adverse determination on the merits of the affected issue(s).

In re Viselman v. Itsy Bitsy Entertainment Co., Inc.

New York App. Div. 1st Dep't, 2005.
19 A.D.3d 186

▪ PER CURIAM.

Order and judgment (one paper), Supreme Court, New York County (Robert D. Lippmann, J.), entered January 7, 2005, which denied petitioner's application to vacate an arbitration, and dismissed the petition, unanimously affirmed, without costs.

The evidence supporting the award, and the panel's finding that the company in which petitioner seeks to recover an equity interest was rendered worthless in part because of petitioner's actions, meets the standard of *Matter of Andros Cia. Maritima* [*Marc Rich & Co.*] (579 F2d 691, 704 [2d Cir, 1978]). Nor was petitioner denied a " 'fundamentally fair hearing' " (Fine v Bear Stearns & Co., 765 F Supp 824, 828–29 [SDNY 1991]) by the panel's refusal to fully enforce disclosure directives made at the outset of the hearing. However, the appeal is not frivolous and we reject respondents' request to impose sanctions.

[B] The Requirement of a Hearing and Pre-Hearing Motions

Schlessinger v. Rosenfeld, Meyer & Susman

Court of Appeal of California, Second Appellate District, Division One, 1995.
40 Cal. App. 4th 1096.

- MASTERSON, ASSOCIATE JUSTICE.

Gary Schlessinger, an attorney, and Rosenfeld, Meyer & Susman (RM&S), his former law firm, could not agree on the payment due Schlessinger upon his resignation from the partnership. Pursuant to the partnership agreement, the dispute proceeded to arbitration before the American Arbitration Association. The arbitrator disposed of the principal issues by way of two motions for summary adjudication and ultimately rendered an award in favor of RM&S.

Schlessinger petitioned the superior court to vacate the arbitration award on the ground that the arbitrator had refused to hear evidence material to the controversy. In the petition, he asserted that the California Arbitration Act (Code Civ. Proc., § 1280–1294.2) precluded the use of summary adjudication motions in an arbitration proceeding. The trial court dismissed the petition. We conclude that the arbitrator could entertain such motions and affirm.

BACKGROUND

Schlessinger was a partner at RM&S from January 1, 1966, through May 12, 1993, at which time he resigned from the partnership. In 1975, Schlessinger and other partners at RM&S had entered into a written partnership agreement (the agreement) governing their practice of law. The agreement provided that partners who left the firm were to be paid for their interest in the firm's anticipated revenues from work in progress and receivables (the "agreed sum") and for their capital account. The amount of the agreed sum was reduced in accordance with a specified formula if the departing partner engaged in competition with the firm.

After Schlessinger left RM&S, he began competing with the firm. RM&S calculated the agreed sum by making the specified reductions in Schlessinger's share of anticipated revenues. Schlessinger contended that the reductions constituted unlawful tolls on competition. When the parties could not resolve this dispute, RM&S filed a demand for arbitration with the American Arbitration Association (AAA) pursuant to article 13 of the agreement. Schlessinger responded with a counter-demand for arbitration. The parties retained counsel for purposes of the arbitration.

Under AAA rules, the matter was assigned to Arbitrator Winslow Christian, a retired justice of the Court of Appeal. On November 18, 1993, the arbitrator held a preliminary hearing to determine the arbitration procedure. After consultation with counsel and the consideration of written submissions, the arbitrator issued "procedural order number one," which stated in part, "The parties are invited, but not required, to present initial summary judgment motions, tendering any issues framed by the pleadings which, in the judgment of counsel, can be resolved on declarations." The order provided for a briefing schedule, with argument to be conducted by a telephone conference call.

The parties filed cross-motions for summary adjudication on the question of whether the agreement's tolls on competition were valid. On December 13, 1993, the arbitrator conducted a telephonic hearing on the motions. The following day, he issued a three-page ruling denying Schlessinger's motion and granting RM&S's motion in part. The arbitrator noted that the parties had submitted declarations, memoranda of points and authorities, and other documents in support of their respective positions. He ruled that under *Howard v. Babcock* (1993) 6 Cal. 4th 409, "an agreement between law partners may lawfully exact from a withdrawing partner a *reasonable* toll for competing with his former law firm." The arbitrator also found that the issue of the tolls' "reasonableness" could not be resolved on the basis of the motions and would have to await the taking of evidence. He concluded that the toll provisions of the agreement "are valid if they are reasonable."

The parties then submitted proposals as to the further course of the proceedings. On December 22, 1993, the arbitrator conducted a telephone conference call with counsel on that subject. On January 3, 1994, he issued "procedural order number two," WHICH STATED IN

PART: "In the interest of economy and expedition in the disposition of this proceeding, . . . the single issue of reasonableness of the 'toll' for competition . . . will be tried first. Pending further order, discovery will be limited to the reasonableness of the 'toll.' " With the scope of discovery so limited, the arbitrator established deadlines for the taking of depositions and for each party to serve and respond to one set of contention interrogatories and a document demand. He also set a deadline for any additional summary adjudication motions and, absent such a motion, scheduled a trial date. Schlessinger deposed two RM&S partners, and RM&S took Schlessinger's deposition.

In February 1994, Schlessinger filed a motion for summary adjudication contending that the tolls were unreasonable as a matter of law. Shortly thereafter, RM&S filed a cross-motion on the same issue. In support of his motion and in opposition to RM&S's motion, Schlessinger submitted, among other things, memoranda of points and authorities and evidence consisting of two declarations from himself, a declaration from a certified public accountant, a declaration from his attorney, excerpts from the two depositions he had taken, and portions of his own deposition. The evidence supporting RM&S's motion consisted primarily of declarations from the two partners whom Schlessinger had deposed and of Schlessinger's deposition testimony.

On March 31, 1994, the arbitrator held a telephonic hearing on this second round of summary adjudication motions. In mid-April, he issued a three-page ruling, denying Schlessinger's motion and granting RM&S's motion. The ruling quoted *Howard v. Babcock*, supra, 6 Cal. 4th at page 425, for the proposition that "[t]hese tolls on competition are valid if 'at the time of the agreement [they were] reasonably calculated to compensate the firm for losses that may be caused by the withdrawing partner's competition.' " Applying this standard, the arbitrator reviewed the evidence submitted on the motions and concluded that the tolls were reasonable as a matter of law.

In light of the arbitrator's rulings on the two summary adjudication motions, the parties were able to resolve the remaining issue by stipulation. In July 1994, the arbitrator issued an award in RM&S's favor which incorporated the summary adjudication rulings.

In November 1994, Schlessinger filed a petition in superior court to vacate the arbitration award. The petition asserted that the award was invalid because Schlessinger's "rights were substantially prejudiced . . . by the refusal of the arbitrator[] to hear evidence material to the controversy or by other conduct of the arbitrator[] contrary to the provisions of this [Act]." (Code Civ. Proc., § 1286.2, subd. (e)). In particular, Schlessinger claimed that the California Arbitration Act (the Act) required the arbitrator to conduct a hearing at which witnesses appeared and presented live testimony, thus precluding the use of summary adjudication motions. The trial court dismissed the petition. Schlessinger filed a timely appeal.

DISCUSSION

The contention that the arbitrator lacked authority to entertain summary adjudication motions requires that we interpret provisions of the Act, the AAA rules, and the agreement. In construing statutory provisions, we follow well-established principles: First, " 'the court should ascertain the intent of the Legislature so as to effectuate the purpose of the law' ". . . . Secondly, the provision must be given a reasonable and common sense interpretation consistent with the apparent purpose and intention of the lawmakers, practical rather than technical in nature, which upon application will result in wise policy rather than mischief or absurdity. . . . " 'The court should take into account matters such as context, the object in view, the evils to be remedied, the history of the times and of legislation upon the same subject, public policy, and contemporaneous construction. . . .' " (DeYoung v. City of San Diego (1983) 147 Cal. App. 3d 11, 17–18.) To determine intent, we first look to the statutory language, giving effect to its plain meaning. We also resort to the plain meaning of the language in the agreement and the AAA rules.

Neither the agreement, the Act, nor the AAA rules incorporate the state's summary adjudication statute (§ 437c). Nor do any of those sources expressly provide for such a motion. However, the lack of explicit authorization does not mean summary adjudication motions are precluded. While an authorizing statute may be necessary to permit summary adjudication motions in an action at law, the "rules of judicial procedure need not be observed [in an arbitration]." (§ 1282.2, subd.

(d)). We conclude that the arbitrator had implicit authority to rule on such motions. We begin by examining the statutes on which Schlessinger relied in seeking to vacate the award.

A. *The Statutory Basis of Schlessinger's Petition*

An arbitration award must be vacated if the rights of a party were substantially prejudiced by the arbitrator's "refusal . . . to *hear* evidence material to the controversy." (§ 1286.2, subd. (e), italics added). Schlessinger contends that the arbitrator did not "hear" any evidence because he disposed of the principal issues by way of summary adjudication motions. According to Schlessinger, an arbitrator "hears" evidence only if he learns of it through his auditory sense; thus, the evidence had to be presented orally through witnesses.

An award must also be set aside if the arbitrator engaged in prejudicial conduct contrary to any of the Act's provisions. (§ 1286.2, subd. (e)). Schlessinger asserts that one provision of the Act required a hearing at which he could cross-examine witnesses. (See § 1282.2, subd. (d)). He claims that the arbitrator violated this provision because the summary adjudication motions deprived him of the right of cross-examination. We disagree with these contentions.

B. *The Arbitrator's Duty to "Hear" the Evidence*

Under section 1286.2, subdivision (e), the arbitrator's obligation "to hear evidence" does not mean that the evidence must be orally presented or that live testimony is required. "Legally speaking the admission of evidence is to hear it." (Gonzales v. Interinsurance Exchange (1978) 84 Cal. App. 3d 58, 63.) An arbitrator "hears" evidence by providing a "legal hearing," that is, by affording an "opportunity to . . . present one's side of a case." (Webster's Third New Internat. Dict. (1981) p. 1044, col. 2 [defining "hear" and "hearing"]). An arbitrator also "hears" a matter by "consider[ing] a motion upon presentation thereof by counsel." (Ballentine's Law Dict. (3d ed. 1969) p. 552, col. 2). Thus, a "hearing" does not necessarily include "an opportunity to present live testimony or be subject to cross examination." (Buxton v. Lynaugh (5th Cir. 1989) 879 F.2d 140, 145). "Unless required by the express language, or the context of the particular rule, the use of the word 'hearing' does not necessarily contemplate either a personal appearance or an oral presentation to the court." (Classic Promotions, Inc. v. Shafer (Tex.App. 1993) 846 S.W.2d 948, 950).

We decline to read section 1286.2, subdivision (e), as requiring that an arbitrator always resolve disputes through the oral presentation of evidence or the taking of live testimony. To do otherwise would lead to anomalous results. The purpose of arbitration, as reflected in the Act, is to provide a "speedy and relatively inexpensive means of dispute resolution." (Moncharsh v. Heily & Blase (1992) 3 Cal. 4th 1, 9). Having chosen arbitration over civil litigation, a party should "reap the advantages that flow from the use of that nontechnical, *summary procedure*." (Id. at p. 11, italics added).

Yet, Schlessinger's position would require full-blown trials even where, as here, one of the parties believes that no material facts are in dispute. In a case where a legal issue or defense could possibly be resolved on undisputed facts, the purpose of the arbitration process would be defeated by precluding a summary judgment or summary adjudication motion and instead requiring a lengthy trial. Moreover, taking Schlessinger's argument to its logical extreme, an arbitrator could not consider any documentary evidence, with or without a trial, unless one of the parties first read it to him. The Act certainly does not countenance such a wasteful use of the parties' resources and the arbitrator's time.

C. *Schlessinger's Alleged Right to Cross-examine Witnesses*

We reject Schlessinger's argument that section 1282.2, subdivision (d), mandated a hearing at which witnesses presented live testimony and were subject to cross-examination. While that portion of the Act entitles a party to cross-examine witnesses *if* they appear at a hearing, it does not give a party an absolute right to present oral testimony in every case. Indeed, section 1282.2, subdivision (c), states that the arbitrator "shall rule on . . . questions of hearing procedure and shall exercise all powers relating to the conduct of the hearing." This language is sufficiently broad to permit an arbitrator to conduct a hearing on a summary adjudication motion in lieu of a hearing with oral testimony.

Equally important, all of the provisions of section 1282.2 are prefaced with the words "[u]nless the arbitration agreement otherwise provides." Thus, even if section 1282.2, subdivision (d), mandates a hearing with live testimony, the introductory language of the statute permits the parties to adopt a different procedure. They did so here. The partnership agreement required application of AAA rules to the parties' arbitration. Consistent with Rule 10, the arbitrator held a "preliminary hearing" at which he was authorized to "specify the issues to be resolved, to [have the parties] stipulate to uncontested facts, and *to consider any other matters that will expedite the arbitration proceedings*." (Rule 10, italics added). Further, while Rule 29 describes the method for conducting a "hearing," including the questioning of witnesses, it also provides that "[t]he arbitrator has the discretion to vary this procedure." Significantly, Rule 32 permits the arbitrator to "receive and consider the evidence of witnesses by affidavit." We believe that these rules implicitly sanctioned the use of summary adjudication motions.

Finally, Schlessinger's position, if correct, would exalt form over substance. Where, through discovery, the parties have pretrial access to pertinent witnesses and information, a summary adjudication motion may provide an efficient means of evaluating the same evidence that would otherwise be presented at a more time-consuming trial. Had the summary adjudication motions not been made, RM&S could have presented its case at trial by calling two of its partners as witnesses (the ones who executed the declarations) and by reading from Schlessinger's deposition transcript. Schlessinger could have cross-examined the RM&S witnesses (whom he had already deposed) and could have taken the stand himself. At the close of the testimony, the arbitrator would have decided that RM&S's evidence alone was sufficient, that Schlessinger's evidence was irrelevant or cumulative, that no material facts were in dispute, and that RM&S was entitled to prevail. In other words, the inefficient use of a trial would have accomplished the same result as a summary adjudication motion. Neither the Act nor the AAA rules require a trial in such circumstances.

D. *Non-California Authorities*

While no California case has addressed the issue before us, other authorities shed some light on the question. For instance, a number of decisions by arbitrators indicate that they occasionally consider motions for summary judgment. (See, e.g., Eastern Air Lines, Inc., 79 Lab. Arb. Rep. (BNA 1982) 61, 64, fn. 3 ["a summary judgment is extraordinary (although not unheard of) in arbitration proceedings"]; Pantsmaker, Inc., 83 Lab. Arb. Rep. 753, 759 (BNA 1984) [considering and denying union's motion for summary judgment]; City of Pasadena, 96 Lab. Arb. Rep. 26, 29 (BNA 1990) [denying grievant's summary judgment motion and ordering trial on the merits].).

Commentators, on the other hand, generally assume or conclude that such motions are not available in an arbitration proceeding. (See, e.g., Mathiason & Uppal, Evaluating and Using Employer-Initiated Arbitration Policies and Agreements: Preparing the Workplace for the Twenty-First Century, in Employment Discrimination and Civil Rights Actions in Federal and State Courts (ALI-ABA 1994) 875, 919 [noting that California Arbitration Act does not provide for motion practice]; Knight et al., Cal. Practice Guide: Alternative Dispute Resolution (The Rutter Group 1994) P 4.4, pp. 4-1 to 4-2 [mentioning unavailability of summary judgment motions as a disadvantage of contractual arbitration proceedings]). But none of these secondary authorities has considered whether the Act, in conjunction with AAA rules, permits the use of summary judgment or summary adjudication motions.

* * * *

More in line with our thinking is *Stifler v. Weiner* (1985) 62 Md. App. 1, which concerned whether a motion for "summary disposition" is available under Maryland's Health Claims Arbitration Act (Md. Code Ann., Cts. & Jud. Proc., § 3-2A-01 et seq.). In concluding that such a motion is permissible, the court reasoned: "Although there is no provision in the statute for summary disposition . . . , we see no reason why a claim cannot be adjudicated on that basis in those instances where it may be susceptible to such treatment. If, for example, as here, limitations has clearly run on the claim, there is no reason to waste time, effort, and money on a full-scale trial on the merits of the claim." (62 Md. App. at p. 24.)

In sum, we conclude that the arbitrator had authority under the Act and AAA rules to entertain the parties' cross-motions for summary adjudication.

E. *Judicial Review of the Arbitrator's Decision*

Having concluded that the arbitrator could rule on summary adjudication motions, we next decide whether the arbitration award should be vacated based on his rulings.

In general, ". . . courts may not interfere with arbitration awards. Courts may not examine the merits of the controversy, the sufficiency of the evidence supporting the award, or the reasoning supporting the decision. . . . A court may not set aside an arbitration award even if the arbitrator made an error in law or fact. . . ." (Santa Clara-San Benito etc. Elec. Contractors' Assn. v. Local Union No. 332 (1974) 40 Cal. App. 3d 431, 437, citations omitted.) As explained more recently by our Supreme Court: "[I]t is the general rule that, with narrow exceptions, an arbitrator's decision cannot be reviewed for errors of fact or law. In reaffirming this general rule, we recognize there is a risk that the arbitrator will make a mistake. That risk, however, is acceptable for two reasons. First, by voluntarily submitting to arbitration, the parties have agreed to bear that risk in return for a quick, inexpensive, and conclusive resolution of their dispute. . . . A second reason why we tolerate the risk of an erroneous decision is because the Legislature has reduced the risk to the parties of such a decision by providing for judicial review in circumstances involving serious problems with the award itself, or with the fairness of the arbitration process." (*Moncharsh v. Heily & Blase*, supra, 3 Cal. 4th at pp. 11–12.).

Moncharsh's reference to the narrow, statutory exceptions permitting judicial review of arbitration awards brings us back to section 1286.2, subdivision (e). As our earlier discussion indicates, the arbitrator did not "refuse to hear evidence" or otherwise contravene the Act merely because he entertained motions for summary adjudication. However, our conclusion that the arbitrator had the authority to rule on such motions does not end the inquiry. Section 1286.2, subdivision (e), ensures that a party is not "unfairly deprived of a fair opportunity to present his or her side of the dispute." (*Moncharsh*, supra, 3 Cal. 4th at p. 13.) Here, Schlessinger argues that the arbitrator committed two principal errors in granting the summary adjudication motions: he found that there were no disputed issues of material fact, and he precluded Schlessinger from offering certain material evidence in opposition to the motions.

As to the first alleged error, *Moncharsh* makes clear that we cannot examine the arbitration award for errors of fact or law. (See 3 Cal. 4th at pp. 11–12.) Indeed, "the existence of an error of law apparent on the face of the award that causes substantial injustice does not provide grounds for judicial review." (Id. at p. 33.) Thus, even if the arbitrator erred in concluding that there were no disputed issues of material fact, the trial court properly refused to vacate the award on that basis.

Schlessinger's second contention—that the arbitrator did not permit him to offer material evidence—could be made in virtually every case where the arbitrator has excluded some evidence or placed limitations on discovery. Further, such a challenge would be available regardless of how the case was decided—by motion or trial. Plainly, this type of attack on the arbitrator's decision, if not properly limited, could swallow the rule that arbitration awards are generally not reviewable on the merits. Accordingly, a challenge to an arbitrator's evidentiary rulings or limitations on discovery should not provide a basis for vacating an award unless the error *substantially prejudiced* a party's ability to present *material* evidence in support of its case. (§ 1286.2, subd. (e).)

As more fully explained by one Court of Appeal:

> "In the typical arbitration, an arbitrator must make numerous decisions about admission of evidence and in doing so may exclude material evidence. No doubt there will often be aggrieved parties who believe they have been 'substantially prejudiced.' Decisions about materiality cannot be made without familiarity with the issues and evidence in the arbitration. If the superior court must, with or without a transcript of the arbitration, routinely review the arbitrator's decision on materiality before reaching the question of substantial prejudice, the legislative goal of arbitral finality will be unattainable. Instead of saving time and money, the arbitration will be supplemented by lengthy and costly judicial second-guessing of the arbitrator. . . . We do not accept the suggestion . . . that section 1286.2, subdivision (e), provides a back door to *Moncharsh* through which parties

> may routinely test the validity of legal theories of arbitrators. Instead, we interpret section 1286.2, subdivision (e), as a safety valve in private arbitration that permits a court to intercede *when an arbitrator has prevented a party from fairly presenting its case*. . . . Where, as here, a party complains of excluded material evidence, the reviewing court should generally focus first on prejudice, not materiality. To find substantial prejudice the court must accept for purposes of analysis, the arbitrator's legal theory and conclude that the arbitrator might well have made a different award had the evidence been allowed."

(Hall v. Superior Court (1993) 18 Cal. App. 4th 427, 438–39, italics added.)

In this case, we have no trouble concluding that Schlessinger was permitted to fairly present his side of the dispute. On the first round of cross-motions for summary adjudication, the parties filed declarations and memoranda of points and authorities concerning whether the tolls on competition were valid. In partially granting RM&S's motion, the arbitrator simply held that the tolls were valid *if* they were reasonable. This ruling was based on *Howard v. Babcock*, supra, 6 Cal. 4th 409, in which the high court made the same determination based on the face of the contract before it. (Id. at pp. 419, 425–26.) Thus, the arbitrator's first ruling addressed a pure question of law that could be resolved on the basis of the agreement alone. Schlessinger therefore suffered no prejudice from the fact that the first summary adjudication ruling was made before the parties commenced discovery.

As to the second round of cross-motions, the arbitrator permitted the parties to engage in discovery before they sought to summarily adjudicate the issue of the tolls' reasonableness. In connection with these motions, Schlessinger submitted considerable evidence from several sources. RM&S's motion was based on Schlessinger's deposition testimony and the declarations of two of its partners, both of whom Schlessinger had deposed. Given the legal theory used by the arbitrator, as established in *Howard v. Babcock*, supra, 6 Cal. 4th 409, we cannot say that a different result might have been reached had Schlessinger been allowed to conduct additional discovery. Even if Schlessinger had engaged in further discovery, we do not believe he would have uncovered any new *material* evidence. Accordingly, we find that Schlessinger was not precluded from offering any material evidence and that he had a fair opportunity to present his case.

In closing, we caution that our holding should not be taken as an endorsement of motions for summary judgment or summary adjudication in the arbitration context. By concluding that, under the Act and AAA rules, the arbitrator was permitted to entertain summary adjudication motions, we do not suggest that he was required to do so.

NOTE

1. FINRA now severely restricts the grant of dismissal applications before claimant is given an evidentiary hearing. *See* Rule 12504.

[C] Availability of Witnesses

Tempo Shain Corp. v. Bertek, Inc.

United States Court of Appeals, Second Circuit, 1997.
120 F.3d 16.

- PARKER, CIRCUIT JUDGE.

Neptune Plus Corporation ("Neptune"), an affiliate of Tempo Shain Corporation ("Tempo Shain"), entered into an agreement with Bertek, Inc. ("Bertek") to purchase a license agreement from Gelman Sciences, Inc. ("Gelman") for a patented process to treat materials to enhance their repellency characteristics. Under the agreement, Bertek was to manufacture the treated material, which Neptune intended to sell to the apparel and footwear industries. Disagreements arose and the parties entered arbitration to resolve claims brought by Neptune against Bertek for fraudulent inducement to contract and breach of contract. Bertek counterclaimed with its own fraudulent inducement and breach of contract charges.

Bertek intended to call Wayne Pollock, former President of Bertek's Laminated Products Division, as a witness to provide what Bertek considered to be crucial testimony concerning the negotiations and dealings between the parties about which it claims only Pollock could testify. Pollock became temporarily unavailable to testify, however, after his wife was diagnosed with a recurrence of cancer. The arbitration panel was advised that Pollock remained willing to testify, but that the expected duration of his unavailability was indeterminate. Bertek urged the panel to keep the record open until Pollock could testify either in person or by deposition.

After deliberation, the panel concluded the hearings without waiting for Pollock's testimony. The arbitrators stated:

> We as arbitrators have to decide does Mr. Pollock have any information that if he was here in person and you fellows are banging him with questions that some new information comes out that we haven't heard or is it going to be a rehash of what we've heard from other witnesses.

The question on appeal is whether the panel's refusal to continue the hearings to allow Pollock to testify amounts to fundamental unfairness and misconduct sufficient to vacate the arbitration award pursuant to section 10(a)(3) of the Act. We believe that it did, and therefore vacate the court's endorsement of the award.

* * * *

The district court was correct that arbitration panel determinations are generally accorded great deference under the FAA. Judicial review of arbitration awards is necessarily narrowly limited. Ethyl Corp. v. United Steelworkers of America, AFL-CIO-CLC, 768 F.2d 180, 183 (7th Cir. 1985). Undue judicial intervention would inevitably judicialize the arbitration process, thus defeating the objective of providing an alternative to judicial dispute resolution. See id. at 183–84.

Federal courts may vacate an arbitration award only in limited circumstances as proscribed by section 10(a) of the Act, 9 U.S.C. §

10(a). Section 10(a)(3) provides that a federal court may vacate an arbitration award if "the arbitrators were guilty of misconduct in refusing to postpone the hearing, upon sufficient cause shown, or in refusing to hear evidence pertinent and material to the controversy[,] or of any other misbehavior by which the rights of the party have been prejudiced." 9 U.S.C. § 0(a)(3). In this case, we are primarily concerned with whether the arbitration panel committed misconduct in refusing to hear evidence pertinent or material to the controversy.

Courts have interpreted section 10(a)(3) to mean that except where fundamental fairness is violated, arbitration determinations will not be opened up to evidentiary review. In making evidentiary determinations, an arbitrator "need not follow all the niceties observed by the federal courts." Bell Aerospace Co. Div. of Textron v. Local 516, 500 F.2d 921, 923 (2d Cir. 1974). However, although not required to hear all the evidence proffered by a party, an arbitrator "must give each of the parties to the dispute an adequate opportunity to present its evidence and argument." Hoteles Condado Beach v. Union De Tronquistas Local 901, 763 F.2d 34, 39 (1st Cir. 1985). "Federal courts do not superintend arbitration proceedings. Our review is restricted to determining whether the procedure was fundamentally unfair." See Teamsters, Local Union 657 v. Stanley Structures, Inc., 735 F.2d 903, 906 (5th Cir. 1984); accord Concourse Beauty School, Inc. v. Polakov, 685 F.Supp. 1311, 1318 (S.D.N.Y. 1988) ("The misconduct must amount to a denial of fundamental fairness of the arbitration proceeding in order to warrant vacating the award." (quoting Transit Cas. Co. v. Trenwick Reinsurance Co., 659 F.Supp. 1346, 1354 (S.D.N.Y. 1987), aff'd mem., 841 F.2d 1117 (2d Cir. 1988))).

We find that there was no reasonable basis for the arbitration panel to determine that Pollock's omitted testimony would be cumulative with regard to the fraudulent inducement claims. Said differently, the panel excluded evidence plainly "pertinent and material to the controversy," 9 U.S.C. § 10(a)(3). The panel did not indicate in what respects Pollock's testimony would be cumulative. . . . [T]here is nothing to suggest that Pollock's intended testimony concerning appellees' fraudulent inducement claim and Bertek's counterclaim for fraudulent inducement was addressed by the documents admitted into evidence.

Because Bertek's alleged misrepresentations were not

documented, appellees' unsupported oral testimony concerning such representations was unrebutted because Pollock, who allegedly made the representations on Bertek's behalf, was not allowed to testify, and he is the only person who could have done so.

* * * *

On the facts of this case, the panel's refusal to continue the hearings to allow Pollock to testify amounts to fundamental unfairness and misconduct sufficient to vacate the award pursuant to section 10(a)(3) of the FAA. For the reasons stated above, we vacate the district court's endorsement of the arbitration award and remand for further proceeding consistent with this opinion.

§ 6.02 REVIEW ON THE MERITS

Arbitral Injustice — Rethinking the Manifest Disregard Standard for Judicial Review of Awards

By Nicholas R. Weiskopf*

INTRODUCTION

Despite long-standing resistance to such an idea, virtually all American courts today claim the power to upset commercial awards reflecting deliberate arbitral rejection of those basic rules of law which would apply in court. Nonetheless, and confusingly, there remain those principles of arbitration law designed to insulate awards from such review. In the vernacular, "something has to give."

After all, there is still widespread recognition that arbitrators may do what they perceive to be essential justice at the expense of legal doctrine possibly requiring a different result. Basic arbitral groundrules have and continue to reflect that expectation. Accordingly, if a court is

---

* © Nicholas R. Weiskopf, reprinted from the University of Louisville Law Review, Volume 46 Number 2, Winter Issue 2007. Footnotes omitted.

asked to compel arbitration, it is not supposed to consider whether the underlying claim has any conceivable merit. Nor should it matter that the claim would not be cognizable under established doctrine. Similarly, once there has been arbitration, a court is ordinarily expected to confirm any award even if it believes it to be wrong. It has been said that even awards "clearly erroneous both in logic and result" must be confirmed. The arbitral statutes do not even mention fundamental error as a basis for remand to arbitration. There would hence appear to be no room for judicial consideration of the merits of an arbitral claim, either before or after it has gone to the arbitrators. As New York's highest court explained thirty years ago:

> In arbitration parties seek the resolution of differences . . . free from the requirements and expectations familiar to judicial proceedings with respect both to the formulation of pleadings and causes of action and to historical and current legal theories as to the availability of remedies. The awards of arbitrators are not subject to judicial review for errors of law or of fact. . . . Submissions are for determinations based on the Ad hoc application of broad principles of justice and fairness in the particular instance.

It is not that simple. In the past few decades, the United States Supreme Court, while adopting sweeping new policies in favor of arbitration, has endeavored to counterbalance them with assurances that courts have sufficient residual controls to prevent the more obvious forms of arbitral injustice. The Court's extraordinary embrace of arbitration has had several components. First, using an extremely broad definition of "interstate commerce," it has extended the preemptive reach of the Federal Arbitration Act ("FAA"), and the underlying federal law of arbitration, to the full current constitutional limit, creating a breadth of application which Congress could not possibly have envisioned at the time it enacted that statute in 1925. Second, operating under the FAA, the Court has overruled its own earlier decisions so as to conclude that so-called "public" statutory claims for workplace discrimination, securities fraud, RICO, and antitrust are covered by conventional predispute agreements to arbitrate, even under contracts of adhesion where the obligation to arbitrate is presented on a "take it or leave it" basis. Third, the Supreme Court has used principles of preemption consistently to strike down state legislative attempts to shield certain types of claims from compulsory arbitration. In doing all this, the

Supreme Court, without meaningful underlying exposition, has assured that courts may reject arbitral awards for "manifest disregard," and, more specifically, that arbitration must be adequate to protect substantive rights created by statute. All of this broadscale expansion of arbitration and arbitrability has stirred up residual concerns about arbitral process. In the past several years there have been hundreds of statutory but also common law cases that discuss "manifest disregard of the law," and the power of the courts to guard against it.

Caselaw doctrine usually evolves slowly, and in a somewhat orderly progression. However, in the series of steps just described, the Supreme Court, in relatively sudden fashion, has stood significant parts of the federal law of arbitration on their head. This has left it to the lower courts to scramble to formulate the rules and concepts needed to refine and implement what the highest court has covered with broad brush. The predictable price has been inconsistency, and resulting confusion. To this day, the courts cannot agree on what a showing of "manifest disregard" actually requires. The "manifest disregard" standard of review has done little to predict which awards are ripe for judicial rejection on the merits, and this has resulted in a roulette-like waste of judicial and party resources.

This article describes and suggests possible solutions to the problems of definition and application of "manifest disregard" which have confronted the courts. Certain predispositions can be stated up front. As to statutory claims in which there is a perceived and particularly strong public interest in enforcement, there are reasons to argue for a standard of review that is more rigorous than any used at present. That standard could require that any denial of relief be supported by substantial evidence, with the presumably rare pure issues of law regarding statutory coverage to be revisited *de novo* so that no arbitrator is free to reject a *prima facie* case of statutorily proscribed behavior for legal insufficiency. As to common law claims, there is much to be said for precluding any review on the merits unless the parties have actually provided for it in their agreement to arbitrate. However, it is likely that some form of "manifest disregard" will be with us for some time. If so, that standard of review must be refined if it is to have any appreciable utility.

I. An Overview

Given the rarity with which "manifest disregard" has actually been applied to reject an award on its merits, some might think of it as a shibboleth. The Seventh Circuit, while admitting that it and other courts have recognized "manifest disregard," has said

> We can understand neither the need for the formula nor the role that it plays in judicial review of arbitration (we suspect none – that it is just words).

That may be, but a year after this pronouncement, in 1995, the United States Supreme Court, in dictum, reaffirmed its allegiance to "manifest disregard" as an "unusual circumstance" under which a court would set an award aside.

The concept of "manifest disregard" was first used by the United States Supreme Court in 1953 to explain its refusal to compel arbitration of securities law claims—the "manifest disregard" standard, because it would not reach erroneous arbitral "interpretations" of the law, would be insufficient to protect adequately against arbitrators reaching wrong results in such cases. In its present form, most lower court formulations of "manifest disregard" have both an objective and subjective component—the award must be inconsistent with fundamental legal principles brought to the arbitrator's attention, but the arbitrator must also have acted with scienter in negating those rules. Because most awards are unreasoned, the party challenging the award would typically establish intent to disregard the law by inference from the absence of any conceivable justification for it. Several courts, however, have limited "manifest disregard" to issues of law, thereby rejecting the idea that even blatantly wrong factual determinations should also be a basis for upsetting an award.

One could readily question whether a requirement of arbitral scienter makes sense, or instead obfuscates required distinction between an arbitral desire to do equity and the rejection of doctrine in order to reach an unjust result. There is also the question of whether arbitral factual error should be totally excluded when it comes to fashioning any standard of review. There must also be recognition that a difficulty in formulating any unitary standard of review stems from competing, and often very conceptions about what arbitrators are expected to do. This confusion is not entirely systemic, because, as we shall see, attitudes about the goals of arbitration are often geared to the type of claim being arbitrated. The more types of claims that are held arbitrable, the greater the potential for inconsistency.

One also must remember that there is caselaw recognition that the parties themselves can set their own contractual groundrules for review. What then is the appropriate interplay between arbitrators, the courts, and the prerogatives of the parties themselves? Should review standards be more intrusive in adhesory situations where the weaker party will have no say on that subject, or is something close to arbitral finality an essentially neutral default rule so long as the arbitral system employed is unbiased?

Leaving aside for the moment the issues posed when the parties purport to set their own contractual ground rules, it could be argued, as a matter of efficiency, that courts which so rarely reject awards for "manifest disregard" should not bother with any review on the merits. Every dispute resolution system has infirmities. The courts can and sometimes do get things seriously wrong as well. Juries are known to disregard instructions the judge gives them on the applicable law. Also, but for arbitration, some claims would not be heard at all—going to court may be too expensive or too complicated. Similarly, making more intense review on the merits available in adhesory contexts, unless it were to operate solely in favor of disappointed claimants, might well encourage losing institutional respondents more actively to resist confirmation, thereby overwhelming the claimant. A sampling of recent cases would suggest, for instance, that brokerage respondents challenge awards against them more often than do their customers challenge denials of relief.

Despite these considerations, today's courts never seem to tire from giving reminders that it is they who have the ultimate responsibility to insure that exercises of arbitral power comply with some fundamental standard. Indeed, the courts appear uncomfortable with what could be construed as contractual attempts totally to insulate awards from review on the merits. History tells us that private dispute resolution is not an inherently governmental function, but when it comes to commercial arbitration, one can see from the cases that judges sometimes feel acutely a conflict between not wanting to let go of supervision and not wanting to stand in the way—it is the classic quandary of a caretaker, even a largely self-appointed one. While the courts have backed away from such attitudes, arbitral departures from the law, and some would say compulsory arbitration in and of itself, can still be said to pose serious challenges to the best interests of our society at large. Fears in this regard, which can readily extend to all types of claims, are based largely on the conception that even the subtler sorts of contractual adhesion usually translate out to uneven arbitral playing fields, with the courts and juries, despite infirmities, being the best equalizers. In any event, and despite the rarity of actual refusals to confirm, the "eye of the needle" continues to beckon. A party to a significant business arbitration has to anticipate that the dispute may well ultimately wind up in active court litigation in connection with attempted confirmation or an application to vacate.

[A] Contract Cases

These cases, particularly those outside the consumer area, fall squarely within the traditional ambit of mercantile arbitration. Some early decisions suggest that an arbitrator must apply the contract as written, that she cannot "rewrite" the contract of the parties. In later cases, that view is not very apparent. We also see many unsuccessful attempts to attack arbitral "misreads" of a contract as acts of bias, as exceeding of arbitral authority, or as violations of public policy. These "side door" attempts have not fared well, but there are exceptions on the state level. Would their reasoning be preempted under current standards?

In re Arbitration Between Granite Worsted Mills, Inc.

New York Court of Appeals, 1969.
25 N.Y.2d 451.

- BURKE, J.

Granite Worsted Mills, Inc. ('Seller') made two sales of certain cloth goods to Aaronson Cowen, Ltd. ('Buyer') to be used in the manufacture of sport coats. In each case, sales agreements were employed which included broad arbitration clauses and clauses which limited the buyer's damages for defective goods. Paragraph 12 of each of the sales agreements contained the following language: 'ARBITRATION. Any controversy or claim arising out of or relating to this contract shall be settled by arbitration.'

With respect to the goods delivered pursuant to each of the sales agreements, the buyer complained to the seller that there were defects and thereafter filed a demand for arbitration of the dispute according to the terms of the sales agreements. The total purchase price for the goods shipped under both agreements was less than $1,000 but the buyer's demand for damages amounted to more than $7,000. Paragraph 6 of each of the sales agreements provided as follows: "Defective Goods. . . . . Buyer shall not be entitled to claim or recover consequential damages for defective goods (whether the defect be latent or otherwise), nor for manufacturing, processing or selling expenses or for the loss of contemplated use or profits; and in all events Buyer's damages shall not exceed the difference in value on date of delivery between goods specified and goods actually delivered.' (Emphasis added.) The parties proceeded to arbitration and the arbitrator made an award in the amount of $3,780.51.

It is clear that an arbitrator's award may be vacated only upon the grounds specified in the statute (CPLR 7511 subd. (b)) and that, if the party moving to vacate cannot establish one of the statutory grounds, the award must be confirmed. In this case, the seller moved to vacate under CPLR 7511 (subd. (b), par. 1, cl. (iii)) which provides that an award shall be vacated if the moving party's rights were prejudiced by the fact that 'an arbitrator, or agency or person making the award exceeded his power'. The case law applying this subdivision makes it clear that a mere error committed by the arbitrator as to questions of fact or law is insufficient to establish that excess of power necessary to vacate the award. The mere statement of that rule does not, however, resolve the issue tendered for decision in the present case. That issue, simply stated, is whether, when an arbitrator makes an award which on its face and without express mention of the fact ignores an express provision of the contract limiting damages, he is guilty of 'mere error' or whether he has in fact exceeded his powers.

* * * *

[W]here it is clear from the face of the award itself or from an examination of the computations made by the arbitrator that the arbitrator has included an element of damages specifically excluded by the contract pursuant to which he obtained his very authority to act, he exceeds his powers under the contract and the award thus made must be vacated upon proper application. In the present case, the award itself demonstrates that the arbitrator ignored the provision of the contract providing a formula for the computation of the buyer's damages and specifically excluding consequential damages since the award amounted to more than $3,700 whereas the total purchase price for both sales was only $984.

* * * *

There is no doubt that an arbitrator, if he so decides, may indeed refuse to enforce such a damage limitation clause on the ground of unconscionability or on other grounds and today's decision does not in any way limit that power. What is required, however, is that the award indicate that he has in fact deliberately and intentionally exercised that power so that judicial review can proceed without the need for speculation as to what has in fact occurred in the arbitral tribunal. Since the award in this case is insufficient in this respect, it can only be concluded that the arbitrator has exceeded his powers in making it and the order of the Appellate Division reversing that of Special Term and confirming the award should be reversed and the matter remitted to the arbitrator for further proceedings in accordance with this opinion.

- BREITEL, J., dissenting.

The sales agreements in suit included a "broad" arbitration clause covering "(a)ny controversy or claim arising out of or relating to (the) contract." Thus the parties chose arbitration rather than the courts to resolve the disputes which might arise between them, and, as a corollary, the arbitrators were vested with the power to interpret the agreement between the parties.

The only part of the agreement bearing an arbitration clause which is not determinable by the arbitrators alone is the arbitration clause itself. It is always open to judicial censorship to determine whether or not the arbitration clause limits the scope of the arbitrator's powers. But this does not mean that every direction in the over-all agreement is a limitation on the arbitrators' powers. On the contrary, the agreement is addressed to the arbitrators and there is no judicial review of their errors in failing to follow such direction, if the failure amounts to no more than an error of law. As it has often been said, the arbitrators' awards are not reviewable before the courts for errors of law or fact, and obviously a misinterpretation of a written agreement is an error of law and no worse.

This, of course, is the latter-day rule of a court less hostile to the private forum of arbitration than were the courts of another day. Indeed, the leading practice treatise states: 'As noted under CPLR 7501, however, the arbitrator's power to interpret the agreement is now so great and relatively free of judicial control . . . that earlier cases vacating awards because an arbitrator exceeded his power should not be heavily relied upon. Typical of the more recent tendency is *Matter of National Cash Register Co.* (*Wilson*), in which the Court of Appeals pointed out that arbitrators exceeded their powers within the meaning of the statute only if 'they gave a completely irrational construction to the provisions (of the agreement) in dispute and, in effect made a new contract for the parties' in the rendering of an award. Thus, if there is any possible way of construing the agreement to encompass the dispute and the arbitrator so construes it in assuming jurisdiction, the courts would seem to lack authority to review the determination. . . . Such a conclusion makes arbitration clauses exceedingly dangerous, no matter how circumscribed they appear to be. But it is a logical outgrowth of the tendency to make the arbitrator the judge of his own jurisdiction once validity of the arbitration clause is determined.'

Coming to the precise question in this case, it is quite clear, as the Appellate Division majority held, that the arbitrators were doing no more than interpreting and applying the agreement before them. Because it was possible for the arbitrators to have found the consequential damage clause unconscionable, it cannot be said that their construction was so perverse as to amount to misconduct. Their award is beyond judicial review, not because this or any other court might agree with their view of the consequential damage clause, but because no court may say that a rational tribunal, especially one endowed with equitable powers, could not reach the same conclusion as did the arbitrators.

It is difficult, of course, to resist the temptation to look over the shoulders of the arbitrators, as it is also difficult to envisage as reasonable any system of interpretation that does not conform to one's own. Nevertheless, arbitration is an alternative forum governed to a large extent by its own principles, and not limited by the rules of evidence, the rules of law, or even the canons of construction in the reading of documents . . . .

Accordingly, I dissent and vote to affirm the order of the Appellate Division.

NOTES

1. What if the damage limitation were in the arbitration clause itself? In the materials to follow, trace whether courts accept the idea that the arbitrator must comply with the directives in an arbitration provision or else act in excess of their powers, a statutory ground for vacation of awards. What of a directive in an arbitration clause that "the arbitrator must apply the plain meaning of this contract?"

2. How viable is the majority opinion approach that an arbitrator must explain departure from contractual provision given that awards are typically unreasoned?

3. Note the remand in *Granite*. What flexibility does the arbitrator have upon remand?

Integrated Sales, Inc. v. Maxell Corp of America

New York Supreme Court, Appellate Division, 1st Dep't, 1983.
94 A.D.2d 221.

- SULLIVAN, J.

For several years petitioner Integrated Sales, Inc. had been the exclusive, and apparently successful, sales representative of respondent Maxell Corporation of America for its consumer audio products in the Ohio, western Pennsylvania and West Virginia region. According to Integrated in 1977 it had surpassed all of Maxell's monthly sales targets, doubled the number of sales in its tri-State territory and sold $629,586 of Maxell-manufactured audiotape, an increase of almost 25% over the previous year. In 1978 it achieved 114% of its annual quota and doubled its sales to $1,757,653. By the end of 1979 it had more than tripled Maxell's accounts and expanded the number of sales locations twelvefold. Utilizing its own employees and funds Integrated recruited and trained a network of dealers, consisting of discount houses, drug store chains and record shops. As a result of its efforts, Integrated estimates that Maxell, over the next 10 years, will earn more than $30,000,000 from sales in the Ohio, West Virginia and western Pennsylvania region. Notwithstanding, on October 15, 1979, Maxell, without stating any reason, terminated the relationship, effective 30 days thereafter.

Almost one year earlier, on December 29, 1978, the parties had executed a sales representative agreement which provided in paragraph 3 that the "relationship" was to "continue until either [party] decide[s] for any reason that we should no longer do business together." Additionally, paragraph 18 gave Maxell the power to terminate the agreement at its sole option on 30 days' written notice, and paragraph 23 absolved either party from damages resulting from termination of the agreement. The agreement also contained a broad arbitration clause providing for arbitration in accordance with the Commercial Rules of the American Arbitration Association. The agreement and performance thereunder were to be governed by the laws of the State of New York. In April, 1981, 17 months after termination, Integrated served a demand for arbitration, claiming that Maxell had not paid certain back commissions and other amounts due, and that it had wrongfully terminated the agreement. The amounts of damages sought was not specified.

At the arbitration hearing Integrated contended that the reason for the termination was its refusal to pay bribes to Maxell's former national sales manager, now deceased, who had himself been discharged by Maxell after Integrated's termination. Through witnesses and documents Integrated described a corrupt scheme in which the former sales manager and a coterie of Maxell officials and consultants played a central role. Apparently, these individuals pressured sales representatives such as Integrated, as well as Maxell suppliers and employees, to make payments to their wholly owned company for the ostensible purpose of purchasing shares of stock. The stock was worthless. Throughout the arbitration hearings Maxell, alleging an absolute right of termination under the sales representative agreement, maintained that its reason for terminating Integrated was not properly before the arbitrator. Nevertheless, Maxell presented witnesses in an effort to establish a non-corrupt reason for the termination. Integrated offered evidence that it sustained damages of $1,500,000.

After taking testimony from 17 witnesses, divided almost equally between the parties, during five days of hearings, and viewing 80 exhibits, the arbitrator, a New York attorney selected by the American Arbitration Association, found that Maxell had wrongfully terminated the sales representative agreement, and awarded Integrated $500,000 in damages with interest. The arbitrator did not write an opinion explaining the basis of his award since the parties had previously stipulated that none was necessary. Special Term confirmed the award and, rejecting the argument that the arbitrator had exceeded his power (see CPLR 7511, subd [b], par 1, cl [iii]), the only basis for vacatur asserted by Maxell, denied its cross motion to vacate. We agree with Special Term and affirm.

In support of its argument that the arbitrator exceeded his authority Maxell contends that the claims of corrupt motive are irrelevant to the termination of an agreement terminable at will and that, in any event, the express contractual limitation on damages contained in the sales representative agreement bars an award for wrongful termination. Thus, it reasons, in fashioning an award in damages for wrongful termination the arbitrator effectively rewrote the parties' agreement by creating obligations to which they had never agreed.

In the absence of fraud, corruption or other misconduct, an arbitration award may not be impeached because of arbitrator error as to the law or facts. "An arbitrator's paramount responsibility is to reach an equitable result, and the courts will not assume the role of overseers to mold the award to conform to their sense of justice. Thus, an arbitrator's award will not be vacated for errors of law and fact committed by the arbitrator . . . and '[e]ven where the arbitrator states an intention to apply a law, and then misapplies it." ' (Matter of Sprinzen [Nomberg], 46 NY2d 623, 629, citing Matter of Associated Teachers of Huntington v Board of Educ., 33 NY2d 229, 235.) Nor may a court set aside an arbitration award merely because it believes that the arbitrator's interpretation of a contract "disregards the apparent, or even the plain, meaning of the words." (Matter of Adelstein v Ortiz Funeral Home Corp., 75 AD2d 529, 530, affd 52 NY2d 997.) "Parties who agree to refer contract disputes to arbitration must recognize that " '[a]rbitrators may do justice' " and [that] the award may well reflect the spirit rather than the letter of the agreement" (Matter of Local Div. 1179, Amalgamated Tr. Union, AFL-CIO [Green Bus Lines], 50 NY2d 1007, 1009, citing Rochester City School Dist. v Rochester Teachers Assn., 41 NY2d 578, 582). Moreover, "in the absence of contrary public policy . . . or an express provision in the arbitration agreement otherwise limiting his authority", an arbitrator has the power to fashion appropriate remedies including reformation of a contract. (Matter of SCM Corp. [Fisher Park Lane Co.], 40 NY2d 788, 794.)

New York courts have uniformly held that an arbitrator exceeds his powers only when he ignores specific limitations on the powers delegated to him in the arbitration clause or he gives a completely irrational construction to the provisions of the parties' agreement, thereby effectively rewriting it. (Lentine v Fundaro, 29 NY2d 382, 385–86, and cases cited therein; 8 Weinstein-Korn-Miller, NY Civ Prac, par 7511.11 et seq.) The sales representative agreement between Maxell and Integrated contained an arbitration clause which conferred broad power on the arbitrator to determine the issues submitted to him. Moreover, since the arbitration was to be held in accordance with the Commercial Rules of the American Arbitration Association, and rule 43 provides that "[t]he Arbitrator may grant any remedy or relief which [he] deems just and equitable and within the scope of the agreement of the parties," the arbitrator had broad equitable power to mold an award which, in his view, was just and proper. (See United Buying Serv. Int. Corp. v United Buying Serv. of Northeastern N.Y., 38 AD2d 75, 79.) Any question as to what is "just and equitable" (rule 43) is for the arbitrator to decide, since "[t]he Arbitrator shall interpret and apply these Rules insofar as they relate to the [his] powers and duties" (rule 53).

Since it is clear that the arbitrator acted within the broad terms of the powers conferred upon him, the only remaining test in determining the issue of excess of arbitral power is whether his award constitutes, at most, a mere error of law, that is, a result different from that which a court would have rendered had the issue been before it or complete irrationality and, in effect, a rewriting of the parties' agreement (Matter of National Cash Register Co. [Wilson], 8 NY2d 377, 383). According to its interpretation Maxell could, without cause or even for corrupt cause, terminate the agreement at any time and that, furthermore, no damages could be assessed against it under any circumstance.

"Arbitrators may do justice . . . [S]hort of 'complete irrationality', 'they may fashion the law to fit the facts before them' " (*Lentine v Fundaro*, supra, at p 386, citing Matter of Exercycle Corp. [Maratta], 9 NY2d 329, 336; see also, Matter of Spectrum Fabrics Corp. [Main St. Fashions], 285 App Div 710). In *Lentine* (p 386) the court hinted that an arbitrator "might rationally refuse to apply [an equal division of assets] provision unless the original contributions were in fact equal, because otherwise the result would be unjust and violate the spirit of the agreement." Precisely such a situation is presented here. Integrated alleges, and it is not disputed, that evidence of a complicated scheme of kickback, bribery and securities fraud was presented to the arbitrator as the reason for its termination. In such circumstances the arbitrator could find that enforcement of the termination-at-will clause would have resulted in an injustice and violated the spirit of the agreement. When two parties contract with each other good faith and fair dealing are presumed (O'Neil Supply Co. v Petroleum Heat & Power Co., 280 NY 50, 54–55). Bribe solicitation and consequent termination for refusal to pay demonstrates a breach of the implied covenant, and would afford a rational basis for the arbitrator's refusal to enforce the termination-at-will provision.

Moreover, Integrated argued to the arbitrator that Maxell

officials had, to its detriment, misled it into believing that only poor performance would justify termination. Thus, it contended, Maxell was equitably estopped from terminating the sales representative agreement without good cause. Additional support for Integrated's reliance on the representations of Maxell's officials can be found in the agreement itself, which provides for termination on the ground, inter alia, of unsatisfactory performance with respect quota. A provision for termination for cause detracts, of course, from Maxell's argument that the agreement was terminable at will. This point was also urged upon the arbitrator. Each provision of a contract should be read, where possible, to give meaning and effect to the other parts (Corhill Corp. v S.D. Plants, Inc., 9 NY2d 595, 599), and any ambiguity must be construed against the party who drafted the agreement (Rentways, Inc. v O'Neill Milk & Cream Co., 308 NY 342, 348). Thus, the arbitrator had further support for his refusal to enforce the termination-at-will clause.

In *Matter of Granite Worsted Mills* (*Cowen*) (25 NY2d 451, 457) the Court of Appeals reaffirmed an arbitrator's power to refuse to enforce contractual limitations provided, however, that the award indicates that "he has in fact deliberately and intentionally exercised that power so that judicial review can proceed without the need for speculation as to what has in fact occurred in the arbitral tribunal." There, the underlying agreement limited damages to the total sales price of the goods involved. The arbitrator exceeded the limitation by awarding consequential damages, and it was uncertain whether he made a computational error or refused to enforce the damage limitation clause because of unconscionability, as argued, or on other grounds. The Court of Appeals remitted the matter to the arbitrator for an explanation.

But we need not speculate here. It is clear from the post hearing briefs that the issues of the terminability at will of the agreement and the enforceability of the damage limitation provision were presented to the arbitrator. His refusal to enforce these contractual provisions must be viewed, especially in light of his use of the term "wrongfully terminated," as a considered determination. His finding that the relationship was wrongfully terminated necessarily carries with it a rejection of Maxell's claim that the agreement was terminable at will, since that was the only argument offered as a complete defense to the termination, even if the reasons therefore were shown to have violated public policy. Inasmuch as the award of damages was for wrongful termination, not for unpaid commissions or for any other claim, it is clear that the arbitrator exercised the broad power vested in him and refused to enforce the damage limitation precisely because the termination was wrongful. No further expression, written or otherwise, was needed as a manifestation of his reasoning. Indeed, the parties specifically authorized the arbitrator to dispense with an opinion.

NOTES

1. What has happened to the idea that departure from contract text requires explanation?

2. Several courts have limited the power to terminate at-will employees for public policy reasons. Does that help explain the result in the last case?

In re I/S Stavborg v. National Metal Converters, Inc.

United States Court of Appeals, Second Circuit, 1974.
500 F.2d 424.

- OAKES, CIRCUIT JUDGE.

National Metal Converters, Inc., appeals from an order entered August 2, 1973, by the district court granting I/S Stavborg's motion to confirm a 2-1 arbitration award made May 3, 1973, in New York City. Appellant raises two main issues on this appeal: (1) whether the district court had jurisdiction to enter judgment on the award under the Federal Arbitration Act, 9 U.S.C. §1 et seq., when the parties did not explicitly agree to the entry of judgment on an award in the arbitration agreement; and (2) whether the decision of the majority of the arbitrators should be reversed on grounds of its being either 'clearly erroneous' or 'manifestly in disregard' of the applicable law. We find that the district court did have jurisdiction to enter judgment on the award, and, not without some doubt, affirm the award.

* * * *

II. Review of the Arbitral Award.

Appellant's other claims may be stated variously that the arbitrators' decision was 'clearly erroneous,' or was 'in manifest disregard of the applicable law,' or amounted to a 'reformation' of the charter party agreement. Although interpretation of the charter party agreement here in issue is clearly a matter of federal maritime law, 'the charter party is merely a contract, subject in general to all the rules and requirements of contract law.' G. Gilmore & C. Black, The Law of Admiralty 172 (1957). The same authors have also observed that 'a single short (and often, to the uninitiate, obscure) expression may refer to a whole set of complicated practices perfectly familiar to those who deal regularly in such matters . . .,' id., and they conclude that 'In such a field, it is not surprising that arbitration . . . has largely taken the place of litigation."

* * * *

In dispute below, then, was the responsibility for the payment of freight in a situation where the consignee, Rosal, had failed to make it. Appellant contended that it was the intent of the parties that the charterer was obligated to pay only to the extent the owner was unable to obtain payment by exercise of its lien. Appellant relies on clause 8 of the charter party, which reads in pertinent part as follows:

> Owners (appellee) shall have a lien on the cargo for freight . . . Charterers (appellant) also remain responsible for freight . . ., but only to such extent as the Owners have been unable to obtain payment thereof by exercising the lien on the cargo.

The clear import of this clause, taken alone, is that appellant remained responsible for payment of freight only to the extent that the appellee was unable to recoup freight by means of execution of the lien it held on the cargo. As a practical matter, this clause would cast the burden of taking affirmative action to secure payment of the freight due upon the only party to the agreement guaranteed to have a representative at the scene where the cargo is discharged (the owner's ship's captain). Despite this clause, the owner, aware of the fact that the freight was not prepaid and that the consignee was "initially obligated to pay the freight," did not seek to obtain payment by exercise of its lien on the cargo.

Appellee argues, and the majority of the arbitrators apparently found, that clause 1 of the charter party contradicts clause 8 and therefore the true intent of the parties must be otherwise ascertained. Clause 1 in pertinent part reads as follows:

Freight to be telegraphically remitted to Owners by Messrs. Rosal E. Madrid, the Receivers. Charterers to remain fully responsible for fulfillment of charter party.

* * * *

As we view it, the majority, in effect, read clause 8 out of the charter party. It seems rather anomalous, but had the arbitral majority failed to render a written opinion in this case, our ability—ignoring the question of our power—to review that decision would be greatly limited. See Sobel v. Hertz, Warner & Co., 469 F.2d 1211, 1214–15 (2d Cir. 1972). Indeed, the AAA apparently discourages the practice of written arbitral opinions in order to insulate the arbitral process from any judicial review. Faced, however, with a reasoned opinion that is, in our view, clearly erroneous both in logic and result, we are confronted with the question whether it is nevertheless our obligation under the Federal Arbitration Act to affirm the award.

* * * *

All of appellant's claims here reduce to the proposition that the arbitrators misconstrued the contract. The arbitral majority justified reading clause 8 out of the charter party by considering clause 1 to conflict with it and then by placing heavy reliance on the August 30 letter from appellant's president, supra, which seemed to acknowledge that appellant was responsible for the freight given Rosal's failure to pay. In a court of law, this evidence would probably not have been properly admitted if, as we feel to be the case, the intent of the parties were made abundantly clear from within the four corners of the charter party. Even if admitted it should have been entitled to little or no weight since the letter was delivered when the discharge was almost complete and the check accompanying the letter was to be held in escrow pending effort by the owner to secure payment from the consignee. We see no basis, however, to reverse the award even though it is based on a clearly erroneous interpretation of the contract. Whatever arbitrators' mistakes of law may be corrected, simple misinterpretations of contracts do not appear one of them.

Judgment affirmed.

- MANSFIELD, CIRCUIT JUDGE, dissenting.

I must respectfully dissent.

I agree with Judge Oakes' statement that a majority of the arbitrators have "read Clause 8 out of the charter party." However, I cannot agree with his conclusion that appellant's claims here 'reduce to the proposition that the arbitrators misconstrued the contract' and that the arbitrators' decision, which he concedes to be 'clearly erroneous,' was based upon a 'misinterpretation of the contract.'

The pertinent provisions of the charter party contract are crystal clear and there is no conflict between them. Clause 8 plainly and unambiguously provides that 'Charterers shall also remain responsible for freight . . . but only to such extent as the Owners have been unable to obtain payment thereof by exercising the lien on the cargo.' There is not the slightest conflict between this specific obligation and the Charterer's general duty, as set forth in Clause 1 of the contract, 'to remain fully responsible for fulfillment of charter party.' The charter party obviously obligated the charterer to perform various obligations, including payment of freight according to the terms and conditions of Clause 8, and other specific duties according to the terms of other paragraphs of the agreement (e.g., stowage of cargo, payment of demurrage, wharfage, literage, subletting, lay days, etc.).

Thus, the Charterer here assumed full responsibility for fulfillment of the charter party, including the obligation to pay the freight upon the owner's compliance with Clause 8, and the Owner obligated itself first to seek payment 'by exercising the lien on the cargo.' The Owner clearly failed to perform this latter obligation, which was a condition precedent to its exacting payment from the Charterer. The

Owner should either have obtained payment of the freight from the consignee prior to or at the time of discharge or, upon completing discharge, have petitioned the court for an order placing the cargo under lien. It did neither. Its failure to perform its obligation was not excused by the existence of the Charterer's August 30, 1972 letter to its broker enclosing a check for the freight, since the letter, aside from its not being part of the contract between the parties, was to be held in escrow pending the Owner's fulfillment of its obligation to secure payment from the consignee.

Although we are obligated to avoid frustrating the purpose of arbitration, which is to resolve disputes quickly and inexpensively by minimizing judicial review or interference, we may not go so far as to countenance a wholly baseless and irrational award. To do so would be to deny due process. Our guideline was well stated by the Supreme Court in United Steel Workers, supra, where it said:

> Nevertheless, an arbitrator is confined to interpretation and application of the collective bargaining agreement; he does not sit to dispense his own brand of industrial justice. He may of course look for guidance from many sources, yet his award is legitimate only so long as it draws its essence from the collective bargaining agreement. When the arbitrator's words manifest an infidelity to this obligation, courts have no choice but to refuse enforcement of the award. (363 U.S. at 597).

Since the arbitrators' award fails to draw its essence from the charter party contract and is wholly baseless and irrational, I would reverse the decision of the district court and direct the entry of judgment vacating the award.

Sweeney v. Herman Management, Inc.

New York Supreme Court, Appellate Division, 1st Dep't, 1982.
85 A.D.2d 34.

- FEIN, J.

In March 1976 Bernard H. Lange was appointed receiver in

foreclosure proceedings of premises 1921-35 7th Avenue, Manhattan. Respondent Herman Management (Herman) was subsequently retained by Lange as manager of the premises. Later that year Herman, on behalf of Lange, signed a collective bargaining agreement with a service employees union, represented herein by petitioner. The agreement was a union pre-printed form, designed for signature by a representative of the union on the one hand, and by an agent on behalf of the employer on the other. A representative of Herman signed on behalf of the "employer", "As agent for Bernard H. Lange as Receiver".

Paragraph 1(a) of Article VII of the agreement provided in pertinent part that in the event of any

> sale, lease, transfer or assignment of control, occupancy or operation of the premises ... the Employer, be he seller, lessor, transferor, assignor or otherwise, shall, as a condition of the transfer require the transferee to agree in writing to adopt this agreement and offer employment to all employees of the Employer. Without in any way limiting the other rights and remedies of the Union, anyone failing to adhere to the foregoing provisions shall pay, in addition to such further damages as may be found by the Arbitrator, six (6) months pay for the benefit of the employees as liquidated damages to them.

At the foreclosure sale held in 1977 by the court-appointed referee, the property was bid in by Bankers Trust Company, the mortgagee, to whom the property was conveyed by referee's deed. Bankers Trust Company then sold the property to World Muslim Organization. The referee's deed contained no reference to the agreement signed by petitioner and Herman. Neither the mortgagee nor the new owner signed any further agreements with the union. However, World Muslim Organization, the new owner, signed the following agreement with Bankers Trust:

> The Purchaser agrees to assume and carry out the terms of any labor contract covering said buildings.

The new owner did hire all nine of the employees covered in the collective bargaining agreement, but fired them all three days after assuming ownership. This arbitration proceeding was then commenced against Herman, the managing agent, for violation of the agreement. In the formal notice of intention to arbitrate, the union's complaint director asserted that the new owner, which had discharged the union employees, "took title to the premises from Milton Herman Management, the prior owner, who did not require the new owner to sign a contract and offer the members employment in accordance with Article VII of the Union contract."

The arbitrator found that Herman had entered into a valid contract with the union, assuming liability for performance thereunder; that the new owner's firing of the union members constituted non-compliance with Article VII of the agreement; and that "in effect a 'clear' agreement was made to avoid the terms of the Agreement," thus rendering Herman liable for six months' pay for these employees, as liquidated damages.

Plainly petitioner and the arbitrator ignored the facts that there had been a foreclosure sale, a referee's deed to Bankers Trust (the mortgagee), and an arm's length conveyance by Bankers Trust to World Muslim organization, and that Herman had no role in these conveyances and could not legally have had any voice in the terms thereof. Under these circumstances it was contrary to the facts and plainly irrational to find that Herman had entered into "a 'clear' agreement . . . to avoid the terms of the Agreement."

The principle has long been established that an agent acting on behalf of a disclosed principal will not be personally bound, absent clear and explicit evidence of the agent's intention to substitute or add his personal liability for or to that of his principal. (Mencher v. Weiss, 306 N.Y. 1, 4 Hall v. Lauderdale, 46 N.Y. 70; Matter of Littlejohn & Co. [Fah Sang Co.], 20 A.D.2d 697, 441 N.Y.S.2d 735; see Savoy Record Co. v. Cardinal Export Corp., 15 N.Y.2d 1, 4, where the manner of the agent's subscription was similar to the subscription by respondent herein ["As agent on Behalf of"].) Indeed, the burden has historically been on the party seeking to bind the agent exclusively, to overcome the presumption that the agent's act was solely on behalf of the disclosed principal (*Hall v. Lauderdale*, supra; RKO-Stanley Warner Theatres v. Plaza Pictures, 54 A.D.2d 623, 624).

Here the arbitrator and Special Term relied upon the use in the signature block of the word "Employer", which they construed in contradistinction to the "owner" of the premises. But while it may be customary in the industry for a managing agent to exercise immediate supervisory control over the hiring and firing of service employees, such custom could not add to the power of the court-appointed receiver in foreclosure or the court-appointed referee who conveyed the premises by referee's deed pursuant to the terms of the referee's foreclosure sale. It is not shown how Herman could in any lawful way affect or condition the terms of such conveyance. Moreover, it was the new owner of the premises, not respondent, which independently and summarily fired the employees in the face of its commitment to retain them. The court cannot close its eyes to an attempt to hold an agent, such as Herman, liable under these circumstances.

It is plain from the face of the contract and its signature page that petitioner knew it was contracting with Herman as agent of a disclosed principal, Bernard H. Lange as Receiver, not as owner. It is thus clear that the parties negotiating here were the union and the agent of a court-appointed receiver, with limited powers, awaiting a foreclosure sale, terminable upon such sale.

* * * *

Here the arbitrator's decision was irrational in several respects, and as such should have been vacated by Special Term. First, the arbitrator overlooked the fact that Herman entered into the contract with petitioner as agent for a receiver, ignoring Herman's limited agency status and lack of power to transfer any control over the premises. In coming to his conclusion the arbitrator had to disregard the fact that Herman never had any power to enforce this agreement. Moreover he gave no weight to the fact that the new owner unilaterally fired the employees after giving written assurance that it would adhere to existing union contracts. The arbitrator also disregarded petitioner's misstatement of fact in the notice of intention to arbitrate, which named respondent as the "prior owner" of the premises. And finally, the arbitrator found that respondent had somehow entered into "a 'clear' agreement" to avoid the terms of the collective bargaining agreement.

Such an agreement of avoidance—we are not even told with whom respondent reached it—was necessarily created by the arbitrator out of whole cloth, for there is absolutely no evidence in the record to support such a conclusion. Palpably, as a matter of fact and law, Herman could not enter into any such contract or agreement, since the new owner was a purchaser from one whose title came from a referee's deed. The arbitrator took a contract with arguable terms and, by ignoring and misinterpreting some facts and adding new ones, created non-existent legal duties and an entirely new contract with different obligations. The award was completely irrational.

NOTE

1. A subspecies of review on the merits is judicial scrutiny of an award for compliance with "public policy," a concept not referenced in the FAA or the typical state statute. The following case discusses this sort of analysis.

In re Arbitration Between Sprinzen & Nomberg

New York Court of Appeals, 1979.
46 N.Y.2d 623.

- JASEN, J.

This appeal requires us to determine whether an arbitrator's award which enforces the terms of a restrictive covenant of employment is unenforceable as being contrary to public policy.

Respondent Murray Nomberg was employed by the petitioner Local 1115 Joint Board in April, 1973 as a business agent in its health-care division. Nomberg's responsibilities included, among other tasks, the negotiation of collective bargaining agreements, the processing of members' grievances, and the general organization of employees at various facilities. Practically all of Nomberg's service occurred in New Jersey, although he did, on occasion, work in Connecticut and Pennsylvania.

Upon commencement of his employment with Local 1115 in April 1973, Nomberg signed an agreement which contained a restrictive covenant. The terms of such covenant provided for a perpetual prohibition against the divulgence of the identity and addresses of union members or the terms and conditions embodied in the union agreements or the revelation of any information obtained by Nomberg during the course of his employment. Further, Nomberg agreed that "(u)pon the termination of his employment . . . he shall not directly or indirectly, within the States of New York, Pennsylvania, New Jersey and Connecticut . . . enter into or engage in organizing workers, either as an individual or as a part of a labor organization, for a period of five (5) years after the date of termination of his employment hereunder." The agreement also contained a sweeping arbitration clause which prescribed that "(a)ll complaints, disputes whatsoever of whatever kind or nature . . . concerning any provision of this contract . . . or otherwise . . . shall be submitted for arbitration" pursuant to a clearly delineated process.

In February, 1976, Nomberg left Local 1115 and began employment as a business representative for Local 144 of the Hotel, Hospital, Nursing Home and Allied Services Union, a union also involved in organizing and representing employees in the health-care field. With Local 144, Nomberg's geographical responsibilities included only Manhattan and Staten Island, areas with which he had no previous dealings.

Petitioner Local 1115 demanded arbitration to compel compliance with the terms of the restrictive covenant and to enjoin Nomberg from employment as a business representative for Local 144. The parties proceeded to arbitration, where Nomberg, after unsuccessfully contesting the partiality of the arbitrator named in the April, 1973 agreement, walked out of the hearing, refusing to participate further. After petitioner presented its case, the arbitrator ruled that Local 1115 was entitled to the relief sought and issued an award enjoining Nomberg from working for Local 144 until February 6, 1981, five years after his employment ceased with Local 1115, and further restrained Nomberg from engaging in any of the other practices and acts specifically prohibited by the restrictive covenant.

Petitioner moved to confirm the arbitrator's award, and Nomberg cross-moved to vacate the same, contending that his rights were prejudiced by the arbitrator's partiality and that the award itself was unjust. Special Term confirmed the award and denied Nomberg's cross motion in all respects. On appeal, the Appellate Division, with two Justices dissenting, reversed and vacated the award, holding that "the arbitration award under the circumstances of this case (is) in contravention of public policy". There should be a reversal and the judgment of Special Term confirming the award of the arbitrator reinstated.

Controversies involving questions of public policy can rarely, if ever, be resolved by the blind application of sedentary legal principles. The very nature of the concept of public policy itself militates against any attempt to define its ingredients in a manner which would allow one to become complacent in the thought that those precepts which society so steadfastly embraces today will continue to serve as the foundation upon which society will function tomorrow. Public policy, like society, is continually evolving and those entrusted with its implementation must respond to its ever-changing demands.

Over the years, courts have had not infrequent occasion to test restrictive covenants against the fabric of prevailing public policy. While it has been consistently asserted that the policy considerations against depriving the public of a person's industry and precluding an individual from pursuing his occupation, thereby preventing him from supporting himself and his family, must be weighed against the enforcement of such covenants, no hard-and-fast rules have yet been formulated and courts have been continuously engaged in the ongoing task of determining what restrictions are reasonable given the peculiar circumstances and context of each individual case.

In furtherance of the laudable purposes served by permitting consenting parties to submit controversies to arbitration, the law has adopted a policy of noninterference, with few exceptions, in this mode of dispute resolution. Quite simply, it can be said that the arbitrator is not bound to abide by, absent a contrary provision in the arbitration agreement, those principles of substantive law or rules of procedure which govern the traditional litigation process. An arbitrator's paramount responsibility is to reach an equitable result, and the courts will not assume the role of overseers to mold the award to conform to their sense of justice. Thus, an arbitrator's award will not be vacated for errors of law and fact committed by the arbitrator.

Despite this policy of according an arbitrator seemingly unfettered discretion in matters submitted to him by the consent of the parties, it is the established law in this State that an award which is violative of public policy will not be permitted to stand. (Garrity v. Lyle Stuart, Inc., 40 N.Y.2d 354, 357, Supra.) The courts, however, must exercise due restraint in this regard, for the preservation of the arbitration process and the policy of allowing parties to choose a nonjudicial forum, embedded in freedom to contract principles, must not be disturbed by courts, acting under the guise of public policy, wishing to decide the dispute on its merits, for arguably every controversy has at its core some issue requiring the application, or weighing, of policy considerations. Thus, there are now but a few matters of concern which have been recognized as so intertwined with overriding public policy considerations as to either place them beyond the bounds of the arbitration process itself or mandate the vacatur of awards which do violence to the principles upon which such matters rest.

Some examples would be instructive. It has been held that an arbitrator is without power to award punitive damages, a sanction reserved solely to the State (Garrity v. Lyle Stuart, Inc., 40 N.Y.2d 354, supra; Matter of Publishers' Assn. of N. Y. City (Newspaper Union), 280 App.Div. 500), and that an agreement to arbitrate, when sought to be enforced by a lender, cannot divest the courts of their responsibility to determine whether a purported sales agreement is in fact a usurious loan, and thus illegal.

* * * *

These illustrations of instances where courts will intervene in the arbitration process are, without apparent exception, cases in which public policy considerations, embodied in statute or decisional law, prohibit, in an absolute sense, particular matters being decided or certain relief being granted by an arbitrator. Stated another way, the courts must be able to examine an arbitration agreement or an award on its face, without engaging in extended factfinding or legal analysis, and conclude that public policy precludes its enforcement. This is so because, as has been previously noted, an arbitrator is free to apply his own sense of law and equity to the facts as he has found them to be in resolving a controversy.

Applying these principles to this case, we now hold that disputes involving restrictive covenants of employment can be, by mutual consent of the parties, submitted to arbitration, and an arbitrator's award which specifically enforces such covenants, even to the extent of enjoining an individual from engaging in like employment for a reasonable period of years in the future, will not be vacated on public policy grounds.

Here, the parties, by reason of a broad arbitration clause contained in their signed agreement, submitted the issue of the enforceability of the restrictive covenant to arbitration, clearly a proper forum for the resolution of their dispute in this private matter. By so doing, the parties placed upon the arbitrator, not the courts, the responsibility of passing upon the merits of their controversy with the expectation that a just, yet practical, result would be reached. While there may be some doubt whether we would have enforced the restrictive covenant now before us had this dispute been adjudicated in the courts, such consideration is irrelevant to the disposition of this case, for courts will not second-guess the factual findings or the legal conclusions of the arbitrator. The utility of the arbitration process itself is derived from its autonomy, and courts must honor the choice of the parties to have their controversy decided within this framework. Insofar as public policy considerations do not absolutely preclude the enforcement of restrictive covenants of future employment for a reasonable period of time or related business concerns, we conclude that the arbitrator had the power to pass upon the issue of both the reasonableness and the necessity of the restrictions imposed upon the employee. Having thus concluded, and acknowledging the wide latitude afforded arbitrators in formulating just relief, the award rendered should not now be disturbed.

[B] Statutory Cases

Remember the various admonitions in *Wilko*, *Gilmer*, *Shearson* and *Mitsubishi* that a statutory complainant in arbitration cannot lose essential protections? One would think that judicial review in these cases would be correspondingly intensified. Apparently, despite their raising his question, the courts have still backed away from review on the merits.

Dawahare v. Spencer

United States Court of Appeals, Sixth Circuit, 2000.
210 F.3d 666.

▪ GIBSON, CIRCUIT JUDGE.

Woodrow Dawahare appeals from the district court's denial of his motion to vacate the arbitration award he obtained against Adam Spencer and Dean Witter Reynolds, Inc. Dawahare argues that because the damages awarded were grossly inadequate and bore no relationship to the evidence submitted, the award itself shows evident partiality. Further, he argues that the arbitrators manifestly disregarded the law of damages. We affirm the district court's confirmation of the award.

* * * *

Dawahare also argues that the substantial disparity between the damages awarded and the damages evidence presented establishes a manifest disregard of the law of damages. He asserts that the common law entitles him to recover all losses proximately caused by the wrongful acts of the liable parties. Our review for manifest disregard of the law does not open the door to extensive review of arbitral awards.

An arbitration decision "must fly in the face of established legal precedent" for us to find manifest disregard of the law. An arbitration panel acts with manifest disregard if "(1) the applicable legal principle is clearly defined and not subject to reasonable debate; and (2) the arbitrators refused to heed that legal principle." Thus, to find manifest disregard a court must find two things: the relevant law must be clearly defined and the arbitrator must have consciously chosen not to apply it. Arbitrators are not required to explain their decisions. If they choose not to do so, it is all but impossible to determine whether they acted with manifest disregard for the law.

* * * *

Chief Judge Martin, concurring in *Federated Department Stores, Inc. v. J.V.B. Industries, Inc.*, 894 F.2d 862 (6th Cir. 1990), recognized the problems inherent in reviewing an arbitration award for manifest disregard of the law where the arbitrators fail to state a reason for their decision. He stated that courts are forced to participate in a "judicial snipe hunt" with the parties arguing about law that may or may not have been disregarded by the arbitrators. See id. at 871. He would allow reversal when there are no reasons given for an arbitration decision and the record is insufficient to show that the arbitrators did not manifestly disregard the law. See id. No panel of this court has adopted this reasoning.

The arbitrators' decision in this case outlined the parties' contentions and discussed the claims and evidence in some detail for some three-and-a-half, single-spaced pages. The monetary award simply designated the amount of damages without detailed explanation. It is difficult to say that the arbitrators refused to heed a clearly defined legal principle. Dawahare points to nothing in the record that shows the arbitrators' awareness of the common law that he alleges to be applicable. This is not a case where one of the parties clearly stated the law and the arbitrators expressly chose not to follow it.

Since Supreme Court dictum established the manifest disregard of the law standard forty-seven years ago, see *Wilko v. Swan*, 346 U.S. 427, 436 (1953), overruled on other grounds; *Rodriguez de Quijas v. Shearson/American Express, Inc.*, 490 U.S. 477 (1989), only two federal courts of appeals have used it to vacate arbitration decisions. Dawahare understandably cites to these cases, but to no avail, as both cases are easily distinguished from the case before us.

The Second Circuit held that an arbitration panel that denied relief on an ADEA claim showed manifest disregard by ignoring "the law or the evidence or both" where the plaintiff presented strong evidence that he was fired because of his age. Halligan v. Piper Jaffray, Inc., 148 F.3d 197, 204 (2d Cir. 1998), cert. denied, 526 U.S. 1034 (1999). The court pointed out that the parties explained the applicable law to the arbitrators. See id. at 204. This is important because manifest disregard requires awareness of the relevant law. Here, Dawahare points to nothing in the record that indicates the arbitration panel was aware of the law he alleges it ignored. Also, the *Halligan* court particularly emphasized the importance of assuring plaintiffs with employment discrimination claims a forum in which to effectively vindicate their statutory rights. See 148 F.3d at 201–03.

In *Montes v. Shearson Lehman Brothers, Inc.*, 128 F.3d 1456

(11th Cir. 1997), the Eleventh Circuit reversed the district court's confirmation of an arbitration award because the arbitration panel acted in manifest disregard of the law. An employee sued her former employer for overtime pay pursuant to the Fair Labor Standards Act, and the dispute went to arbitration. The employer's attorney repeatedly urged the arbitration panel to disregard the FLSA when making its decision and the panel denied the employee's claim. Because there was no evidence the arbitrators rejected the urging and because there was a lack of factual support for the ruling, the court remanded with instructions to refer the case to a new arbitration panel. The concurrence emphasized that the decision was narrowly limited to the unusual facts of the case. See id. Here, there is no evidence that Spencer, Smith Barney, or Dean Witter urged the arbitrators to disregard the applicable law.

* * * *

Dawahare's argument on manifest disregard of the law is premised on the fact that the only damages evidence was his expert's opinion that he had sustained damages in excess of $600,000. In essence, he argues that the arbitrators were compelled to accept this testimony and award that amount. We agree with the district court's observation that "expert testimony, even if uncontradicted, may be believed in its entirety, in part, or not at all." See also Quinones-Pacheco v. American Airlines, Inc., 979 F.2d 1, 5 (1st Cir. 1992) (fact finder not ordinarily bound by uncontradicted expert opinion testimony, particularly where testimony "lacks great convictive force" in context of evidence as a whole); Gregg v. U.S. Indus., Inc., 887 F.2d 1462, 1469–70 (11th Cir. 1989) (expert testimony is not conclusive and need not be accepted). The court also pointed out that the expert's opinion had been impeached on cross-examination and that there was evidence that Dawahare maintained substantial control over his investments. For us to hold that the arbitration panel was compelled to accept Dawahare's expert's damages evidence would be to disregard the fact finder's responsibility to evaluate testimony.

We decline to adopt Dawahare's suggestion that we engage in a more extensive review of arbitration awards. To do so would undermine the goal of the arbitration process: to resolve disputes efficiently while avoiding extended litigation.

Smith Barney requests attorneys' fees and double the costs incurred in this appeal, arguing that Dawahare's appeal is frivolous. We deny Smith Barney's motion for sanctions. For the foregoing reasons, the judgment of the district court is affirmed.

DiRussa v. Dean Witter Reynolds Inc.

United States Court of Appeal, Second Circuit, 1997.
121 F.3d 818.

- FEINBERG, CICUIT JUDGE.

* * * *

In May 1992, DiRussa was demoted by Dean Witter from the position of Branch Manager of its Ridgewood, New Jersey office to the position of Account Executive in the Morristown, New Jersey office. DiRussa was then 58 years old. DiRussa objected to the demotion and challenged it through arbitration before the National Association of Securities Dealers, Inc. (NASD), as required under the terms of his employment. DiRussa claimed that defendants had discriminated against him based on his age in violation of ADEA and the New Jersey Law Against Discrimination (NJLAD), N.J. Stat. Ann. 10:5-1 et seq.

As set forth in the arbitrators' award, defendants maintained that DiRussa was demoted because of (1) the poor performance of the Ridgewood branch compared to competitors in the same geographic area, (2) his inappropriate conduct with supervisors and subordinates, and (3) his failure to adequately explain to Solari and Robert Dwyer, Dean Witter's National Director of Sales, how he intended to increase his branch's performance. DiRussa countered that these reasons were pretextual, offering evidence that, despite his "competent and conscientious" performance as Branch Manager, he was demoted because of his age. DiRussa introduced testimony during the arbitration that, among other things, Solari and Dwyer "back-dated" a memorandum from them to DiRussa requesting information from DiRussa regarding improvement of his branch and surreptitiously placed that memorandum in DiRussa's personnel file without ever transmitting it to him.

In March 1995, after holding hearings on seven days between June and December 1994 at which both sides were represented by counsel, the arbitrators awarded DiRussa $200,000 in compensatory damages jointly and severally against both defendants and an additional $20,000 against Solari. Although the arbitrators acknowledged in the award that DiRussa also sought, among other things, punitive damages and "attorney's fees and costs of suit pursuant to the ADEA and NJLAD," the award explicitly denied all other relief.

In June 1995, DiRussa filed this complaint in the district court seeking to modify the award to include $249,050.10 in attorney's fees, and to increase the amount of damages awarded.

* * * *

DiRussa argues that the award should be modified because the arbitrators engaged in "manifest disregard of the law" by failing to award attorney's fees under the ADEA and NJLAD. Although we have often recognized this judicially-created ground for modifying or vacating an arbitration award, e.g., Merrill Lynch, Pierce, Fenner & Smith, Inc. v. Bobker, 808 F.2d 930, 933 (2d Cir. 1986) (citing Wilko v. Swan, 346 U.S. 427, 436–37 (1953)); Carte Blanche (Singapore) Pte., Ltd. v. Carte Blanche Int'l, Ltd., 888 F.2d 260, 265 (2d Cir. 1989), we have also emphasized that the reach of the manifest disregard doctrine is "severely limited." Government of India v. Cargill Inc., 867 F.2d 130, 133 (2d Cir. 1989). Indeed, we have cautioned that manifest disregard "clearly means more than error or misunderstanding with respect to the law." *Bobker*, 808 F.2d at 933.

> The error must have been obvious and capable of being readily and instantly perceived by the average person qualified to serve as an arbitrator. Moreover, the term "disregard" implies that the arbitrator appreciates the existence of a clearly governing legal principle but decides to ignore or pay no attention to it.

Id. Thus, to modify or vacate an award on this ground, a court must find both that (1) the "arbitrators knew of a governing legal principle yet refused to apply it or ignored it altogether," and (2) the "law ignored by the arbitrators . . . [was] 'well defined, explicit, and clearly applicable' " to the case. Folkways Music Publishers, Inc. v. Weiss, 989 F.2d 108, 112 (2d Cir. 1993) (internal citations omitted); *Bobker*, 808 F.2d at 933–34.

As an initial matter, DiRussa argues that the manifest disregard standard, which gives extreme deference to arbitrators, should not apply in cases where arbitrators construe federal statutes rather than decide simply the usual issues in typical commercial or labor disputes. See Gilmer v. Interstate/Johnson Lane Corp., 500 U.S. 20, 23 (1991) (holding for the first time that ADEA claims are subject to compulsory arbitration). In support of this argument, DiRussa cites *Cole v. Burns Int'l Sec. Servs.*, 105 F.3d 1465 (D.C.Cir. 1997) (upholding order compelling arbitration of Title VII claim), in which the D.C. Circuit expressed its view that

> [t]he nearly unlimited deference paid to arbitration awards in the context of collective bargaining is not required, and not appropriate, in the context of employees' statutory claims [because] [i]n this context, the Supreme Court has assumed that arbitration awards are subject to judicial review sufficiently rigorous to ensure compliance with statutory law.

Id. at 1468–69; cf. Chisolm v. Kidder, Peabody Asset Management, Inc., 966 F.Supp. 218, 223–28 (S.D.N.Y.1997) (discussing but rejecting argument that a "different manifest disregard standard" should apply to statutory claims).

(1) <u>Attorney's Fees Under the ADEA</u>

Section 626(b) of the ADEA, 29 U.S.C. §626(b), incorporates by reference 29 U.S.C. §216(b) of the Fair Labor Standards Act, which states, in relevant part, that "[t]he court . . . shall, in addition to any judgment awarded to the plaintiff, . . . allow a reasonable attorney's fee to be paid by the defendant, and costs of the action." (emphasis added); see Hagelthorn v. Kennecott Corp., 710 F.2d 76, 86 (2d Cir.1983) (award of attorney's fees to prevailing plaintiff is mandatory). The district court found that "it is difficult to imagine a more 'well defined, explicit and clearly applicable' provision of governing law than the ADEA's mandate that successful age discrimination claimants such as plaintiff recover attorney's fees." *DiRussa*, 936 F.Supp. at 106. With this much of

DiRussa's argument we agree.

However, we also agree with the district court's conclusion that the arbitrators did not manifestly disregard the law, because there is no persuasive evidence that the arbitrators actually knew of—and intentionally disregarded—the mandatory aspect of the ADEA's fee provision. The arbitrators did not state their reasons for denying DiRussa attorney's fees, nor were they required to do so. We are thus faced with the "difficult task" of inferring from the facts of the case whether the arbitrators "appreciate[d] the existence of a clearly governing legal principle but decide[d] to ignore or pay no attention to it." *Standard Microsystems*, 103 F.3d at 12–13 (internal quotes and citations omitted).

DiRussa argues that we should assume that the arbitrators knew that the ADEA mandated attorney's fees to prevailing plaintiffs because he indicated several times during the arbitration that he was "entitled" to such fees under that statute. We observe that DiRussa stated on several occasions, including the statement of his claims that the arbitrators received into evidence at the first hearing, that he sought attorney's fees under both the ADEA and NJLAD. Similarly, DiRussa argued in his opening statement to the arbitrators, and in his "Brief in Support of [His] Application for Punitive Damages, Liquidated Damages and Attorney's Fees," that he was "entitled to" attorney's fees under the ADEA.

However, DiRussa misses the point. The arbitrators obviously knew that DiRussa was requesting attorney's fees under the ADEA (and NJLAD) because they stated in their award that DiRussa sought "attorney's fees and costs of suit pursuant to the ADEA and NJLAD." Nevertheless, at no point did DiRussa communicate—either by written submission or orally—to the arbitrators that the ADEA mandated such an award to a prevailing party. Indeed, in what is apparently the only brief DiRussa submitted to the arbitrators regarding attorney's fees, he focused exclusively on NJLAD's provisions regarding the "lodestar" calculation of attorney's fees and whether upward enhancement of that figure was warranted. Nowhere in this submission does DiRussa either explain that the ADEA requires an award of attorney's fees or quote the language of the relevant ADEA section, which clearly communicates that principle. In view of DiRussa's failure to inform the arbitrators of the relevant legal standard, we are hard-pressed to infer that they consciously disregarded the ADEA's fee provisions.

DiRussa insists that his use of the phrase "entitled to" when discussing attorney's fees under the ADEA indicated to the arbitrators that they had no discretion to deny such fees. It is true that the phrase "entitled to" could convey the idea that as a matter of law attorney's fees were required once the arbitrators awarded DiRussa damages for age discrimination. However, it is equally plausible that the arbitrators interpreted the phrase as a statement of DiRussa's belief that the arbitrators should exercise discretion to award him fees because he was particularly deserving of such an award. Indeed, it would not be surprising for them to assume this latter meaning in view of the fact that "many" statutes providing for attorney's fees to prevailing parties leave the decision whether to award such fees to the discretion of the decision-maker, in this case the arbitrators.

Finally, DiRussa counters that although there is no direct evidence that the arbitrators consciously ignored this provision of the ADEA, "[t]he controlling legal principle and subsequent error is so obvious to the average qualified arbitrator that any different conclusion is absurd." We disagree. We sympathize with the district court's view that "the securities industry, having persuaded the Supreme Court in *Gilmer* to require arbitration of employees' ADEA claims, should be required to supply arbitrators who know what the ADEA says about attorney's fees." 936 F.Supp. at 107. But the remedy for that does not lie with us. Moreover, "knowing" all of the provisions of a particular statutory scheme without assistance from the parties is a daunting task, even for a skilled lawyer or judge. DiRussa argues that "[a] competent and conscientious panel, knowing it was being called upon to enforce federal and state anti-discrimination statutes, would be sure to review these statutes in order to ensure its compliance therewith and would request briefing from the parties on any issue on which it was unclear." While this would be a prudent course of action for arbitrators dealing with statutory claims, we agree with the district court that their failure to do so did not constitute manifest disregard of the law.

* * * *

B. *Other Grounds for Modification*

DiRussa contends that "the Panel's power and authority was

defined by the ADEA (and NJLAD) and that power and authority was exceeded when the Panel, having found a violation of the ADEA, decided not to award a statutorily required remedy." This argument misapprehends the scope of § 10(a)(4). "We have consistently accorded the narrowest reading to section 10(d) [currently section 10(a)(4)], especially when it has been invoked in the context of the arbitrators' alleged failure to correctly decide a question which all concede to have been properly submitted in the first instance." Fahnestock & Co., Inc. v. Waltman, 935 F.2d 512, 515 (2d Cir. 1991) (internal quotes and citations omitted); Matter of Andros Compania Maritima, S.A., 579 F.2d 691, 703 (2d Cir. 1978). Our inquiry under § 10(a)(4) thus focuses on whether the arbitrators had the power, based on the parties' submissions or the arbitration agreement, to reach a certain issue, not whether the arbitrators correctly decided that issue. *Fahnestock*, 935 F.2d at 515–16.

In this case, the parties clearly submitted to the arbitrators the issue whether DiRussa was entitled to attorney's fees. Thus, though the arbitrators denied such relief, they did not "exceed their powers" as that phrase has been interpreted in our cases. Indeed, we agree with defendants that DiRussa's real objection appears to be that the arbitrators committed an obvious legal error in denying him attorney's fees. Section 10(a)(4) was not intended to apply to such a situation.

DiRussa also argues that enforcement of the award without modification to include attorney's fees violates public policy. The Supreme Court has instructed that a court may refuse to enforce an arbitration award on this ground only when such enforcement would "violate some explicit public policy that is well defined and dominant, and is to be ascertained by reference to the laws and legal precedents and not from general considerations of supposed public interests." United Paperworkers Int'l v. Misco, Inc., 484 U.S. 29, 43 (1987) (internal quotes and citations omitted); Newsday, Inc. v. Long Island Typographical Union, 915 F.2d 840, 844 (2d Cir. 1990). This rarely-used ground for reversal "derives from the basic notion that no court will lend its aid to one who founds a cause of action upon an immoral or illegal act." *Misco*, 484 U.S. at 42. The party seeking to prevent enforcement of the award must "clearly show[ ]" a violation of public policy. Id. at 43.

DiRussa claims that the award conflicts with two such policies. He first argues that awarding attorney's fees to victims of employment discrimination encourages private litigants to pursue their rights and thus contributes to the eradication of employment discrimination generally. See *Christiansburg*, 434 U.S. at 416. Second, DiRussa relies on the Supreme Court's repeated statement that " '[b]y agreeing to arbitrate a statutory claim, a party does not forgo the substantive rights afforded by the statute; it only submits to their resolution in an arbitral, rather than a judicial, forum.' " E.g., *Gilmer*, 500 U.S. at 26 (citing Motors Co. v. Soler Chrysler-Plymouth Inc., 473 U.S. 614, 628 (1985)); Rodriguez de Quijas v. Shearson/American Express, Inc., 490 U.S. 477, 481 (1989). DiRussa argues that these decisions express a public policy that arbitration awards must include all remedies mandated by statutory law.

Although we agree that the "policies" on which DiRussa relies are important, his argument misapprehends the scope of our power to vacate an award based on a violation of public policy. In Newsday, for instance, the arbitrators found that an employee described by the district court as a "chronic sexual harasser" had not been discharged for just cause and ordered his reinstatement. *Newsday*, 915 F.2d at 843–44. On appeal, we vacated the award because it ordered Newsday to retain the employee in violation of Title VII's strong prohibitions against sexual harassment in the workplace and "perpetuate[d] a hostile, intimidating and offensive work environment." Id. at 844–45. Other courts have vacated awards as against public policy to prevent conduct that is particularly harmful to society and egregious in nature, such as when the conduct required by the award would jeopardize public health and safety. E.g., Iowa Elec. Light & Power Co. v. Local Union 204, 834 F.2d 1424, 1425, 1428 (8th Cir. 1987) (vacating award reinstating machinist in nuclear power plant discharged for "deliberately violating important federally-mandated safety regulations").

In contrast, DiRussa contends in effect that arbitration awards violate public policy whenever an arbitrator erroneously interprets federal statutory law. Whether to vacate an arbitration award based on this type of broadly-stated public policy poses a difficult question, and it is far from clear under the cases cited above where to draw the line in determining whether the public policy allegedly violated is important enough to require us to vacate an award. However innocent DiRussa's argument seems on its face, it could allow a court to vacate an arbitration award any time it disagreed with the arbitrator's interpretation of federal statutory law. We doubt that the Supreme Court intended to invite this type of plenary review of arbitration awards when it held in *Gilmer* that statutory claims pursuant to the ADEA were arbitrable.

The key issue is actually not whether to expand the "public policy" ground for reversal of arbitration awards but whether a standard of review less deferential than "manifest disregard" may be appropriate when certain federal statutory rights are involved, as described in our discussion in II A above. For reasons there stated, we decline to address that question in this case. On this record, DiRussa has not shown that the award clearly violates public policy.

In sum, we find no ground on which to modify the arbitration award to include attorney's fees. We emphasize that we do not condone defendants' conduct here in demoting DiRussa, nor do we applaud an arbitration award that evinces some ignorance of the governing legal principles. However, we feel constrained by our precedents and policies regarding the limited scope of judicial review of arbitration awards to affirm the district court's order confirming the award.

* * * *

Porzig v. Dresdner, Kleinwort, Benson, North America LLC

United States Court of Appeals, Second Circuit, 2007.
497 F.3d 133.

- HALL, CIRCUIT JUDGE.

Bernhard Porzig seeks vacatur of a modified arbitration award. The award was the result of Porzig's success in an underlying arbitration proceeding in which Porzig had alleged intentional age discrimination in violation of State and Federal laws. On appeal, Porzig asserts that the award he received for attorney's fees was issued in manifest disregard of the law. We find that a portion of the award in this case was issued in violation of the Federal Arbitration Act and that additional significant portions were issued in manifest disregard of the law based on the convergence of multiple factors implicating the integrity of the award. Accordingly, we vacate the order of the District Court, and remand to that court for further proceedings.

I. Factual and Procedural Background

Porzig was hired as Vice President of Central Bank Sales by Dresdner Securities, a subsidiary of Dresdner Bank, in December 1995. As a condition of his employment, Porzig was required by the NASD, the industry self-regulatory organization, to sign and execute a standard "U-4" form containing an agreement to arbitrate any future disputes.

* * * *

In January of 1998, Porzig was fired. Initially, he filed an action against the Defendants Dresdner, Kleinwort, Benson, North America LLC and Dresdner Bank ("Dresdner") in the Southern District of New York making a claim under the Age Discrimination in Employment Act ("ADEA"), 29 U.S.C. §623, et. seq. Upon motion by Dresdner, the District Court stayed the action because the dispute was subject to the arbitration provisions of the agreement Porzig had signed upon entering employment. Thereafter, the parties submitted their dispute to a three member Arbitration Panel ("Panel") at the NASD.

The Panel concluded that "age was a factor" in Dresdners' decision to terminate Porzig's employment. The Panel awarded Porzig \$96,200 in compensatory damages, plus \$27,679 of interest, and \$96,200 in punitive damages. Contrary to statutory requirements, the Panel did not award Porzig attorney's fees or costs and, in fact, assessed \$13,840.75 against Porzig in forum, filing, and arbitrators' fees (hereinafter the "Original Award").

Porzig appealed the Original Award to the Southern District of New York, seeking a modification to provide him an award of attorney's fees and costs and to vacate the Panel's assessment against him of the various fees. The District Court (Jones, J.) concluded the arbitrators had acted in manifest disregard of the law with respect to attorney's fees, finding there had been "ample evidence to support the conclusion that the arbitrators were made aware of the applicable law but either refused to apply it or ignored it altogether." The court remanded the case to the

Panel to determine the reasonable attorney's fees to which Porzig was entitled and to fashion a new award. Although in its initial order the District Court denied Porzig's motion to vacate or modify the award as to costs, it subsequently granted his motion when it reconsidered its decision on that point. Concluding on the motion to reconsider that the arbitrators had in fact disregarded the law with respect to costs "just as they did with respect to attorney's fees," the court vacated the original award as to costs and instructed the Panel also to modify the award and assess the $13,840.75 in costs against Defendants, not Porzig.

On remand, Porzig submitted to the Panel a fee application that consisted of an Attorney Affirmation and a Memorandum of Law. The application included detailed billing records outlining each fee request delineated on a spreadsheet that set out the date of the service, a description of the service, the time spent, and the rate charged, documenting a total of $249,996.95 in attorney's fees and $12,050.09 in costs. The billing records included entries for the representation Attorney Michael K. O'Donnell had provided before the District Court successfully arguing Porzig's right to receive attorney's fees and costs. Porzig explicitly informed the Panel that he was entitled to attorney's fees to compensate him for the time his attorney spent preparing the fee application and for litigating the fee claim. In support of this position, he cited *Gagne v. Maher*, 594 F.2d 336, 344 (2d Cir. 1979), aff'd on other grounds, 448 U.S. 122 (1980), which clearly states that attorneys are to be recompensed for time spent litigating attorney's fees.

For their part, Dresdner filed an affidavit in opposition to Porzig's fee application arguing contrary to law, see Blanchard v. Bergeron, 489 U.S. 87 (1989), that Porzig's contingency fee arrangement with Mr. O'Donnell "should set the maximum limit ($73,359.67) on the amount Porzig can recover under the fee-shifting statute."

The Panel issued its modified arbitration award (hereinafter "Modified Award") on May 19, 2004. The Modified Award granted Porzig's application in part, ostensibly awarding $75,000 for attorney's fees and $8,500 in costs. It stated:

> [Defendants] are jointly and severally liable for and shall pay to Respondent's counsel, Mr. O'Donnell, the sum of

> $75,000.00 for reasonable attorneys' fees (which sum includes interest from the date of the award of damages to Respondent) in the above matter, and an additional sum of $8,500.00, the reasonable amount of costs and disbursements, for a total amount of $83,500.00.

Porzig again appealed to the District Court from that Modified Award, requesting the court vacate that award with respect to attorney's fees and again remand the issue to the Panel with instructions that it use the lodestar method of calculation to determine the reasonable fees . . . .

This Court has repeatedly recognized the strong deference appropriately due arbitral awards and the arbitral process, and has limited its review of arbitration awards in obeisance to that process, see, e.g., Halligan v. Jaffray, Inc., 148 F.3d 197, 200 (2d Cir. 1998) (noting the strong judicial support of "the use of arbitration as a device to resolve disputes"). The value of arbitration lies in its efficiency and cost-effectiveness as a process for resolving disputes outside the courts, and its tendency to foster a less acrimonious process. See DiRussa v. Dean Witter Reynolds, Inc., 121 F.3d 818, 821 (2d Cir. 1997); National Broadcasting Co., Inc. v. Bear Stearns & Co., Inc., 165 F.3d 184, 190–91 (2d Cir. 1999). To encourage and support the use of arbitration by consenting parties, this Court, therefore, uses an extremely deferential standard of review for arbitral awards. See *Duferco*, 333 F.3d at 388.

A decision of an arbitrator, however, is not totally impervious to judicial review. The FAA provides four statutory grounds for vacatur in situations that involve, generally, impropriety on the part of the arbitrators. In addition, a court may vacate an award if it exhibits a "manifest disregard of the law." Goldman v. Architectural Iron Co., 306 F.3d 1214, 1216 (2d Cir. 2002) (quoting *DiRussa*, 121 F.3d at 821). Our review under the doctrine of manifest disregard of the law is highly deferential and such relief is appropriately rare. An arbitral award may be vacated for manifest disregard only where a petitioner can demonstrate "both that (1) the arbitrators knew of a governing legal principle yet refused to apply it or ignored it altogether, and (2) the law ignored by the arbitrators was well-defined, explicit, and clearly applicable to the case."

Other Circuits have recognized additional, nonstatutory bases upon which a reviewing court may vacate an arbitrator's award, including where the awards are "completely irrational," *Hoffman v.*

Cargill Inc., 236 F.3d 458, 461 (8th Cir. 2001) (internal quotation omitted). To the extent our sister courts may have broadened somewhat the path to vacatur of an arbitration award, we decline to wander from the narrow one embodied in our own jurisprudence. Thus, we will vacate an award only upon finding a violation of one of the four statutory bases, or, more rarely, if we find a panel has acted in manifest disregard of the law. See *Wallace*, 378 F.3d at 189.

That said, in our review of this case we find several issues that cause us great concern. We examine them in more depth below, but, generally, the following factors cloud the presumption of validity of the award: (1) the district court concluded the original attorney's fee award was issued in manifest disregard of the law and vacated the award; (2) the same Panel on remand acted without authority with respect to a portion of the award; (3) Porzig accurately explained to the arbitrators the controlling law with regard to attorney's fees, while the Defendants advanced several misstatements of law to the Panel—including one on the very point of law on which the district court had found manifest disregard; (4) the Panel did not explain how it came up with a fee award virtually identical to the contingent fee. Taken individually, in all likelihood, such circumstances would not have overcome the deference owed to the Panel's award. Taken together, however, these circumstances create, if not the perfect storm, then a disturbance ample enough to give us pause. Upon careful reflection, and mindful of the importance that the arbitration process plays in dispute resolution today and the narrow lens through which we examine such awards, we conclude the award here was issued partially in violation of the enabling statute and partially in manifest disregard of law and must be vacated.

* * * *

In ascertaining the amount of reasonable attorney's fees to which a successful claimant is entitled, arbitration panels use the same fee calculation methods as the courts—generally the "lodestar"[5] analysis by which the decision maker considers all of the case-specific variables courts have identified as relevant to the reasonableness of the attorney's fees. See Arbor Hill Concerned Citizens Neighborhood Ass'n v. County of Albany, 493 F.3d 11 & n.4 (2d Cir. 2007); see also Hensley v.

Eckerhart, 461 U.S. 424, 440 (1983) (discussing fee calculation); Blum v. Stenson, 465 U.S. 886, 888 (1984) (same). The presumptively reasonable fee analysis involves determining the reasonable hourly rate for each attorney and the reasonable number of hours expended, and multiplying the two figures together to obtain the presumptively reasonable fee award. Courts are regularly called upon to conduct a reasonable fee analysis even though a lawyer may have taken the case on a contingent fee. See, e.g., Blanchard v. Bergeron, 489 U.S. 87 (1989); Luciano v. Olsten Corp., 109 F.3d 111 (2d Cir. 1997); Dominic v. Consol. Edison Co. of New York, Inc., 822 F.2d 1249 (2d Cir. 1987). Generally when reviewing analyses of reasonable attorney's fees, we have the benefit of being able to examine the methodology used by a district court to ensure that court applied the law correctly. While arbitral panels may, but are not required to, explain their reasoning, when the circumstances that exist in this case are present—namely, where a court has already taken the rare and extreme step of vacating the original award for being issued in manifest disregard of law, where the Panel on remand has acted plainly outside its authority with respect to one facet of the award, and where we do not have the benefit of being able to examine the Panel's analytical methodology on the very issue that required the original vacatur and remand—we may consider that absence of explanation when deciding whether the Panel has acted in manifest disregard of the law. *Halligan*, 148 F.3d at 204 ("[W]e believe that when a reviewing court is inclined to hold that an arbitration panel manifestly disregarded the law, the failure of the arbitrators to explain the award can be taken into account.").

It is true that a reviewing authority may consider the contingency fee paid in determining a reasonable attorney's fee, *Johnson v. Ga. Highway Express, Inc.*, 488 F.2d 714, 718 (5th Cir. 1974), it is also undisputed, however, that the contingency fee may not serve as a cap on an attorney fee award, *Blanchard*, 489 U.S. at 90 (1989). Porzig carefully and accurately explained to the arbitral panel the prevailing law as to the manner in which a contingency fee may be considered in a fee calculation. Cf. *DiRussa*, 121 F.3d at 823 (finding plaintiff had not explained to the arbitrators that attorney's fees were *mandated* under the statute).

In addition, both Porzig and the District Court made clear to the Panel that it was not only obliged to award Porzig attorney's fees under the ADEA, see Hagelthorn v. Kennecott Corp., 710 F.2d 76, 86 (2d Cir. 1983); accord Lightfoot v. Union Carbide Corp., 110 F.3d 898, 913 (2d Cir. 1997), it was also obliged to award fees for pursuing that statutory right to fees. As we stated in *Gagne*,

> If an attorney is required to expend time litigating his fee claim, yet may not be compensated for that time, the attorney's effective rate for all the hours expended on the case will be correspondingly decreased.... Such a result would not comport with the purpose behind most statutory fee authorizations, [v]iz, the encouragement of attorneys to represent indigent clients and to act as private attorneys general in vindicating congressional policies.

Despite the settled jurisprudence with respect to the mandatory requirement both that attorney's fees be awarded for successful claims brought under the ADEA and that attorney's fees be awarded for litigation enforcing the right to those fees, Dresdner nonetheless made two problematic arguments to the Panel: (1) "an award of attorneys' fees may . . . be unnecessary to achieve the purposes of the statutory fee-shifting provision," and (2) the contingency fee "should set the maximum limit . . . on the amount Porzig can recover under the fee-shifting statute." The first flies in the face of the district court's determination that the Panel had already manifestly disregarded the law when it first refused to award attorney's fees. The second is contrary to a position already established by the Supreme Court. See *Blanchard*, 489 U.S. 87.

In this case, the Panel, stating it had considered "numerous factors" when fashioning the award, awarded Porzig $83,500.00 in attorney's fees and costs. This award is remarkably similar to the $82,437.81 contingent fee Attorney O'Donnell stated he had already received from Porzig. The Panel did not indicate whether it had considered the fact that Porzig was required to appeal the Original Award to the District Court or the time Attorney O'Donnell spent on the fee application. This similarity in amount between the original contingency fee and the Modified Award, viewed in light of the (now vacated) portion of the order requiring Attorney O'Donnell to reimburse that contingency fee, and seen against the backdrop of the litigation history of the Panel's inquiry into that fee, suggests that the Defendants' misstatement of the law with respect to contingent fees influenced the Panel in its final determination. Moreover, it is apparent the Panel failed to award Porzig any attorney's fees whatsoever for the time his attorney spent in District Court successfully litigating his statutory right to the fees or for the attorney time spent relitigating the issue in front of the Panel after remand from the District Court—fees which, as had been made clear to the Panel, were mandatory.

In this case, because of the lack of any transparent fee calculation analysis by the Panel, which handicaps our ability to review the reasonableness of the Modified Award, the numerous incorrect representations regarding the applicable law made by the Defendants to the Panel, the fact that the Panel issued the original award in manifest disregard of the law, and the fact that the Panel issued a portion of the present award without authority, we conclude that the Modified Award was issued in manifest disregard of the law.

NOTES

1. Based on the type of reasoning used in the last case, most courts require that arbitral "disregard" of the law be deliberate. Is a *scienter* requirement a good idea? Does it show concern for arbitral bias as opposed to getting a just result—bad mistakes can be innocent. What about arbitral power deliberately to depart from strict rules of law to do essential justice? Look again at the *SCM Corporation* case, *supra* at page 19. Does the power to do essential justice at the expense of fixed rules of law extend to statutory cases? Should it?

2. Many cases insist that a showing for arbitral scienter for review purposes requires proof that the arbitrator(s) were told specifically what the law is. *E.g.*, Goldman v. Architectural Iron Co., 306 F.3d 1214, 1216 (2d Cir. 2002) ("An arbitrator (even an arbitrator who is a lawyer) . . . is ordinarily assumed to be a blank slate unless educated in the law by the parties.").

3. Does a *scienter* requirement for vacating awards make it more or less likely that arbitrators will opt to issue detailed reasoned awards?

4. Every so often, a court, contrary to expectations based on other episodes, vacates an award. The case that follows is an example.

Halligan v. Piper Jaffray, Inc.

United States Court of Appeals, Second Circuit, 1998.
148 F.3d 197.

- FEINBERG, CIRCUIT JUDGE.

Irene Halligan (Mrs. Halligan), as executrix for the Estate of Theodore Halligan (Halligan), appeals from orders dated April 14, June 10 and June 16, 1997 of the United States District Court for the Southern District of New York, Kimba M. Wood, J. The orders of April 14 and June 10 respectively refused to vacate and then confirmed an arbitration award in favor of defendants Piper Jaffray, Inc. (Piper) and Marvin Geisness, Halligan's sales partner, on Halligan's claim, among others, that defendants had terminated his employment in violation of the Age Discrimination in Employment Act (ADEA), 29 U.S.C. §621 et seq. The order of June 16, 1997, dismissed as barred by res judicata Mrs. Halligan's federal complaint based on the same underlying facts as the ADEA claim in arbitration.

Mrs. Halligan argues, among other things, that the award reflected "manifest disregard" of the law. We agree, and accordingly reverse the orders of the district court.

I. Background

Halligan was hired by Piper in 1973 as a salesman of equity investments to financial institutions. As a condition of employment, Halligan was required by the industry self-regulatory organization, the National Association of Securities Dealers (NASD), to sign a standard form (U-4) containing an agreement to arbitrate any future disputes. In 1988, Tad Piper succeeded his father as CEO of Piper. Mrs. Halligan contends that thereafter Halligan was forced from his job in December 1992 by Tad Piper and Halligan's supervisor, Bruce Huber, because of his age and despite his continuing high performance.

In October 1993, Halligan submitted his ADEA claim, along with other claims, to arbitration before a panel of NASD arbitrators. Before he could complete his own re-direct testimony, however, his health deteriorated and in early 1995 the arbitrators were advised that Halligan was unable to testify further. By stipulation, the arbitrators struck his re-direct testimony from the record and continued the proceeding. Halligan's direct testimony had been subject to cross-examination and was not stricken. After his death, Mrs. Halligan continued the arbitration.

During the arbitration hearings, Halligan presented the arbitrators with very strong evidence of age-based discrimination. Piper for its part has conceded throughout that Halligan was "basically qualified." Piper principally contended that Halligan had chosen to retire; it also argued that performance and health issues justified its conduct.

Before leaving Piper in December 1992, Halligan was making nearly $500,000 per year. He ranked fifth out of 25 institutional salesmen. He was ranked first from 1987 through 1991, and had consistently been among Piper's top salesmen. He testified as to repeated discriminatory statements by Tad Piper, Huber, and Halligan's younger partner Geisness. For example, Halligan testified that at a meeting on August 27, 1992, Tad Piper told him "you're too old. Our clients are young and they want young salesmen," and Huber told him "we want you out of here quickly." Tad Piper and Huber denied making such remarks. Halligan also testified that during a telephone conversation on September 10, 1992, Huber told him that "we want you out of Piper Jaffray by the end of the year," and that "if you don't leave, we will fire you." Halligan testified that he then asked if he could stay for the remainder of the year, and that Huber agreed. Huber testified that during the conversation, Halligan asked him what he should do. He testified that he advised Halligan to resign, and that Halligan agreed "then that's what it will be." Huber admitted that Halligan had never requested his advice before. There were no witnesses to this conversation.

Halligan's evidence also included his notes of this and other conversations, a witness who testified that he had seen Halligan recording notes, and several witnesses who heard Halligan say he was being "fired." In addition, Halligan called many witnesses who testified that Piper personnel had expressed their intention to oust Halligan on account of his age. John Dockendorff, a former client and later competitor, testified that in 1989 (the year after Tad Piper became CEO) Huber attempted to recruit him (in Dockendorff's words) to "learn as much as I could about [Halligan's] accounts," because Halligan "would get put out to pasture because he was getting old." All Piper personnel denied having made such statements, although their testimony was occasionally inconsistent or ambiguous. Halligan presented testimonials from current and former clients and colleagues who testified that Halligan was among the best in his field. Halligan refused to provide Piper with a letter of resignation. He also refused an offer of a retirement party and refused to write a letter to his clients saying he was retiring. On November 23, 1992, Halligan's lawyer sent a letter threatening suit if Halligan was terminated. In addition, Halligan testified that he approached Huber in November and asked him if he could keep his job. Huber replied that plans had already been made to close the New York office. Apparently, those plans consisted simply of termination notices to two support staff. Halligan's accounts were thereafter assigned to two younger men. Halligan testified that he unsuccessfully looked for a new job after leaving Piper.

Piper principally argued that it gave Halligan the options of retiring, agreeing to a new percentage split with Geisness or being assigned a new group of accounts, and that Halligan agreed to retire in the phone conversation on September 10, 1992. Piper also contended its conduct was justified by concerns over Halligan's performance and health. Halligan had surgery for oral cancer twice (in 1990 and 1991), but returned to work each time after approximately two weeks. Halligan conceded that the surgeries had caused slight speech impairment, but offered various witnesses who testified that Halligan was always able to perform his job. Piper discounted Halligan's objective evidence of performance, arguing that Halligan's accounts had more inherent potential and that the rankings failed to reflect the contributions that other employees had made to Halligan's success. In addition, Huber testified that he thought Halligan needed to develop accounts more effectively (although Huber was unable to identify specific accounts) and use the firm's research and other resources more efficiently. Piper submitted various memoranda related to these concerns, and offered testimony by various witnesses who, with the exception of one employee who had recently retired, were all Piper officers or major shareholders. Piper discounted the testimonials in favor of Halligan, arguing that it was not his clients and former colleagues whose expectations Halligan had to satisfy.

Huber was the only witness testifying that in the September 10th telephone conversation Halligan accepted the "option" of retirement, and Huber was contradicted as to key elements of his testimony by other Piper witnesses. For example, Huber testified that Geisness was not informed of the August 27 meeting before it took place, but both Tad Piper and Geisness testified to the contrary. Geisness testified that when he discussed this meeting with Huber, he asked Huber to keep the New York office open.

In March 1996, after extensive hearings, the arbitrators rendered a written award setting forth the claims and defenses of each party, and denying any relief to the Halligans. The award did not contain any explanation or rationale for the result.

In June 1996, Mrs. Halligan petitioned the district court to vacate the award under § 10(a) of the Federal Arbitration Act (FAA), 9 U.S.C. §10(a). She argued, among other things, that given the very strong evidence of discrimination and the clear description of the applicable law presented to the arbitrators, the award reflected manifest disregard of the law.

Piper agreed that the law governing the claim was generally not disputed by the parties, but argued in response that it was not the function of the court to review the merits of the decision and that the arbitrators' award was supported by the evidence Piper presented. Piper cross-petitioned the district court to confirm the award.

The district judge refused to vacate the award. She stated in the order of April 14, 1997 that

> [h]ere, the determination of what constitutes "direct evidence" [of discrimination] . . . is a

> difficult one to make. In addition, the record . . . does not indicate the Panel's awareness, prior to its determinations, of the standards for burdens of proof . . . . [T]he Panel was faced with the task of evaluating conflicting witness testimony, and where it did not issue a written opinion, I cannot conclude that the panel did in fact disregard the parties' burdens of proof . . . . [C]rediting one witness over another does not constitute manifest disregard of the law [and] this Court's role is not to second-guess the fact-finding done by the Panel. Because there is factual as well as legal support for the Panel's ultimate conclusion, I determine that the Panel did not manifestly disregard the law . . . . (internal citations and footnote omitted).

The judge granted Piper's cross-petition to confirm the award in her order of June 10, 1997.

In addition to petitioning to vacate the arbitration award, in October 1996 Mrs. Halligan had filed a complaint in the district court based upon the same underlying facts and raising the ADEA claim. Piper moved to dismiss this complaint on grounds of res judicata, and the district court granted the motion in its order dated June 16, 1997.

II. Analysis

Mrs. Halligan argues in this court, among other things, that the arbitrators' award reflected manifest disregard of the law. Piper argues in response, among other things, that it is not the function of this court to reassess the evidence or make judgments about witness credibility and that the district court was able to adequately review the award—even in the absence of a written explanation—by inferring from the record grounds that support the arbitrators' award. We have also received amicus briefs from the Equal Employment Opportunity Commission (EEOC) and the Securities Industry Association (SIA).

A. *Arbitrability of ADEA Claims*

This appeal arises in a context that has become increasingly important in the federal courts. The use of arbitration as a device to resolve disputes has received strong judicial support in the last few decades, both in labor management disputes and also in disputes involving ordinary commercial contracts. However, one aspect of the increased use of arbitration has recently engendered greater scrutiny and controversy—the use of mandatory pre-dispute arbitration agreements to resolve statutory claims of employment discrimination. Such agreements require an individual, as a condition of employment, to agree in advance to arbitration of future claims alleging violation of a statute prohibiting discrimination in employment. The arbitration award here arose out of such an agreement.

In *Gilmer v. Interstate/Johnson Lane Corp.*, 500 U.S. 20 (1991), the Supreme Court found for the first time that an employee could be held to his pre-dispute agreement to arbitrate his claim under the ADEA, the same statute upon which the Halligans rely. The Court relied on a line of cases, commencing with *Mitsubishi Motors Corp. v. Soler Chrysler-Plymouth, Inc.*, 473 U.S. 614 (1985), that held enforceable pre-dispute arbitration agreements as applied to claims under various federal statutes, including the securities acts and RICO. In *Mitsubishi*, the Court had enforced an agreement between two corporations to arbitrate claims under the federal antitrust laws, on the premise that "[b]y agreeing to arbitrate a statutory claim, a party does not forgo the substantive rights afforded by the statute; it only submits to their resolution in an arbitral, rather than a judicial, forum." Id., 473 U.S. at 628. In *Gilmer*, which quoted this language, the Court held that an employee, who had been required to sign a form containing an agreement to arbitrate as a condition of employment, had not shown that Congress intended to preclude the waiver of a judicial forum for ADEA claims. 500 U.S. at 26. Again quoting from *Mitsubishi*, the Court stated that "[s]o long as the prospective litigant effectively may vindicate [his or her] statutory cause of action in the arbitral forum, the statute will continue to serve both its remedial and deterrent function." Id. at 28.

The Court also noted in *Gilmer* the contention "that judicial review of arbitration decisions is too limited" to adequately protect statutory rights. Id. at 32 n. 4, the Court rejected that argument, stating that "although judicial scrutiny of arbitration awards necessarily is limited, such review is sufficient to ensure that arbitrators comply with the requirements of the statute." *Gilmer*, 500 U.S. at 32 n.4. The employee in Gilmer also generally challenged the procedures usually employed in arbitration. The Court stated that these "claimed procedural inadequacies" are "best left for resolution in specific cases." Id. at 33.

B. *Standard of Review of Award*

The parties agree that review of arbitration awards is generally governed by the FAA. The relevant statutory language is reproduced in the margin. In addition, relying on an observation by the Supreme Court in *Wilko v. Swan*, 346 U.S. 427, 436–37 (1953), this court has also recognized that an arbitration award may be vacated if it is in "manifest disregard of the law." See e.g., Carte Blanche (Singapore) Pte., Ltd. v. Carte Blanche Int'l, Ltd., 888 F.2d 260, 265 (2d Cir. 1989); Merrill Lynch, Pierce, Fenner & Smith, Inc. v. Bobker, 808 F.2d 930, 933 (2d Cir. 1986). We have also pointed out, however, that the reach of the doctrine is "severely limited." Government of India v. Cargill, Inc., 867 F.2d 130, 133 (2d Cir. 1989). Indeed, we have cautioned that manifest disregard "clearly means more than error or misunderstanding with respect to the law." *Bobker*, 808 F.2d at 933. We have further noted that to modify or vacate an award on this ground, a court must find both that (1) the arbitrators knew of a governing legal principle yet refused to apply it or ignored it altogether, and (2) the law ignored by the arbitrators was well defined, explicit, and clearly applicable to the case. Dirussa v. Dean Witter Reynolds Inc., 121 F.3d 818, 821 (2d Cir. 1997), cert. denied, 522 U.S. 1049 (1998).

This case also arises in the context of other developments. In the aftermath of *Gilmer*, as we have already noted, mandatory binding arbitration of employment discrimination disputes as a condition of employment has caused increased controversy. Attention has focused on, among other things, whether additional procedural requirements are necessary to ensure that employees will be able, in the words of *Gilmer*, to "effectively . . . vindicate" their statutory rights in arbitration. 500 U.S. at 28; see, e.g., Commission on the Future of Worker-Management Relations, Report and Recommendations (1994) (Dunlop Report); EEOC Policy Statement on Mandatory Binding Arbitration of Employment Discrimination Disputes as a Condition of Employment, No. 915.002 (July 10, 1997); Samuel Estreicher, Predispute Agreements to Arbitrate

Statutory Employment Claims, 72 N.Y.U. L. Rev. 1344, 1352–59 (1997). The major independent arbitration agencies have formulated due process standards for the adjudication of these disputes. See, e.g., National Academy of Arbitrators, Guidelines on Arbitration of Statutory Claims Under Employer-Promulgated Systems (Statement adopted May 21, 1997); American Arbitration Association, National Rules for the Resolution of Employment Disputes (1996, as amended 1997); JAMS/ENDISPUTE, Six Principles of Neutrality and Fairness for Employment Dispute Resolution Practice (1995).

Industry self-regulatory organizations (SRO's) like the NASD have been singled out for criticism because, among other reasons, the role they play in determining the pool of available arbitrators and selecting the arbitrators who will hear a particular discrimination claim against a member firm of the SRO calls into question the impartiality of the arbitrators selected. See, e.g., Rosenberg v. Merrill Lynch, Pierce, Fenner & Smith, Inc., 995 F.Supp. 190, 206–12 (D.Mass. 1998) (appeal pending) (discussing possibility of institutional bias due to industry influence over arbitration before SRO's and, in particular, under the rules of the New York Stock Exchange); George Nicolau, Gilmer v. Interstate/Johnson Lane Corp.: Its Ramifications and Implications for Employees, Employers and Practitioners, 1 U. Pa. J. Lab. & Emp. L. 175, 183.

Mrs. Halligan argues that the NASD has undue influence here. Under the NASD's Code of Arbitration Procedure, a pool of arbitrators "from within and without the securities industry" is selected by a National Arbitration Committee, a body appointed annually by the Board of Governors "of such size and composition, including representation from the public at large, as [the Board] shall deem appropriate and in the public interest." NASD Code of Arbitration Procedure § 2. The composition of particular panels is then determined by a Director of Arbitration who is also appointed by the Board of Governors, and the Director has discretion to allow the Executive Committee of the National Arbitration Committee to appoint the panel for a case directly. Id. at §§ 3–4. Each party is allowed a single peremptory challenge as of right. Id. at § 22.

In response to criticism, the NASD has recently filed a proposed rule change with the Securities and Exchange Commission under which its member organizations would not be required to condition employment on an employee's agreement to arbitrate these disputes. Notice of Filing of Proposed Change by the NASD Relating to the Arbitration of Employment Discrimination Claims, 62 F.R. 66164 (December 17, 1997). The filing promises further unspecified rule changes to enhance the fairness of the procedures applied by the NASD in this context. There have also been bills introduced in Congress that would prevent pre-dispute waiver of a judicial forum. See the Civil Rights Procedures Protection Act of 1997, S. 63, H.R. 983, 105th Cong. (1997).

In addition, the federal courts have shown growing concern over the problem. For example, the D.C. Circuit has recently emphasized the necessity of adequate review in enforcing a mandatory, pre-dispute agreement to arbitrate Title VII discrimination claims. Cole v. Burns Int'l Sec. Serv., 105 F.3d 1465 (D.C. Cir. 1997). Similarly, in *Prudential Ins. Co. of Am. v. Lai*, 42 F.3d 1299 (9th Cir. 1994), the Ninth Circuit held that waivers of a judicial forum for statutory employment discrimination claims must be "knowing and voluntary" and refused to enforce an agreement to arbitrate that did not meet that standard. See also Chisolm v. Kidder, Peabody Asset Management, 966 F. Supp. 218, 225–26 (S.D.N.Y. 1997) (appeal pending) (thorough review of relevant authorities); *Rosenberg*, 995 F. Supp. 190 (holding employee could not be compelled to arbitrate her claim given questions as to the voluntary nature of her agreement to arbitrate and procedural deficiencies in the proposed arbitral forum). Given our disposition of this appeal on the merits of the award issued in this case, with one exception discussed below we do not address Mrs. Halligan's generalized challenge to arbitrations conducted under the aegis of the NASD.

C. *Application of Standard of Review*

We turn now to review of the district court's decision in this case. Mrs. Halligan argued in the district court and repeats to us that the arbitration award reflected manifest disregard of the law. Mrs. Halligan makes a strong case for that proposition. Quite simply, Halligan presented overwhelming evidence that Piper's conduct after Tad Piper became CEO was motivated by age discrimination. Halligan testified to repeated discriminatory statements, and offered contemporaneous notes supporting his version of events, which were in turn backed by the testimony of a witness who saw him making notes. Halligan also presented the testimony of numerous other witnesses who testified that Piper personnel admitted that the company wanted Halligan out. Halligan presented powerful evidence of his performance, in the form of quantitative sales rankings and relevant witness testimony. Notwithstanding Piper's testimony as to Halligan's performance and health, Piper conceded before the arbitrators—and continues to do so—that Halligan's continuing performance was not so unsatisfactory as to justify discharge. Indeed, its principal argument has been that Halligan retired voluntarily. Halligan also made a very strong showing that he did not choose the "option" of quitting but was fired. The strength of Halligan's showing of discriminatory motive is most probative of whether Piper took discriminatory action, i.e., fired him. In addition, the circumstantial evidence surrounding his departure, e.g., his statements to various witnesses about his being "fired," his refusal to write to his clients announcing his "resignation," his retention of counsel, is consistent only with a finding that Halligan was pushed out of his job.

Moreover, this is not a case like *DiRussa* where we refused to find "manifest disregard" because *DiRussa* had not sufficiently brought the governing law to the attention of the arbitrators. There is no such problem here. The record indicates that counsel for both parties generally agreed on the applicable law (and still do on appeal), and explained it to the arbitrators. It is true that the district court stated that the record "does not indicate the Panel's awareness, prior to its determinations, of the standards for burdens of proof." If this observation meant that counsel did not explain the law sufficiently to the arbitrators, it is not correct. Perhaps the district court meant that the arbitrators did not state that they were ignoring the relevant standards for burdens of proof. That is true, but we doubt whether even under a strict construction of the meaning of manifest disregard, it is necessary for arbitrators to state that they are deliberately ignoring the law. See DeGaetano v. Smith Barney, Inc., 983 F. Supp. 459, 463 (S.D.N.Y. 1997).

In view of the strong evidence that Halligan was fired because of his age and the agreement of the parties that the arbitrators were correctly advised of the applicable legal principles, we are inclined to hold that they ignored the law or the evidence or both. Moreover, the arbitrators did not explain their award. It is true that we have stated repeatedly that arbitrators have no obligation to do so. E.g., Sobel v. Hertz, Warner & Co., 469 F.2d 1211, 1214 (2d Cir. 1972). But in *Gilmer*, when the Supreme Court ruled that an employee could be forced to assert an ADEA claim in an arbitral forum, the Court did so on the assumptions that the claimant would not forgo the substantive rights afforded by the statute, that the arbitration agreement simply changed the forum for enforcement of those rights and that a claimant could effectively vindicate his or her statutory rights in the arbitration. 500 U.S. at 26, 28. This case puts those assumptions to the test. The Court also stated in *Gilmer* that "claimed procedural inadequacies" in arbitration "are best left for resolution in specific cases," 500 U.S. at 33. At least in the circumstances here, we believe that when a reviewing court is inclined to hold that an arbitration panel manifestly disregarded the law, the failure of the arbitrators to explain the award can be taken into account. Having done so, we are left with the firm belief that the arbitrators here manifestly disregarded the law or the evidence or both.

Piper argues that the arbitration panel resolved the case in accordance with substantive ADEA law; for example, it credited Piper's witnesses rather than Halligan's. Had the arbitrators offered that explanation of the award, on this record it would have been extremely hard to accept—but they did not do even that. There is some authority permitting discretionary remand of a case to the arbitrators for a written explanation of their award. Siegel v. Titan Indus. Corp., 779 F.2d 891, 894 (2d Cir. 1985)(per curiam). But in view of the entire record here, we see no persuasive reason for doing so.

We want to make clear that we are not holding that arbitrators should write opinions in every case or even in most cases. We merely observe that where a reviewing court is inclined to find that arbitrators manifestly disregarded the law or the evidence and that an explanation, if given, would have strained credulity, the absence of explanation may reinforce the reviewing court's confidence that the arbitrators engaged in manifest disregard.

For the reasons stated above, we reverse the district court's orders of April 14, 1997 and June 10, 1997 respectively refusing to vacate and then confirming the award. We also reverse the order of June 16, 1997 dismissing the complaint filed in the district court by Mrs. Halligan because there is no enforceable award to bar the suit on res judicata principles. We remand to the district court for further proceedings consistent with this opinion.

NOTES

1. Is there such a thing as "manifest disregard . . . of the evidence?" The Second Circuit has since opined that there is not. Westerbeke Corp. v. Daihatsu Motor Co., Ltd., 304 F.3d 200, 213 n.9 (2d Cir. 2002). Is an issue of meeting the burden of proof one of law or something else?

2. There was obviously conflicting evidence and credibility issues in *Halligan*—why take a rare stand in such a case? Note the refusal to remand to the arbitrators—who will determine damages, and how?

3. Several reviewing courts have rued the absence of a reasoned award. For an amusing judicial expression of frustration with unreasoned awards, see *Perini Corp. v. Great Bay Hotel & Casino, Inc.*, 610 A.2d 364, 392 (N.J. 1992) (Wilentz, C.J., concurring)—"There are no reasons, no findings of fact, no conclusions of law. For all we know the arbitrators concluded that the sun rises in the west, that the earth is flat, and damages have nothing to do with the intentions of the parties or the foreseeability of the consequences of breach." Is the *Halligan* Court correct to take the lack of such an award into account?

In re Arbitration Between UBS Warburg LLC & Auerbach, Pollak & Richardson

New York Supreme Court, 1st Dep't, 2001.
2001 WL 1586978.

- RAMOS, J.S.C.

Petitioner UBS Warburg LLC ("UBS"), moves to vacate an arbitration award dated August 8, 2000. Respondent Auerbach, Pollak & Richardson, Inc. ("APR") cross-moves to confirm.

UBS is a financial services firm that provides, inter alia, securities clearing services to independent retail broker-dealers such as

APR. The parties entered into a written agreement dated December 4, 1995 wherein UBS agreed to provide certain securities clearing services to APR. In conformity with NYSE Rule 382, the parties identified and allocated the essential responsibilities and duties for their roles as a clearing firm and broker.

APR filed a claim before the New York Stock Exchange against UBS seeking damages allegedly arising out of the breach of a clearing agreement, allegedly grossly negligent performance of clearing functions in enabling previously canceled stock certificates to be negotiated, and bad faith conduct toward APR after the discovery of fraud. APR also sought punitive damages and reimbursements of legal fees, costs and expenses for prosecuting its arbitration claim. UBS counterclaimed for a declaratory judgment regarding the propriety of its actions. UBS also sought recovery of termination fees and recovery for reimbursement of legal fees, costs and expenses in connection with the action.

The agreement allocated to APR the responsibility of ascertaining and documenting all information necessary to insure regulatory compliance. In addition, the agreement provides that APR shall be responsible to screen, accept, or reject orders. Finally, the agreement places full responsibility upon APR to ensure proper delivery of securities by stating:

> [UBS] will receive and deliver all funds and securities in connection with transactions for [APR] Customer Accounts in accordance with [APR's] instructions to [UBS], provided that *[APR] shall be responsible for advising [APR's] Customers of their obligations to deliver funds or securities in connection with each* transaction . . . and *shall be responsible for any failure of any [APR] Customer to fulfill such obligation.*

In the event that a customer fails to abide by his or her obligation to, inter alia, deliver securities, UBS is expressly authorized to charge APR's propriety accounts "all amounts owing to [UBS] by or on account of [APR]." UBS's ability to make charges to APR's accounts is subject to unlimited discretion by UBS "irrespective of whether [APR's]

Account or assets with [UBS] are sufficient to satisfy the debt".

The agreement limited the liability of UBS to losses for which it was the sole responsible party, which losses had resulted only from its gross negligence or bad faith. The provision states:

> [APR] agrees [UBS] shall not have any liability (whether direct or indirect, in contract or tort or otherwise) to [APR] in connection with any matter referred to in this Agreement except for such liability for losses, claims, damages, or liabilities incurred by [APR] that are finally judicially determined to have arisen solely out of the gross negligence or bad faith of [UBS] in performing the services which are the subject of this agreement.

In April 1998, Turgut Ozaydin ("Ozaydin"), a new APR customer, produced for sale nine fraudulent Marsh & McLennan ("Marsh") stock certificates. An APR representative opened the Ozaydin account despite never having met the person, nor verifying any of the information provided by Ozaydin. The APR representative never inquired as to Ozaydin's net worth despite the reason given for the sale being the need to pay off alleged loans. APR executed nine separate 1,000 share transactions in the Ozaydin account.

After each transaction Ozaydin delivered to APR a stock certificate representing 1,000 shares. Each of these certificates bore tiny perforations forming a date. An APR employee recognized the perforated dating on the certificates but did not realize that it indicated the stock certificates had been canceled. After receiving the certificates, APR forwarded the certificates to UBS which also did not realize that the certificates had been canceled.

Upon receipt of the first certificate, UBS contacted APR to obtain a stock power since the stock was in the name of Kentras Industries. Ozaydin completed a Statement of Sole Proprietor wherein he stated that he was the sole proprietor of Kentras Industries. When UBS received from APR the Statement of Sole Proprietor, it attached a medallion guarantee to each certificate which constituted a warranty by UBS that, *inter alia,* Ozaydin's signature was authentic and that Ozaydin and Kentras Industries are the same. After applying the medallion guarantee to each certificate, UBS forwarded the shares to the

Depository Trust Corporation ("DTC"). Ozaydin's account was eventually credited a total of $798,291.51 for the nine fraudulent certificates.

DTC confirmed that the certificates where in negotiable form and sent them to Marsh's registered transfer agent, The Bank of New York ("BONY"). On or before March 23, 1998, BONY obtained information that indicated that the shares had been canceled in July 1983. Despite this information, BONY did not notify DTC or UBS of the fraudulent transaction until June 9, 1998. On this date, UBS was notified that one of the certificates was invalid. On June 10, 1998, BONY notified UBS that all of the certificates were canceled. UBS then notified APR on that same day that Ozaydin had failed to deliver securities covering Ozaydin's sales of 9,000 shares of Marsh stock. UBS also sent APR a letter acknowledging the problems they had already experienced with two of the certificates.

In a meeting conducted on June 12, 1998, UBS asserted its rights under the agreement for any losses which resulted from the Ozaydin transactions. On June 12, 1998, UBS received written confirmation that all of the shares of stock were invalid because they had been previously canceled. UBS then purchased 9,000 shares in the open market to replace the undelivered shares fraudulently sold in the Ozaydin account and demanded immediate payment from APR for the amount expended to replace the invalid Marsh stock. APR denied any responsibility.

What occurred after this point is relevant based upon the award of consequential damages resulting from APR being required to cease operations due to its failure to comply with the SEC's net capital rule. The net capital rule set forth in SEC Rule 15c3-1 (17 CFR § 240.15c3-1) required APR to maintain a certain level of liquid assets on account. Based upon a proper application of the net capital rule, it is undisputable that APR fell below the SEC mandated net capital requirements because of the fraudulent transfer of stock and was required by operation of law to cease trading. This is apparent from the communications the NASD faxed to APR which cited the NYSE Interpretation Handbook stating:

> Deficits in unsecured and partly secured introduced accounts shall be deducted by the

> carrying broker-dealer and the introducing broker when the clearing agreement states that such deficits are the liability of the introducing broker-dealer.

As the parties agreement contains a provision which assigns liability to APR, *both* UBS and APR were required to take a charge against their net capital under applicable regulations. APR did not maintain proper net capital and was required to cease trading until the company was infused with additional capital.

UBS has noted that this was not the first time that APR had problems complying with the net capital rule. Indeed, the dissenting arbitrator found that the cessation of APR's operations were a direct result of APR's chronic under-funding of the company. In an unrelated matter, APR violated the net capital rule based upon a $300,000 settlement with a former customer on June 10, 1998. Although APR notified the NASD of the violation, it apparently did not cease operations as required. This violation was apparently not cured until the June 11, 1998 when APR's parent infused the company with $300,000.

UBS has cited to another net capital violation which is of greater significance to this action as it implicates the ability of APR to assert in good faith the legal argument that contingent liabilities did not require a charge to net capital. In 1997, APR failed to take a charge against its net capital after it agreed to guarantee a bank line of credit for its corporate parent. The NASD apparently censured APR for violating the net capital rule, ruling that contingent liability required a charge to net capital even if the likelihood of incurring actual liability was remote. This earlier experience before the NASD implicitly impacts APR's assertion that no claim on net capital was required because actual liability on 7,000 of the shares was not demanded by those who bought the fraudulent shares.

The present dispute was submitted to arbitration in accordance with Clearing Agreement ¶ 17[b] which states:

> Any disputes hereunder shall be submitted to arbitration in New York, New York pursuant to the constitution and rules of the NYSE.

The Clearing Agreement is governed by New York law. (Clearing Agreement ¶ 17 [h]). The arbitration panel heard testimony from 30 witnesses and reviewed over 500 exhibits during the course of

64 hearing sessions. The arbitration panel also presided over 11 days of discovery hearings prior to the arbitration hearing.

Although not dispositive here, this Court finds that the voluminous proofs submitted in the arbitration support a finding that UBS had an overwhelming case on the merits based not just on the parties agreement, but also pursuant to well-established statutes and regulations. Relevant here is that had the arbitration panel acted in a rational manner and considered the applicable statutes and regulations, it might have understood the strength of UBS's case. However, the arbitration panel not only misapplied the applicable law, it stated that it was going to ignore the law. This conclusion is implicit from the record and the following commentary:

> [Counsel for UBS]: I have a question about the briefs . . . . We're going to be citing case law and regulatory authorities in the brief. Would it be useful for the panel for us to supply copies of the things that we cite, so that you don't have to look them up yourselves?
>
> [Counsel for APR]: I don't believe we have an objection to that. I think it's really a question of what the panel would want.
>
> If you are going to be reading these cases—
>
> [Arbitrator]: I am not. I'm not going to read it.
>
> This very same arbitrator was not merely dispensing with redundant information, she was ignorant of the rule. She stated:
>
> [Arbitrator]: Excuse me, but I never heard of a rule that says in accounting that you have to enter prospective charge [sic] just because you know it is going to come down.
>
> [Counsel for UBS]: Well, Ms. Kunzler, I could give you of the uniform net capital rule, 15c3-1, and the uniform net capital rule specifically says you have to take a charge against liabilities that you know you have, even though you haven't been called to put up the money.

In reviewing the arbitration award, this Court is faced with one of the two arbitrators which voted in the majority stating that she did not know a basic regulation impacting on strong public policy and that she would refuse to read the law so that she could properly apply or refuse to apply the rule. She deliberately avoided knowing the applicable laws and regulations.

In addition to the express statement by an arbitration panel member that the cases and regulatory authorities would not be read, the panel held executive session and then sua sponte prohibited the parties from citing more than *three* decisions in their post-hearing briefs. The arbitration panel refused to alter this bizarre limitation without any explanation even after a written request was made. The arbitration panel also refused to permit UBS to provide legal authority that contradicted APR's state law claim that good faith and fair dealing required UBS to waive its contractual right to recoup the funds that it expended to "cover."

Despite an overwhelming case by UBS on the merits, a two-member majority awarded APR damages in the amount of $5,694,002. This award was comprised of three components: 1) $381,893 representing 50% of the actual losses resulting from the sale of fraudulent securities; 2) $3.5 Million in consequential damages; and 3) $1,695,709 in attorneys' fees, costs and expert witness fees and other expenses of $116,400. The third member of the arbitration panel concurred on the award of $381,892.62, but dissented on the award of consequential damages and attorneys fees.

In rendering the award, the majority found that UBS had engaged in bad faith by demanding immediate payment for the 9,000 shares despite such a demand being permitted under the terms of the agreement. In making this determination, the panel found that the demand was vindictive in nature. Assuming that the immediate demand was unreasonable, the panel does not state how this would relieve APR from eventually paying for the cost of obtaining replacement shares for the fraudulent shares of stock, as provided by the parties' agreement.

> The arbitration panel also found as evidence of bad faith that UBS informed the NASD that APR was operating in violation of the net capital rule.

> In awarding APR attorneys' fees, the majority did not base the award on any statute or contractual provision. Instead, the panel premised the award on the following logic:
>
> Claimant should not have had to bring this case—it should have been settled between the parties and Respondent should have agreed immediately to take some responsibility for the loss.
>
> This fee was awarded despite UBS arguing from the outset of the arbitration proceedings that the panel lacked the power to award APR fees.

In dissenting, the minority member of the panel found that UBS was not "grossly negligent", but found that the circumstances supported UBS and APR should split the cost of purchasing the 9,000 shares in the market. This was an equitable conclusion since the same arbitrator found that "[Ozaydin's] failure to deliver good securities was [APR's] responsibility, and . . . [UBS] had a right, under the Clearing Agreement, to demand immediate repayment for the buy-in of all 9,000 shares."

The dissenting member rejected the award of consequential damages by finding that any consequential damage was the result of APR's undercapitalization. The minority panel member noted that APR required 10 cash infusions of over $1 Million. In addition, three senior officers of APR departed the company and founded a competing broker-dealer. The dissenting arbitrator found that the facts presented did not support a finding of bad faith. In addition, the dissenting member rejected the award for attorneys' fees noting that the parties' Clearing Agreement did not provide for the reimbursement of APR's attorneys' fees.

As the parties have agreed to have the arbitration agreement governed in accordance with New York law, the only basis for vacating that award is found within the confines of the Civil Practice Law & Rules ("CPLR") and governing case law. (Hackett v. Milbank, Tweed, Hadley & McCloy, 86 N.Y.2d 146, 154 [1995]). In *Hackett*, the Court of Appeals set forth the standard for vacating an arbitration award under

New York law. An arbitration award can be vacated under CPLR 7511 if:

> (1) the rights of a party were prejudiced by corruption, fraud or misconduct in procuring the award, or by the partiality of the arbitrator; (2) the arbitrator exceeded his or her power or failed to make a final and definite award; or (3) the arbitration suffered from an unwaived procedural defect. Even where the arbitrator makes a mistake of fact or law, or disregards the plain words of the parties' agreement, the award is not subject to vacatur "unless the court concludes that it is totally irrational or violative of a strong public policy" and thus in excess of the arbitrator's powers.

(*Hackett* at 154–55). Based upon the parties' submissions, the arbitration award is vacated in its entirety, unless APR will consent to a reduction of the award to the sum of $381,892.62. That branch of the parties dispute pertaining to the allocation of the expense of purchasing shares of stock in the market to cover the fraudulent shares will be presented to a new arbitration panel.

The award must be vacated based upon the arbitration panel's irrational refusal to even consider the applicable law which governed the dispute. While an award will not be vacated because a court disagrees with the arbitration panel's application of the law, *Silverman v. Benmor Coats, Inc.*, 61 N.Y.2d 299 [1984], this Court finds that the arbitration panel, at a minimum, must have at least considered the law which it erroneously applied. The arbitration award of consequential damages despite the application of the net capital rule set forth in SEC Rule 15c3-1 (17 CFR § 240.15c3-1) demonstrates that the panel not only acted irrationally, but also exhibited a manifest disregard for well-established public policy. The net capital rule is "a derivation of net worth, excluding certain non-liquid, non-secured assets and other adjustments the SEC determine necessary to protect the investment community and its customers." (Mishkin v. Ensminger, 247 B.R. 51 [SDNY 1999]). Once a broker-dealer fails to meet the net capital ratio required by the SEC Rule, it is required to immediately cease operations until it resumes compliance. Until such time as the broker-dealer resumes compliance with the net capital rule, it is not permitted to operate in the regulated securities market.

The arbitration panel's award of consequential damages was irrational based upon the application of SEC Rule 15c3-1. This is without this Court considering the parties' agreement which only permits a finding of liability if UBS was "solely" responsible for a loss.

This Court also notes that APR does not even contest that a violation of the net capital rule required it to cease operations as a matter of law until it regained a proper net equity ratio. (See In re Gerhauser, Admin. Pro. No. 3-9519, 1998 SEC LEXIS 2402 (Nov. 4, 1998). A plain reading of the net capital rule (and the parties' agreement) indicates that APR was required to take an immediate charge against its net capital once the fraud was uncovered. (Id.). Despite the clear legal mandate of APR to cease operations based upon its failure to maintain proper net equity, the arbitration panel improperly found that APR should have been permitted to continue its operations because only a certain percentage of fraudulent shares were called.

Having determined that the arbitration panel could not rationally award consequential damages based upon any application of SEC Rule 15c3-1, the Court also finds that the arbitration panel award contravenes strong public policy because it is premised on profits APR could not have obtained by lawful compliance with the net capital rule. (Cochran v. Dellfava, 136 Misc.2d 38 [City of Rochester Court 1987]) ("For no court should be required to serve as a paymaster of the wages of crime, or referee between thieves."). As stated by one court:

> The net capital rule is one of the most important weapons in the [SEC's] arsenal to protect investors. By limiting the ratio of a broker's indebtedness to his capital, the rule operates to assure confidence and safety to the investing public.

* * * *

Accordingly, it is

ORDERED that the petition to vacate the arbitration award is granted and the cross-petition to confirm the award is denied unless the respondent consents to the lesser award as provided above; and it is further

ORDERED that the portion of arbitration pertaining to the allocation for the costs associated with the purchase of shares of stock in the market is referred back for a new arbitration proceeding before a new arbitration panel; and it is further

ORDERED that the claims for consequential damages and attorney's fees are dismissed with prejudice.

Motor Vehicle Accident Indemnification Corp. v. Aetna Casualty & Surety Co.

Court of Appeals of New York, 1996.
89 N.Y.2d 214.

- LEVINE, J.

* * * *

Here, however, the obligation to arbitrate arises not through voluntary agreement, but through statutory mandate (see, Insurance Law § 5105[b]; § 5221[b][6]). Where arbitration is compulsory, our decisional law imposes closer judicial scrutiny of the arbitrator's determination under CPLR 7511(b) (see, Mount St. Mary's Hosp. v. Catherwood, 26 N.Y.2d 493; Matter of Furstenberg [Aetna Cas. & Sur. Co.], 49 N.Y.2d 757). To be upheld, an award in a compulsory arbitration proceeding must have evidentiary support and cannot be arbitrary and capricious (*Matter of Furstenberg [Aetna Cas. & Sur. Co.]*, supra; Matter of Central Gen. Hosp. v. Hanover Ins. Co., 49 N.Y.2d 950; Matter of Garcia v. Federal Ins. Co., 46 N.Y.2d 1040, rev'g 61 A.D.2d 236).

* * * *

§ 6.03 THE FAA IN STATE COURT POST-AWARD PROCEEDINGS

Must a State Court apply the FAA (assuming the case involves interstate commerce) in post-award proceedings? We shall see that the answer to this question may impact on the right of the parties to provide for broadened judicial review of awards.

Hall Street Associates, L.L.C., v. Mattel, Inc.

Supreme Court of the United States, 2008.
128 S. Ct. 1396.

▪ SOUTER, J.

The Federal Arbitration Act (FAA or Act), 9 U.S.C. §1 et seq., provides for expedited judicial review to confirm, vacate, or modify arbitration awards. §§ 9-11 (2000 ed. and Supp. V). The question here is whether statutory grounds for prompt vacatur and modification may be supplemented by contract. We hold that the statutory grounds are exclusive.

I

This case began as a lease dispute between landlord, petitioner Hall Street Associates, L.L.C., and tenant, respondent Mattel, Inc. The property was used for many years as a manufacturing site, and the leases provided that the tenant would indemnify the landlord for any costs resulting from the failure of the tenant or its predecessor lessees to follow environmental laws while using the premises.

Tests of the property's well water in 1998 showed high levels of trichloroethylene (TCE), the apparent residue of manufacturing discharges by Mattel's predecessors between 1951 and 1980. After the Oregon Department of Environmental Quality (DEQ) discovered even more pollutants, Mattel stopped drawing from the well and, along with one of its predecessors, signed a consent order with the DEQ providing for cleanup of the site.

After Mattel gave notice of intent to terminate the lease in 2001, Hall Street filed this suit, contesting Mattel's right to vacate on the date it gave, and claiming that the lease obliged Mattel to indemnify Hall Street for costs of cleaning up the TCE, among other things. Following a bench trial before the United States District Court for the District of Oregon, Mattel won on the termination issue, and after an unsuccessful try at mediating the indemnification claim, the parties proposed to submit to arbitration. The District Court was amenable, and the parties drew up an arbitration agreement, which the court approved and entered as an order. One paragraph of the agreement provided that

> [t]he United States District Court for the District of Oregon may enter judgment upon any award, either by confirming the award or by vacating, modifying or correcting the award. The Court shall vacate, modify or correct any award: (i) where the arbitrator's findings of facts are not supported by substantial evidence, or (ii) where the arbitrator's conclusions of law are erroneous.

Arbitration took place, and the arbitrator decided for Mattel. In particular, he held that no indemnification was due, because the lease obligation to follow all applicable federal, state, and local environmental laws did not require compliance with the testing requirements of the Oregon Drinking Water Quality Act (Oregon Act); that Act the arbitrator characterized as dealing with human health as distinct from environmental contamination.

Hall Street then filed a District Court Motion for Order Vacating, Modifying And/Or Correcting the arbitration decision, App. 4, on the ground that failing to treat the Oregon Act as an applicable environmental law under the terms of the lease was legal error. The District Court agreed, vacated the award, and remanded for further consideration by the arbitrator. The court expressly invoked the standard of review chosen by the parties in the arbitration agreement, which included review for legal error, and cited *LaPine Technology Corp. v. Kyocera Corp.*, 130 F.3d 884, 889 (9th Cir. 1997), for the proposition that the FAA leaves the parties "free . . . to draft a contract that sets rules for arbitration and dictates an alternative standard of review."

On remand, the arbitrator followed the District Court's ruling that the Oregon Act was an applicable environmental law and amended the decision to favor Hall Street. This time, each party sought modification, and again the District Court applied the parties' stipulated standard of review for legal error, correcting the arbitrator's calculation of interest but otherwise upholding the award. Each party then appealed to the Court of Appeals for the Ninth Circuit, where Mattel switched horses and contended that the Ninth Circuit's recent en banc action overruling *LaPine in Kyocera Corp. v. Prudential-Bache Trade Servs., Inc.*, 341 F.3d 987, 1000 (2003), left the arbitration agreement's provision for judicial review of legal error unenforceable. Hall Street countered that *Kyocera* (the later one) was distinguishable, and that the agreement's judicial review provision was not severable from the submission to arbitration.

The Ninth Circuit reversed in favor of Mattel in holding that, "[u]nder *Kyocera* the terms of the arbitration agreement controlling the mode of judicial review are unenforceable and severable." 113 Fed. Appx. 272, 272–73 (2004) . . . .

After the District Court again held for Hall Street and the Ninth Circuit again reversed, we granted certiorari to decide whether the grounds for vacatur and modification provided by §§ 10 and 11 of the FAA are exclusive. 550 U.S. 968 (2007). We agree with the Ninth Circuit that they are, but vacate and remand for consideration of independent issues.

II

Congress enacted the FAA to replace judicial indisposition to arbitration with a "national policy favoring [it] and plac[ing] arbitration agreements on equal footing with all other contracts." Buckeye Check Cashing, Inc. v. Cardegna, 546 U.S. 440, 443 (2006). As for jurisdiction over controversies touching arbitration, the Act does nothing, being "something of an anomaly in the field of federal-court jurisdiction" in bestowing no federal jurisdiction but rather requiring an independent jurisdictional basis. Moses H. Cone Memorial Hospital v. Mercury Constr. Corp., 460 U.S. 1, 25, n.32 (1983); see, e.g., 9 U.S.C. §4 (providing for action by a federal district court "which, save for such [arbitration] agreement, would have jurisdiction under title 28"). But in cases falling within a court's jurisdiction, the Act makes contracts to arbitrate "valid, irrevocable, and enforceable," so long as their subject involves "commerce." § 2. And this is so whether an agreement has a broad reach or goes just to one dispute, and whether enforcement be sought in state court or federal. See ibid.; Southland Corp. v. Keating, 465 U.S. 1, 15–16, (1984).

The Act also supplies mechanisms for enforcing arbitration awards: a judicial decree confirming an award, an order vacating it, or an order modifying or correcting it. §§ 9–11. An application for any of these orders will get streamlined treatment as a motion, obviating the separate contract action that would usually be necessary to enforce or tinker with an arbitral award in court. § 6. Under the terms of § 9, a court "must" confirm an arbitration award "unless" it is vacated, modified, or corrected "as prescribed" in §§ 10 and 11. Section 10 lists grounds for vacating an award, while § 11 names those for modifying or correcting one.[4]

The Courts of Appeals have split over the exclusiveness of these statutory grounds when parties take the FAA shortcut to confirm, vacate, or modify an award, with some saying the recitations are exclusive, and others regarding them as mere threshold provisions open to expansion by agreement.[5] As mentioned already, when this litigation started, the Ninth Circuit was on the threshold side of the split, see *LaPine,* 130 F.3d at 889, from which it later departed en banc in favor of the exclusivity view, see *Kyocera*, 341 F.3d at 1000, which it followed in this case, see 113 Fed. Appx., at 273. We now hold that §§ 10 and 11 respectively provide the FAA's exclusive grounds for expedited vacatur and modification.

III

Hall Street makes two main efforts to show that the grounds set out for vacating or modifying an award are not exclusive, taking the position, first, that expandable judicial review authority has been accepted as the law since *Wilko v. Swan*, 346 U.S. 427 (1953). This, however, was not what *Wilko* decided, which was that § 14 of the Securities Act of 1933 voided any agreement to arbitrate claims of violations of that Act, see id., at 437–38, a holding since overruled by *Rodriguez de Quijas v. Shearson/American Express, Inc.*, 490 U.S. 477, 484 (1989). Although it is true that the Court's discussion includes some language arguably favoring Hall Street's position, arguable is as far as it goes.

The *Wilko* Court was explaining that arbitration would undercut the Securities Act's buyer protections when it remarked (citing FAA § 10) that "[p]ower to vacate an [arbitration] award is limited," 346 U.S., at 436, and went on to say that "the interpretations of the law by the arbitrators in contrast to manifest disregard [of the law] are not subject, in the federal courts, to judicial review for error in interpretation," id., at 436–37. Hall Street reads this statement as recognizing "manifest disregard of the law" as a further ground for vacatur on top of those listed in § 10, and some Circuits have read it the same way. See, e.g., McCarthy v. Citigroup Global Markets, Inc., 463 F.3d 87, 91 (CA1 2006). Hall Street sees this supposed *addition to § 10 as* the camel's nose: If judges can add grounds to vacate (or modify), so can contracting parties.

But this is too much for *Wilko* to bear. Quite apart from its leap from a supposed judicial expansion by interpretation to a private expansion by contract, Hall Street overlooks the fact that the statement it relies on expressly rejects just what Hall Street asks for here, general review for an arbitrator's legal errors. Then there is the vagueness of *Wilko*'s phrasing. Maybe the term "manifest disregard" was meant to name a new ground for review, but maybe it merely referred to the § 10 grounds collectively, rather than adding to them. See, e.g., *Mitsubishi Motors Corp.* Or, as some courts have thought, "manifest disregard" may have been. We, when speaking as a Court, have merely taken the *Wilko* language as we found it, without embellishment, see *First Options of Chicago, Inc. v. Kaplan*, 514 U.S. shorthand for § 10(a)(3) or § 10(a)(4), the subsections authorizing vacatur when the arbitrators were "guilty of misconduct" or "exceeded their powers." See, e.g., *Kyocera*, supra, at 997, 938, 942 (1995), and now that its meaning is implicated, we see no reason to accord it the significance that Hall Street urges.

Second, Hall Street says that the agreement to review for legal error ought to prevail simply because arbitration is a creature of contract, and the FAA is "motivated, first and foremost, by a congressional desire to enforce agreements into which parties ha[ve] entered." Dean Witter Reynolds Inc. v. Byrd, 470 U.S. 213, 220 (1985). But, again, we think the argument comes up short. Hall Street is certainly right that the FAA lets parties tailor some, even many features of arbitration by contract, including the way arbitrators are chosen, what their qualifications should be, which issues are arbitrable, along with procedure and choice of substantive law. But to rest this case on the general policy of treating arbitration agreements as enforceable as such would be to beg the question, which is whether the FAA has textual features at odds with enforcing a contract to expand judicial review following the arbitration.

To that particular question we think the answer is yes, that the text compels a reading of the §§ 10 and 11 categories as exclusive. To begin with, even if we assumed §§ 10 and 11 could be supplemented to some extent, it would stretch basic interpretive principles to expand the stated grounds to the point of evidentiary and legal review generally. Sections 10 and 11, after all, address egregious departures from the parties' agreed-upon arbitration: "corruption," "fraud," "evident partiality," "misconduct," "misbehavior," "exceed[ing] . . . powers," "evident material miscalculation," "evident material mistake," "award[s] upon a matter not submitted," the only ground with any softer focus is "imperfect[ions]," and a court may correct those only if they go to "[a] matter of form not affecting the merits." Given this emphasis on extreme arbitral conduct, the old rule of ejusdem generis has an implicit lesson to teach here. Under that rule, when a statute sets out a series of specific items ending with a general term, that general term is con fined to covering subjects comparable to the specifics it follows. Since a general term included in the text is normally so limited, then surely a statute with no textual hook for expansion cannot authorize contracting parties to supplement review for specific instances of outrageous conduct with review for just any legal error. "Fraud" and a mistake of law are not cut from the same cloth.

That aside, expanding the detailed categories would rub too much against the grain of the § 9 language, where provision for judicial confirmation carries no hint of flexibility. On application for a n order confirming the arbitration award, the court "must grant" the order "unless the award is vacated, modified, or corrected as prescribed in sections 10 and 11 of this title." There is nothing malleable about "must grant," which unequivocally tells courts to grant confirmation in all cases, except when one of the "prescribed" exceptions applies. This does not sound remotely like a provision meant to tell a court what to do just in case the parties say nothing else.

In fact, anyone who thinks Congress might have understood § 9 as a default provision should turn back to § 5 for an example of what Congress thought a default provision would look like:

> "[i]f in the agreement provision be made for a method of naming or appointing an arbitrator . . . such method shall be followed; but if no method be provided therein, or if a method be provided and any party thereto shall fail to avail himself of such method, . . . then upon the application of either party to the controversy the court shall designate and appoint an arbitrator . . . ."

"[I]f no method be provided" is a far cry from "must grant . . . unless" in § 9.

Instead of fighting the text, it makes more sense to see the three provisions, §§ 9–11, as substantiating a national policy favoring arbitration with just the limited review needed to maintain arbitration's essential virtue of resolving disputes straightaway. Any other reading opens the door to the full-bore legal and evidentiary appeals that can "rende[r] informal arbitration merely a prelude to a more cumbersome and time-consuming judicial review process," *Kyocera*, 341 F.3d at 998; cf. Ethyl Corp. v. United Steelworkers of America, 768 F.2d 180, 184 (CA7 1985), and bring arbitration theory to grief in post-arbitration process . . . .

IV

In holding that §§ 10 and 11 provide exclusive regimes for the review provided by the statute, we do not purport to say that they exclude more searching review based on authority outside the statute as well. The FAA is not the only way into court for parties wanting review of arbitration awards: They may contemplate enforcement under state statutory or common law, for example, where judicial review of different scope is arguable. But here we speak only to the scope of the expeditious judicial review under §§ 9, 10, and 11, deciding nothing about other possible avenues for judicial enforcement of arbitration awards . . . .

One unusual feature, however, prompted some of us to question whether the case should be approached another way. The arbitration agreement was entered into in the course of district-court litigation, was submitted to the District Court as a request to deviate from the standard sequence of trial procedure, and was adopted by the District Court as an order. Hence a question raised by this Court at oral argument: should the agreement be treated as an exercise of the District Court's authority to manage its cases under Federal Rules of Civil Procedure 16? Supplemental briefing at the Court's behest joined issue on the question, and it appears that Hall Street suggested something along these lines in the Court of Appeals, which did not address the suggestion.

We are, however, in no position to address the question now, beyond noting the claim of relevant case management authority independent of the FAA. The parties' supplemental arguments on the subject in this Court implicate issues of waiver and the relation of the FAA both to Rule 16 and the Alternative Dispute Resolution Act of 1998, 28 U.S.C. §651 et seq., none of which has been considered previously in this litigation, or could be well addressed for the first time here. We express no opinion on these matters beyond leaving them open for Hall Street to press on remand. If the Court of Appeals finds they are open, the court may consider whether the District Court's authority to manage litigation independently warranted that court's order on the mode of resolving the indemnification issues remaining in this case.

* * * *

Although we agree with the Ninth Circuit that the FAA confines its expedited judicial review to the grounds listed in 9 U.S.C. §§ 10 and 11, we vacate the judgment and remand the case for proceedings consistent with this opinion.

It is so ordered.

▪ STEVENS, J., dissenting (with whom KENNEDY, J., joins).

May parties to an ongoing lawsuit agree to submit their dispute to arbitration subject to the caveat that the trial judge should refuse to enforce an award that rests on an erroneous conclusion of law? Prior to Congress' enactment of the Federal Arbitration Act (FAA or Act) in 1925, the answer to that question would surely have been "Yes." Today, however, the Court holds that the FAA does not merely authorize the vacation or enforcement of awards on specified grounds, but also forbids enforcement of perfectly reasonable judicial review provisions in arbitration agreements fairly negotiated by the parties and approved by the district court. Because this result conflicts with the primary purpose of the FAA and ignores the historical context in which the Act was passed, I respectfully dissent.

Prior to the passage of the FAA, American courts were generally hostile to arbitration. They refused, with rare exceptions, to order specific enforcement of executory agreements to arbitrate. Section 2 of the FAA responded to this hostility by making written arbitration agreements "valid, irrevocable, and enforceable." 9 U.S.C. §2. This section, which is the centerpiece of the FAA, reflects Congress' main goal in passing the legislation: "to abrogate the general common-law rule against specific enforcement of arbitration agreements," *Southland*, 465 U.S. at 18, (Stevens, J., concurring in part and dissenting in part), and to "ensur[e] that private arbitration agreements are enforced according to their terms," *Volt*, 489 U.S. at 478. Given this settled understanding of the core purpose of the FAA, the interests favoring enforceability of parties' arbitration agreements are stronger today than before the FAA was enacted. As such, there is more—and certainly not less—reason to give effect to parties' fairly negotiated decisions to provide for judicial review of arbitration awards for errors of law . . . .

This Court now agrees with the Ninth Circuit's (most recent) interpretation of the FAA as setting forth the exclusive grounds for modification or vacation of an arbitration award under the statute. As I read the Court's opinion, it identifies two possible reasons for reaching this result: (1) a *supposed quid pro quo bargain between Congress and litigants that conditions expedited federal enforcement* of arbitration awards on acceptance of a statutory limit on the scope of judicial review of such awards; and (2) an assumption that Congress intended to include the words "and no other" in the grounds specified in §§ 10 and 11 for the vacatur and modification of awards. Neither reason is persuasive . . . .

Even if I thought the narrow issue presented in this case were as debatable as the conflict among the courts of appeals suggests, I would rely on a presumption of overriding importance to resolve the debate and rule in favor of petitioner's position that the FAA permits the statutory grounds for vacatur and modification of an award to be supplemented by contract . . . .

Accordingly, . . . I respectfully dissent from the Court's interpretation of the FAA, and would direct the Court of Appeals to affirm the judgment of the District Court enforcing the arbitrator's final award.

- BREYER, J., dissenting.

The question presented in this case is whether "the Federal Arbitration Act . . . *precludes* a federal court from enforcing" an arbitration agreement that gives the court the power to set aside an arbitration award that embodies an arbitrator's mistake about the law. Like the majority and Justice Stevens, and primarily for the reasons they set forth, I believe that the Act does not *preclude* enforcement of such an agreement. See ante, (opinion of the Court) (The Act "is not the only way into court for parties wanting review of arbitration awards"); ante, (Stevens, J., dissenting) (The Act is a "shield meant to protect parties from hostile courts, not a sword with which to cut down parties' 'valid, irrevocable and enforceable' agreements to arbitrate their disputes subject to judicial review for errors of law' ").

At the same time, I see no need to send the case back for further judicial decisionmaking. The agreement here was entered into with the consent of the parties and the approval of the District Court. Aside from the Federal Arbitration Act itself, 9 U.S.C. §1 et seq., respondent below pointed to no statute, rule, or other relevant public policy that the agreement might violate. The Court has now rejected its argument that the agreement violates the Act, and I would simply remand the case with instructions that the Court of Appeals affirm the District Court's judgment enforcing the arbitrator's final award.

NOTES

1. The majority made a point to explain that it was "deciding nothing about other possible avenues for judicial enforcement of arbitration awards." Is this dictum "opening the door" for states to allow broadened review in their courts? Is the reasoning behind this potential expanded review based on an absence of preemption, i.e., that the FAA doe not preempt broadened judicial review in state courts? If yes, would this latitude apply to state courts cases that find themselves in federal court on account of diversity?

2. Although the Court refrained from deciding whether broad judicial review encourages or discourages arbitration, it is a question worthy of some thought. If *Hall Street*'s judicial review limitation is not applicable in state courts, *see* note 1, then it may be necessary to determine whether broad judicial review is hostile to arbitration. Does the courts' interest in expediting the arbitral review process hinge on whether broadened review is hostile?

3. Put another way, what if parties choose a state law of arbitration that recognizes a right to expand judicial review. Would this choice of state law be preempted under *Volt*, supra page 209 given the tenor of the *Hall Street* opinion?

4. Upon remand, the Ninth Circuit "concluded that *Hall Street Associates, L.L.C.* has preserved the issue of sources of authority, other than the Federal Arbitration Act, through which a court may enforce an arbitration award. *Hall St. Assocs. v. Mattel Inc.*, 531 F.3d 1019, 1020 (9th Cir. 2008). The court therefore, "remanded [the case] to the district court to make such determinations and conduct such hearings as may be consistent with the Supreme Court's decision." *Id.* Did the Ninth Circuit properly interpret the Supreme Court's holding?

5. Particularly if parties to a case involving interstate commerce can nonetheless opt for review under a state's statutory review standards, it will become important to use the requisite language in the arbitration

provision. Along similar lines, under section 9 of the FAA, its post-award procedures apply where "the parties in their agreement have agreed that a judgment of the court shall be entered upon the award . . . . " There are cases that hold that absent such language, and absent incorporation of tribunal rules providing for such entry, statutory confirmation procedures do not apply. One such case, decided before the AAA amended its rules to provide for entry, is Varley v. Tarrytown Assocs,, Inc., 477 F.2d 208 (1973). Accord, Local Union No. 387 v. Roberts Dairy, 294 F. Supp.2d 1050 (S.D. Iowa 2003). Other decisions, however, often gloss over this point. In the absence of statutory confirmation procedures, the award is treated as a common law arbitration award which can only be confirmed by a plenary contract action. Arbitration pursuant to an oral agreement to do so is also referenced as "common law arbitration."

* * * *

Hall Street has great significance for two reasons. For one, it opens the door to expanded review where parties specifically provide for state law to govern and such law permits them to opt for review for errors of law or fact. Also important is that the opinion suggests that "manifest disregard" may never have been intended to be an extra statutory basis to vacate, as opposed to a subspecies of gross arbitral misconduct such as "abuse" of arbitral power, which is a statutory basis to refuse confirmation. Let us deal with these points in turn.

[A] The Aftermath of *Hall Street* — Expanded Review in State Court

Hall Street holds that, under the FAA in federal court, the parties cannot escape limited review by contract. FAA section 9, by its terms, applies to the federal courts and has the "must confirm" language emphasized by Justice Souter in his opinion. Most arbitral awards, however, are reviewed by state courts because of the lack of independent subject matter jurisdiction in the federal courts under the FAA. Presumably, notwithstanding diversity, the parties can contractually provide that the state courts alone will deal with post-award proceedings.

Providing for review of awards under state law, without more, typically would accomplish little, because state law grounds to vacate often parrot those under the FAA. This is true even in states which have retained forms of so-called "common law arbitration" not subject to statute. *See generally* Weiskopf & Mulqueen, *Hall Street, Judicial Review of Arbitral Awards, and Federal Preemption*, 29 REV. LITIG. 361 (2010). However, state law may be more flexible in permitting enforcement of an express party-provision for expanded review.

To the extent common law arbitration exists at the state level, there is old authority, from the famed Justice Story no less, that "If the parties wish to reserve the law for the decision of the court, they may stipulate to that effect . . . ." Klein v. Catara, 14 F. Cas. 732, 735 (C.C.D. Mass. 1814).

What about review in state court in the far more common situation where state statute applies. First, it is critical to understand that there is some state court precedent, post-*Hall Street*, that the FAA's confirmation provisions do not apply in state court. The question then becomes whether a party provision for extended review violates state statutory policy. If not, and despite the reference to state law review in *Hall Street*, there is also still the theoretical possibility that, to the extent state law would otherwise permit expanded review, it is preempted as "hostile" to federal policy in cases involving interstate commerce. Obviously, case opinions in this area can make for difficult reading.

Cable Connection, Inc., v. DIRECTV, Inc.

Supreme Court of California, 2008.
190 P.3d 586.

- CORRIGAN, J.

The United States Supreme Court has held that the Federal Arbitration Act does not permit the parties to expand the scope of review by agreement. (Hall Street Associates, L.L.C. v. Mattel, Inc. (2008) 552 U.S. 576, (Hall Street)). However, the high court went on to say that federal law does not preclude "more searching review based on authority outside the [federal] statute," including "state statutory or common law."

The California rule is that the parties may obtain judicial review of the merits by express agreement. There is a statutory as well as a contractual basis for this rule; one of the grounds for review of an arbitration award is that "[t]he arbitrators exceeded their powers." Here, the parties agreed that "[t]he arbitrators shall not have the power to commit errors of law or legal reasoning, and the award may be vacated or corrected on appeal to a court of competent jurisdiction for any such error." This contract provision is enforceable under state law, and we reverse the contrary ruling of the Court of Appeal.

The CAA and the FAA provide only limited grounds for judicial review of an arbitration award. Under both statutes, courts are authorized to vacate an award if it was (1) procured by corruption, fraud, or undue means; (2) issued by corrupt arbitrators; (3) affected by prejudicial misconduct on the part of the arbitrators; or (4) in excess of the arbitrators' powers.

As noted at the outset, and discussed further below, in *Moncharsh* we declared that " 'in the absence of some limiting clause in the arbitration agreement, the merits of the award, either on questions of fact or of law, may not be reviewed except as provided in the statute.' "

Nevertheless, when the issue has been squarely presented, no Court of Appeal has enforced a contract clause calling for judicial review of an arbitration award on its merits.

Before the *Hall Street* decision was handed down, the federal circuits were split on whether the FAA grounds for judicial review are exclusive. The First, Third, Fourth, Fifth, and Sixth Circuits held or indicated that contract provisions for expanded review of arbitration awards were enforceable. The Seventh, Eighth, Ninth, and Tenth Circuits took the opposite view. As we discuss next, a majority of the Supreme Court in *Hall Street* decided the FAA was intended to provide exclusive criteria for review of arbitration awards.

Hall Street and the Question of Preemption

The *Hall Street* case arose from an arbitration agreement negotiated during litigation, to resolve an indemnification claim. The agreement was approved and entered as an order by the trial court. It provided: " 'The Court shall vacate, modify or correct any award: (i) where the arbitrator's findings of facts are not supported by substantial evidence, or (ii) where the arbitrator's conclusions of law are erroneous.' "

Despite this strict reading of the FAA, the *Hall Street* majority left the door ajar for alternate routes to an expanded scope of review. "In holding that §§ 10 and 11 provide exclusive regimes for the review provided by the statute, we do not purport to say that they exclude more searching review based on authority outside the statute as well. The FAA is not the only way into court for parties wanting review of arbitration awards: they may contemplate enforcement under state statutory or common law, for example, where judicial review of different scope is arguable. But here we speak only to the scope of the expeditious judicial review under §§ 9, 10, and 11, deciding nothing about other possible avenues for judicial enforcement of arbitration awards."

Furthermore, the *Hall Street* majority recognized that the trial court's case management authority under rule 16 of the Federal Rules of Civil Procedure might support its order adopting the parties' agreement to review of the merits. However, it remanded for further proceedings on this point, concluding that it was "in no position to address the question now, beyond noting the claim of relevant case management authority independent of the FAA."

The dealers in this case urge us to follow the rationale of the *Hall Street* majority. They contend that any other construction of the CAA would result in its preemption by the FAA. Alternatively, they argue that *Hall Street* provides a persuasive analysis of the FAA that should be applied to the similar CAA provisions governing judicial review. We consider first the question of preemption, because if the dealers are correct on that point, it would be fruitless to consider alternate interpretations of state law.

Section 2 of the FAA, declaring the enforceability of arbitration agreements, "create[s] a body of federal substantive law of arbitrability, applicable to any arbitration agreement within the coverage of the Act." (Moses H. Cone Hospital v. Mercury Constr. Corp. (1983) 460 U.S. 1, 24). The FAA governs agreements in contracts involving interstate commerce, like those in this case. (Southland Corp. v. Keating, supra, 465 U.S. at pp. 10–11; Cronus Investments, Inc. v. Cocierge Services (2005) 35 Cal.4th 376, 383–84 (Cronus)). The United States Supreme Court has frequently held that state laws invalidating arbitration agreements on grounds applicable only to arbitration provisions contravene the policy of enforceability established by section 2 of the FAA, and are therefore preempted.

However, "the United States Supreme Court does not read the FAA's procedural provisions to apply to state court proceedings." (*Cronus*, supra, 35 Cal.4th at p. 389). Sections 3 and 4 of the FAA, governing stays of litigation and petitions to enforce arbitration agreements, do not apply in state court. As we have noted, the provisions for judicial review of arbitration awards in sections 10 and 11 of the FAA are directed to "the United States court in and for the district where the award was made." We have held that similar language in sections 3 and 4 of the FAA reflects Congress's intent to limit the application of those provisions to federal courts.

Before *Hall Street*, we would have had no difficulty concluding that enforcing agreements for judicial review on the merits is consistent with the fundamental purpose of the FAA. The high court has made it clear that the FAA does not "prevent[ ] the enforcement of agreements to arbitrate under different rules than those set forth in the Act itself. Indeed, such a result would be quite inimical to the FAA's primary purpose of ensuring that private agreements to arbitrate are enforced according to their terms. Arbitration under the Act is a matter of consent, not coercion, and parties are generally free to structure their arbitration agreements as they see fit. Just as they may limit by contract the issues which they will arbitrate [citation], so too may they specify by contract the rules under which that arbitration will be con-ducted. Where . . . the parties have agreed to abide by state rules of arbitration, enforcing those rules according to the terms of the agreement is fully consistent with the goals of the FAA . . . . By permitting the courts to "rigorously enforce" such agreements according to their terms [citation], we give effect to the contractual rights and expectations of the parties, without doing violence to the policies behind by the FAA." (*Volt*, supra, 489 U.S. at p. 479).

The court has repeatedly ruled that the terms of the parties' agreement are controlling over considerations of expediency in the dispute resolution process. "After all, the basic objective in this area is not to resolve disputes in the quickest manner possible, no matter what the parties' wishes, but to ensure that commercial arbitration agreements, like other contracts, 'are enforced according to their terms,' and according to the intentions of the parties." (First Options of Chicago, Inc. v. Kaplan (1995) 514 U.S. 938, 947; see also *Volt*, supra, 489 U.S. at p. 479, Dean Witter Reynolds Inc. v. Byrd (1985) 470 U.S. 213, 220–21). The court has viewed the federal policy served by the FAA as "at bottom a policy guaranteeing the enforcement of private contractual arrangements." (*Mitsubishi Motors v. Soler Chrysler-Plymouth*, supra, 473 U.S. at p. 625; see also, e.g., Mastrobuono v. Shearson Lehman Hutton, Inc. (1995) 514 U.S. 52, 58).

We do not believe the *Hall Street* majority intended to declare a policy with preemptive effect in all cases involving interstate commerce. *Hall Street* was a federal case governed by federal law; the court considered no question of competing state law. It reviewed the application of FAA provisions for judicial review that speak only to the federal courts. The court unanimously left open other avenues for judicial review, including those provided by state statutory or common law. While the court, of course, decided nothing about the viability of these alternatives, their mention in the majority opinion indicates that *Hall Street's* holding on the effect of the FAA is a limited one.

We conclude that the *Hall Street* holding is restricted to proceedings to review arbitration awards under the FAA, and does not require state law to conform with its limitations. Furthermore, a reading of the CAA that permits the enforcement of agreements for merits review is fully consistent with the FAA "policy guaranteeing the enforcement of private contractual arrangements." (*Mitsubishi Motors v. Soler Chrysler-Plymouth*, supra, 473 U.S. at p. 625; see 9 U.S.C. § 2.).

Brookfield Country Club, Inc. v. St. James-Brookfield, LLC

Supreme Court of Georgia, 2010.
287 Ga. 408.

▪ THOMPSON, J.

Brookfield is a non-profit corporation established in 1991 to own and operate a country club in Roswell. . . .

In 2000 Brookfield leased the country club property to St. James pursuant to a long-term lease and an incorporated management agreement (the lease). . . .

The terms of the lease . . . required the parties to submit all disputes "to negotiation and, if necessary mediation and arbitration." That arbitration provision specified that the arbitrator be bound by the strict terms of the lease and also provided for court vacatur of the arbitrator's award "if the court finds the arbitrator's award is not consistent with applicable law or not supported by a preponderance of the evidence . . . all in addition to grounds for vacation of an award as set forth in the Georgia Arbitration Code [OCGA § 9-9-1 et seq. (Arbitration Code)]." The lease further specified that in case of conflict between the lease provisions and the Arbitration Code, "the provisions of the lease shall control."

The pivotal question presented by this case is whether parties to an arbitration agreement may by contract modify the scope of the trial court's review of an arbitrator's award to include grounds for vacatur that are not set forth in the Arbitration Code. This issue presents two countervailing legal concepts-the rights of parties to set the terms of their contract, against the firmly established principle that the expansion of judicial review of arbitration awards beyond that created by statute would frustrate the "expeditious and final resolution of disputes by means that circumvent the time and expense associated with civil litigation." Greene v. Hundley, 266 Ga. 592, 597(3) (1996). See also Hardin Constr. Group v. Fuller Enterprises, 265 Ga. 770, 771 (1995) ("the role of the trial court should be limited so that the purpose of avoiding litigation by resorting to arbitration is not frustrated").

OCGA § 9-9-13(b) of the Arbitration Code sets forth five statutory grounds for vacating an arbitration award upon the application of a party subject to the award, as follows:

> The award shall be vacated on the application of a party who either participated in the arbitration or was served with a demand for arbitration if the court finds that the rights of that party were prejudiced by:
>
> (1) Corruption, fraud, or misconduct in procuring the award;
>
> (2) Partiality of an arbitrator appointed as a neutral;
>
> (3) An overstepping by the arbitrators of their authority or such imperfect execution of it that a final and definite award upon the subject matter submitted was not made;
>
> (4) A failure to follow the procedure of this part, unless the party applying to vacate the award continued with the arbitration with notice of this failure and without objection; or
>
> (5) The arbitrator's manifest disregard of the law.

Our appellate courts have consistently found that the statutory grounds for vacatur enumerated in OCGA § 9-9-13(b) are the exclusive means by which a court may vacate an arbitration award.

With these principles in mind we consider whether the statutory grounds for vacatur may be expanded by contract, an issue addressed for the first time in Georgia in *Brookfield*, supra. "Because our state arbitration code closely tracks federal arbitration law, we look to federal cases for guidance in construing our own statutes." ABCO Builders v. Progressive Plumbing, 282 Ga. 308, 309 (2007). In *Hall Street*, 552 U.S. 576 (2008), the United States Supreme Court considered whether the grounds for vacatur and modification of arbitration awards set forth in the Federal Arbitration Act (FAA), are exclusive, or whether they can be modified by contract. The Court resolved a split among the federal circuits by holding that §§ 10 and 11 of the FAA, listing grounds for vacating an arbitration award and those for modifying or correcting one, are the exclusive grounds for such action.

Georgia's Arbitration Code demands that a "court shall confirm an award upon application of a party . . . unless the award is vacated or modified by the court as provided in this part." The federal statute has a similar provision. Under 9 USC § 9, a court "must" confirm an arbitration award "unless" it is vacated, modified, or corrected "as prescribed" in the FAA. As the Court observed in *Hall Street*, to allow contractual expansion of §§ 10 and 11,

> would rub too much against the grain of the § 9 language, where provision for judicial confirmation carries no hint of flexibility.... There is nothing malleable about "must grant," which unequivocally tells courts to grant confirmation in all cases, except when one of the "prescribed" exceptions applies. This does not sound remotely like a provision meant to tell a court what to do just in case the parties say nothing else.

Id., 552 U.S. at 587. In similar fashion, this language can be applied to the mandatory feature of OCGA § 9-9-12, which directs the court to confirm an award unless the statutory grounds for vacatur are established.

While *Hall Street* is not dispositive of the scope of judicial review available under state law, the vast majority of states have followed its lead. Having examined the reasoning and logic of *Hall Street* and the decisions of other courts adopting its rationale, we find those cases to be consistent with the statutory and interpretative law of this state, and therefore persuasive. We also reiterate that arbitration in this state is no longer governed by common law, but is wholly a creature of statute, and thus it is the role of the legislature, not this Court, to augment any fundamental changes in the nature of the proceeding. Here the parties' decision to arbitrate grievances expresses their intent to by-pass the judicial system and thus avoid potential delays at the trial and appellate levels.

* * * *

[B] The Aftermath of *Hall Street* — The Ongoing Viability of Manifest Disregard

Supreme Court treatment of "manifest disregard" in *Hall Street* is a real puzzler. The suggestion there that "manifest disregard" may simply be a subspecies of abuse of arbitral power, or perhaps of bias, may not mean very much, at least in those courts which have required deliberate arbitral rejection of controlling legal principles before "manifest disregard" can be found. Most courts faced with the issue have simply said that 'manifest disregard" is a form of abuse of arbitral power, and then gone on with the traditional analysis. *See, e.g.*, Comedy Club In. v. Improv W. Assocs., 553 F.3d 1277, 1290 (9th Cir. 2009) (defining manifest disregard as 'shorthand" for abuse of power); *See generally* Richard Reuben, *Personal Autonomy and Vacatur After Hall Street*, 113 PENN ST. L. REV. 1103 (2009); Weiskopf & Mulqueen, *supra*, 29 REV. LITIG. at 369–70. *But see* Ramos-Santiago v. United Parcel Serv., 524 F.3d 120, 124 n.3 (1st Cir. 2008) (manifest disregard no longer grounds to vacate).

The Supreme Court continues to flirt with "manifest disregard." In its *Stolt-Nielsen* opinion, *supra* at 362, it again, even more ambiguously, expressly refuses to "decide whether 'manifest disregard' survives . . . as an independent ground for review or as a judicial gloss on the enumerated grounds for vacatur set for in 9 U.S.C. § 10." Interestingly, the dissent in the case speaks in terms of whether arbitrators abuse their power in opening a case to class action treatment absent specific provision for it by the parties. "Abuse of power" may simply be the new vernacular for purposeful gross arbitral error. If so, earlier cases to the contrary become outmoded in this respect.

§ 6.04 THE PRECLUSIVE EFFORTS OF ARBITRAL AWARDS

Commercial arbitral awards, even when reasoned, are not reported and essentially lack *stare decisis* precedential significance. That does not mean, however, that arbitral determinations are not preclusive as between the parties. Principles of res judicata and collateral estoppel are both applicable to awards, but some courts require that awards be confirmed before they may be given preclusive effect. The first two cases here deal with the converse situation, however—the preclusive effect of court judgments in subsequent arbitrations. The last case deals with the preclusive effect of arbitral awards in subsequent court litigation between the same parties or their "privies."

Collins v. D.R. Horton, Inc.

United States Court of Appeals, Ninth Circuit, 2007.
505 F.3d 874.

- BEA, CIRCUIT JUDGE.

We have "not specifically addressed whether arbitrators are bound by prior federal court decisions under the doctrines of collateral estoppel and/or res judicata[.]" Collins v. Horton, 361 F. Supp. 2d 1085, 1097 (D. Ariz. 2005). Other circuits, however, have held that where the prerequisites for collateral estoppel are satisfied arbitrators must give preclusive effect to prior federal judgments. See, e.g., Aircraft Braking Sys. Corp. v. Local 856, 97 F.3d 155, 159 (6th Cir. 1996); Miller v. Runyon, 77 F.3d 189, 193 (7th Cir. 1996); John Morrell & Co. v. Local Union 304A, 913 F.2d 544 (8th Cir. 1990). We agree: "Arbitrators are not free to ignore the preclusive effect of prior judgments under the doctrines of res judicata and collateral estoppel, although they generally are entitled to determine in the first instance whether to give the prior judicial determination preclusive effect." *Aircraft Braking Sys. Corp.*, 97 F.3d at 159; see also Miller Brewing Co. v. Fort Worth Distrib. Co., 781 F.2d 494, 499 (5th Cir. 1986) (reasoning that parties should be barred from seeking relief from an arbitration panel if res judicata principles would bar relief in federal court because an arbitration award involves the entry of judgment by a court).

Miller Brewing Co. v. Fort Worth Distributing Co.

United States Court of Appeals, Fifth Circuit, 1986.
781 F.2d 494.

- GOLDBERG, CIRCUIT JUDGE.

This case has been brewing far too long. Things came to a head when plaintiff-appellee Fort Worth Distributing Company went into state court in 1980 to prevent Miller Brewing Company from terminating a distributorship agreement between the two companies. After having its state court suit dismissed with prejudice for want of prosecution, however, Fort Worth Distributing now invokes an arbitration clause in order to pursue essentially the same claim. We find Fort Worth Distributing's case flat and stale at this juncture, and direct the district court to grant Miller Brewing's application for a stay of arbitration.

* * * *

III. Waiver of Arbitration

We first consider whether FWDC has waived its right to arbitration by invoking the judicial process and forcing Miller to expend substantial amounts of time and money defending itself in that forum. Waiver of arbitration is not a favored finding, and there is a presumption against it. As the Supreme Court stated in *Moses H. Cone*, 460 U.S. 1, 24 (1983), "questions of arbitrability must be addressed with a healthy regard for the federal policy favoring arbitration." See 9 U.S.C. § 2. Nevertheless, under appropriate circumstances a waiver of arbitration may be found. Even in stressing the policy favoring arbitrability the *Moses Cone* Court noted that "Congress' clear intent, in the Arbitration Act, [was] to move the parties to an arbitrable dispute out of court and into arbitration as quickly and easily as possible." 460 U.S. at 22. Here, of course, FWDC's first step was to move the parties *into* court; its belated attempt to arbitrate 3 1/2 years later, after losing in court, can hardly be seen as moving the parties into arbitration "as quickly and easily as possible."

Waiver will be found when the party seeking arbitration substantially invokes the judicial process to the detriment or prejudice of the other party. "The right to arbitration, like any other contract right, can be waived. A party waives his right to arbitrate when he actively participates in a lawsuit or takes other action inconsistent with that right." Cornell & Co. v. Barber & Ross Co., 360 F.2d 512, 513 (D.C. Cir. 1966) (footnotes omitted); accord Burton-Dixie Corp. v. Timothy McCarthy Const. Co., 436 F.2d 405, 407–08 (5th Cir. 1971). As this court noted in *E.C. Ernst, Inc. v. Manhattan Const. Co.*, 559 F.2d 268, 269 (5th Cir. 1977), "When one party reveals a disinclination to resort to arbitration on any phase of suit involving all parties, those parties are prejudiced by being forced to bear the expenses of a trial . . . . Substantially invoking the litigation machinery qualifies as the kind of prejudice . . . that is the essence of waiver."

FWDC has demonstrated a clear and unmistakable "disinclination" to arbitrate, and has done so to the substantial detriment and prejudice of Miller. FWDC's Original Petition in the Texas court suit against miller did not rely on or even mention the arbitration clause. Only in January, 1981—nearly eight months after bringing its state court suit—did FWDC announce its intention to arbitrate. Thereafter, however, "Neither Miller nor FWDC took steps to cause the American Arbitration Association to schedule a hearing until FWDC did so on September 22, 1984."

While its demand for arbitration lay dormant for 3 1/2 years, FWDC was busily pursuing its legal remedies. Lawsuits were filed, at one time or another, in state trial court, the state court of appeals, federal district court, and this court. Of course, Miller had to participate and defend its interests in all these actions. The record reveals that numerous depositions were taken, and that Miller paid over $85,000 in legal fees and expended more than 300 hours of its own employees' time defending the FWDC claims.

* * * *

Even more significant, perhaps, is the prejudice to Miller's legal position that resulted from FWDC's actions. A party to arbitration does not have a right to the pre-trial discovery procedures that are used in a case at law. A party "may not invoke arbitration and yet seek pre-trial discovery going to the merits . . . . Any attempt to go to the merits and to retain still the right to arbitration is clearly impermissible." Graig Shipping Co. v. Midland Overseas Shipping Corp., 259 F. Supp. 929,

931 (S.D.N.Y. 1966). There is every indication that Miller's position would be prejudiced and compromised in arbitration by FWDC's use of pre-trial discovery going to the merits.

* * * *

IV. Res Judicata

Even if the waiver considerations outlined above did not apply, we would still have good grounds for enjoining arbitration proceedings in this case. The doctrine of res judicata, as developed by Texas courts, ensures that when a court of competent jurisdiction has entered a final judgment on the merits of a case, the parties are bound as to all claims that were raised or that *could* have been raised. The Texas Supreme Court has declared:

> [T]he rule of res judicata in Texas bars litigation of all issues connected with a cause of action or defense which, with the use of diligence, might have been tried in a former action as well as those which were actually tried .... Stated differently, a party cannot relitigate matters which he might have interposed, but failed to do so, in an action between the same parties or their privies in reference to the same subject matter.

Anchor Glass Container Corp. v. Buschmeier

United States Court of Appeals, Seventh Circuit, 2005.
426 F.3d 872.

- SYKES, CIRCUIT JUDGE.

Anchor Glass Container Corporation ("Anchor") loaned its parent company, G&G Investments, Inc. ("G & G"), approximately \$ 17 million needed by G & G to make an initial installment payment toward the purchase of a German glass company known as Kommanditgessellschaft in Firma Hermann Heye ("Heye"). When the deal went sour after the initial \$ 17 million had been paid, G & G proceeded to arbitration on the question of whether Heye's principal shareholder, Petra Buschmeier, would be required to return the initial payment. The arbitration panel eventually ruled in favor of Mrs. Buschmeier. In the present case, Anchor has sued Petra Buschmeier and her husband, Ulrich, seeking the return of the same $ 17 million that was at issue in the arbitration proceeding. The district court dismissed the action, holding that there was sufficient identity in the causes of action and the parties that the arbitration award was res judicata as to Anchor's claims. Anchor appeals and we affirm.

I. Background

In the spring of 1998, G & G, backed by a consortium of Canadian coinvestors, entered into negotiations with Petra and Ulrich Buschmeier for the acquisition of Heye, a German limited partnership. One of the principal negotiators acting on behalf of G & G was Richard Deneau, president and CEO of Anchor, a subsidiary of G & G. Petra Buschmeier owned a 60.1% interest in Heye, and Ulrich Buschmeier owned another 1.02%. In the course of the negotiations, the Buschmeiers represented to G & G that any sale of Heye would require the Buschmeiers to first purchase the interests of minority shareholders as well as the usufructuary rights of Petra Buschmeier's mother. The Buschmeiers indicated they had agreements in place that would allow them to force the sale of those interests but that time was of the essence because of an impending deadline within which a sale of minority interests could be compelled.

On September 5, 1998, G & G executed an agreement to purchase Heye. The agreement required payment in three installments, the first of which—a payment of approximately $17 million—was due within three days. This sum was to be paid directly to Petra Buschmeier for use in purchasing her mother's usufructuary rights. The second payment was due a week later and the final payment a month after that. The purchase agreement also contained an arbitration clause which stipulated that "all disputes arising in connection with this Agreement shall be finally settled under the Rules of Arbitration of the International Chamber of Commerce by three arbitrators appointed in accordance with said rules."

Apparently G & G's execution of the purchase agreement and

the tight payment schedule to which it had committed caught its Canadian coinvestors completely off-guard. The day before the first payment was due, certain coinvestors reported that their boards would not authorize the release of the money needed to fund the initial installment until additional due diligence was performed. G & G asked the Buschmeiers for an extension of the initial payment due date in order to placate the demands of the coinvestors and secure the financial records they required. The Buschmeiers refused to extend the deadline.

In an effort to meet the deadline and save the deal, G & G turned to its subsidiary, Anchor, for a $17 million bridge loan. Anchor agreed to loan G & G the funds for the initial installment, provided that Deneau receive assurances that the initial payment would be returned if G & G and its coinvestors were unable to complete the acquisition of Heye under the terms of the September 5 agreement. To this end, Ulrich Buschmeier and Deneau had telephone conversations on September 7 and 8 in which Mr. Buschmeier allegedly promised that the initial payment would be repaid in the event the transaction was not completed. Buschmeier also apparently reiterated that the deadline for making the initial payment could not be extended due to the impending expiration of Heye's agreements with its minority shareholders. Deneau and his German counsel then drafted a letter for Ulrich Buschmeier's signature dated September 8, 1998, addressed from Buschmeier to G & G's CEO, in which Buschmeier confirmed that "this first installment . . . will be repaid to G & G Investments, Inc., if for any reason, or without reason, the transfer of the Sold Interest [in Heye] . . . does not occur." Buschmeier signed the letter and returned it to Anchor's German counsel. Thus reassured, Anchor immediately borrowed $ 17,330,026.37 against its revolving line of credit and wired the funds directly into the personal bank account of Petra Buschmeier, thereby meeting G & G's September 8 deadline for making the first payment.

When the deadline for making the second payment arrived one week later, G & G's Canadian investors still had not completed their due diligence. The Buschmeiers once again declined to extend the payment deadline. Following a series of events irrelevant to the present suit, G & G's Canadian investors completely withdrew from participation in the proposed acquisition of Heye. G & G attempted to secure replacement financing and negotiations to save the deal ensued, but none of these efforts bore fruit. By February 1999 all parties considered the deal to be dead. When Petra Buschmeier made it clear she had no intention of refunding the $17 million due to G & G's breach of the payment schedule, a substantial volume of litigation ensued.

Pursuant to the arbitration clause in the purchase agreement, G & G requested arbitration before the International Chamber of Commerce ("ICC") on the question of whether the September 8 letter, drafted by Deneau and his attorney and signed by Ulrich Buschmeier, modified the terms of the purchase agreement such that Petra Buschmeier was required to return the initial payment. G & G's position was that the September 8 letter amended the original purchase agreement and amounted to an exit clause, entitling it to rescind the agreement and obtain the return of the money if the sale went uncompleted for any reason whatsoever—including, as ultimately occurred, G & G's own inability to timely secure financing. Petra Buschmeier took the position that the September 8 letter had no effect on the parties' obligations established in the purchase agreement, and that the letter was intended to require the return of the first installment *only* if the ultimate transfer of Heye became impossible because of *her own* failure to meet her obligations, most notably the possibility that she would be unable to purchase shares from the minority shareholders of Heye.

* * * *

After the hearings concluded but before the arbitrators rendered their decision, Anchor commenced the present action against the Buschmeiers, seeking return of the initial installment payment on theories of breach of contract, fraud, promissory estoppel, conversion, and unjust enrichment. Less than a month after this suit was filed, the ICC issued a final arbitration decision, denying G & G's claim for a refund and sustaining Petra Buschmeier's counterclaim for damages.

* * * *

Armed with the arbitration decision in its favor, the Buschmeiers moved to dismiss Anchor's lawsuit on the pleadings, arguing that there was sufficient identity of the parties and the causes of action such that the arbitration award against G & G was res judicata as to Anchor's claims. The district court held that Pennsylvania law governed the res judicata analysis and the arbitration award was res judicata with respect to Anchor's claims and therefore dismissed the action. Anchor appeals.

* * * *

Discussion

* * * *

B. *Res Judicata Effect of the ICC Arbitration.*

In Pennsylvania application of the doctrine of res judicata generally requires that the two actions possess the following common elements: (1) identity of the thing sued upon, (2) identity of the cause of action, (3) identity of the parties, and (4) identity of the capacity of the parties.

* * * *

1. Identity of the Causes of Action.

Anchor argues that the arbitration was limited to a single issue of contract interpretation—whether the September 8 letter constituted an amendment to the purchase agreement—and that its claims in this case, by contrast, are predicated *not* on the September 8 letter but on "oral representations" made by Ulrich Buschmeier directly to Anchor during preletter telephone conversations on September 7 and 8, 1998. Thus (the argument goes), Anchor's claims in this suit are grounded on different claims for relief—fraud, promissory estoppel, conversion, and unjust enrichment—and a different evidentiary foundation, namely, oral representations made by Mr. Buschmeier.

Anchor's argument draws too fine a distinction between the claims res judicata insulates from relitigation and those that are excluded from the doctrine's scope. In Pennsylvania, as elsewhere, the causes of action litigated in the first action need not be *identical* to those in a subsequent action for res judicata to be successfully invoked. Rather, identity of the causes of action is evaluated by reference to the similarity of the acts complained of, the demand for recovery, and the identity of "witnesses, documents and facts alleged."

* * * *

Applying these principles here, we agree with the district court that there is sufficient identity of the causes of action in the arbitration and the present action for res judicata to apply. The ultimate relief sought in the two actions—return of the $ 17 million installment payment—is identical, as is the alleged wrongful conduct of the Buschmeiers in refusing to refund the payment. The underlying events, the surrounding facts, the witnesses, and the documents giving rise to the claims in the respective actions are the same.

* * * *

2. Identity of the Parties.

The third element of res judicata under Pennsylvania law is identity of the parties in the two actions. Literal identity is once again not required; "the doctrine of res judicata applies to and is binding, not only on actual parties to the litigations, but also to those who are in privity with them." Day v. Volkswagenwerk Aktiengesellschaft, 464 A.2d 1313, 1317 (Pa. Super. 1983) . . . .

* * * *

NOTE

1. Decisions diverge on whether an award must be confirmed before it can have preclusive effect in court. One approach is that an award offered for preclusive purposes in court is subject to defenses that might defeat confirmation, but none other. Hybert v. Sherson Lehman / American Express, Inc., 688 F. Supp. 320 (N.D. Ill. 198); *cf. In re* Robinson, 256 B.R. 482 (S.D. Ohio 2000), aff'd 262 B. R. 722, aff'd 326 F.3d 767.

APPENDICES TABLE OF CONTENTS

Appendix 1:
THE FEDERAL ARBITRATION ACT

CHAPTER 1. GENERAL PROVISIONS

Section 1. "Maritime transactions" and "commerce" defined; exceptions to operation of title

"Maritime transactions", as herein defined, means charter parties, bills of lading of water carriers, agreements relating to wharfage, supplies furnished vessels or repairs to vessels, collisions, or any other matters in foreign commerce which, if the subject of controversy, would be embraced within admiralty jurisdiction; "commerce", as herein defined, means commerce among the several States or with foreign nations, or in any Territory of the United States or in the District of Columbia, or between any such Territory and another, or between any such Territory and any State or foreign nation, or between the District of Columbia and any State or Territory or foreign nation, but nothing herein contained shall apply to contracts of employment of seamen, railroad employees, or any other class of workers engaged in foreign or interstate commerce.

Section 2. Validity, irrevocability, and enforcement of agreements to arbitrate

A written provision in any maritime transaction or a contract evidencing a transaction involving commerce to settle by arbitration a controversy thereafter arising out of such contract or transaction, or the refusal to perform the whole or any part thereof, or an agreement in writing to submit to arbitration an existing controversy arising out of such a contract, transaction, or refusal, shall be valid, irrevocable, and enforceable, save upon such grounds as exist at law or in equity for the revocation of any contract.

Section 3. Stay of proceedings where issue therein referable to arbitration

If any suit or proceeding be brought in any of the courts of the United States upon any issue referable to arbitration under an agreement in writing for such arbitration, the court in which such suit is pending, upon being satisfied that the issue involved in such suit or proceeding is referable to arbitration under such an agreement, shall on application of one of the parties stay the trial of the action until such arbitration has been had in accordance with the terms of the agreement, providing the applicant for the stay is not in default in proceeding with such arbitration.

Section 4. Failure to arbitrate under agreement; petition to United States court having jurisdiction for order to compel arbitration; notice and service thereof; hearing and determination

A party aggrieved by the alleged failure, neglect, or refusal of another to arbitrate under a written agreement for arbitration may petition any United States district court which, save for such agreement, would have jurisdiction under Title 28, in a civil action or in admiralty of the subject matter of a suit arising out of the controversy between the parties, for an order directing that such arbitration proceed in the manner provided for in such agreement. Five days' notice in writing of such application shall be served upon the party in default. Service thereof shall be made in the manner provided by the Federal Rules of Civil Procedure. The court shall hear the parties, and upon being satisfied that the making of the agreement for arbitration or the failure to comply therewith is not in issue, the court shall make an order directing the parties to proceed to arbitration in accordance with the terms of the agreement. The hearing and proceedings, under such agreement, shall be within the district in which the petition for an order directing such arbitration is filed. If the making of the arbitration agreement or the failure, neglect, or refusal to perform the same be in issue, the court shall proceed summarily to the trial thereof. If no jury trial be demanded by the party alleged to be in default, or if the matter in dispute is within admiralty jurisdiction, the court shall hear and determine such issue. Where such an issue is raised, the party alleged to be in default may, except in cases of admiralty, on or before the return day of the notice of application, demand a jury trial of such issue, and upon such demand the court shall make an order referring the issue or issues to a jury in the manner provided by the Federal Rules of Civil Procedure, or may specially call a jury for that purpose. If the jury find that no agreement in writing for arbitration was made or that there is no default in proceeding thereunder, the proceeding shall be dismissed. If the jury find that an agreement for arbitration was made in writing and that there is a default in proceeding thereunder, the court shall make an order summarily directing the parties to proceed with the arbitration in accordance with the terms thereof.

Section 5. Appointment of arbitrators or umpire

If in the agreement provision be made for a method of naming or appointing an arbitrator or arbitrators or an umpire, such method shall be followed; but if no method be provided therein, or if a method be provided and any party thereto shall fail to avail himself of such method, or if for any other reason there shall be a lapse in the naming of an arbitrator or arbitrators or umpire, or in filling a vacancy, then upon the application of either party to the controversy the court shall designate and appoint an arbitrator or arbitrators or umpire, as the case may require, who shall act under the said agreement with the same force and effect as if he or they had been specifically named therein; and unless otherwise provided in the agreement the arbitration shall be by a single arbitrator.

Section 6. Application heard as motion

Any application to the court hereunder shall be made and heard in the manner provided by law for the making and hearing of motions, except as otherwise herein expressly provided.

Section 7. Witnesses before arbitrators; fees; compelling attendance

The arbitrators selected either as prescribed in this title or otherwise, or a majority of them, may summon in writing any person to attend before them or any of them as a witness and in a proper case to bring with him or them any book, record, document, or paper which may be deemed material as evidence in the case. The fees for such attendance shall be the same as the fees of witnesses before masters of the United States courts. Said summons shall issue in the name of the arbitrator or arbitrators, or a majority of them, and shall be signed by the arbitrators, or a majority of them, and shall be directed to the said person and shall be served in the same manner as subpoenas to appear and testify before the court; if any person or persons so summoned to testify shall refuse or neglect to obey said summons, upon petition the United States district court for the district in which such arbitrators, or a majority of them, are sitting may compel the attendance of such person or persons before said arbitrator or arbitrators, or punish said person or persons for contempt in the same manner provided by law for securing the attendance of witnesses or their punishment for neglect or refusal to attend in the courts of the United States.

Section 8. Proceedings begun by libel in admiralty and seizure of vessel or property

If the basis of jurisdiction be a cause of action otherwise justiciable in admiralty, then, notwithstanding anything herein to the contrary, the party claiming to be aggrieved may begin his proceeding hereunder by libel and seizure of the vessel or other property of the other party according to the usual course of admiralty proceedings, and the court shall then have jurisdiction to direct the parties to proceed with the arbitration and shall retain jurisdiction to enter its decree upon the award

Section 9. Award of arbitrators; confirmation; jurisdiction; procedure

If the parties in their agreement have agreed that a judgment of the court shall be entered upon the award made pursuant to the arbitration, and shall specify the court, then at any time within one year after the award is made any party to the arbitration may apply to the court so specified for an order confirming the award, and thereupon the court must grant such an order unless the award is vacated, modified, or corrected as prescribed in sections 10 and 11 of this title. If no court is specified in the agreement of the parties, then such application may be made to the United States court in and for the district within which such award was made. Notice of the application shall be served upon the adverse party, and thereupon the court shall have jurisdiction of such party as though he had appeared generally in the proceeding. If the adverse party is a resident of the district within which the award was made, such service shall be made upon the adverse party or his attorney as prescribed by law for service of notice of motion in an action in the same court. If the adverse party shall be a nonresident, then the notice of the application shall be served by the marshal of any district within which the adverse party may be found in like manner as other process of the court.

Section 10. Same; vacation; grounds; rehearing

(a) In any of the following cases the United States court in and for the district wherein the award was made may make an order vacating the award upon the application of any party to the arbitration--

(1) where the award was procured by corruption, fraud, or undue means;

(2) where there was evident partiality or corruption in the arbitrators, or either of them;

(3) where the arbitrators were guilty of misconduct in refusing to postpone the hearing, upon sufficient cause shown, or in refusing to hear evidence pertinent and material to the controversy; or of any other misbehavior by which the rights of any party have been prejudiced; or

(4) where the arbitrators exceeded their powers, or so imperfectly executed them that a mutual, final, and definite award upon the subject matter submitted was not made.

(b) If an award is vacated and the time within which the agreement required the award to be made has not expired, the court may, in its discretion, direct a rehearing by the arbitrators.

(c) The United States district court for the district wherein an award was made that was issued pursuant to section 580 of title 5 may make an order vacating the award upon the application of a person, other than a party to the arbitration, who is adversely affected or aggrieved by the award, if the use of arbitration or the award is clearly inconsistent with the factors set forth in section 572 of title 5.

Section 11. Same; modification or correction; grounds; order

In either of the following cases the United States court in and for the district wherein the award was made may make an order modifying or correcting the award upon the application of any party to the arbitration-

(a) Where there was an evident material miscalculation of figures or an evident material mistake in the description of any person, thing, or property referred to in the award.

(b) Where the arbitrators have awarded upon a matter not submitted to them, unless it is a matter not affecting the merits of the decision upon the matter submitted.

(c) Where the award is imperfect in matter of form not affecting the merits of the controversy.

The order may modify and correct the award, so as to effect the intent thereof and promote justice between the parties.

Section 12. Notice of motions to vacate or modify; service; stay of proceedings

Notice of a motion to vacate, modify, or correct an award must be served upon the adverse party or his attorney within three months after the award is filed or delivered. If the adverse party is a resident of the district within which the award was made, such service shall be made upon the adverse party or his attorney as prescribed by law for service of notice of motion in an action in the same court. If the adverse party shall be a nonresident then the notice of the application shall be served by the marshal of any district within which the adverse party may be found in like manner as other process of the court. For the purposes of the motion any judge who might make an order to stay the proceedings in an action brought in the same court may make an order, to be served with the notice of motion, staying the proceedings of the adverse party to enforce the award.

Section 13. Papers filed with order on motions; judgment; docketing; force and effect; enforcement

The party moving for an order confirming, modifying, or correcting an award shall, at the time such order is filed with the clerk for the entry of judgment thereon, also file the following papers with the clerk:

(a) The agreement; the selection or appointment, if any, of an additional arbitrator or umpire; and each written extension of the time, if any, within which to make the award.

(b) The award.

(c) Each notice, affidavit, or other paper used upon an application to confirm, modify, or correct the award, and a copy of each order of the court upon such an application.

The judgment shall be docketed as if it was rendered in an action.

The judgment so entered shall have the same force and effect, in all respects, as, and be subject to all the provisions of law relating to, a judgment in an action; and it may be enforced as if it had been rendered in an action in the court in which it is entered.

Section 14. Contracts not affected

This title shall not apply to contracts made prior to January 1, 1926.

Section 15. Inapplicability of the Act of State doctrine

Enforcement of arbitral agreements, confirmation of arbitral awards, and execution upon judgments based on orders confirming such awards shall not be refused on the basis of the Act of State doctrine.

Section 16. Appeals

(a) An appeal may be taken from--

(1) an order--

(A) refusing a stay of any action under section 3 of this title,

(B) denying a petition under section 4 of this title to order arbitration to proceed,

(C) denying an application under section 206 of this title to compel arbitration,

(D) confirming or denying confirmation of an award or partial award, or

(E) modifying, correcting, or vacating an award;

(2) an interlocutory order granting, continuing, or modifying an injunction against an arbitration that is subject to this title; or

(3) a final decision with respect to an arbitration that is subject to this title.

(b) Except as otherwise provided in section 1292(b) of title 28, an appeal may not be taken from an interlocutory order--

(1) granting a stay of any action under section 3 of this title;

(2) directing arbitration to proceed under section 4 of this title;

(3) compelling arbitration under section 206 of this title; or

(4) refusing to enjoin an arbitration that is subject to this title.

CHAPTER 2. CONVENTION ON THE RECOGNITION AND ENFORCEMENT OF FOREIGN ARBITRAL AWARDS

Section 201. Enforcement of Convention

The Convention on the Recognition and Enforcement of Foreign Arbitral Awards of June 10, 1958, shall be enforced in United States courts in accordance with this chapter.

Section 202. Agreement or award falling under the Convention

An arbitration agreement or arbitral award arising out of a legal relationship, whether contractual or not, which is considered as commercial, including a transaction, contract, or agreement described in section 2 of this title, falls under the Convention. An agreement or award arising out of such a relationship which is entirely between citizens of the United States shall be deemed not to fall under the Convention unless that relationship involves property located abroad, envisages performance or enforcement abroad, or has some other reasonable relation with one or more foreign states. For the purpose of this section a corporation is a citizen of the United States if it is incorporated or has its principal place of business in the United States.

Section 203. Jurisdiction; amount in controversy

An action or proceeding falling under the Convention shall be deemed to arise under the laws and treaties of the United States. The district courts of the United States (including the courts enumerated in section 460 of title 28) shall have original jurisdiction over such an action or proceeding, regardless of the amount in controversy.

Section 204. Venue

An action or proceeding over which the district courts have jurisdiction pursuant to section 203 of this title may be brought in any such court in which save for the arbitration agreement an action or proceeding with respect to the controversy between the parties could be brought, or in such court for the district and division which embraces the place designated in the agreement as the place of arbitration if such place is within the United States.

Section 205. Removal of cases from State courts

Where the subject matter of an action or proceeding pending in a State court relates to an arbitration agreement or award falling under the Convention, the defendant or the defendants may, at any time before the trial thereof, remove such action or proceeding to the district court of the United States for the district and division embracing the place where the action or proceeding is pending. The procedure for removal of causes otherwise provided by law shall apply, except that the ground for removal provided in this section need not appear on the face of the complaint but may be shown in the petition for removal. For the purposes of Chapter 1 of this title any action or proceeding removed under this section shall be deemed to have been brought in the district court to which it is removed.

Section 206. Order to compel arbitration; appointment of arbitrators

A court having jurisdiction under this chapter may direct that arbitration be held in accordance with the agreement at any place therein provided for, whether that place is within or without the United States. Such court may also appoint arbitrators in accordance with the provisions of the agreement.

Section 207. Award of arbitrators; confirmation; jurisdiction; proceeding

Within three years after an arbitral award falling under the Convention is made, any party to the arbitration may apply to any court having jurisdiction under this chapter for an order confirming the award as against any other party to the arbitration. The court shall confirm the award unless it finds one of the grounds for refusal or deferral of recognition or enforcement of the award specified in the said Convention.

Section 208. Chapter 1; residual application

Chapter 1 applies to actions and proceedings brought under this chapter to the extent that chapter is not in conflict with this chapter or the Convention as ratified by the United States.

CHAPTER 3. INTER-AMERICAN CONVENTION ON INTERNATIONAL COMMERCIAL ARBITRATION

Section 301. Enforcement of Convention

The Inter-American Convention on International Commercial Arbitration of January 30, 1975, shall be enforced in United States courts in accordance with this chapter.

Section 302. Incorporation by reference

Sections 202, 203, 204, 205, and 207 of this title shall apply to this chapter as if specifically set forth herein, except that for the purposes of this chapter "the Convention" shall mean the Inter-American Convention.

Section 303. Order to compel arbitration; appointment of arbitrators; locale

(a) A court having jurisdiction under this chapter may direct that arbitration be held in accordance with the agreement at any place therein provided for, whether that place is within or without the United States. The court may also appoint arbitrators in accordance with the provisions of the agreement.

(b) In the event the agreement does not make provision for the place of arbitration or the appointment of arbitrators, the court shall direct that the arbitration shall be held and the arbitrators be appointed in accordance with Article 3 of the Inter-American Convention.

Section 304. Recognition and enforcement of foreign arbitral decisions and awards; reciprocity

Arbitral decisions or awards made in the territory of a foreign State shall, on the basis of reciprocity, be recognized and enforced under this chapter only if that State has ratified or acceded to the Inter-American Convention.

Section 305. Relationship between the Inter-American Convention and the Convention on the Recognition and Enforcement of Foreign Arbitral Awards of June 10, 1958

When the requirements for application of both the Inter-American Convention and the Convention on the Recognition and Enforcement of Foreign Arbitral Awards of June 10, 1958, are met, determination as to which Convention applies shall, unless otherwise expressly agreed, be made as follows:

(1) If a majority of the parties to the arbitration agreement are citizens of a State or States that have ratified or acceded to the Inter-American Convention and are member States of the Organization of American States, the Inter-American Convention shall apply.

(2) In all other cases the Convention on the Recognition and Enforcement of Foreign Arbitral Awards of June 10, 1958, shall apply.

Section 306. Applicable rules of Inter-American Commercial Arbitration Commission

(a) For the purposes of this chapter the rules of procedure of the Inter-American Commercial Arbitration Commission referred to in Article 3 of the Inter-American Convention shall, subject to subsection (b) of this section, be those rules as promulgated by the Commission on July 1, 1988.

(b) In the event the rules of procedure of the Inter-American Commercial Arbitration Commission are modified or amended in accordance with the procedures for amendment of the rules of that Commission, the Secretary of State, by regulation in accordance with section 553 of title 5, consistent with the aims and purposes of this Convention, may prescribe that such modifications or amendments shall be effective for purposes of this chapter.

Section 307. Chapter 1; residual application

Chapter 1 applies to actions and proceedings brought under this chapter to the extent chapter 1 is not in conflict with this chapter or the Inter-American Convention as ratified by the United States.

Appendix 2:

NEW YORK CPLR ARTICLES 7501–14

Article 7501. Effect of arbitration agreement

A written agreement to submit any controversy thereafter arising or any existing controversy to arbitration is enforceable without regard to the justiciable character of the controversy and confers jurisdiction on the courts of the state to enforce it and to enter judgment on an award. In determining any matter arising under this article, the court shall not consider whether the claim with respect to which arbitration is sought is tenable, or otherwise pass upon the merits of the dispute.

Article 7502. Applications to the court; venue; statutes of limitation; provisional remedies

(a) Applications to the court; venue. A special proceeding shall be used to bring before a court the first application arising out of an arbitrable controversy which is not made by motion in a pending action

(i) The proceeding shall be brought in the court and county specified in the agreement. If the name of the county is not specified, proceedings to stay or bar arbitration shall be brought in the county where the party seeking arbitration resides or is doing business, and other proceedings affecting arbitration are to be brought in the county where at least one of the parties resides or is doing business or where the arbitration was held or is pending.

(ii) If there is no county in which the proceeding may be brought under paragraph (i) of this subdivision, the proceeding may be brought in any county.

(iii) Notwithstanding the entry of judgment, all subsequent applications shall be made by motion in the special proceeding or action in which the first application was made.

(iv) If an application to confirm an arbitration award made within the one year as provided by section seventy-five hundred ten of this article, or an application to vacate or modify an award made within the ninety days as provided by subdivision (a) of section seventy-five hundred eleven of this article, was denied or dismissed solely on the ground that it was made in the form of a motion captioned in an earlier special proceeding having reference to the arbitration instead of as a distinct special proceeding, the time in which to apply to confirm the award and the time in which to apply to vacate or modify the award may, notwithstanding that the applicable period of time has expired, be made at any time within ninety days after the effective date of this paragraph, and may be made in whatever form is appropriate (motion or special proceeding) pursuant to this subdivision.

(b) Limitation of time. If, at the time that a demand for arbitration was made or a notice of intention to arbitrate was served, the claim sought to be arbitrated would have been barred by limitation of time had it been asserted in a court of the state, a party may assert the limitation as a bar to the arbitration on an application to the court as provided in section Article 7503 or subdivision (b) of section Article 7511. The failure to assert such bar by such application shall not preclude its assertion before the arbitrators, who may, in their sole discretion, apply or not apply the bar. Except as provided in subdivision (b) of section Article 7511, such exercise of discretion by the arbitrators shall not be subject to review by a court on an application to confirm, vacate or modify the award.

(c) Provisional remedies. The supreme court in the county in which an arbitration is pending or in a county specified in subdivision (a) of this section, may entertain an application for an order of attachment or for a preliminary injunction in connection with an arbitration that is pending or that is to be commenced inside or outside this state, whether or not it is subject to the United Nations convention on the recognition and enforcement of foreign arbitral awards, but only upon the ground that the award to which the applicant may be entitled may be rendered ineffectual without such provisional relief. The provisions of articles 62 and 63 of this chapter shall apply to the application, including those relating to undertakings and to the time for commencement of an action (arbitration shall be deemed an action for this purpose), except that the sole ground for the granting of the remedy shall be as stated above. If an arbitration is not commenced within thirty days of the granting of the provisional relief, the order granting such relief shall expire and be null and void and costs, including reasonable attorney's fees, awarded to the respondent. The court may reduce or expand this period of time for good cause shown. The form of the application shall be as provided in subdivision (a) of this section.

Article 7503. Application to compel or stay arbitration; stay of action; notice of intention to arbitrate

(a) Application to compel arbitration; stay of action. A party aggrieved by the failure of another to arbitrate may apply for an order compelling arbitration. Where there is no substantial question whether a valid agreement was made or complied with, and the claim sought to be arbitrated is not barred by limitation under subdivision (b) of section Article 7502, the court shall direct the parties to arbitrate. Where any such question is raised, it shall be tried forthwith in said court. If an issue claimed to be arbitrable is involved in an action pending in a court having jurisdiction to hear a motion to compel arbitration, the application shall be made by motion in that action. If the application is granted, the order shall operate to stay a pending or subsequent action, or so much of it as is referable to arbitration.
(b) Application to stay arbitration. Subject to the provisions of subdivision (c), a party who has not participated in the arbitration and who has not made or been served with an

application to compel arbitration, may apply to stay arbitration on the ground that a valid agreement was not made or has not been complied with or that the claim sought to be arbitrated is barred by limitation under subdivision (b) of section Article 7502.

(c) Notice of intention to arbitrate. A party may serve upon another party a demand for arbitration or a notice of intention to arbitrate, specifying the agreement pursuant to which arbitration is sought and the name and address of the party serving the notice, or of an officer or agent thereof if such party is an association or corporation, and stating that unless the party served applies to stay the arbitration within twenty days after such service he shall thereafter be precluded from objecting that a valid agreement was not made or has not been complied with and from asserting in court the bar of a limitation of time. Such notice or demand shall be served in the same manner as a summons or by registered or certified mail, return receipt requested. An application to stay arbitration must be made by the party served within twenty days after service upon him of the notice or demand, or he shall be so precluded. Notice of such application shall be served in the same manner as a summons or by registered or certified mail, return receipt requested. Service of the application may be made upon the adverse party, or upon his attorney if the attorney's name appears on the demand for arbitration or the notice of intention to arbitrate. Service of the application by mail shall be timely if such application is posted within the prescribed period. Any provision in an arbitration agreement or arbitration rules which waives the right to apply for a stay of arbitration is hereby declared null and void.

Article 7504. Court appointment of arbitrator

If the arbitration agreement does not provide for a method of appointment of an arbitrator, or if the agreed method fails or for any reason is not followed, or if an arbitrator fails to act and his successor has not been appointed, the court, on application of a party, shall appoint an arbitrator.

Article 7505. Powers of arbitrator

An arbitrator and any attorney of record in the arbitration proceeding has the power to issue subpoenas. An arbitrator has the power to administer oaths.

Article 7506. Hearing

(a) Oath of arbitrator. Before hearing any testimony, an arbitrator shall be sworn to hear and decide the controversy faithfully and fairly by an officer authorized to administer an oath.
(b) Time and place. The arbitrator shall appoint a time and place for the hearing and notify the parties in writing personally or by registered or certified mail not less than eight days before the hearing. The arbitrator may adjourn or postpone the hearing. The court, upon application of any party, may direct the arbitrator to proceed promptly with the hearing and determination of the controversy.
(c) Evidence. The parties are entitled to be heard, to present evidence and to cross-examine witnesses. Notwithstanding the failure of a party duly notified to appear, the arbitrator may hear and determine the controversy upon the evidence produced.
(d) Representation by attorney. A party has the right to be represented by an attorney and may claim such right at any time as to any part of the arbitration or hearings which have not taken place. This right may not be waived. If a party is represented by an attorney, papers to be served on the party shall be served upon his attorney.
(e) Determination by majority. The hearing shall be conducted by all the arbitrators, but a majority may determine any question and render an award.
(f) Waiver. Except as provided in subdivision (d), a requirement of this section may be waived by written consent of the parties and it is waived if the parties continue with the arbitration without objection.

Article 7507. Award; form; time; delivery
Except as provided in section Article 7508, the award shall be in writing, signed and affirmed by the arbitrator making it within the time fixed by the agreement, or, if the time is not fixed, within such time as the court orders. The parties may in writing

extend the time either before or after its expiration. A party waives the objection that an award was not made within the time required unless he notifies the arbitrator in writing of his objection prior to the delivery of the award to him. The arbitrator shall deliver a copy of the award to each party in the manner provided in the agreement, or, if no provision is so made, personally or by registered or certified mail, return receipt requested.

Article 7508. Award by confession

(a) When available. An award by confession may be made for money due or to become due at any time before an award is otherwise made. The award shall be based upon a statement, verified by each party, containing an authorization to make the award, the sum of the award or the method of ascertaining it, and the facts constituting the liability.
(b) Time of award. The award may be made at any time within three months after the statement is verified.
(c) Person or agency making award. The award may be made by an arbitrator or by the agency or person named by the parties to designate the abitrator [arbitrator] .[1]

Article 7509. Modification of award by arbitrator

On written application of a party to the arbitrators within twenty days after delivery of the award to the applicant, the arbitrators may modify the award upon the grounds stated in subdivision (c) of section Article 7511. Written notice of the application shall be given to other parties to the arbitration. Written objection to modification must be served on the arbitrators and other parties to the arbitration within ten days of receipt of the notice. The arbitrators shall dispose of any application made under this section in writing, signed and acknowledged by them, within thirty days after either written objection to modification has been served on them or the time for serving said objection has expired, whichever is earlier. The parties may in writing extend the time for such disposition either before or after its expiration.

Article 7510. Confirmation of award

The court shall confirm an award upon application of a party made within one year after its delivery to him, unless the award is vacated or modified upon a ground specified in section Article 7511.

Article 7511. Vacating or modifying award

(a) When application made. An application to vacate or modify an award may be made by a party within ninety days after its delivery to him.

(b) Grounds for vacating.

1. The award shall be vacated on the application of a party who either participated in the arbitration or was served with a notice of intention to arbitrate if the court finds that the rights of that party were prejudiced by:

(i) corruption, fraud or misconduct in procuring the award; or

(ii) partiality of an arbitrator appointed as a neutral, except where the award was by confession; or

(iii) an arbitrator, or agency or person making the award exceeded his power or so imperfectly executed it that a final and definite award upon the subject matter submitted was not made; or

(iv) failure to follow the procedure of this article, unless the party applying to vacate the award continued with the arbitration with notice of the defect and without objection.

2. The award shall be vacated on the application of a party who neither participated in the arbitration nor was served with a notice of intention to arbitrate if the court finds that:

(i) the rights of that party were prejudiced by one of the grounds specified in paragraph one; or

(ii) a valid agreement to arbitrate was not made; or

(iii) the agreement to arbitrate had not been complied with; or

(iv) the arbitrated claim was barred by limitation under subdivision (b) of section Article 7502.

(c) Grounds for modifying. The court shall modify the award if:

1. there was a miscalculation of figures or a mistake in the description of any person, thing or property referred to in the award; or
2. the arbitrators have awarded upon a matter not submitted to them and the award may be corrected without affecting the merits of the decision upon the issues submitted; or
3. the award is imperfect in a matter of form, not affecting the merits of the controversy.

(d) Rehearing. Upon vacating an award, the court may order a rehearing and determination of all or any of the issues either before the same arbitrator or before a new arbitrator appointed in accordance with this article. Time in any provision limiting the time for a hearing or award shall be measured from the date of such order or rehearing, whichever is appropriate, or a time may be specified by the court.
(e) Confirmation. Upon the granting of a motion to modify, the court shall confirm the award as modified; upon the denial of a motion to vacate or modify, it shall confirm the award.

Article 7512. Death or incompetency of a party

Where a party dies after making a written agreement to submit a controversy to arbitration, the proceedings may be begun or continued upon the application of, or upon notice to, his executor or administrator or, where it relates to real property, his distributee or devisee who has succeeded to his interest in the real property. Where a committee of the property or of the person of a party to such an agreement is appointed, the proceedings may be continued upon the application of, or notice to, the committee. Upon the death or incompetency of a party, the court may extend the time within which an application to confirm, vacate or modify the award or to stay arbitration must be made. Where a party has died since an award was delivered, the proceedings thereupon are the same as where a party dies after a verdict.

Article 7513. Fees and expenses

Unless otherwise provided in the agreement to arbitrate, the arbitrators' expenses and fees, together with other expenses, not including attorney's fees, incurred in the conduct of the arbitration, shall be paid as provided in the award. The court, on application, may reduce or disallow any fee or expense it finds excessive or allocate it as justice requires.

Article 7514. Judgment on an award

(a) Entry. A judgment shall be entered upon the confirmation of an award.
(b) Judgment-roll. The judgment-roll consists of the original or a copy of the agreement and each written extention [extension] of time within which to make an award; the statement required by section Article 7508 where the award was by confession; the award; each paper submitted to the court and each order of the court upon an application under sections Article 7510 and Article 7511; and a copy of the judgment.

Appendix 3: UNIFORM ARBITRATION ACT

(Last Revisions Completed Year 2000)
Drafted by the
NATIONAL CONFERENCE OF COMMISSIONERS
ON UNIFORM STATE LAWS

APPROVED AND RECOMMENDED FOR ENACTMENT
IN ALL THE STATES
at its

ANNUAL CONFERENCE
MEETING IN ITS ONE-HUNDRED-AND-NINTH YEAR
ST. AUGUSTINE, FLORIDA

JULY 28 - AUGUST 4, 2000

PREFATORY NOTE

The Uniform Arbitration Act (UAA), promulgated in 1955, has been one of the most successful Acts of the National Conference of Commissioners on Uniform State Laws. Forty-nine jurisdictions have arbitration statutes; 35 of these have adopted the UAA and 14 have adopted substantially similar legislation. A primary purpose of the 1955 Act was to insure the enforceability of agreements to arbitrate in the face of oftentimes hostile state law. That goal has been accomplished. Today arbitration is a primary mechanism favored by courts and parties to resolve disputes in many areas of the law. This growth in arbitration caused the Conference to appoint a Drafting Committee to consider revising the Act in light of the increasing use of arbitration, the greater complexity of many disputes resolved by arbitration, and the developments of the law in this area.

The UAA did not address many issues which arise in modern arbitration cases. The statute provided no guidance as to (1) who decides the arbitrability of a dispute and by what criteria; (2) whether a court or arbitrators may issue provisional remedies; (3) how a party can initiate an arbitration proceeding; (4) whether arbitration proceedings may be consolidated; (5) whether arbitrators are required to disclose facts reasonably likely to affect impartiality; (6) what extent arbitrators or an arbitration organization are immune from civil actions; (7) whether arbitrators or representatives of arbitration organizations may be required to testify in another proceeding; (8) whether arbitrators have the discretion to order discovery, issue protective orders, decide motions for summary dispositions, hold prehearing conferences and otherwise manage the arbitration process; (9) when a court may enforce a preaward ruling by an arbitrator; (10) what remedies an arbitrator may award, especially in regard to attorney's fees, punitive damages or other exemplary relief; (11) when a court can award attorney's fees and costs to arbitrators and arbitration organizations; (12) when a court can award attorney's fees and costs to a prevailing party in an appeal of an arbitrator's award; and (13) which sections of the UAA would not be waivable, an important matter to insure fundamental fairness to the parties will be preserved, particularly in those instances where one party may have significantly less bargaining power than another; and (14) the use of electronic information and other modern means of technology in the arbitration process. The Revised Uniform Arbitration Act (RUAA) examines all of these issues and provides state legislatures with a more up-to-date statute to resolve disputes through arbitration.

There are a number of principles that the Drafting Committee agreed upon at the outset of its consideration of a revision to the UAA. First, arbitration is a consensual process in which autonomy of the parties who enter into arbitration agreements should be given primary consideration, so long as their agreements conform to notions of fundamental fairness. This approach provides parties with the opportunity in most instances to shape the arbitration process to their own particular needs. In most instances the RUAA provides a default mechanism if the parties do not have a specific agreement on a particular issue. Second, the underlying reason many parties choose arbitration is the relative speed, lower cost, and greater efficiency of the process. The law should take these factors, where applicable, into account. For example, Section 10 allows consolidation of issues involving multiple parties. Such a provision can be of special importance in adhesion situations where there are numerous persons with essentially the same claims against a party to the arbitration agreement. Finally, in most cases parties intend the decisions of arbitrators to be final with minimal court involvement unless there is clear unfairness or a denial of justice. This contractual nature of arbitration means that the provision to vacate awards in Section 23 is limited. This is so even where an arbitrator may award attorney's fees, punitive damages or other exemplary relief under Section 21. Section 14 insulates arbitrators from unwarranted litigation to insure their independence by providing them with immunity.

Other new provisions are intended to reflect developments in arbitration law and to insure that the process is a fair one. Section 12 requires arbitrators to make important disclosures to the parties. Section 8 allows courts to grant provisional remedies in certain circumstances to protect the integrity of the arbitration process. Section 17 includes limited rights to discovery while recognizing the importance of expeditious arbitration proceedings.

In light of a number of decisions by the United States Supreme Court concerning the Federal Arbitration Act (FAA), any revision of the UAA must take into account the doctrine of preemption. The rule of preemption, whereby FAA standards and the emphatically pro-arbitration perspective of the FAA control, applies in both the federal courts and the state courts. To date, the preemption-related opinions of the Supreme Court have centered in large part on the two key issues that arise at the front end of the arbitration process - enforcement of the agreement to arbitrate and issues of substantive arbitrability. *Prima Paint Corp. v. Flood & Conklin Mfg. Co.*, 388 U.S. 35 (1967); *Moses H. Cone Mem'l Hosp. v. Mercury Constr. Corp.*, 460 U.S. 1 (1983); *Southland Corp. v. Keating*, 465 U.S. 2 (1984); *Perry v. Thomas*, 482 U.S. 483 (1987); *Allied-Bruce Terminix Cos. v. Dobson*, 513 U.S. 265 (1995); *Doctor's Assocs. v. Cassarotto*, 517 U.S. 681 (1996). That body of case law establishes that state law of any ilk, including adaptations of the RUAA, mooting or limiting contractual agreements to arbitrate must yield to the pro-arbitration public policy voiced in Sections 2, 3, and 4 of the FAA.

The other issues to which the FAA speaks definitively lie at the back end of the arbitration process. The standards and procedure for vacatur, confirmation and modification of arbitration awards are the subject of Sections 9, 10, 11, and 12 of the FAA. In contrast to the "front end" issues of enforceability and substantive arbitrability, there is no definitive Supreme Court case law speaking to the preemptive effect, if any, of the FAA with regard to these "back end" issues. This dimension of FAA preemption of state arbitration law is further complicated by the strong majority view among the United States Circuit Courts of Appeals that the Section 10(a) standards are not the exclusive grounds for vacatur.

Nevertheless, the Supreme Court's unequivocal stand to date as to the preemptive effect of the FAA provides strong reason to believe that a similar result will obtain with regard to Section 10(a) grounds for vacatur. If it does, and if the Supreme Court eventually determines that the Section 10(a) standards are the sole grounds for vacatur of commercial arbitration awards, FAA preemption of conflicting state law with regard to the "back end" issues of vacatur (and confirmation and modification) would be certain. If the Court takes the opposite tack and holds that the Section 10(a) grounds are not the exclusive criteria for vacatur, the preemptive effect of Section 10(a) would most likely be limited to the rule that state arbitration acts cannot eliminate, limit or modify any of the four grounds of party and arbitrator misconduct set out in Section 10(a). Any definitive federal "common law," pertaining to the nonstatutory grounds for vacatur other than those set out in Section 10(a), articulated by the Supreme Court or established as a clear majority rule by the United States Courts of Appeals, likely would preempt contrary state law. A holding by the Supreme Court that the Section 10(a) grounds are not exclusive would also free the States to codify other grounds for vacatur beyond those set out in Section 10(a). These various, currently nonstatutory grounds for vacatur are discussed at length in the Section C to the Comment to Section 23.

An important caveat to the general rule of FAA preemption is found in *Volt Information Sciences, Inc. v. Stanford Univiversity*, 489 U.S. 468 (1989) and *Mastrobuono v. Shearson Lehman Hutton, Inc.*, 514 U.S. 52 (1995). The focus in these cases is on the effect of FAA preemption on choice-of-law provisions routinely included in commercial contracts. *Volt* and *Mastrobuono* establish that a clearly expressed contractual agreement by the parties to an arbitration contract to conduct their arbitration under state law rules effectively trumps the preemptive effect of the FAA. If the parties elect to govern their contractual arbitration mechanism by the law of a particular State and thereby limit the issues that they will arbitrate or the procedures under which the arbitration will be conducted, their bargain will be honored - as long as the state law principles invoked by the choice-of-law provision do not conflict with the FAA's prime directive that agreements to arbitrate be enforced. *See, e.g., ASW Allstate Painting & Constr. Co. v. Lexington Ins. Co.*, 188 F.3d 307 (5th Cir. 1999); *Russ Berrie & Co. v. Gantt*, 988 S.W.2d 713 (Tex. Ct. App. 1999). It is in these situations that the RUAA will have most impact. Section 4(a) of the RUAA also explicitly provides that the parties to an arbitration agreement may waive or vary the terms of the Act to the extent otherwise permitted by law. Thus, when parties choose to contractually specify the procedures to be followed under their arbitration agreement, the RUAA contemplates that the contractually-established procedures will control over contrary state law, except with regard to issues designated as "nonwaivable" in Section 4(b) and (c) of the RUAA.

The contractual election to proceed under state law instead of the FAA will be honored presuming that the state law is not antithetical to the pro-arbitration public policy of the FAA. *Southland* and *Terminix* leave no doubt that anti-arbitration state law provisions will be struck down because preempted by the federal arbitration statute.

Besides arbitration contracts where the parties choose to be governed by state law, there are other areas of arbitration law where the FAA does not preempt state law, in the absence of definitive federal law set out in the FAA or determined by the federal courts. First, the Supreme Court has made clear its belief that ascertaining when a particular contractual agreement to arbitrate is enforceable is a matter to be decided under the general contract law principles of each State. The sole limitation on state law in that regard is the Court's assertion that the enforceability of arbitration agreements must be determined by the same standards as are used for all other contracts. *Terminix*, 513 U.S. at 281 (1995) (quoting *Volt*, 489 U.S. at 474 (1989)) and quoted in *Cassarotto*, 517 U.S. 681, 685 (1996); and *Cassarotto*, 517 U.S. at 688 (quoting *Scherk v. Alberto-Culver Co.*, 417 U.S. 506, 511 (1974)). Arbitration agreements may not be invalidated under state laws applicable only to arbitration provisions. *Id.* The FAA will preempt state law that does not place arbitration agreements on an "equal footing" with other contracts.

During the course of its deliberations the Drafting Committee considered at length another issue with strong preemption undertones - the question of whether the RUAA should explicitly sanction contractual provisions for "opt-in" review of challenged arbitration awards beyond that presently contemplated by the FAA and current state arbitration acts. "Opt-in" provisions of two types are in limited use today. The first variant permits a party who is dissatisfied with the arbitral result to petition directly to a designated state court and stipulates that the court may vacate challenged awards, typically for errors of law or fact. The second type of "opt-in" contractual provision establishes an appellate arbitral mechanism to which challenged arbitration awards can be submitted for review, again most typically for errors of law or fact.

As explained in detail in Section B of the Comment to Section 23, there were a number of reasons that resulted in the decision not to include statutory sanction of the "opt-in" device for expanded judicial review in the RUAA: (1) the current uncertainty as to the legality of a state statutory sanction of the "opt-in" device, (2) the "disconnect" between the Act's purpose of fostering the use of arbitration as a final and binding alternative to traditional litigation in a court of law, and (3) the inclusion of a statutory provision that would permit the parties to contractually render arbitration decidedly non-final and non-binding. Simply stated, the potential gain to be realized by codifying a right to opt-into expanded judicial review that has not yet been definitively confirmed to exist does not outweigh the potential threat that adoption of an opt-in statutory provision would create for the integrity and viability of the RUAA as a template for state arbitration acts.

Unlike the "opt-in" judicial review mechanism, there are few, if any, legal concerns raised by statutory sanction of "opt-in" provisions for appellate arbitral review. Nevertheless, as explained in the Section B of the Comments to Section 23, because the current, contract-based view of arbitration establishes that the parties are free to design the inner workings of their arbitration procedures in any manner they see fit, the Drafting Committee determined that codification of that right in the RUAA would add nothing of substance to the existing law of arbitration.

The decision not to statutorily sanction either form of the "opt-in" device in the RUAA leaves the issue of the legal propriety of this means for securing review of awards to the developing case law under the FAA and state arbitration statutes. Parties remain free, within the constraints imposed by the existing and developing law, to agree to contractual provisions for arbitral or judicial review of challenged awards.

It is likely that matters not addressed in the FAA are also open to regulation by the States. State law provisions regulating purely procedural dimensions of the arbitration process (*e.g.*, discovery [RUAA Section 17], consolidation of claims [RUAA Section 10], and arbitrator immunity [RUAA Section 14]) likely will not be subject to preemption. Less certain is the effect of FAA preemption with regard to substantive issues like the authority of arbitrators to award punitive damages (RUAA Section 21) and the standards for arbitrator disclosure of potential conflicts of interest (RUAA Section 12) that have a significant impact on the integrity and/or the adequacy of the arbitration process. These "borderline" issues are not purely procedural in nature but unlike the "front end" and "back end" issues they do not go to the essence of the agreement to arbitrate or effectuation of the arbitral result. Although there is no concrete guidance in the case law, preemption of state law dealing with such matters seems unlikely as long as it cannot be characterized as anti-arbitration or as intended to limit the enforceability or viability of agreements to arbitrate.

The subject of international arbitration is not specifically addressed in the RUAA. Twelve States have passed arbitration statutes directed to international arbitration. Seven States have based their statutes on the Model Arbitration Law proposed in 1985 by the United Nations Commission on International Trade Law (UNCITRAL). Other States have approached international arbitration in a variety of ways, such as adopting parts of the UNCITRAL Model Law together with provisions taken directly from the 1958 United Nations Convention on Recognition and Enforcement of Foreign Arbitral Awards (commonly referred to as the New York Convention) or by devising their own international arbitration provisions.

Any provisions of these state international arbitration statutes that are inconsistent with the New York Convention, to which the United States adhered in 1970 (terms of the New York Convention can be found at 9 U.S.C. § 201), or with the federal legislation in Chapter 2 of Title 9 of the United States Code are preempted. Chapter 2 creates federal-question jurisdiction in the federal district courts for any case "falling under the [New York] Convention" and permits removal of any such case from a state court to the federal court "at any time prior to trial." 9 U.S.C. §§ 203, 205. The statute covers any commercial agreement to arbitrate and the resultant arbitration award unless the matter involves only American citizens and has no reasonable relationship to any foreign country and the courts have broadly applied the statute. Therefore, it is unlikely that state arbitration law will have major application to an international case. There are two instances where state arbitration law might apply in the international context: (1) where the parties designate a specific state arbitration law to govern the international arbitration and (2) where all parties to an arbitration proceeding involving an international transaction decide to proceed on a matter in state court and do not exercise their rights of removal under Chapter 2 of Title 9 and the relevant provision of state arbitration law is not preempted by federal arbitration law or the New York Convention. In these relatively rare cases, the state courts will refer to the RUAA unless the State has enacted a special international arbitration law.

Because few international cases are likely to be dealt with in state courts and because of the diversity of state law already enacted for international cases, the Drafting Committee decided not to address international arbitration as a specific subject in the revision of the UAA; however, the Committee utilized provisions of the UNCITRAL Model Law, the New York Convention, and the 1996 English Arbitration Act as sources of statutory language for the RUAA.

The members of the Drafting Committee to revise the Uniform Arbitration Act wish to acknowledge our deep indebtedness and appreciation to Professor Stephen Hayford and Professor Thomas Stipanowich who devoted extensive amounts of time by providing invaluable advice throughout the entire drafting process.

UNIFORM ARBITRATION ACT

SECTION 1. DEFINITIONS.

In this [Act]:

(1) "Arbitration organization" means an association, agency, board, commission, or other entity that is neutral and initiates, sponsors, or administers an arbitration proceeding or is involved in the appointment of an arbitrator.

(2) "Arbitrator" means an individual appointed to render an award, alone or with others, in a controversy that is subject to an agreement to arbitrate.

(3) "Court" means [a court of competent jurisdiction in this State].

(4) "Knowledge" means actual knowledge.

(5) "Person" means an individual, corporation, business trust, estate, trust, partnership, limited liability company, association, joint venture, government; governmental subdivision, agency, or instrumentality; public corporation; or any other legal or commercial entity.

(6) "Record" means information that is inscribed on a tangible medium or that is stored in an electronic or other medium and is retrievable in perceivable form.

SECTION 2. NOTICE.

(a) Except as otherwise provided in this [Act], a person gives notice to another person by taking action that is reasonably necessary to inform the other person in ordinary course, whether or not the other person acquires knowledge of the notice.

(b) A person has notice if the person has knowledge of the notice or has received notice.

(c) A person receives notice when it comes to the person's attention or the notice is delivered at the person's place of residence or place of business, or at another location held out by the person as a place of delivery of such communications.

SECTION 3. WHEN [ACT] APPLIES.

(a) This [Act] governs an agreement to arbitrate made on or after [the effective date of this [Act]].

(b) This [Act] governs an agreement to arbitrate made before [the effective date of this [Act]] if all the parties to the agreement or to the arbitration proceeding so agree in a record.

(c) On or after [a delayed date], this [Act] governs an agreement to arbitrate whenever made.

SECTION 4. EFFECT OF AGREEMENT TO ARBITRATE; NONWAIVABLE PROVISIONS.

(a) Except as otherwise provided in subsections (b) and (c), a party to an agreement to arbitrate or to an arbitration proceeding may waive or, the parties may vary the effect of, the requirements of this [Act] to the extent permitted by law.

(b) Before a controversy arises that is subject to an agreement to arbitrate, a party to the agreement may not:

(1) waive or agree to vary the effect of the requirements of Section 5(a), 6(a), 8, 17(a), 17(b), 26, or 28;

(2) agree to unreasonably restrict the right under Section 9 to notice of the initiation of an arbitration proceeding;

(3) agree to unreasonably restrict the right under Section 12 to disclosure of any facts by a neutral arbitrator; or

(4) waive the right under Section 16 of a party to an agreement to arbitrate to be represented by a lawyer at any proceeding or hearing under this [Act], but an employer and a labor organization may waive the right to representation by a lawyer in a labor arbitration.

(c) A party to an agreement to arbitrate or arbitration proceeding may not waive, or the parties may not vary the effect of, the requirements of this section or Section 3(a) or (c), 7, 14, 18, 20(d) or (e), 22, 23, 24, 25(a) or (b), 29, 30, 31, or 32.

SECTION 5. [APPLICATION] FOR JUDICIAL RELIEF.

(a) Except as otherwise provided in Section 28, an [application] for judicial relief under this [Act] must be made by [motion] to the court and heard in the manner provided by law or rule of court for making and hearing [motions].

(b) Unless a civil action involving the agreement to arbitrate is pending, notice of an initial [motion] to the court under this [Act] must be served in the manner provided by law for the service of a summons in a civil action. Otherwise, notice of the motion must be given in the manner provided by law or rule of court for serving [motions] in pending cases.

SECTION 6. VALIDITY OF AGREEMENT TO ARBITRATE.

(a) An agreement contained in a record to submit to arbitration any existing or subsequent controversy arising between the parties to the agreement is valid, enforceable, and irrevocable except upon a ground that exists at law or in equity for the revocation of a contract.

(b) The court shall decide whether an agreement to arbitrate exists or a controversy is subject to an agreement to arbitrate.

(c) An arbitrator shall decide whether a condition precedent to arbitrability has been fulfilled and whether a contract containing a valid agreement to arbitrate is enforceable.

(d) If a party to a judicial proceeding challenges the existence of, or claims that a controversy is not subject to, an agreement to arbitrate, the arbitration proceeding may continue pending final resolution of the issue by the court, unless the court otherwise orders.

SECTION 7. [MOTION] TO COMPEL OR STAY ARBITRATION.

(a) On [motion] of a person showing an agreement to arbitrate and alleging another person's refusal to arbitrate pursuant to the agreement:

> (1) if the refusing party does not appear or does not oppose the [motion], the court shall order the parties to arbitrate; and
>
> (2) if the refusing party opposes the [motion], the court shall proceed summarily to decide the issue and order the parties to arbitrate unless it finds that there is no enforceable agreement to arbitrate.

(b) On [motion] of a person alleging that an arbitration proceeding has been initiated or threatened but that there is no agreement to arbitrate, the court shall proceed summarily to decide the issue. If the court finds that there is an enforceable agreement to arbitrate, it shall order the parties to arbitrate.

(c) If the court finds that there is no enforceable agreement, it may not pursuant to subsection (a) or (b) order the parties to arbitrate.

(d) The court may not refuse to order arbitration because the claim subject to arbitration lacks merit or grounds for the claim have not been established.

(e) If a proceeding involving a claim referable to arbitration under an alleged agreement to arbitrate is pending in court, a [motion] under this section must be made in that court. Otherwise a [motion] under this section may be made in any court as provided in Section 27.

(f) If a party makes a [motion] to the court to order arbitration, the court on just terms shall stay any judicial proceeding that involves a claim alleged to be subject to the arbitration until the court renders a final decision under this section.

(g) If the court orders arbitration, the court on just terms shall stay any judicial proceeding that involves a claim subject to the arbitration. If a claim subject to the arbitration is severable, the court may limit the stay to that claim.

SECTION 8. PROVISIONAL REMEDIES.

(a) Before an arbitrator is appointed and is authorized and able to act, the court, upon [motion] of a party to an arbitration proceeding and for good cause shown, may enter an order for provisional remedies to protect the effectiveness of the arbitration proceeding to the same extent and under the same conditions as if the controversy were the subject of a civil action.

(b) After an arbitrator is appointed and is authorized and able to act:

(1) the arbitrator may issue such orders for provisional remedies, including interim awards, as the arbitrator finds necessary to protect the effectiveness of the arbitration proceeding and to promote the fair and expeditious resolution of the controversy, to the same extent and under the same conditions as if the controversy were the subject of a civil action and

(2) a party to an arbitration proceeding may move the court for a provisional remedy only if the matter is urgent and the arbitrator is not able to act timely or the arbitrator cannot provide an adequate remedy.

(c) A party does not waive a right of arbitration by making a [motion] under subsection (a) or (b).

SECTION 9. INITIATION OF ARBITRATION.

(a) A person initiates an arbitration proceeding by giving notice in a record to the other parties to the agreement to arbitrate in the agreed manner between the parties or, in the absence of agreement, by certified or registered mail, return receipt requested and obtained, or by service as authorized for the commencement of a civil action. The notice must describe the nature of the controversy and the remedy sought.

(b) Unless a person objects for lack or insufficiency of notice under Section 15(c) not later than the beginning of the arbitration hearing, the person by appearing at the hearing waives any objection to lack of or insufficiency of notice.

SECTION 10. CONSOLIDATION OF SEPARATE ARBITRATION PROCEEDINGS.

(a) Except as otherwise provided in subsection (c), upon [motion] of a party to an agreement to arbitrate or to an arbitration proceeding, the court may order consolidation of separate arbitration proceedings as to all or some of the claims if:

(1) there are separate agreements to arbitrate or separate arbitration proceedings between the same persons or one of them is a party to a separate agreement to arbitrate or a separate arbitration proceeding with a third person;

(2) the claims subject to the agreements to arbitrate arise in substantial part from the same transaction or series of related transactions;

(3) the existence of a common issue of law or fact creates the possibility of conflicting decisions in the separate arbitration proceedings; and

(4) prejudice resulting from a failure to consolidate is not outweighed by the risk of undue delay or prejudice to the rights of or hardship to parties opposing consolidation.

(b) The court may order consolidation of separate arbitration proceedings as to some claims and allow other claims to be resolved in separate arbitration proceedings.

(c) The court may not order consolidation of the claims of a party to an agreement to arbitrate if the agreement prohibits consolidation.

SECTION 11. APPOINTMENT OF ARBITRATOR; SERVICE AS A NEUTRAL ARBITRATOR.

(a) If the parties to an agreement to arbitrate agree on a method for appointing an arbitrator, that method must be followed, unless the method fails. If the parties have not agreed on a method, the agreed method fails, or an arbitrator appointed fails or is unable to act and a successor has not been appointed, the court, on [motion] of a party to the arbitration proceeding, shall appoint the arbitrator. An arbitrator so appointed has all the powers of an arbitrator designated in the agreement to arbitrate or appointed pursuant to the agreed method.

(b) An individual who has a known, direct, and material interest in the outcome of the arbitration proceeding or a known, existing, and substantial relationship with a party may not serve as an arbitrator required by an agreement to be neutral.

SECTION 12. DISCLOSURE BY ARBITRATOR.

(a) Before accepting appointment, an individual who is requested to serve as an arbitrator, after making a reasonable inquiry, shall disclose to all parties to the agreement to arbitrate and arbitration proceeding and to any other arbitrators any known facts that a reasonable person would consider likely to affect the impartiality of the arbitrator in the arbitration proceeding, including:

(1) a financial or personal interest in the outcome of the arbitration proceeding; and

(2) an existing or past relationship with any of the parties to the agreement to arbitrate or the arbitration proceeding, their counsel or representatives, a witness, or another arbitrators.

(b) An arbitrator has a continuing obligation to disclose to all parties to the agreement to arbitrate and arbitration proceeding and to any other arbitrators any facts that the arbitrator learns after accepting appointment which a reasonable person would consider likely to affect the impartiality of the arbitrator.

(c) If an arbitrator discloses a fact required by subsection (a) or (b) to be disclosed and a party timely objects to the appointment or continued service of the arbitrator based upon the fact disclosed, the objection may be a ground under Section 23(a)(2) for vacating an award made by the arbitrator.

(d) If the arbitrator did not disclose a fact as required by subsection (a) or (b), upon timely objection by a party, the court under Section 23(a)(2) may vacate an award.

(e) An arbitrator appointed as a neutral arbitrator who does not disclose a known, direct, and material interest in the outcome of the arbitration proceeding or a known, existing, and substantial relationship with a party is presumed to act with evident partiality under Section 23(a)(2).

(f) If the parties to an arbitration proceeding agree to the procedures of an arbitration organization or any other procedures for challenges to arbitrators before an award is made, substantial compliance with those procedures is a condition precedent to a [motion] to vacate an award on that ground under Section 23(a)(2).

SECTION 13. ACTION BY MAJORITY.

If there is more than one arbitrator, the powers of an arbitrator must be exercised by a majority of the arbitrators, but all of them shall conduct the hearing under Section 15(c).

SECTION 14. IMMUNITY OF ARBITRATOR; COMPETENCY TO TESTIFY; ATTORNEY'S FEES AND COSTS.

(a) An arbitrator or an arbitration organization acting in that capacity is immune from civil liability to the same extent as a judge of a court of this State acting in a judicial capacity.

(b) The immunity afforded by this section supplements any immunity under other law.

(c) The failure of an arbitrator to make a disclosure required by Section 12 does not cause any loss of immunity under this section.

(d) In a judicial, administrative, or similar proceeding, an arbitrator or representative of an arbitration organization is not competent to testify, and may not be required to produce records as to any statement, conduct, decision, or ruling occurring during the arbitration proceeding, to the same extent as a judge of a court of this State acting in a judicial capacity. This subsection does not apply:

(1) to the extent necessary to determine the claim of an arbitrator, arbitration organization, or representative of the arbitration organization against a party to the arbitration proceeding; or

(2) to a hearing on a [motion] to vacate an award under Section 23(a)(1) or (2) if the [movant] establishes prima facie that a ground for vacating the award exists.

(e) If a person commences a civil action against an arbitrator, arbitration organization, or representative of an arbitration organization arising from the services of the arbitrator, organization, or representative or if a person seeks to compel an arbitrator or a representative of an arbitration organization to testify or produce records in violation of subsection (d), and the court decides that the arbitrator, arbitration organization, or representative of an arbitration organization is immune from civil liability or that the arbitrator or representative of the organization is not competent to testify, the court shall award to the arbitrator, organization, or representative reasonable attorney's fees and other reasonable expenses of litigation.

SECTION 15. ARBITRATION PROCESS.

(a) An arbitrator may conduct an arbitration in such manner as the arbitrator considers appropriate for a fair and expeditious disposition of the proceeding. The authority conferred upon the arbitrator includes the power to hold conferences with the parties to the arbitration proceeding before the hearing and, among other matters, determine the admissibility, relevance, materiality and weight of any evidence.

(b) An arbitrator may decide a request for summary disposition of a claim or particular issue:

(1) if all interested parties agree; or

(2) upon request of one party to the arbitration proceeding if that party gives notice to all other parties to the proceeding, and the other parties have a reasonable opportunity to respond.

(c) If an arbitrator orders a hearing, the arbitrator shall set a time and place and give notice of the hearing not less than five days before the hearing begins. Unless a party to the arbitration proceeding makes an objection to lack or insufficiency of notice not later than the beginning of the hearing, the party's appearance at the hearing waives the objection. Upon request of a party to the arbitration proceeding and for good cause shown, or upon the arbitrator's own initiative, the arbitrator may adjourn the hearing from time to time as necessary but may not postpone the hearing to a time later than that fixed by the agreement to arbitrate for making the award unless the parties to the arbitration proceeding consent to a later date. The arbitrator may hear and decide the controversy upon the evidence produced although a party who was duly notified of the arbitration proceeding did not appear. The court, on request, may direct the arbitrator to conduct the hearing promptly and render a timely decision.

(d) At a hearing under subsection (c), a party to the arbitration proceeding has a right to be heard, to present evidence material to the controversy, and to cross-examine witnesses appearing at the hearing.

(e) If an arbitrator ceases or is unable to act during the arbitration proceeding, a replacement arbitrator must be appointed in accordance with Section 11 to continue the proceeding and to resolve the controversy.

SECTION 16. REPRESENTATION BY LAWYER.

A party to an arbitration proceeding may be represented by a lawyer.

SECTION 17. WITNESSES; SUBPOENAS; DEPOSITIONS; DISCOVERY.

(a) An arbitrator may issue a subpoena for the attendance of a witness and for the production of records and other evidence at any hearing and may administer oaths. A subpoena must be served in the manner for service of subpoenas in a civil action and, upon [motion] to the court by a party to the arbitration proceeding or the arbitrator, enforced in the manner for enforcement of subpoenas in a civil action.

(b) In order to make the proceedings fair, expeditious, and cost effective, upon request of a party to or a witness in an arbitration proceeding, an arbitrator may permit a deposition of any witness to be taken for use as evidence at the hearing, including a witness who cannot be subpoenaed for or is unable to attend a hearing. The arbitrator shall determine the conditions under which the deposition is taken.

(c) An arbitrator may permit such discovery as the arbitrator decides is appropriate in the circumstances, taking into account the needs of the parties to the arbitration proceeding and other affected persons and the desirability of making the proceeding fair, expeditious, and cost effective.

(d) If an arbitrator permits discovery under subsection (c), the arbitrator may order a party to the arbitration proceeding to comply with the arbitrator's discovery-related orders, issue subpoenas for the attendance of a witness and for the production of records and other evidence at a discovery proceeding, and take action against a noncomplying party to the extent a court could if the controversy were the subject of a civil action in this State.

(e) An arbitrator may issue a protective order to prevent the disclosure of privileged information, confidential information, trade secrets, and other information protected from disclosure to the extent a court could if the controversy were the subject of a civil action in this State.

(f) All laws compelling a person under subpoena to testify and all fees for attending a judicial proceeding, a deposition, or a discovery proceeding as a witness apply to an arbitration proceeding as if the controversy were the subject of a civil action in this State.

(g) The court may enforce a subpoena or discovery-related order for the attendance of a witness within this State and for the production of records and other evidence issued by an arbitrator in connection with an arbitration proceeding in another State upon conditions determined by the court so as to make the arbitration proceeding fair, expeditious, and cost effective. A subpoena or discovery-related order issued by an arbitrator in another State must be served in the manner provided by law for service of subpoenas in a civil action in this State and, upon [motion] to the court by a party to the arbitration proceeding or the arbitrator, enforced in the manner provided by law for enforcement of subpoenas in a civil action in this State.

SECTION 18. JUDICIAL ENFORCEMENT OF PREAWARD RULING BY ARBITRATOR.

If an arbitrator makes a preaward ruling in favor of a party to the arbitration proceeding, the party may request the arbitrator to incorporate the ruling into an award under Section 19. A prevailing party may make a [motion] to the court for an expedited order to confirm the award under Section 22, in which case the court shall summarily decide the [motion]. The court shall issue an order to confirm the award unless the court vacates, modifies, or corrects the award under Section 23 or 24.

SECTION 19. AWARD.

(a) An arbitrator shall make a record of an award. The record must be signed or otherwise authenticated by any arbitrator who concurs with the award. The arbitrator or the arbitration organization shall give notice of the award, including a copy of the award, to each party to the arbitration proceeding.

(b) An award must be made within the time specified by the agreement to arbitrate or, if not specified therein, within the time ordered by the court. The court may extend or the parties to the arbitration proceeding may agree in a record to extend the time. The court or the parties may do so within or after the time specified or ordered. A party waives any objection that an award was not timely made unless the party gives notice of the objection to the arbitrator before receiving notice of the award.

SECTION 20. CHANGE OF AWARD BY ARBITRATOR.

(a) On [motion] to an arbitrator by a party to an arbitration proceeding, the arbitrator may modify or correct an award:

(1) upon a ground stated in Section 24(a)(1) or (3);

(2) because the arbitrator has not made a final and definite award upon a claim submitted by the parties to the arbitration proceeding; or

(3) to clarify the award.

(b) A [motion] under subsection (a) must be made and notice given to all parties within 20 days after the movant receives notice of the award.

(c) A party to the arbitration proceeding must give notice of any objection to the [motion] within 10 days after receipt of the notice.

(d) If a [motion] to the court is pending under Section 22, 23, or 24, the court may submit the claim to the arbitrator to consider whether to modify or correct the award:

(1) upon a ground stated in Section 24(a)(1) or (3);

(2) because the arbitrator has not made a final and definite award upon a claim submitted by the parties to the arbitration proceeding; or

(3) to clarify the award.

(e) An award modified or corrected pursuant to this section is subject to Sections 19(a), 22, 23, and 24.

SECTION 21. REMEDIES; FEES AND EXPENSES OF ARBITRATION PROCEEDING.

(a) An arbitrator may award punitive damages or other exemplary relief if such an award is authorized by law in a civil action involving the same claim and the evidence produced at the hearing justifies the award under the legal standards otherwise applicable to the claim.

(b) An arbitrator may award reasonable attorney's fees and other reasonable expenses of arbitration if such an award is authorized by law in a civil action involving the same claim or by the agreement of the parties to the arbitration proceeding.

(c) As to all remedies other than those authorized by subsections (a) and (b), an arbitrator may order such remedies as the arbitrator considers just and appropriate under the circumstances of the arbitration proceeding. The fact that such a remedy could not or would not be granted by the court is not a ground for refusing to confirm an award under Section 22 or for vacating an award under Section 23.

(d) An arbitrator's expenses and fees, together with other expenses, must be paid as provided in the award.

(e) If an arbitrator awards punitive damages or other exemplary relief under subsection (a), the arbitrator shall specify in the award the basis in fact justifying and the basis in law authorizing the award and state separately the amount of the punitive damages or other exemplary relief.

SECTION 22. CONFIRMATION OF AWARD.

After a party to an arbitration proceeding receives notice of an award, the party may make a [motion] to the court for an order confirming the award at which time the court shall issue a confirming order unless the award is modified or corrected pursuant to Section 20 or 24 or is vacated pursuant to Section 23.

SECTION 23. VACATING AWARD.

(a) Upon [motion] to the court by a party to an arbitration proceeding, the court shall vacate an award made in the arbitration proceeding if:

> (1) the award was procured by corruption, fraud, or other undue means;
>
> (2) there was:
>
> > (A) evident partiality by an arbitrator appointed as a neutral arbitrator;
> >
> > (B) corruption by an arbitrator; or
> >
> > (C) misconduct by an arbitrator prejudicing the rights of a party to the arbitration proceeding;
>
> (3) an arbitrator refused to postpone the hearing upon showing of sufficient cause for postponement, refused to consider evidence material to the controversy, or otherwise conducted the hearing contrary to Section 15, so as to

prejudice substantially the rights of a party to the arbitration proceeding;

(4) an arbitrator exceeded the arbitrator's powers;

(5) there was no agreement to arbitrate, unless the person participated in the arbitration proceeding without raising the objection under Section 15(c) not later than the beginning of the arbitration hearing; or

(6) the arbitration was conducted without proper notice of the initiation of an arbitration as required in Section 9 so as to prejudice substantially the rights of a party to the arbitration proceeding.

(b) A [motion] under this section must be filed within 90 days after the [movant] receives notice of the award pursuant to Section 19 or within 90 days after the [movant] receives notice of a modified or corrected award pursuant to Section 20, unless the [movant] alleges that the award was procured by corruption, fraud, or other undue means, in which case the [motion] must be made within 90 days after the ground is known or by the exercise of reasonable care would have been known by the [movant].

(c) If the court vacates an award on a ground other than that set forth in subsection (a)(5), it may order a rehearing. If the award is vacated on a ground stated in subsection (a)(1) or (2), the rehearing must be before a new arbitrator. If the award is vacated on a ground stated in subsection (a)(3), (4), or (6), the rehearing may be before the arbitrator who made the award or the arbitrator's successor. The arbitrator must render the decision in the rehearing within the same time as that provided in Section 19(b) for an award.

(d) If the court denies a [motion] to vacate an award, it shall confirm the award unless a [motion] to modify or correct the award is pending.

SECTION 24. MODIFICATION OR CORRECTION OF AWARD.

(a) Upon [motion] made within 90 days after the [movant] receives notice of the award pursuant to Section 19 or within 90 days after the [movant] receives notice of a modified or corrected award pursuant to Section 20, the court shall modify or correct the award if:

(1) there was an evident mathematical miscalculation or an evident mistake in the description of a person, thing, or property referred to in the award;

(2) the arbitrator has made an award on a claim not submitted to the arbitrator and the award may be corrected

without affecting the merits of the decision upon the claims submitted; or

(3) the award is imperfect in a matter of form not affecting the merits of the decision on the claims submitted.

(b) If a [motion] made under subsection (a) is granted, the court shall modify or correct and confirm the award as modified or corrected. Otherwise, unless a motion to vacate is pending, the court shall confirm the award.

(c) A [motion] to modify or correct an award pursuant to this section may be joined with a [motion] to vacate the award.

SECTION 25. JUDGMENT ON AWARD; ATTORNEY'S FEES AND LITIGATION EXPENSES.

(a) Upon granting an order confirming, vacating without directing a rehearing, modifying, or correcting an award, the court shall enter a judgment in conformity therewith. The judgment may be recorded, docketed, and enforced as any other judgment in a civil action.

(b) A court may allow reasonable costs of the [motion] and subsequent judicial proceedings.

(c) On [application] of a prevailing party to a contested judicial proceeding under Section 22, 23, or 24, the court may add reasonable attorney's fees and other reasonable expenses of litigation incurred in a judicial proceeding after the award is made to a judgment confirming, vacating without directing a rehearing, modifying, or correcting an award.

SECTION 26. JURISDICTION.

(a) A court of this State having jurisdiction over the controversy and the parties may enforce an agreement to arbitrate.

(b) An agreement to arbitrate providing for arbitration in this State confers exclusive jurisdiction on the court to enter judgment on an award under this [Act].

SECTION 27. VENUE.

A [motion] pursuant to Section 5 must be made in the court of the [county] in which the agreement to arbitrate specifies the arbitration hearing is to be held or, if the hearing has been held, in the court of the [county] in which it was held. Otherwise, the [motion] may be made in the court of any [county] in which an adverse party resides or has a place of business or, if no adverse party has a residence or place of business in this State, in the court of any [county] in this

State. All subsequent [motions] must be made in the court hearing the initial [motion] unless the court otherwise directs.

SECTION 28. APPEALS.

(a) An appeal may be taken from:

(1) an order denying a [motion] to compel arbitration;

(2) an order granting a [motion] to stay arbitration;

(3) an order confirming or denying confirmation of an award;

(4) an order modifying or correcting an award;

(5) an order vacating an award without directing a rehearing; or

(6) a final judgment entered pursuant to this [Act].

(b) An appeal under this section must be taken as from an order or a judgment in a civil action.

SECTION 29. UNIFORMITY OF APPLICATION AND CONSTRUCTION.

In applying and construing this uniform act, consideration must be given to the need to promote uniformity of the law with respect to its subject matter among States that enact it.

SECTION 30. RELATIONSHIP TO ELECTRONIC SIGNATURES IN GLOBAL AND NATIONAL COMMERCE ACT. The provisions of this Act governing the legal effect, validity, and enforceability of electronic records or electronic signatures, and of contracts performed with the use of such records or signatures conform to the requirements of Section 102 of the Electronic Signatures in Global and National Commerce Act.

SECTION 31. EFFECTIVE DATE.

This [Act] takes effect on [effective date].

SECTION 32. REPEAL.

Effective on [delayed date should be the same as that in Section 3(c)], the [Uniform Arbitration Act] is repealed.

SECTION 33. SAVINGS CLAUSE.

This [Act] does not affect an action or proceeding commenced or right accrued before this [Act] takes effect. Subject to Section 3 of this [Act], an arbitration agreement made before the effective date of this [Act] is governed by the [Uniform Arbitration Act].

Appendix 4:
AAA: COMMERCIAL ARBITRATION RULES AND MEDIATION

TABLE OF CONTENTS

M-13. Exclusion of Liability

M-14. Interpretation and Application of Procedures

M-15. Deposits

M-16. Expenses

M-17. Cost of Mediation

COMMERCIAL ARBITRATION RULES

R-1. Agreement of Parties
R-2. AAA and Delegation of Duties
R-3. National Roster of Arbitrators
R-4. Initiation under an Arbitration Provision in a Contract
R-5. Initiation under a Submission
R-6. Changes of Claim
R-7. Jurisdiction
R-8. Mediation
R-9. Administrative Conference
R-10. Fixing of Locale
R-11. Appointment from National Roster
R-12. Direct Appointment by a Party
R-13. Appointment of Chairperson by Party-Appointed Arbitrators or Parties
R-14. Nationality of Arbitrator
R-15. Number of Arbitrators
R-16. Disclosure
R-17. Disqualification of Arbitrator
R-18. Communication with Arbitrator
R-19. Vacancies
R-20. Preliminary Hearing
R-21. Exchange of Information
R-22. Date, Time, and Place of Hearing
R-23. Attendance at Hearings
R-24. Representation
R-25. Oaths
R-26. Stenographic Record
R-27. Interpreters
R-28. Postponements
R-29. Arbitration in the Absence of a Party or Representative
R-30. Conduct of Proceedings

EXPEDITED PROCEDURES

PROCEDURES FOR LARGE, COMPLEX COMMERCIAL DISPUTES

OPTIONAL RULES FOR EMERGENCY MEASURES OF PROTECTION

ADMINISTRATIVE FEES

IMPORTANT NOTICE

These rules and any amendment of them shall apply in the form in effect at the time the administrative filing requirements are met for a demand for arbitration or submission agreement received by the AAA. To ensure that you have the most current information, see our Web Site at www.adr.org.

INTRODUCTION

Each year, many millions of business transactions take place. Occasionally, disagreements develop over these business transactions. Many of these disputes are resolved by arbitration, the voluntary submission of a dispute to an impartial person or persons for final and binding determination. Arbitration has proven to be an effective way to resolve these disputes privately, promptly, and economically.

The American Arbitration Association (AAA), a not-for-profit, public service organization, offers a broad range of dispute resolution services to business executives, attorneys, individuals, trade associations, unions, management, consumers, families, communities, and all levels of government. Services are available through AAA headquarters in New York and through offices located in major cities throughout the United States. Hearings may be held at locations convenient for the parties and are not limited to cities with AAA offices. In addition, the AAA serves as a center for education and training, issues specialized publications, and conducts research on all forms of out-of-court dispute settlement.

Standard Arbitration Clause

The parties can provide for arbitration of future disputes by inserting the following clause into their contracts:

> *Any controversy or claim arising out of or relating to this contract, or the breach thereof, shall be settled by arbitration administered by the American Arbitration Association under its Commercial Arbitration Rules, and judgment on the award rendered by the arbitrator(s) may be entered in any court having jurisdiction thereof.*

Arbitration of existing disputes may be accomplished by use of the following:

> *We, the undersigned parties, hereby agree to submit to arbitration administered by the American Arbitration Association under its Commercial Arbitration Rules the following controversy: (describe briefly) We further agree that the above controversy be submitted to (one) (three) arbitrator(s). We further agree that we will faithfully observe this agreement and the rules, that we will abide by and perform any award rendered by the arbitrator(s), and that a judgment of any court having jurisdiction may be entered on the award.*

In transactions likely to require emergency interim relief, the parties may wish to add to their clause the following language:

The parties also agree that the AAA Optional Rules for Emergency Measures of Protection shall apply to the proceedings.

These Optional Rules may be found below.

The services of the AAA are generally concluded with the transmittal of the award. Although there is voluntary compliance with the majority of awards, judgment on the award can be entered in a court having appropriate jurisdiction if necessary.

Administrative Fees

The AAA charges a filing fee based on the amount of the claim or counterclaim. This fee information, which is included with these rules, allows the parties to exercise control over their administrative fees.

The fees cover AAA administrative services; they do not cover arbitrator compensation or expenses, if any, reporting services, or any post-award charges incurred by the parties in enforcing the award.

Mediation

The parties might wish to submit their dispute to mediation prior to arbitration. In mediation, the neutral mediator assists the parties in reaching a settlement but does not have the authority to make a binding decision or award. Mediation is administered by the AAA in accordance with its Commercial Mediation Procedures. There is no additional administrative fee where parties to a pending arbitration attempt to mediate their dispute under the AAA's auspices.

If the parties want to adopt mediation as a part of their contractual dispute settlement procedure, they can insert the following mediation clause into their contract in conjunction with a standard arbitration provision:

If a dispute arises out of or relates to this contract, or the breach thereof, and if the dispute cannot be settled through negotiation, the parties agree first to try in good faith to settle the dispute by mediation administered by the American Arbitration Association under its Commercial Mediation

Procedures before resorting to arbitration, litigation, or some other dispute resolution procedure.

If the parties want to use a mediator to resolve an existing dispute, they can enter into the following submission:

The parties hereby submit the following dispute to mediation administered by the American Arbitration Association under its Commercial Mediation Procedures. (The clause may also provide for the qualifications of the mediator(s), method of payment, locale of meetings, and any other item of concern to the parties.)

Large, Complex Cases

Unless the parties agree otherwise, the procedures for Large, Complex Commercial Disputes, which appear in this pamphlet, will be applied to all cases administered by the AAA under the Commercial Arbitration Rules in which the disclosed claim or counterclaim of any party is at least $500,000 exclusive of claimed interest, arbitration fees and costs.

The key features of these procedures include:

- a highly qualified, trained Roster of Neutrals;
- a mandatory preliminary hearing with the arbitrators, which may be conducted by teleconference;
- broad arbitrator authority to order and control discovery, including depositions;
- presumption that hearings will proceed on a consecutive or block basis.

COMMERCIAL MEDIATION PROCEDURES

M-1. Agreement of Parties

Whenever, by stipulation or in their contract, the parties have provided for mediation or conciliation of existing or future disputes under the auspices of the American Arbitration Association (AAA) or under these procedures, the parties and their representatives, unless agreed otherwise in writing, shall be deemed to have made these procedural guidelines, as amended and in effect as of the date of filing of a request for mediation, a part of their agreement and designate the AAA as the administrator of their mediation.

The parties by mutual agreement may vary any part of these procedures including, but not limited to, agreeing to conduct the mediation via telephone or other electronic or technical means.

M-2. Initiation of Mediation

Any party or parties to a dispute may initiate mediation under the AAA's auspices by making a request for mediation to any of the AAA's regional offices or case management centers via telephone, email, regular mail or fax. Requests for mediation may also be filed online via WebFile at www.adr.org.

The party initiating the mediation shall simultaneously notify the other party or parties of the request. The initiating party shall provide the following information to the AAA and the other party or parties as applicable:

i. A copy of the mediation provision of the parties' contract or the parties' stipulation to mediate.

ii. The names, regular mail addresses, email addresses, and telephone numbers of all parties to the dispute and representatives, if any, in the mediation.

iii. A brief statement of the nature of the dispute and the relief requested.

iv. Any specific qualifications the mediator should possess.

Where there is no preexisting stipulation or contract by which the parties have provided for mediation of existing or future disputes under the auspices of the AAA, a party may request the AAA to invite another party to participate in "mediation by voluntary submission". Upon receipt of such a request, the AAA will contact the other party or parties involved in the dispute and attempt to obtain a submission to mediation.

M-3. Representation

Subject to any applicable law, any party may be represented by persons of the party's choice. The names and addresses of such persons shall be communicated in writing to all parties and to the AAA.

M-4. Appointment of the Mediator

Parties may search the online profiles of the AAA's Panel of Mediators at www.aaamediation.com in an effort to agree on a mediator. If the parties have not agreed to the appointment of a mediator and have not provided any other method of appointment, the mediator shall be appointed in the following manner:

i. Upon receipt of a request for mediation, the AAA will send to each party a list of mediators from the AAA's Panel of Mediators. The parties are encouraged to agree to a mediator from the submitted list and to advise the AAA of their agreement.

ii. If the parties are unable to agree upon a mediator, each party shall strike unacceptable names from the list, number the remaining names in order of preference, and return the list to the AAA. If a party does not return the list within the time specified, all mediators on the list shall be deemed acceptable. From among the mediators who have been mutually approved by the parties, and in accordance with the designated order of mutual preference, the AAA shall invite a mediator to serve.

iii. If the parties fail to agree on any of the mediators listed, or if acceptable mediators are unable to serve, or if for any other reason the appointment cannot be made from the submitted list, the AAA shall have the authority to make the appointment from among other members of the Panel of Mediators without the submission of additional lists.

M-5. Mediator's Impartiality and Duty to Disclose

AAA mediators are required to abide by the Model Standards of Conduct for Mediators in effect at the time a mediator is appointed to a case. Where there is a conflict between the Model Standards and any provision of these Mediation Procedures, these Mediation Procedures shall govern. The Standards require mediators to (i) decline a mediation if the mediator cannot conduct it in an impartial manner, and (ii) disclose, as soon as practicable, all actual and potential conflicts of interest that are reasonably known to the mediator and could reasonably be seen as raising a question about the mediator's impartiality.

Prior to accepting an appointment, AAA mediators are required to make a reasonable inquiry to determine whether there are any facts that a reasonable individual would consider likely to create a potential or actual conflict of interest for the mediator. AAA mediators are required to disclose any circumstance likely to create a presumption of bias or prevent a resolution of the parties' dispute within the time-frame desired by the parties. Upon receipt of such disclosures, the AAA shall immediately communicate the disclosures to the parties for their comments.

The parties may, upon receiving disclosure of actual or potential conflicts of interest of the mediator, waive such conflicts and proceed with the mediation. In the event that a party disagrees as to whether the mediator shall serve, or in the event that the mediator's conflict of interest might reasonably be viewed as undermining the integrity of the mediation, the mediator shall be replaced.

M-6. Vacancies

If any mediator shall become unwilling or unable to serve, the AAA will appoint another mediator, unless the parties agree otherwise, in accordance with section M-4.

M-7. Duties and Responsibilities of the Mediator

i. The mediator shall conduct the mediation based on the principle of party self-determination. Self-determination is the act of coming to a voluntary, uncoerced decision in which each party makes free and informed choices as to process and outcome.

ii. The mediator is authorized to conduct separate or ex parte meetings and other communications with the parties and/or their representatives, before, during, and after any scheduled mediation conference. Such communications may be conducted via telephone, in writing, via email, online, in person or otherwise.

iii. The parties are encouraged to exchange all documents pertinent to the relief requested. The mediator may request the exchange of memoranda on issues, including the underlying interests and the history of the parties' negotiations. Information that a party wishes to keep confidential may be sent to the mediator, as necessary, in a separate communication with the mediator.

iv. The mediator does not have the authority to impose a settlement on the parties but will attempt to help them reach a satisfactory resolution of their dispute. Subject to the discretion of the mediator, the mediator may make oral or written recommendations for settlement to a party privately or, if the parties agree, to all parties jointly.

v. In the event a complete settlement of all or some issues in dispute is not achieved within the scheduled mediation session(s), the mediator may continue to communicate with the parties, for a period of time, in an ongoing effort to facilitate a complete settlement.

vi. The mediator is not a legal representative of any party and has no fiduciary duty to any party.

M-8. Responsibilities of the Parties

The parties shall ensure that appropriate representatives of each party, having authority to consummate a settlement, attend the mediation conference.

Prior to and during the scheduled mediation conference session(s) the parties and their representatives shall, as appropriate to each party's circumstances, exercise their best efforts to prepare for and engage in a meaningful and productive mediation.

M-9. Privacy

Mediation sessions and related mediation communications are private proceedings. The parties and their representatives may attend mediation sessions. Other persons may attend only with the permission of the parties and with the consent of the mediator.

M-10. Confidentiality

Subject to applicable law or the parties' agreement, confidential information disclosed to a mediator by the parties or by other participants (witnesses) in the course of the mediation shall not be divulged by the mediator. The mediator shall maintain the confidentiality of all information obtained in the mediation, and all records, reports, or other documents received by a mediator while serving in that capacity shall be confidential.

The mediator shall not be compelled to divulge such records or to testify in regard to the mediation in any adversary proceeding or judicial forum.

The parties shall maintain the confidentiality of the mediation and shall not rely on, or introduce as evidence in any arbitral, judicial, or other proceeding the following, unless agreed to by the parties or required by applicable law:

i. Views expressed or suggestions made by a party or other participant with respect to a possible settlement of the dispute;
ii. Admissions made by a party or other participant in the course of the mediation proceedings;
iii. Proposals made or views expressed by the mediator; or
iv. The fact that a party had or had not indicated willingness to accept a proposal for settlement made by the mediator.

M-11. No Stenographic Record

There shall be no stenographic record of the mediation process.

M-12. Termination of Mediation

The mediation shall be terminated:

i. By the execution of a settlement agreement by the parties; or

ii. By a written or verbal declaration of the mediator to the effect that further efforts at mediation would not contribute to a resolution of the parties' dispute; or

iii. By a written or verbal declaration of all parties to the effect that the mediation proceedings are terminated; or

iv. When there has been no communication between the mediator and any party or party's representative for 21 days following the conclusion of the mediation conference.

M-13. Exclusion of Liability

Neither the AAA nor any mediator is a necessary party in judicial proceedings relating to the mediation. Neither the AAA nor any mediator shall be liable to any party for any error, act or omission in connection with any mediation conducted under these procedures.

M-14. Interpretation and Application of Procedures

The mediator shall interpret and apply these procedures insofar as they relate to the mediator's duties and responsibilities. All other procedures shall be interpreted and applied by the AAA.

M-15. Deposits

Unless otherwise directed by the mediator, the AAA will require the parties to deposit in advance of the mediation conference such sums of money as it, in consultation with the mediator, deems necessary to cover the costs and expenses of the mediation and shall render an accounting to the parties and return any unexpended balance at the conclusion of the mediation.

M-16. Expenses

All expenses of the mediation, including required traveling and other expenses or charges of the mediator, shall be borne equally by the parties unless they agree otherwise. The expenses of participants for either side shall be paid by the party requesting the attendance of such participants.

M-17. Cost of the Mediation

There is no filing fee to initiate a mediation or a fee to request the AAA to invite parties to mediate.

The cost of mediation is based on the hourly mediation rate published on the mediator's AAA profile. This rate covers both mediator compensation and an allocated portion for the AAA's services. There is a four-hour minimum charge for a mediation conference. Expenses referenced in Section M-16 may also apply.

If a matter submitted for mediation is withdrawn or cancelled or results in a settlement after the agreement to mediate is filed but prior to the mediation conference the cost is $250 plus any mediator time and charges incurred.

The parties will be billed equally for all costs unless they agree otherwise.

If you have questions about mediation costs or services visit our website at www.adr.org or contact your local AAA office.

Conference Room Rental

The costs described above do not include the use of AAA conference rooms. Conference rooms are available on a rental basis. Please contact your local AAA office for availability and rates.

COMMERCIAL ARBITRATION RULES

R-1. Agreement of Parties*+

(a) The parties shall be deemed to have made these rules a part of their arbitration agreement whenever they have provided for arbitration by the American Arbitration Association (hereinafter AAA) under its Commercial Arbitration Rules or for arbitration by the AAA of a domestic commercial dispute without specifying particular rules. These rules and any amendment of them shall apply in the form in effect at the time the administrative requirements are met for a demand for arbitration or submission agreement received by the AAA. The parties, by written agreement, may vary the procedures set forth in these rules. After appointment of the arbitrator, such modifications may be made only with the consent of the arbitrator.

(b) Unless the parties or the AAA determines otherwise, the Expedited Procedures shall apply in any case in which no disclosed claim or counterclaim exceeds $75,000, exclusive of interest and arbitration fees and costs. Parties may also agree to use these procedures in larger cases. Unless the parties agree otherwise, these procedures will not apply in cases involving more than two parties. The Expedited Procedures shall be applied as described in Sections E-1 through E-10 of these rules, in addition to any other portion of these rules that is not in conflict with the Expedited Procedures.

(c) Unless the parties agree otherwise, the Procedures for Large, Complex Commercial Disputes shall apply to all cases in which the disclosed claim or counterclaim of any party is at least $500,000, exclusive of claimed interest, arbitration fees and costs. Parties may also agree to use the Procedures in cases involving claims or counterclaims under $500,000, or in nonmonetary cases. The Procedures for Large, Complex Commercial Disputes shall be applied as described in Sections L-1 through L-4 of these rules, in addition to any other portion of these rules that is not in conflict with the Procedures for Large, Complex Commercial Disputes.

(d) All other cases shall be administered in accordance with Sections R-1 through R-54 of these rules.

* The AAA applies the *Supplementary Procedures for Consumer-Related Disputes* to arbitration clauses in agreements between individual consumers and businesses where the business has a standardized, systematic application of arbitration clauses with customers and where the terms and conditions of the purchase of standardized, consumable goods or services are nonnegotiable or primarily non-negotiable in most or all of its terms, conditions, features, or choices. The product or service must be for personal or household use. The AAA will have the discretion to apply or not to apply the Supplementary Procedures and the parties will be able to bring any disputes concerning the application or non-application to the attention of the arbitrator. Consumers are not prohibited from seeking relief in a small claims court for disputes or claims within the scope of its jurisdiction, even in consumer arbitration cases filed by the business.

+ A dispute arising out of an employer promulgated plan will be administered under the AAA's Employment Arbitration Rules and Mediation Procedures.

R-2. AAA and Delegation of Duties

When parties agree to arbitrate under these rules, or when they provide for arbitration by the AAA and an arbitration is initiated under these rules, they thereby authorize the AAA to administer the arbitration. The authority and duties of the AAA are prescribed in the agreement of the parties and in these rules, and may be carried out through such of the AAA's representatives as it may direct. The AAA may, in its discretion, assign the administration of an arbitration to any of its offices.

R-3. National Roster of Arbitrators

The AAA shall establish and maintain a National Roster of Commercial Arbitrators ("National Roster") and shall appoint arbitrators as provided in these rules. The term "arbitrator" in these rules refers to the arbitration panel, constituted for a particular case, whether composed of one or more arbitrators, or to an individual arbitrator, as the context requires.

R-4. Initiation under an Arbitration Provision in a Contract

(a) Arbitration under an arbitration provision in a contract shall be initiated in the following manner:

(i) The initiating party (the "claimant") shall, within the time period, if any, specified in the contract(s), give to the other party (the "respondent") written notice of its intention to arbitrate (the "demand"), which demand shall contain a statement setting forth the nature of the dispute, the names and addresses of all other parties, the amount involved, if any, the remedy sought, and the hearing locale requested.

(ii) The claimant shall file at any office of the AAA two copies of the demand and two copies of the arbitration provisions of the contract, together with the appropriate filing fee as provided in the schedule included with these rules.

(iii) The AAA shall confirm notice of such filing to the parties.

(b) A respondent may file an answering statement in duplicate with the AAA within 15 days after confirmation of notice of filing of the demand is sent by the AAA. The respondent shall, at the time of any such filing, send a copy of the answering statement to the claimant. If a counterclaim is asserted, it shall contain a statement setting forth the nature of the counterclaim, the amount involved, if any, and the remedy sought. If a counterclaim is made, the party making the counterclaim shall forward to the AAA with the answering statement the appropriate fee provided in the schedule included with these rules.

(c) If no answering statement is filed within the stated time, respondent will be deemed to deny the claim. Failure to file an answering statement shall not operate to delay the arbitration.

(d) When filing any statement pursuant to this section, the parties are encouraged to provide descriptions of their claims in sufficient detail to make the circumstances of the dispute clear to the arbitrator.

R-5. Initiation under a Submission

Parties to any existing dispute may commence an arbitration under these rules by filing at any office of the AAA two copies of a written submission to arbitrate under these rules, signed by the parties. It shall contain a statement of the nature of the dispute, the names and addresses of all parties, any claims and counterclaims, the amount involved, if any, the remedy sought, and the hearing locale requested, together with the appropriate filing fee as provided in the schedule included with these rules. Unless the parties state otherwise in the submission, all claims and counterclaims will be deemed to be denied by the other party.

R-6. Changes of Claim

After filing of a claim, if either party desires to make any new or different claim or counterclaim, it shall be made in writing and filed with the AAA. The party asserting such a claim or counterclaim shall provide a copy to the other party, who shall have 15 days from the date of such transmission within which to file an answering statement with the AAA. After the arbitrator is appointed, however, no new or different claim may be submitted except with the arbitrator's consent.

R-7. Jurisdiction

(a) The arbitrator shall have the power to rule on his or her own jurisdiction, including any objections with respect to the existence, scope or validity of the arbitration agreement.

(b) The arbitrator shall have the power to determine the existence or validity of a contract of which an arbitration clause forms a part. Such an arbitration clause shall be treated as an agreement independent of the other terms of the contract. A decision by the arbitrator that the contract is null and void shall not for that reason alone render invalid the arbitration clause.

(c) A party must object to the jurisdiction of the arbitrator or to the arbitrability of a claim or counterclaim no later than the filing of the answering statement to the claim or counterclaim that gives rise to the objection. The arbitrator may rule on such objections as a preliminary matter or as part of the final award.

R-8. Mediation

At any stage of the proceedings, the parties may agree to conduct a mediation conference under the Commercial Mediation Procedures in order to facilitate settlement. The mediator shall not be an arbitrator appointed to the case. Where the parties to a pending arbitration agree to mediate under the AAA's rules, no additional administrative fee is required to initiate the mediation.

R-9. Administrative Conference

At the request of any party or upon the AAA's own initiative, the AAA may conduct an administrative conference, in person or by telephone, with the parties and/or their representatives. The conference may address such issues as arbitrator selection, potential mediation of the dispute, potential exchange of information, a timetable for hearings and any other administrative matters.

R-10. Fixing of Locale

The parties may mutually agree on the locale where the arbitration is to be held. If any party requests that the hearing be held in a specific locale and the other party files no objection thereto within 15 days after notice of the request has been sent to it by the AAA, the locale shall be the one requested. If a party objects to the locale requested by the other party, the AAA shall have the power to determine the locale, and its decision shall be final and binding.

R-11. Appointment from National Roster

(a) If the parties have not appointed an arbitrator and have not provided any other method of appointment, the arbitrator shall be appointed in the following manner: The AAA shall send simultaneously to each party to the dispute an identical list of 10 (unless the AAA decides that a different number is appropriate) names of persons chosen from the National Roster. The parties are encouraged to agree to an arbitrator from the submitted list and to advise the AAA of their agreement.

(b) If the parties are unable to agree upon an arbitrator, each party to the dispute shall have 15 days from the transmittal date in which to strike names objected to, number the remaining names in order of preference, and return the list to the AAA. If a party does not return the list within the time specified, all persons named therein shall be deemed acceptable. From among the persons who have been approved on both lists, and in accordance with the designated order of mutual preference, the AAA shall invite the acceptance of an arbitrator to serve. If the parties fail to agree on any of the persons named, or if acceptable arbitrators are unable to act, or if for any other reason the appointment cannot be made from the submitted lists, the AAA shall have the power to make the appointment from among other members of the National Roster without the submission of additional lists.

(c) Unless the parties agree otherwise when there are two or more claimants or two or more respondents, the AAA may appoint all the arbitrators.

R-12. Direct Appointment by a Party

(a) If the agreement of the parties names an arbitrator or specifies a method of appointing an arbitrator, that designation or method shall be followed. The notice of appointment, with the name and address of the arbitrator, shall be filed with the AAA by the appointing party. Upon the request of any appointing party, the AAA shall submit a list of members of the National Roster from which the party may, if it so desires, make the appointment.

(b) Where the parties have agreed that each party is to name one arbitrator, the arbitrators so named must meet the standards of Section R-17 with respect to impartiality and independence unless the parties have specifically agreed pursuant to Section R-17(a) that the party-appointed arbitrators are to be non-neutral and need not meet those standards.

(c) If the agreement specifies a period of time within which an arbitrator shall be appointed and any party fails to make the appointment within that period, the AAA shall make the appointment.

(d) If no period of time is specified in the agreement, the AAA shall notify the party to make the appointment. If within 15 days after such notice has been sent, an arbitrator has not been appointed by a party, the AAA shall make the appointment.

R-13. Appointment of Chairperson by Party-Appointed Arbitrators or Parties

(a) If, pursuant to Section R-12, either the parties have directly appointed arbitrators, or the arbitrators have been appointed by the AAA, and the parties have authorized them to appoint a chairperson within a specified time and no appointment is made within that time or any agreed extension, the AAA may appoint the chairperson.

(b) If no period of time is specified for appointment of the chairperson and the party-appointed arbitrators or the parties do not make the appointment within 15 days from the date of the appointment of the last party-appointed arbitrator, the AAA may appoint the chairperson.

(c) If the parties have agreed that their party-appointed arbitrators shall appoint the chairperson from the National Roster, the AAA shall furnish to the party-appointed arbitrators, in the manner provided in Section R-11, a list selected from the National Roster, and the appointment of the chairperson shall be made as provided in that Section.

R-14. Nationality of Arbitrator

Where the parties are nationals of different countries, the AAA, at the request of any party or on its own initiative, may appoint as arbitrator a national of a country other than that of any of the parties. The request must be made before the time set for the appointment of the arbitrator as agreed by the parties or set by these rules.

R-15. Number of Arbitrators

If the arbitration agreement does not specify the number of arbitrators, the dispute shall be heard and determined by one arbitrator, unless the AAA, in its discretion, directs that three arbitrators be appointed. A party may request three arbitrators in the demand or answer, which request the AAA will consider in exercising its discretion regarding the number of arbitrators appointed to the dispute.

R-16. Disclosure

(a) Any person appointed or to be appointed as an arbitrator shall disclose to the AAA any circumstance likely to give rise to justifiable doubt as to the arbitrator's impartiality or independence, including any bias or any financial or personal interest in the result of the arbitration or any past or present relationship with the parties or their representatives. Such obligation shall remain in effect throughout the arbitration.

(b) Upon receipt of such information from the arbitrator or another source, the AAA shall communicate the information to the parties and, if it deems it appropriate to do so, to the arbitrator and others.

(c) In order to encourage disclosure by arbitrators, disclosure of information pursuant to this Section R-16 is not to be construed as an indication that the arbitrator considers that the disclosed circumstance is likely to affect impartiality or independence.

R-17. Disqualification of Arbitrator

(a) Any arbitrator shall be impartial and independent and shall perform his or her duties with diligence and in good faith, and shall be subject to disqualification for

(i) partiality or lack of independence,

(ii) inability or refusal to perform his or her duties with diligence and in good faith, and

(iii) any grounds for disqualification provided by applicable law. The parties may agree in writing, however, that arbitrators directly appointed by a party pursuant to Section R-12 shall be nonneutral, in which case such arbitrators need not be impartial or independent and shall not be subject to disqualification for partiality or lack of independence.

(b) Upon objection of a party to the continued service of an arbitrator, or on its own initiative, the AAA shall determine whether the arbitrator should be disqualified under the grounds set out above, and shall inform the parties of its decision, which decision shall be conclusive.

R-18. Communication with Arbitrator

(a) No party and no one acting on behalf of any party shall communicate ex parte with an arbitrator or a candidate for arbitrator concerning the arbitration, except that a party, or someone acting on behalf of a party, may communicate ex parte with a candidate for direct appointment pursuant to Section R-12 in order to advise the candidate of the general nature of the controversy and of the anticipated proceedings and to discuss the candidate's qualifications, availability, or independence in relation to the parties or to discuss the suitability of candidates for selection as a third arbitrator where the parties or party-designated arbitrators are to participate in that selection.

(b) Section R-18(a) does not apply to arbitrators directly appointed by the parties who, pursuant to Section R-17(a), the parties have agreed in writing are non-neutral. Where the parties have so agreed under Section R-17(a), the AAA shall as an administrative practice suggest to the parties that they agree further that Section R-18(a) should nonetheless apply prospectively.

R-19. Vacancies

(a) If for any reason an arbitrator is unable to perform the duties of the office, the AAA may, on proof satisfactory to it, declare the office vacant. Vacancies shall be filled in accordance with the applicable provisions of these rules.

(b) In the event of a vacancy in a panel of neutral arbitrators after the hearings have commenced, the remaining arbitrator or arbitrators may continue with the hearing and determination of the controversy, unless the parties agree otherwise.

(c) In the event of the appointment of a substitute arbitrator, the panel of arbitrators shall determine in its sole discretion whether it is necessary to repeat all or part of any prior hearings.

R-20. Preliminary Hearing

(a) At the request of any party or at the discretion of the arbitrator or the AAA, the arbitrator may schedule as soon as practicable a preliminary hearing with the parties and/or their representatives. The preliminary hearing may be conducted by telephone at the arbitrator's discretion.

(b) During the preliminary hearing, the parties and the arbitrator should discuss the future conduct of the case, including clarification of the issues and claims, a schedule for the hearings and any other preliminary matters.

R-21. Exchange of Information

(a) At the request of any party or at the discretion of the arbitrator, consistent with the expedited nature of arbitration, the arbitrator may direct

i) the production of documents and other information, and

ii) the identification of any witnesses to be called.

(b) At least five business days prior to the hearing, the parties shall exchange copies of all exhibits they intend to submit at the hearing.

(c) The arbitrator is authorized to resolve any disputes concerning the exchange of information.

R-22. Date, Time, and Place of Hearing

The arbitrator shall set the date, time, and place for each hearing. The parties shall respond to requests for hearing dates in a timely manner, be cooperative in scheduling the earliest practicable date, and adhere to the established hearing schedule. The AAA shall send a notice of hearing to the parties at least 10 days in advance of the hearing date, unless otherwise agreed by the parties.

R-23. Attendance at Hearings

The arbitrator and the AAA shall maintain the privacy of the hearings unless the law provides to the contrary. Any person having a direct interest in the arbitration is entitled to attend hearings. The arbitrator shall otherwise have the power to require the exclusion of any witness, other than a party or other essential person, during the testimony of any other witness. It shall be discretionary with the arbitrator to determine the propriety of the attendance of any other person other than a party and its representatives.

R-24. Representation

Any party may be represented by counsel or other authorized representative. A party intending to be so represented shall notify the other party and the AAA of the name and address of the representative at least three days prior to the date set for the hearing at which that person is first to appear. When such a representative initiates an arbitration or responds for a party, notice is deemed to have been given.

R-25. Oaths

Before proceeding with the first hearing, each arbitrator may take an oath of office and, if required by law, shall do so. The arbitrator may require witnesses to testify under oath administered by any duly qualified person and, if it is required by law or requested by any party, shall do so.

R-26. Stenographic Record

Any party desiring a stenographic record shall make arrangements directly with a stenographer and shall notify the other parties of these arrangements at least three days in advance of the hearing. The requesting party or parties shall pay the cost of the record. If the transcript is agreed by the parties, or determined by the arbitrator to be the official record of the proceeding, it must be provided to the arbitrator and made available to the other parties for inspection, at a date, time, and place determined by the arbitrator.

R-27. Interpreters

Any party wishing an interpreter shall make all arrangements directly with the interpreter and shall assume the costs of the service.

R-28. Postponements

The arbitrator may postpone any hearing upon agreement of the parties, upon request of a party for good cause shown, or upon the arbitrator's own initiative.

R-29. Arbitration in the Absence of a Party or Representative

Unless the law provides to the contrary, the arbitration may proceed in the absence of any party or representative who, after due notice, fails to be present or fails to obtain a postponement. An award shall not be made solely on the default of a party. The arbitrator shall require the party who is present to submit such evidence as the arbitrator may require for the making of an award.

R-30. Conduct of Proceedings

(a) The claimant shall present evidence to support its claim. The respondent shall then present evidence to support its defense. Witnesses for each party shall also submit to questions from the arbitrator and the adverse party. The arbitrator has the discretion to vary this procedure, provided that the parties are treated with equality and that each party has the right to be heard and is given a fair opportunity to present its case.

(b) The arbitrator, exercising his or her discretion, shall conduct the proceedings with a view to expediting the resolution of the dispute and may direct the order of proof, bifurcate proceedings and direct the parties to focus their presentations on issues the decision of which could dispose of all or part of the case.

(c) The parties may agree to waive oral hearings in any case.

R-31. Evidence

(a) The parties may offer such evidence as is relevant and material to the dispute and shall produce such evidence as the arbitrator may deem necessary to an understanding and determination of the dispute. Conformity to legal rules of evidence shall not be necessary. All evidence shall be taken in the presence of all of the arbitrators and all of the parties, except where any of the parties is absent, in default or has waived the right to be present.

(b) The arbitrator shall determine the admissibility, relevance, and materiality of the evidence offered and may exclude evidence deemed by the arbitrator to be cumulative or irrelevant.

(c) The arbitrator shall take into account applicable principles of legal privilege, such as those involving the confidentiality of communications between a lawyer and client.

(d) An arbitrator or other person authorized by law to subpoena witnesses or documents may do so upon the request of any party or independently.

R-32. Evidence by Affidavit and Post-hearing Filing of Documents or Other Evidence

(a) The arbitrator may receive and consider the evidence of witnesses by declaration or affidavit, but shall give it only such weight as the arbitrator deems it entitled to after consideration of any objection made to its admission.

(b) If the parties agree or the arbitrator directs that documents or other evidence be submitted to the arbitrator after the hearing, the documents or other evidence shall be filed with the AAA for transmission to the arbitrator. All parties shall be afforded an opportunity to examine and respond to such documents or other evidence.

R-33. Inspection or Investigation

An arbitrator finding it necessary to make an inspection or investigation in connection with the arbitration shall direct the AAA to so advise the parties. The arbitrator shall set the date and time and the AAA shall notify the parties. Any party who so desires may be present at such an inspection or investigation. In the event that one or all parties are not present at the inspection or investigation, the arbitrator shall make an oral or written report to the parties and afford them an opportunity to comment.

R-34. Interim Measures

(a) The arbitrator may take whatever interim measures he or she deems necessary, including injunctive relief and measures for the protection or conservation of property and disposition of perishable goods.

(b) Such interim measures may take the form of an interim award, and the arbitrator may require security for the costs of such measures.

(c) A request for interim measures addressed by a party to a judicial authority shall not be deemed incompatible with the agreement to arbitrate or a waiver of the right to arbitrate.

R-35. Closing of Hearing

The arbitrator shall specifically inquire of all parties whether they have any further proofs to offer or witnesses to be heard. Upon receiving negative replies or if satisfied that the record is complete, the arbitrator shall declare the hearing closed. If briefs are to be filed, the hearing shall b e declared closed as of the final date set by the arbitrator for the receipt of briefs. If documents are to be filed as provided in Section R-32 and the date set for their receipt is later than that set for the receipt of briefs, the later date shall be the closing date of the hearing. The time limit within which the arbitrator is required to make the award shall commence, in the absence of other agreements by the parties, upon the closing of the hearing.

R-36. Reopening of Hearing

The hearing may be reopened on the arbitrator's initiative, or upon application of a party, at any time before the award is made. If reopening the hearing would prevent the making of the award within the specific time agreed on by the parties in the contract(s) out of which the controversy has arisen, the matter may not be reopened unless the parties agree on an extension of time. When no specific date is fixed in the contract, the arbitrator may reopen the hearing and shall have 30 days from the closing of the reopened hearing within which to make an award.

R-37. Waiver of Rules

Any party who proceeds with the arbitration after knowledge that any provision or requirement of these rules has not been complied with and who fails to state an objection in writing shall be deemed to have waived the right to object.

R-38. Extensions of Time

The parties may modify any period of time by mutual agreement. The AAA or the arbitrator may for good cause extend any period of time established by these rules, except the time for making the award. The AAA shall notify the parties of any extension.

R-39. Serving of Notice

(a) Any papers, notices, or process necessary or proper for the initiation or continuation of an arbitration under these rules, for any court action in connection therewith, or for the entry of judgment on any award made under these rules may be served on a party by mail addressed to the party, or its representative at the last known address or by personal service, in or outside the state where the arbitration is to be held, provided that reasonable opportunity to be heard with regard to the dispute is or has been granted to the party.

(b) The AAA, the arbitrator and the parties may also use overnight delivery or electronic facsimile transmission (fax), to give the notices required by these rules. Where all parties and the arbitrator agree, notices may be transmitted by electronic mail (E-mail), or other methods of communication.

(c) Unless otherwise instructed by the AAA or by the arbitrator, any documents submitted by any party to the AAA or to the arbitrator shall simultaneously be provided to the other party or parties to the arbitration.

R-40. Majority Decision

When the panel consists of more than one arbitrator, unless required by law or by the arbitration agreement, a majority of the arbitrators must make all decisions.

R-41. Time of Award

The award shall be made promptly by the arbitrator and, unless otherwise agreed by the parties or specified by law, no later than 30 days from the date of closing the hearing, or, if oral hearings have been waived, from the date of the AAA's transmittal of the final statements and proofs to the arbitrator.

R-42. Form of Award

(a) Any award shall be in writing and signed by a majority of the arbitrators. It shall be executed in the manner required by law.

(b) The arbitrator need not render a reasoned award unless the parties request such an award in writing prior to appointment of the arbitrator or unless the arbitrator determines that a reasoned award is appropriate.

R-43. Scope of Award

(a) The arbitrator may grant any remedy or relief that the arbitrator deems just and equitable and within the scope of the agreement of the parties, including, but not limited to, specific performance of a contract.

(b) In addition to a final award, the arbitrator may make other decisions, including interim, interlocutory, or partial rulings, orders, and awards. In any interim, interlocutory, or partial award, the arbitrator may assess and apportion the fees, expenses, and compensation related to such award as the arbitrator determines is appropriate.

(c) In the final award, the arbitrator shall assess the fees, expenses, and compensation provided in Sections R-49, R-50, and R-51. The arbitrator may apportion such fees, expenses, and compensation among the parties in such amounts as the arbitrator determines is appropriate.

(d) The award of the arbitrator(s) may include:

(i) interest at such rate and from such date as the arbitrator(s) may deem appropriate; and

(ii) an award of attorneys' fees if all parties have requested such an award or it is authorized by law or their arbitration agreement.

R-44. Award upon Settlement

If the parties settle their dispute during the course of the arbitration and if the parties so request, the arbitrator may set forth the terms of the settlement in a "consent award." A consent award must include an allocation of arbitration costs, including administrative fees and expenses as well as arbitrator fees and expenses.

R-45. Delivery of Award to Parties

Parties shall accept as notice and delivery of the award the placing of the award or a true copy thereof in the mail addressed to the parties or their representatives at the last known addresses, personal or electronic service of the award, or the filing of the award in any other manner that is permitted by law.

R-46. Modification of Award

Within 20 days after the transmittal of an award, any party, upon notice to the other parties, may request the arbitrator, through the AAA, to correct any clerical, typographical, or computational errors in the award. The arbitrator is not empowered to redetermine the merits of any claim already decided. The other parties shall be given 10 days to respond to the request. The arbitrator shall dispose of the request within 20 days after transmittal by the AAA to the arbitrator of the request and any response thereto.

R-47. Release of Documents for Judicial Proceedings

The AAA shall, upon the written request of a party, furnish to the party, at the party's expense, certified copies of any papers in the AAA's possession that may be required in judicial proceedings relating to the arbitration.

R-48. Applications to Court and Exclusion of Liability

(a) No judicial proceeding by a party relating to the subject matter of the arbitration shall be deemed a waiver of the party's right to arbitrate.

(b) Neither the AAA nor any arbitrator in a proceeding under these rules is a necessary or proper party in judicial proceedings relating to the arbitration.

(c) Parties to an arbitration under these rules shall be deemed to have consented that judgment upon the arbitration award may be entered in any federal or state court having jurisdiction thereof.

(d) Parties to an arbitration under these rules shall be deemed to have consented that neither the AAA nor any arbitrator shall be liable to any party in any action for damages or injunctive relief for any act or omission in connection with any arbitration under these rules.

R-49. Administrative Fees

As a not-for-profit organization, the AAA shall prescribe an initial filing fee and a case service fee to compensate it for the cost of providing administrative services. The fees in effect when the fee or charge is incurred shall be applicable. The filing fee shall be advanced by the party or parties making a claim or counterclaim, subject to final apportionment by the arbitrator in the award. The AAA may, in the event of extreme hardship on the part of any party, defer or reduce the administrative fees.

R-50. Expenses

The expenses of witnesses for either side shall be paid by the party producing such witnesses. All other expenses of the arbitration, including required travel and other expenses of the arbitrator, AAA representatives, and any witness and the cost of any proof produced at the direct request of the arbitrator, shall be borne equally by the parties, unless they agree otherwise or unless the arbitrator in the award assesses such expenses or any part thereof against any specified party or parties.

R-51. Neutral Arbitrator's Compensation

(a) Arbitrators shall be compensated at a rate consistent with the arbitrator's stated rate of compensation.

(b) If there is disagreement concerning the terms of compensation, an appropriate rate shall be established with the arbitrator by the AAA and confirmed to the parties.

(c) Any arrangement for the compensation of a neutral arbitrator shall be made through the AAA and not directly between the parties and the arbitrator.

R-52. Deposits

The AAA may require the parties to deposit in advance of any hearings such sums of money as it deems necessary to cover the expense of the arbitration, including the arbitrator's fee, if any, and shall render an accounting to the parties and return any unexpended balance at the conclusion of the case.

R-53. Interpretation and Application of Rules

The arbitrator shall interpret and apply these rules insofar as they relate to the arbitrator's powers and duties. When there is more than one arbitrator and a difference arises among them concerning the meaning or application of these rules, it shall be decided by a majority vote. If that is not possible, either an arbitrator or a party may refer the question to the AAA for final decision. All other rules shall be interpreted and applied by the AAA.

R-54. Suspension for Nonpayment

If arbitrator compensation or administrative charges have not been paid in full, the AAA may so inform the parties in order that one of them may advance the required payment. If such payments are not made, the arbitrator may order the suspension or termination of the proceedings. If no arbitrator has yet been appointed, the AAA may suspend the proceedings.

EXPEDITED PROCEDURES

E-1. Limitation on Extensions

Except in extraordinary circumstances, the AAA or the arbitrator may grant a party no more than one seven-day extension of time to respond to the demand for arbitration or counterclaim as provided in Section R-4.

E-2. Changes of Claim or Counterclaim

A claim or counterclaim may be increased in amount, or a new or different claim or counterclaim added, upon the agreement of the other party, or the consent of the arbitrator. After the arbitrator is appointed, however, no new or different claim or counterclaim may be submitted except with the arbitrator's consent. If an increased claim or counterclaim exceeds $75,000, the case will be administered under the regular procedures unless all parties and the arbitrator agree that the case may continue to be processed under the Expedited Procedures.

E-3. Serving of Notices

In addition to notice provided by Section R-39(b), the parties shall also accept notice by telephone. Telephonic notices by the AAA shall subsequently be confirmed in writing to the parties. Should there be a failure to confirm in writing any such oral notice, the proceeding shall nevertheless be valid if notice has, in fact, been given by telephone.

E-4. Appointment and Qualifications of Arbitrator

(a) The AAA shall simultaneously submit to each party an identical list of five proposed arbitrators drawn from its National Roster from which one arbitrator shall be appointed.

(b) The parties are encouraged to agree to an arbitrator from this list and to advise the AAA of their agreement. If the parties are unable to agree upon an arbitrator, each party may strike two names from the list and return it to the AAA within seven days from the date of the AAA's mailing to the parties. If for any reason the appointment of an arbitrator cannot be made from the list, the AAA may make the appointment from other members of the panel without the submission of additional lists.

(c) The parties will be given notice by the AAA of the appointment of the arbitrator, who shall be subject to disqualification for the reasons specified in Section R-17. The parties shall notify the AAA within seven days of any objection to the arbitrator appointed. Any such objection shall be for cause and shall be confirmed in writing to the AAA with a copy to the other party or parties.

E-5. Exchange of Exhibits

At least two business days prior to the hearing, the parties shall exchange copies of all exhibits they intend to submit at the hearing. The arbitrator shall resolve disputes concerning the exchange of exhibits.

E-6. Proceedings on Documents

Where no party's claim exceeds $10,000, exclusive of interest and arbitration costs, and other cases in which the parties agree, the dispute shall be resolved by submission of documents, unless any party requests an oral hearing, or the arbitrator determines that an oral hearing is necessary. The arbitrator shall establish a fair and equitable procedure for the submission of documents.

E-7. Date, Time, and Place of Hearing

In cases in which a hearing is to be held, the arbitrator shall set the date, time, and place of the hearing, to be scheduled to take place within 30 days of confirmation of the arbitrator's appointment. The AAA will notify the parties in advance of the hearing date.

E-8. The Hearing

(a) Generally, the hearing shall not exceed one day. Each party shall have equal opportunity to submit its proofs and complete its case. The arbitrator shall determine the order of the hearing, and may require further submission of documents within two days after the hearing. For good cause shown, the arbitrator may schedule additional hearings within seven business days after the initial day of hearings.

(b) Generally, there will be no stenographic record. Any party desiring a stenographic record may arrange for one pursuant to the provisions of Section R-26.

E-9. Time of Award

Unless otherwise agreed by the parties, the award shall be rendered not later than 14 days from the date of the closing of the hearing or, if oral hearings have been waived, from the date of the AAA's transmittal of the final statements and proofs to the arbitrator.

E-10. Arbitrator's Compensation

Arbitrators will receive compensation at a rate to be suggested by the AAA regional office.

PROCEDURES FOR LARGE, COMPLEX COMMERCIAL DISPUTES

L-1. Administrative Conference

Prior to the dissemination of a list of potential arbitrators, the AAA shall, unless the parties agree otherwise, conduct an administrative conference with the parties and/or their attorneys or other representatives by conference call. The conference will take place within 14 days after the commencement of the arbitration. In the event the parties are unable to agree on a mutually acceptable time for the conference, the AAA may contact the parties individually to discuss the issues contemplated herein. Such administrative conference shall be conducted for the following purposes and for such additional purposes as the parties or the AAA may deem appropriate:

(a) to obtain additional information about the nature and magnitude of the dispute and the anticipated length of hearing and scheduling;

(b) to discuss the views of the parties about the technical and other qualifications of the arbitrators;

(c) to obtain conflicts statements from the parties; and

(d) to consider, with the parties, whether mediation or other non-adjudicative methods of dispute resolution might be appropriate.

L-2. Arbitrators

(a) Large, Complex Commercial Cases shall be heard and determined by either one or three arbitrators, as may be agreed upon by the parties. If the parties are unable to agree upon the number of arbitrators and a claim or counterclaim involves at least $1,000,000, then three arbitrator(s) shall hear and determine the case. If the parties are unable to agree on the number of arbitrators and each claim and counterclaim is less than $1,000,000, then one arbitrator shall hear and determine the case.

(b) The AAA shall appoint arbitrator(s) as agreed by the parties. If they are unable to agree on a method of appointment, the AAA shall appoint arbitrators from the Large, Complex Commercial Case Panel, in the manner provided in the Regular Commercial Arbitration Rules. Absent agreement of the parties, the arbitrator(s) shall not have served as the mediator in the mediation phase of the instant proceeding.

L-3. Preliminary Hearing

As promptly as practicable after the selection of the arbitrator(s), a preliminary hearing shall be held among the parties and/or their attorneys or other representatives and the arbitrator(s). Unless the parties agree otherwise, the preliminary hearing will be conducted by telephone conference call rather than in person. At the preliminary hearing the matters to be considered shall include, without limitation:

(a) service of a detailed statement of claims, damages and defenses, a statement of the issues asserted by each party and positions with respect thereto, and any legal authorities the parties may wish to bring to the attention of the arbitrator(s);

(b) stipulations to uncontested facts;

(c) the extent to which discovery shall be conducted;

(d) exchange and premarking of those documents which each party believes may be offered at the hearing;

(e) the identification and availability of witnesses, including experts, and such matters with respect to witnesses including their biographies and expected testimony as may be appropriate;

(f) whether, and the extent to which, any sworn statements and/or depositions may be introduced;

(g) the extent to which hearings will proceed on consecutive days;

(h) whether a stenographic or other official record of the proceedings shall be maintained;

(i) the possibility of utilizing mediation or other non-adjudicative methods of dispute resolution; and

(j) the procedure for the issuance of subpoenas.

By agreement of the parties and/or order of the arbitrator(s), the pre-hearing activities and the hearing procedures that will govern the arbitration will be memorialized in a Scheduling and Procedure Order.

L-4. Management of Proceedings

(a) Arbitrator(s) shall take such steps as they may deem necessary or desirable to avoid delay and to achieve a just, speedy and cost-effective resolution of Large, Complex Commercial Cases.

(b) Parties shall cooperate in the exchange of documents, exhibits and information within such party's control if the arbitrator(s) consider such production to be consistent with the goal of achieving a just, speedy and cost-effective resolution of a Large, Complex Commercial Case.

(c) The parties may conduct such discovery as may be agreed to by all the parties provided, however, that the arbitrator(s) may place such limitations on the conduct of such discovery as the arbitrator(s) shall deem appropriate. If the parties cannot agree on production of documents and other information, the arbitrator(s), consistent with the expedited nature of arbitration, may establish the extent of the discovery.

(d) At the discretion of the arbitrator(s), upon good cause shown and consistent with the expedited nature of arbitration, the arbitrator(s) may order depositions of, or the propounding of interrogatories to, such persons who may possess information determined by the arbitrator(s) to be necessary to determination of the matter.

(e) The parties shall exchange copies of all exhibits they intend to submit at the hearing 10 business days prior to the hearing unless the arbitrator(s) determine otherwise.

(f) The exchange of information pursuant to this rule, as agreed by the parties and/or directed by the arbitrator(s), shall be included within the Scheduling and Procedure Order.

(g) The arbitrator is authorized to resolve any disputes concerning the exchange of information.

(h) Generally hearings will be scheduled on consecutive days or in blocks of consecutive days in order to maximize efficiency and minimize costs.

OPTIONAL RULES FOR EMERGENCY MEASURES OF PROTECTION

O-1. Applicability

Where parties by special agreement or in their arbitration clause have adopted these rules for emergency measures of protection, a party in need of emergency relief prior to the constitution of the panel shall notify the AAA and all other parties in writing of the nature of the relief sought and the reasons why such relief is required on an emergency basis. The application shall also set forth the reasons why the party is entitled to such relief. Such notice may be given by facsimile transmission, or other reliable means, but must include a statement certifying that all other parties have been notified or an explanation of the steps taken in good faith to notify other parties.

O-2. Appointment of Emergency Arbitrator

Within one business day of receipt of notice as provided in Section O-1, the AAA shall appoint a single emergency arbitrator from a special AAA panel of emergency arbitrators designated to rule on emergency applications. The emergency arbitrator shall immediately disclose any circumstance likely, on the basis of the facts disclosed in the application, to affect such arbitrator's impartiality or independence. Any challenge to the appointment of the emergency arbitrator must be made within one business day of the communication by the AAA to the parties of the appointment of the emergency arbitrator and the circumstances disclosed.

O-3. Schedule

The emergency arbitrator shall as soon as possible, but in any event within two business days of appointment, establish a schedule for consideration of the application for emergency relief. Such schedule shall provide a reasonable opportunity to all parties to be heard, but may provide for proceeding by telephone conference or on written submissions as alternatives to a formal hearing.

O-4. Interim Award

If after consideration the emergency arbitrator is satisfied that the party seeking the emergency relief has shown that immediate and irreparable loss or damage will result in the absence of emergency relief, and that such party is entitled to such relief, the emergency arbitrator may enter an interim award granting the relief and stating the reasons therefore.

O-5. Constitution of the Panel

Any application to modify an interim award of emergency relief must be based on changed circumstances and may be made to the emergency arbitrator until the panel is constituted; thereafter such a request shall be addressed to the panel. The emergency arbitrator shall have no further power to act after the panel is constituted unless the parties agree that the emergency arbitrator is named as a member of the panel.

O-6. Security

Any interim award of emergency relief may be conditioned on provision by the party seeking such relief of appropriate security.

O-7. Special Master

A request for interim measures addressed by a party to a judicial authority shall not be deemed incompatible with the agreement to arbitrate or a waiver of the right to arbitrate. If the AAA is directed by a judicial authority to nominate a special master to consider and report on an application for emergency relief, the AAA shall proceed as provided in Section O-1 of this article and the references to the emergency arbitrator shall be read to mean the special master, except that the special master shall issue a report rather than an interim award.

O-8. Costs

The costs associated with applications for emergency relief shall initially be apportioned by the emergency arbitrator or special master, subject to the power of the panel to determine finally the apportionment of such costs.

ADMINISTRATIVE FEES

The administrative fees of the AAA are based on the amount of the claim or counterclaim. Arbitrator compensation is not included in this schedule. Unless the parties agree otherwise, arbitrator compensation and administrative fees are subject to allocation by the arbitrator in the award.

In an effort to make arbitration costs reasonable for consumers, the AAA has a separate fee schedule for consumer-related disputes. Please refer to Section C-8 of the *Supplementary Procedures for Consumer-Related Disputes* when filing a consumer-related claim.

The AAA applies the *Supplementary Procedures for Consumer-Related Disputes* to arbitration clauses in agreements between individual consumers and businesses where the business has a standardized, systematic application of arbitration clauses with customers and where the terms and conditions of the purchase of standardized, consumable goods or services are non-negotiable or primarily non-negotiable in most or all of its terms, conditions, features, or choices. The product or service must be for personal or household use. The AAA will have the discretion to apply or not to apply the Supplementary Procedures and the parties will be able to bring any disputes concerning the application or non-application to the attention of the arbitrator. Consumers are not prohibited from seeking relief in a small claims court for disputes or claims within the scope of its jurisdiction, even in consumer arbitration cases filed by the business.

Pilot Flexible Fee Schedule

Recognizing the continued fragility of the business environment and wishing to provide cost-saving alternatives to parties filing an arbitration case, the American Arbitration Association is offering an optional fee payment schedule that parties may choose instead of the Standard Fee Schedule. It is a pilot that will be available on cases filed through May 30, 2010 (1) , and is intended to give parties added flexibility in both filing and in selection of arbitrators. Please call 1-800-778-7879 or your nearest office if you have questions.

A non-refundable Initial Filing Fee is payable in full by a filing party when a claim, counterclaim, or additional claim is filed. Upon receipt of the Demand for Arbitration, the AAA will promptly initiate the case and notify all parties as well as establish the due date for filing of an Answer, which may include a Counterclaim. In order to proceed with the further administration of the arbitration and appointment of the arbitrator(s), the appropriate, non-refundable Proceed Fee outlined below must be paid. If a Proceed Fee is not submitted within ninety (90) days of the filing of the Claimant's Demand for Arbitration, the Association will administratively close the file and notify all parties. *No refunds or refund schedule will apply to the Filing or Proceed Fees once received.*

Savings for Mutual Arbitrator Appointment by Parties : Proceed Fees may be reduced by fift y (50) percent where parties mutually select and appoint their arbitrator(s) without the AAA providing a list of arbitrators and an appointment process. Parties must provide the Case Manager with the appropriate stipulations and information pertaining to arbitrator(s) that have been mutually selected and have accepted their appointment(s). Forms for confirmation of arbitrators mutually selected and appointed by the parties are available through the Case Manager or AAA regional office.

The Flexible Fee Schedule below also may be utilized for the filing of counterclaims. However, as with the Claimant's claim, the counterclaim will not be presented to the arbitrator until the Proceed Fee is paid.

A Final Fee will be incurred for all claims and/or counterclaims that proceed to their first hearing. This fee will be payable in advance when the first hearing is scheduled, but will be refunded at the conclusion of the case if no hearings have occurred. However, if the Association is not notified of a cancellation at least 24 hours before the time of the scheduled hearing, the Final Fee will remain due and will not be refunded.

All fees for the Pilot Flexible Fee Schedule, effective June 1, 2009 to May 30, 2010, will be billed in accordance with the schedule below:

Amount of Claim	Initial Filing Fee	Proceed Fee	Final Fee
Above $0 to $10,000	$300	$550*	$200
Above $10,000 to $75,000	$500	$600*	$300
Above $75,000 to $150,000	$500	$1,500*	$750
Above $150,000 to $300,000	$500	$2,525*	$1,250
Above $300,000 to $500,000	$1,000	$3,750*	$1,750
Above $500,000 to $1,000,000	$1,000	$5,600*	$2,500
Above $1,000,000 to $5,000,000	$1,000	$7,800*	$3,250
Above $5,000,000 to $10,000,000	$2,000	$9,000*	$4,000
Above $10,000,000	$2,500	$11,500* plus .01% of claim amount over $10,000,000 up to $65,000	$6,000
Nonmonetary**	$1,000	$2,750*	$1,250
Consent Award***			

(1) The Pilot Flexible Fee Schedule is subject to change or cancellation at any time prior to the date of May 30, 2010.

*Where an arbitrator has been pre-selected and appointed by the parties, the Proceed Fee will be reduced by fifty percent (50%).

**This fee is applicable only when a claim or counterclaim is not for a monetary amount. Where a monetary claim amount is not known, parties will be required to state a range of claims or be subject to the highest possible filing fee (see fee range for claims above $10,000,000.00).

***The AAA may assist the parties with the appointment of an arbitrator for the sole purpose of having their Consent Award signed. For more information, please contact your local AAA office, case management center, or our Customer Service desk at 1-800-778-7879.

All fees are subject to increase if the amount of a claim or counterclaim is modified after the initial filing date. Fees are subject to decrease if the amount of a claim or counterclaim is modified before the first hearing.

The minimum fees for any case having three or more arbitrators are $1,000 for the Initial Filing Fee; $3,750 for the Proceed Fee; and $1,750 for the Final Fee.

Under the Flexible Fee Schedule, a party's obligation to pay the Proceed Fee shall remain in effect regardless of any agreement of the parties to stay, postpone or otherwise modify the arbitration proceedings. Parties that, through mutual agreement, have held their case in abeyance for one year will be assessed an annual abeyance fee of $300. If a party refuses to pay the assessed fee, the other party or parties may pay the entire fee on behalf of all parties, otherwise the matter will be closed.

Note: The date of receipt by the AAA of the demand/notice for arbitration will be used to calculate the ninety(90)-day time limit for payment of the Proceed Fee.

Standard Fee Schedule

An Initial Filing Fee is payable in full by a filing party when a claim, counterclaim, or additional claim is filed. A Case Service Fee will be incurred for all cases that proceed to their first hearing. This fee will be payable in advance at the time that the first hearing is scheduled. This fee will be refunded at the conclusion of the case if no hearings have occurred. However, if the Association is not notified at least 24 hours before the time of the scheduled hearing, the Case Service Fee will remain due and will not be refunded.

All fees for the Standard Fee Schedule, effective January 1, 2010, will be billed in accordance with the schedules below:

Amount of Claim	Initial Filing Fee	Case Service Fee
Above $0 to $10,000	$775	$200
Above $10,000 to $75,000	$975	$300
Above $75,000 to $150,000	$1,850	$750
Above $150,000 to $300,000	$2,800	$1,250
Above $300,000 to $500,000	$4,350	$1,750
Above $500,000 to $1,000,000	$6,200	$2,500
Above $1,000,000 to $5,000,000	$8,200	$3,250
Above $5,000,000 to $10,000,000	$10,200	$4,000
Above $10,000,000	*	*
Nonmonetary Claims**	$3,350	$1,250

** For information regarding the fee schedule for claims in excess of $10 million, see below.*
*** This fee is applicable when a claim or counterclaim is not for a monetary amount. Where a monetary claim amount is not known, parties will be required to state a range of claims or be subject to a filing fee of $10,200.*

Standard Fee Schedule for Claims in Excess of $10 Million

The following is the Standard Fee Schedule for use in disputes involving claims in excess of $10 million. If you have any questions, please consult your local AAA office or case management center.

Claim Size	Fee	Case Service Fee
$10 million and above	Base fee of $12,800 plus .01% of the	$6,000

	amount of claim above $10 million	
	Filing fees capped at $65,000	

Fees are subject to increase if the amount of a claim or counterclaim is modified after the initial filing date. Fees are subject to decrease if the amount of a claim or counterclaim is modified before the first hearing.

The minimum fees for any case having three or more arbitrators are $2,800 for the filing fee, plus a $1,250 Case Service Fee. Expedited Procedures are applied in any case where no disclosed claim or counterclaim exceeds $75,000, exclusive of interest and arbitration costs.

Parties on cases filed under the Standard Fee Schedule that are held in abeyance for one year will be assessed an annual abeyance fee of $300. If a party refuses to pay the assessed fee, the other party or parties may pay the entire fee on behalf of all parties, otherwise the matter will be administratively closed.

Refund Schedule

The AAA offers a refund schedule on filing fees connected with the Standard Fee Schedule. For cases with claims up to $75,000, a minimum filing fee of $350 will not be refunded. For all other cases, a minimum fee of $600 will not be refunded. Subject to the minimum fee requirements, refunds will be calculated as follows:

- 100% of the filing fee, above the minimum fee, will be refunded if the case is settled or withdrawn within five calendar days of filing.
- > 50% of the filing fee will be refunded if the case is settled or withdrawn between six and 30 calendar days of filing.
- > 25% of the filing fee will be refunded if the case is settled or withdrawn between 31 and 60 calendar days of filing.
- No refund will be made once an arbitrator has been appointed (this includes one arbitrator on a three-arbitrator panel). No refunds will be granted on awarded cases.

Note: The date of receipt of the demand for arbitration with the AAA will be used to calculate refunds of filing fees for both claims and counterclaims.

Hearing Room Rental

The fees described above do not cover the cost of hearing rooms, which are available on a rental basis. Check with the AAA for availability and rates.

Appendix 5:

THE CODE OF ETHICS FOR ARBITRATORS IN COMMERCIAL DISPUTES

Approved by the American Bar Association House of Delegates on February 9, 2004
Approved by the Executive Committee of the Board of Directors of the AAA
The Code of Ethics for Arbitrators in Commercial Disputes was originally prepared in 1977 by a joint committee consisting of a special committee of the American Arbitration Association and a special committee of the American Bar Association. The Code was revised in 2003 by an ABA Task Force and special committee of the AAA. Both the original 1977 Code and the 2003Revision have been approved and recommended by both organizations.

Preamble

The use of arbitration to resolve a wide variety of disputes has grown extensively and forms a significant part of the system of justice on which our society relies for a fair determination of legal rights. Persons who act as arbitrators therefore undertake serious responsibilities to the public, as well as to the parties. Those responsibilities include important ethical obligations. Few cases of unethical behavior by commercial arbitrators have arisen. Nevertheless, this Code sets forth generally accepted standards of ethical conduct for the guidance of arbitrators and parties in commercial disputes, in the hope of contributing to the maintenance of high standards and continued confidence in the process of arbitration. This Code provides ethical guidelines for many types of arbitration but does not apply to labor arbitration, which is generally conducted under the Code of Professional Responsibility for Arbitrators of Labor-Management Disputes.

There are many different types of commercial arbitration. Some proceedings are conducted under arbitration rules established by various organizations and trade associations, while others are conducted without such rules. Although most proceedings are arbitrated pursuant to voluntary agreement of the parties, certain types of disputes are submitted to arbitration by reason of particular laws. This Code is intended to apply to all such proceedings in which disputes or claims are submitted for decision to one or more arbitrators appointed in a manner provided by an agreement of the parties, by applicable arbitration rules, or by law. In all such cases, the persons who have the power to decide should observe fundamental standards of ethical conduct. In this Code, all such persons are called "arbitrators," although in some types of proceeding they might be called "umpires," "referees," "neutrals," or have some other title.

Arbitrators, like judges, have the power to decide cases. However, unlike full-time judges, arbitrators are usually engaged in other occupations before, during, and after the time that they serve as arbitrators. Often, arbitrators are purposely chosen from the same trade or industry as the parties in order to bring special knowledge to the task of deciding. This Code recognizes these fundamental differences between arbitrators and judges. In those instances where this Code has been approved and recommended by organizations that provide, coordinate, or administer services of arbitrators, it provides ethical standards for the members of their respective panels of arbitrators. However, this Code does not form a part of the arbitration rules of any such organization unless its rules so provide.

Note on Neutrality

In some types of commercial arbitration, the parties or the administering institution provide for three or more arbitrators. In some such proceedings, it is the practice for each party, acting alone, to appoint one arbitrator (a "party-appointed arbitrator") and for one additional arbitrator to be designated by the party-appointed arbitrators, or by the parties, or by an independent institution or individual. The sponsors of this Code believe that it is preferable for all arbitrators – including any party-appointed arbitrators – to be neutral, that is, independent and impartial, and to comply with the same ethical standards. This expectation generally is essential in arbitrations where the parties, the nature of the dispute, or the enforcement of any resulting award may have international aspects. However, parties in certain domestic arbitrations in the United States may prefer that party-appointed arbitrators be non-neutral and governed by special ethical considerations. These special ethical considerations appear in Canon X of this Code. This Code establishes a presumption of neutrality for all arbitrators, including partyappointed arbitrators, which applies unless the parties' agreement, the arbitration rules agreed to by the parties or applicable laws provide otherwise. This Code requires all party-appointed arbitrators, whether neutral or not, to make pre-appointment disclosures of any facts which might affect their neutrality, independence, or impartiality. This Code also requires all party-appointed arbitrators to ascertain and disclose as soon as practicable whether the parties intended for them to serve as neutral or not. If any doubt or uncertainty exists, the party-appointed arbitrators should serve as neutrals unless and until such doubt or uncertainty is resolved in accordance with Canon IX. This Code expects all arbitrators, including those serving under Canon X, to preserve the integrity and fairness of the process.

Note on Construction

Various aspects of the conduct of arbitrators, including some matters covered by this Code, may also be governed by agreements of the parties, arbitration rules to which the parties have agreed, applicable law, or other applicable ethics rules, all of which should be consulted by the arbitrators. This Code does not take the place of or supersede such laws, agreements, or arbitration rules to which the parties have agreed and should be read in conjunction with other rules of ethics. It does not establish new or additional grounds for judicial review of arbitration awards.

All provisions of this Code should therefore be read as subject to contrary provisions of applicable law and arbitration rules. They should also be read as subject to contrary agreements of the parties. Nevertheless, this Code imposes no obligation on any arbitrator to act in a manner inconsistent with the arbitrator's fundamental duty to preserve the integrity and fairness of the arbitral process. Canons I through VIII of this Code apply to all arbitrators. Canon IX applies to all party-appointed arbitrators, except that certain party-appointed arbitrators are exempted by Canon X from compliance with certain provisions of Canons I-IX related to impartiality and independence, as specified in Canon X.

CANON I. AN ARBITRATOR SHOULD UPHOLD THE INTEGRITY AND FAIRNESS OF THE ARBITRATION PROCESS.

A. An arbitrator has a responsibility not only to the parties but also to the process of arbitration itself, and must observe high standards of conduct so that the integrity and fairness of the process will be preserved. Accordingly, an arbitrator should recognize a responsibility to the public, to the parties whose rights will be decided, and to all other participants in the proceeding. This responsibility may include pro bono service as an arbitrator where appropriate.

B. One should accept appointment as an arbitrator only if fully satisfied:

(1) that he or she can serve impartially;

(2) that he or she can serve independently from the parties, potential witnesses,

and the other arbitrators;

(3) that he or she is competent to serve; and

(4) that he or she can be available to commence the arbitration in accordance with the requirements of the proceeding and thereafter to devote the time and attention to its completion that the parties are reasonably entitled to expect.

C. After accepting appointment and while serving as an arbitrator, a person shouldavoid entering into any business, professional, or personal relationship, or acquiring any financial or personal interest, which is likely to affect impartiality or which might reasonably create the appearance of partiality. For a reasonable period of time after the decision of a case, persons who have served as arbitrators should avoid entering into any such relationship, or acquiring any such interest, in circumstances which might reasonably create the appearance that they had been influenced in the arbitration by the anticipation or expectation of the relationship or interest. Existence of any of the matters or circumstances described in this paragraph C does not render it unethical for one to serve as an arbitrator where the parties have consented to the arbitrator's appointment or continued services following full disclosure of the relevant facts in accordance with Canon II.

D. Arbitrators should conduct themselves in a way that is fair to all parties and should not be swayed by outside pressure, public clamor, and fear of criticism or self-interest. They should avoid conduct and statements that give the appearance of partiality toward or against any party.

E. When an arbitrator's authority is derived from the agreement of the parties, an arbitrator should neither exceed that authority nor do less than is required to exercise that authority completely. Where the agreement of the parties sets forth procedures to be followed in conducting the arbitration or refers to rules to be followed, it is the obligation of the arbitrator to comply with such procedures or rules. An arbitrator has no ethical obligation to comply with any agreement, procedures or rules that are unlawful or that, in the arbitrator's judgment, would be inconsistent with this Code.

F. An arbitrator should conduct the arbitration process so as to advance the fair and efficient resolution of the matters submitted for decision. An arbitrator should make all reasonable efforts to prevent delaying tactics, harassment of parties or other participants, or other abuse or disruption of the arbitration process.

G. The ethical obligations of an arbitrator begin upon acceptance of the appointment and continue throughout all stages of the proceeding. In addition, as set forth in this Code, certain ethical obligations begin as soon as a person is requested to serve as an arbitrator and certain ethical obligations continue after the decision in the proceeding has been given to the parties.

H. Once an arbitrator has accepted an appointment, the arbitrator should not withdraw or abandon the appointment unless compelled to do so by unanticipated circumstances that would render it impossible or impracticable to continue. When an arbitrator is to be compensated for his or her services, the arbitrator may withdraw if the parties fail or refuse to provide for payment of the compensation as agreed.

I. An arbitrator who withdraws prior to the completion of the arbitration, whether upon the arbitrator's initiative or upon the request of one or more of the parties, should take reasonable steps to protect the interests of the parties in the arbitration, including return of evidentiary materials and protection of confidentiality.

Comment to Canon I

A prospective arbitrator is not necessarily partial or prejudiced by having acquired knowledge of the parties, the applicable law or the customs and practices of the business involved. Arbitrators may also have special experience or expertise in the areas of business, commerce, or technology which are involved in the arbitration. Arbitrators do not contravene this Canon if, by virtue of such experience or expertise, they have views on certain general issues likely to arise in the arbitration, but an arbitrator may not have prejudged any of the specific factual or legal determinations to be addressed during the arbitration.

During an arbitration, the arbitrator may engage in discourse with the parties or their counsel, draw out arguments or contentions, comment on the law or evidence, make interim rulings, and otherwise control or direct the arbitration. These activities are integral parts of an arbitration. Paragraph D of Canon I is not intended to preclude or limit either full discussion of the issues during the course of the arbitration or the arbitrator's management of the proceeding.

CANON II. AN ARBITRATOR SHOULD DISCLOSE ANY INTEREST OR RELATIONSHIP LIKELY TO AFFECT IMPARTIALITY OR WHICH MIGHT CREATE AN APPEARANCE OF PARTIALITY.

A. Persons who are requested to serve as arbitrators should, before accepting,

disclose:

(1) Any known direct or indirect financial or personal interest in the outcome

of the arbitration;

(2) Any known existing or past financial, business, professional or personal relationships which might reasonably affect impartiality or lack of independence in the eyes of any of the parties. For example, prospective arbitrators should disclose any such relationships which they personally have with any party or its lawyer, with any co-arbitrator, or with any individual whom they have been told will be a witness. They should also disclose any such relationships involving their families or household members or their current employers, partners, or professional or business associates that can be ascertained by reasonable efforts;

(3) The nature and extent of any prior knowledge they may have of the dispute; and

(4) Any other matters, relationships, or interests which they are obligated to disclose by the agreement of the parties, the rules or practices of an institution, or applicable law regulating arbitrator disclosure.

B. Persons who are requested to accept appointment as arbitrators should make a reasonable effort to inform themselves of any interests or relationships described in paragraph A.

C. The obligation to disclose interests or relationships described in paragraph A is a continuing duty which requires a person who accepts appointment as an arbitrator to disclose, as soon as practicable, at any stage of the arbitration, any such interests or relationships which may arise, or which are recalled or discovered.

D. Any doubt as to whether or not disclosure is to be made should be resolved in favor of disclosure.

E. Disclosure should be made to all parties unless other procedures for disclosure are provided in the agreement of the parties, applicable rules or practices of an institution, or by law. Where more than one arbitrator has been appointed, each should inform the others of all matters disclosed.

F. When parties, with knowledge of a person's interests and relationships, nevertheless desire that person to serve as an arbitrator, that person may properly serve.

G. If an arbitrator is requested by all parties to withdraw, the arbitrator must do so. If an arbitrator is requested to withdraw by less than all of the parties because of alleged partiality, the arbitrator should withdraw unless either of the following circumstances exists:

> (1) An agreement of the parties, or arbitration rules agreed to by the parties, or applicable law establishes procedures for determining challenges to arbitrators, in which case those procedures should be followed; or
>
> (2) In the absence of applicable procedures, if the arbitrator, after carefully considering the matter, that the reason for the challenge is not substantial, and that he or she can nevertheless act and decide the case impartially and fairly.

H. If compliance by a prospective arbitrator with any provision of this Code would require disclosure of confidential or privileged information, the prospective arbitrator should either:

> (1) Secure the consent to the disclosure from the person who furnished the information or the holder of the privilege; or

(2) Withdraw.

CANON III. AN ARBITRATOR SHOULD AVOID IMPROPRIETY OR THE APPEARANCE OF IMPROPRIETY IN COMMUNICATING WITH PARTIES.

A. If an agreement of the parties or applicable arbitration rules establishes the manner or content of communications between the arbitrator and the parties, the arbitrator should follow those procedures notwithstanding any contrary provision of paragraphs B and C.

B. An arbitrator or prospective arbitrator should not discuss a proceeding with any party in the absence of any other party, except in any of the following circumstances:

(1) When the appointment of a prospective arbitrator is being considered, the prospective arbitrator:

(a) may ask about the identities of the parties, counsel, or witnesses and the general nature of the case; and

(b) may respond to inquiries from a party or its counsel designed to determine his or her suitability and availability for the appointment. In any such dialogue, the prospective arbitrator may receive information from a party or its counsel disclosing the general nature of the dispute but should not permit them to discuss the merits of the case.

(2) In an arbitration in which the two party-appointed arbitrators are expected to appoint the third arbitrator, each party-appointed arbitrator may consult with the party who appointed the arbitrator concerning the choice of the third arbitrator;

(3) In an arbitration involving party-appointed arbitrators, each party-appointed arbitrator may consult with the party who appointed the arbitrator concerning arrangements for

any compensation to be paid to the party appointed arbitrator. Submission of routine written requests for payment of compensation and expenses in accordance with such arrangements and written communications pertaining solely to such requests need not be sent to the other party;

(4) In an arbitration involving party-appointed arbitrators, each party-appointed arbitrator may consult with the party who appointed the arbitrator concerning the status of the arbitrator (i.e., neutral or non-neutral), as contemplated by paragraph C of Canon IX;

(5) Discussions may be had with a party concerning such logistical matters as setting the time and place of hearings or making other arrangements for the conduct of the proceedings. However, the arbitrator should promptly inform each other party of the discussion and should not make any final determination concerning the matter discussed before giving each absent party an opportunity to express the party's views; or

(6) If a party fails to be present at a hearing after having been given due notice, or if all parties expressly consent, the arbitrator may discuss the case with any party who is present.

C. Unless otherwise provided in this Canon, in applicable arbitration rules or in an agreement of the parties, whenever an arbitrator communicates in writing with one party, the arbitrator should at the same time send a copy of the communication to every other party, and whenever the arbitrator receives any written communication concerning the case from one party which has not already been sent to every other party, the arbitrator should send or cause it to be sent to the other parties.

CANON IV. AN ARBITRATOR SHOULD CONDUCT THE PROCEEDINGS FAIRLY AND DILIGENTLY.

A. An arbitrator should conduct the proceedings in an even-handed manner. The arbitrator should be patient and courteous to the parties, their representatives, and the witnesses and should encourage similar conduct by all participants.

B. The arbitrator should afford to all parties the right to be heard and due notice of the time and place of any hearing. The arbitrator should allow each party a fair opportunity to present its evidence and arguments.

C. The arbitrator should not deny any party the opportunity to be represented by counsel or by any other person chosen by the party.

D. If a party fails to appear after due notice, the arbitrator should proceed with the arbitration when authorized to do so, but only after receiving assurance that appropriate notice has been given to the absent party.

E. When the arbitrator determines that more information than has been presented by the parties is required to decide the case, it is not improper for the arbitrator to ask questions, call witnesses, and request documents or other evidence, including expert testimony.

F. Although it is not improper for an arbitrator to suggest to the parties that they discuss the possibility of settlement or the use of mediation, or other dispute resolution processes, an arbitrator should not exert pressure on any party to settle or to utilize other dispute resolution processes. An arbitrator should not be present or otherwise participate in settlement discussions or act as a mediator unless requested to do so by all parties.

G. Co-arbitrators should afford each other full opportunity to participate in all aspects of the proceedings.

Comment to paragraph G

Paragraph G of Canon IV is not intended to preclude one arbitrator from acting in limited circumstances (e.g., ruling on discovery issues) where authorized by the agreement of the parties, applicable rules or law, nor does it preclude a majority of the arbitrators from proceeding with any aspect of the arbitration if an arbitrator is unable or unwilling to participate and such action is authorized by the agreement of the parties or applicable rules or law. It also does not preclude ex parte requests for interim relief.

CANON V. AN ARBITRATOR SHOULD MAKE DECISIONS IN A JUST, INDEPENDENT AND DELIBERATE MANNER.

A. The arbitrator should, after careful deliberation, decide all issues submitted for determination. An arbitrator should decide no other issues.

B. An arbitrator should decide all matters justly, exercising independent judgment, and should not permit outside pressure to affect the decision.

C. An arbitrator should not delegate the duty to decide to any other person.

D. In the event that all parties agree upon a settlement of issues in dispute and request the arbitrator to embody that agreement in an award, the arbitrator may do so, but is not required to do so unless satisfied with the propriety of the terms of settlement. Whenever an arbitrator embodies a settlement by the parties in an award, the arbitrator should state in the award that it is based on an agreement of the parties.

CANON VI. AN ARBITRATOR SHOULD BE FAITHFUL TO THE RELATIONSHIP OF TRUST AND CONFIDENTIALITY INHERENT IN THAT OFFICE.

A. An arbitrator is in a relationship of trust to the parties and should not, at any time, use confidential information acquired during the arbitration proceeding to gain personal advantage or advantage for others, or to affect adversely the interest of another.

B. The arbitrator should keep confidential all matters relating to the arbitration proceedings and decision. An arbitrator may obtain help from an associate, a research assistant or other persons in connection with reaching his or her decision if the arbitrator informs the parties of the use of such assistance and such persons agree to be bound by the provisions of this Canon.

C. It is not proper at any time for an arbitrator to inform anyone of any decision in advance of the time it is given to all parties. In a proceeding in which there is more than one arbitrator, it is not proper at any time for an arbitrator to inform anyone about the substance of the deliberations of the arbitrators. After an arbitration award has been made, it is not proper for an arbitrator to assist in proceedings to enforce or challenge the award.

D. Unless the parties so request, an arbitrator should not appoint himself or herself to a separate office related to the subject matter of the dispute, such as receiver or trustee, nor should a panel of arbitrators appoint one of their number to such an office.

CANON VII. AN ARBITRATOR SHOULD ADHERE TO STANDARDS OF INTEGRITY AND FAIRNESS WHEN MAKING ARRANGEMENTS FOR COMPENSATION AND REIMBURSEMENT OF EXPENSES.

A. Arbitrators who are to be compensated for their services or reimbursed for their expenses shall adhere to standards of integrity and fairness in making arrangements for such payments.

B. Certain practices relating to payments are generally recognized as tending to preserve the integrity and fairness of the arbitration process. These practices include:

> (1) Before the arbitrator finally accepts appointment, the basis of payment, including any cancellation fee, compensation in the event of withdrawal and compensation for study and preparation time, and all other charges, should be established. Except for arrangements for the compensation of party-appointed arbitrators, all parties should be informed in writing of the terms established.

(2) In proceedings conducted under the rules or administration of an institution that is available to assist in making arrangements for payments, communication related to compensation should be made through the institution. In proceedings where no institution has been engaged by the parties to administer the arbitration, any communication with arbitrators (other than party appointed arbitrators) concerning payments should be in the presence of all parties; and

(3) Arbitrators should not, absent extraordinary circumstances, request increases in the basis of their compensation during the course of a proceeding.

CANON VIII. AN ARBITRATOR MAY ENGAGE IN ADVERTISING OR PROMOTION OF ARBITRAL SERVICES WHICH IS TRUTHFUL AND ACCURATE.

A. Advertising or promotion of an individual's willingness or availability to serve as an arbitrator must be accurate and unlikely to mislead. Any statements about the quality of the arbitrator's work or the success of the arbitrator's practice must be truthful.

B. Advertising and promotion must not imply any willingness to accept an appointment otherwise than in accordance with this Code.

Comment to Canon VIII
This Canon does not preclude an arbitrator from printing, publishing, or disseminating advertisements conforming to these standards in any electronic or print medium, from making personal presentations to prospective users of arbitral services conforming to such standards or from responding to inquiries concerning the arbitrator's availability, qualifications, experience, or fee arrangements.

CANON IX. ARBITRATORS APPOINTED BY ONE PARTY HAVE A DUTY TO DETERMINE AND DISCLOSE THEIR STATUS AND TO COMPLY WITH THIS CODE, EXCEPT AS EXEMPTED BY CANON X.

A. In some types of arbitration in which there are three arbitrators, it is customary for each party, acting alone, to appoint one arbitrator. The third arbitrator is then appointed by agreement either of the parties or of the two arbitrators, or failing such agreement, by an independent institution or individual. In tripartite arbitrations to which this Code applies, all three arbitrators are presumed to be neutral and are expected to observe the same standards as the third arbitrator.

B. Notwithstanding this presumption, there are certain types of tripartite arbitration in which it is expected by all parties that the two arbitrators appointed by the parties may be predisposed toward the party appointing them. Those arbitrators, referred to in this Code as "Canon X arbitrators," are not to be held to the standards of neutrality and independence applicable to other arbitrators. Canon X describes the special ethical obligations of party-appointed arbitrators who are not expected to meet the standard of neutrality.

C. A party-appointed arbitrator has an obligation to ascertain, as early as possible but not later than the first meeting of the arbitrators and parties, whether the parties have agreed that the party-appointed arbitrators will serve as neutrals or whether they shall be subject to Canon X, and to provide a timely report of their conclusions to the parties and other arbitrators:

> (1) Party-appointed arbitrators should review the agreement of the parties, the applicable rules and any applicable law bearing upon arbitrator neutrality. In reviewing the agreement of the parties, party-appointed arbitrators should consult any relevant express terms of the written or oral arbitration agreement. It may also be appropriate for them to inquire into agreements that have not been expressly set forth, but which may be implied from an established course of dealings of the parties or well-recognized custom and usage in their trade or profession;

(2) Where party-appointed arbitrators conclude that the parties intended for the party-appointed arbitrators not to serve as neutrals, they should so inform the parties and the other arbitrators. The arbitrators may then act as provided in Canon X unless or until a different determination of their status is made by the parties, any administering institution or the arbitral panel; and

(3) Until party-appointed arbitrators conclude that the party-appointed arbitrators were not intended by the parties to serve as neutrals, or if the party-appointed arbitrators are unable to form a reasonable belief of their status from the foregoing sources and no decision in this regard has yet been made by the parties, any administering institution, or the arbitral panel, they should observe all of the obligations of neutral arbitrators set forth in this Code.

D. Party-appointed arbitrators not governed by Canon X shall observe all of the obligations of Canons I through VIII unless otherwise required by agreement of the parties, any applicable rules, or applicable law.

CANON X. EXEMPTIONS FOR ARBITRATORS APPOINTED BY ONE PARTY WHO ARE NOT SUBJECT TO RULES OF NEUTRALITY.

Canon X arbitrators are expected to observe all of the ethical obligations prescribed by this Code except those from which they are specifically excused by Canon X.

A. *Obligations under Canon I*
Canon X arbitrators should observe all of the obligations of Canon I subject only to the following provisions:

(1) Canon X arbitrators may be predisposed toward the party who appointed them but in all other respects are obligated to act in good faith and with integrity and fairness. For example, Canon X arbitrators should not engage in delaying tactics or harassment of any party or witness and should not

knowingly make untrue or misleading statements to the other arbitrators; and

(2) The provisions of subparagraphs B(1), B(2), and paragraphs C and D of Canon I, insofar as they relate to partiality, relationships, and interests are not applicable to Canon X arbitrators.

B. *Obligations under Canon II*

(1) Canon X arbitrators should disclose to all parties, and to the other arbitrators, all interests and relationships which Canon II requires be disclosed. Disclosure as required by Canon II is for the benefit not only of the party who appointed the arbitrator, but also for the benefit of the other parties and arbitrators so that they may know of any partiality which may exist or appear to exist; and

(2) Canon X arbitrators are not obliged to withdraw under paragraph G of Canon II if requested to do so only by the party who did not appoint them.

C. *Obligations under Canon III*

Canon X arbitrators should observe all of the obligations of Canon III subject only to the following provisions:

(1) Like neutral party-appointed arbitrators, Canon X arbitrators may consult with the party who appointed them to the extent permitted in paragraph B of Canon III;

(2) Canon X arbitrators shall, at the earliest practicable time, disclose to the other arbitrators and to the parties whether or not they intend to communicate with their appointing parties. If they have disclosed the intention to engage in such communications, they may thereafter communicate with their appointing parties concerning any other aspect of the case, except as provided in paragraph (3).

(3) If such communication occurred prior to the time they were appointed as arbitrators, or prior to the first hearing or other meeting of the parties with the arbitrators, the Canon X arbitrator should, at or before the first hearing or meeting of the arbitrators with the parties, disclose the fact that such communication has taken place. In complying with the

provisions of this subparagraph, it is sufficient that there be disclosure of the fact that such communication has occurred without disclosing the content of the communication. A single timely disclosure of the Canon X arbitrator's intention to participate in such communications in the future is sufficient;

(4) Canon X arbitrators may not at any time during the arbitration:

(a) disclose any deliberations by the arbitrators on any matter or issue submitted to them for decision;

(b) communicate with the parties that appointed them concerning any matter or issue taken under consideration by the panel after the record is closed or such matter or issue has been submitted for decision; or

(c) disclose any final decision or interim decision in advance of the time that it is disclosed to all parties.

(5) Unless otherwise agreed by the arbitrators and the parties, a Canon X arbitrator may not communicate orally with the neutral arbitrator concerning any matter or issue arising or expected to arise in the arbitration in the absence of the other Canon X arbitrator. If a Canon X arbitrator communicates in writing with the neutral arbitrator, he or she shall simultaneously provide a copy of the written communication to the other Canon X arbitrator;

(6) When Canon X arbitrators communicate orally with the parties that appointed them concerning any matter on which communication is permitted under this Code, they are not obligated to disclose the contents of such oral communications to any other party or arbitrator; and

(7) When Canon X arbitrators communicate in writing with the party who appointed them concerning any matter on which communication is permitted under this Code, they are not required to send copies of any such written communication to any other party or arbitrator.

D. *Obligations under Canon IV*

Canon X arbitrators should observe all of the obligations of Canon IV.

E. *Obligations under Canon V*

Canon X arbitrators should observe all of the obligations of Canon V, except that they may be predisposed toward deciding in favor of the party who appointed them.

F. *Obligations under Canon VI*

Canon X arbitrators should observe all of the obligations of Canon VI.

G. *Obligations Under Canon VII*

Canon X arbitrators should observe all of the obligations of Canon VII.

H. *Obligations Under Canon VIII*

Canon X arbitrators should observe all of the obligations of Canon VIII.

I. *Obligations Under Canon IX*

The provisions of paragraph D of Canon IX are inapplicable to Canon X arbitrators, except insofar as the obligations are also set forth in this Canon.

APPENDIX 6:

FINRA CODE OF ARBITRATION PROCEDURE FOR CUSTOMER DISPUTES

12000. CODE OF ARBITRATION PROCEDURE FOR CUSTOMER DISPUTES

PART I: INTERPRETIVE MATERIAL, DEFINITIONS, ORGANIZATION AND AUTHORITY

- **IM-12000. Failure to Act Under Provisions of Code of Arbitration Procedure for Customer Disputes**

  It may be deemed conduct inconsistent with just and equitable principles of trade and a violation of Rule 2010 for a member or a person associated with a member to:

  (a) fail to submit a dispute for arbitration under the Code as required by the Code;

  (b) fail to comply with any injunctive order issued pursuant to the Code;

  (c) fail to appear or to produce any document in his possession or control as directed pursuant to provisions of the Code;

(d) fail to honor an award, or comply with a written and executed settlement agreement, obtained in connection with an arbitration submitted for disposition pursuant to the rules applicable to the arbitration of disputes before FINRA or other dispute resolution forum selected by the parties where timely motion has not been made to vacate or modify such award pursuant to applicable law; or

(e) fail to comply with a written and executed settlement agreement, obtained in connection with a mediation submitted for disposition pursuant to the procedures specified by FINRA.

All awards shall be honored by a cash payment to the prevailing party of the exact dollar amount stated in the award. Awards may not be honored by crediting the prevailing party's account with the dollar amount of the award, unless authorized by the express terms of the award or consented to in writing by the parties. Awards shall be honored upon receipt thereof, or within such other time period as may be prescribed by the award.

It may be deemed conduct inconsistent with just and equitable principles of trade and a violation of Rule 2010 for a member to require associated persons to waive the arbitration of disputes contrary to the provisions of the Code of Arbitration Procedure.

- **12100. Definitions**

Unless otherwise defined in the Code, terms used in the Rules and interpretive material, if defined in the FINRA By-Laws, shall have the meaning as defined in the FINRA By-Laws.

(a) Associated Person

The term "associated person" or "associated person of a member" means a person associated with a member, as that term is defined in paragraph (r).

(b) Award

An award is a document stating the disposition of a case.

(c) Board

The term "Board" means the Board of Directors of FINRA Dispute Resolution, Inc.

(d) Claim

The term "claim" means an allegation or request for relief.

(e) Claimant

The term "claimant" means a party that files the statement of claim that initiates an arbitration under Rule 12302.

(f) Code

The term "Code" means the Code of Arbitration Procedure for Customer Disputes. For disputes involving only industry parties, see the Code of Arbitration Procedure for Industry Disputes.

(g) Counterclaim

The term "counterclaim" means a claim asserted against a claimant by a respondent.

(h) Cross Claim

The term "cross claim" means a claim asserted by a respondent against another already-named respondent.

(i) Customer

A customer shall not include a broker or dealer.

(j) Day

Except as otherwise provided, the term "day" means calendar day. If a deadline specified in the Code falls on a Saturday, Sunday or any FINRA holiday, the deadline is extended until the next business day.

(k) Director

The term "Director" means the Director of FINRA Dispute Resolution. Unless the Code provides that the Director may not delegate a specific function, the term includes FINRA staff to whom the Director has delegated authority.

(l) Dispute

The term "dispute" means a dispute, claim or controversy. A dispute may consist of one or more claims.

(m) Hearing

The term "hearing" means the hearing on the merits of an arbitration under Rule 12600.

(n) Hearing Session

The term "hearing session" means any meeting between the parties and arbitrator(s) of four hours or less, including a hearing or a prehearing conference.

(o) Member

For purposes of the Code, the term "member" means any broker or dealer admitted to membership in FINRA, whether or not the membership has been terminated or cancelled; and any broker or dealer admitted to membership in a self-regulatory organization that, with FINRA consent, has required its members to arbitrate pursuant to the Code and/or to be treated as members of FINRA for purposes of the Code, whether or not the membership has been terminated or cancelled.

(p) Non-Public Arbitrator

The term "non-public arbitrator" means a person who is otherwise qualified to serve as an arbitrator and:

(1) is, or within the past five years, was:

(A) associated with, including registered through, a broker or a dealer (including a government securities broker or dealer or a municipal securities dealer);

(B) registered under the Commodity Exchange Act;

(C) a member of a commodities exchange or a registered futures association; or

(D) associated with a person or firm registered under the Commodity Exchange Act;

(2) is retired from, or spent a substantial part of a career engaging in, any of the business activities listed in paragraph (p)(1);

(3) is an attorney, accountant, or other professional who has devoted 20 percent or more of his or her professional work, in the last two years, to clients who are engaged in any of the business activities listed in paragraph (p)(1); or

(4) is an employee of a bank or other financial institution and effects transactions in securities, including government or municipal securities, and commodities futures or options or supervises or monitors the compliance with the securities and commodities laws of employees who engage in such activities.

For purposes of this rule, the term "professional work" shall not include mediation services performed by mediators who are also arbitrators, provided that the mediator acts in the capacity of a mediator and does not represent a party in the mediation.

(q) Panel

The term "panel" means the arbitration panel, whether it consists of one or more arbitrators.

(r) Person Associated with a Member

The term "person associated with a member" means:

(1) A natural person who is registered or has applied for registration under the Rules of FINRA; or

(2) A sole proprietor, partner, officer, director, or branch manager of a member, or other natural person occupying a similar status or performing similar functions, or a natural person engaged in the investment banking or securities business who is directly or indirectly controlling or controlled by a member, whether or not any such person is registered or exempt from registration with FINRA under the By-Laws or the Rules of FINRA.

For purposes of the Code, a person formerly associated with a member is a person associated with a member.

(s) Pleadings

A pleading is a statement describing a party's causes of action or defenses. Documents that are considered pleadings are: a statement of claim, an answer, a counterclaim, a cross claim, a third party claim, and any replies.

(t) Prehearing Conference

The term "prehearing conference" means any hearing session, including an Initial Prehearing Conference, that takes place before the hearing on the merits begins.

(u) Public Arbitrator

The term "public arbitrator" means a person who is otherwise qualified to serve as an arbitrator and:

(1) is not engaged in the conduct or activities described in paragraphs (p)(1)–(4);

(2) was not engaged in the conduct or activities described in paragraphs (p)(1)–(4) for a total of 20 years or more;

(3) is not an investment adviser;

(4) is not an attorney, accountant, or other professional whose firm derived 10 percent or more of its annual revenue in the past two years from any persons or entities listed in paragraphs (p)(1)–(4);

(5) is not an attorney, accountant, or other professional whose firm derived $50,000 or more in annual revenue in the past two years from professional services rendered to any persons or entities listed in paragraph (p)(1) relating to any customer disputes concerning an investment account or transaction, including but not limited to, law firm fees, accounting firm fees, and consulting fees;

(6) is not employed by, and is not the spouse or an immediate family member of a person who is employed by, an entity that directly or indirectly controls, is controlled by, or is under common control with, any partnership, corporation, or other organization that is engaged in the securities business;

(7) is not a director or officer of, and is not the spouse or an immediate family member of a person who is a director or officer of, an entity that directly or indirectly controls, is controlled by, or is under common control with, any partnership, corporation, or other organization that is engaged in the securities business; and

(8) is not the spouse or an immediate family member of a person who is engaged in the conduct or activities described in paragraphs (p)(1)–(4). For purposes of this rule, the term immediate family member means:

(A) a person's parent, stepparent, child, or stepchild;

(B) a member of a person's household;

(C) an individual to whom a person provides financial support of more than 50 percent of his or her annual income; or

(D) a person who is claimed as a dependent for federal income tax purposes.

For purposes of this rule, the term "revenue" shall not include mediation fees received by mediators who are also arbitrators, provided that the mediator acts in the capacity of a mediator and does not represent a party in the mediation.

(v) Respondent

The term "respondent" means a party against whom a statement of claim or third party claim has been filed. A claimant against whom a counterclaim has been filed is not a respondent for purposes of the Code.

(w) Statement of Claim

The term "statement of claim" means the initial or amended claim filed by the party or parties initiating the arbitration.

(x) Submission Agreement

The term "Submission Agreement" means the FINRA Submission Agreement. The FINRA Submission Agreement is a document that parties must sign at the outset of an arbitration in which they agree to submit to arbitration under the Code.

(y) Third Party Claim

The term "third party claim" means a claim asserted against a party not already named in the statement of claim or any other previous pleading.

- **12101. Applicability of Code and Incorporation by Reference**

(a) Applicability of Code

The Code applies to any dispute between a customer and a member or associated person of a member that is submitted to arbitration under Rule 12200 or 12201.

(b) Incorporation by Reference

When a dispute is submitted to arbitration under the Code pursuant to an arbitration agreement, the Code is incorporated by reference into the agreement.

- **12102. National Arbitration and Mediation Committee**

(a) Pursuant to Section III of the Plan of Allocation and Delegation of Functions by FINRA to Subsidiaries ("Delegation Plan"), the Board shall appoint a National Arbitration and Mediation Committee ("NAMC").

(1) The NAMC shall consist of no fewer than 10 and no more than 25 members. At least 50 percent of the NAMC shall be Non-Industry members.

(2) The Chairperson of the Board shall name the chairperson of the NAMC.

(b) Pursuant to the Delegation Plan, the NAMC shall have the authority to recommend rules, regulations, procedures and amendments relating to arbitration, mediation, and other dispute resolution matters to the Board. The NAMC shall also establish and maintain rosters of neutrals composed of persons from within and outside of the securities industry. All matters recommended by the NAMC to the Board must have been approved by a quorum, which shall consist of a majority of the NAMC, including at least 50 percent of the Non-Industry committee members. If at least 50 percent of the Non-Industry committee members are either (i) present at or (ii) have filed a waiver of attendance for a meeting after receiving an agenda prior to such meeting, the requirement that at least 50 percent of the Non-Industry committee members be present to constitute the quorum shall be waived. The NAMC has such other power and authority as is necessary to carry out the purposes of the Code.

(c) The NAMC may meet as frequently as necessary, but must meet at least once a year.

- **12103. Director of Dispute Resolution**

  (a) The Board shall appoint a Director of Dispute Resolution. The Director shall perform all the administrative duties relating to arbitrations submitted under the Code. The Director may delegate his or her duties when it is appropriate, unless the Code provides otherwise.

  (b) The Director shall consult with the NAMC at the NAMC's request.

  (c) The President of FINRA Dispute Resolution may perform the Director's duties. If the Director is unable to perform his or her duties, the President of FINRA Dispute Resolution may appoint an interim Director.

- **12104. Effect of Arbitration on FINRA Regulatory Activities**

  (a) Submitting a dispute to arbitration under the Code does not limit or preclude any right, action or determination by FINRA that it would otherwise be authorized to adopt, administer or enforce.

  (b) Only at the conclusion of an arbitration, any arbitrator may refer to FINRA for disciplinary investigation any matter that has come to the arbitrator's attention during and in connection with the arbitration, either from the record of the proceeding or from material or communications related to the arbitration, which the arbitrator has reason to believe may constitute a violation of NASD or FINRA rules, the federal securities laws, or other applicable rules or laws.

- **12105. Agreement of the Parties**
(a) Except as provided in paragraph (b), if the Code provides that the parties may agree to modify a provision of the Code, or a decision of the Director or the panel, the written agreement of all named parties is required.
(b) If the Director or the panel determines that a named party is inactive in the arbitration, or has failed to respond after adequate notice has been given, the Director or the panel may determine that the written agreement of that party is not required while the party is inactive or not responsive. For purposes of this rule, an inactive party could be, but is not limited to: (1) a party that does not answer; (2) a party that answers and then fails to respond to correspondence sent by the Director; (3) a party that answers and then fails to respond to correspondence sent by the panel in cases involving direct communication under Rule 12211; or (4) a party that does not attend pre-hearing conferences.

PART II: GENERAL ARBITRATION RULES

- **12200. Arbitration Under an Arbitration Agreement or the Rules of FINRA**
Parties must arbitrate a dispute under the Code if:
• Arbitration under the Code is either:
(1) Required by a written agreement, or
(2) Requested by the customer;
• The dispute is between a customer and a member or associated person of a member; and
• The dispute arises in connection with the business activities of the member or the associated person, except disputes involving the insurance business activities of a member that is also an insurance company.

- **12201. Elective Arbitration**
  Parties may arbitrate a dispute under the Code if:
  • The parties agree in writing to submit the dispute to arbitration under the Code after the dispute arises; and
  • The dispute is between a customer and a member, associated person of a member, or other related party; and
  • The dispute arises in connection with the business activities of a member or an associated person, except disputes involving the insurance business activities of a member that is also an insurance company.

- **12202. Claims Against Inactive Members**
  A claim by or against a member in one of the following categories is ineligible for arbitration under the Code unless the customer agrees in writing to arbitrate after the claim arises:
  • A member whose membership is terminated, suspended, cancelled or revoked;
  • A member that has been expelled from FINRA; or
  • A member that is otherwise defunct.

- **12203. Denial of FINRA Forum**
  (a) The Director may decline to permit the use of the FINRA arbitration forum if the Director determines that, given the purposes of FINRA and the intent of the Code, the subject matter of the dispute is inappropriate, or that accepting the matter would pose a risk to the health or safety of arbitrators, staff, or parties or their representatives. Only the Director or the President of FINRA Dispute Resolution may exercise the Director's authority under this rule.
  (b) Disputes that arise out of transactions in a readily identifiable market may be referred to the arbitration forum for that market, if the claimant agrees.

- **12204. Class Action Claims**
  (a) Class action claims may not be arbitrated under the Code.
  (b) Any claim that is based upon the same facts and law, and involves the same defendants as in a court-certified class action or a

putative class action, or that is ordered by a court for class-wide arbitration at a forum not sponsored by a self-regulatory organization, shall not be arbitrated under the Code, unless the party bringing the claim files with FINRA one of the following:

(1) a copy of a notice filed with the court in which the class action is pending that the party will not participate in the class action or in any recovery that may result from the class action, or has withdrawn from the class according to any conditions set by the court; or

(2) a notice that the party will not participate in the class action or in any recovery that may result from the class action.

(c) The Director will refer to a panel any dispute as to whether a claim is part of a class action, unless a party asks the court hearing the class action to resolve the dispute within 10 days of receiving notice that the Director has decided to refer the dispute to a panel.

(d) A member or associated person may not enforce any arbitration agreement against a member of a certified or putative class action with respect to any claim that is the subject of the certified or putative class action until:

- The class certification is denied;
- The class is decertified;
- The member of the certified or putative class is excluded from the class by the court; or
- The member of the certified or putative class elects not to participate in the class or withdraws from the class according to conditions set by the court, if any.

This paragraph does not otherwise affect the enforceability of any rights under this Code or any other agreement.

- **12205. Shareholder Derivative Actions**
  Shareholder derivative actions may not be arbitrated under the Code.

- **12206. Time Limits**
  (a) Time Limitation on Submission of Claims
  No claim shall be eligible for submission to arbitration under the Code where six years have elapsed from the occurrence or event giving rise to the claim. The panel will resolve any questions regarding the eligibility of a claim under this rule.

(b) Dismissal under Rule

Dismissal of a claim under this rule does not prohibit a party from pursuing the claim in court. By filing a motion to dismiss a claim under this rule, the moving party agrees that if the panel dismisses a claim under this rule, the non-moving party may withdraw any remaining related claims without prejudice and may pursue all of the claims in court.

(1) Motions under this rule must be made in writing, and must be filed separately from the answer, and only after the answer is filed.

(2) Unless the parties agree or the panel determines otherwise, parties must serve motions under this rule at least 90 days before a scheduled hearing, and parties have 30 days to respond to the motion.

(3) Motions under this rule will be decided by the full panel.

(4) The panel may not grant a motion under this rule unless an in-person or telephonic prehearing conference on the motion is held or waived by the parties. Prehearing conferences to consider motions under this rule will be recorded as set forth in Rule 12606.

(5) If the panel grants a motion under this rule (in whole or part), the decision must be unanimous, and must be accompanied by a written explanation.

(6) If the panel denies a motion under this rule, a party may not re-file the denied motion, unless specifically permitted by panel order.

(7) If the party moves to dismiss on multiple grounds including eligibility, the panel must decide eligibility first.

- If the panel grants the motion to dismiss the case on eligibility grounds on all claims, it shall not rule on any other grounds for the motion to dismiss.
- If the panel grants the motion to dismiss on eligibility grounds on some, but not all claims, and the party against whom the motion was granted elects to move the case to court, the panel shall not rule on any other ground for dismissal for 15 days from the date of service of the panel's decision to grant the motion to dismiss on eligibility grounds.
- If a panel dismisses any claim on eligibility grounds, the panel must record the dismissal on eligibility grounds on the face of its order and any subsequent award the panel may issue.

• If the panel denies the motion to dismiss on eligibility grounds, it shall rule on the other bases for the motion to dismiss the remaining claims in accordance with the procedures set forth in Rule 12504(a).

(8) If the panel denies a motion under this rule, the panel must assess forum fees associated with hearings on the motion against the moving party.

(9) If the panel deems frivolous a motion filed under this rule, the panel must also award reasonable costs and attorneys' fees to any party that opposed the motion.

(10) The panel also may issue other sanctions under Rule 12212 if it determines that a party filed a motion under this rule in bad faith.

(c) Effect of Rule on Time Limits for Filing Claim in Court

The rule does not extend applicable statutes of limitations; nor shall the six-year time limit on the submission of claims apply to any claim that is directed to arbitration by a court of competent jurisdiction upon request of a member or associated person. However, when a claimant files a statement of claim in arbitration, any time limits for the filing of the claim in court will be tolled while FINRA retains jurisdiction of the claim.

(d) Effect of Filing a Claim in Court on Time Limits for Filing in Arbitration

If a party submits a claim to a court of competent jurisdiction, the six-year time limitation will not run while the court retains jurisdiction of the claim matter.

- **12207. Extension of Deadlines**

  (a) The parties may agree in writing to extend or modify any deadline for:

  • Serving an answer;

  • Returning arbitrator or chairperson lists;

  • Responding to motions; or

  • Exchanging documents or witness lists.

  If the parties agree to extend or modify a deadline under this rule, they must notify the Director of the new deadline in writing.

(b) The panel may extend or modify any deadline listed in paragraph (a), or any other deadline set by the panel, either on its own initiative or upon motion of a party.

(c) The Director may extend or modify any deadline or time period set by the Code for good cause. The Director may also extend or modify any deadline or time period set by the panel in extraordinary circumstances.

- **12208. Representation of Parties**

(a) Representation by a Party

Parties may represent themselves in an arbitration held in a United States hearing location. A member of a partnership may represent the partnership; and a bona fide officer of a corporation, trust, or association may represent the corporation, trust, or association.

(b) Representation by an Attorney

At any stage of an arbitration proceeding held in a United States hearing location, all parties shall have the right to be represented by an attorney at law in good standing and admitted to practice before the Supreme Court of the United States or the highest court of any state of the United States, the District of Columbia, or any commonwealth, territory, or possession of the United States, unless state law prohibits such representation.

(c) Representation by Others

Parties may be represented in an arbitration by a person who is not an attorney, unless:

• state law prohibits such representation, or

• the person is currently suspended or barred from the securities industry in any capacity, or

• the person is currently suspended from the practice of law or disbarred.

(d) Qualifications of Representative

Issues regarding the qualifications of a person to represent a party in arbitration are governed by applicable law and may be determined by an appropriate court or other regulatory agency. In the absence of a court order, the arbitration proceeding shall not be stayed or otherwise delayed pending resolution of such issues.

- **12209. Legal Proceedings**
  During an arbitration, no party may bring any suit, legal action, or proceeding against any other party that concerns or that would resolve any of the matters raised in the arbitration.

- **12210. Ex Parte Communications**
  (a) Except as provided in Rule 12211, no party, or anyone acting on behalf of a party, may communicate with any arbitrator outside of a scheduled hearing or conference regarding an arbitration unless all parties or their representatives are present.
  (b) No party, or anyone acting on behalf of a party, may send or give any written motion, request, submission or other materials directly to any arbitrator, unless the arbitrators and the parties agree, or the Code provides otherwise.

- **12211. Direct Communication Between Parties and Arbitrators**
  (a) This rule provides procedures under which parties and arbitrators may communicate directly.
  (b) Only parties that are represented by counsel may use direct communication under this rule. If, during the proceeding, a party chooses to appear *pro se* (without counsel), this rule shall no longer apply.

  (c) All arbitrators and all parties must agree to the use of direct communication during the Initial Prehearing Conference or a later conference or hearing before it can be used.

  (d) Parties may send the arbitrators only items that are listed in an order.

  (e) Parties may send items by regular mail, overnight courier, facsimile, or email. All the arbitrators and parties must have facsimile or email capability before such a delivery method may be used.

  (f) Copies of all materials sent to arbitrators must also be sent at the same time and in the same manner to all parties and the Director. Materials that exceed 15 pages, however, shall be sent to the Director only by regular mail or overnight courier.

(g) The Director must receive copies of any orders and decisions made as a result of direct communications among the parties and the arbitrators.

(h) Parties may not communicate orally with any of the arbitrators outside the presence of all parties.

(i) Any party or arbitrator may terminate the direct communication order at any time, after giving written notice to the other arbitrators and the parties.

- **12212. Sanctions**

(a) The panel may sanction a party for failure to comply with any provision in the Code, or any order of the panel or single arbitrator authorized to act on behalf of the panel.
Unless prohibited by applicable law, sanctions may include, but are not limited to:

- Assessing monetary penalties payable to one or more parties;
- Precluding a party from presenting evidence;
- Making an adverse inference against a party;
- Assessing postponement and/or forum fees; and
- Assessing attorneys' fees, costs and expenses.

(b) The panel may initiate a disciplinary referral at the conclusion of an arbitration.

(c) The panel may dismiss a claim, defense or arbitration with prejudice as a sanction for material and intentional failure to comply with an order of the panel if prior warnings or sanctions have proven ineffective.

- **12213. Hearing Locations**

(a) U.S. Hearing Location
(1) The Director will decide which of FINRA's hearing locations will be the hearing location for the arbitration. Generally, the Director will select the hearing location closest to the customer's residence at the time of the events giving rise to the dispute, unless the hearing location closest to the customer's residence is in a different state, in which case the customer may request a hearing location in the customer's state of residence at the time of the events giving rise to the dispute.

(2) Before arbitrator lists are sent to the parties under Rule 12403, the parties may agree in writing to a hearing location other than the one selected by the Director.

(3) The Director may change the hearing location upon motion of a party, as set forth in Rule 12503.

(4) After the panel is appointed, the panel may decide a motion relating to changing the hearing location.

(b) Foreign Hearing Location

(1) If the Director and all parties agree, parties may have their hearing in a foreign hearing location and conducted by foreign arbitrators, provided that the foreign arbitrators have:

(A) met FINRA background qualifications for arbitrators;

(B) received training on FINRA arbitration rules and procedures; and

(C) satisfied at least the same training and testing requirements as those arbitrators who serve in U. S. locations of FINRA.

(2) The parties shall pay an additional surcharge for each day of hearings held in a foreign hearing location. The amount of the surcharge will be determined by the Director and must be agreed to by the parties before the foreign hearing location may be used. This surcharge shall be specified in the agreement to use a foreign hearing location and shall be apportioned equally among the parties, unless they agree otherwise. The foreign arbitrators shall have the authority to apportion this surcharge as provided in Rule 12902(c).

- **12214. Payment of Arbitrators**

  (a) Except as provided in paragraph (b) and in Rule 12800, FINRA will pay the panel an honorarium, as follows:

  • $200 to each arbitrator for each hearing session in which he or she participates;

  • an additional $75 per day to the chairperson for each hearing on the merits;

  • $50 for travel to a hearing session that is postponed pursuant to Rule 12601; and

  • $100 for each arbitrator if a hearing session other than a prehearing conference is postponed within three business days before a scheduled hearing session pursuant to Rules 12601(a)(2) and (b)(2).

(b) The Director may authorize a higher or additional honorarium for the use of a foreign hearing location.

(c) Payment for Deciding Discovery-Related Motions Without a Hearing Session

(1) FINRA will pay each arbitrator an honorarium of $200 to decide a discovery-related motion without a hearing session. This paragraph does not apply to cases administered under Rule 12800.

(2) For purposes of paragraph (c)(1), a discovery-related motion and any replies or other correspondence relating to the motion shall be considered to be a single motion.

(3) The panel will allocate the cost of the honoraria under paragraph (c)(1) to the parties pursuant to Rule 12902(c).

(d) Payment for Deciding Contested Subpoena Requests Without a Hearing Session

(1) The honorarium for deciding one or more contested motions requesting the issuance of a subpoena without a hearing session shall be $200. The honorarium shall be paid on a per case basis to each arbitrator who decides the contested motion(s). The parties shall not be assessed more than $600 in fees under this paragraph in any arbitration proceeding. The honorarium shall not be paid for cases administered under Rule 12800.

(2) For purposes of paragraph (d)(1), a contested motion requesting the issuance of a subpoena shall include a motion requesting the issuance of a subpoena, the draft subpoena, a written objection from the party opposing the issuance of the subpoena, and any other documents supporting a party's position.

(3) The panel will allocate the cost of the honorarium under paragraph (d)(1) to the parties pursuant to Rule 12902(c).

(e) Payment for Explained Decisions

(1) The chairperson who is responsible for writing an explained decision pursuant to Rule 12904(g) will receive an additional honorarium of $400. The panel will allocate the cost of the honorarium under Rule 12904(g) to the parties.

(2) If the panel decides on its own to write an explained decision, then no panel member will receive the additional honorarium of $400.

PART III: INITIATING AND RESPONDING TO CLAIMS

- **12300. Filing and Serving Documents**

(a) Initial statements of claim must be filed with the Director, with enough copies for each other party and each arbitrator. The number of arbitrators is determined in accordance with Rule 12401. The Director will serve the statement of claim on the other parties, and send copies of the statement of claim to each arbitrator.

(b) The parties must serve all other pleadings and other documents directly on each other party. Parties must serve all pleadings on all parties at the same time and in the same manner, unless the parties agree otherwise.

(c) Unless the Code provides otherwise, parties must also file all pleadings and other documents with the Director, with additional copies for each arbitrator. Pleadings and other documents must be filed with the Director at the same time and in the same manner in which they are served on the other parties. Parties filing pleadings and other documents with the Director must include a certificate of service stating the names of the parties served, the date and method of service, and the address(es) to which service was made.

(d) Pleadings and other documents may be filed and served by: first class mail; overnight mail or delivery service; hand delivery; facsimile; or any other method, including electronic mail, that is approved or required by the panel.

(e) Filing and service are accomplished on the date of mailing either by first-class postage prepaid mail or overnight mail service, or, in the case of other means of service, on the date of delivery. Whenever pleadings and other documents must be filed with the Director and served on the other parties, filing and service must occur on the same day and in the same manner, unless the parties agree or the panel directs otherwise.

(f) A party must inform the Director and all other parties in writing of any change of address during an arbitration.

- **12301. Service on Associated Persons**

(a) The Director will serve the initial statement of claim on an associated person directly at the person's residential address or usual place of abode. If service cannot be completed at the person's residential address or usual place of abode, the Director will serve the initial statement of claim on the associated person at the person's business address.
(b) If a member and a person currently associated with the member are named as respondents to the same arbitration, and the Director cannot complete service as provided in paragraph (a), then the Director may serve the member with the initial statement of claim on behalf of the associated person. If service is made on the member, the member must serve the associated person, even if the member will not be representing the associated person in the arbitration. If the member is not representing the associated person in the arbitration, the member must notify, and provide the associated person's current address to, all parties and the Director.

- **12302. Filing an Initial Statement of Claim**

(a) Filing Claim with the Director
To initiate an arbitration, a claimant must file the following with the Director:

- Signed and dated Submission Agreement; and
- A statement of claim specifying the relevant facts and remedies requested.

The claimant may include any additional documents supporting the statement of claim. The claimant may file the documents: (1) in hard copy; or (2) electronically through the Online Arbitration Claim Filing system that can be accessed at www.finra.org.

(b) Number of Copies

If not submitted electronically, the claimant must file enough copies of the statement of claim, and the signed Submission Agreement, and any additional materials, for the Director, each arbitrator and each other party.

(c) Fees

At the time the statement of claim is filed, the claimant must pay all required filing fees.

(d) Service by Director

Unless the statement of claim is deficient under Rule 12307, the Director will send a copy of the Submission Agreement, the statement of claim, and any additional materials filed by the claimant, to each other party, and to each arbitrator once the panel has been appointed.

- **12303. Answering the Statement of Claim**

  (a) Respondent(s) must directly serve each other party with the following documents within 45 days of receipt of the statement of claim:

  • Signed and dated Submission Agreement; and

  • An answer specifying the relevant facts and available defenses to the statement of claim.

  The respondent may include any additional documents supporting the answer to the statement of claim. Parties that fail to answer in the time provided may be subject to default proceedings under Rule 12801.

  (b) The answer to the statement of claim may include any counterclaims against the claimant, cross claims against other respondents, or third party claims, specifying all relevant facts and remedies requested, as well as any additional documents supporting such claim. When serving a third party claim, the respondent must provide each new respondent with copies of all documents previously served by any party, or sent to the parties by the Director.

  (c) At the same time that the answer to the statement of claim is served on the other parties, the respondent must file copies of the Submission Agreement, the answer to the statement of claim, and any additional documents, with the Director, with enough copies for the Director and each arbitrator.

  (d) If the answer to the statement of claim contains any counterclaims, cross claims or third party claims, the respondent must pay all required filing fees.

- **12304. Answering Counterclaims**

  (a) A claimant must directly serve any answer to a counterclaim on each other party within 20 days of receipt of the counterclaim. At the

same time, the claimant must file the answer to the counterclaim with the Director with additional copies for each arbitrator.
(b) The answer must include the relevant facts and available defenses to the counterclaim. The claimant may include any additional documents supporting the answer to the counterclaim.

- **12305. Answering Cross Claims**
  (a) A respondent must directly serve an answer to a cross claim on each other party within 20 days from the date that the respondent's answer to the statement of claim is due, or from the receipt of the cross claim, whichever is later. At the same time, the respondent must file the answer to the cross claim with the Director with additional copies for each arbitrator.
  (b) The answer must include the relevant facts and available defenses to the cross claim. The respondent may include any additional documents supporting the answer to the cross claim.

- **12306. Answering Third Party Claims**
  (a) A party responding to a third party claim must directly serve all other parties with the following documents within 45 days of receipt of the third party claim:
  • Signed and dated Submission Agreement; and
  • An answer specifying the relevant facts and available defenses to the third party claim.

  The respondent may include any additional documents supporting the answer to the third party claim.

  (b) The answer to the third party claim may also include any counterclaims, cross claims, or third party claims, specifying all relevant facts and remedies requested. The answer may also include any additional documents supporting such claim. When serving a third party claim, the respondent must provide each new respondent with copies of all documents previously served by any party, or sent to the parties by the Director.

  (c) At the same time that the answer to the third party claim is served on the other parties, the third party respondent must also file copies of the Submission Agreement, the answer to the third party claim, and any additional documents, with the Director, with additional copies for each arbitrator.

(d) If the answer to the third party claim contains any counterclaim, cross claim or third party claim, the party must also pay all required filing fees.

- **12307. Deficient Claims**

(a) The Director will not serve any claim that is deficient. The reasons a claim may be deficient include the following:

• A Submission Agreement was not filed by each claimant;

• The Submission Agreement was not properly signed and dated;

• The Submission Agreement does not name all parties named in the claim;

• The claimant did not file the correct number of copies of the Submission Agreement, statement of claim or supporting documents for service on respondents and for the arbitrators;

• The claim does not specify the customer's home address at the time of the events giving rise to the dispute;

• The claim does not specify the claimant's or the claimant's representative's current address; or

• The claimant did not pay all required filing fees, unless the Director deferred the fees.

(b) The Director will notify the claimant in writing if the claim is deficient. If the deficiency is corrected within 30 days from the time the claimant receives notice, the claim will be considered filed on the date the initial statement of claim was filed with the Director under Rule 12300(a). If all deficiencies are not corrected within 30 days, the Director will close the case without serving the claim, and will refund part of the filing fee in the amount indicated in the schedule under Rule 12900(c).

(c) The panel will not consider any counterclaim, cross claim or third party claim that is deficient. The reasons a counterclaim, cross claim or third party claim may be deficient include the reasons listed in paragraph (a). The Director will notify the party making the counterclaim, cross claim or third party claim of the any deficiencies in writing. If all deficiencies are not corrected within 30 days from the time the party making the counterclaim, cross claim or third party claim receives notice of the deficiency, the panel will proceed with the arbitration as though the deficient counterclaim, cross claim or third party claim had not been made.

- **12308. Loss of Defenses Due to Untimely or Incomplete Answer**

  (a) If a party does not answer within the time period specified in the Code, the panel may, upon motion, bar that party from presenting any defenses or facts at the hearing, unless the time to answer was extended in accordance with the Code. The party may also be subject to default proceedings under Rule 12801, if the conditions of Rule 12801(a) apply.

  (b) If a party answers a claim that alleges specific facts and contentions with a general denial, or fails to include defenses or relevant facts in its answer that were known to it at the time the answer was filed, the panel may bar that party from presenting the omitted defenses or facts at the hearing.

- **12309. Amending Pleadings**

  (a) Before Panel Appointment

  Except as provided in paragraph (c), a party may amend a pleading at any time before the panel has been appointed.

  (1) To amend a statement of claim that has been filed but not yet served by the Director, the claimant must file the amended claim with the Director, with additional copies for each arbitrator and each other party. The Director will then serve the amended claim in accordance with Rules 12300 and 12301.

  (2) To amend any other pleading, a party must serve the amended pleading on each party. At the same time, the party must file the amended pleading with the Director, with additional copies for each arbitrator. If a pleading is amended to add a party to the arbitration, the party amending the pleading must provide each new party with copies of all documents previously served by any party, or sent to the parties by the Director.

  (b) After Panel Appointment

  Once a panel has been appointed, a party may only amend a pleading if the panel grants a motion to amend in accordance with Rule 12503. Motions to amend a pleading must include a copy of the proposed amended pleading. If the panel grants the motion to amend, the amended pleading does not need to be re-served on the other parties, the Director, or the panel, unless the panel determines otherwise.

(c) Amendments to Add Parties

Once the ranked arbitrator lists are due to the Director under Rule 12404(c), no party may amend a pleading to add a new party to the arbitration until a panel has been appointed and the panel grants a motion to add the party. Motions to add a party after panel appointment must be served on all parties, including the party to be added, and the party to be added may respond to the motion in accordance with Rule 12503 without waiving any rights or objections under the Code.

(d) Responding to an Amended Pleading

Any party may file a response to an amended pleading, provided the response is filed and served within 20 days of receipt of the amended pleading, unless the panel determines otherwise.

- **12310. Answering Amended Claims**

  (a) If a claim is amended before it has been answered, the respondent's original time to answer is extended by 20 days.
  (b) If a claim is amended after it has been answered, but before a panel has been appointed, the respondent has 20 days from the time the amended claim is served to serve an amended answer.

  (c) If a claim is amended after a panel has been appointed, the respondent has 20 days from the time the respondent receives notice that the panel has granted the motion to amend the claim to serve an amended answer.

  (d) The amended answer must be directly served on each other party. At the same time, the amended answer must also be filed with the Director, with additional copies for each arbitrator.

  (e) If the amended claim adds a new party to the arbitration, the new party's answer is governed by Rule 12306.

- **12311. Amendments to Amount in Dispute**

  If an amended pleading increases the amount in dispute, all filing fees, surcharges and process fees required by the Code will be recalculated based on the new amount in dispute.

- **12312. Multiple Claimants**
  (a) One or more parties may join multiple claims together in the same arbitration if the claims contain common questions of law or fact and:
  • The claims assert any right to relief jointly and severally; or
  • The claims arise out of the same transaction or occurrence, or series of transactions or occurrences.
  (b) After all responsive pleadings have been served, claims joined together under paragraph (a) of this rule may be separated into two or more arbitrations by the Director before a panel is appointed, or by the panel after the panel is appointed. A party whose claims were separated by the Director may make a motion to the panel in the lowest numbered case to reconsider the Director's decision.

- **12313. Multiple Respondents**
  (a) One or more parties may name one or more respondents in the same arbitration if the claims contain any questions of law or fact common to all respondents and:
  • The claims are asserted against the respondents jointly and severally; or
  • The claims arise out of the same transaction or occurrence, or series of transactions or occurrences.
  (b) After all responsive pleadings have been served, claims joined together under paragraph (a) of this rule may be separated into two or more arbitrations by the Director before a panel is appointed, or by the panel after the panel is appointed. A party whose claims were separated by the Director may make a motion to the panel in the lowest numbered case to reconsider the Director's decision.

- **12314. Combining Claims**
  Before ranked arbitrator lists are due to the Director under Rule 12404(c), the Director may combine separate but related claims into one arbitration. Once a panel has been appointed, the panel may reconsider the Director's decision upon motion of a party.

PART IV: APPOINTMENT, DISQUALIFICATION, AND AUTHORITY OF ARBITRATORS

- **12400. Neutral List Selection System and Arbitrator Rosters**

(a) Neutral List Selection System

The Neutral List Selection System is a computer system that generates, on a random basis, lists of arbitrators from FINRA's rosters of arbitrators for the selected hearing location for each proceeding. The parties will select their panel through a process of striking and ranking the arbitrators on lists generated by the Neutral List Selection System.

(b) Arbitrator Rosters

FINRA maintains the following roster of arbitrators:

• A roster of non-public arbitrators as defined in Rule 12100(p);

• A roster of public arbitrators as defined in Rule 12100(u); and

• A roster of arbitrators who are eligible to serve as chairperson of a panel as described in paragraph (c). Arbitrators who are eligible to serve as chairperson will also be included in the roster of public arbitrators, but will only appear on one list in a case.

(c) Eligibility for Chairperson Roster

In customer disputes, chairpersons must be public arbitrators. Arbitrators are eligible for the chairperson roster if they have completed chairperson training provided by FINRA and:

• Have a law degree and are a member of a bar of at least one jurisdiction and have served as an arbitrator through award on at least two arbitrations administered by a self-regulatory organization in which hearings were held; or

• Have served as an arbitrator through award on at least three arbitrations administered by a self-regulatory organization in which hearings were held.

- **12401. Number of Arbitrators**

(a) Claims of $25,000 or Less

If the amount of a claim is $25,000 or less, exclusive of interest and expenses, the panel will consist of one arbitrator and the claim is subject to the simplified arbitration procedures under Rule 12800.

(b) Claims of More Than $25,000 Up To $100,000

If the amount of a claim is more than $25,000 but not more than $100,000, exclusive of interest and expenses, the panel will consist of one arbitrator unless the parties agree in writing to three arbitrators.

(c) Claims of More Than $100,000; Unspecified or Non-Monetary Claims

If the amount of a claim is more than $100,000, exclusive of interest and expenses, or is unspecified, or if the claim does not request money damages, the panel will consist of three arbitrators, unless the parties agree in writing to one arbitrator.

- **12402. Composition of Arbitration Panels**
  (a) If the panel consists of one arbitrator, the arbitrator will be a public arbitrator selected from the public chairperson roster, unless the parties agree in writing otherwise.
  (b) If the panel consists of three arbitrators, one will be a non-public arbitrator and two will be public arbitrators, one of whom will be selected from the public chairperson roster, unless the parties agree in writing otherwise.

- **12403. Generating and Sending Lists to the Parties**
  (a) Generating Lists
  (1) If the panel consists of one arbitrator, the Neutral List Selection System will generate a list of 10 public arbitrators from the FINRA chairperson roster.

  (2) If the panel consists of three arbitrators, the Neutral List Selection System will generate:

  • A list of 10 arbitrators from the FINRA non-public arbitrator roster;

  • A list of 10 arbitrators from the FINRA public arbitrator roster; and

  • A list of 10 public arbitrators from the FINRA chairperson roster.

(3) If the panel consists of three arbitrators, the Neutral List Selection System will generate the chairperson list first. Chair-qualified arbitrators who were not selected for the chairperson list will be eligible for selection on the public list. An individual arbitrator cannot appear on both the chairperson list and the public list for the same case.

(4) The Neutral List Selection System will exclude arbitrators from the lists based upon current conflicts of interest identified within the Neutral List Selection System.

(b) Sending Lists to Parties

(1) The Director will send the lists generated by the Neutral List Selection System to all parties at the same time, within approximately 30 days after the last answer is due. The parties will also receive employment history for the past 10 years and other background information for each arbitrator listed.

(2) If a party requests additional information about an arbitrator, the Director will request the additional information from the arbitrator, and will send any response to all of the parties at the same time. When a party requests additional information, the Director may, but is not required to, toll the time for parties to return the ranked lists under Rule 12404(c).

- **12404. Striking and Ranking Arbitrators**
  (a) Each separately represented party may strike up to four of the arbitrators from each list for any reason by crossing through the names of the arbitrators. At least six names must remain on each list.
  (b) Each separately represented party shall rank all remaining arbitrators on the lists in order of preference, with a "1" indicating the party's first choice, a "2" indicating the party's second choice, and so on. Each list of arbitrators must be ranked separately.

  (c) The ranked lists must be returned to the Director no more than 20 days after the date upon which the Director sent the lists to the parties. If the Director does not receive a party's ranked lists within that time, the Director will proceed as though the party did not want to strike any arbitrator or have any preferences among the listed arbitrators.

- **12405. Combining Lists**
For each arbitrator classification (public, non-public, and chairperson), the Director will prepare combined ranked lists of arbitrators based on the parties' numerical rankings, as follows:
• The Director will add the rankings of all claimants together, and the rankings of all respondents together, to produce separate combined ranked lists for the claimants and the respondents.
• The Director will then add the combined rankings of claimants and the respondents together, to produce a single combined ranking number for each arbitrator, excluding all arbitrators stricken by a party.
• The Director will create separate combined ranked lists for each arbitrator classification in cases with both public and non-public arbitrators.

- **12406. Appointment of Arbitrators; Discretion to Appoint Arbitrators Not on List**
(a) If the panel consists of one arbitrator, the Director will appoint the highest-ranked available arbitrator from the combined chairperson list.
(b) If the panel consists of three arbitrators, the Director will appoint:
• The highest-ranked available non-public arbitrator from the combined non-public arbitrator list;
• The highest-ranked available public arbitrator from the combined public arbitrator list, and
• The highest-ranked available public arbitrator from the combined chairperson list, who will serve as chairperson of the panel.
(c) If the number of arbitrators available to serve from the combined list(s) is not sufficient to fill an initial panel, the Director will appoint one or more arbitrators of the required classification to complete the panel from names generated randomly by the Neutral List Selection System. If the Director must appoint a non-public arbitrator, the Director may not appoint a non-public arbitrator as defined in Rule 12100(p)(2) or (3), unless the parties agree otherwise. The Director will provide the parties information about the arbitrators as provided in Rule 12403 and the parties will have the right to challenge the arbitrators as provided in Rule 12410.

(d) Appointment of arbitrators occurs when the Director sends notice to the parties of the names of the arbitrators on the panel. Before making any decision as an arbitrator or attending a hearing session, the arbitrators must execute FINRA's arbitrator oath or affirmation.

- **12407. Additional Parties**
  (a) If a party is added to an arbitration after the Director sends the lists generated by the Neutral List Selection System to the parties, but before parties must return the ranked lists to the Director, the Director will send the lists to the newly added party, with employment history for the past 10 years and other background information for each arbitrator listed. The newly added party may rank and strike the arbitrators in accordance with Rule 12404. If the newly added party returns the lists within 20 days after the date upon which the Director sent the lists to the party, the Director will include the new party's lists when combining rankings under Rule 12405. If the Director does not receive the list within that time, the Director will proceed as though the party did not want to strike any arbitrator or have any preference among the listed arbitrators.
  (b) Once the ranked lists are due to the Director under Rule 12404, no party may amend a pleading to add a new party to the arbitration until a panel is appointed and grants a motion to add the party. Motions to add a party must be served on all parties, including the party to be added, and the party to be added may respond to the motion in accordance with Rule 12503 without waiving any rights or objections under the Code. If the panel grants the motion to add the party, the newly added party may not strike and rank the arbitrators, but may challenge an arbitrator for cause in accordance with Rule 12410.

- **12408. Disclosures Required of Arbitrators**
  (a) Before appointing arbitrators to a panel, the Director will notify the arbitrators of the nature of the dispute and the identity of the parties. Each potential arbitrator must make a reasonable effort to learn of, and must disclose to the Director, any circumstances which might preclude the arbitrator from rendering an objective and impartial determination in the proceeding, including:

(1) Any direct or indirect financial or personal interest in the outcome of the arbitration;

(2) Any existing or past financial, business, professional, family, social, or other relationships or circumstances with any party, any party's representative, or anyone who the arbitrator is told may be a witness in the proceeding, that are likely to affect impartiality or might reasonably create an appearance of partiality or bias;

(3) Any such relationship or circumstances involving members of the arbitrator's family or the arbitrator's current employers, partners, or business associates; and

(4) Any existing or past service as a mediator for any of the parties in the case for which the arbitrator has been selected.

(b) The obligation to disclose interests, relationships, or circumstances that might preclude an arbitrator from rendering an objective and impartial determination described in paragraph (a) is a continuing duty that requires an arbitrator who accepts appointment to an arbitration proceeding to disclose, at any stage of the proceeding, any such interests, relationships, or circumstances that arise, or are recalled or discovered.

(c) The Director will inform the parties to the arbitration of any information disclosed to the Director under this rule unless the arbitrator who disclosed the information declines appointment or voluntarily withdraws from the panel as soon as the arbitrator learns of any interest, relationship or circumstance that might preclude the arbitrator from rendering an objective and impartial determination in the proceeding, or the Director removes the arbitrator.

- **12409. Arbitrator Recusal**
  Any party may ask an arbitrator to recuse himself or herself from the panel for good cause. Requests for arbitrator recusal are decided by the arbitrator who is the subject of the request.

- **12410. Removal of Arbitrator by Director**
  (a) Before First Hearing Session Begins
  Before the first hearing session begins, the Director may remove an arbitrator for conflict of interest or bias, either upon request of a party or on the Director's own initiative.

(1) The Director will grant a party's request to remove an arbitrator if it is reasonable to infer, based on information known at the time of the request, that the arbitrator is biased, lacks impartiality, or has a direct or indirect interest in the outcome of the arbitration. The interest or bias must be definite and capable of reasonable demonstration, rather than remote or speculative. Close questions regarding challenges to an arbitrator by a customer under this rule will be resolved in favor of the customer.

(2) The Director must first notify the parties before removing an arbitrator on the Director's own initiative. The Director may not remove the arbitrator if the parties agree in writing to retain the arbitrator within five days of receiving notice of the Director's intent to remove the arbitrator.

(b) After First Hearing Session Begins

After the first hearing session begins, the Director may remove an arbitrator based only on information required to be disclosed under Rule 12408 that was not previously known by the parties. The Director may exercise this authority upon request of a party or on the Director's own initiative. Only the Director or the President of FINRA Dispute Resolution may exercise the Director's authority under this paragraph (b).

- **12411. Replacement of Arbitrators**

(a) If an arbitrator is removed, or becomes otherwise unable or unwilling to serve, the Director will appoint a replacement arbitrator in accordance with this rule, unless the parties agree in writing to proceed with only the remaining arbitrators.

(b) The Director will appoint as a replacement arbitrator the arbitrator who is the most highly ranked available arbitrator of the required classification remaining on the combined list.

(c) If there are no available arbitrators of the required classification on the consolidated list, the Director will appoint an arbitrator of the required classification to complete the panel from names generated by the Neutral List Selection System. The Director will provide the parties information about the arbitrator as provided in Rule 12403, and the parties shall have the right to object to the arbitrator as provided in Rule 12410.

(d) If the Director must appoint a non-public arbitrator under paragraph (c), the Director may not appoint a non-public arbitrator as defined in Rule 12100(p)(2) or (3), unless the parties agree otherwise.

- **12412. Director's Discretionary Authority**
  The Director may exercise discretionary authority and make any decision that is consistent with the purposes of the Code to facilitate the appointment of arbitrators and the resolution of arbitrations.

- **12413. Jurisdiction of Panel and Authority to Interpret the Code**
  The panel has the authority to interpret and determine the applicability of all provisions under the Code. Such interpretations are final and binding upon the parties.

- **12414. Determinations of Arbitration Panel**
  All rulings and determinations of the panel must be made by a majority of the arbitrators, unless the parties agree, or the Code or applicable law provides, otherwise.

PART V: PREHEARING PROCEDURES AND DISCOVERY

- **12500. Initial Prehearing Conference**
  (a) After the panel is appointed, the Director will schedule an Initial Prehearing Conference before the panel, except as provided in paragraph (c) of this rule.

  (b) The Initial Prehearing Conference will generally be held by telephone. Unless the parties agree otherwise, the Director must notify each party of the time and place of the Initial Prehearing Conference at least 20 days before it takes place.

  (c) At the Initial Prehearing Conference, the panel will set discovery, briefing, and motions deadlines, schedule subsequent hearing sessions, and address other preliminary matters. The parties may agree to forgo the Initial Prehearing Conference only if they jointly provide the Director with the following information, in writing, with additional copies for each arbitrator, before the Initial Prehearing Conference is scheduled to be held:

- A statement that the parties accept the panel;
- Whether any other prehearing conferences will be held, and if so, for each prehearing conference, a minimum of four mutually agreeable dates and times, and whether the chairperson or the full panel will preside;
- A minimum of four sets of mutually agreeable hearing dates;
- A discovery schedule;
- A list of all anticipated motions, with filing and response due dates; and
- A determination regarding whether briefs will be submitted, and, if so, the due date for the briefs and any reply briefs.

o **12501. Other Prehearing Conferences**

(a) A prehearing conference may be scheduled upon the joint request of the parties or at the discretion of the Director. The Director will set the time and place of the prehearing conference and appoint a person to preside.

(b) At a party's request, or at the discretion of the panel, the panel may schedule one or more additional prehearing conferences regarding any outstanding preliminary matters, including:

- Discovery disputes;
- Motions;
- Witness lists and subpoenas;
- Stipulations of fact;
- Unresolved scheduling issues;
- Contested issues on which the parties will submit briefs; and
- Any other matter that will simplify or expedite the arbitration.

(c) The panel will determine the time and place of any additional prehearing conferences. Prehearing conferences will generally be held by telephone. Unless the full panel is required under Rule 12503, prehearing conferences may be held before a single arbitrator, generally the chairperson.

- **12502. Recording Prehearing Conferences**

  (a) Prehearing conferences will not be recorded unless the panel determines otherwise, either on its own initiative or upon motion of a party.

  (b) If a prehearing conference is recorded, it may be recorded using any of the methods discussed under Rule 12606. The Director will provide a copy of the recording to any party upon request for a nominal fee.

- **12503. Motions**

  (a) Motions

  (1) A party may make motions in writing, or orally during any hearing session. Before making a motion, a party must make an effort to resolve the matter that is the subject of the motion with the other parties. Every motion, whether written or oral, must include a description of the efforts made by the moving party to resolve the matter before making the motion.

  (2) Written motions are not required to be in any particular form, and may take the form of a letter, legal motion, or any other form that the panel decides is acceptable. Written motions must be served directly on each other party, at the same time and in the same manner. Written motions must also be filed with the Director, with additional copies for each arbitrator, at the same time and in the same manner in which they are served on the parties.

  (3) Written motions must be served at least 20 days before a scheduled hearing, unless the panel decides otherwise.

  (4) Motions to amend a pleading after panel appointment pursuant to Rule 12309(b) must be accompanied by copies of the proposed amended pleading when the motion is served on the other parties and filed with the Director. If the panel grants the motion, the amended pleading does not have to be served again, unless the panel determines otherwise. If a party moves to amend a pleading to add a party, the motion must be served on all parties, including the party to be added, and the party to be added may respond to the motion in accordance with Rule 12309(c) without waiving any rights or objections under the Code.

  (b) Responding to Motions

Parties have 10 days from the receipt of a written motion to respond to the motion, unless the moving party agrees to an extension of time, or the Director or the panel decides otherwise. Responses to written motions must be served directly on each other party, at the same time and in the same manner. Responses to written motions must also be filed with the Director, with additional copies for each arbitrator, at the same time and in the same manner in which they are served on the parties.

(c) Authority to Decide Motions

(1) The Director decides motions relating to use of the forum under Rule 12203 and removal of an arbitrator under Rule 12410.

(2) Motions relating to combining or separating claims or arbitrations, or changing the hearing location, are decided by the Director before a panel is appointed, and by the panel after the panel is appointed.

(3) Discovery-related motions are decided by one arbitrator, generally the chairperson. The arbitrator may refer such motions to the full panel either at his or her own initiative, or at the request of a party. The arbitrator must refer motions relating to privilege to the full panel at the request of a party.

(4) Motions for arbitrator recusal under Rule 12409 are decided by the arbitrator who is the subject of the request.

(5) The full panel decides all other motions, including motions relating to the eligibility of a claim under Rule 12206, unless the Code provides or the parties agree otherwise.

- **12504. Motions to Dismiss**

(a) Motions to Dismiss Prior to Conclusion of Case in Chief

(1) Motions to dismiss a claim prior to the conclusion of a party's case in chief are discouraged in arbitration.

(2) Motions under this rule must be made in writing, and must be filed separately from the answer, and only after the answer is filed.

(3) Unless the parties agree or the panel determines otherwise, parties must serve motions under this rule at least 60 days before a scheduled hearing, and parties have 45 days to respond to the motion.

(4) Motions under this rule will be decided by the full panel.

(5) The panel may not grant a motion under this rule unless an in-person or telephonic prehearing conference on the motion is held or waived by the parties. Prehearing conferences to consider motions under this rule will be recorded as set forth in Rule 12606.

(6) The panel cannot act upon a motion to dismiss a party or claim under paragraph (a) of this rule, unless the panel determines that:

(A) the non-moving party previously released the claim(s) in dispute by a signed settlement agreement and/or written release; or

(B) the moving party was not associated with the account(s), security(ies), or conduct at issue.

(7) If the panel grants a motion under this rule (in whole or part), the decision must be unanimous, and must be accompanied by a written explanation.

(8) If the panel denies a motion under this rule, the moving party may not re-file the denied motion, unless specifically permitted by panel order.

(9) If the panel denies a motion under this rule, the panel must assess forum fees associated with hearings on the motion against the moving party.

(10) If the panel deems frivolous a motion filed under this rule, the panel must also award reasonable costs and attorneys' fees to any party that opposed the motion.

(11) The panel also may issue other sanctions under Rule 12212 if it determines that a party filed a motion under this rule in bad faith.

(b) Motions to Dismiss After Conclusion of Case in Chief

A motion to dismiss made after the conclusion of a party's case in chief is not subject to the procedures set forth in paragraph (a).

(c) Motions to Dismiss Based on Eligibility

A motion to dismiss based on eligibility filed under Rule 12206 will be governed by that rule.

(d) Motions to Dismiss Based on Failure to Comply with Code or Panel Order

A motion to dismiss based on failure to comply with any provision in the Code, or any order of the panel or single arbitrator filed under Rule 12212 will be governed by that rule.

(e) Motions to Dismiss Based on Discovery Abuse

A motion to dismiss based on discovery abuse filed under Rule 12511 will be governed by that rule.

- **12505. Cooperation of Parties in Discovery**
  The parties must cooperate to the fullest extent practicable in the exchange of documents and information to expedite the arbitration.

- **12506. Document Production Lists**
  (a) Applicability of Document Production Lists

  When the Director serves the statement of claim, the Director will notify parties of the location of the FINRA Discovery Guide and Document Production Lists on FINRA's Web site, but will provide a copy to the parties upon request. Document Production Lists 1 and 2 describe the documents that are presumed to be discoverable in all arbitrations between a customer and a member or associated person. Other Document Production Lists may also apply, depending on the specific cause(s) of action alleged.

  (b) Time for Responding to Document Production Lists

  (1) Unless the parties agree otherwise, within 60 days of the date that the answer to the statement of claim is due, or, for parties added by amendment or third party claim, within 60 days of the date that their answer is due, parties must either:

  • Produce to all other parties all documents in their possession or control that are described in the Document Production Lists 1 and 2, and any other Document Production List that is applicable based on the cause(s) of action alleged;

  • Identify and explain the reason that specific documents described in Document Production Lists 1 and 2, and any other Document Production List that is applicable based on the cause(s) of action alleged, cannot be produced within the required time, and state when the documents will be produced; or

  • Object as provided in Rule 12508.

  (2) A party must act in good faith when complying with subparagraph (1) of this rule. "Good faith" means that a party must use its best efforts to produce all documents required or agreed to be produced. If a document cannot be produced in the required time, a

party must establish a reasonable timeframe to produce the document.

(c) Redacted Information

For purposes of this rule and Rule 12507, if a party redacts any portion of a document prior to production, the redacted pages (or range of pages) shall be labeled "redacted."

- **12507. Other Discovery Requests**

(a) Making Other Discovery Requests

(1) Parties may also request additional documents or information from any party by serving a written request directly on the party. Requests for information are generally limited to identification of individuals, entities, and time periods related to the dispute; such requests should be reasonable in number and not require narrative answers or fact finding. Standard interrogatories are generally not permitted in arbitration.

(2) Other discovery requests may be served:

• On the claimant, or any respondent named in the initial statement of claim, 45 days or more after the Director serves the statement of claim; and

• On any party subsequently added to the arbitration, 45 days or more after the statement of claim is served on that party.

At the same time, the party must serve copies of the request on all other parties. Any request for documents or information not described in applicable Document Production Lists should be specific, and relate to the matter in controversy.

(b) Responding to Other Discovery Requests

(1) Unless the parties agree otherwise, within 60 days from the date a discovery request other than the Document Production Lists is received, the party receiving the request must either:

• Produce the requested documents or information to all other parties;

• Identify and explain the reason that specific requested documents or information cannot be produced within the required time, and state when the documents will be produced; or

• Object as provided in Rule 12508.

(2) A party must act in good faith when complying with subparagraph (1) of this rule. "Good faith" means that a party must use its best efforts to produce all documents or information required or agreed to be produced. If a document or information cannot be produced in the required time, a party must establish a reasonable timeframe to produce the document or information.

- **12508. Objecting to Discovery; Waiver of Objection**

  (a) If a party objects to producing any document described in Document Production Lists 1 or 2, any other applicable Document Production List, or any document or information requested under Rule 12507, it must specifically identify which document or requested information it is objecting to and why. Objections must be in writing, and must be served on all other parties at the same time and in the same manner. Objections should not be filed with the Director. Parties must produce all applicable listed documents, or other requested documents or information not specified in the objection.

  (b) Any objection not made within the required time is waived unless the panel determines that the party had substantial justification for failing to make the objection within the required time.

  (c) In making any rulings on objections, arbitrators may consider the relevance of documents or discovery requests and the relevant costs and burdens to parties to produce this information.

- **12509. Motions to Compel Discovery**

  (a) A party may make a motion asking the panel to order another party to produce documents or information if the other party has:

  • Failed to comply with Rule 12506 or 12507; or

  • Objected to the production of documents or information under Rule 12508.

  (b) Motions to compel discovery must be made, and will be decided, in accordance with Rule 12503. Such motions must include the disputed document request or list, a copy of any objection thereto, and a description of the efforts of the moving party to resolve the issue before making the motion.

- **12510. Depositions**

  Depositions are strongly discouraged in arbitration. Upon motion of a party, the panel may permit depositions, but only under very limited circumstances, including:

  • To preserve the testimony of ill or dying witnesses;

  • To accommodate essential witnesses who are unable or unwilling to travel long distances for a hearing and may not otherwise be required to participate in the hearing;

  • To expedite large or complex cases; and

  • If the panel determines that extraordinary circumstances exist.

- **12511. Discovery Sanctions**

  (a) Failure to cooperate in the exchange of documents and information as required under the Code may result in sanctions. The panel may issue sanctions against any party in accordance with Rule 12212(a) for:

  • Failing to comply with the discovery provisions of the Code, unless the panel determines that there is substantial justification for the failure to comply; or

  • Frivolously objecting to the production of requested documents or information.

  (b) The panel may dismiss a claim, defense or proceeding with prejudice in accordance with Rule 12212(c) for intentional and material failure to comply with a discovery order of the panel if prior warnings or sanctions have proven ineffective.

- **12512. Subpoenas**

  (a) To the fullest extent possible, parties should produce documents and make witnesses available to each other without the use of subpoenas. Arbitrators shall have the authority to issue subpoenas for the production of documents or the appearance of witnesses.

  (b) A party may make a written motion requesting that an arbitrator issue a subpoena to a party or a non-party. The motion must include a draft subpoena and must be filed with the Director, with an additional copy for the arbitrator. The requesting party must serve the motion and draft subpoena on each other party, at the same time and in the same manner as on the Director. The requesting party may not serve the motion or draft subpoena on a non-party.

(c) If a party receiving a motion and draft subpoena objects to the scope or propriety of the subpoena, that party shall, within 10 calendar days of service of the motion, file written objections with the Director, with an additional copy for the arbitrator, and shall serve copies on all other parties at the same time and in the same manner as on the Director. The party that requested the subpoena may respond to the objections within 10 calendar days of receipt of the objections. After considering all objections, the arbitrator responsible for deciding discovery-related motions shall rule promptly on the issuance and scope of the subpoena.

(d) If the arbitrator issues a subpoena, the party that requested the subpoena must serve the subpoena at the same time and in the same manner on all parties and, if applicable, on any non-party receiving the subpoena.

(e) Any party that receives documents in response to a subpoena served on a non-party shall provide notice to all other parties within five days of receipt of the documents. Thereafter, any party may request copies of such documents and, if such a request is made, the documents must be provided within 10 calendar days following receipt of the request.

- **12513. Authority of Panel to Direct Appearances of Associated Person Witnesses and Production of Documents Without Subpoenas**

(a) Upon motion of a party, the panel may order the following without the use of subpoenas:

• The appearance of any employee or associated person of a member of FINRA; or

• The production of any documents in the possession or control of such persons or members.

(b) Unless the panel directs otherwise, the party requesting the appearance of witnesses by, or the production of documents from, non-parties under this rule shall pay the reasonable costs of the appearance and/or production.

- **12514. Prehearing Exchange of Documents and Witness Lists, and Explained Decision Requests**

  (a) Documents and Other Materials

  At least 20 days before the first scheduled hearing date, all parties must provide all other parties with copies of all documents and other materials in their possession or control that they intend to use at the hearing that have not already been produced. The parties should not file the documents with the Director or the arbitrators before the hearing.

  (b) Witness Lists

  At least 20 days before the first scheduled hearing date, all parties must provide each other party with the names and business affiliations of all witnesses they intend to present at the hearing. At the same time, all parties must file their witness lists with the Director, with enough copies for each arbitrator.

  (c) Exclusion of Documents or Witnesses

  Parties may not present any documents or other materials not produced and or any witnesses not identified in accordance with this rule at the hearing, unless the panel determines that good cause exists for the failure to produce the document or identify the witness. Good cause includes the need to use documents or call witnesses for rebuttal or impeachment purposes based on developments during the hearing. Documents and lists of witnesses in defense of a claim are not considered rebuttal or impeachment information and, therefore, must be exchanged by the parties.

  (d) Explained Decision Request

  At least 20 days before the first scheduled hearing date, all parties must submit to the panel any joint request for an explained decision under Rule 12904(g).

PART VI: HEARINGS; EVIDENCE; CLOSING THE RECORD

- **12600. Required Hearings**

  (a) Hearings will be held, unless:

- The arbitration is administered under Rule 12800 or Rule 12801;
- The parties agree otherwise in writing; or
- The arbitration has been settled, withdrawn or dismissed.

(b) The panel will decide the time and date of the hearing at the initial prehearing conference or otherwise in another manner.

(c) The Director will notify the parties of the time and place at least 20 days before the hearing begins, unless the parties agree to a shorter time.

- **12601. Postponement of Hearings**

(a) Postponement of Hearings

(1) When a Hearing Shall Be Postponed

A hearing shall be postponed by agreement of the parties.

(2) When a Hearing May Be Postponed

A hearing may be postponed:

- By the Director, in extraordinary circumstances;
- By the panel, in its own discretion; or
- By the panel, upon motion of a party.

The panel may not grant a motion to postpone a hearing made within 10 days of the date that the hearing is scheduled to begin, unless the panel determines that good cause exists.

(b) Postponement Fees

(1) Except as otherwise provided, a postponement fee will be charged for each postponement agreed to by the parties, or granted upon request of one or more parties. The fee will equal the applicable hearing session fee under Rule 12902. The panel may allocate the fee among the party or parties that agreed to or requested the postponement. The panel may also assess part or all of any postponement fees against a party that did not request the postponement, if the panel determines that the non-requesting party caused or contributed to the need for the postponement. The panel may waive the fees.

(2) If a postponement request is made by one or more parties and granted within three business days before a scheduled hearing session, the party or parties making the request shall pay an additional fee of $100 per arbitrator. If more than one party requests

the postponement, the arbitrators shall allocate the $100 per arbitrator fee among the requesting parties. The arbitrators may allocate all or portion of the $100 per arbitrator fee to the non-requesting party or parties, if the arbitrators determine that the non-requesting party or parties caused or contributed to the need for the postponement. In the event that a request results in the postponement of consecutively scheduled hearing sessions, the additional fee will be assessed only for the first of the consecutively scheduled hearing sessions. In the event that an extraordinary circumstance prevents a party or parties from making a timely postponement request, arbitrators may use their discretion to waive the fee, provided verification of such circumstance is received.

(3) No postponement fee will be charged if a hearing is postponed:

- Because the parties agree to submit the matter to mediation administered through FINRA, except that the parties shall pay the additional fees described in Rule 12601(b)(2) for late postponement requests;
- By the panel in its own discretion; or
- By the Director in extraordinary circumstances.

(c) Dismissal of Arbitration Due to Multiple Postponements

If all parties jointly request, or agree to, more than two postponements, the panel may dismiss the arbitration without prejudice.

- **12602. Attendance at Hearings**

  (a) The parties and their representatives are entitled to attend all hearings. Absent persuasive reasons to the contrary, expert witnesses should be permitted to attend all hearings.

  (b) An attorney for a non-party witness may attend a hearing while that non-party witness is testifying. Unless otherwise authorized by the panel, the attorney's role is limited to the assertion of recognized privileges, such as the attorney client and work product privileges, and the privilege against self-incrimination. The attorney must be in good standing and admitted to practice before the Supreme Court of the United States or the highest court of any state of the United States, the District of Columbia, or any commonwealth, territory, or possession of the United States, unless state law prohibits such representation.

(c) The panel will decide who else may attend any or all of the hearings.

- **12603. Failure to Appear**
  If a party fails to appear at a hearing after having been notified of the time, date and place of the hearing, the panel may determine that the hearing may go forward, and may render an award as though all parties had been present.

- **12604. Evidence**
  (a) The panel will decide what evidence to admit. The panel is not required to follow state or federal rules of evidence.

  (b) Production of documents in discovery does not create a presumption that the documents are admissible at the hearing. A party may state objections to the introduction of any document as evidence at the hearing to the same extent that any other objection may be raised in arbitration.

- **12605. Witness Oath**
  All witnesses must testify under oath or affirmation.

- **12606. Record of Proceedings**
  (a) Tape, Digital, or Other Recording

  (1) Except as provided in paragraph (b), the Director will make a tape, digital, or other recording of every hearing. The Director will provide a copy of the recording to any party upon request for a nominal fee.

  (2) The panel may order the parties to provide a transcription of the recording. If the panel orders a transcription, copies of the transcription must be provided to each arbitrator and each party. The panel will determine which party or parties must pay the cost of making the transcription and copies.

  (3) The recording is the official record of the proceeding, even if it is transcribed.

(b) Stenographic Record

(1) Any party may make a stenographic record of the hearing. Even if a stenographic record is made, the tape, digital, or other recording will be the official record of the proceeding, unless the panel determines otherwise. If the panel determines in advance that the stenographic record will be the official record, the Director will not record the hearing.

(2) If the stenographic record is the official record of the proceeding, a copy must be provided to the Director, each arbitrator, and each other party. The cost of making and copying the stenographic record will be borne by the party electing to make the stenographic record, unless the panel decides that one or more other parties should bear all or part of the costs.

- **12607. Order of Presentation of Evidence and Arguments**
  Generally, the claimant shall present its case, followed by the respondent's defense. The panel has the discretion to vary the order in which the hearing is conducted, provided that each party is given a fair opportunity to present its case.

- **12608. Closing the Record**
  (a) The panel will decide when the record is closed. Once the record is closed, no further submissions will be accepted from any party.

  (b) In cases in which no hearing is held, the record is presumed to be closed when the Director sends the pleadings to the panel, unless the panel requests, or agrees to accept, additional submissions from any party. If so, the record is presumed to be closed when the last such submission is due.

  (c) In cases in which a hearing is held, the panel will generally close the record at the end of the last hearing session, unless the panel requests, or agrees to accept, additional submissions from any party. If so, the panel will inform the parties when the submissions are due and when the record will close.

- **12609. Reopening the Record**

The panel may reopen the record on its own initiative or upon motion of any party at any time before the award is rendered, unless prohibited by applicable law.

PART VII: TERMINATION OF AN ARBITRATION BEFORE AWARD

- **12700. Dismissal of Proceedings Prior to Award**

(a) The panel must dismiss an arbitration or a claim at the joint request of the parties to that arbitration or claim. The dismissal will be with or without prejudice, depending on the request of the parties.

(b) The panel may dismiss a claim or an arbitration:

- Upon motion of a party under Rule 12206; or
- On its own initiative under Rule 12212(c) or Rule 12601(c).

- **12701. Settlement**

(a) Parties to an arbitration may agree to settle their dispute at any time. Parties who settle must notify the Director. The Director will continue to administer the arbitration, and fees may continue to accrue, until the Director receives written notice of the settlement. The parties do not need to disclose the terms of the settlement agreement to the Director or to FINRA Dispute Resolution, but members and associated persons may have reporting obligations under the rules of FINRA.

(b) Settling parties will remain responsible for fees incurred under the Code. If parties to a settlement fail to agree on the allocation of any outstanding fees, those fees will be divided equally among the settling parties, except member surcharges and prehearing and hearing process fees required by the Code, which will remain the responsibility of the member party or parties.

- **12702. Withdrawal of Claims**

(a) Before a claim has been answered by a party, the claimant may withdraw the claim against that party with or without prejudice.

(b) After a claim has been answered by a party, the claimant may only withdraw it against that party with prejudice unless the panel decides, or the claimant and that party agree, otherwise.

PART VIII: SIMPLIFIED ARBITRATION AND DEFAULT PROCEEDINGS

- **12800. Simplified Arbitration**

(a) Applicability of Rule

This rule applies to arbitrations involving $25,000 or less, exclusive of interest and expenses. Except as otherwise provided in this rule, all provisions of the Code apply to such arbitrations.

(b) Single Arbitrator

All arbitrations administered under this rule will be decided by a single public arbitrator appointed from the FINRA chairperson roster in accordance with the Neutral List Selection System, unless the parties agree in writing otherwise.

(c) Hearings

(1) No hearing will be held in arbitrations administered under this rule unless the customer requests a hearing.

(2) If no hearing is held, no initial prehearing conference or other prehearing conference will be held, and the arbitrator will render an award based on the pleadings and other materials submitted by the parties. If a hearing is held, the regular provisions of the Code relating to prehearings and hearings, including fee provisions, will apply.

(d) Discovery and Additional Evidence

(1) Document Production Lists, described in Rule 12506, do not apply to arbitrations subject to this rule. However, the arbitrator may, in his or her discretion, choose to use relevant portions of the Document Production Lists in a manner consistent with the expedited nature of simplified proceedings.

(2) The parties may request documents and other information from each other. All requests for the production of documents and other information must be served on all other parties, and filed with the

Director, within 30 days from the date that the last answer is due. Any response or objection to a discovery request must be served on all other parties and filed with the Director within 10 days of the receipt of the requests. The arbitrator will resolve any discovery disputes.

(e) Increases in Amount in Dispute

If any pleading increases the amount in dispute to more than $25,000, the arbitration will no longer be administered under this rule, and the regular provisions of the Code will apply. If an arbitrator has been appointed, that arbitrator will remain on the panel. If a three-arbitrator panel is required or requested under Rule 12401, the remaining arbitrators will be appointed by the Director in accordance with Rule 12406(b). If no arbitrator has been appointed, the entire panel will be appointed in accordance with the Neutral List Selection System.

(f) Arbitrator Honoraria

FINRA will pay the arbitrator an honorarium of $125 for each arbitration administered under this rule.

- **12801. Default Proceedings**

(a) Applicability of Rule

A claimant may request default proceedings against any respondent that falls within one of the following categories and fails to file an answer within the time provided by the Code.

- A member whose membership has been terminated, suspended, canceled, or revoked;
- A member that has been expelled from the FINRA;
- A member that is otherwise defunct; or
- An associated person whose registration is terminated, revoked, or suspended.

(b) Initiating Default Proceedings

(1) To initiate default proceedings against one or more respondents that fail to file a timely answer, the claimant must notify the Director in writing and must send a copy of the notification to all other parties at the same time and in the same manner as the notification was sent to the Director. If there is more than one claimant, all claimants must

agree in writing to proceed under this rule against a defaulting respondent before this rule may be used.

(2) If the Director receives written notice from the claimant and determines that the requirements for proceeding under this rule have been met, the Director will:

- Notify all parties that the claim against the defaulting respondent will proceed under this rule; and
- Appoint a single arbitrator in accordance with the Neutral List Selection System to consider the statement of claim and other documents presented by the claimant.

(c) Hearings

No hearing shall be held. The arbitrator may request additional information from the claimant before rendering an award.

(d) Amendments to Increase Relief Requested

Claimants may not amend a claim to increase the relief requested from the defaulting respondent after the Director has notified the parties that the claim will proceed under this rule.

(e) Awards

(1) The arbitrator may not issue an award based solely on the nonappearance of a party. Claimants must present a sufficient basis to support the making of an award. The arbitrator may not award damages in an amount greater than the damages requested in the statement of claim, and may not award any other relief that was not requested in the statement of claim.

(2) The default award shall have no effect on any non-defaulting party.

(f) Respondent's Answer

If a defaulting respondent files an answer after the Director has notified the parties that the claim against that respondent will proceed under this rule but before an award has been issued, the proceedings against that respondent under this rule will be terminated and the claim against that respondent will proceed under the regular provisions in the Code.

- **12805. Expungement of Customer Dispute Information under Rule 2080**

In order to grant expungement of customer dispute information under Rule 2080, the panel must:

(a) Hold a recorded hearing session (by telephone or in person) regarding the appropriateness of expungement. This paragraph will apply to cases administered under Rule 12800 even if a customer did not request a hearing on the merits.

(b) In cases involving settlements, review settlement documents and consider the amount of payments made to any party and any other terms and conditions of a settlement.

(c) Indicate in the arbitration award which of the Rule 2080 grounds for expungement serve(s) as the basis for its expungement order and provide a brief written explanation of the reason(s) for its finding that one or more Rule 2080 grounds for expungement applies to the facts of the case.

(d) Assess all forum fees for hearing sessions in which the sole topic is the determination of the appropriateness of expungement against the parties requesting expungement relief.

PART IX: FEES AND AWARDS

- **12900. Fees Due When a Claim Is Filed**

(a) Fees for Claims Filed by Customers, Associated Persons and Other Non-Members

(1) Customers, associated persons, and other non-members who file a claim, counterclaim, cross claim or third party claim must pay a filing fee in the amount indicated in the schedule below. The Director may defer payment of all or part of the filing fee on a showing of financial hardship. If payment of the fee is not deferred, failure to pay the required amount will result in a deficiency under Rule 12307.

Filing Fees for Claims Filed by Customers, Associated Persons, and Other Non-Members

Amount of Claim (exclusive of interest and expenses)	Filing Fee
$.01 to $1,000	$50

$1,000.01 to $2,500	$75
$2,500.01 to $5,000	$175
$5,000.01 to $10,000	$325
$10,000.01 to $25,000	$425
$25,000.01 to $50,000	$600
$50,000.01 to $100,000	$975
$100,000.01 to $500,000	$1,425
$500,000.01 to $1 million	$1,575
Over $ 1 million	$1,800
Non-Monetary/Not Specified	$1,250

(2) If the claim does not request or specify money damages, the Director may determine that the filing fee should be more or less than the amount specified in the schedule above, but in any event, the amount of the filing fee may not be less than $50 or more than $1,800.

(b) Fees for Claims Filed by Members

(1) Members filing a claim, counterclaim, cross claim, or third party claim must pay a filing fee in the amount indicated in the schedule below. Failure to pay the required amount will result in a deficiency under Rule 12307.

Fees for Claims Filed by Members

Amount of Claim (exclusive of interest and expenses)	**Filing Fee**
$.01 to $1,000	$225
$1,000.01 to $2,500	$350
$2,500.01 to $5,000	$525
$5,000.01 to $10,000	$750
$10,000.01 to $25,000	$1,050
$25,000.01 to $50,000	$1,450
$50,000.01 to $100,000	$1,750
$100,000.01 to $500,000	$2,125
$500,000.01 to $1,000,000	$2,450
$1,000,000.01 to $5,000,000	$3,200
Over $5,000,000	$3,700
Non-Monetary/Not Specified	$1,500

(2) If the claim does not request or specify money damages, the Director may determine that the filing fee should be more or less than the amount specified in the schedule above, but in any event, the filing fee may not be less than $225 or more than $3,700.

(c) Partial Refund of Filing Fee

(1) If a claim is settled or withdrawn more than 10 days before the date that the hearing on the merits under Rule 12600 is scheduled to begin, a party paying a filing fee will receive a partial refund of the filing fee in the amount indicated in the schedule below, less any other fees or costs assessed against the party under the Code, including any hearing session fees assessed under Rule 12902. No refund will be paid if FINRA receives notice that a claim is settled or withdrawn within 10 days of the date that the hearing on the merits under Rule 12600 is scheduled to begin.

Partial Refund for Settlement or Withdrawal More Than 10 Days Before Hearing on the Merits

Amount of Claim (exclusive of interest and expenses)	Refund
$.01 to $1,000	$25
$1,000.01 to $2,500	$50
$2,500.01 to $5,000	$125
$5,000.01 to $10,000	$250
$10,000.01 to $25,000	$300
$25,000.01 to $50,000	$450
$50,000.01 to $100,000	$750
$100,000.01 to $500,000	$1,125
Over $500,000	$1,200
Non-monetary/Not specified	$1,000

(2) If the claim does not request or specify money damages, and the Director determines that the hearing session fee should be a different amount than the amount specified in the schedule in Rule 12902, the amount of the refund will be the amount of the hearing session fee determined by the Director, less any fees or costs assessed against the party under the Code, including any hearing session fees assessed under Rule 12902.

(d) Reimbursement of Filing Fees

In the award, the panel may order a party to reimburse another party for all or part of any filing fee paid.

- **12901. Member Surcharge**

(a) Member Surcharge

(1) A surcharge in the amount indicated in the schedule below will be assessed against each member that:

- Files a claim, counterclaim, cross claim, or third party claim under the Code;
- Is named as a respondent in a claim, counterclaim, cross claim, or third party claim filed and served under the Code; or
- Employed, at the time the dispute arose, an associated person who is named as a respondent in a claim, counterclaim, cross claim, or third party claim filed and served under the Code.

Member Surcharge

Amount in Dispute	**Surcharge (exclusive of interest and expenses)**
Up to $2,500	$150
$2,500.01–$5,000	$200
$5,000.01–$10,000	$325
$10,000.01–$25,000	$425
$25,000.01–$30,000	$600
$30,000.01–$50,000	$875
$50,000.01–$100,000	$1,100
$100,000.01–$500,000	$1,700
$500,000.01–$1,000,000	$2,250
$1,000,000.01–$5,000,000	$2,800
$5,000,000.01–$10,000,000	$3,350
Over $10,000,000	$3,750
Non-Monetary/Not Specified	$1,500

(2) If the claim does not request or specify money damages, the Director may determine that the member surcharge should be more or less than the amount specified in the schedule above, but in any event the amount of the member surcharge may not be less than $150 or more than $3,750.

(3) If the claim is filed by the member, the surcharge is due when the claim is filed. If the claim is filed against the member, or against an associated person employed by the member at the time of the events giving rise to the dispute, the surcharge is due when the claim is served in accordance with Rule 12300.

(4) No member shall be assessed more than a single surcharge in any arbitration. The panel may not reallocate a surcharge paid by a member to any other party.

(b) Refund of Member Surcharge

(1) The Director will refund the surcharge paid by a member in an arbitration filed by a customer if the panel:

- Denies all of a customer's claims against the member or associated person; and
- Allocates all fees assessed pursuant to Rule 12902(a) against the customer.

(2) The Director may also refund or waive the member surcharge in extraordinary circumstances.

- **12902. Hearing Session Fees, and Other Costs and Expenses**

(a) Hearing Session Fees

(1) Hearing session fees will be charged for each hearing session. The total amount chargeable to the parties for each hearing session is based on the amount in dispute, as specified in the schedule below. In the award, the panel will determine the amount of each hearing session fee that each party must pay.

Hearing Session Fees

Amount of Claim	Hearing Session W/ One Arbitrator	Hearing Session W/ Three Arbitrators
Up to $2,500	$50	N/A
$2,500.01 to $5,000	$125	N/A
$5,000.01 to $10,000	$250	N/A
$10,000.01 to $25,000	$450	N/A
$25,000.01 to $50,000	$450	$600
$50,000.01 to $100,000	$450	$750
$100,000.01 to	$450	$1,125

$500,000		
Over $500,000	$450	$1,200
Unspecified Damages	$450	$1,000

(2) If the claim does not request or specify money damages, the Director may determine that the hearing session fee should be more or less than the amount specified in the schedule above, but in any event the hearing session fee shall not be less than $50 or more than $1,200 for each hearing session.

(3) If there is more than one claim in a proceeding, the amount of hearing session fees will be based on the largest claim in the proceeding. If any claims are joined or combined under Rules 12312, 12313, or 12314, the amount of those claims will be aggregated and they will be treated as one claim for purposes of this paragraph.

(4) If hearing session fees are allocated against a customer in connection with a claim filed by a member or associated person, the amount of hearing session fees the customer must pay must be based on the amount actually awarded to the member or associated person, rather than on the amount claimed by the member or associated person. No hearing session fees may be assessed against a customer in connection with a claim filed by a member that is dismissed; however, in cases where there is also a customer claim, the customer may be assessed a filing fee under Rule 12900(a), and may be subject to hearing session fees.

(b) Payment of Hearing Session Fees

(1) The panel may assess the hearing session fees in the award, or may require the parties to pay hearing session fees during the course of the arbitration. The total amount that the panel may require the parties to pay for each hearing session during the course of an arbitration may not exceed the total amount chargeable to the parties for each hearing session under the schedule to paragraph (a) of this rule.

(2) Any interim hearing session fee payments made by a party under this rule will be deducted from the total amount of hearing session fees assessed against that party in the award. If the amount of interim payments is more than the amount assessed against the party in the award, the balance will be refunded to that party.

(3) In the award, the amount of one hearing session fee will be deducted from the total amount of hearing session fees assessed against the party who paid the filing fee. If this amount is more than any fees, costs, and expenses assessed against this party under the Code, the balance will be refunded to the party.

(c) Assessment of Other Costs and Expenses in Award

In its award, the panel must also determine the amount of any costs and expenses incurred by the parties under the Code or that are within the scope of the agreement of the parties, and which party or parties will pay those costs and expenses.

(d) Assessment of Hearing Session Fees, Costs, and Expenses in Case of Settlement or Withdrawal

If a claim is settled or withdrawn:

• The parties will be subject to an assessment of hearing session fees for hearing sessions already held.

• If FINRA receives a settlement or withdrawal notice 10 days or fewer prior to the date that the hearing on the merits under Rule 12600 is scheduled to begin, parties that paid a filing fee under Rule 12900 will not be entitled to any refund of the filing fee.

• The parties will also be responsible for any fee or costs incurred under Rules 12502, 12513, 12601, or 12606 in connection with such hearings. If a case is settled or withdrawn and the parties' agreement fails to allocate such fees and costs, the fees and costs will be allocated as provided by Rule 12701(b).

(e) Refund Payments

Any refunds of fees or costs incurred under the Code will be paid directly to the named parties, even if a non-party made a payment on behalf of the named parties.

- **12903. Process Fees Paid by Members**

(a) Each member that is a party to an arbitration in which more than $25,000, exclusive of interest and expenses, is in dispute must pay:

• A non-refundable prehearing process fee of $750, due at the time the parties are sent arbitrator lists in accordance with Rule 12403(b); and

• A non-refundable hearing process fee, due when the parties are notified of the date and location of the hearing on the merits under Rule 12600, as set forth in the schedule below.

Hearing Process Fee Schedule

Amount of Claim (exclusive of interest and expenses)	**Hearing Process Fee**
$1–$25,000	$ 0
$25,000.01–$50,000	$1,000
$50,000.01–$100,000	$1,700
$100,000.01–$500,000	$2,750
$500,000.01–$1,000,000	$4,000
$1,000,000.01–$5,000,000	$5,000
More than $5,000,000	$5,500
Non-Monetary/Not Specified	$2,200

(b) If an associated person of a member is a party, the member that employed the associated person at the time the dispute arose will be charged the process fees, even if the member is not a party. No member shall be assessed more than one prehearing and one hearing process fee in any arbitration.

(c) The panel may not reallocate to any other party any prehearing and hearing process fees paid by a member.

o **12904. Awards**

(a) All awards shall be in writing and signed by a majority of the arbitrators or as required by applicable law. Such awards may be entered as a judgment in any court of competent jurisdiction.

(b) Unless the applicable law directs otherwise, all awards rendered under the Code are final and are not subject to review or appeal.

(c) The Director will serve a copy of the award on each party, or the representative of the party. The Director will serve the award by using any method available and convenient to the parties and the Director, and that is reasonably expected to cause the award to be delivered to all parties, or their representative, on the same day. Methods the Director may use include, but are not limited to, first class, registered or certified mail, hand delivery, and facsimile or other electronic transmission.

(d) The panel shall endeavor to render an award within 30 business days from the date the record is closed.

(e) The award shall contain the following:

- The names of the parties;
- The name of the parties' representatives, if any;
- An acknowledgement by the arbitrators that they have each read the pleadings and other materials filed by the parties;
- A summary of the issues, including the type(s) of any security or product, in controversy;
- The damages and other relief requested;
- The damages and other relief awarded;
- A statement of any other issues resolved;
- The allocation of forum fees and any other fees allocable by the panel;
- The names of the arbitrators;
- The dates the claim was filed and the award rendered;
- The number and dates of hearing sessions;
- The location of the hearings; and
- The signatures of the arbitrators.

(f) The award may contain a rationale underlying the award.

(g) Explained Decisions

(1) This paragraph (g) applies only when all parties jointly request an explained decision.

(2) An explained decision is a fact-based award stating the general reason(s) for the arbitrators' decision. Inclusion of legal authorities and damage calculations is not required.

(3) Parties must make any request for an explained decision no later than the time for the prehearing exchange of documents and witness lists under Rule 12514(d).

(4) The chairperson of the panel will be responsible for writing the explained decision.

(5) The chairperson will receive an additional honorarium of $400 for writing the explained decision, as required by this paragraph (g). The panel will allocate the cost of the chairperson's honorarium to the parties as part of the final award.

(6) This paragraph (g) will not apply to simplified cases decided without a hearing under Rule 12800 or to default cases conducted under Rule 12801.

(h) All awards shall be made publicly available.

(i) Fees and assessments imposed by the arbitrators under the Code shall be paid immediately upon the receipt of the award by the parties. Payment of such fees shall not be deemed ratification of the award by the parties.

(j) All monetary awards shall be paid within 30 days of receipt unless a motion to vacate has been filed with a court of competent jurisdiction. An award shall bear interest from the date of the award:

- If not paid within 30 days of receipt;
- If the award is the subject of a motion to vacate which is denied; or
- As specified by the panel in the award.

Interest shall be assessed at the legal rate, if any, then prevailing in the state where the award was rendered, or at a rate set by the arbitrator(s).

- **12905. Submissions After a Case Has Closed**

(a) Parties may not submit documents to arbitrator(s) in cases that have been closed except under the following limited circumstances:

(1) as ordered by a court;

(2) at the request of any party within 10 days of service of an award or notice that a matter has been closed, for typographical or computational errors, or mistakes in the description of any person or property referred to in the award; or

(3) if all parties agree and submit documents within 10 days of (1) service of an award or (2) notice that a matter has been closed.

(b) Parties must make requests under this rule in writing to the Director and must include the basis relied on under this rule for the request. The Director will forward documents submitted pursuant to paragraph (a)(1), along with any responses from other parties, to the arbitrators. The Director will determine if submissions made pursuant to paragraphs (a)(2) and (a)(3) comply with the grounds enumerated in the rule. If the Director determines that the request complies with paragraphs (a)(2) and (a)(3), the Director will forward the documents, along with any responses from other parties, to the arbitrators. The arbitrators may decline to consider requests that the Director forwards to them under paragraphs (a)(2) and (a)(3).

(c) Unless the arbitrators rule within 10 days after the Director forwards the documents to the arbitrators pursuant to a request made under paragraphs (a)(2) and (a)(3), the request shall be deemed considered and denied.

(d) Requests under this rule do not extend the time period for payment of any award pursuant to Rule 12904.

Appendix 7:

THE NEW YORK CONVENTION — CONVENTION ON THE RECOGNITION AND ENFORCEMENT OF FOREIGN ARBITRAL AWARDS

Article I

1. This Convention shall apply to the recognition and enforcement of arbitral awards made in the territory of a State other than the State where the recognition and enforcement of such awards are sought, and arising out of differences between persons, whether physical or legal. It shall also apply to arbitral awards not considered as domestic awards in the State where their recognition and enforcement are sought.

2. The term "arbitral awards" shall include not only awards made by arbitrators appointed for each case but also those made by permanent arbitral bodies to which the parties have submitted.

3. When signing, ratifying or acceding to this Convention, or notifying extension under article X hereof, any State may on the basis of reciprocity declare that it will apply the Convention to the recognition and enforcement of awards made only in the territory of another Contracting State. It may also declare that it will apply the Convention only to differences arising out of legal relationships, whether contractual or not, which are considered as commercial under the national law of the State making such declaration.

Article II

1. Each Contracting State shall recognize an agreement in writing under which the parties undertake to submit to arbitration all or any differences which have arisen or which may arise between them in respect of a defined legal relationship, whether contractual or not, concerning a subject matter capable of settlement by arbitration.

2. The term "agreement in writing" shall include an arbitral clause in a contract or an arbitration agreement, signed by the parties or contained in an exchange of letters or telegrams.

3. The court of a Contracting State, when seized of an action in a matter in respect of which the parties have made an agreement within the meaning of this article, shall, at the request of one of the parties, refer the parties to arbitration, unless it finds that the said agreement is null and void, inoperative or incapable of being performed.

Article III

Each Contracting State shall recognize arbitral awards as binding and enforce them in accordance with the rules of procedure of the territory where the award is relied upon, under the conditions laid down in the following articles. There shall not be imposed substantially more onerous conditions or higher fees or charges on the recognition or enforcement of arbitral awards to which this Convention applies than are imposed on the recognition or enforcement of domestic arbitral awards.

Article IV

1. To obtain the recognition and enforcement mentioned in the preceding article, the party applying for recognition and enforcement shall, at the time of the application, supply:

(a) The duly authenticated original award or a duly certified copy thereof;
(b) The original agreement referred to in article II or a duly certified copy thereof.

2. If the said award or agreement is not made in an official language of the country in which the award is relied upon, the party applying for recognition and enforcement of the award shall produce a translation of these documents into such language. The translation shall be certified by an official or sworn translator or by a diplomatic or consular agent.

Article V

1. Recognition and enforcement of the award may be refused, at the request of the party against whom it is invoked, only if that party furnishes to the competent authority where the recognition and enforcement is sought, proof that:

> (a) The parties to the agreement referred to in article II were, under the law applicable to them, under some incapacity, or the said agreement is not valid under the law to which the parties have subjected it or, failing any indication thereon, under the law of the country where the award was made; or
> (b) The party against whom the award is invoked was not given proper notice of the appointment of the arbitrator or of the arbitration proceedings or was otherwise unable to present his case; or
> (c) The award deals with a difference not contemplated by or not falling within the terms of the submission to arbitration, or it contains decisions on matters beyond the scope of the submission to arbitration, provided that, if the decisions on matters submitted to arbitration can be separated from those not so submitted, that part of the award which contains decisions on matters submitted to arbitration may be recognized and enforced; or
> (d) The composition of the arbitral authority or the arbitral procedure was not in accordance with the agreement of the parties, or, failing such agreement, was not in accordance with the law of the country where the arbitration took place; or
> (e) The award has not yet become binding, on the parties, or has been set aside or suspended by a competent authority of the country in which, or under the law of which, that award was made.

2. Recognition and enforcement of an arbitral award may also be refused if the competent authority in the country where recognition and enforcement is sought finds that:

> (a) The subject matter of the difference is not capable of settlement by arbitration under the law of that country; or
> (b) The recognition or enforcement of the award would be contrary to the public policy of that country.

Article VI

If an application for the setting, aside or suspension of the award has been made to a competent authority referred to in article V (1) (e), the authority before which the award is sought to be relied upon may, if it considers it proper, adjourn the decision on the enforcement of the award and may also, on the application of the party claiming, enforcement of the award, order the other party to give suitable security.

Article VII

1. The provisions of the present Convention shall not affect the validity of multilateral or bilateral agreements concerning the recognition and enforcement of arbitral awards entered into by the Contracting States nor deprive any interested party of any right he may have to avail himself of an arbitral award in the manner and to the extent allowed by the law or the treaties of the country where such award is sought to be relied upon.

2. The Geneva Protocol on Arbitration Clauses of 1923 and the Geneva Convention on the Execution of Foreign Arbitral Awards of 1927 shall cease to have effect between Contracting States on their becoming bound and to the extent that they become bound, by this convention.

Article VIII

1. This Convention shall be open until 31 December 1958 for signature on behalf of any Member of the United Nations and also on behalf of any other State which is or hereafter becomes a member of any specialized agency of the United Nations, or which is or hereafter becomes a party to the Statute of the International Court of Justice, or any other State to which an invitation has been addressed by the General Assembly of the United Nations.

2. This Convention shall be ratified and the instrument of ratification shall be deposited with the Secretary-General of the United Nations.

Article IX

1. This Convention shall be open for accession to all States referred to in article VIII.

2. Accession shall be effected by the deposit of an instrument of accession with the Secretary-General of the United Nations.

Article X

1. Any State may, at the time of signature, ratification or accession, declare that this Convention shall extend to all or any of the territories for the international relations of which it is responsible. Such a declaration shall take effect when the Convention enters into force for the State concerned.

2. At any time thereafter any such extension shall be made by notification addressed to the Secretary-General of the United Nations and shall take effect as from the ninetieth day after the day of receipt by the Secretary-General of the United Nations of this notification, or as from the date of entry into force of the Convention for the State concerned, whichever is the later.

3. With respect to those territories to which this Convention is not extended at the time of signature, ratification or accession, each State concerned shall consider the possibility of taking the necessary steps in order to extend the application of this Convention to such territories, subject, where necessary for constitutional reasons, to the consent of the Governments of such territories.

Article XI

In the case of a federal or non-unitary State, the following provisions shall apply:

(a) With respect to those articles of this Convention that come within the legislative jurisdiction of the federal authority, the obligations of the federal Government shall to this extent be the same as those of Contracting States which are not federal States;

(b) With respect to those articles of this Convention that come within the legislative jurisdiction of constituent states or provinces which are not, under the constitutional system of the federation, bound to take legislative action, the federal Government shall bring such articles with a favourable recommendation to the notice of the appropriate authorities of constituent states or provinces at the earliest possible moment;

(c) A federal State Party to this Convention shall, at the request of any other Contracting State transmitted through the Secretary-General of the United Nations, supply a statement of the law and practice of the federation and its constituent units in regard to any particular provision of this Convention, showing the extent to which effect has been given to that provision by legislative or other action.

Article XII

1. This Convention shall come into force on the ninetieth day following the date of deposit of the third instrument of ratification or accession.

2. For each State ratifying or acceding to this Convention after the deposit of the third instrument of ratification or accession, this Convention shall enter into force on the ninetieth day after deposit by such State of its instrument of ratification or accession.

Article XIII

1. Any Contracting State may denounce this Convention by a written notification to the Secretary-General of the United Nations. Denunciation shall take effect one year after the date of receipt of the notification by the Secretary-General.

2. Any State which has made a declaration or notification under article X may, at any time thereafter, by notification to the Secretary-General of the United Nations, declare that this Convention shall cease to extend to the territory concerned one year after the date of the receipt of the notification by the Secretary-General.

3. This Convention shall continue to be applicable to arbitral awards in respect of which recognition or enforcement proceedings have been instituted before the denunciation takes effect.

Article XIV

A Contracting State shall not be entitled to avail itself of the present Convention against other Contracting States except to the extent that it is itself bound to apply the Convention.

Article XV

The Secretary-General of the United Nations shall notify the States contemplated in article VIII of the following:

(a) Signatures and ratifications in accordance with article VIII;
(b) Accessions in accordance with article IX;
(c) Declarations and notifications under articles I, X and XI;
(d) The date upon which this Convention enters into force in accordance with article XII;

(e) Denunciations and notifications in accordance with article XIII.

Article XVI

1. This Convention, of which the Chinese, English, French, Russian and Spanish texts shall be equally authentic, shall be deposited in the archives of the United Nations.

2. The Secretary-General of the United Nations shall transmit a certified copy of this Convention to the States contemplated in article VIII.

INDEX*

A

* The Index cites to section and subsections as well as specific cases and Appendices (abbreviated as "App.") when appropriate. Cites to both a case and notes ("n." or "nn.") references the notes immediately following the case. "Notes" refers to all of the notes following the case.

D

E

F

P

R

S

T

W

CPSIA information can be obtained at www.ICGtesting.com
Printed in the USA
240965LV00005B/124/P